THE WONDER WOMAN CHRONICLES
VOLUME TWO

**ALL STORIES WRITTEN BY WILLIAM MOULTON MARSTON.
ALL COVERS AND STORY ART BY HARRY G. PETER.**

*These stories were originally untitled and are titled here for reader convenience.

The comics reprinted in this volume were produced in a time when racism played a larger role
in society and popular culture, both consciously and unconsciously.

WONDER WOMAN CREATED BY WILLIAM MOULTON MARSTON

Sheldon Mayer EDITOR – ORIGINAL SERIES
Ian Sattler DIRECTOR – EDITORIAL, SPECIAL PROJECTS AND ARCHIVAL EDITIONS
Scott Nybakken EDITOR ☆ **Robbin Brosterman** DESIGN DIRECTOR – BOOKS

Eddie Berganza EXECUTIVE EDITOR ☆ **Bob Harras** VP – EDITOR IN CHIEF

Diane Nelson PRESIDENT ☆ **Dan DiDio** and **Jim Lee** CO-PUBLISHERS ☆ **Geoff Johns** CHIEF CREATIVE OFFICER ☆ **John Rood** EXECUTIVE VP – SALES, MARKETING AND BUSINESS DEVELOPMENT ☆ **Amy Genkins** SENIOR VP – BUSINESS AND LEGAL AFFAIRS ☆ **Nairi Gardiner** Senior VP – FINANCE ☆ **Jeff Boison** VP – PUBLISHING OPERATIONS ☆ **Mark Chiarello** VP – ART DIRECTION AND DESIGN ☆ **John Cunningham** VP – MARKETING ☆ **Terri Cunningham** VP – TALENT RELATIONS AND SERVICES ☆ **Alison Gill** SENIOR VP – MANUFACTURING AND OPERATIONS ☆ **David Hyde** VP – PUBLICITY ☆ **Hank Kanalz** SENIOR VP – DIGITAL **Jay Kogan** VP – BUSINESS AND LEGAL AFFAIRS, PUBLISHING ☆ **Jack Mahan** VP – BUSINESS AFFAIRS, TALENT ☆ **Nick Napolitano** VP – MANUFACTURING ADMINISTRATION ☆ **Sue Pohja** VP – BOOK SALES ☆ **Courtney Simmons** SENIOR VP – PUBLICITY ☆ **Bob Wayne** SENIOR VP – SALES

THE WONDER WOMAN CHRONICLES VOLUME TWO Published by DC Comics. Cover and compilation Copyright © 2011 DC Comics. All Rights Reserved. Originally published in single magazine form in SENSATION COMICS 10-14, WONDER WOMAN 2-3 and COMIC CAVALCADE 1. Copyright 1942, 1943 DC Comics. All Rights Reserved. All characters, their distinctive likenesses and related elements featured in this publication are trademarks of DC Comics. The stories, characters and incidents featured in this publication are entirely fictional. DC Comics does not read or accept unsolicited submissions of ideas, stories or artwork.

DC Comics, 1700 Broadway, New York, NY 10019
A Warner Bros. Entertainment Company
Printed by RR Donnelley, Willard, OH, USA. 10/28/11.
First Printing.
ISBN: 978-1-4012-3240-5

Cover art by Harry G. Peter.

Black and white reconstruction on cover and interior art by Rick Keene.
Color reconstruction on cover and interior art by Patricia Mulvihill and Digital Chameleon.

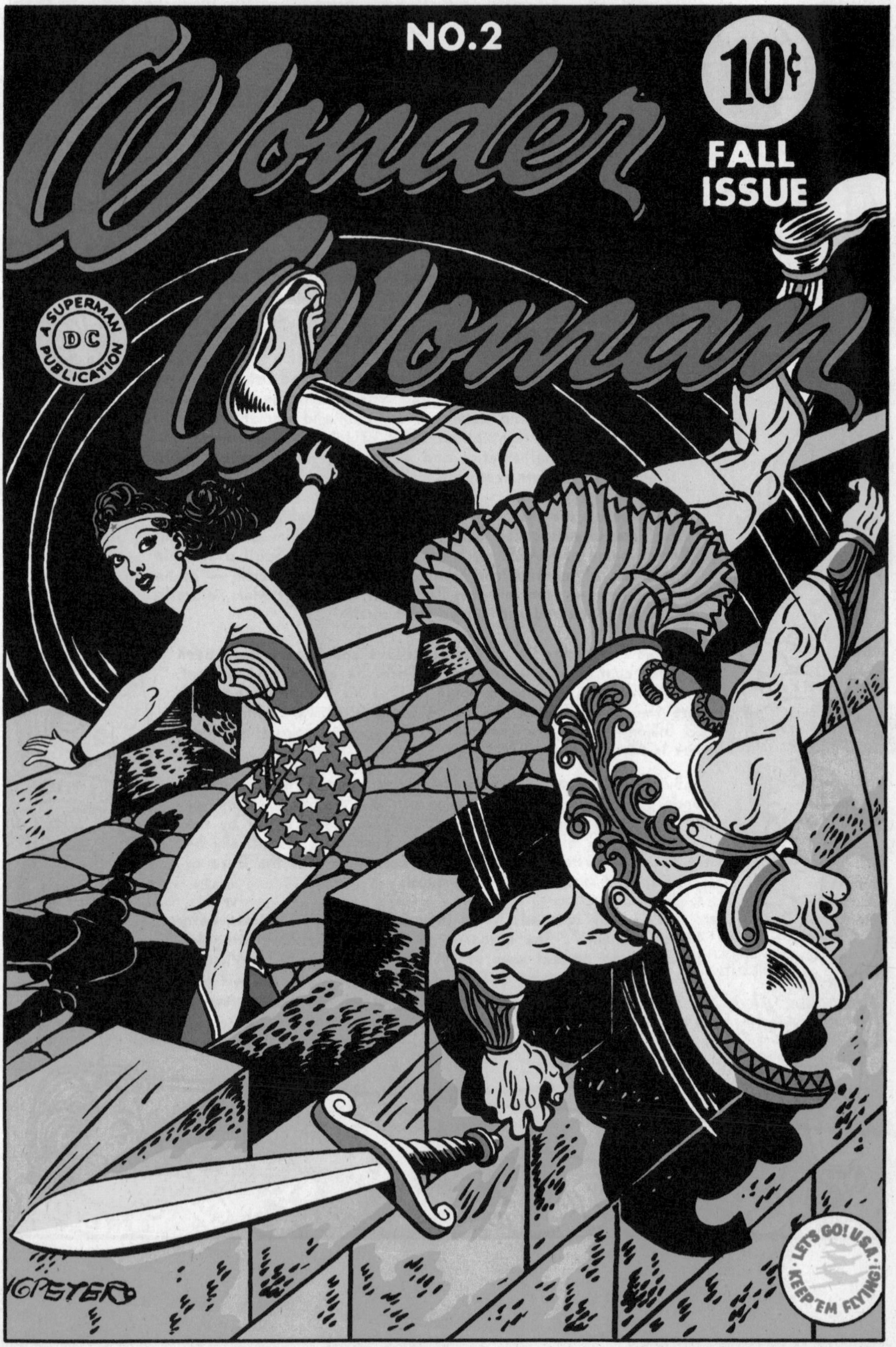
NO.2
Wonder Woman
10¢
FALL ISSUE
A SUPERMAN DC PUBLICATION
LET'S GO! U.S.A. KEEP 'EM FLYING!
H.G. PETER

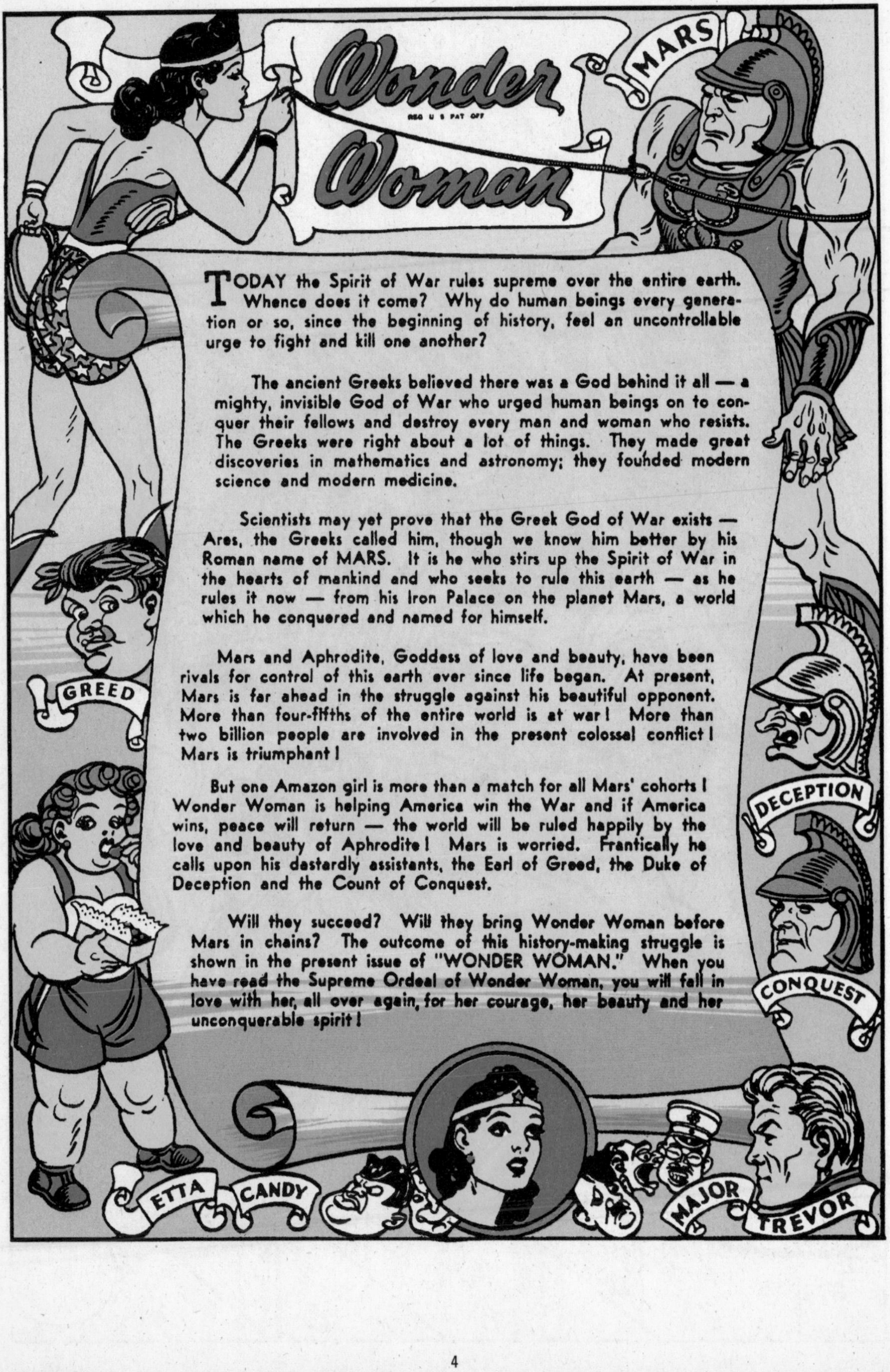
Wonder Woman
REG U S PAT OFF
MARS
GREED
DECEPTION
CONQUEST
ETTA
CANDY
MAJOR
TREVOR

TODAY the Spirit of War rules supreme over the entire earth. Whence does it come? Why do human beings every generation or so, since the beginning of history, feel an uncontrollable urge to fight and kill one another?

The ancient Greeks believed there was a God behind it all — a mighty, invisible God of War who urged human beings on to conquer their fellows and destroy every man and woman who resists. The Greeks were right about a lot of things. They made great discoveries in mathematics and astronomy; they founded modern science and modern medicine.

Scientists may yet prove that the Greek God of War exists — Ares, the Greeks called him, though we know him better by his Roman name of MARS. It is he who stirs up the Spirit of War in the hearts of mankind and who seeks to rule this earth — as he rules it now — from his Iron Palace on the planet Mars, a world which he conquered and named for himself.

Mars and Aphrodite, Goddess of love and beauty, have been rivals for control of this earth ever since life began. At present, Mars is far ahead in the struggle against his beautiful opponent. More than four-fifths of the entire world is at war! More than two billion people are involved in the present colossal conflict! Mars is triumphant!

But one Amazon girl is more than a match for all Mars' cohorts! Wonder Woman is helping America win the War and if America wins, peace will return — the world will be ruled happily by the love and beauty of Aphrodite! Mars is worried. Frantically he calls upon his dastardly assistants, the Earl of Greed, the Duke of Deception and the Count of Conquest.

Will they succeed? Will they bring Wonder Woman before Mars in chains? The outcome of this history-making struggle is shown in the present issue of "WONDER WOMAN." When you have read the Supreme Ordeal of Wonder Woman, you will fall in love with her, all over again, for her courage, her beauty and her unconquerable spirit!

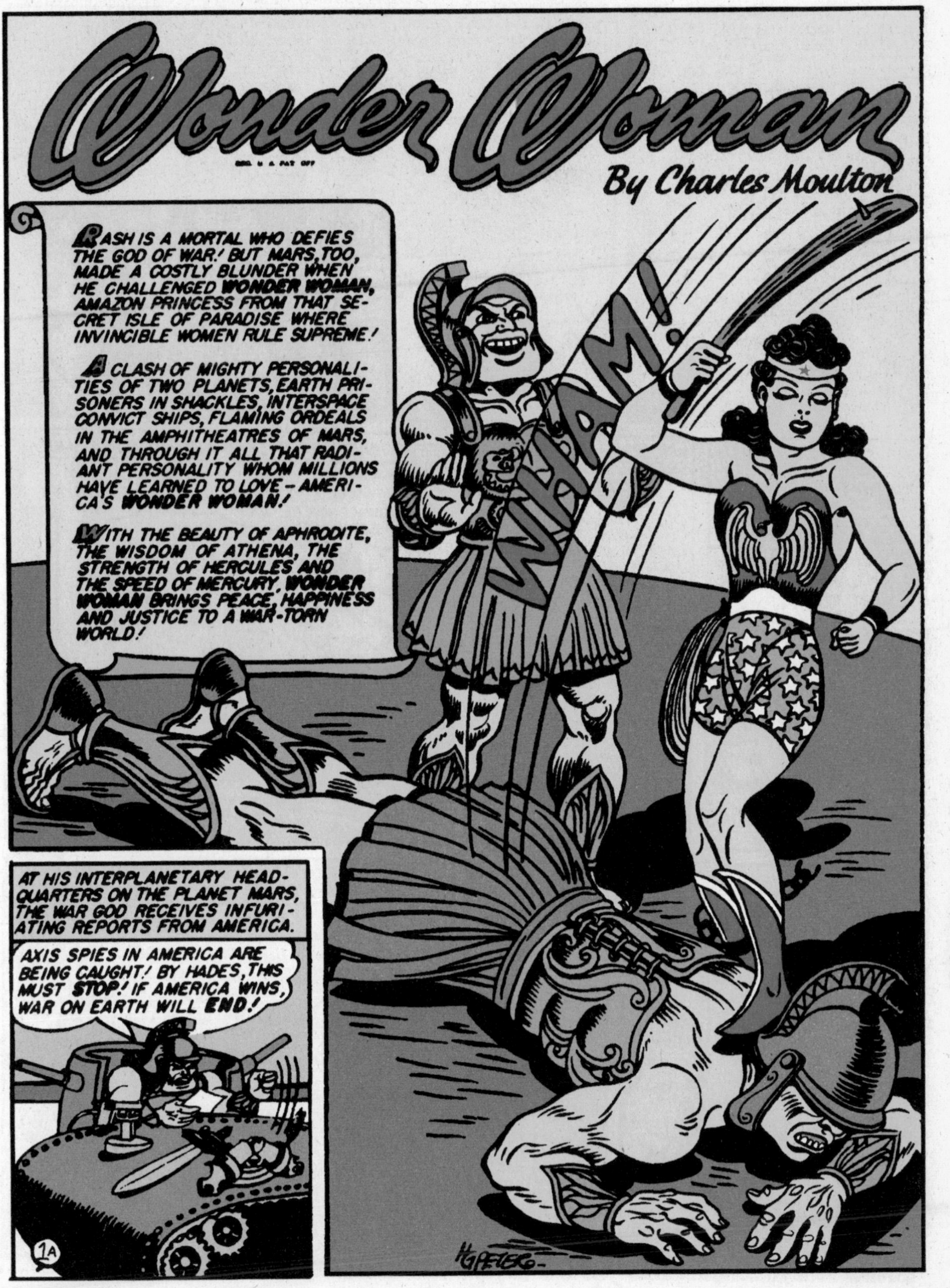
Wonder Woman
By Charles Moulton
RASH IS A MORTAL WHO DEFIES THE GOD OF WAR! BUT MARS, TOO, MADE A COSTLY BLUNDER WHEN HE CHALLENGED WONDER WOMAN, AMAZON PRINCESS FROM THAT SECRET ISLE OF PARADISE WHERE INVINCIBLE WOMEN RULE SUPREME!
A CLASH OF MIGHTY PERSONALITIES OF TWO PLANETS, EARTH PRISONERS IN SHACKLES, INTERSPACE CONVICT SHIPS, FLAMING ORDEALS IN THE AMPHITHEATRES OF MARS, AND THROUGH IT ALL THAT RADIANT PERSONALITY WHOM MILLIONS HAVE LEARNED TO LOVE — AMERICA'S WONDER WOMAN!
WITH THE BEAUTY OF APHRODITE, THE WISDOM OF ATHENA, THE STRENGTH OF HERCULES AND THE SPEED OF MERCURY, WONDER WOMAN BRINGS PEACE, HAPPINESS AND JUSTICE TO A WAR-TORN WORLD!
WHAM!
AT HIS INTERPLANETARY HEADQUARTERS ON THE PLANET MARS, THE WAR GOD RECEIVES INFURIATING REPORTS FROM AMERICA.
AXIS SPIES IN AMERICA ARE BEING CAUGHT! BY HADES, THIS MUST STOP! IF AMERICA WINS, WAR ON EARTH WILL END!
1A
HG PETER

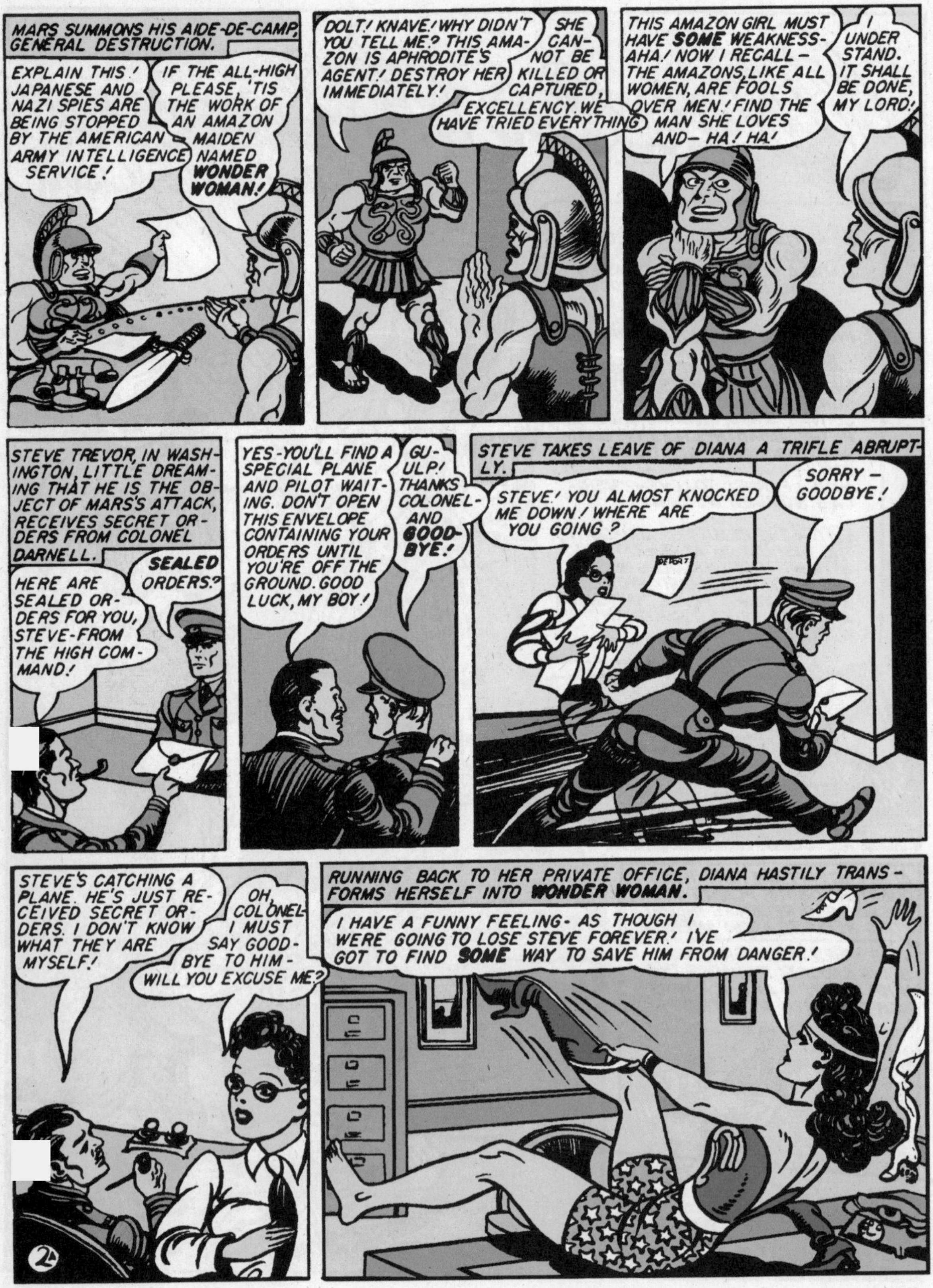

MARS SUMMONS HIS AIDE-DE-CAMP, GENERAL DESTRUCTION.
EXPLAIN THIS! JAPANESE AND NAZI SPIES ARE BEING STOPPED BY THE AMERICAN ARMY INTELLIGENCE SERVICE!
IF THE ALL-HIGH PLEASE, 'TIS THE WORK OF AN AMAZON MAIDEN NAMED **WONDER WOMAN!**
DOLT! KNAVE! WHY DIDN'T YOU TELL ME? THIS AMAZON IS APHRODITE'S AGENT! DESTROY HER IMMEDIATELY!
SHE CANNOT BE KILLED OR CAPTURED, EXCELLENCY. WE HAVE TRIED EVERYTHING
THIS AMAZON GIRL MUST HAVE **SOME** WEAKNESS-AHA! NOW I RECALL- THE AMAZONS, LIKE ALL WOMEN, ARE FOOLS OVER MEN! FIND THE MAN SHE LOVES AND- HA! HA!
I UNDERSTAND. IT SHALL BE DONE, MY LORD!
STEVE TREVOR, IN WASHINGTON, LITTLE DREAMING THAT HE IS THE OBJECT OF MARS'S ATTACK, RECEIVES SECRET ORDERS FROM COLONEL DARNELL.
HERE ARE SEALED ORDERS FOR YOU, STEVE-FROM THE HIGH COMMAND!
SEALED ORDERS?
YES-YOU'LL FIND A SPECIAL PLANE AND PILOT WAITING. DON'T OPEN THIS ENVELOPE CONTAINING YOUR ORDERS UNTIL YOU'RE OFF THE GROUND. GOOD LUCK, MY BOY!
GULP! THANKS COLONEL- AND **GOOD-BYE!**
STEVE TAKES LEAVE OF DIANA A TRIFLE ABRUPTLY.
STEVE! YOU ALMOST KNOCKED ME DOWN! WHERE ARE YOU GOING?
SORRY - GOODBYE!
STEVE'S CATCHING A PLANE. HE'S JUST RECEIVED SECRET ORDERS. I DON'T KNOW WHAT THEY ARE MYSELF!
OH, COLONEL- I MUST SAY GOODBYE TO HIM- WILL YOU EXCUSE ME?
RUNNING BACK TO HER PRIVATE OFFICE, DIANA HASTILY TRANSFORMS HERSELF INTO **WONDER WOMAN**.
I HAVE A FUNNY FEELING- AS THOUGH I WERE GOING TO LOSE STEVE FOREVER! I'VE GOT TO FIND **SOME** WAY TO SAVE HIM FROM DANGER!
2

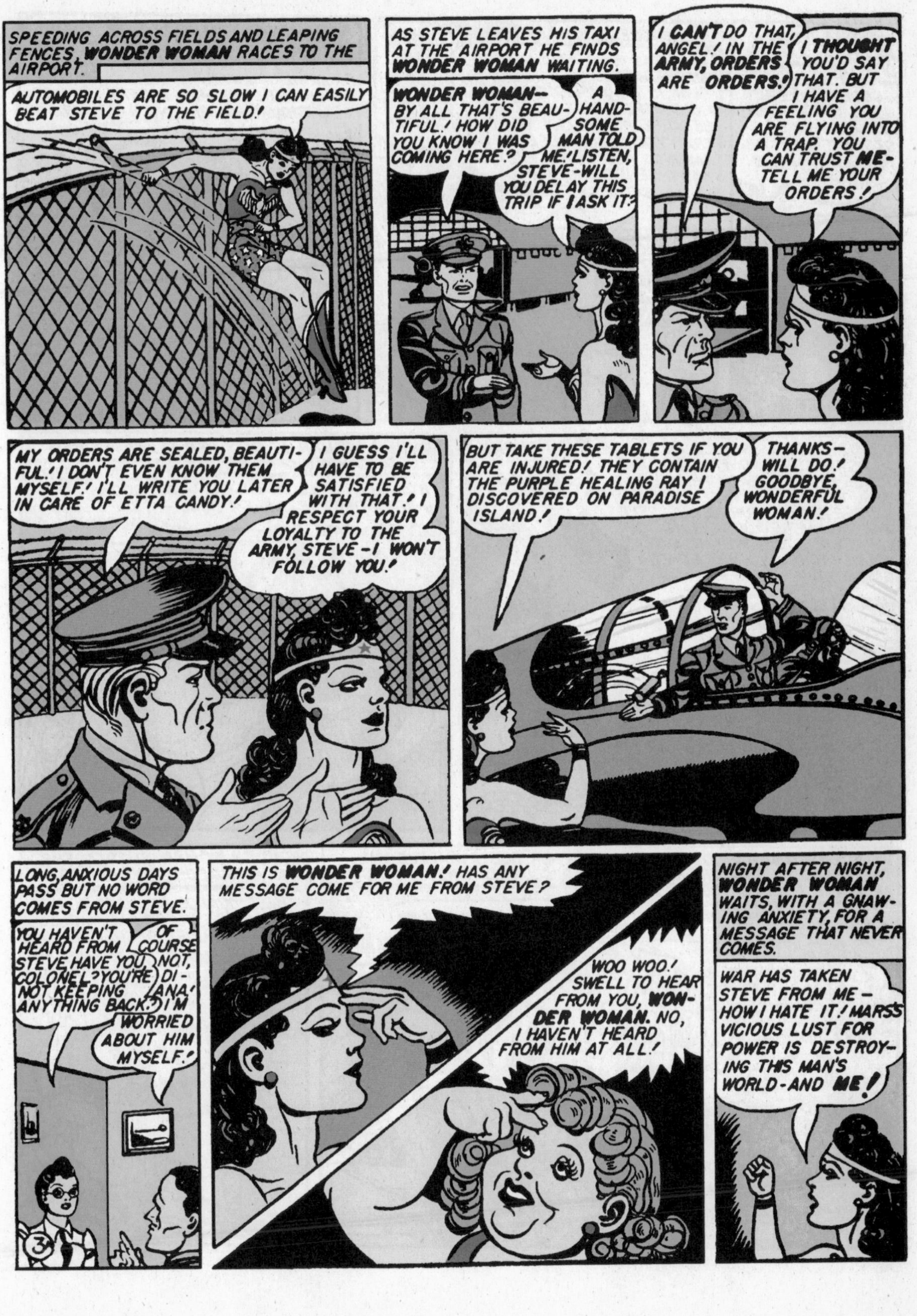
SPEEDING ACROSS FIELDS AND LEAPING FENCES, WONDER WOMAN RACES TO THE AIRPORT.
AUTOMOBILES ARE SO SLOW I CAN EASILY BEAT STEVE TO THE FIELD!
AS STEVE LEAVES HIS TAXI AT THE AIRPORT HE FINDS WONDER WOMAN WAITING.
WONDER WOMAN-- BY ALL THAT'S BEAUTIFUL! HOW DID YOU KNOW I WAS COMING HERE?
A HANDSOME MAN TOLD ME! LISTEN, STEVE-WILL YOU DELAY THIS TRIP IF I ASK IT?
I CAN'T DO THAT, ANGEL! IN THE ARMY, ORDERS ARE ORDERS!
I THOUGHT YOU'D SAY THAT. BUT I HAVE A FEELING YOU ARE FLYING INTO A TRAP. YOU CAN TRUST ME-TELL ME YOUR ORDERS!
MY ORDERS ARE SEALED, BEAUTIFUL! I DON'T EVEN KNOW THEM MYSELF! I'LL WRITE YOU LATER IN CARE OF ETTA CANDY!
I GUESS I'LL HAVE TO BE SATISFIED WITH THAT! I RESPECT YOUR LOYALTY TO THE ARMY, STEVE-I WON'T FOLLOW YOU!
BUT TAKE THESE TABLETS IF YOU ARE INJURED! THEY CONTAIN THE PURPLE HEALING RAY I DISCOVERED ON PARADISE ISLAND!
THANKS-WILL DO! GOODBYE, WONDERFUL WOMAN!
LONG, ANXIOUS DAYS PASS BUT NO WORD COMES FROM STEVE.
YOU HAVEN'T HEARD FROM STEVE HAVE YOU, COLONEL? YOU'RE NOT KEEPING ANYTHING BACK?
OF COURSE NOT, DIANA! I'M WORRIED ABOUT HIM MYSELF!
THIS IS WONDER WOMAN! HAS ANY MESSAGE COME FOR ME FROM STEVE?
WOO WOO! SWELL TO HEAR FROM YOU, WONDER WOMAN. NO, I HAVEN'T HEARD FROM HIM AT ALL!
NIGHT AFTER NIGHT, WONDER WOMAN WAITS, WITH A GNAWING ANXIETY, FOR A MESSAGE THAT NEVER COMES.
WAR HAS TAKEN STEVE FROM ME - HOW I HATE IT! MARS'S VICIOUS LUST FOR POWER IS DESTROYING THIS MAN'S WORLD-AND ME!

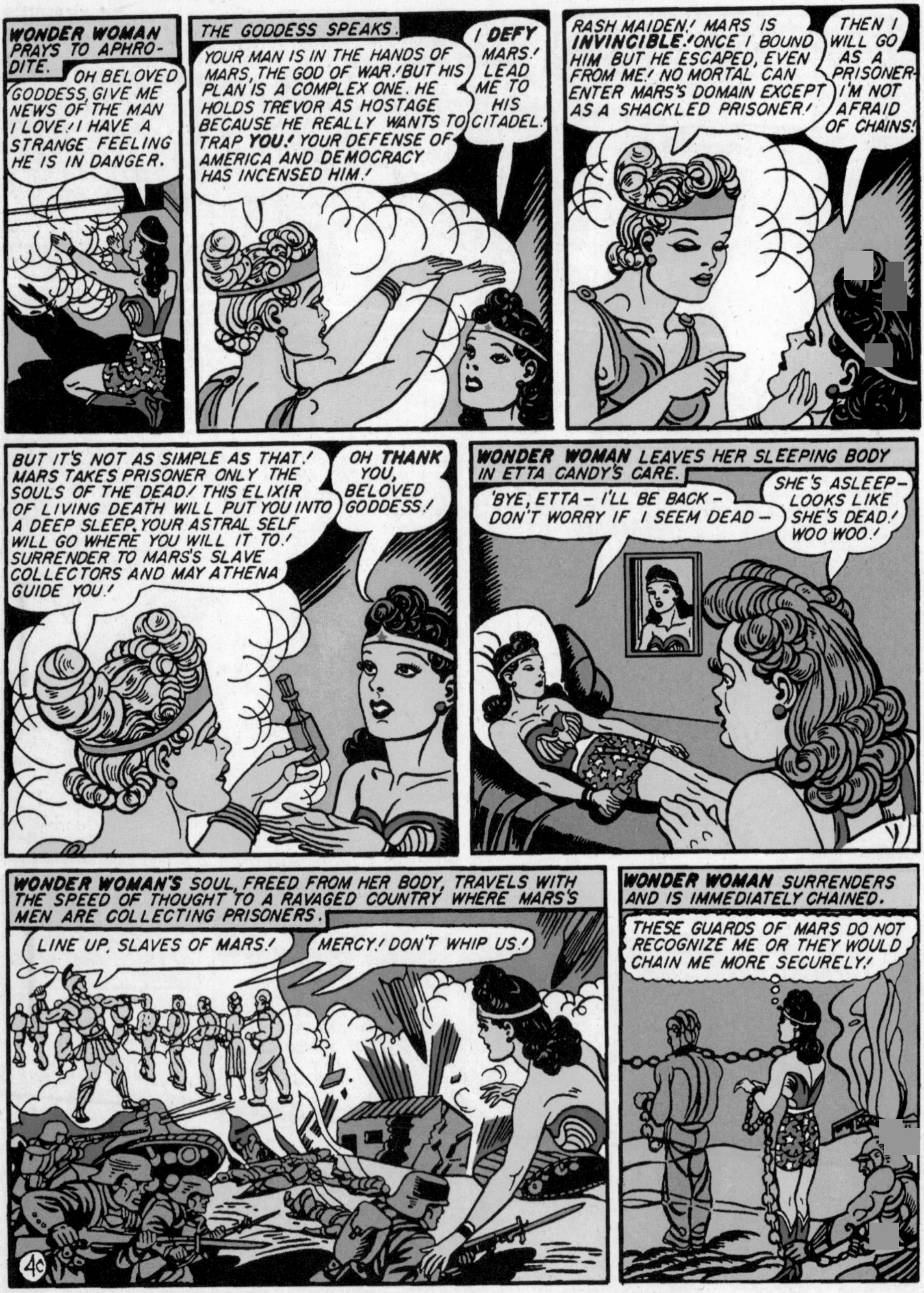

WONDER WOMAN PRAYS TO APHRODITE.
OH BELOVED GODDESS, GIVE ME NEWS OF THE MAN I LOVE! I HAVE A STRANGE FEELING HE IS IN DANGER.
THE GODDESS SPEAKS.
YOUR MAN IS IN THE HANDS OF MARS, THE GOD OF WAR! BUT HIS PLAN IS A COMPLEX ONE. HE HOLDS TREVOR AS HOSTAGE BECAUSE HE REALLY WANTS TO TRAP YOU! YOUR DEFENSE OF AMERICA AND DEMOCRACY HAS INCENSED HIM!
I DEFY MARS! LEAD ME TO HIS CITADEL!
RASH MAIDEN! MARS IS INVINCIBLE! ONCE I BOUND HIM BUT HE ESCAPED, EVEN FROM ME! NO MORTAL CAN ENTER MARS'S DOMAIN EXCEPT AS A SHACKLED PRISONER!
THEN I WILL GO AS A PRISONER- I'M NOT AFRAID OF CHAINS!
BUT IT'S NOT AS SIMPLE AS THAT! MARS TAKES PRISONER ONLY THE SOULS OF THE DEAD! THIS ELIXIR OF LIVING DEATH WILL PUT YOU INTO A DEEP SLEEP. YOUR ASTRAL SELF WILL GO WHERE YOU WILL IT TO! SURRENDER TO MARS'S SLAVE COLLECTORS AND MAY ATHENA GUIDE YOU!
OH THANK YOU, BELOVED GODDESS!
WONDER WOMAN LEAVES HER SLEEPING BODY IN ETTA CANDY'S CARE.
'BYE, ETTA - I'LL BE BACK - DON'T WORRY IF I SEEM DEAD -
SHE'S ASLEEP- LOOKS LIKE SHE'S DEAD! WOO WOO!
WONDER WOMAN'S SOUL, FREED FROM HER BODY, TRAVELS WITH THE SPEED OF THOUGHT TO A RAVAGED COUNTRY WHERE MARS'S MEN ARE COLLECTING PRISONERS.
LINE UP, SLAVES OF MARS!
MERCY! DON'T WHIP US!
4c
WONDER WOMAN SURRENDERS AND IS IMMEDIATELY CHAINED.
THESE GUARDS OF MARS DO NOT RECOGNIZE ME OR THEY WOULD CHAIN ME MORE SECURELY!

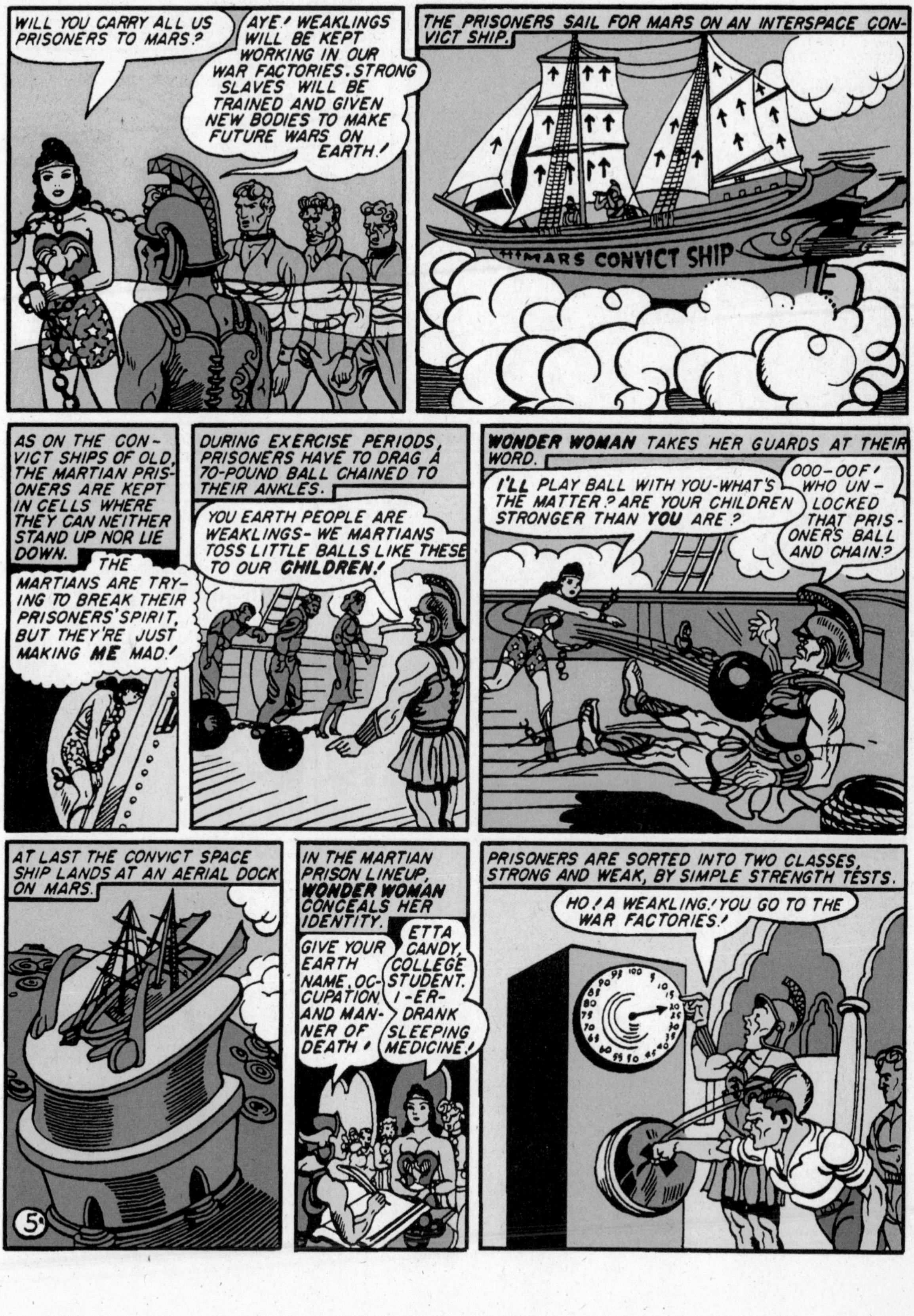
WILL YOU CARRY ALL US PRISONERS TO MARS?
AYE! WEAKLINGS WILL BE KEPT WORKING IN OUR WAR FACTORIES. STRONG SLAVES WILL BE TRAINED AND GIVEN NEW BODIES TO MAKE FUTURE WARS ON EARTH!
THE PRISONERS SAIL FOR MARS ON AN INTERSPACE CONVICT SHIP.
MARS CONVICT SHIP
AS ON THE CONVICT SHIPS OF OLD, THE MARTIAN PRISONERS ARE KEPT IN CELLS WHERE THEY CAN NEITHER STAND UP NOR LIE DOWN.
THE MARTIANS ARE TRYING TO BREAK THEIR PRISONERS' SPIRIT, BUT THEY'RE JUST MAKING ME MAD!
DURING EXERCISE PERIODS, PRISONERS HAVE TO DRAG A 70-POUND BALL CHAINED TO THEIR ANKLES.
YOU EARTH PEOPLE ARE WEAKLINGS- WE MARTIANS TOSS LITTLE BALLS LIKE THESE TO OUR CHILDREN!
WONDER WOMAN TAKES HER GUARDS AT THEIR WORD.
I'LL PLAY BALL WITH YOU-WHAT'S THE MATTER? ARE YOUR CHILDREN STRONGER THAN YOU ARE?
OOO-OOF! WHO UNLOCKED THAT PRISONER'S BALL AND CHAIN?
AT LAST THE CONVICT SPACE SHIP LANDS AT AN AERIAL DOCK ON MARS.
5
IN THE MARTIAN PRISON LINEUP, WONDER WOMAN CONCEALS HER IDENTITY.
GIVE YOUR EARTH NAME, OCCUPATION AND MANNER OF DEATH!
ETTA CANDY, COLLEGE STUDENT. I-ER-DRANK SLEEPING MEDICINE!
PRISONERS ARE SORTED INTO TWO CLASSES, STRONG AND WEAK, BY SIMPLE STRENGTH TESTS.
HO! A WEAKLING! YOU GO TO THE WAR FACTORIES!

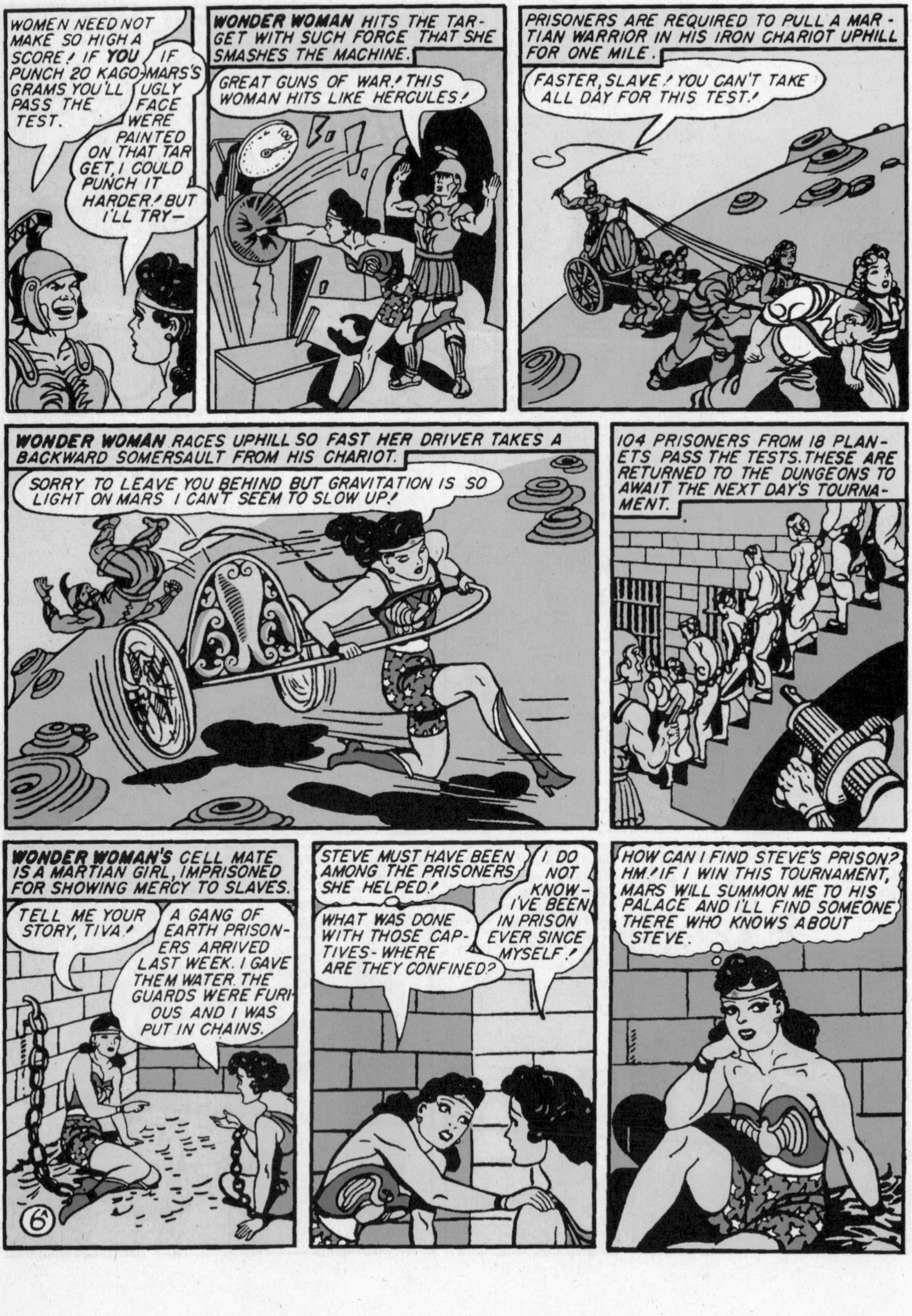
WOMEN NEED NOT MAKE SO HIGH A SCORE! IF YOU PUNCH 20 KAGO-GRAMS YOU'LL PASS THE TEST.
IF MARS'S UGLY FACE WERE PAINTED ON THAT TARGET, I COULD PUNCH IT HARDER! BUT I'LL TRY—
WONDER WOMAN HITS THE TARGET WITH SUCH FORCE THAT SHE SMASHES THE MACHINE.
GREAT GUNS OF WAR! THIS WOMAN HITS LIKE HERCULES!
PRISONERS ARE REQUIRED TO PULL A MARTIAN WARRIOR IN HIS IRON CHARIOT UPHILL FOR ONE MILE.
FASTER, SLAVE! YOU CAN'T TAKE ALL DAY FOR THIS TEST!
WONDER WOMAN RACES UPHILL SO FAST HER DRIVER TAKES A BACKWARD SOMERSAULT FROM HIS CHARIOT.
SORRY TO LEAVE YOU BEHIND BUT GRAVITATION IS SO LIGHT ON MARS I CAN'T SEEM TO SLOW UP!
104 PRISONERS FROM 18 PLANETS PASS THE TESTS. THESE ARE RETURNED TO THE DUNGEONS TO AWAIT THE NEXT DAY'S TOURNAMENT.
WONDER WOMAN'S CELL MATE IS A MARTIAN GIRL, IMPRISONED FOR SHOWING MERCY TO SLAVES.
TELL ME YOUR STORY, TIVA!
A GANG OF EARTH PRISONERS ARRIVED LAST WEEK. I GAVE THEM WATER. THE GUARDS WERE FURIOUS AND I WAS PUT IN CHAINS.
6
STEVE MUST HAVE BEEN AMONG THE PRISONERS SHE HELPED!
WHAT WAS DONE WITH THOSE CAPTIVES- WHERE ARE THEY CONFINED?
I DO NOT KNOW- I'VE BEEN IN PRISON EVER SINCE MYSELF!
HOW CAN I FIND STEVE'S PRISON? HM! IF I WIN THIS TOURNAMENT, MARS WILL SUMMON ME TO HIS PALACE AND I'LL FIND SOMEONE THERE WHO KNOWS ABOUT STEVE.

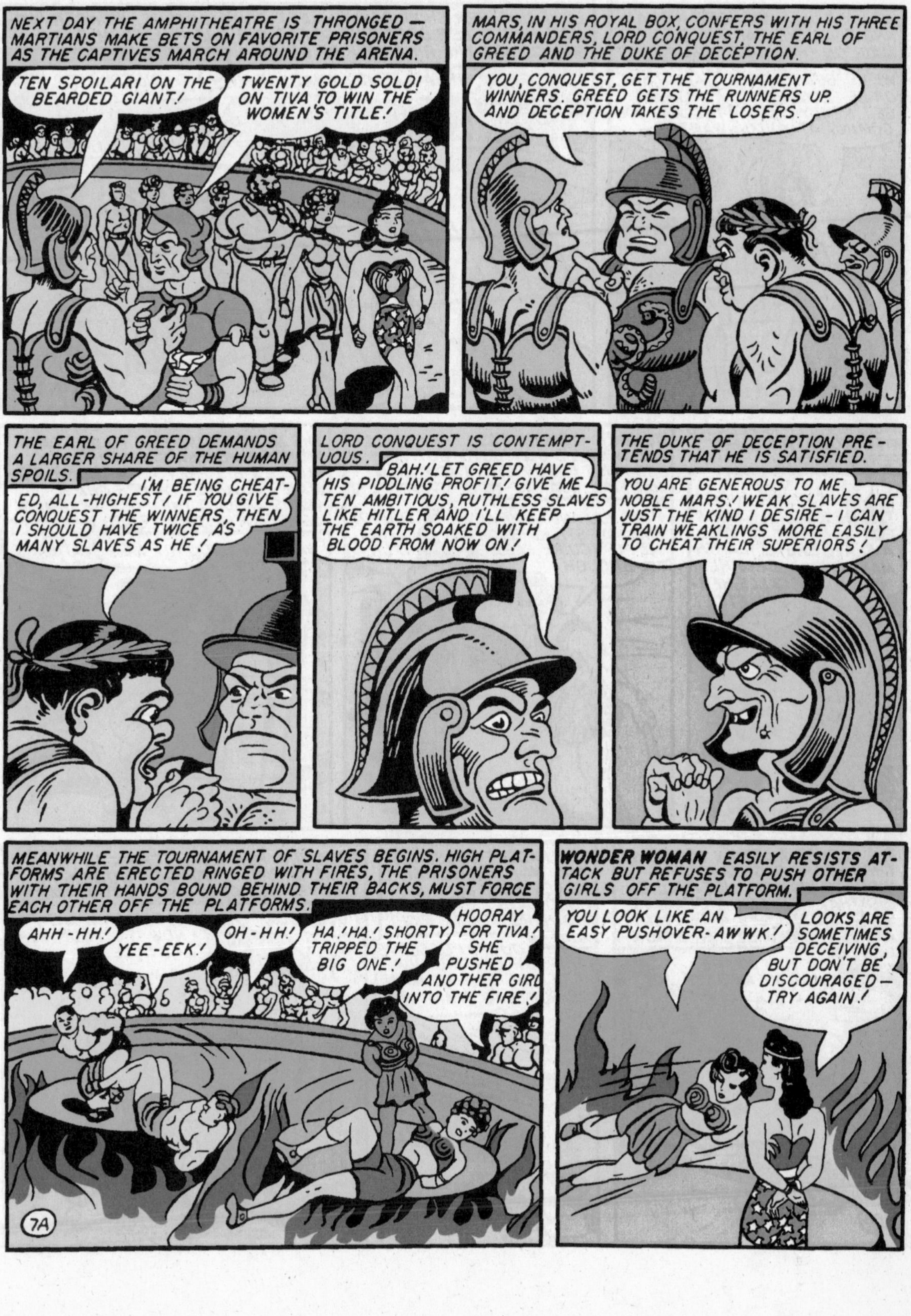
NEXT DAY THE AMPHITHEATRE IS THRONGED — MARTIANS MAKE BETS ON FAVORITE PRISONERS AS THE CAPTIVES MARCH AROUND THE ARENA.
TEN SPOILARI ON THE BEARDED GIANT!
TWENTY GOLD SOLDI ON TIVA TO WIN THE WOMEN'S TITLE!
MARS, IN HIS ROYAL BOX, CONFERS WITH HIS THREE COMMANDERS, LORD CONQUEST, THE EARL OF GREED AND THE DUKE OF DECEPTION.
YOU, CONQUEST, GET THE TOURNAMENT WINNERS. GREED GETS THE RUNNERS UP. AND DECEPTION TAKES THE LOSERS.
THE EARL OF GREED DEMANDS A LARGER SHARE OF THE HUMAN SPOILS.
I'M BEING CHEATED, ALL-HIGHEST! IF YOU GIVE CONQUEST THE WINNERS, THEN I SHOULD HAVE TWICE AS MANY SLAVES AS HE!
LORD CONQUEST IS CONTEMPTUOUS.
BAH! LET GREED HAVE HIS PIDDLING PROFIT! GIVE ME TEN AMBITIOUS, RUTHLESS SLAVES LIKE HITLER AND I'LL KEEP THE EARTH SOAKED WITH BLOOD FROM NOW ON!
THE DUKE OF DECEPTION PRETENDS THAT HE IS SATISFIED.
YOU ARE GENEROUS TO ME, NOBLE MARS! WEAK SLAVES ARE JUST THE KIND I DESIRE - I CAN TRAIN WEAKLINGS MORE EASILY TO CHEAT THEIR SUPERIORS!
MEANWHILE THE TOURNAMENT OF SLAVES BEGINS. HIGH PLATFORMS ARE ERECTED RINGED WITH FIRES, THE PRISONERS WITH THEIR HANDS BOUND BEHIND THEIR BACKS, MUST FORCE EACH OTHER OFF THE PLATFORMS.
AHH-HH!
YEE-EEK!
OH-HH!
HA! HA! SHORTY TRIPPED THE BIG ONE!
HOORAY FOR TIVA! SHE PUSHED ANOTHER GIRL INTO THE FIRE!
7A
WONDER WOMAN EASILY RESISTS ATTACK BUT REFUSES TO PUSH OTHER GIRLS OFF THE PLATFORM.
YOU LOOK LIKE AN EASY PUSHOVER- AWWK!
LOOKS ARE SOMETIMES DECEIVING, BUT DON'T BE DISCOURAGED — TRY AGAIN!

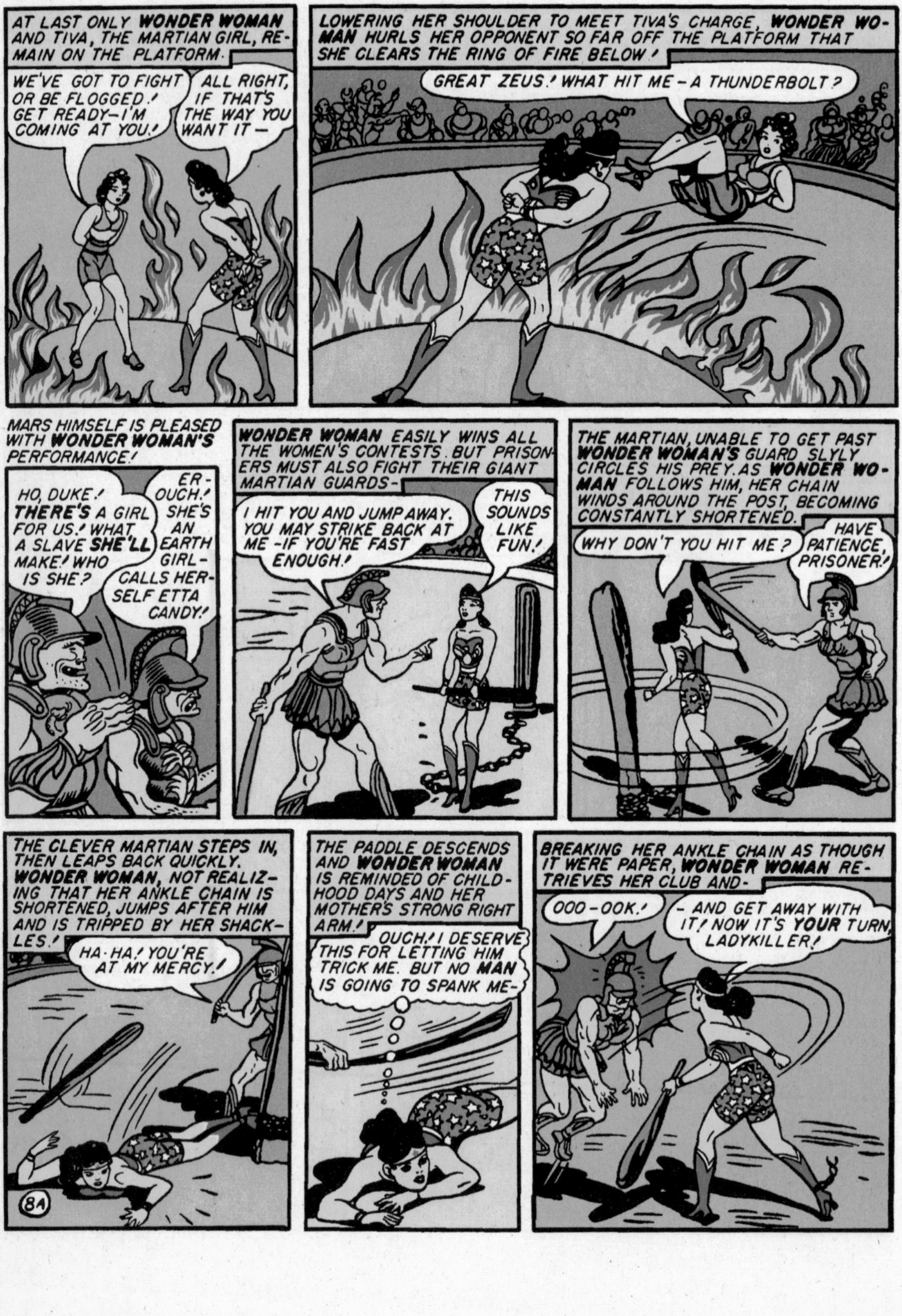
AT LAST ONLY WONDER WOMAN AND TIVA, THE MARTIAN GIRL, REMAIN ON THE PLATFORM.
WE'VE GOT TO FIGHT OR BE FLOGGED! GET READY—I'M COMING AT YOU!
ALL RIGHT, IF THAT'S THE WAY YOU WANT IT —
LOWERING HER SHOULDER TO MEET TIVA'S CHARGE, WONDER WOMAN HURLS HER OPPONENT SO FAR OFF THE PLATFORM THAT SHE CLEARS THE RING OF FIRE BELOW!
GREAT ZEUS! WHAT HIT ME — A THUNDERBOLT?
MARS HIMSELF IS PLEASED WITH WONDER WOMAN'S PERFORMANCE!
HO, DUKE! THERE'S A GIRL FOR US! WHAT A SLAVE SHE'LL MAKE! WHO IS SHE?
ER-OUCH! SHE'S AN EARTH GIRL- CALLS HERSELF ETTA CANDY!
WONDER WOMAN EASILY WINS ALL THE WOMEN'S CONTESTS. BUT PRISONERS MUST ALSO FIGHT THEIR GIANT MARTIAN GUARDS-
I HIT YOU AND JUMP AWAY. YOU MAY STRIKE BACK AT ME -IF YOU'RE FAST ENOUGH!
THIS SOUNDS LIKE FUN!
THE MARTIAN, UNABLE TO GET PAST WONDER WOMAN'S GUARD SLYLY CIRCLES HIS PREY. AS WONDER WOMAN FOLLOWS HIM, HER CHAIN WINDS AROUND THE POST, BECOMING CONSTANTLY SHORTENED.
WHY DON'T YOU HIT ME?
HAVE PATIENCE, PRISONER!
THE CLEVER MARTIAN STEPS IN, THEN LEAPS BACK QUICKLY. WONDER WOMAN, NOT REALIZING THAT HER ANKLE CHAIN IS SHORTENED, JUMPS AFTER HIM AND IS TRIPPED BY HER SHACKLES!
HA-HA! YOU'RE AT MY MERCY!
8A
THE PADDLE DESCENDS AND WONDER WOMAN IS REMINDED OF CHILDHOOD DAYS AND HER MOTHER'S STRONG RIGHT ARM!
OUCH! I DESERVE THIS FOR LETTING HIM TRICK ME. BUT NO MAN IS GOING TO SPANK ME-
BREAKING HER ANKLE CHAIN AS THOUGH IT WERE PAPER, WONDER WOMAN RETRIEVES HER CLUB AND-
OOO-OOK!
- AND GET AWAY WITH IT! NOW IT'S YOUR TURN, LADYKILLER!

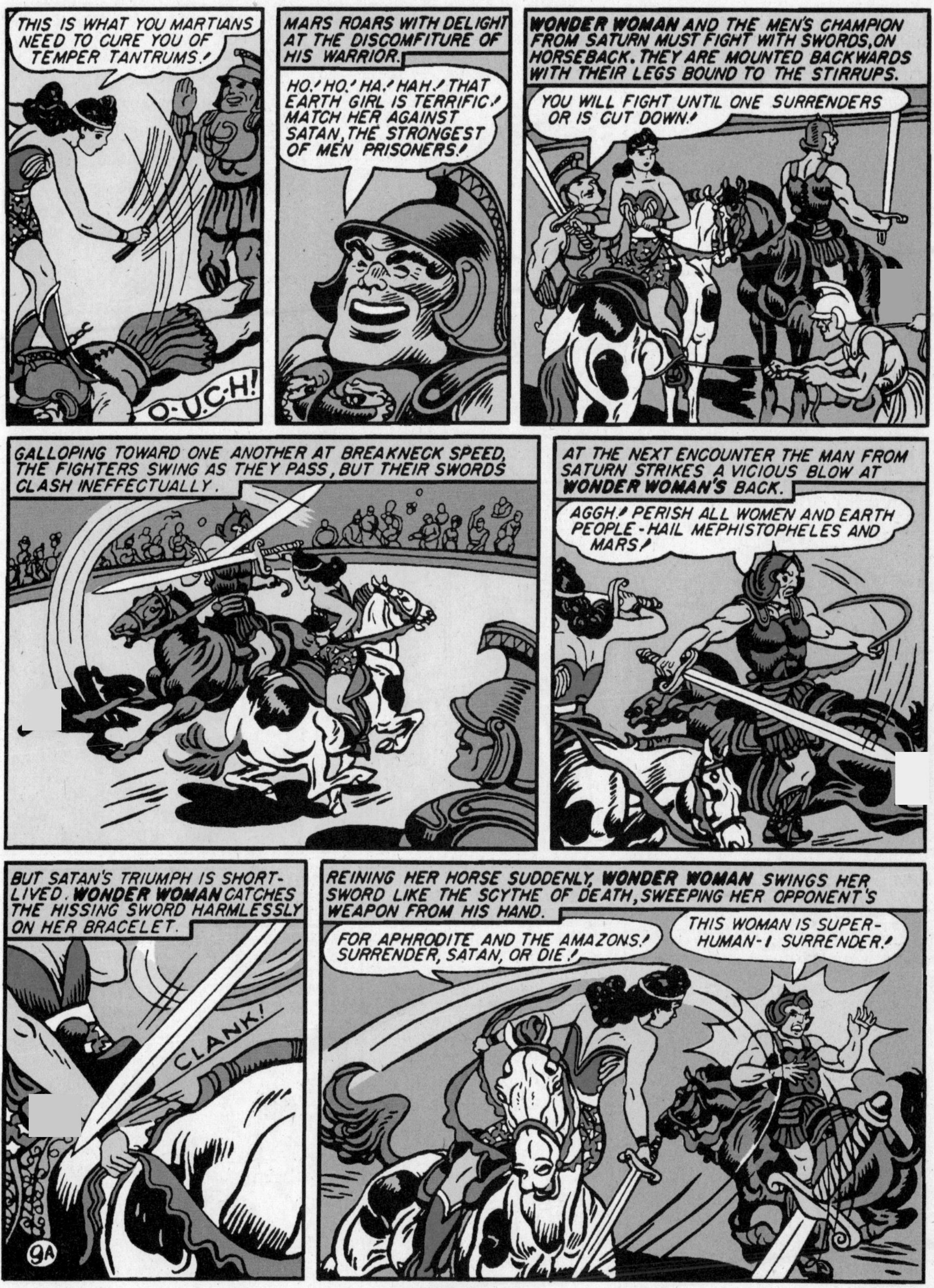
THIS IS WHAT YOU MARTIANS NEED TO CURE YOU OF TEMPER TANTRUMS!
O-U-C-H!
MARS ROARS WITH DELIGHT AT THE DISCOMFITURE OF HIS WARRIOR.
HO! HO! HA! HAH! THAT EARTH GIRL IS TERRIFIC! MATCH HER AGAINST SATAN, THE STRONGEST OF MEN PRISONERS!
WONDER WOMAN AND THE MEN'S CHAMPION FROM SATURN MUST FIGHT WITH SWORDS, ON HORSEBACK. THEY ARE MOUNTED BACKWARDS WITH THEIR LEGS BOUND TO THE STIRRUPS.
YOU WILL FIGHT UNTIL ONE SURRENDERS OR IS CUT DOWN!
GALLOPING TOWARD ONE ANOTHER AT BREAKNECK SPEED, THE FIGHTERS SWING AS THEY PASS, BUT THEIR SWORDS CLASH INEFFECTUALLY.
AT THE NEXT ENCOUNTER THE MAN FROM SATURN STRIKES A VICIOUS BLOW AT WONDER WOMAN'S BACK.
AGGH! PERISH ALL WOMEN AND EARTH PEOPLE - HAIL MEPHISTOPHELES AND MARS!
BUT SATAN'S TRIUMPH IS SHORT-LIVED. WONDER WOMAN CATCHES THE HISSING SWORD HARMLESSLY ON HER BRACELET.
CLANK!
9A
REINING HER HORSE SUDDENLY, WONDER WOMAN SWINGS HER SWORD LIKE THE SCYTHE OF DEATH, SWEEPING HER OPPONENT'S WEAPON FROM HIS HAND.
FOR APHRODITE AND THE AMAZONS! SURRENDER, SATAN, OR DIE!
THIS WOMAN IS SUPER-HUMAN - I SURRENDER!

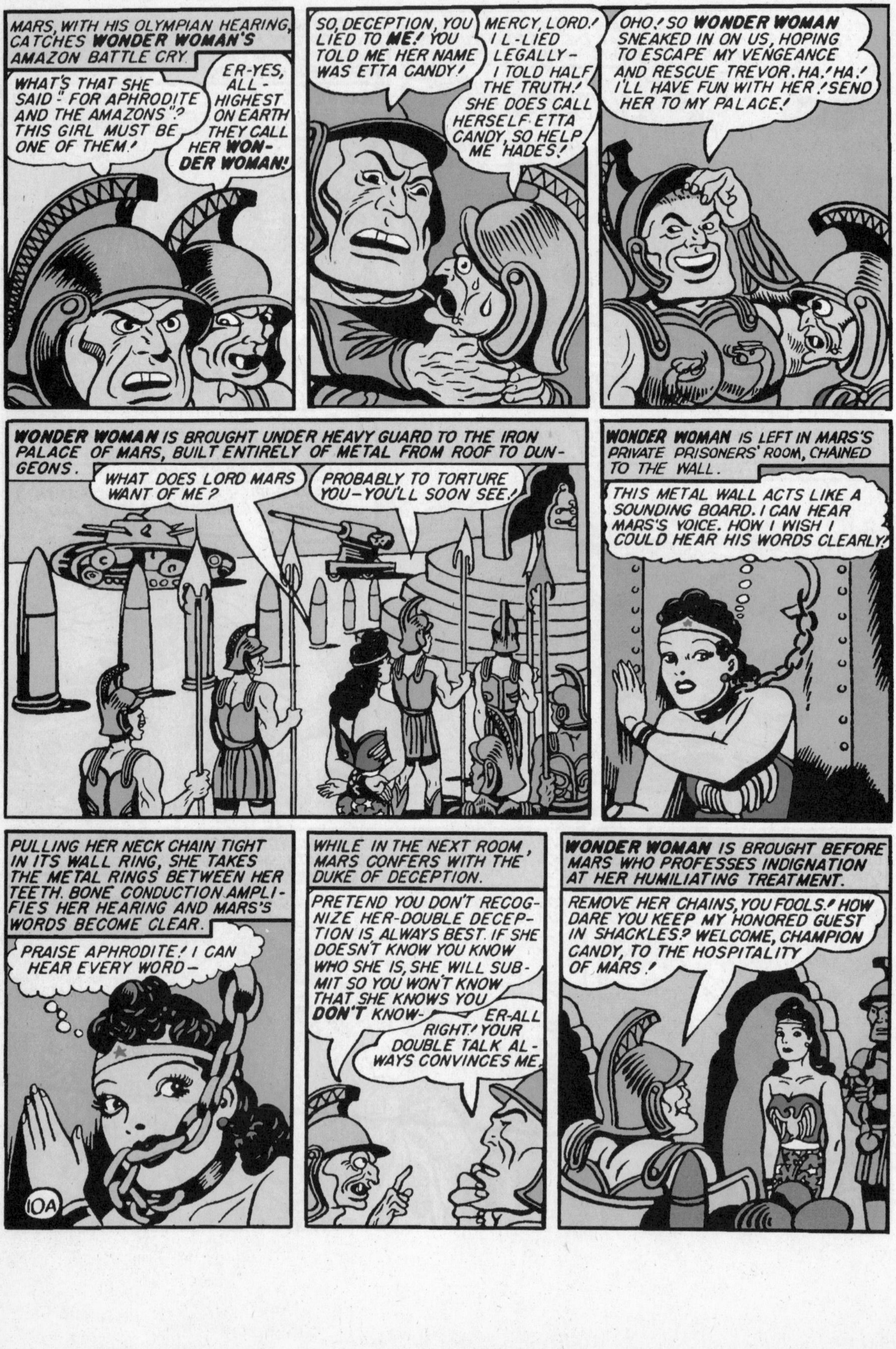
MARS, WITH HIS OLYMPIAN HEARING, CATCHES **WONDER WOMAN'S** AMAZON BATTLE CRY.
WHAT'S THAT SHE SAID - "FOR APHRODITE AND THE AMAZONS"? THIS GIRL MUST BE ONE OF THEM!
ER-YES, ALL-HIGHEST ON EARTH THEY CALL HER **WONDER WOMAN!**
SO, DECEPTION, YOU LIED TO **ME!** YOU TOLD ME HER NAME WAS ETTA CANDY!
MERCY, LORD! I L-LIED LEGALLY - I TOLD HALF THE TRUTH! SHE DOES CALL HERSELF ETTA CANDY, SO HELP ME HADES!
OHO! SO **WONDER WOMAN** SNEAKED IN ON US, HOPING TO ESCAPE MY VENGEANCE AND RESCUE TREVOR. HA! HA! I'LL HAVE FUN WITH HER! SEND HER TO MY PALACE!
WONDER WOMAN IS BROUGHT UNDER HEAVY GUARD TO THE IRON PALACE OF MARS, BUILT ENTIRELY OF METAL FROM ROOF TO DUNGEONS.
WHAT DOES LORD MARS WANT OF ME?
PROBABLY TO TORTURE YOU-YOU'LL SOON SEE!
WONDER WOMAN IS LEFT IN MARS'S PRIVATE PRISONERS' ROOM, CHAINED TO THE WALL.
THIS METAL WALL ACTS LIKE A SOUNDING BOARD. I CAN HEAR MARS'S VOICE. HOW I WISH I COULD HEAR HIS WORDS CLEARLY!
PULLING HER NECK CHAIN TIGHT IN ITS WALL RING, SHE TAKES THE METAL RINGS BETWEEN HER TEETH. BONE CONDUCTION AMPLIFIES HER HEARING AND MARS'S WORDS BECOME CLEAR.
PRAISE APHRODITE! I CAN HEAR EVERY WORD-
10A
WHILE IN THE NEXT ROOM, MARS CONFERS WITH THE DUKE OF DECEPTION.
PRETEND YOU DON'T RECOGNIZE HER-DOUBLE DECEPTION IS ALWAYS BEST. IF SHE DOESN'T KNOW YOU KNOW WHO SHE IS, SHE WILL SUBMIT SO YOU WON'T KNOW THAT SHE KNOWS YOU **DON'T** KNOW-
ER-ALL RIGHT! YOUR DOUBLE TALK ALWAYS CONVINCES ME.
WONDER WOMAN IS BROUGHT BEFORE MARS WHO PROFESSES INDIGNATION AT HER HUMILIATING TREATMENT.
REMOVE HER CHAINS, YOU FOOLS! HOW DARE YOU KEEP MY HONORED GUEST IN SHACKLES? WELCOME, CHAMPION CANDY, TO THE HOSPITALITY OF MARS!

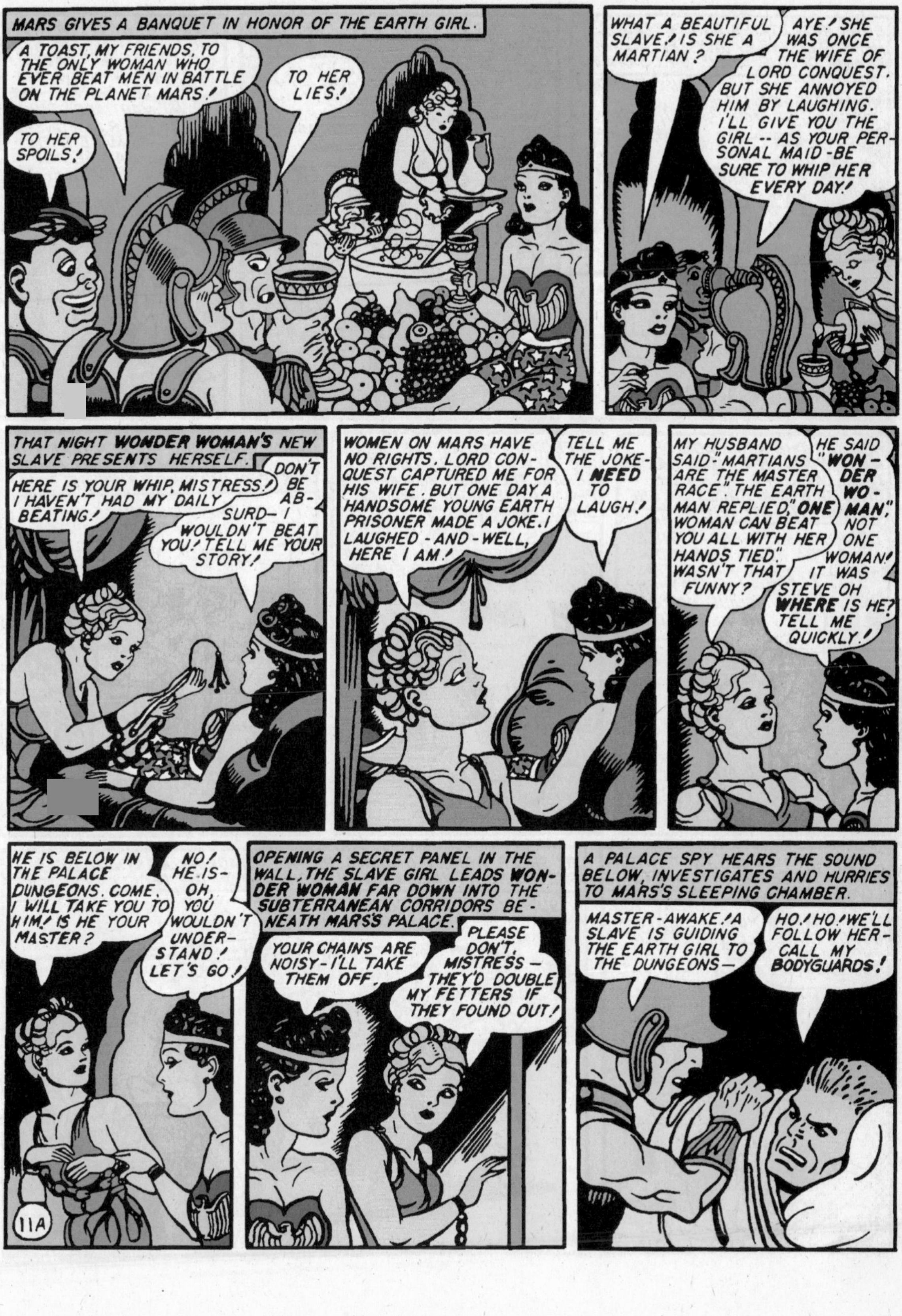
MARS GIVES A BANQUET IN HONOR OF THE EARTH GIRL.
A TOAST, MY FRIENDS, TO THE ONLY WOMAN WHO EVER BEAT MEN IN BATTLE ON THE PLANET MARS!
TO HER LIES!
TO HER SPOILS!
WHAT A BEAUTIFUL SLAVE! IS SHE A MARTIAN?
AYE! SHE WAS ONCE THE WIFE OF LORD CONQUEST. BUT SHE ANNOYED HIM BY LAUGHING. I'LL GIVE YOU THE GIRL -- AS YOUR PERSONAL MAID - BE SURE TO WHIP HER EVERY DAY!
THAT NIGHT WONDER WOMAN'S NEW SLAVE PRESENTS HERSELF.
HERE IS YOUR WHIP, MISTRESS! I HAVEN'T HAD MY DAILY BEATING!
DON'T BE AB- SURD- I WOULDN'T BEAT YOU! TELL ME YOUR STORY!
WOMEN ON MARS HAVE NO RIGHTS. LORD CONQUEST CAPTURED ME FOR HIS WIFE. BUT ONE DAY A HANDSOME YOUNG EARTH PRISONER MADE A JOKE. I LAUGHED - AND - WELL, HERE I AM!
TELL ME THE JOKE - I NEED TO LAUGH!
MY HUSBAND SAID-"MARTIANS ARE THE MASTER RACE." THE EARTH MAN REPLIED, "ONE WOMAN CAN BEAT YOU ALL WITH HER HANDS TIED." WASN'T THAT FUNNY?
HE SAID "WONDER WOMAN," NOT ONE WOMAN! IT WAS STEVE OH WHERE IS HE? TELL ME QUICKLY!
HE IS BELOW IN THE PALACE DUNGEONS. COME. I WILL TAKE YOU TO HIM! IS HE YOUR MASTER?
NO! HE IS- OH, YOU WOULDN'T UNDERSTAND! LET'S GO!
11A
OPENING A SECRET PANEL IN THE WALL, THE SLAVE GIRL LEADS WONDER WOMAN FAR DOWN INTO THE SUBTERRANEAN CORRIDORS BENEATH MARS'S PALACE.
YOUR CHAINS ARE NOISY - I'LL TAKE THEM OFF.
PLEASE DON'T, MISTRESS - THEY'D DOUBLE MY FETTERS IF THEY FOUND OUT!
A PALACE SPY HEARS THE SOUND BELOW, INVESTIGATES AND HURRIES TO MARS'S SLEEPING CHAMBER.
MASTER - AWAKE! A SLAVE IS GUIDING THE EARTH GIRL TO THE DUNGEONS -
HO! HO! WE'LL FOLLOW HER - CALL MY BODYGUARDS!

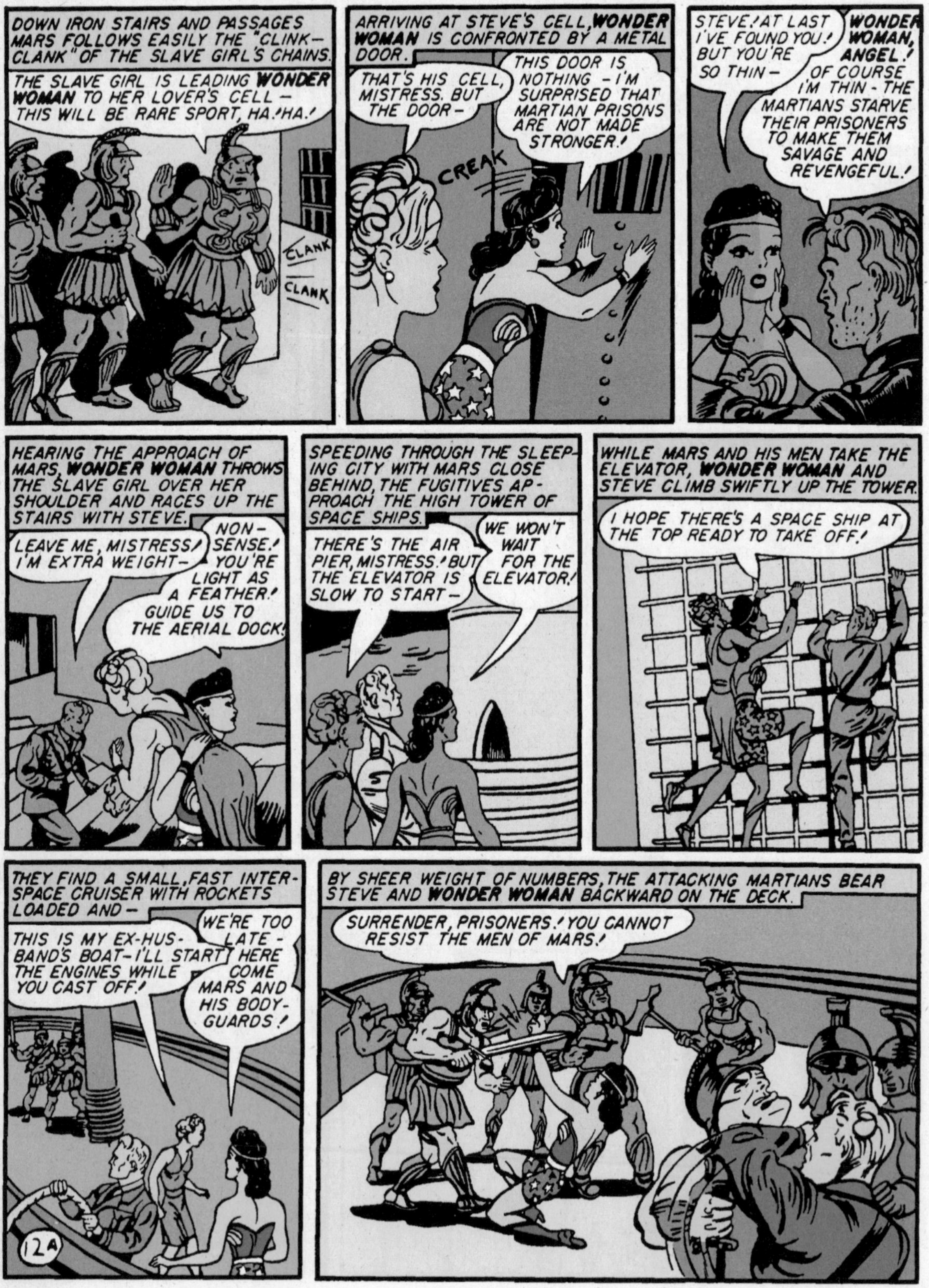
DOWN IRON STAIRS AND PASSAGES MARS FOLLOWS EASILY THE "CLINK-CLANK" OF THE SLAVE GIRL'S CHAINS.
THE SLAVE GIRL IS LEADING **WONDER WOMAN** TO HER LOVER'S CELL — THIS WILL BE RARE SPORT, HA! HA!
CLANK
CLANK
ARRIVING AT STEVE'S CELL, **WONDER WOMAN** IS CONFRONTED BY A METAL DOOR.
THAT'S HIS CELL, MISTRESS. BUT THE DOOR —
THIS DOOR IS NOTHING — I'M SURPRISED THAT MARTIAN PRISONS ARE NOT MADE STRONGER!
CREAK
STEVE! AT LAST I'VE FOUND YOU! BUT YOU'RE SO THIN —
WONDER WOMAN, ANGEL! OF COURSE I'M THIN - THE MARTIANS STARVE THEIR PRISONERS TO MAKE THEM SAVAGE AND REVENGEFUL!
HEARING THE APPROACH OF MARS, **WONDER WOMAN** THROWS THE SLAVE GIRL OVER HER SHOULDER AND RACES UP THE STAIRS WITH STEVE.
LEAVE ME, MISTRESS! I'M EXTRA WEIGHT —
NONSENSE! YOU'RE LIGHT AS A FEATHER! GUIDE US TO THE AERIAL DOCK!
SPEEDING THROUGH THE SLEEPING CITY WITH MARS CLOSE BEHIND, THE FUGITIVES APPROACH THE HIGH TOWER OF SPACE SHIPS.
THERE'S THE AIR PIER, MISTRESS! BUT THE ELEVATOR IS SLOW TO START —
WE WON'T WAIT FOR THE ELEVATOR!
WHILE MARS AND HIS MEN TAKE THE ELEVATOR, **WONDER WOMAN** AND STEVE CLIMB SWIFTLY UP THE TOWER.
I HOPE THERE'S A SPACE SHIP AT THE TOP READY TO TAKE OFF!
THEY FIND A SMALL, FAST INTER-SPACE CRUISER WITH ROCKETS LOADED AND —
THIS IS MY EX-HUSBAND'S BOAT — I'LL START THE ENGINES WHILE YOU CAST OFF!
WE'RE TOO LATE — HERE COME MARS AND HIS BODYGUARDS!
12A
BY SHEER WEIGHT OF NUMBERS, THE ATTACKING MARTIANS BEAR STEVE AND **WONDER WOMAN** BACKWARD ON THE DECK.
SURRENDER, PRISONERS! YOU CANNOT RESIST THE MEN OF MARS!

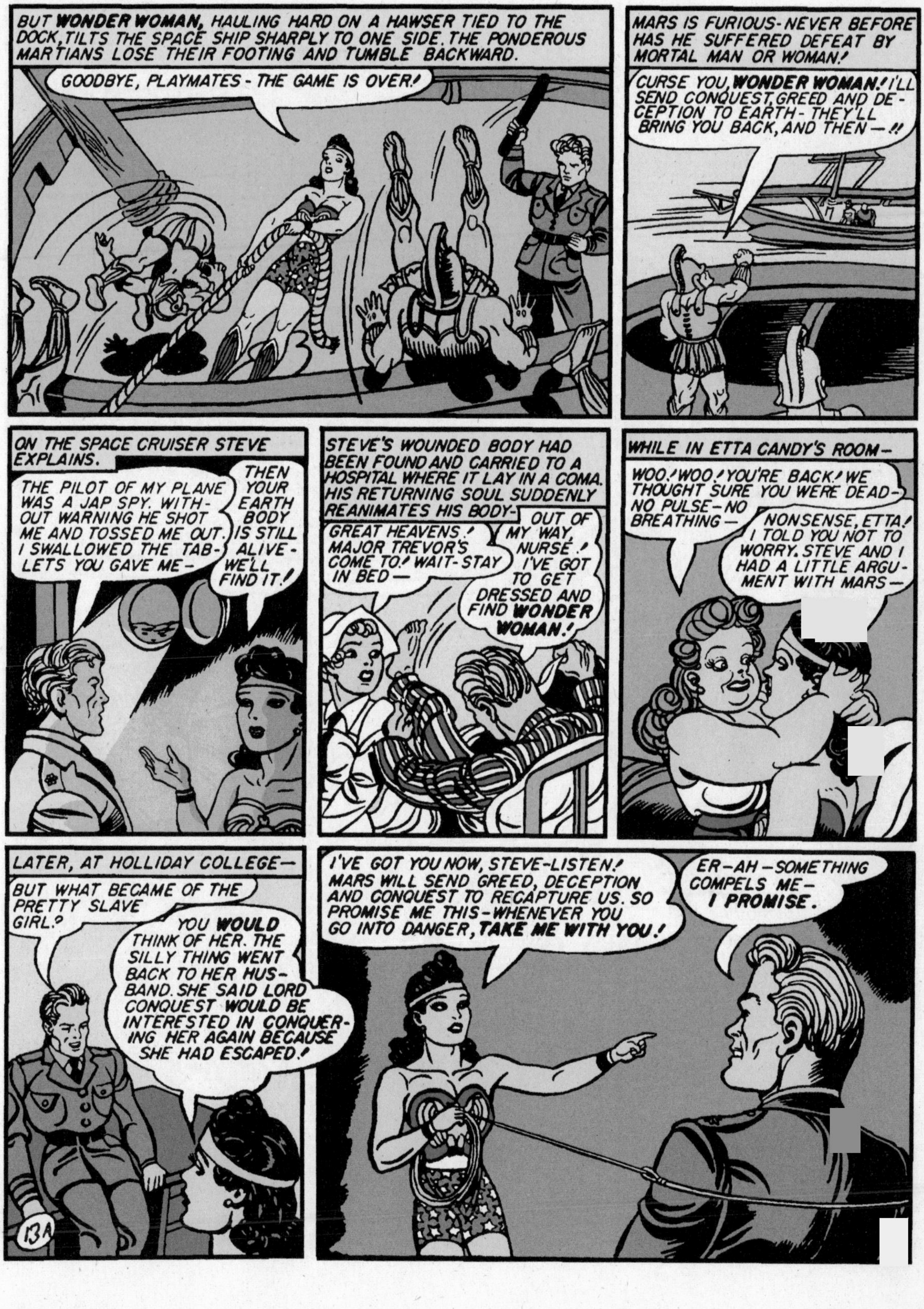

BUT WONDER WOMAN, HAULING HARD ON A HAWSER TIED TO THE DOCK, TILTS THE SPACE SHIP SHARPLY TO ONE SIDE. THE PONDEROUS MARTIANS LOSE THEIR FOOTING AND TUMBLE BACKWARD.
GOODBYE, PLAYMATES - THE GAME IS OVER!
MARS IS FURIOUS - NEVER BEFORE HAS HE SUFFERED DEFEAT BY MORTAL MAN OR WOMAN!
CURSE YOU, WONDER WOMAN! I'LL SEND CONQUEST, GREED AND DECEPTION TO EARTH - THEY'LL BRING YOU BACK, AND THEN —!!
ON THE SPACE CRUISER STEVE EXPLAINS.
THE PILOT OF MY PLANE WAS A JAP SPY. WITHOUT WARNING HE SHOT ME AND TOSSED ME OUT. I SWALLOWED THE TABLETS YOU GAVE ME—
THEN YOUR EARTH BODY IS STILL ALIVE - WE'LL FIND IT!
STEVE'S WOUNDED BODY HAD BEEN FOUND AND CARRIED TO A HOSPITAL WHERE IT LAY IN A COMA. HIS RETURNING SOUL SUDDENLY REANIMATES HIS BODY-
GREAT HEAVENS! MAJOR TREVOR'S COME TO! WAIT - STAY IN BED —
OUT OF MY WAY, NURSE! I'VE GOT TO GET DRESSED AND FIND WONDER WOMAN!
WHILE IN ETTA CANDY'S ROOM—
WOO! WOO! YOU'RE BACK! WE THOUGHT SURE YOU WERE DEAD - NO PULSE - NO BREATHING—
NONSENSE, ETTA! I TOLD YOU NOT TO WORRY. STEVE AND I HAD A LITTLE ARGUMENT WITH MARS—
LATER, AT HOLLIDAY COLLEGE—
BUT WHAT BECAME OF THE PRETTY SLAVE GIRL?
YOU WOULD THINK OF HER. THE SILLY THING WENT BACK TO HER HUSBAND. SHE SAID LORD CONQUEST WOULD BE INTERESTED IN CONQUERING HER AGAIN BECAUSE SHE HAD ESCAPED!
13A
I'VE GOT YOU NOW, STEVE - LISTEN! MARS WILL SEND GREED, DECEPTION AND CONQUEST TO RECAPTURE US. SO PROMISE ME THIS - WHENEVER YOU GO INTO DANGER, TAKE ME WITH YOU!
ER-AH - SOMETHING COMPELS ME - I PROMISE.

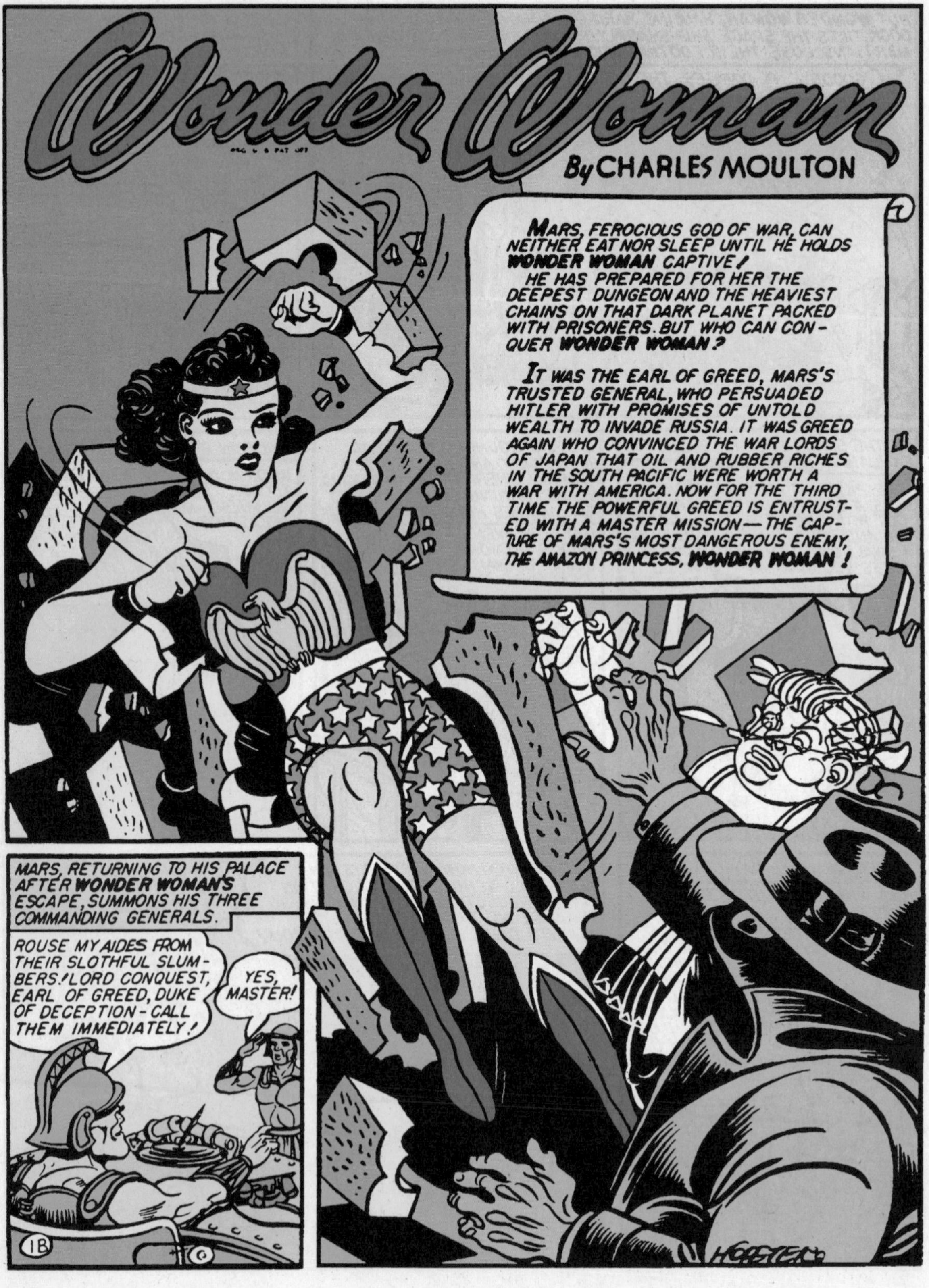

Wonder Woman
By CHARLES MOULTON
MARS, FEROCIOUS GOD OF WAR, CAN NEITHER EAT NOR SLEEP UNTIL HE HOLDS WONDER WOMAN CAPTIVE! HE HAS PREPARED FOR HER THE DEEPEST DUNGEON AND THE HEAVIEST CHAINS ON THAT DARK PLANET PACKED WITH PRISONERS. BUT WHO CAN CONQUER WONDER WOMAN?
IT WAS THE EARL OF GREED, MARS'S TRUSTED GENERAL, WHO PERSUADED HITLER WITH PROMISES OF UNTOLD WEALTH TO INVADE RUSSIA. IT WAS GREED AGAIN WHO CONVINCED THE WAR LORDS OF JAPAN THAT OIL AND RUBBER RICHES IN THE SOUTH PACIFIC WERE WORTH A WAR WITH AMERICA. NOW FOR THE THIRD TIME THE POWERFUL GREED IS ENTRUSTED WITH A MASTER MISSION—THE CAPTURE OF MARS'S MOST DANGEROUS ENEMY, THE AMAZON PRINCESS, WONDER WOMAN!
MARS, RETURNING TO HIS PALACE AFTER WONDER WOMAN'S ESCAPE, SUMMONS HIS THREE COMMANDING GENERALS.
ROUSE MY AIDES FROM THEIR SLOTHFUL SLUMBERS! LORD CONQUEST, EARL OF GREED, DUKE OF DECEPTION - CALL THEM IMMEDIATELY!
YES, MASTER!
1B

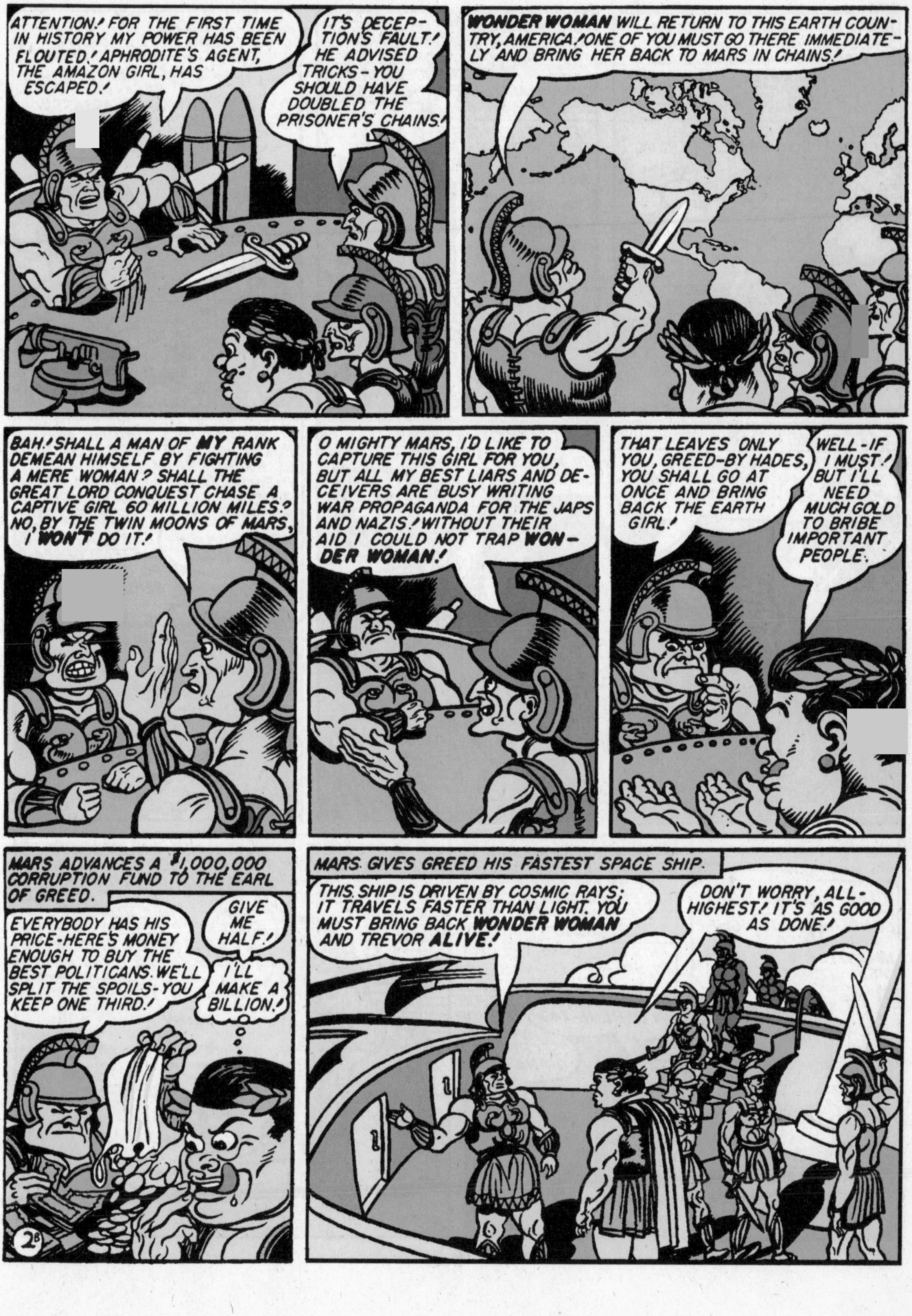
ATTENTION! FOR THE FIRST TIME IN HISTORY MY POWER HAS BEEN FLOUTED! APHRODITE'S AGENT, THE AMAZON GIRL, HAS ESCAPED!
IT'S DECEPTION'S FAULT! HE ADVISED TRICKS - YOU SHOULD HAVE DOUBLED THE PRISONER'S CHAINS!
WONDER WOMAN WILL RETURN TO THIS EARTH COUNTRY, AMERICA! ONE OF YOU MUST GO THERE IMMEDIATELY AND BRING HER BACK TO MARS IN CHAINS!
BAH! SHALL A MAN OF MY RANK DEMEAN HIMSELF BY FIGHTING A MERE WOMAN? SHALL THE GREAT LORD CONQUEST CHASE A CAPTIVE GIRL 60 MILLION MILES? NO, BY THE TWIN MOONS OF MARS, I WON'T DO IT!
O MIGHTY MARS, I'D LIKE TO CAPTURE THIS GIRL FOR YOU, BUT ALL MY BEST LIARS AND DECEIVERS ARE BUSY WRITING WAR PROPAGANDA FOR THE JAPS AND NAZIS! WITHOUT THEIR AID I COULD NOT TRAP WONDER WOMAN!
THAT LEAVES ONLY YOU, GREED-BY HADES, YOU SHALL GO AT ONCE AND BRING BACK THE EARTH GIRL!
WELL - IF I MUST! BUT I'LL NEED MUCH GOLD TO BRIBE IMPORTANT PEOPLE.
MARS ADVANCES A $1,000,000 CORRUPTION FUND TO THE EARL OF GREED.
EVERYBODY HAS HIS PRICE-HERE'S MONEY ENOUGH TO BUY THE BEST POLITICANS. WE'LL SPLIT THE SPOILS-YOU KEEP ONE THIRD!
GIVE ME HALF!
I'LL MAKE A BILLION!
2B
MARS GIVES GREED HIS FASTEST SPACE SHIP.
THIS SHIP IS DRIVEN BY COSMIC RAYS: IT TRAVELS FASTER THAN LIGHT. YOU MUST BRING BACK WONDER WOMAN AND TREVOR ALIVE!
DON'T WORRY, ALL-HIGHEST! IT'S AS GOOD AS DONE!

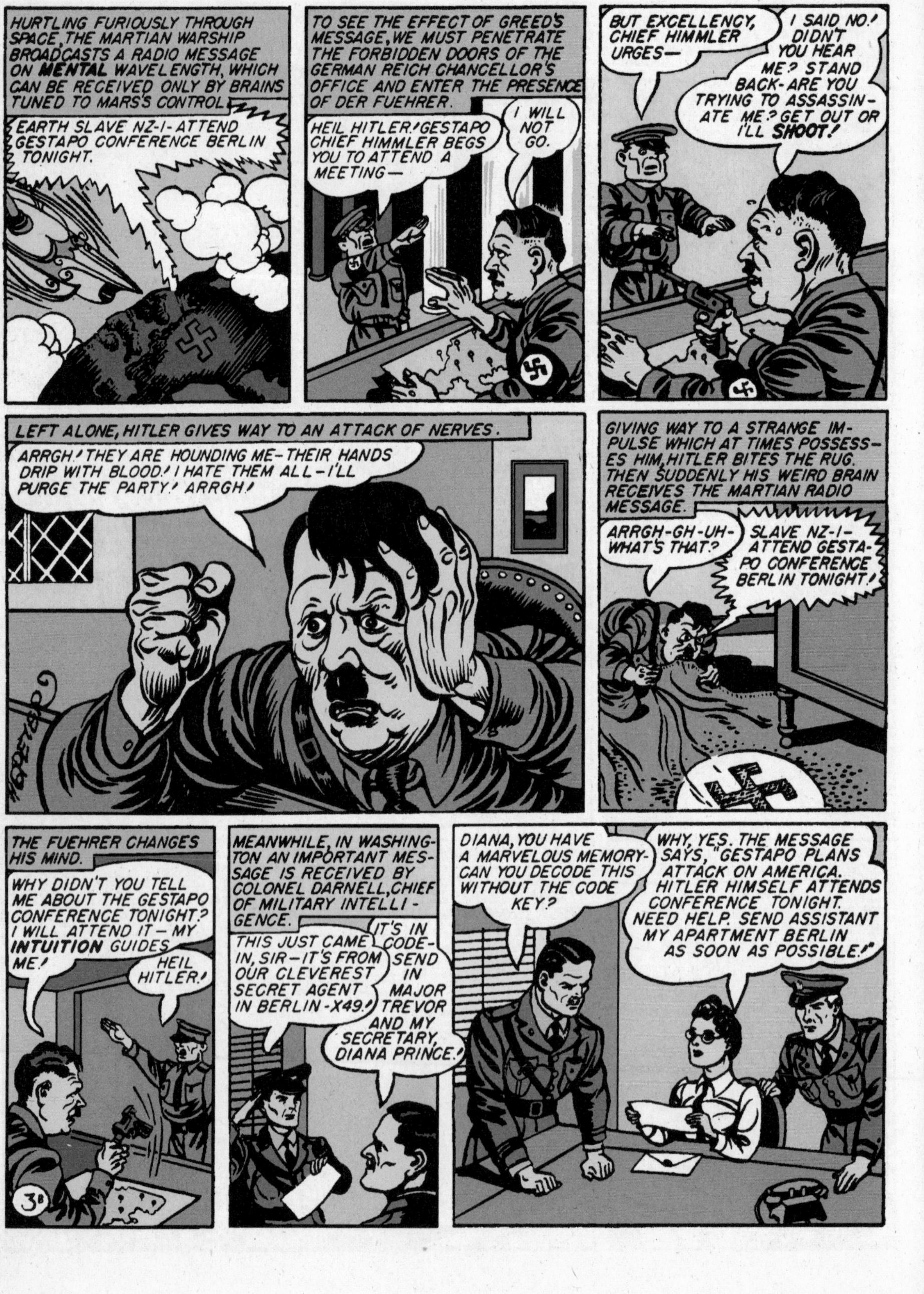
HURTLING FURIOUSLY THROUGH SPACE, THE MARTIAN WARSHIP BROADCASTS A RADIO MESSAGE ON MENTAL WAVELENGTH, WHICH CAN BE RECEIVED ONLY BY BRAINS TUNED TO MARS'S CONTROL.
EARTH SLAVE NZ-1-ATTEND GESTAPO CONFERENCE BERLIN TONIGHT.
TO SEE THE EFFECT OF GREED'S MESSAGE, WE MUST PENETRATE THE FORBIDDEN DOORS OF THE GERMAN REICH CHANCELLOR'S OFFICE AND ENTER THE PRESENCE OF DER FUEHRER.
HEIL HITLER! GESTAPO CHIEF HIMMLER BEGS YOU TO ATTEND A MEETING—
I WILL NOT GO.
BUT EXCELLENCY, CHIEF HIMMLER URGES—
I SAID NO! DIDN'T YOU HEAR ME? STAND BACK-ARE YOU TRYING TO ASSASSIN-ATE ME? GET OUT OR I'LL SHOOT!
LEFT ALONE, HITLER GIVES WAY TO AN ATTACK OF NERVES.
ARRGH! THEY ARE HOUNDING ME-THEIR HANDS DRIP WITH BLOOD! I HATE THEM ALL-I'LL PURGE THE PARTY! ARRGH!
GIVING WAY TO A STRANGE IM-PULSE WHICH AT TIMES POSSESS-ES HIM, HITLER BITES THE RUG. THEN SUDDENLY HIS WEIRD BRAIN RECEIVES THE MARTIAN RADIO MESSAGE.
ARRGH-GH-UH-WHAT'S THAT?
SLAVE NZ-1-ATTEND GESTA-PO CONFERENCE BERLIN TONIGHT!
THE FUEHRER CHANGES HIS MIND.
WHY DIDN'T YOU TELL ME ABOUT THE GESTAPO CONFERENCE TONIGHT? I WILL ATTEND IT—MY INTUITION GUIDES ME!
HEIL HITLER!
MEANWHILE, IN WASHING-TON AN IMPORTANT MES-SAGE IS RECEIVED BY COLONEL DARNELL, CHIEF OF MILITARY INTELLI-GENCE.
THIS JUST CAME IN, SIR—IT'S FROM OUR CLEVEREST SECRET AGENT IN BERLIN-X49!
IT'S IN CODE-SEND IN MAJOR TREVOR AND MY SECRETARY, DIANA PRINCE!
DIANA, YOU HAVE A MARVELOUS MEMORY-CAN YOU DECODE THIS WITHOUT THE CODE KEY?
WHY, YES. THE MESSAGE SAYS, "GESTAPO PLANS ATTACK ON AMERICA. HITLER HIMSELF ATTENDS CONFERENCE TONIGHT. NEED HELP. SEND ASSISTANT MY APARTMENT BERLIN AS SOON AS POSSIBLE!"

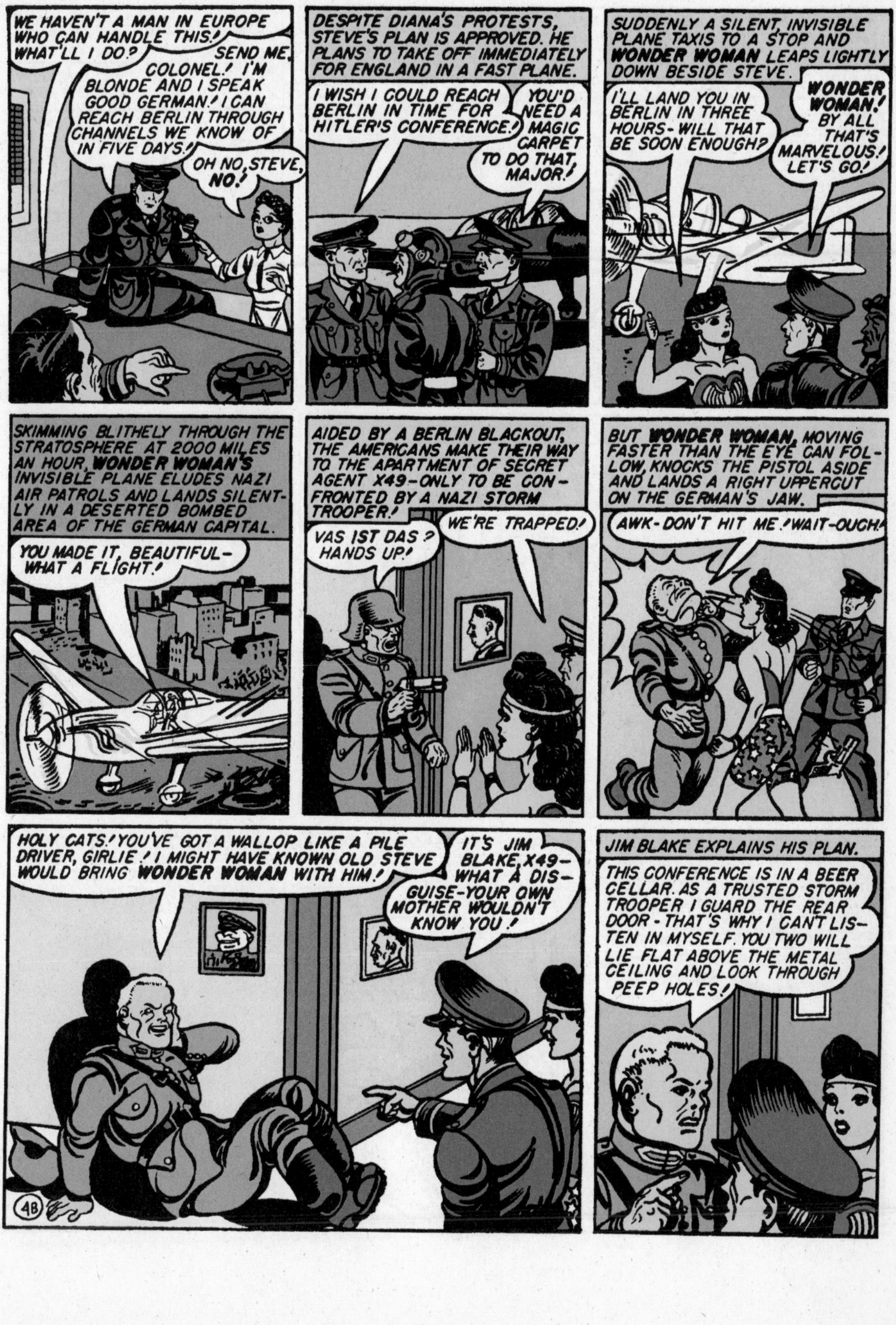
WE HAVEN'T A MAN IN EUROPE WHO CAN HANDLE THIS! WHAT'LL I DO?
SEND ME, COLONEL! I'M BLONDE AND I SPEAK GOOD GERMAN! I CAN REACH BERLIN THROUGH CHANNELS WE KNOW OF IN FIVE DAYS!
OH NO, STEVE, NO!
DESPITE DIANA'S PROTESTS, STEVE'S PLAN IS APPROVED. HE PLANS TO TAKE OFF IMMEDIATELY FOR ENGLAND IN A FAST PLANE.
I WISH I COULD REACH BERLIN IN TIME FOR HITLER'S CONFERENCE!
YOU'D NEED A MAGIC CARPET TO DO THAT, MAJOR!
SUDDENLY A SILENT, INVISIBLE PLANE TAXIS TO A STOP AND WONDER WOMAN LEAPS LIGHTLY DOWN BESIDE STEVE.
I'LL LAND YOU IN BERLIN IN THREE HOURS- WILL THAT BE SOON ENOUGH?
WONDER WOMAN! BY ALL THAT'S MARVELOUS! LET'S GO!
SKIMMING BLITHELY THROUGH THE STRATOSPHERE AT 2000 MILES AN HOUR, WONDER WOMAN'S INVISIBLE PLANE ELUDES NAZI AIR PATROLS AND LANDS SILENTLY IN A DESERTED BOMBED AREA OF THE GERMAN CAPITAL.
YOU MADE IT, BEAUTIFUL- WHAT A FLIGHT!
AIDED BY A BERLIN BLACKOUT, THE AMERICANS MAKE THEIR WAY TO THE APARTMENT OF SECRET AGENT X49-ONLY TO BE CONFRONTED BY A NAZI STORM TROOPER!
VAS IST DAS? HANDS UP!
WE'RE TRAPPED!
BUT WONDER WOMAN, MOVING FASTER THAN THE EYE CAN FOLLOW, KNOCKS THE PISTOL ASIDE AND LANDS A RIGHT UPPERCUT ON THE GERMAN'S JAW.
AWK-DON'T HIT ME! WAIT-OUCH!
HOLY CATS! YOU'VE GOT A WALLOP LIKE A PILE DRIVER, GIRLIE! I MIGHT HAVE KNOWN OLD STEVE WOULD BRING WONDER WOMAN WITH HIM!
IT'S JIM BLAKE, X49- WHAT A DISGUISE-YOUR OWN MOTHER WOULDN'T KNOW YOU!
48
JIM BLAKE EXPLAINS HIS PLAN.
THIS CONFERENCE IS IN A BEER CELLAR. AS A TRUSTED STORM TROOPER I GUARD THE REAR DOOR - THAT'S WHY I CAN'T LISTEN IN MYSELF. YOU TWO WILL LIE FLAT ABOVE THE METAL CEILING AND LOOK THROUGH PEEP HOLES!

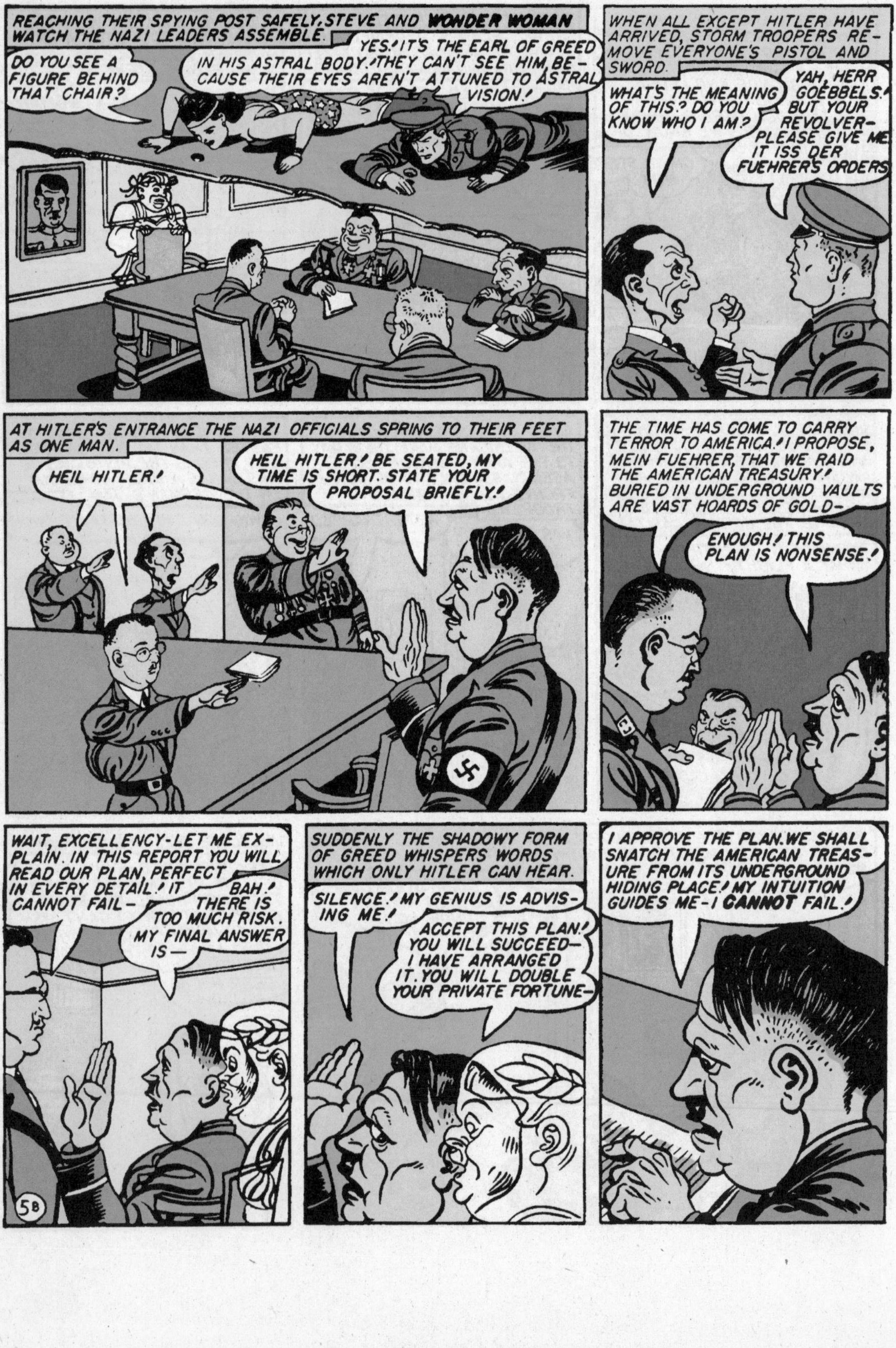
REACHING THEIR SPYING POST SAFELY, STEVE AND WONDER WOMAN WATCH THE NAZI LEADERS ASSEMBLE.
DO YOU SEE A FIGURE BEHIND THAT CHAIR?
YES! IT'S THE EARL OF GREED IN HIS ASTRAL BODY! THEY CAN'T SEE HIM BE-CAUSE THEIR EYES AREN'T ATTUNED TO ASTRAL VISION!
WHEN ALL EXCEPT HITLER HAVE ARRIVED, STORM TROOPERS RE-MOVE EVERYONE'S PISTOL AND SWORD.
WHAT'S THE MEANING OF THIS? DO YOU KNOW WHO I AM?
YAH, HERR GOEBBELS! BUT YOUR REVOLVER-PLEASE GIVE ME! IT ISS DER FUEHRER'S ORDERS!
AT HITLER'S ENTRANCE THE NAZI OFFICIALS SPRING TO THEIR FEET AS ONE MAN.
HEIL HITLER!
HEIL HITLER! BE SEATED, MY TIME IS SHORT. STATE YOUR PROPOSAL BRIEFLY!
THE TIME HAS COME TO CARRY TERROR TO AMERICA! I PROPOSE, MEIN FUEHRER, THAT WE RAID THE AMERICAN TREASURY! BURIED IN UNDERGROUND VAULTS ARE VAST HOARDS OF GOLD-
ENOUGH! THIS PLAN IS NONSENSE!
WAIT, EXCELLENCY-LET ME EX-PLAIN. IN THIS REPORT YOU WILL READ OUR PLAN, PERFECT IN EVERY DETAIL! IT CANNOT FAIL-
BAH! THERE IS TOO MUCH RISK. MY FINAL ANSWER IS—
5B
SUDDENLY THE SHADOWY FORM OF GREED WHISPERS WORDS WHICH ONLY HITLER CAN HEAR.
SILENCE! MY GENIUS IS ADVIS-ING ME!
ACCEPT THIS PLAN! YOU WILL SUCCEED— I HAVE ARRANGED IT. YOU WILL DOUBLE YOUR PRIVATE FORTUNE-
I APPROVE THE PLAN. WE SHALL SNATCH THE AMERICAN TREAS-URE FROM ITS UNDERGROUND HIDING PLACE! MY INTUITION GUIDES ME-I CANNOT FAIL!

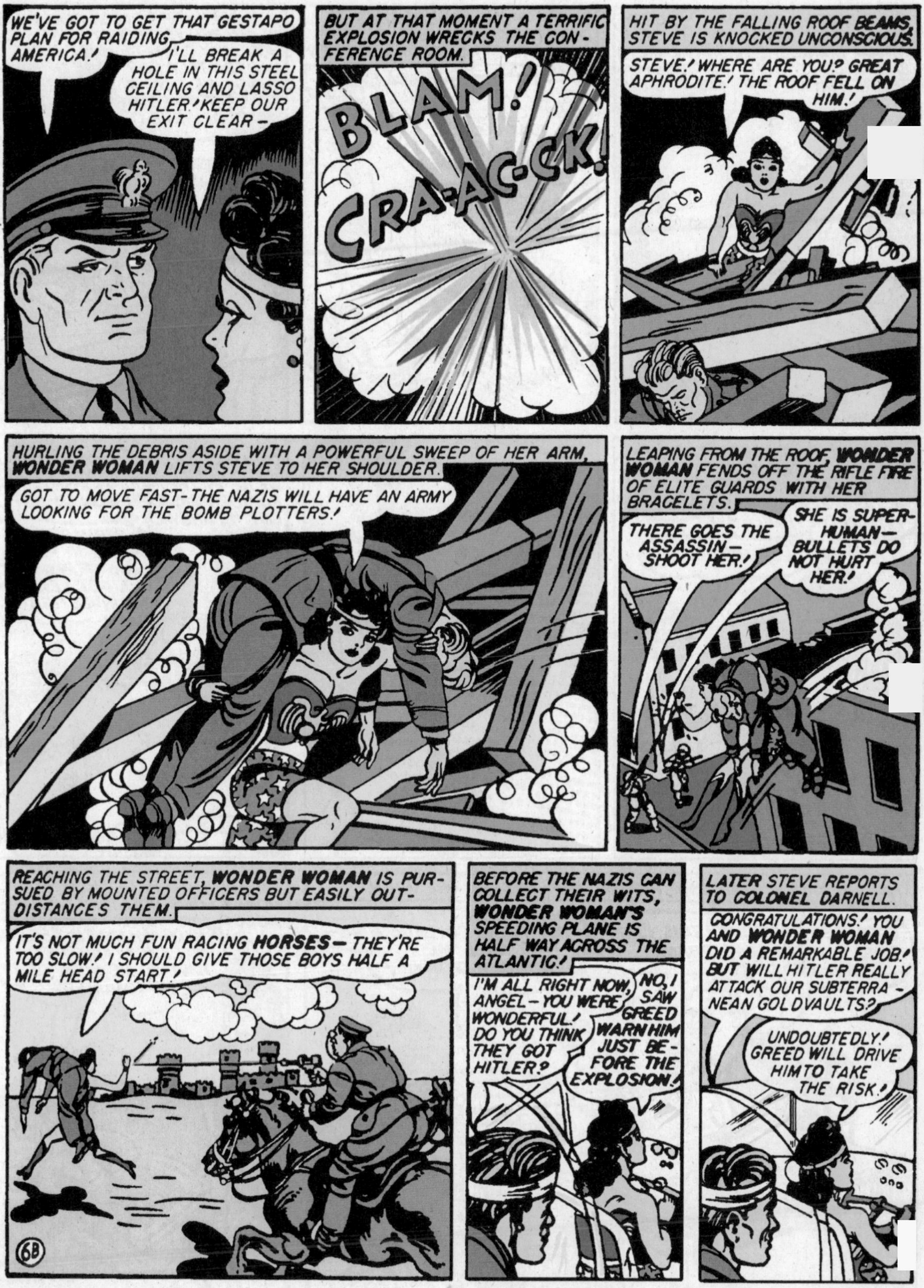

WE'VE GOT TO GET THAT GESTAPO PLAN FOR RAIDING AMERICA!
I'LL BREAK A HOLE IN THIS STEEL CEILING AND LASSO HITLER! KEEP OUR EXIT CLEAR—
BUT AT THAT MOMENT A TERRIFIC EXPLOSION WRECKS THE CONFERENCE ROOM.
BLAM!
CRA-AC-CK!
HIT BY THE FALLING ROOF BEAMS, STEVE IS KNOCKED UNCONSCIOUS.
STEVE! WHERE ARE YOU? GREAT APHRODITE! THE ROOF FELL ON HIM!
HURLING THE DEBRIS ASIDE WITH A POWERFUL SWEEP OF HER ARM, WONDER WOMAN LIFTS STEVE TO HER SHOULDER.
GOT TO MOVE FAST-THE NAZIS WILL HAVE AN ARMY LOOKING FOR THE BOMB PLOTTERS!
LEAPING FROM THE ROOF, WONDER WOMAN FENDS OFF THE RIFLE FIRE OF ELITE GUARDS WITH HER BRACELETS.
THERE GOES THE ASSASSIN—SHOOT HER!
SHE IS SUPER-HUMAN—BULLETS DO NOT HURT HER!
REACHING THE STREET, WONDER WOMAN IS PURSUED BY MOUNTED OFFICERS BUT EASILY OUT-DISTANCES THEM.
IT'S NOT MUCH FUN RACING HORSES—THEY'RE TOO SLOW! I SHOULD GIVE THOSE BOYS HALF A MILE HEAD START!
6B
BEFORE THE NAZIS CAN COLLECT THEIR WITS, WONDER WOMAN'S SPEEDING PLANE IS HALF WAY ACROSS THE ATLANTIC!
I'M ALL RIGHT NOW, ANGEL—YOU WERE WONDERFUL! DO YOU THINK THEY GOT HITLER?
NO, I SAW GREED WARN HIM JUST BEFORE THE EXPLOSION!
LATER STEVE REPORTS TO COLONEL DARNELL.
CONGRATULATIONS! YOU AND WONDER WOMAN DID A REMARKABLE JOB! BUT WILL HITLER REALLY ATTACK OUR SUBTERRANEAN GOLDVAULTS?
UNDOUBTEDLY! GREED WILL DRIVE HIM TO TAKE THE RISK!

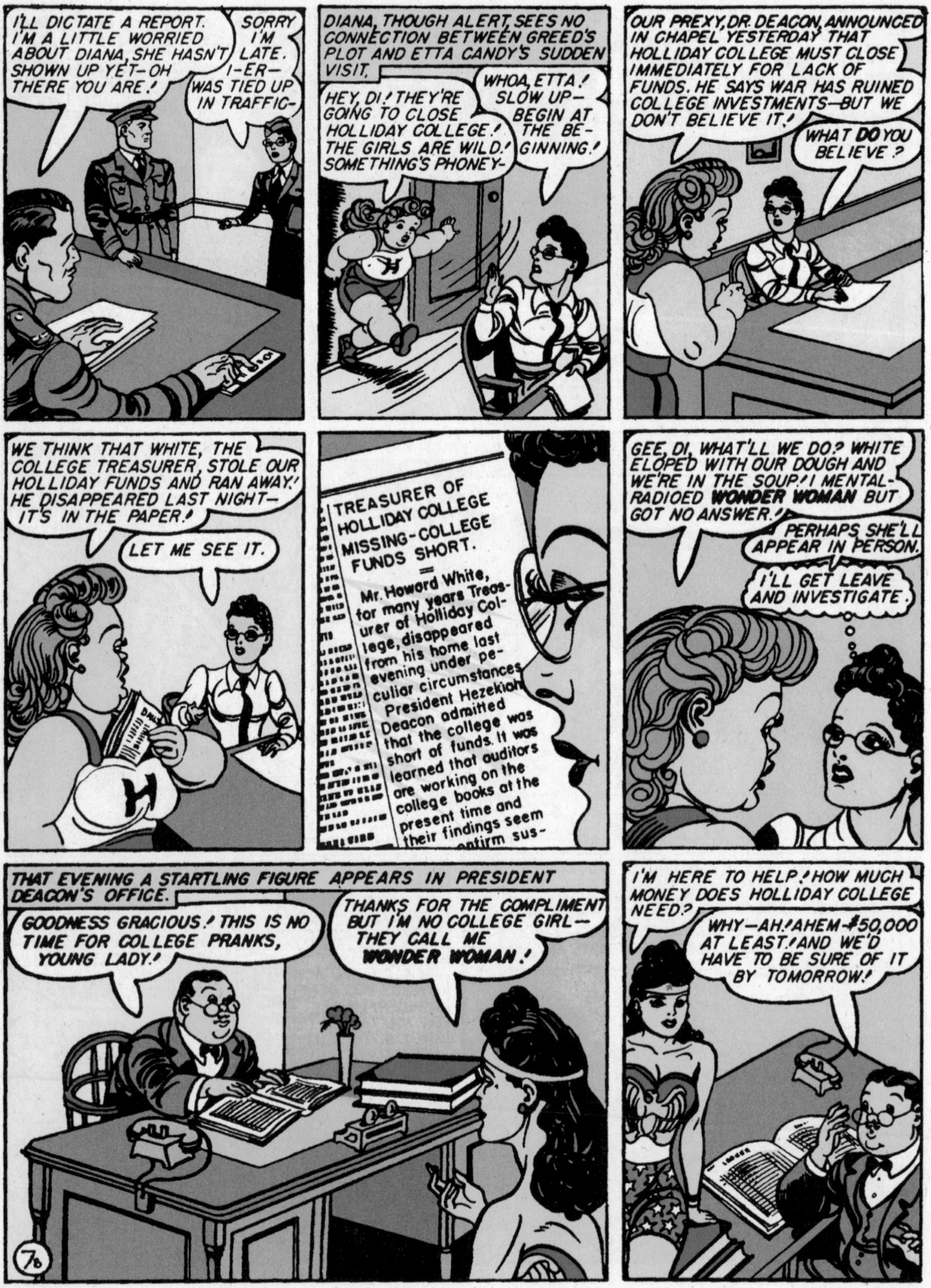
I'LL DICTATE A REPORT. I'M A LITTLE WORRIED ABOUT DIANA, SHE HASN'T SHOWN UP YET–OH THERE YOU ARE!
SORRY I'M LATE. I–ER– WAS TIED UP IN TRAFFIC–
DIANA, THOUGH ALERT, SEES NO CONNECTION BETWEEN GREED'S PLOT AND ETTA CANDY'S SUDDEN VISIT.
HEY, DI! THEY'RE GOING TO CLOSE HOLLIDAY COLLEGE! THE GIRLS ARE WILD! SOMETHING'S PHONEY-
WHOA, ETTA! SLOW UP– BEGIN AT THE BE-GINNING!
OUR PREXY, DR. DEACON, ANNOUNCED IN CHAPEL YESTERDAY THAT HOLLIDAY COLLEGE MUST CLOSE IMMEDIATELY FOR LACK OF FUNDS. HE SAYS WAR HAS RUINED COLLEGE INVESTMENTS—BUT WE DON'T BELIEVE IT!
WHAT DO YOU BELIEVE?
WE THINK THAT WHITE, THE COLLEGE TREASURER, STOLE OUR HOLLIDAY FUNDS AND RAN AWAY! HE DISAPPEARED LAST NIGHT– IT'S IN THE PAPER!
LET ME SEE IT.
TREASURER OF HOLLIDAY COLLEGE MISSING–COLLEGE FUNDS SHORT.
Mr. Howard White, for many years Treasurer of Holliday College, disappeared from his home last evening under peculiar circumstances. President Hezekiah Deacon admitted that the college was short of funds. It was learned that auditors are working on the college books at the present time and their findings seem confirm sus-
GEE, DI, WHAT'LL WE DO? WHITE ELOPED WITH OUR DOUGH AND WE'RE IN THE SOUP! I MENTAL-RADIOED WONDER WOMAN BUT GOT NO ANSWER!
PERHAPS SHE'LL APPEAR IN PERSON.
I'LL GET LEAVE AND INVESTIGATE.
THAT EVENING A STARTLING FIGURE APPEARS IN PRESIDENT DEACON'S OFFICE.
GOODNESS GRACIOUS! THIS IS NO TIME FOR COLLEGE PRANKS, YOUNG LADY!
THANKS FOR THE COMPLIMENT BUT I'M NO COLLEGE GIRL— THEY CALL ME WONDER WOMAN!
7b
I'M HERE TO HELP! HOW MUCH MONEY DOES HOLLIDAY COLLEGE NEED?
WHY–AH! AHEM–$50,000 AT LEAST! AND WE'D HAVE TO BE SURE OF IT BY TOMORROW!

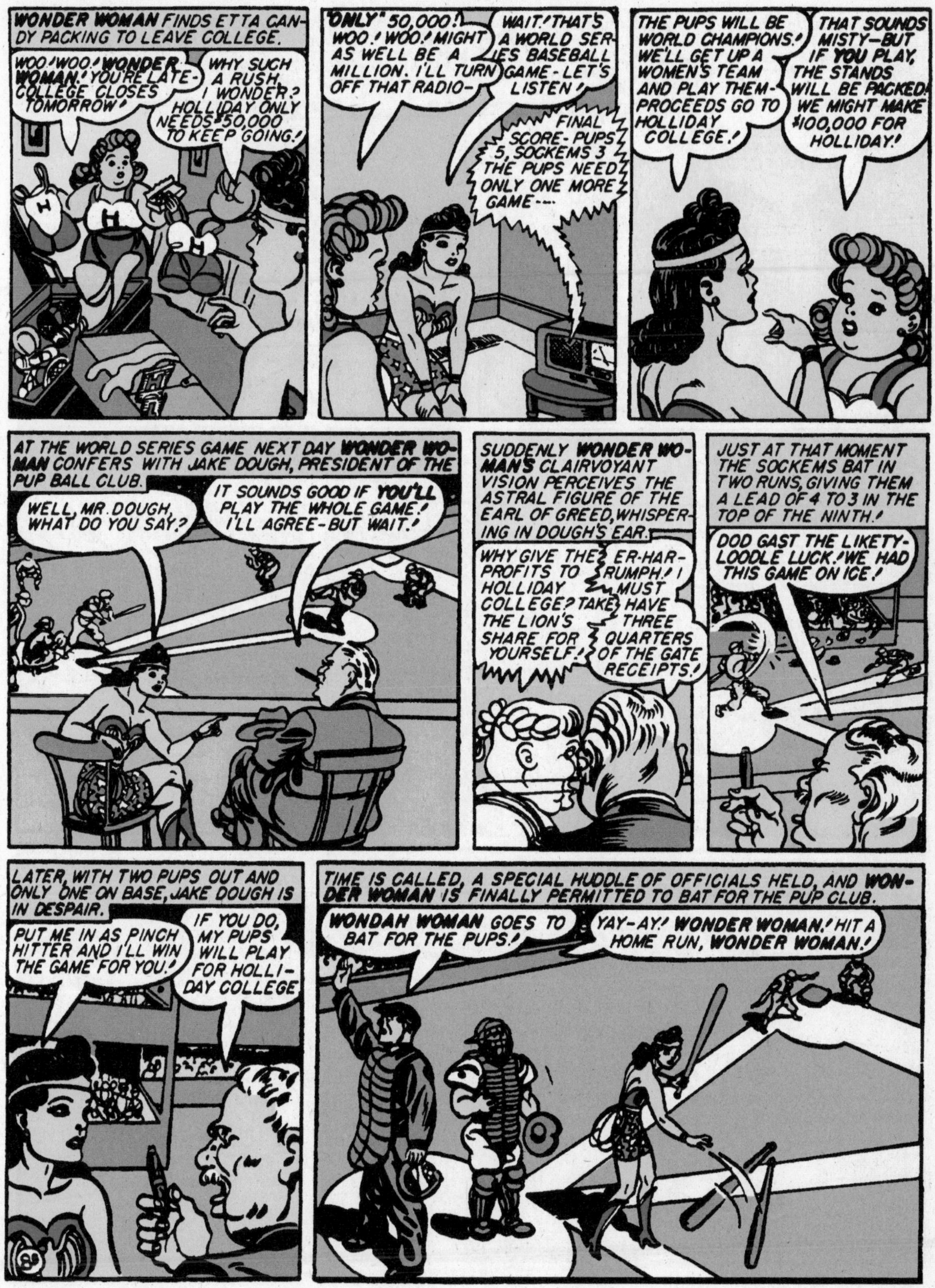

WONDER WOMAN FINDS ETTA CANDY PACKING TO LEAVE COLLEGE.
WOO! WOO! WONDER WOMAN! YOU'RE LATE - COLLEGE CLOSES TOMORROW!
WHY SUCH A RUSH, I WONDER? HOLLIDAY ONLY NEEDS $50,000 TO KEEP GOING!
"ONLY" 50,000! WOO! WOO! MIGHT AS WELL BE A MILLION. I'LL TURN OFF THAT RADIO-
WAIT! THAT'S A WORLD SERIES BASEBALL GAME - LET'S LISTEN!
FINAL SCORE - PUPS 5, SOCKEMS 3 THE PUPS NEED ONLY ONE MORE GAME---
THE PUPS WILL BE WORLD CHAMPIONS! WE'LL GET UP A WOMEN'S TEAM AND PLAY THEM - PROCEEDS GO TO HOLLIDAY COLLEGE!
THAT SOUNDS MISTY—BUT IF YOU PLAY, THE STANDS WILL BE PACKED! WE MIGHT MAKE $100,000 FOR HOLLIDAY!
AT THE WORLD SERIES GAME NEXT DAY WONDER WOMAN CONFERS WITH JAKE DOUGH, PRESIDENT OF THE PUP BALL CLUB.
WELL, MR. DOUGH, WHAT DO YOU SAY?
IT SOUNDS GOOD IF YOU'LL PLAY THE WHOLE GAME! I'LL AGREE - BUT WAIT!
SUDDENLY WONDER WOMAN'S CLAIRVOYANT VISION PERCEIVES THE ASTRAL FIGURE OF THE EARL OF GREED, WHISPERING IN DOUGH'S EAR.
WHY GIVE THE PROFITS TO HOLLIDAY COLLEGE? TAKE THE LION'S SHARE FOR YOURSELF!
ER-HAR-RUMPH! I MUST HAVE THREE QUARTERS OF THE GATE RECEIPTS!
JUST AT THAT MOMENT THE SOCKEMS BAT IN TWO RUNS, GIVING THEM A LEAD OF 4 TO 3 IN THE TOP OF THE NINTH!
DOD GAST THE LIKETY-LOODLE LUCK! WE HAD THIS GAME ON ICE!
LATER, WITH TWO PUPS OUT AND ONLY ONE ON BASE, JAKE DOUGH IS IN DESPAIR.
PUT ME IN AS PINCH HITTER AND I'LL WIN THE GAME FOR YOU!
IF YOU DO, MY PUPS WILL PLAY FOR HOLLIDAY COLLEGE
TIME IS CALLED, A SPECIAL HUDDLE OF OFFICIALS HELD, AND WONDER WOMAN IS FINALLY PERMITTED TO BAT FOR THE PUP CLUB.
WONDAH WOMAN GOES TO BAT FOR THE PUPS!
YAY-AY! WONDER WOMAN! HIT A HOME RUN, WONDER WOMAN!

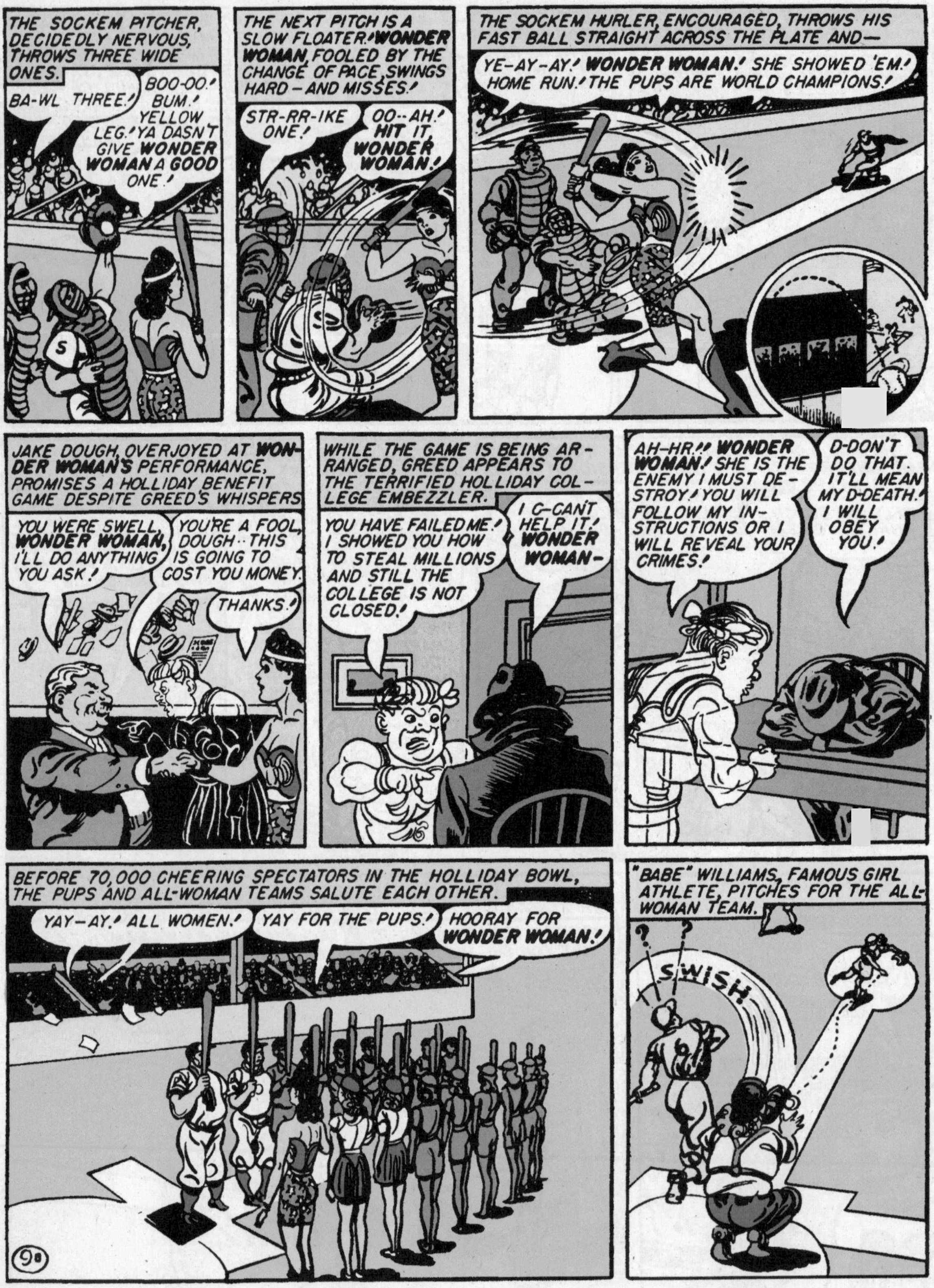

THE SOCKEM PITCHER, DECIDEDLY NERVOUS, THROWS THREE WIDE ONES.
BA-WL THREE!
BOO-OO! BUM! YELLOW LEG! YA DASN'T GIVE WONDER WOMAN A GOOD ONE!
THE NEXT PITCH IS A SLOW FLOATER! WONDER WOMAN, FOOLED BY THE CHANGE OF PACE, SWINGS HARD — AND MISSES!
STR-RR-IKE ONE!
OO--AH! HIT IT, WONDER WOMAN!
THE SOCKEM HURLER, ENCOURAGED, THROWS HIS FAST BALL STRAIGHT ACROSS THE PLATE AND—
YE-AY-AY! WONDER WOMAN! SHE SHOWED 'EM! HOME RUN! THE PUPS ARE WORLD CHAMPIONS!
JAKE DOUGH, OVERJOYED AT WONDER WOMAN'S PERFORMANCE, PROMISES A HOLLIDAY BENEFIT GAME DESPITE GREED'S WHISPERS
YOU WERE SWELL, WONDER WOMAN, I'LL DO ANYTHING YOU ASK!
YOU'RE A FOOL, DOUGH -- THIS IS GOING TO COST YOU MONEY.
THANKS!
WHILE THE GAME IS BEING ARRANGED, GREED APPEARS TO THE TERRIFIED HOLLIDAY COLLEGE EMBEZZLER.
YOU HAVE FAILED ME! I SHOWED YOU HOW TO STEAL MILLIONS AND STILL THE COLLEGE IS NOT CLOSED!
I C-CAN'T HELP IT! WONDER WOMAN-
AH-HR!! WONDER WOMAN! SHE IS THE ENEMY I MUST DESTROY! YOU WILL FOLLOW MY INSTRUCTIONS OR I WILL REVEAL YOUR CRIMES!
D-DON'T DO THAT. IT'LL MEAN MY D-DEATH! I WILL OBEY YOU!
BEFORE 70,000 CHEERING SPECTATORS IN THE HOLLIDAY BOWL, THE PUPS AND ALL-WOMAN TEAMS SALUTE EACH OTHER.
YAY-AY! ALL WOMEN!
YAY FOR THE PUPS!
HOORAY FOR WONDER WOMAN!
9a
"BABE" WILLIAMS, FAMOUS GIRL ATHLETE, PITCHES FOR THE ALL-WOMAN TEAM.
? ?
SWISH

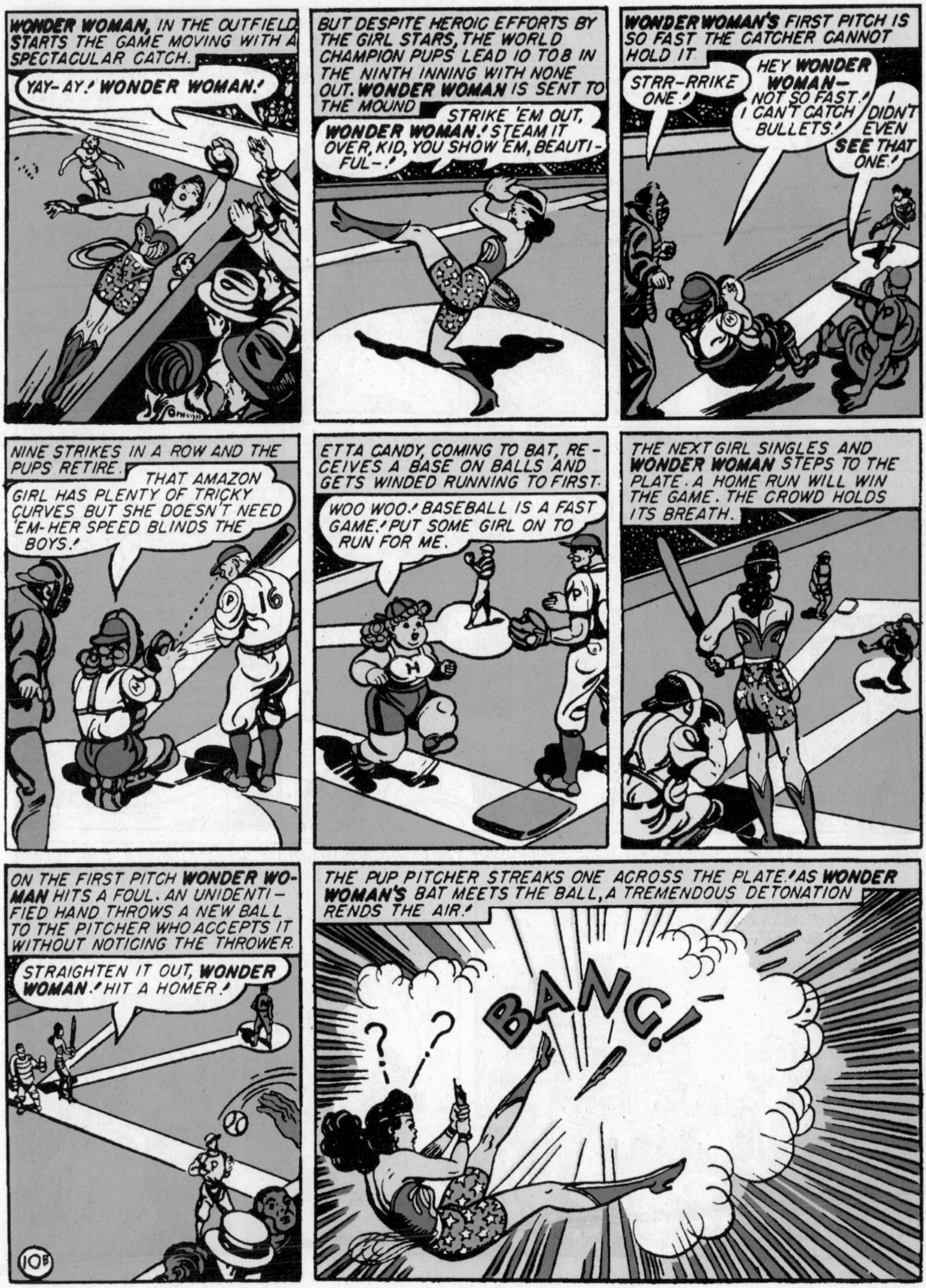
WONDER WOMAN, IN THE OUTFIELD, STARTS THE GAME MOVING WITH A SPECTACULAR CATCH.
YAY-AY! WONDER WOMAN!
BUT DESPITE HEROIC EFFORTS BY THE GIRL STARS, THE WORLD CHAMPION PUPS LEAD 10 TO 8 IN THE NINTH INNING WITH NONE OUT. WONDER WOMAN IS SENT TO THE MOUND.
STRIKE 'EM OUT, WONDER WOMAN! STEAM IT OVER, KID, YOU SHOW 'EM, BEAUTI-FUL-!
WONDER WOMAN'S FIRST PITCH IS SO FAST THE CATCHER CANNOT HOLD IT.
STRR-RRIKE ONE!
HEY WONDER WOMAN— NOT SO FAST! I CAN'T CATCH BULLETS!
I DIDN'T EVEN SEE THAT ONE!
NINE STRIKES IN A ROW AND THE PUPS RETIRE.
THAT AMAZON GIRL HAS PLENTY OF TRICKY CURVES BUT SHE DOESN'T NEED 'EM- HER SPEED BLINDS THE BOYS!
ETTA CANDY, COMING TO BAT, RE-CEIVES A BASE ON BALLS AND GETS WINDED RUNNING TO FIRST.
WOO WOO! BASEBALL IS A FAST GAME! PUT SOME GIRL ON TO RUN FOR ME.
THE NEXT GIRL SINGLES AND WONDER WOMAN STEPS TO THE PLATE. A HOME RUN WILL WIN THE GAME. THE CROWD HOLDS ITS BREATH.
ON THE FIRST PITCH WONDER WO-MAN HITS A FOUL. AN UNIDENTI-FIED HAND THROWS A NEW BALL TO THE PITCHER WHO ACCEPTS IT WITHOUT NOTICING THE THROWER.
STRAIGHTEN IT OUT, WONDER WOMAN! HIT A HOMER!
10B
THE PUP PITCHER STREAKS ONE ACROSS THE PLATE! AS WONDER WOMAN'S BAT MEETS THE BALL, A TREMENDOUS DETONATION RENDS THE AIR!
BANG!
? ?

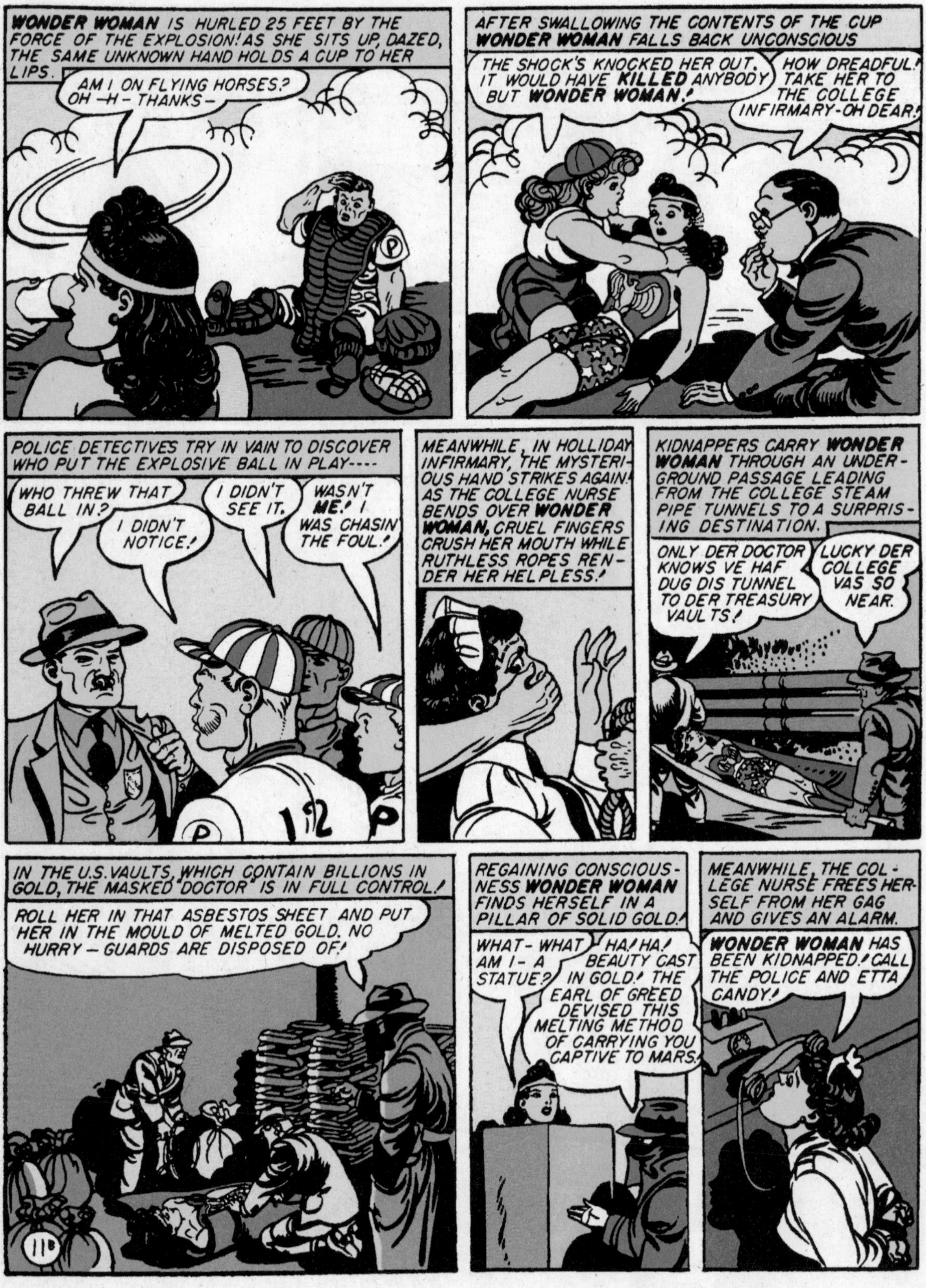

WONDER WOMAN IS HURLED 25 FEET BY THE FORCE OF THE EXPLOSION! AS SHE SITS UP, DAZED, THE SAME UNKNOWN HAND HOLDS A CUP TO HER LIPS.
AM I ON FLYING HORSES? OH -H- THANKS-
AFTER SWALLOWING THE CONTENTS OF THE CUP WONDER WOMAN FALLS BACK UNCONSCIOUS
THE SHOCK'S KNOCKED HER OUT. IT WOULD HAVE KILLED ANYBODY BUT WONDER WOMAN!
HOW DREADFUL! TAKE HER TO THE COLLEGE INFIRMARY-OH DEAR!
POLICE DETECTIVES TRY IN VAIN TO DISCOVER WHO PUT THE EXPLOSIVE BALL IN PLAY----
WHO THREW THAT BALL IN?
I DIDN'T NOTICE!
I DIDN'T SEE IT.
WASN'T ME! I WAS CHASIN' THE FOUL!
MEANWHILE, IN HOLLIDAY INFIRMARY, THE MYSTERIOUS HAND STRIKES AGAIN! AS THE COLLEGE NURSE BENDS OVER WONDER WOMAN, CRUEL FINGERS CRUSH HER MOUTH WHILE RUTHLESS ROPES RENDER HER HELPLESS!
KIDNAPPERS CARRY WONDER WOMAN THROUGH AN UNDERGROUND PASSAGE LEADING FROM THE COLLEGE STEAM PIPE TUNNELS TO A SURPRISING DESTINATION.
ONLY DER DOCTOR KNOWS VE HAF DUG DIS TUNNEL TO DER TREASURY VAULTS!
LUCKY DER COLLEGE VAS SO NEAR.
IN THE U.S. VAULTS, WHICH CONTAIN BILLIONS IN GOLD, THE MASKED "DOCTOR" IS IN FULL CONTROL!
ROLL HER IN THAT ASBESTOS SHEET AND PUT HER IN THE MOULD OF MELTED GOLD. NO HURRY - GUARDS ARE DISPOSED OF!
11B
REGAINING CONSCIOUSNESS WONDER WOMAN FINDS HERSELF IN A PILLAR OF SOLID GOLD!
WHAT- WHAT AM I- A STATUE?
HA! HA! BEAUTY CAST IN GOLD! THE EARL OF GREED DEVISED THIS MELTING METHOD OF CARRYING YOU CAPTIVE TO MARS.
MEANWHILE, THE COLLEGE NURSE FREES HERSELF FROM HER GAG AND GIVES AN ALARM.
WONDER WOMAN HAS BEEN KIDNAPPED! CALL THE POLICE AND ETTA CANDY!

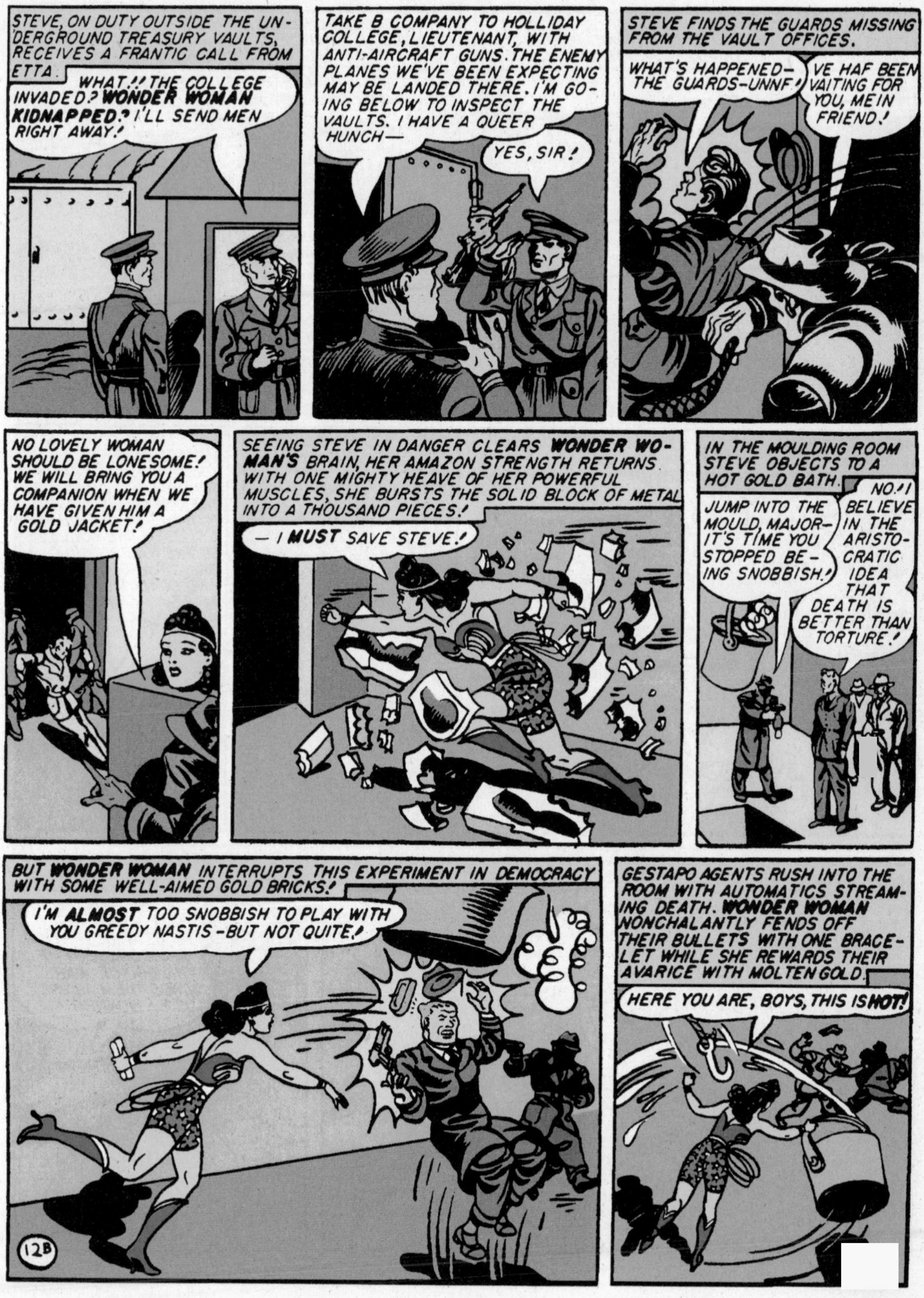
STEVE, ON DUTY OUTSIDE THE UNDERGROUND TREASURY VAULTS, RECEIVES A FRANTIC CALL FROM ETTA.
WHAT!! THE COLLEGE INVADED? WONDER WOMAN KIDNAPPED? I'LL SEND MEN RIGHT AWAY!
TAKE B COMPANY TO HOLLIDAY COLLEGE, LIEUTENANT, WITH ANTI-AIRCRAFT GUNS. THE ENEMY PLANES WE'VE BEEN EXPECTING MAY BE LANDED THERE. I'M GOING BELOW TO INSPECT THE VAULTS. I HAVE A QUEER HUNCH—
YES, SIR!
STEVE FINDS THE GUARDS MISSING FROM THE VAULT OFFICES.
WHAT'S HAPPENED— THE GUARDS—UNNF!
VE HAF BEEN VAITING FOR YOU, MEIN FRIEND!
NO LOVELY WOMAN SHOULD BE LONESOME! WE WILL BRING YOU A COMPANION WHEN WE HAVE GIVEN HIM A GOLD JACKET!
SEEING STEVE IN DANGER CLEARS WONDER WOMAN'S BRAIN, HER AMAZON STRENGTH RETURNS. WITH ONE MIGHTY HEAVE OF HER POWERFUL MUSCLES, SHE BURSTS THE SOLID BLOCK OF METAL INTO A THOUSAND PIECES!
— I MUST SAVE STEVE!
IN THE MOULDING ROOM STEVE OBJECTS TO A HOT GOLD BATH.
JUMP INTO THE MOULD, MAJOR— IT'S TIME YOU STOPPED BEING SNOBBISH!
NO! I BELIEVE IN THE ARISTOCRATIC IDEA THAT DEATH IS BETTER THAN TORTURE!
BUT WONDER WOMAN INTERRUPTS THIS EXPERIMENT IN DEMOCRACY WITH SOME WELL-AIMED GOLD BRICKS!
I'M ALMOST TOO SNOBBISH TO PLAY WITH YOU GREEDY NASTIS—BUT NOT QUITE!
12B
GESTAPO AGENTS RUSH INTO THE ROOM WITH AUTOMATICS STREAMING DEATH. WONDER WOMAN NONCHALANTLY FENDS OFF THEIR BULLETS WITH ONE BRACELET WHILE SHE REWARDS THEIR AVARICE WITH MOLTEN GOLD.
HERE YOU ARE, BOYS, THIS IS HOT!

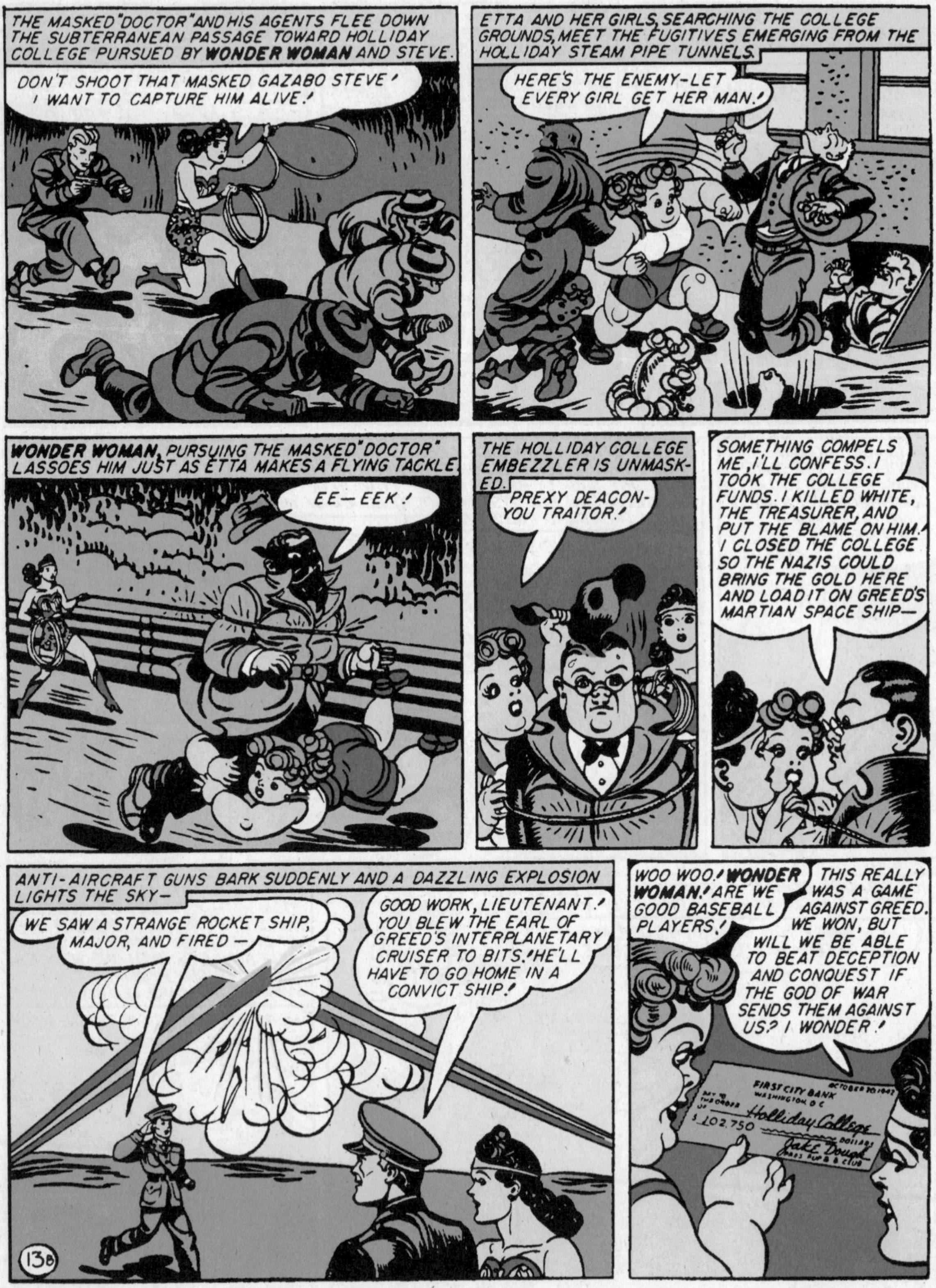
THE MASKED "DOCTOR" AND HIS AGENTS FLEE DOWN THE SUBTERRANEAN PASSAGE TOWARD HOLLIDAY COLLEGE PURSUED BY WONDER WOMAN AND STEVE.
DON'T SHOOT THAT MASKED GAZABO STEVE! I WANT TO CAPTURE HIM ALIVE!
ETTA AND HER GIRLS, SEARCHING THE COLLEGE GROUNDS, MEET THE FUGITIVES EMERGING FROM THE HOLLIDAY STEAM PIPE TUNNELS.
HERE'S THE ENEMY-LET EVERY GIRL GET HER MAN!
WONDER WOMAN, PURSUING THE MASKED "DOCTOR" LASSOES HIM JUST AS ETTA MAKES A FLYING TACKLE.
EE—EEK!
THE HOLLIDAY COLLEGE EMBEZZLER IS UNMASKED.
PREXY DEACON-YOU TRAITOR!
SOMETHING COMPELS ME, I'LL CONFESS. I TOOK THE COLLEGE FUNDS. I KILLED WHITE, THE TREASURER, AND PUT THE BLAME ON HIM. I CLOSED THE COLLEGE SO THE NAZIS COULD BRING THE GOLD HERE AND LOAD IT ON GREED'S MARTIAN SPACE SHIP—
ANTI-AIRCRAFT GUNS BARK SUDDENLY AND A DAZZLING EXPLOSION LIGHTS THE SKY—
WE SAW A STRANGE ROCKET SHIP, MAJOR, AND FIRED—
GOOD WORK, LIEUTENANT! YOU BLEW THE EARL OF GREED'S INTERPLANETARY CRUISER TO BITS! HE'LL HAVE TO GO HOME IN A CONVICT SHIP!
WOO WOO! WONDER WOMAN! ARE WE GOOD BASEBALL PLAYERS!
THIS REALLY WAS A GAME AGAINST GREED. WE WON, BUT WILL WE BE ABLE TO BEAT DECEPTION AND CONQUEST IF THE GOD OF WAR SENDS THEM AGAINST US? I WONDER!
FIRST CITY BANK
Holliday College

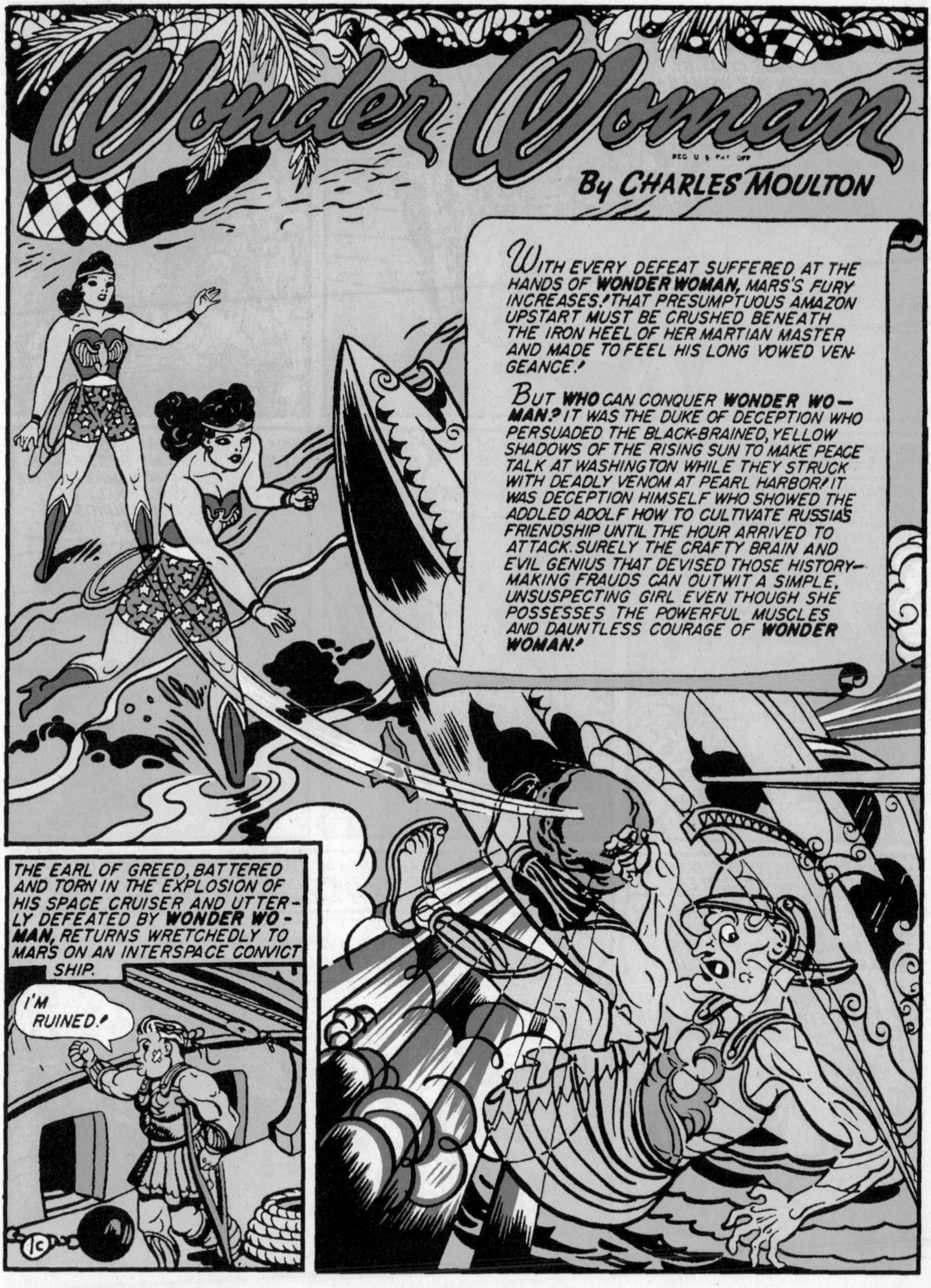

Wonder Woman
REG. U.S. PAT. OFF.
By CHARLES MOULTON
WITH EVERY DEFEAT SUFFERED AT THE HANDS OF WONDER WOMAN, MARS'S FURY INCREASES! THAT PRESUMPTUOUS AMAZON UPSTART MUST BE CRUSHED BENEATH THE IRON HEEL OF HER MARTIAN MASTER AND MADE TO FEEL HIS LONG VOWED VENGEANCE!
BUT WHO CAN CONQUER WONDER WOMAN? IT WAS THE DUKE OF DECEPTION WHO PERSUADED THE BLACK-BRAINED, YELLOW SHADOWS OF THE RISING SUN TO MAKE PEACE TALK AT WASHINGTON WHILE THEY STRUCK WITH DEADLY VENOM AT PEARL HARBOR! IT WAS DECEPTION HIMSELF WHO SHOWED THE ADDLED ADOLF HOW TO CULTIVATE RUSSIA'S FRIENDSHIP UNTIL THE HOUR ARRIVED TO ATTACK. SURELY THE CRAFTY BRAIN AND EVIL GENIUS THAT DEVISED THOSE HISTORY-MAKING FRAUDS CAN OUTWIT A SIMPLE, UNSUSPECTING GIRL EVEN THOUGH SHE POSSESSES THE POWERFUL MUSCLES AND DAUNTLESS COURAGE OF WONDER WOMAN!
THE EARL OF GREED, BATTERED AND TORN IN THE EXPLOSION OF HIS SPACE CRUISER AND UTTERLY DEFEATED BY WONDER WOMAN, RETURNS WRETCHEDLY TO MARS ON AN INTERSPACE CONVICT SHIP.
I'M RUINED!
1c

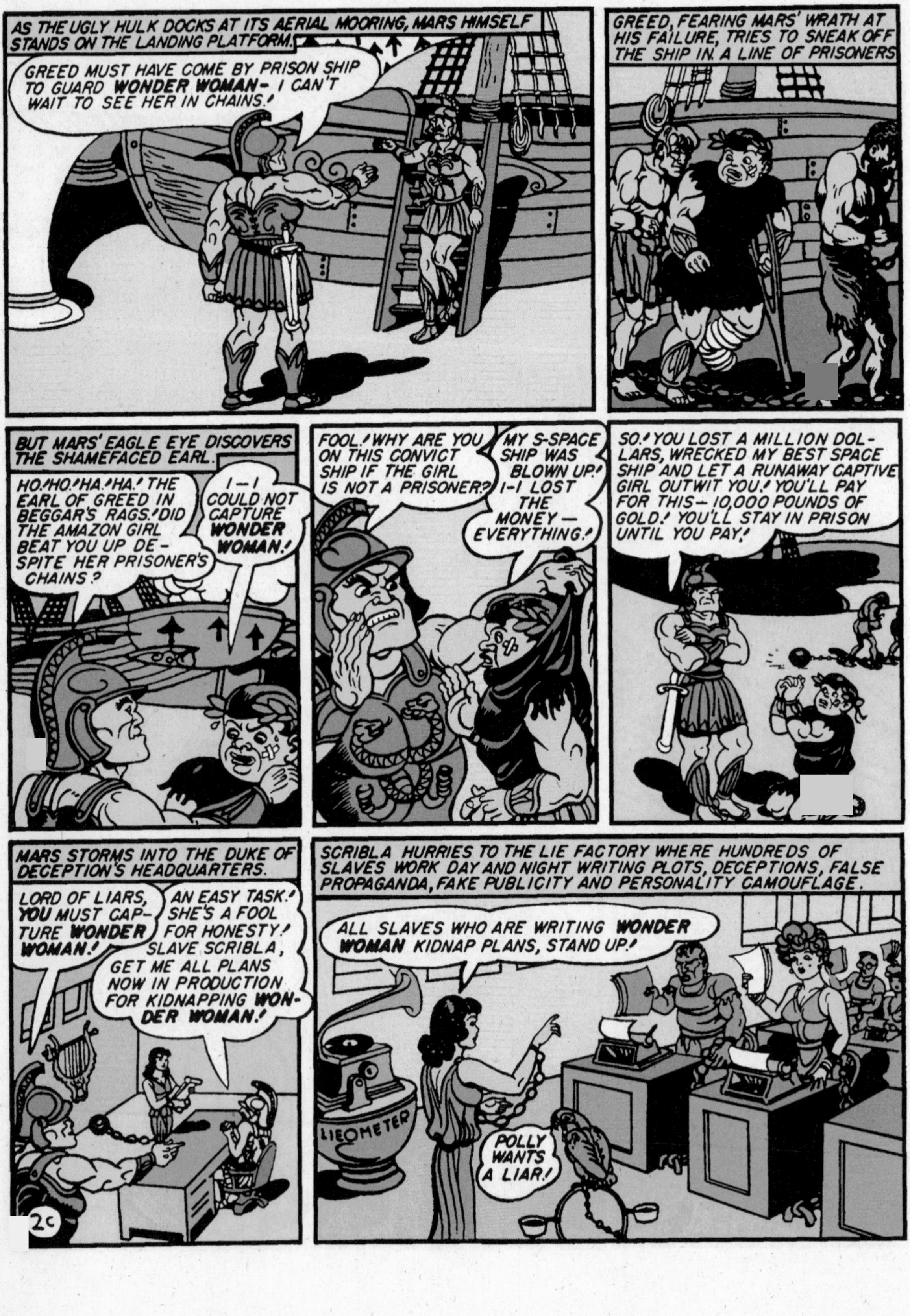

AS THE UGLY HULK DOCKS AT ITS AERIAL MOORING, MARS HIMSELF STANDS ON THE LANDING PLATFORM.
GREED MUST HAVE COME BY PRISON SHIP TO GUARD WONDER WOMAN- I CAN'T WAIT TO SEE HER IN CHAINS!
GREED, FEARING MARS' WRATH AT HIS FAILURE, TRIES TO SNEAK OFF THE SHIP IN A LINE OF PRISONERS
BUT MARS' EAGLE EYE DISCOVERS THE SHAMEFACED EARL.
HO!HO!HA!HA! THE EARL OF GREED IN BEGGAR'S RAGS! DID THE AMAZON GIRL BEAT YOU UP DESPITE HER PRISONER'S CHAINS?
I—I COULD NOT CAPTURE WONDER WOMAN!
FOOL! WHY ARE YOU ON THIS CONVICT SHIP IF THE GIRL IS NOT A PRISONER?
MY S-SPACE SHIP WAS BLOWN UP! I-I LOST THE MONEY— EVERYTHING!
SO! YOU LOST A MILLION DOLLARS, WRECKED MY BEST SPACE SHIP AND LET A RUNAWAY CAPTIVE GIRL OUTWIT YOU! YOU'LL PAY FOR THIS— 10,000 POUNDS OF GOLD! YOU'LL STAY IN PRISON UNTIL YOU PAY!
MARS STORMS INTO THE DUKE OF DECEPTION'S HEADQUARTERS.
LORD OF LIARS, YOU MUST CAPTURE WONDER WOMAN!
AN EASY TASK! SHE'S A FOOL FOR HONESTY! SLAVE SCRIBLA, GET ME ALL PLANS NOW IN PRODUCTION FOR KIDNAPPING WONDER WOMAN!
2C
SCRIBLA HURRIES TO THE LIE FACTORY WHERE HUNDREDS OF SLAVES WORK DAY AND NIGHT WRITING PLOTS, DECEPTIONS, FALSE PROPAGANDA, FAKE PUBLICITY AND PERSONALITY CAMOUFLAGE.
ALL SLAVES WHO ARE WRITING WONDER WOMAN KIDNAP PLANS, STAND UP!
LIEOMETER
POLLY WANTS A LIAR!

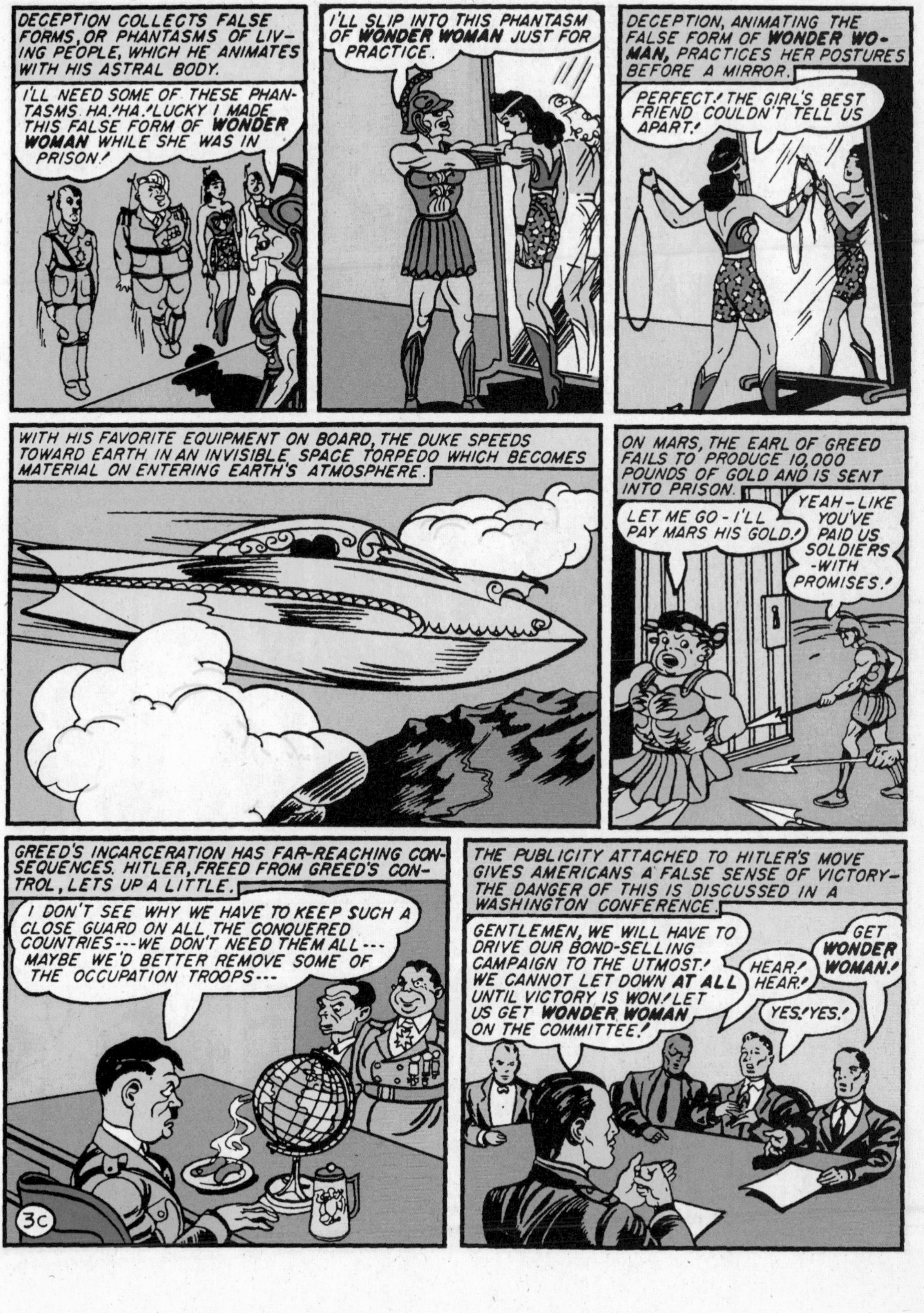
DECEPTION COLLECTS FALSE FORMS, OR PHANTASMS OF LIVING PEOPLE, WHICH HE ANIMATES WITH HIS ASTRAL BODY.
I'LL NEED SOME OF THESE PHANTASMS. HA! HA! LUCKY I MADE THIS FALSE FORM OF WONDER WOMAN WHILE SHE WAS IN PRISON!
I'LL SLIP INTO THIS PHANTASM OF WONDER WOMAN JUST FOR PRACTICE.
DECEPTION, ANIMATING THE FALSE FORM OF WONDER WOMAN, PRACTICES HER POSTURES BEFORE A MIRROR.
PERFECT! THE GIRL'S BEST FRIEND COULDN'T TELL US APART!
WITH HIS FAVORITE EQUIPMENT ON BOARD, THE DUKE SPEEDS TOWARD EARTH IN AN INVISIBLE SPACE TORPEDO WHICH BECOMES MATERIAL ON ENTERING EARTH'S ATMOSPHERE.
ON MARS, THE EARL OF GREED FAILS TO PRODUCE 10,000 POUNDS OF GOLD AND IS SENT INTO PRISON.
LET ME GO - I'LL PAY MARS HIS GOLD!
YEAH - LIKE YOU'VE PAID US SOLDIERS -WITH PROMISES!
GREED'S INCARCERATION HAS FAR-REACHING CONSEQUENCES. HITLER, FREED FROM GREED'S CONTROL, LETS UP A LITTLE.
I DON'T SEE WHY WE HAVE TO KEEP SUCH A CLOSE GUARD ON ALL THE CONQUERED COUNTRIES--- WE DON'T NEED THEM ALL--- MAYBE WE'D BETTER REMOVE SOME OF THE OCCUPATION TROOPS---
3C
THE PUBLICITY ATTACHED TO HITLER'S MOVE GIVES AMERICANS A FALSE SENSE OF VICTORY- THE DANGER OF THIS IS DISCUSSED IN A WASHINGTON CONFERENCE.
GENTLEMEN, WE WILL HAVE TO DRIVE OUR BOND-SELLING CAMPAIGN TO THE UTMOST! WE CANNOT LET DOWN AT ALL UNTIL VICTORY IS WON! LET US GET WONDER WOMAN ON THE COMMITTEE!
HEAR! HEAR!
GET WONDER WOMAN!
YES! YES!

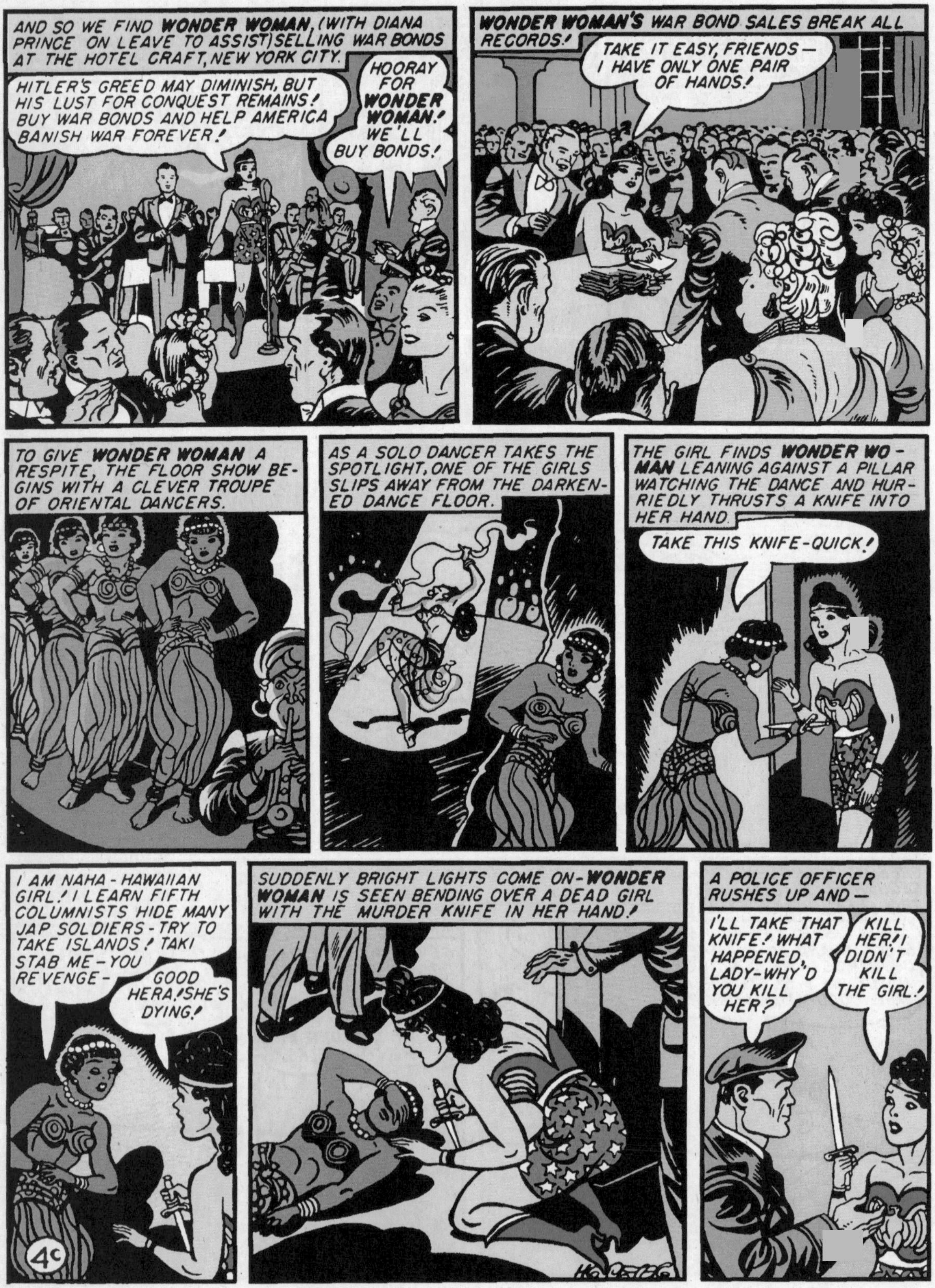
AND SO WE FIND WONDER WOMAN, (WITH DIANA PRINCE ON LEAVE TO ASSIST) SELLING WAR BONDS AT THE HOTEL CRAFT, NEW YORK CITY.
HITLER'S GREED MAY DIMINISH, BUT HIS LUST FOR CONQUEST REMAINS! BUY WAR BONDS AND HELP AMERICA BANISH WAR FOREVER!
HOORAY FOR WONDER WOMAN! WE'LL BUY BONDS!
WONDER WOMAN'S WAR BOND SALES BREAK ALL RECORDS!
TAKE IT EASY, FRIENDS— I HAVE ONLY ONE PAIR OF HANDS!
TO GIVE WONDER WOMAN A RESPITE, THE FLOOR SHOW BEGINS WITH A CLEVER TROUPE OF ORIENTAL DANCERS.
AS A SOLO DANCER TAKES THE SPOTLIGHT, ONE OF THE GIRLS SLIPS AWAY FROM THE DARKENED DANCE FLOOR.
THE GIRL FINDS WONDER WOMAN LEANING AGAINST A PILLAR WATCHING THE DANCE AND HURRIEDLY THRUSTS A KNIFE INTO HER HAND.
TAKE THIS KNIFE-QUICK!
I AM NAHA - HAWAIIAN GIRL! I LEARN FIFTH COLUMNISTS HIDE MANY JAP SOLDIERS - TRY TO TAKE ISLANDS! TAKI STAB ME - YOU REVENGE -
GOOD HERA! SHE'S DYING!
4c
SUDDENLY BRIGHT LIGHTS COME ON - WONDER WOMAN IS SEEN BENDING OVER A DEAD GIRL WITH THE MURDER KNIFE IN HER HAND!
A POLICE OFFICER RUSHES UP AND—
I'LL TAKE THAT KNIFE! WHAT HAPPENED, LADY-WHY'D YOU KILL HER?
KILL HER! I DIDN'T KILL THE GIRL!

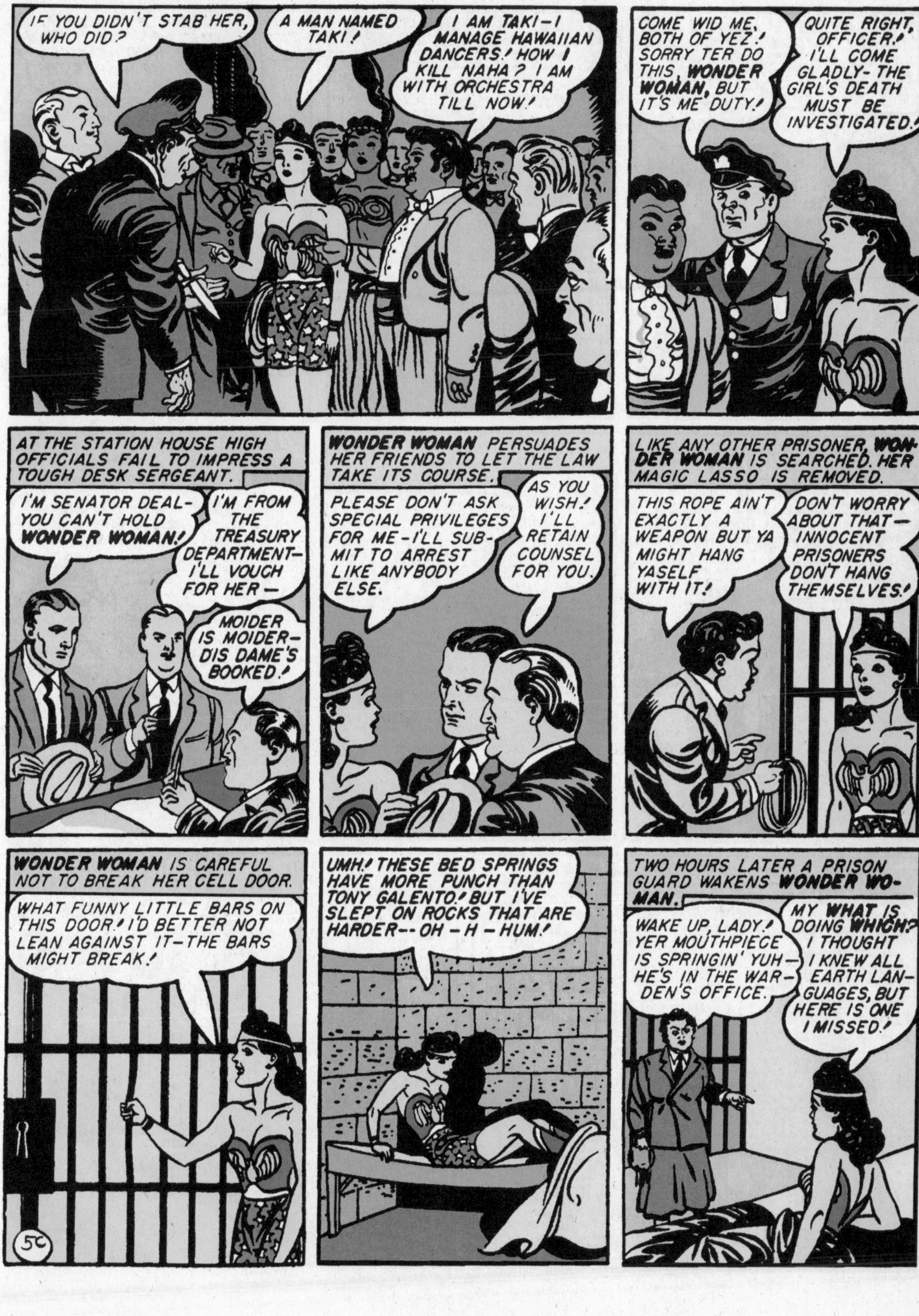
IF YOU DIDN'T STAB HER, WHO DID?
A MAN NAMED TAKI!
I AM TAKI—I MANAGE HAWAIIAN DANCERS! HOW I KILL NAHA? I AM WITH ORCHESTRA TILL NOW!
COME WID ME, BOTH OF YEZ! SORRY TER DO THIS, WONDER WOMAN, BUT IT'S ME DUTY!
QUITE RIGHT, OFFICER! I'LL COME GLADLY- THE GIRL'S DEATH MUST BE INVESTIGATED!
AT THE STATION HOUSE HIGH OFFICIALS FAIL TO IMPRESS A TOUGH DESK SERGEANT.
I'M SENATOR DEAL- YOU CAN'T HOLD WONDER WOMAN!
I'M FROM THE TREASURY DEPARTMENT- I'LL VOUCH FOR HER—
MOIDER IS MOIDER- DIS DAME'S BOOKED!
WONDER WOMAN PERSUADES HER FRIENDS TO LET THE LAW TAKE ITS COURSE.
PLEASE DON'T ASK SPECIAL PRIVILEGES FOR ME-I'LL SUBMIT TO ARREST LIKE ANYBODY ELSE.
AS YOU WISH! I'LL RETAIN COUNSEL FOR YOU.
LIKE ANY OTHER PRISONER, WONDER WOMAN IS SEARCHED. HER MAGIC LASSO IS REMOVED.
THIS ROPE AIN'T EXACTLY A WEAPON BUT YA MIGHT HANG YASELF WITH IT!
DON'T WORRY ABOUT THAT— INNOCENT PRISONERS DON'T HANG THEMSELVES!
WONDER WOMAN IS CAREFUL NOT TO BREAK HER CELL DOOR.
WHAT FUNNY LITTLE BARS ON THIS DOOR! I'D BETTER NOT LEAN AGAINST IT—THE BARS MIGHT BREAK!
5C
UMH! THESE BED SPRINGS HAVE MORE PUNCH THAN TONY GALENTO! BUT I'VE SLEPT ON ROCKS THAT ARE HARDER-- OH - H - HUM!
TWO HOURS LATER A PRISON GUARD WAKENS WONDER WOMAN.
WAKE UP, LADY! YER MOUTHPIECE IS SPRINGIN' YUH— HE'S IN THE WARDEN'S OFFICE.
MY WHAT IS DOING WHICH? I THOUGHT I KNEW ALL EARTH LANGUAGES, BUT HERE IS ONE I MISSED!

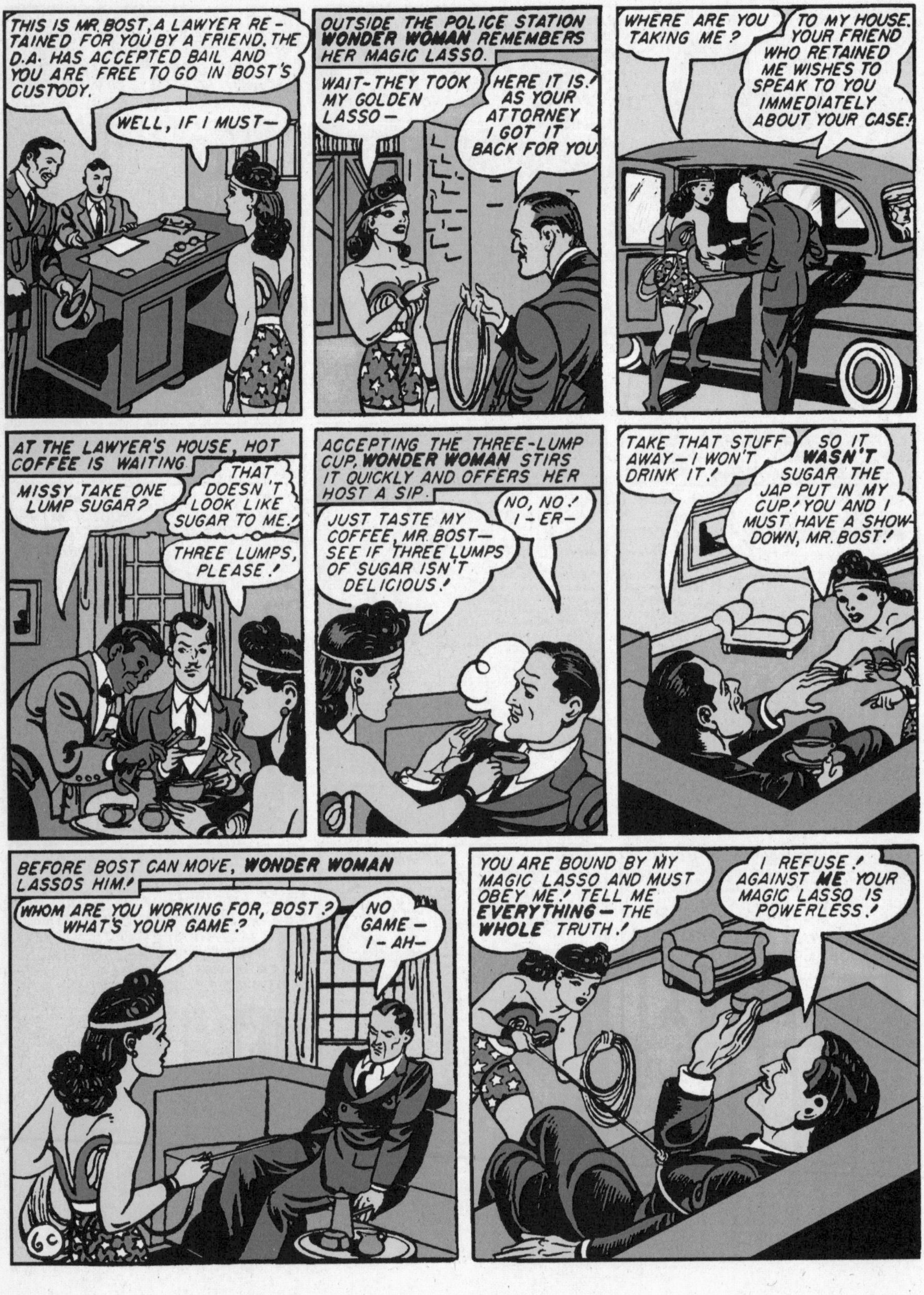
THIS IS MR. BOST, A LAWYER RETAINED FOR YOU BY A FRIEND. THE D.A. HAS ACCEPTED BAIL AND YOU ARE FREE TO GO IN BOST'S CUSTODY.
WELL, IF I MUST—
OUTSIDE THE POLICE STATION WONDER WOMAN REMEMBERS HER MAGIC LASSO.
WAIT-THEY TOOK MY GOLDEN LASSO—
HERE IT IS.! AS YOUR ATTORNEY I GOT IT BACK FOR YOU
WHERE ARE YOU TAKING ME ?
TO MY HOUSE. YOUR FRIEND WHO RETAINED ME WISHES TO SPEAK TO YOU IMMEDIATELY ABOUT YOUR CASE!
AT THE LAWYER'S HOUSE, HOT COFFEE IS WAITING.
MISSY TAKE ONE LUMP SUGAR?
THAT DOESN'T LOOK LIKE SUGAR TO ME.!
THREE LUMPS, PLEASE.!
ACCEPTING THE THREE-LUMP CUP, WONDER WOMAN STIRS IT QUICKLY AND OFFERS HER HOST A SIP.
JUST TASTE MY COFFEE, MR. BOST— SEE IF THREE LUMPS OF SUGAR ISN'T DELICIOUS.!
NO, NO.! I—ER—
TAKE THAT STUFF AWAY—I WON'T DRINK IT.!
SO IT WASN'T SUGAR THE JAP PUT IN MY CUP.! YOU AND I MUST HAVE A SHOW-DOWN, MR. BOST.!
BEFORE BOST CAN MOVE, WONDER WOMAN LASSOS HIM.!
WHOM ARE YOU WORKING FOR, BOST? WHAT'S YOUR GAME?
NO GAME— I—AH—
6C
YOU ARE BOUND BY MY MAGIC LASSO AND MUST OBEY ME.! TELL ME EVERYTHING— THE WHOLE TRUTH.!
I REFUSE.! AGAINST ME YOUR MAGIC LASSO IS POWERLESS.!

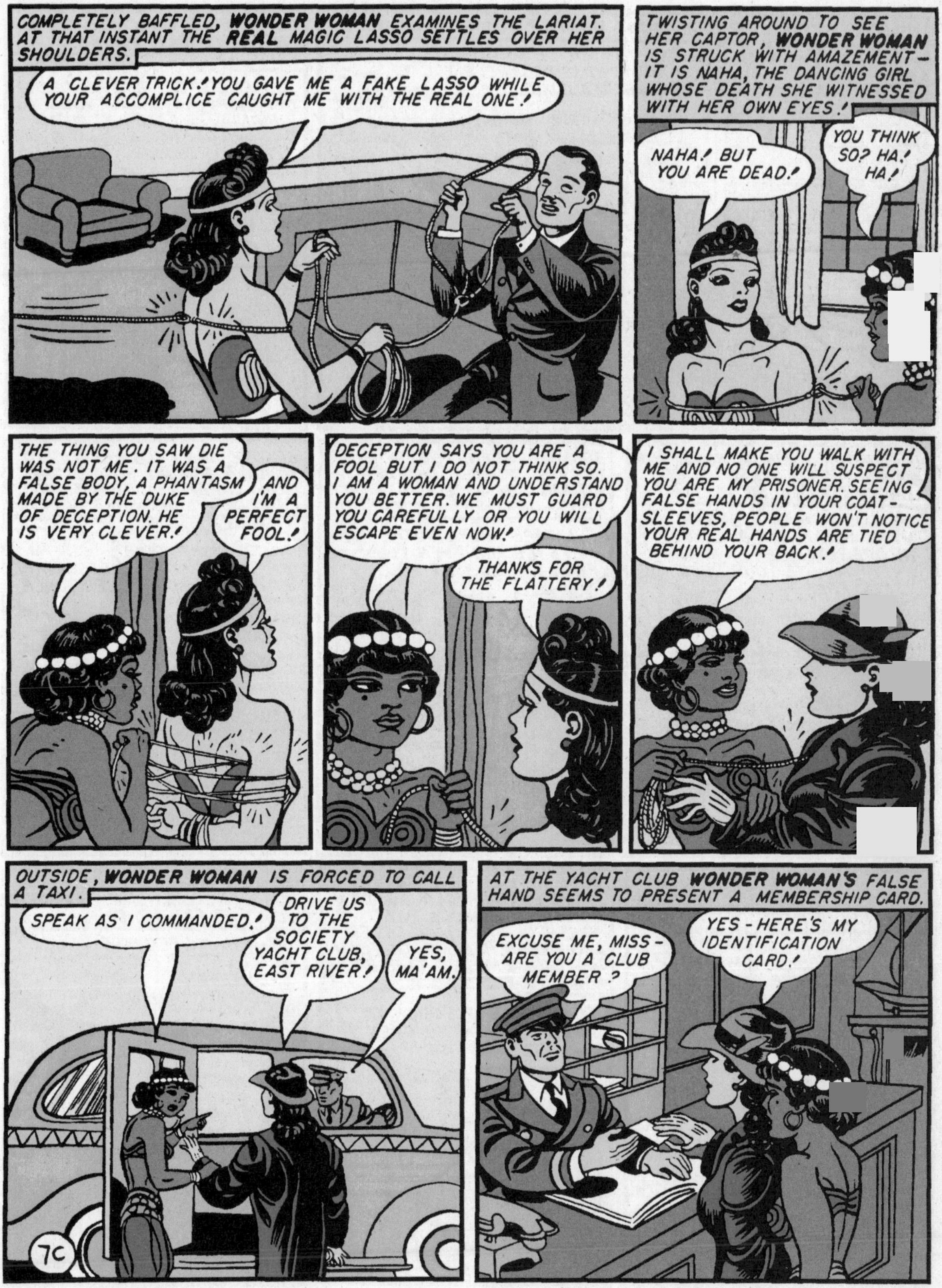
COMPLETELY BAFFLED, WONDER WOMAN EXAMINES THE LARIAT. AT THAT INSTANT THE REAL MAGIC LASSO SETTLES OVER HER SHOULDERS.
A CLEVER TRICK! YOU GAVE ME A FAKE LASSO WHILE YOUR ACCOMPLICE CAUGHT ME WITH THE REAL ONE!
TWISTING AROUND TO SEE HER CAPTOR, WONDER WOMAN IS STRUCK WITH AMAZEMENT— IT IS NAHA, THE DANCING GIRL WHOSE DEATH SHE WITNESSED WITH HER OWN EYES!
NAHA! BUT YOU ARE DEAD!
YOU THINK SO? HA! HA!
THE THING YOU SAW DIE WAS NOT ME. IT WAS A FALSE BODY, A PHANTASM MADE BY THE DUKE OF DECEPTION. HE IS VERY CLEVER!
AND I'M A PERFECT FOOL!
DECEPTION SAYS YOU ARE A FOOL BUT I DO NOT THINK SO. I AM A WOMAN AND UNDERSTAND YOU BETTER. WE MUST GUARD YOU CAREFULLY OR YOU WILL ESCAPE EVEN NOW!
THANKS FOR THE FLATTERY!
I SHALL MAKE YOU WALK WITH ME AND NO ONE WILL SUSPECT YOU ARE MY PRISONER. SEEING FALSE HANDS IN YOUR COAT-SLEEVES, PEOPLE WON'T NOTICE YOUR REAL HANDS ARE TIED BEHIND YOUR BACK!
OUTSIDE, WONDER WOMAN IS FORCED TO CALL A TAXI.
SPEAK AS I COMMANDED!
DRIVE US TO THE SOCIETY YACHT CLUB, EAST RIVER!
YES, MA'AM.
7C
AT THE YACHT CLUB WONDER WOMAN'S FALSE HAND SEEMS TO PRESENT A MEMBERSHIP CARD.
EXCUSE ME, MISS- ARE YOU A CLUB MEMBER ?
YES - HERE'S MY IDENTIFICATION CARD!

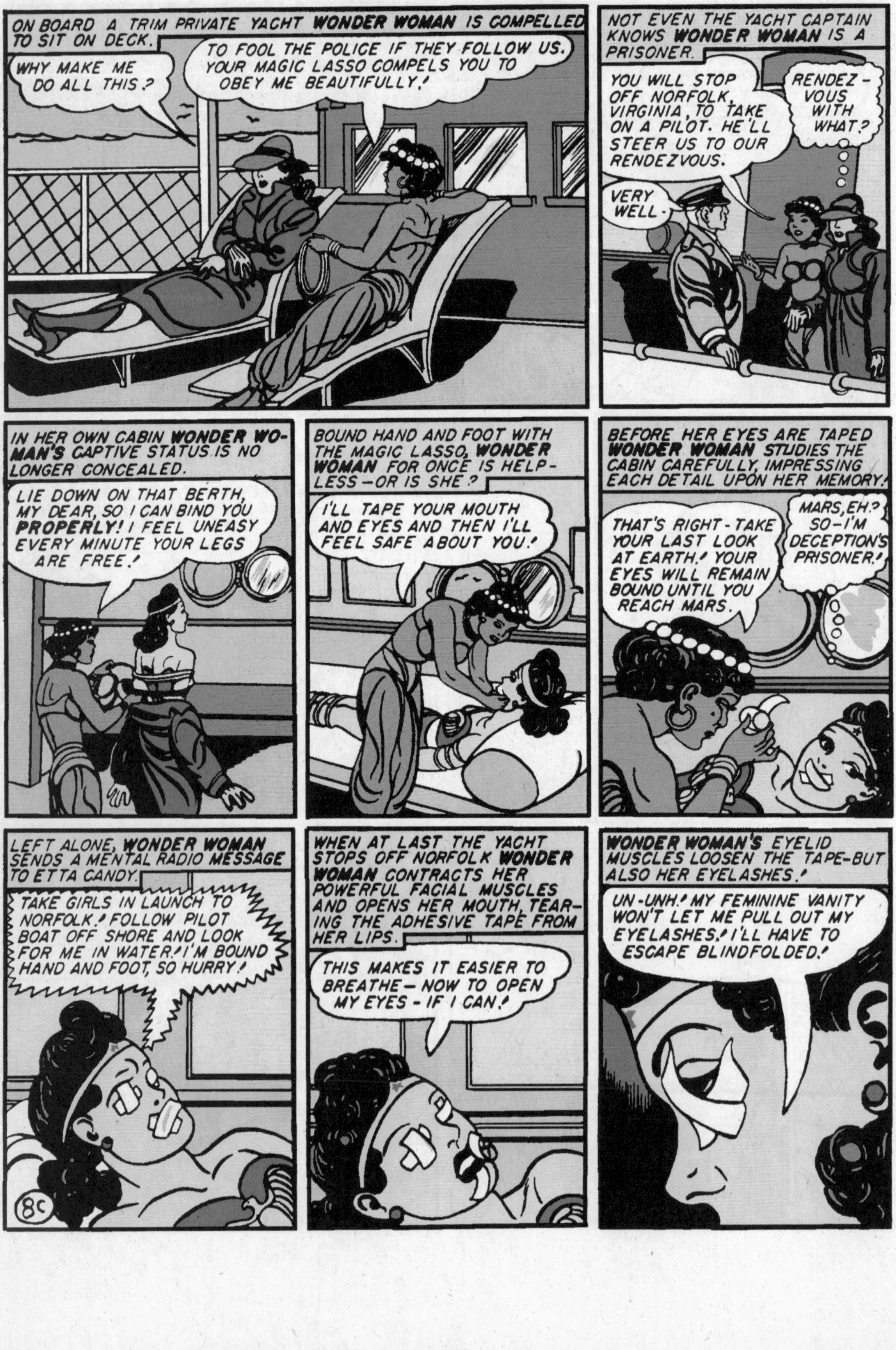
ON BOARD A TRIM PRIVATE YACHT WONDER WOMAN IS COMPELLED TO SIT ON DECK.
WHY MAKE ME DO ALL THIS?
TO FOOL THE POLICE IF THEY FOLLOW US. YOUR MAGIC LASSO COMPELS YOU TO OBEY ME BEAUTIFULLY!
NOT EVEN THE YACHT CAPTAIN KNOWS WONDER WOMAN IS A PRISONER.
YOU WILL STOP OFF NORFOLK, VIRGINIA, TO TAKE ON A PILOT. HE'LL STEER US TO OUR RENDEZVOUS.
RENDEZ-VOUS WITH WHAT?
VERY WELL-
IN HER OWN CABIN WONDER WOMAN'S CAPTIVE STATUS IS NO LONGER CONCEALED.
LIE DOWN ON THAT BERTH, MY DEAR, SO I CAN BIND YOU PROPERLY! I FEEL UNEASY EVERY MINUTE YOUR LEGS ARE FREE!
BOUND HAND AND FOOT WITH THE MAGIC LASSO, WONDER WOMAN FOR ONCE IS HELPLESS—OR IS SHE?
I'LL TAPE YOUR MOUTH AND EYES AND THEN I'LL FEEL SAFE ABOUT YOU!
BEFORE HER EYES ARE TAPED WONDER WOMAN STUDIES THE CABIN CAREFULLY, IMPRESSING EACH DETAIL UPON HER MEMORY!
THAT'S RIGHT-TAKE YOUR LAST LOOK AT EARTH! YOUR EYES WILL REMAIN BOUND UNTIL YOU REACH MARS.
MARS, EH? SO-I'M DECEPTION'S PRISONER!
LEFT ALONE, WONDER WOMAN SENDS A MENTAL RADIO MESSAGE TO ETTA CANDY.
TAKE GIRLS IN LAUNCH TO NORFOLK! FOLLOW PILOT BOAT OFF SHORE AND LOOK FOR ME IN WATER! I'M BOUND HAND AND FOOT, SO HURRY!
8C
WHEN AT LAST THE YACHT STOPS OFF NORFOLK WONDER WOMAN CONTRACTS HER POWERFUL FACIAL MUSCLES AND OPENS HER MOUTH, TEARING THE ADHESIVE TAPE FROM HER LIPS.
THIS MAKES IT EASIER TO BREATHE—NOW TO OPEN MY EYES - IF I CAN!
WONDER WOMAN'S EYELID MUSCLES LOOSEN THE TAPE-BUT ALSO HER EYELASHES!
UN-UNH! MY FEMININE VANITY WON'T LET ME PULL OUT MY EYELASHES! I'LL HAVE TO ESCAPE BLINDFOLDED!

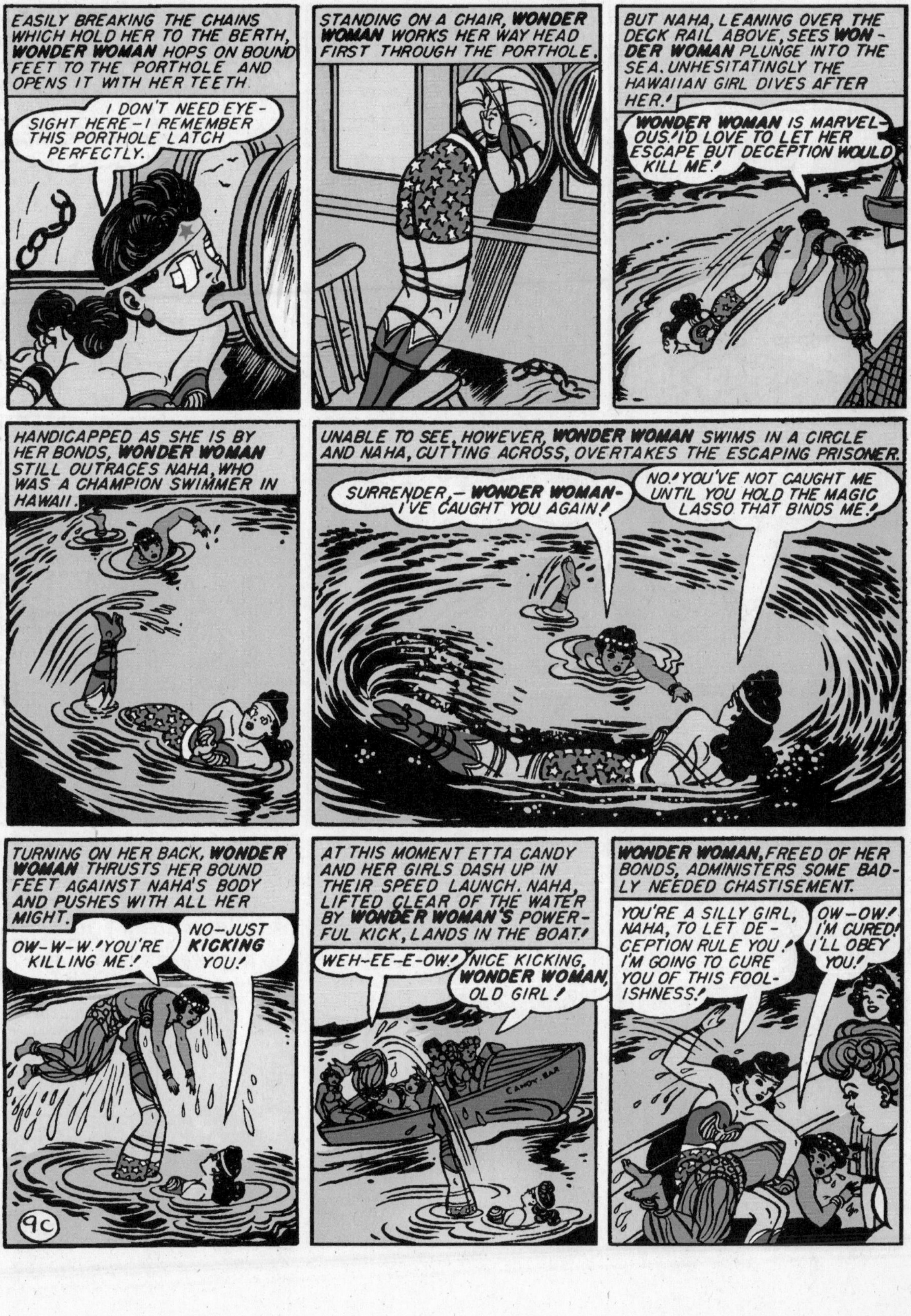
EASILY BREAKING THE CHAINS WHICH HOLD HER TO THE BERTH, WONDER WOMAN HOPS ON BOUND FEET TO THE PORTHOLE AND OPENS IT WITH HER TEETH.
I DON'T NEED EYE-SIGHT HERE—I REMEMBER THIS PORTHOLE LATCH PERFECTLY.
STANDING ON A CHAIR, WONDER WOMAN WORKS HER WAY HEAD FIRST THROUGH THE PORTHOLE.
BUT NAHA, LEANING OVER THE DECK RAIL ABOVE, SEES WONDER WOMAN PLUNGE INTO THE SEA. UNHESITATINGLY THE HAWAIIAN GIRL DIVES AFTER HER!
WONDER WOMAN IS MARVELOUS! I'D LOVE TO LET HER ESCAPE BUT DECEPTION WOULD KILL ME!
HANDICAPPED AS SHE IS BY HER BONDS, WONDER WOMAN STILL OUTRACES NAHA, WHO WAS A CHAMPION SWIMMER IN HAWAII.
UNABLE TO SEE, HOWEVER, WONDER WOMAN SWIMS IN A CIRCLE AND NAHA, CUTTING ACROSS, OVERTAKES THE ESCAPING PRISONER.
SURRENDER,—WONDER WOMAN—I'VE CAUGHT YOU AGAIN!
NO! YOU'VE NOT CAUGHT ME UNTIL YOU HOLD THE MAGIC LASSO THAT BINDS ME!
TURNING ON HER BACK, WONDER WOMAN THRUSTS HER BOUND FEET AGAINST NAHA'S BODY AND PUSHES WITH ALL HER MIGHT.
OW-W-W! YOU'RE KILLING ME!
NO—JUST KICKING YOU!
9C
AT THIS MOMENT ETTA CANDY AND HER GIRLS DASH UP IN THEIR SPEED LAUNCH. NAHA, LIFTED CLEAR OF THE WATER BY WONDER WOMAN'S POWERFUL KICK, LANDS IN THE BOAT!
WEH-EE-E-OW!
NICE KICKING, WONDER WOMAN, OLD GIRL!
CANDY-BAR
WONDER WOMAN, FREED OF HER BONDS, ADMINISTERS SOME BADLY NEEDED CHASTISEMENT.
YOU'RE A SILLY GIRL, NAHA, TO LET DECEPTION RULE YOU! I'M GOING TO CURE YOU OF THIS FOOLISHNESS!
OW-OW! I'M CURED! I'LL OBEY YOU!

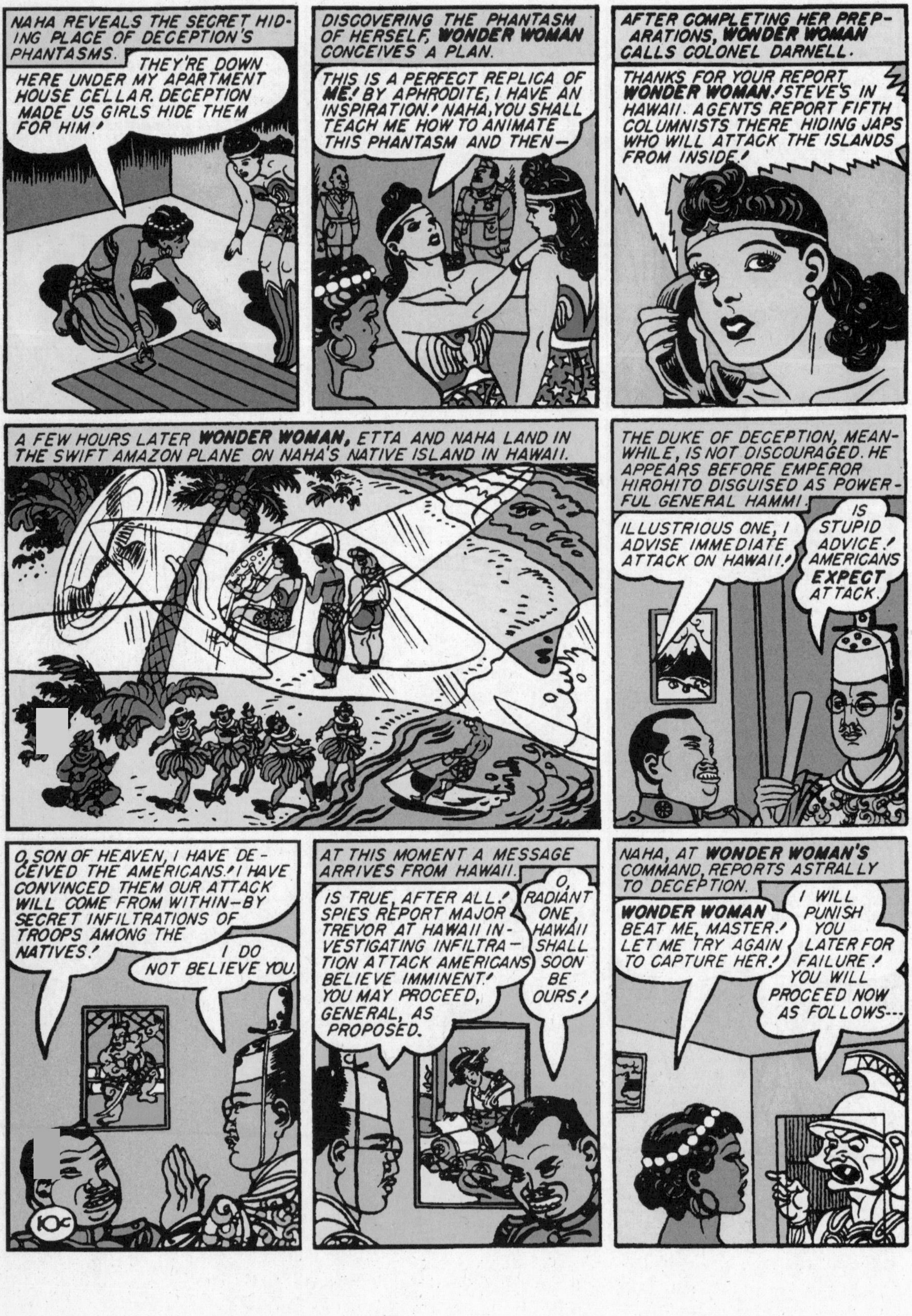
NAHA REVEALS THE SECRET HIDING PLACE OF DECEPTION'S PHANTASMS.
THEY'RE DOWN HERE UNDER MY APARTMENT HOUSE CELLAR. DECEPTION MADE US GIRLS HIDE THEM FOR HIM!
DISCOVERING THE PHANTASM OF HERSELF, WONDER WOMAN CONCEIVES A PLAN.
THIS IS A PERFECT REPLICA OF ME! BY APHRODITE, I HAVE AN INSPIRATION! NAHA, YOU SHALL TEACH ME HOW TO ANIMATE THIS PHANTASM AND THEN—
AFTER COMPLETING HER PREPARATIONS, WONDER WOMAN CALLS COLONEL DARNELL.
THANKS FOR YOUR REPORT WONDER WOMAN! STEVE'S IN HAWAII. AGENTS REPORT FIFTH COLUMNISTS THERE HIDING JAPS WHO WILL ATTACK THE ISLANDS FROM INSIDE!
A FEW HOURS LATER WONDER WOMAN, ETTA AND NAHA LAND IN THE SWIFT AMAZON PLANE ON NAHA'S NATIVE ISLAND IN HAWAII.
THE DUKE OF DECEPTION, MEANWHILE, IS NOT DISCOURAGED. HE APPEARS BEFORE EMPEROR HIROHITO DISGUISED AS POWERFUL GENERAL HAMMI.
ILLUSTRIOUS ONE, I ADVISE IMMEDIATE ATTACK ON HAWAII!
IS STUPID ADVICE! AMERICANS EXPECT ATTACK.
O, SON OF HEAVEN, I HAVE DECEIVED THE AMERICANS! I HAVE CONVINCED THEM OUR ATTACK WILL COME FROM WITHIN—BY SECRET INFILTRATIONS OF TROOPS AMONG THE NATIVES!
I DO NOT BELIEVE YOU.
10¢
AT THIS MOMENT A MESSAGE ARRIVES FROM HAWAII.
IS TRUE, AFTER ALL! SPIES REPORT MAJOR TREVOR AT HAWAII INVESTIGATING INFILTRATION ATTACK AMERICANS BELIEVE IMMINENT! YOU MAY PROCEED, GENERAL, AS PROPOSED.
O, RADIANT ONE, HAWAII SHALL SOON BE OURS!
NAHA, AT WONDER WOMAN'S COMMAND, REPORTS ASTRALLY TO DECEPTION.
WONDER WOMAN BEAT ME, MASTER! LET ME TRY AGAIN TO CAPTURE HER!
I WILL PUNISH YOU LATER FOR FAILURE! YOU WILL PROCEED NOW AS FOLLOWS---

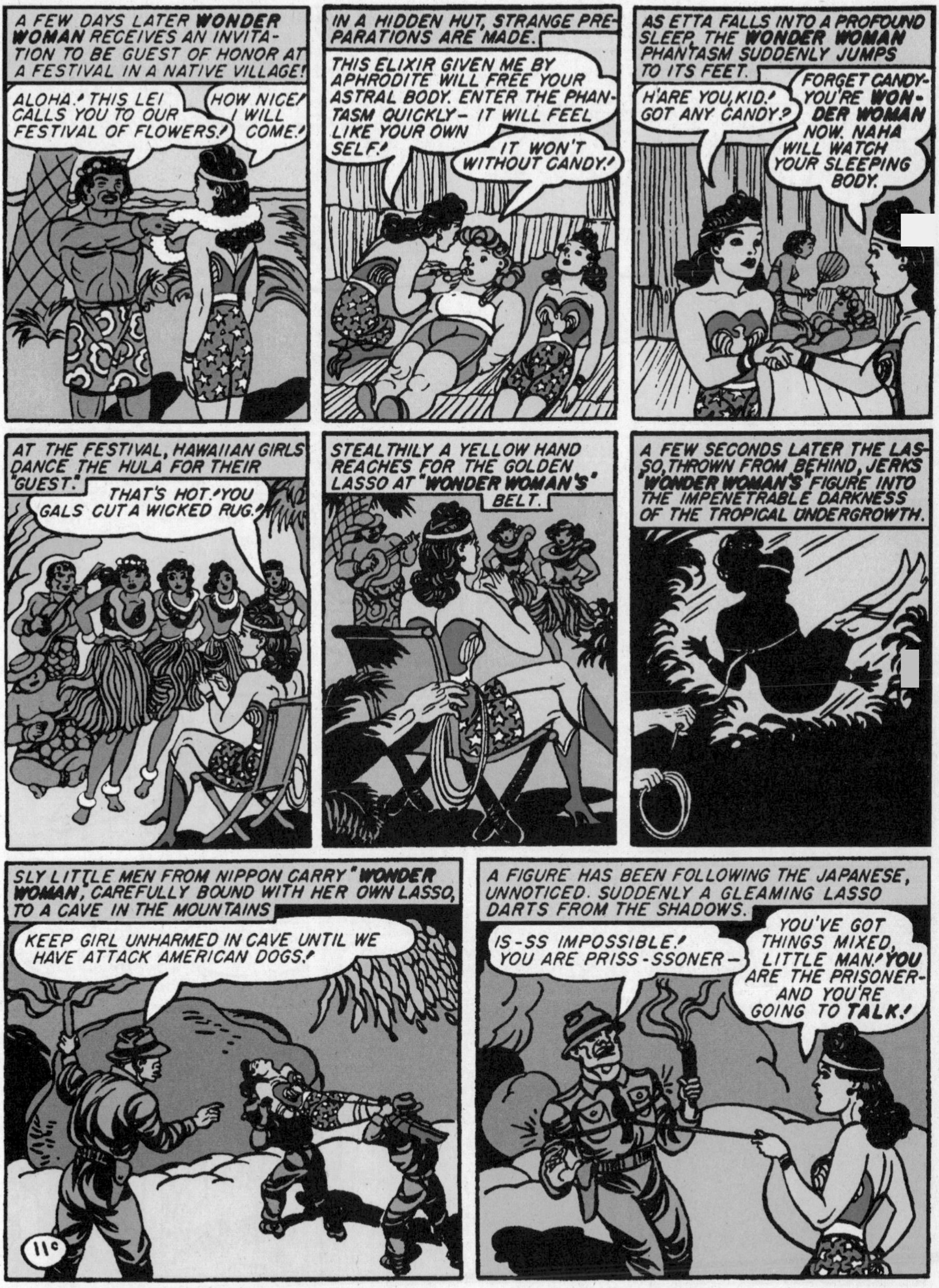
A FEW DAYS LATER WONDER WOMAN RECEIVES AN INVITATION TO BE GUEST OF HONOR AT A FESTIVAL IN A NATIVE VILLAGE!
ALOHA! THIS LEI CALLS YOU TO OUR FESTIVAL OF FLOWERS!
HOW NICE! I WILL COME!
IN A HIDDEN HUT, STRANGE PREPARATIONS ARE MADE.
THIS ELIXIR GIVEN ME BY APHRODITE WILL FREE YOUR ASTRAL BODY. ENTER THE PHANTASM QUICKLY— IT WILL FEEL LIKE YOUR OWN SELF!
IT WON'T WITHOUT CANDY!
AS ETTA FALLS INTO A PROFOUND SLEEP, THE WONDER WOMAN PHANTASM SUDDENLY JUMPS TO ITS FEET.
H'ARE YOU, KID! GOT ANY CANDY?
FORGET CANDY-YOU'RE WONDER WOMAN NOW. NAHA WILL WATCH YOUR SLEEPING BODY.
AT THE FESTIVAL, HAWAIIAN GIRLS DANCE THE HULA FOR THEIR "GUEST."
THAT'S HOT! YOU GALS CUT A WICKED RUG!
STEALTHILY A YELLOW HAND REACHES FOR THE GOLDEN LASSO AT "WONDER WOMAN'S" BELT.
A FEW SECONDS LATER THE LASSO, THROWN FROM BEHIND, JERKS "WONDER WOMAN'S" FIGURE INTO THE IMPENETRABLE DARKNESS OF THE TROPICAL UNDERGROWTH.
SLY LITTLE MEN FROM NIPPON CARRY "WONDER WOMAN", CAREFULLY BOUND WITH HER OWN LASSO, TO A CAVE IN THE MOUNTAINS
KEEP GIRL UNHARMED IN CAVE UNTIL WE HAVE ATTACK AMERICAN DOGS!
11c
A FIGURE HAS BEEN FOLLOWING THE JAPANESE, UNNOTICED. SUDDENLY A GLEAMING LASSO DARTS FROM THE SHADOWS.
IS-SS IMPOSSIBLE! YOU ARE PRISS-SSONER—
YOU'VE GOT THINGS MIXED, LITTLE MAN! YOU ARE THE PRISONER- AND YOU'RE GOING TO TALK!

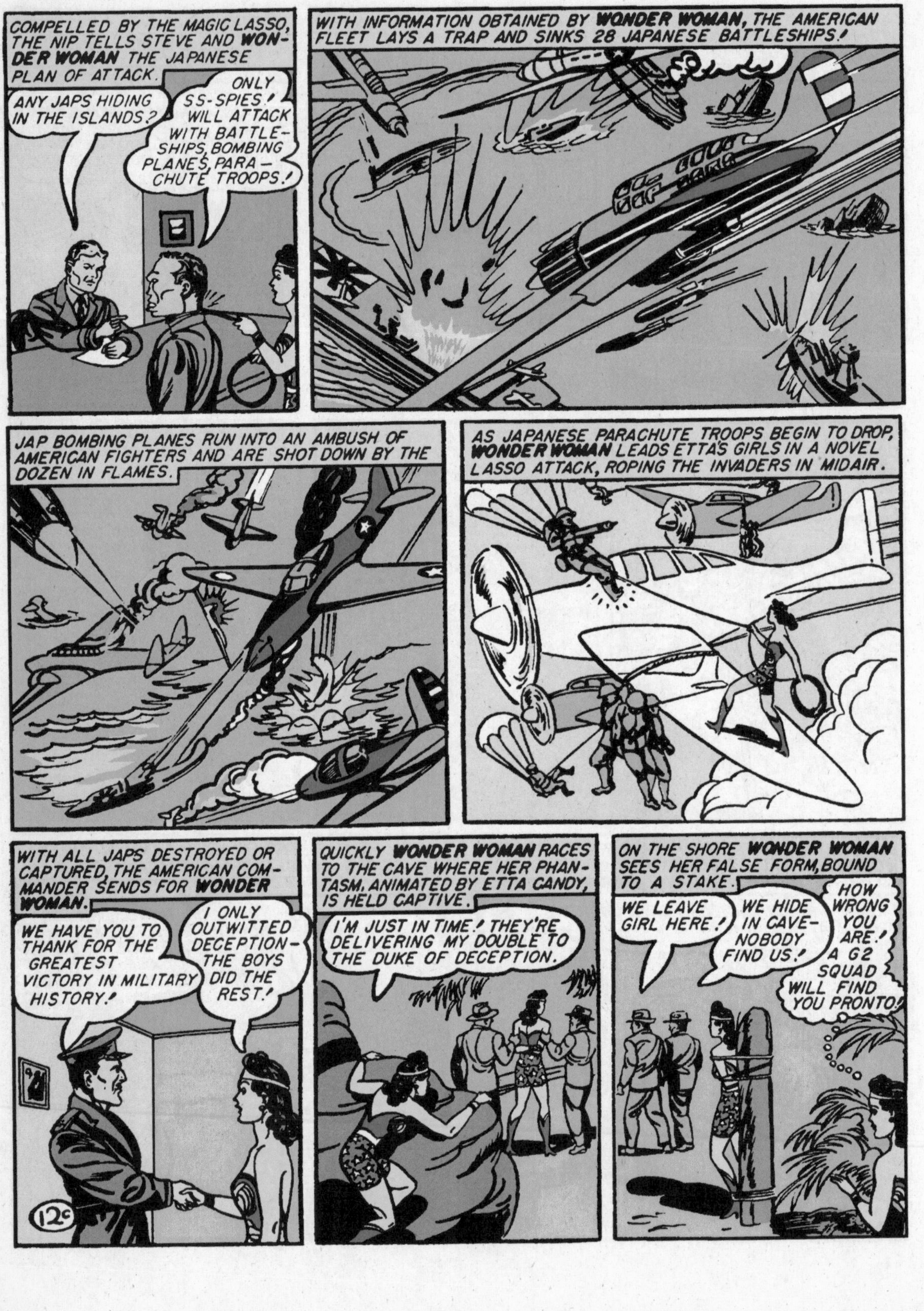
COMPELLED BY THE MAGIC LASSO, THE NIP TELLS STEVE AND WONDER WOMAN THE JAPANESE PLAN OF ATTACK.
ANY JAPS HIDING IN THE ISLANDS?
ONLY SS-SPIES! WILL ATTACK WITH BATTLESHIPS, BOMBING PLANES, PARA-CHUTE TROOPS!
WITH INFORMATION OBTAINED BY WONDER WOMAN, THE AMERICAN FLEET LAYS A TRAP AND SINKS 28 JAPANESE BATTLESHIPS!
JAP BOMBING PLANES RUN INTO AN AMBUSH OF AMERICAN FIGHTERS AND ARE SHOT DOWN BY THE DOZEN IN FLAMES.
AS JAPANESE PARACHUTE TROOPS BEGIN TO DROP, WONDER WOMAN LEADS ETTA'S GIRLS IN A NOVEL LASSO ATTACK, ROPING THE INVADERS IN MIDAIR.
WITH ALL JAPS DESTROYED OR CAPTURED, THE AMERICAN COMMANDER SENDS FOR WONDER WOMAN.
WE HAVE YOU TO THANK FOR THE GREATEST VICTORY IN MILITARY HISTORY!
I ONLY OUTWITTED DECEPTION— THE BOYS DID THE REST!
12¢
QUICKLY WONDER WOMAN RACES TO THE CAVE WHERE HER PHANTASM, ANIMATED BY ETTA CANDY, IS HELD CAPTIVE.
I'M JUST IN TIME! THEY'RE DELIVERING MY DOUBLE TO THE DUKE OF DECEPTION.
ON THE SHORE WONDER WOMAN SEES HER FALSE FORM, BOUND TO A STAKE.
WE LEAVE GIRL HERE!
WE HIDE IN CAVE— NOBODY FIND US!
HOW WRONG YOU ARE! A G2 SQUAD WILL FIND YOU PRONTO!

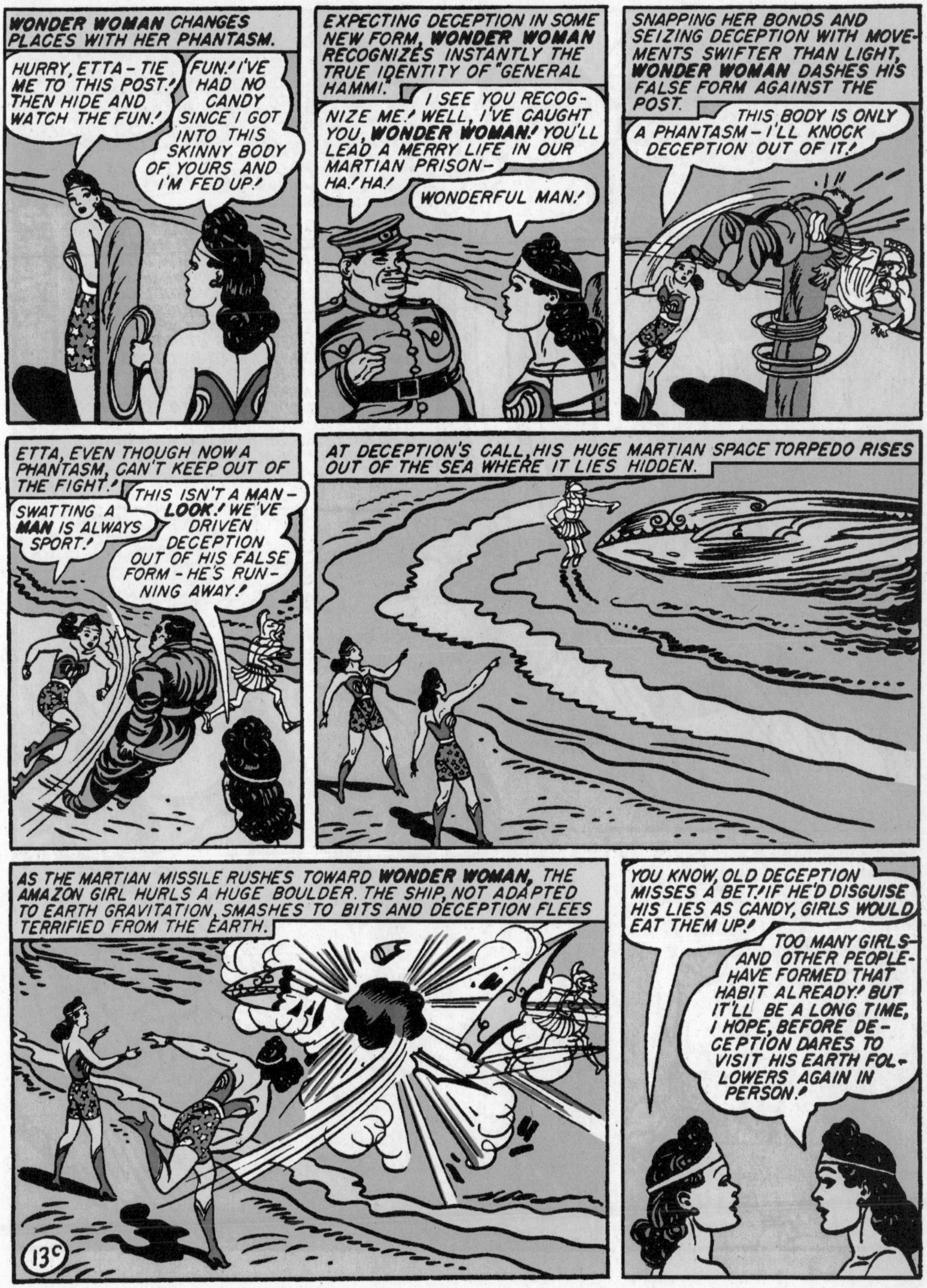
WONDER WOMAN CHANGES PLACES WITH HER PHANTASM.
HURRY, ETTA - TIE ME TO THIS POST! THEN HIDE AND WATCH THE FUN!
FUN! I'VE HAD NO CANDY SINCE I GOT INTO THIS SKINNY BODY OF YOURS AND I'M FED UP!
EXPECTING DECEPTION IN SOME NEW FORM, WONDER WOMAN RECOGNIZES INSTANTLY THE TRUE IDENTITY OF "GENERAL HAMMI."
I SEE YOU RECOGNIZE ME! WELL, I'VE CAUGHT YOU, WONDER WOMAN! YOU'LL LEAD A MERRY LIFE IN OUR MARTIAN PRISON- HA! HA!
WONDERFUL MAN!
SNAPPING HER BONDS AND SEIZING DECEPTION WITH MOVEMENTS SWIFTER THAN LIGHT, WONDER WOMAN DASHES HIS FALSE FORM AGAINST THE POST.
THIS BODY IS ONLY A PHANTASM - I'LL KNOCK DECEPTION OUT OF IT!
ETTA, EVEN THOUGH NOW A PHANTASM, CAN'T KEEP OUT OF THE FIGHT!
SWATTING A MAN IS ALWAYS SPORT!
THIS ISN'T A MAN - LOOK! WE'VE DRIVEN DECEPTION OUT OF HIS FALSE FORM - HE'S RUNNING AWAY!
AT DECEPTION'S CALL, HIS HUGE MARTIAN SPACE TORPEDO RISES OUT OF THE SEA WHERE IT LIES HIDDEN.
AS THE MARTIAN MISSILE RUSHES TOWARD WONDER WOMAN, THE AMAZON GIRL HURLS A HUGE BOULDER. THE SHIP, NOT ADAPTED TO EARTH GRAVITATION, SMASHES TO BITS AND DECEPTION FLEES TERRIFIED FROM THE EARTH.
13C
YOU KNOW, OLD DECEPTION MISSES A BET! IF HE'D DISGUISE HIS LIES AS CANDY, GIRLS WOULD EAT THEM UP!
TOO MANY GIRLS - AND OTHER PEOPLE - HAVE FORMED THAT HABIT ALREADY! BUT IT'LL BE A LONG TIME, I HOPE, BEFORE DECEPTION DARES TO VISIT HIS EARTH FOLLOWERS AGAIN IN PERSON!

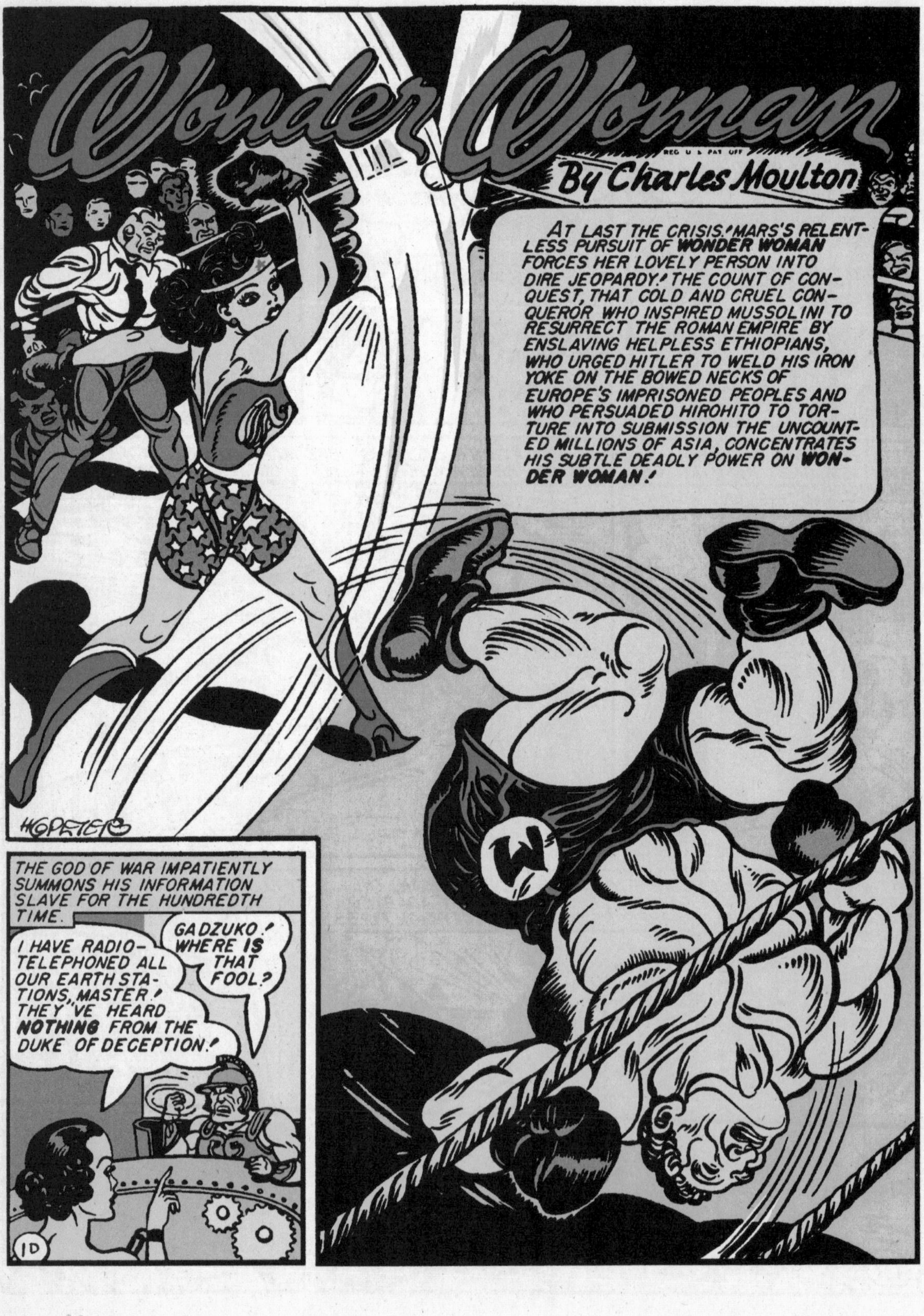
Wonder Woman
REG. U.S. PAT. OFF.
By Charles Moulton
AT LAST THE CRISIS! MARS'S RELENTLESS PURSUIT OF **WONDER WOMAN** FORCES HER LOVELY PERSON INTO DIRE JEOPARDY! THE COUNT OF CONQUEST, THAT COLD AND CRUEL CONQUEROR WHO INSPIRED MUSSOLINI TO RESURRECT THE ROMAN EMPIRE BY ENSLAVING HELPLESS ETHIOPIANS, WHO URGED HITLER TO WELD HIS IRON YOKE ON THE BOWED NECKS OF EUROPE'S IMPRISONED PEOPLES AND WHO PERSUADED HIROHITO TO TORTURE INTO SUBMISSION THE UNCOUNTED MILLIONS OF ASIA, CONCENTRATES HIS SUBTLE DEADLY POWER ON **WONDER WOMAN!**
HG PETER
THE GOD OF WAR IMPATIENTLY SUMMONS HIS INFORMATION SLAVE FOR THE HUNDREDTH TIME.
GADZUKO! WHERE **IS** THAT FOOL?
I HAVE RADIO-TELEPHONED ALL OUR EARTH STATIONS, MASTER! THEY'VE HEARD **NOTHING** FROM THE DUKE OF DECEPTION!
1D

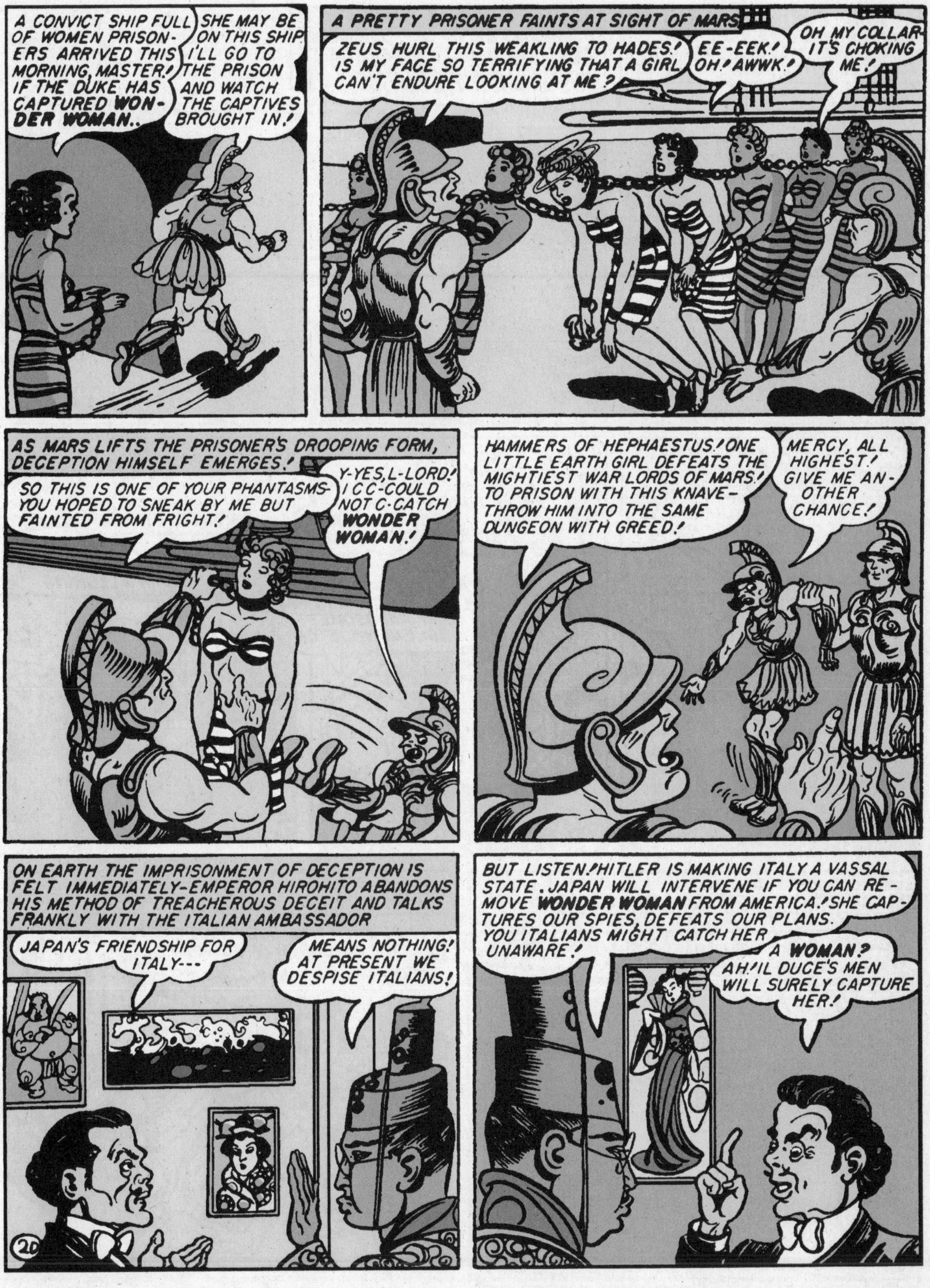
A CONVICT SHIP FULL OF WOMEN PRISONERS ARRIVED THIS MORNING, MASTER! IF THE DUKE HAS CAPTURED WONDER WOMAN..
SHE MAY BE ON THIS SHIP! I'LL GO TO THE PRISON AND WATCH THE CAPTIVES BROUGHT IN!
A PRETTY PRISONER FAINTS AT SIGHT OF MARS
ZEUS HURL THIS WEAKLING TO HADES! IS MY FACE SO TERRIFYING THAT A GIRL CAN'T ENDURE LOOKING AT ME?
EE-EEK! OH! AWWK!
OH MY COLLAR- IT'S CHOKING ME!
AS MARS LIFTS THE PRISONER'S DROOPING FORM, DECEPTION HIMSELF EMERGES!
SO THIS IS ONE OF YOUR PHANTASMS- YOU HOPED TO SNEAK BY ME BUT FAINTED FROM FRIGHT!
Y-YES, L-LORD! I C-C-COULD NOT C-CATCH WONDER WOMAN!
HAMMERS OF HEPHAESTUS! ONE LITTLE EARTH GIRL DEFEATS THE MIGHTIEST WAR LORDS OF MARS! TO PRISON WITH THIS KNAVE- THROW HIM INTO THE SAME DUNGEON WITH GREED!
MERCY, ALL HIGHEST! GIVE ME ANOTHER CHANCE!
ON EARTH THE IMPRISONMENT OF DECEPTION IS FELT IMMEDIATELY-EMPEROR HIROHITO ABANDONS HIS METHOD OF TREACHEROUS DECEIT AND TALKS FRANKLY WITH THE ITALIAN AMBASSADOR
JAPAN'S FRIENDSHIP FOR ITALY---
MEANS NOTHING! AT PRESENT WE DESPISE ITALIANS!
20
BUT LISTEN! HITLER IS MAKING ITALY A VASSAL STATE. JAPAN WILL INTERVENE IF YOU CAN REMOVE WONDER WOMAN FROM AMERICA! SHE CAPTURES OUR SPIES, DEFEATS OUR PLANS. YOU ITALIANS MIGHT CATCH HER UNAWARE!
A WOMAN? AH! IL DUCE'S MEN WILL SURELY CAPTURE HER!

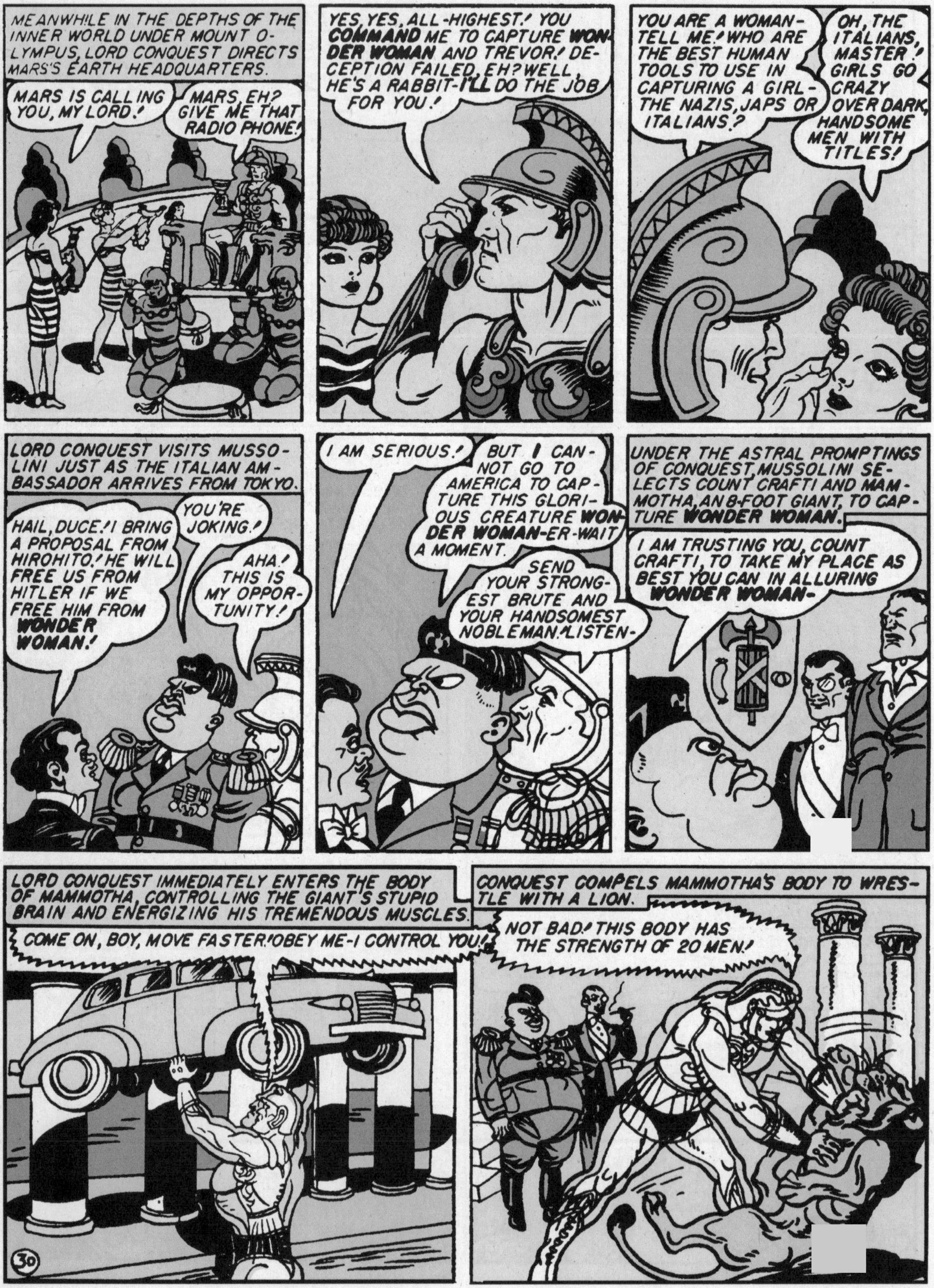
MEANWHILE IN THE DEPTHS OF THE INNER WORLD UNDER MOUNT O-LYMPUS, LORD CONQUEST DIRECTS MARS'S EARTH HEADQUARTERS.
MARS IS CALLING YOU, MY LORD!
MARS, EH? GIVE ME THAT RADIO PHONE!
YES, YES, ALL-HIGHEST! YOU COMMAND ME TO CAPTURE WONDER WOMAN AND TREVOR! DECEPTION FAILED, EH? WELL, HE'S A RABBIT-I'LL DO THE JOB FOR YOU!
YOU ARE A WOMAN-TELL ME! WHO ARE THE BEST HUMAN TOOLS TO USE IN CAPTURING A GIRL-THE NAZIS, JAPS OR ITALIANS?
OH, THE ITALIANS, MASTER! GIRLS GO CRAZY OVER DARK, HANDSOME MEN WITH TITLES!
LORD CONQUEST VISITS MUSSOLINI JUST AS THE ITALIAN AMBASSADOR ARRIVES FROM TOKYO.
HAIL, DUCE! I BRING A PROPOSAL FROM HIROHITO! HE WILL FREE US FROM HITLER IF WE FREE HIM FROM WONDER WOMAN!
YOU'RE JOKING!
AHA! THIS IS MY OPPORTUNITY!
I AM SERIOUS!
BUT I CANNOT GO TO AMERICA TO CAPTURE THIS GLORIOUS CREATURE WONDER WOMAN-ER-WAIT A MOMENT.
SEND YOUR STRONGEST BRUTE AND YOUR HANDSOMEST NOBLEMAN! LISTEN-
UNDER THE ASTRAL PROMPTINGS OF CONQUEST, MUSSOLINI SELECTS COUNT CRAFTI AND MAMMOTHA, AN 8-FOOT GIANT, TO CAPTURE WONDER WOMAN.
I AM TRUSTING YOU, COUNT CRAFTI, TO TAKE MY PLACE AS BEST YOU CAN IN ALLURING WONDER WOMAN-
LORD CONQUEST IMMEDIATELY ENTERS THE BODY OF MAMMOTHA, CONTROLLING THE GIANT'S STUPID BRAIN AND ENERGIZING HIS TREMENDOUS MUSCLES.
COME ON, BOY, MOVE FASTER! OBEY ME-I CONTROL YOU!
30
CONQUEST COMPELS MAMMOTHA'S BODY TO WRESTLE WITH A LION.
NOT BAD! THIS BODY HAS THE STRENGTH OF 20 MEN!

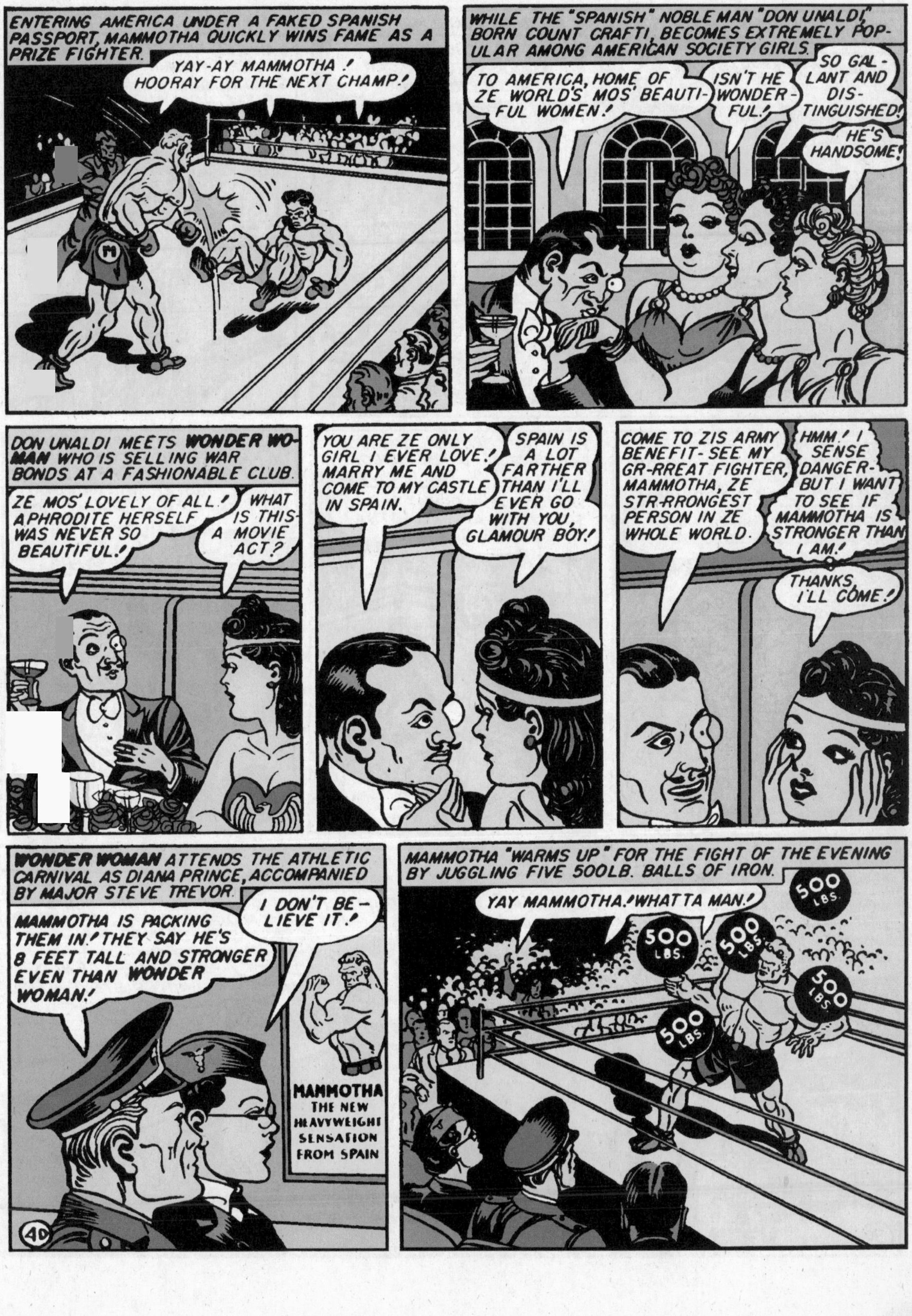

ENTERING AMERICA UNDER A FAKED SPANISH PASSPORT, MAMMOTHA QUICKLY WINS FAME AS A PRIZE FIGHTER.
YAY-AY MAMMOTHA! HOORAY FOR THE NEXT CHAMP!
WHILE THE "SPANISH" NOBLE MAN "DON UNALDI," BORN COUNT CRAFTI, BECOMES EXTREMELY POPULAR AMONG AMERICAN SOCIETY GIRLS.
TO AMERICA, HOME OF ZE WORLD'S MOS' BEAUTIFUL WOMEN!
ISN'T HE WONDERFUL!
SO GALLANT AND DISTINGUISHED!
HE'S HANDSOME!
DON UNALDI MEETS WONDER WOMAN WHO IS SELLING WAR BONDS AT A FASHIONABLE CLUB.
ZE MOS' LOVELY OF ALL! APHRODITE HERSELF WAS NEVER SO BEAUTIFUL!
WHAT IS THIS- A MOVIE ACT?
YOU ARE ZE ONLY GIRL I EVER LOVE! MARRY ME AND COME TO MY CASTLE IN SPAIN.
SPAIN IS A LOT FARTHER THAN I'LL EVER GO WITH YOU, GLAMOUR BOY!
COME TO ZIS ARMY BENEFIT- SEE MY GR-RREAT FIGHTER, MAMMOTHA, ZE STR-RRONGEST PERSON IN ZE WHOLE WORLD.
HMM! I SENSE DANGER- BUT I WANT TO SEE IF MAMMOTHA IS STRONGER THAN I AM!
THANKS, I'LL COME!
WONDER WOMAN ATTENDS THE ATHLETIC CARNIVAL AS DIANA PRINCE, ACCOMPANIED BY MAJOR STEVE TREVOR.
MAMMOTHA IS PACKING THEM IN! THEY SAY HE'S 8 FEET TALL AND STRONGER EVEN THAN WONDER WOMAN!
I DON'T BELIEVE IT!
MAMMOTHA THE NEW HEAVYWEIGHT SENSATION FROM SPAIN
MAMMOTHA "WARMS UP" FOR THE FIGHT OF THE EVENING BY JUGGLING FIVE 500LB. BALLS OF IRON.
YAY MAMMOTHA! WHATTA MAN!
500 LBS.
500 LBS.
500 LBS.
500 LBS.
500 LBS.

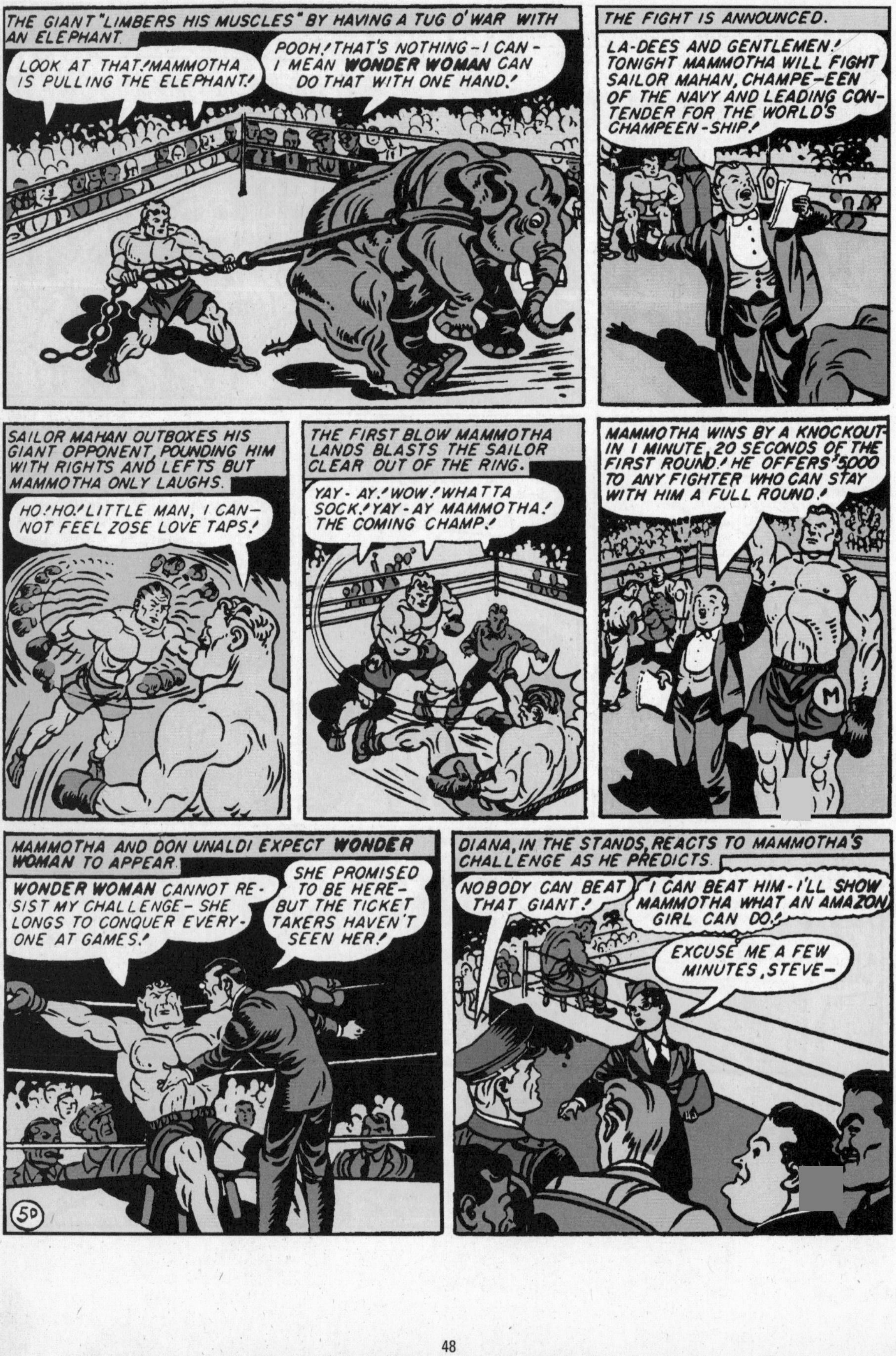

THE GIANT "LIMBERS HIS MUSCLES" BY HAVING A TUG O' WAR WITH AN ELEPHANT.
LOOK AT THAT! MAMMOTHA IS PULLING THE ELEPHANT!
POOH! THAT'S NOTHING - I CAN - I MEAN WONDER WOMAN CAN DO THAT WITH ONE HAND!
THE FIGHT IS ANNOUNCED.
LA-DEES AND GENTLEMEN! TONIGHT MAMMOTHA WILL FIGHT SAILOR MAHAN, CHAMPE-EEN OF THE NAVY AND LEADING CONTENDER FOR THE WORLD'S CHAMPEEN-SHIP!
SAILOR MAHAN OUTBOXES HIS GIANT OPPONENT, POUNDING HIM WITH RIGHTS AND LEFTS BUT MAMMOTHA ONLY LAUGHS.
HO! HO! LITTLE MAN, I CAN-NOT FEEL ZOSE LOVE TAPS!
THE FIRST BLOW MAMMOTHA LANDS BLASTS THE SAILOR CLEAR OUT OF THE RING.
YAY- AY! WOW! WHATTA SOCK! YAY-AY MAMMOTHA! THE COMING CHAMP!
MAMMOTHA WINS BY A KNOCKOUT IN 1 MINUTE, 20 SECONDS OF THE FIRST ROUND! HE OFFERS $5000 TO ANY FIGHTER WHO CAN STAY WITH HIM A FULL ROUND!
M
MAMMOTHA AND DON UNALDI EXPECT WONDER WOMAN TO APPEAR.
WONDER WOMAN CANNOT RESIST MY CHALLENGE - SHE LONGS TO CONQUER EVERYONE AT GAMES!
SHE PROMISED TO BE HERE - BUT THE TICKET TAKERS HAVEN'T SEEN HER!
5D
DIANA, IN THE STANDS, REACTS TO MAMMOTHA'S CHALLENGE AS HE PREDICTS.
NOBODY CAN BEAT THAT GIANT!
I CAN BEAT HIM - I'LL SHOW MAMMOTHA WHAT AN AMAZON GIRL CAN DO!
EXCUSE ME A FEW MINUTES, STEVE -

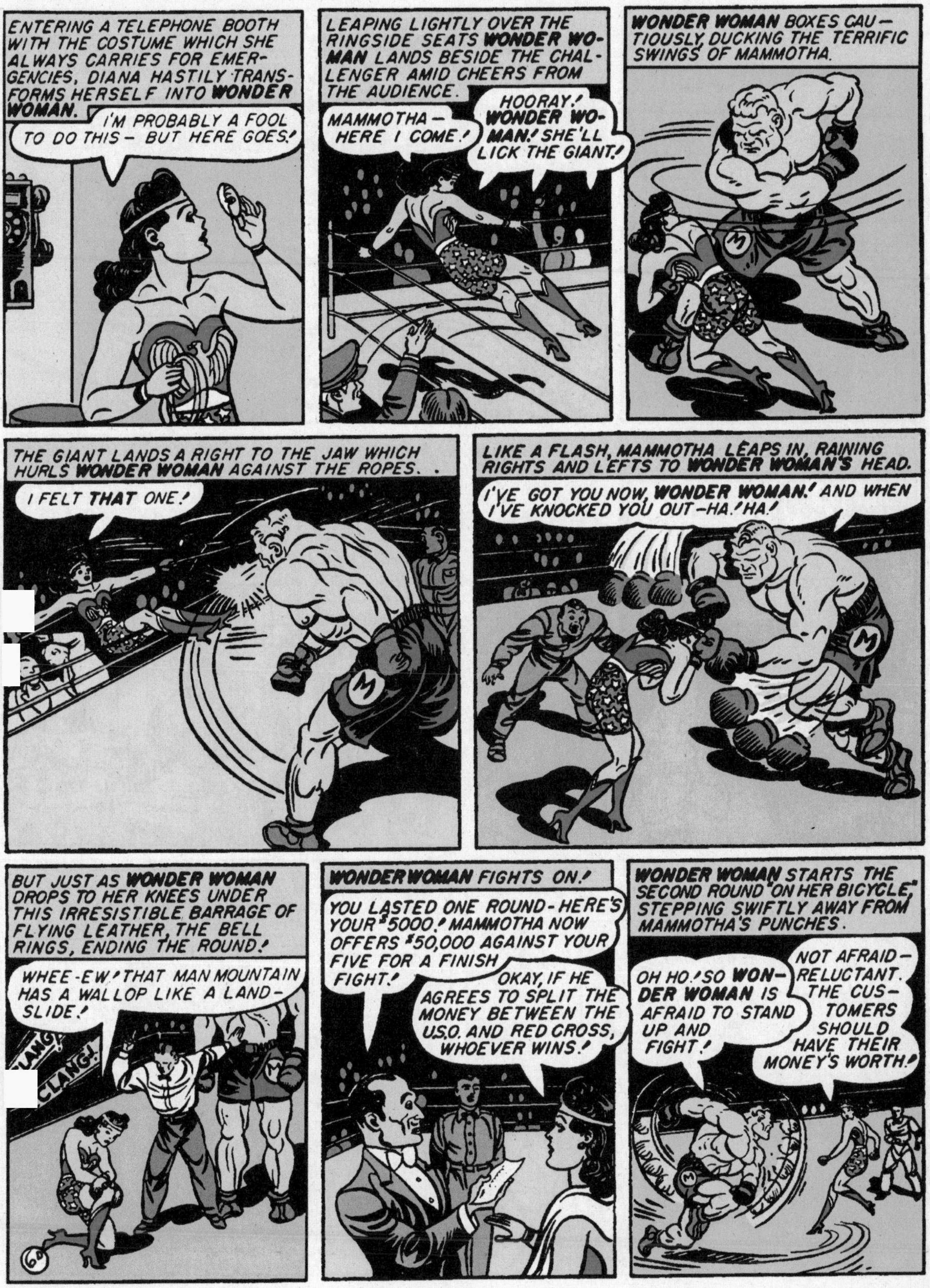
ENTERING A TELEPHONE BOOTH WITH THE COSTUME WHICH SHE ALWAYS CARRIES FOR EMERGENCIES, DIANA HASTILY TRANSFORMS HERSELF INTO WONDER WOMAN.
I'M PROBABLY A FOOL TO DO THIS – BUT HERE GOES!
LEAPING LIGHTLY OVER THE RINGSIDE SEATS WONDER WOMAN LANDS BESIDE THE CHALLENGER AMID CHEERS FROM THE AUDIENCE.
MAMMOTHA – HERE I COME!
HOORAY! WONDER WOMAN! SHE'LL LICK THE GIANT!
WONDER WOMAN BOXES CAUTIOUSLY, DUCKING THE TERRIFIC SWINGS OF MAMMOTHA.
M
THE GIANT LANDS A RIGHT TO THE JAW WHICH HURLS WONDER WOMAN AGAINST THE ROPES.
I FELT THAT ONE!
M
LIKE A FLASH, MAMMOTHA LEAPS IN, RAINING RIGHTS AND LEFTS TO WONDER WOMAN'S HEAD.
I'VE GOT YOU NOW, WONDER WOMAN! AND WHEN I'VE KNOCKED YOU OUT–HA! HA!
M
BUT JUST AS WONDER WOMAN DROPS TO HER KNEES UNDER THIS IRRESISTIBLE BARRAGE OF FLYING LEATHER, THE BELL RINGS, ENDING THE ROUND!
WHEE-EW! THAT MAN MOUNTAIN HAS A WALLOP LIKE A LANDSLIDE!
CLANG!
CLANG!
WONDER WOMAN FIGHTS ON!
YOU LASTED ONE ROUND – HERE'S YOUR $5000! MAMMOTHA NOW OFFERS $50,000 AGAINST YOUR FIVE FOR A FINISH FIGHT!
OKAY, IF HE AGREES TO SPLIT THE MONEY BETWEEN THE U.S.O. AND RED CROSS, WHOEVER WINS!
WONDER WOMAN STARTS THE SECOND ROUND "ON HER BICYCLE," STEPPING SWIFTLY AWAY FROM MAMMOTHA'S PUNCHES.
OH HO! SO WONDER WOMAN IS AFRAID TO STAND UP AND FIGHT!
NOT AFRAID – RELUCTANT. THE CUSTOMERS SHOULD HAVE THEIR MONEY'S WORTH!

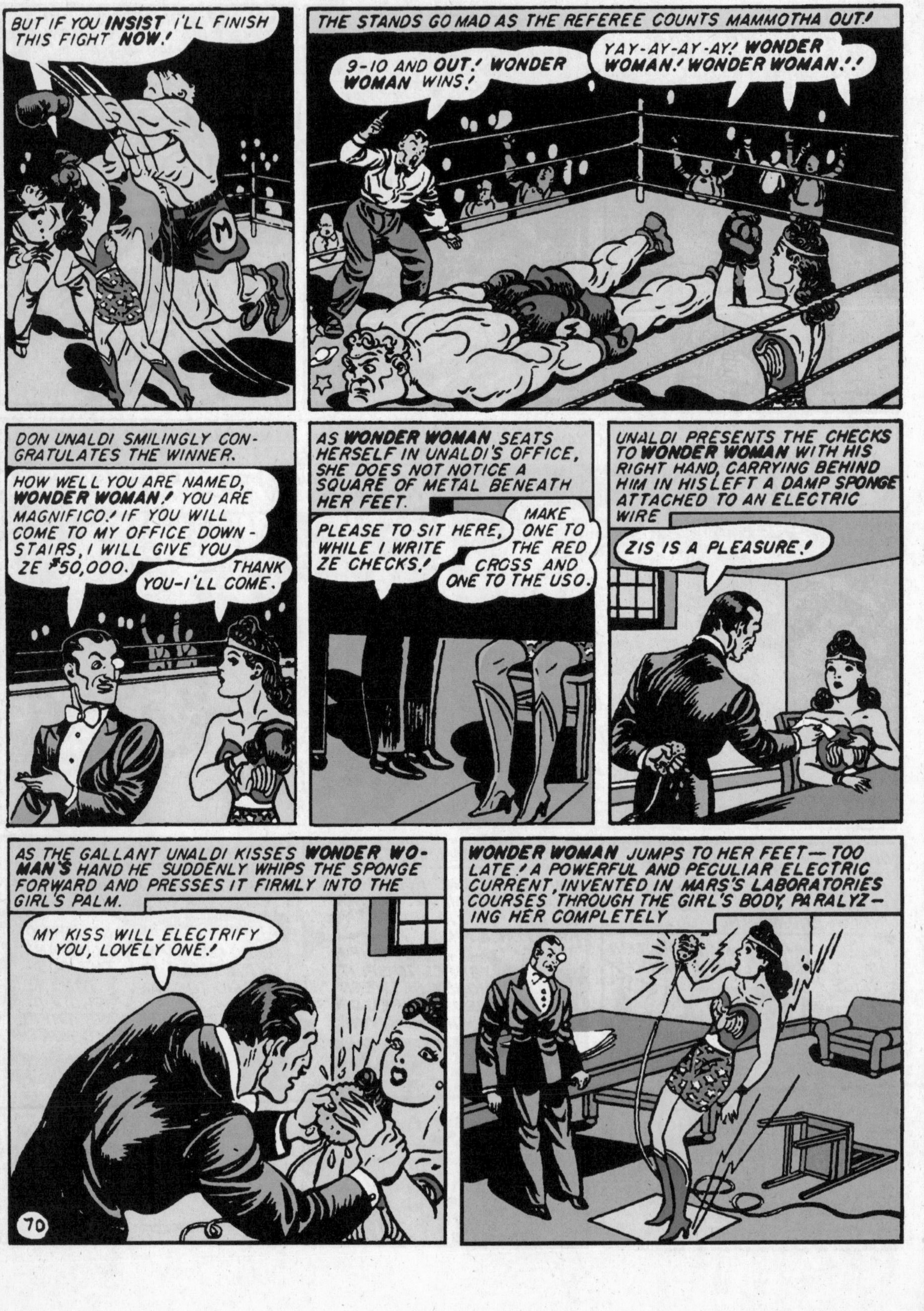
BUT IF YOU INSIST I'LL FINISH THIS FIGHT NOW!
THE STANDS GO MAD AS THE REFEREE COUNTS MAMMOTHA OUT!
9-10 AND OUT! WONDER WOMAN WINS!
YAY-AY-AY-AY! WONDER WOMAN! WONDER WOMAN!!
DON UNALDI SMILINGLY CONGRATULATES THE WINNER.
HOW WELL YOU ARE NAMED, WONDER WOMAN! YOU ARE MAGNIFICO! IF YOU WILL COME TO MY OFFICE DOWNSTAIRS, I WILL GIVE YOU ZE $50,000.
THANK YOU-I'LL COME.
AS WONDER WOMAN SEATS HERSELF IN UNALDI'S OFFICE, SHE DOES NOT NOTICE A SQUARE OF METAL BENEATH HER FEET.
PLEASE TO SIT HERE, WHILE I WRITE ZE CHECKS!
MAKE ONE TO THE RED CROSS AND ONE TO THE USO.
UNALDI PRESENTS THE CHECKS TO WONDER WOMAN WITH HIS RIGHT HAND, CARRYING BEHIND HIM IN HIS LEFT A DAMP SPONGE ATTACHED TO AN ELECTRIC WIRE
ZIS IS A PLEASURE!
AS THE GALLANT UNALDI KISSES WONDER WOMAN'S HAND HE SUDDENLY WHIPS THE SPONGE FORWARD AND PRESSES IT FIRMLY INTO THE GIRL'S PALM.
MY KISS WILL ELECTRIFY YOU, LOVELY ONE!
70
WONDER WOMAN JUMPS TO HER FEET—TOO LATE! A POWERFUL AND PECULIAR ELECTRIC CURRENT, INVENTED IN MARS'S LABORATORIES COURSES THROUGH THE GIRL'S BODY, PARALYZING HER COMPLETELY

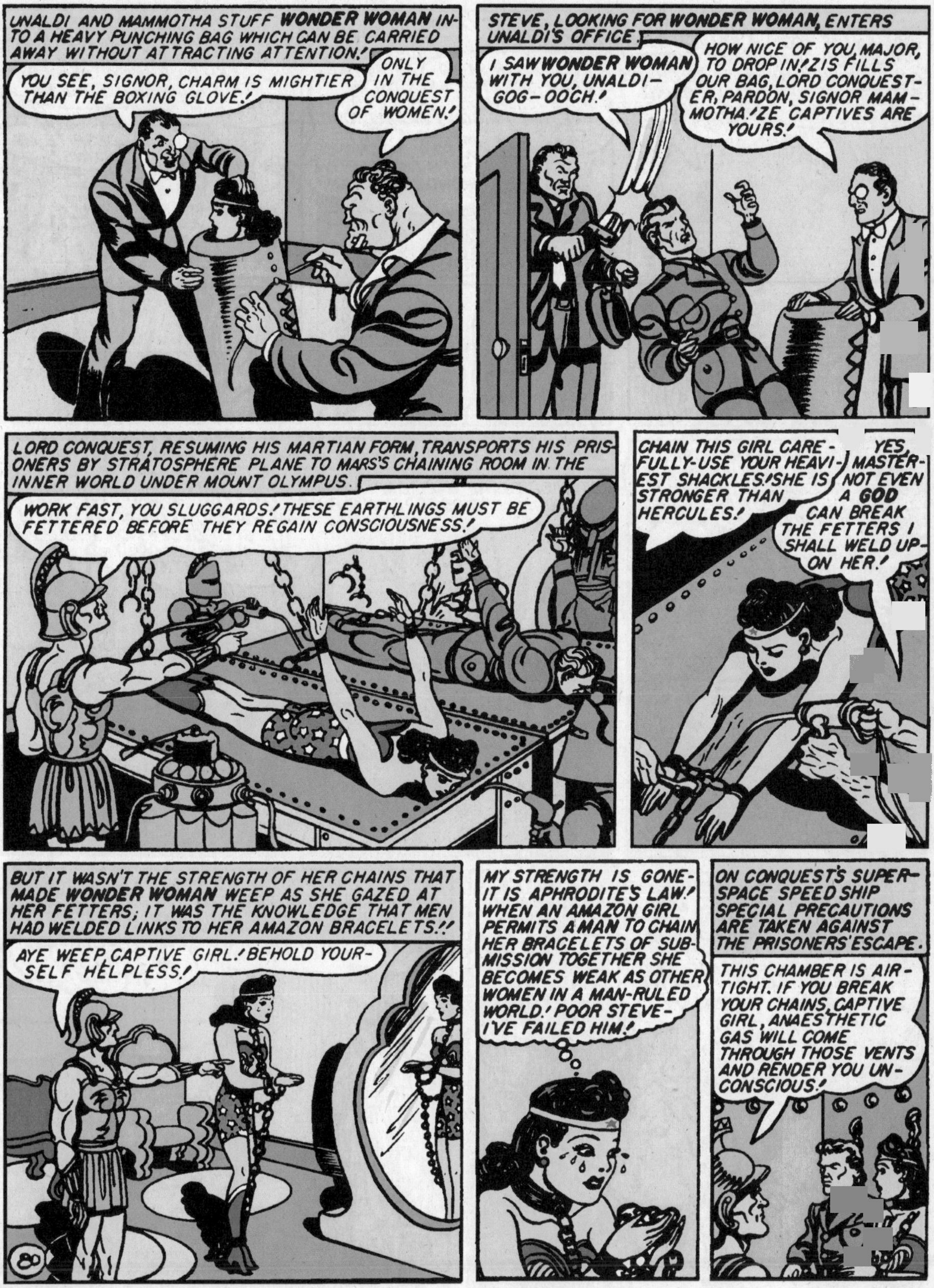

UNALDI AND MAMMOTHA STUFF WONDER WOMAN INTO A HEAVY PUNCHING BAG WHICH CAN BE CARRIED AWAY WITHOUT ATTRACTING ATTENTION!
YOU SEE, SIGNOR, CHARM IS MIGHTIER THAN THE BOXING GLOVE!
ONLY IN THE CONQUEST OF WOMEN!
STEVE, LOOKING FOR WONDER WOMAN, ENTERS UNALDI'S OFFICE.
I SAW WONDER WOMAN WITH YOU, UNALDI-GOG-OOCH!
HOW NICE OF YOU, MAJOR, TO DROP IN! ZIS FILLS OUR BAG, LORD CONQUEST-ER, PARDON, SIGNOR MAMMOTHA! ZE CAPTIVES ARE YOURS!
LORD CONQUEST, RESUMING HIS MARTIAN FORM, TRANSPORTS HIS PRISONERS BY STRATOSPHERE PLANE TO MARS'S CHAINING ROOM IN THE INNER WORLD UNDER MOUNT OLYMPUS.
WORK FAST, YOU SLUGGARDS! THESE EARTHLINGS MUST BE FETTERED BEFORE THEY REGAIN CONSCIOUSNESS!
CHAIN THIS GIRL CAREFULLY-USE YOUR HEAVIEST SHACKLES! SHE IS STRONGER THAN HERCULES!
YES, MASTER-NOT EVEN A GOD CAN BREAK THE FETTERS I SHALL WELD UPON HER!
BUT IT WASN'T THE STRENGTH OF HER CHAINS THAT MADE WONDER WOMAN WEEP AS SHE GAZED AT HER FETTERS; IT WAS THE KNOWLEDGE THAT MEN HAD WELDED LINKS TO HER AMAZON BRACELETS!!
AYE WEEP, CAPTIVE GIRL! BEHOLD YOURSELF HELPLESS!
80
MY STRENGTH IS GONE-IT IS APHRODITE'S LAW! WHEN AN AMAZON GIRL PERMITS A MAN TO CHAIN HER BRACELETS OF SUBMISSION TOGETHER SHE BECOMES WEAK AS OTHER WOMEN IN A MAN-RULED WORLD! POOR STEVE-I'VE FAILED HIM!
ON CONQUEST'S SUPER-SPACE SPEED SHIP SPECIAL PRECAUTIONS ARE TAKEN AGAINST THE PRISONERS' ESCAPE.
THIS CHAMBER IS AIR-TIGHT. IF YOU BREAK YOUR CHAINS, CAPTIVE GIRL, ANAESTHETIC GAS WILL COME THROUGH THOSE VENTS AND RENDER YOU UNCONSCIOUS!

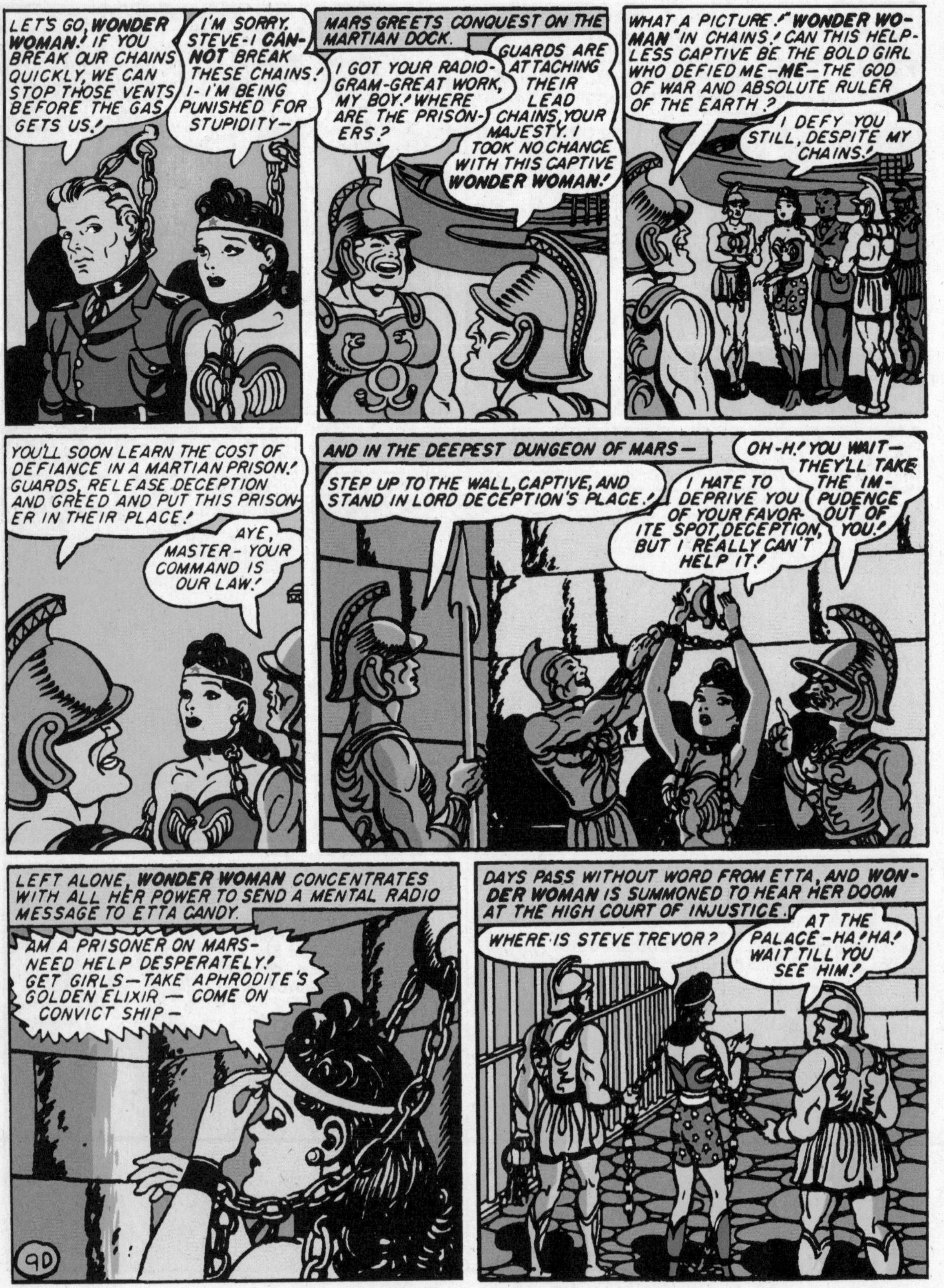
LET'S GO, WONDER WOMAN! IF YOU BREAK OUR CHAINS QUICKLY, WE CAN STOP THOSE VENTS BEFORE THE GAS GETS US!
I'M SORRY, STEVE-I CAN-NOT BREAK THESE CHAINS! I-I'M BEING PUNISHED FOR STUPIDITY—
MARS GREETS CONQUEST ON THE MARTIAN DOCK.
I GOT YOUR RADIO-GRAM-GREAT WORK, MY BOY! WHERE ARE THE PRISON-ERS?
GUARDS ARE ATTACHING THEIR LEAD CHAINS, YOUR MAJESTY. I TOOK NO CHANCE WITH THIS CAPTIVE WONDER WOMAN!
WHAT A PICTURE! "WONDER WO-MAN" IN CHAINS! CAN THIS HELP-LESS CAPTIVE BE THE BOLD GIRL WHO DEFIED ME—ME—THE GOD OF WAR AND ABSOLUTE RULER OF THE EARTH?
I DEFY YOU STILL, DESPITE MY CHAINS!
YOU'LL SOON LEARN THE COST OF DEFIANCE IN A MARTIAN PRISON! GUARDS, RELEASE DECEPTION AND GREED AND PUT THIS PRISON-ER IN THEIR PLACE!
AYE, MASTER- YOUR COMMAND IS OUR LAW!
AND IN THE DEEPEST DUNGEON OF MARS—
STEP UP TO THE WALL, CAPTIVE, AND STAND IN LORD DECEPTION'S PLACE!
I HATE TO DEPRIVE YOU OF YOUR FAVOR-ITE SPOT, DECEPTION, BUT I REALLY CAN'T HELP IT!
OH-H! YOU WAIT— THEY'LL TAKE THE IM-PUDENCE OUT OF YOU!
LEFT ALONE, WONDER WOMAN CONCENTRATES WITH ALL HER POWER TO SEND A MENTAL RADIO MESSAGE TO ETTA CANDY.
AM A PRISONER ON MARS— NEED HELP DESPERATELY! GET GIRLS—TAKE APHRODITE'S GOLDEN ELIXIR — COME ON CONVICT SHIP—
9D
DAYS PASS WITHOUT WORD FROM ETTA, AND WON-DER WOMAN IS SUMMONED TO HEAR HER DOOM AT THE HIGH COURT OF INJUSTICE.
WHERE IS STEVE TREVOR?
AT THE PALACE—HA! HA! WAIT TILL YOU SEE HIM!

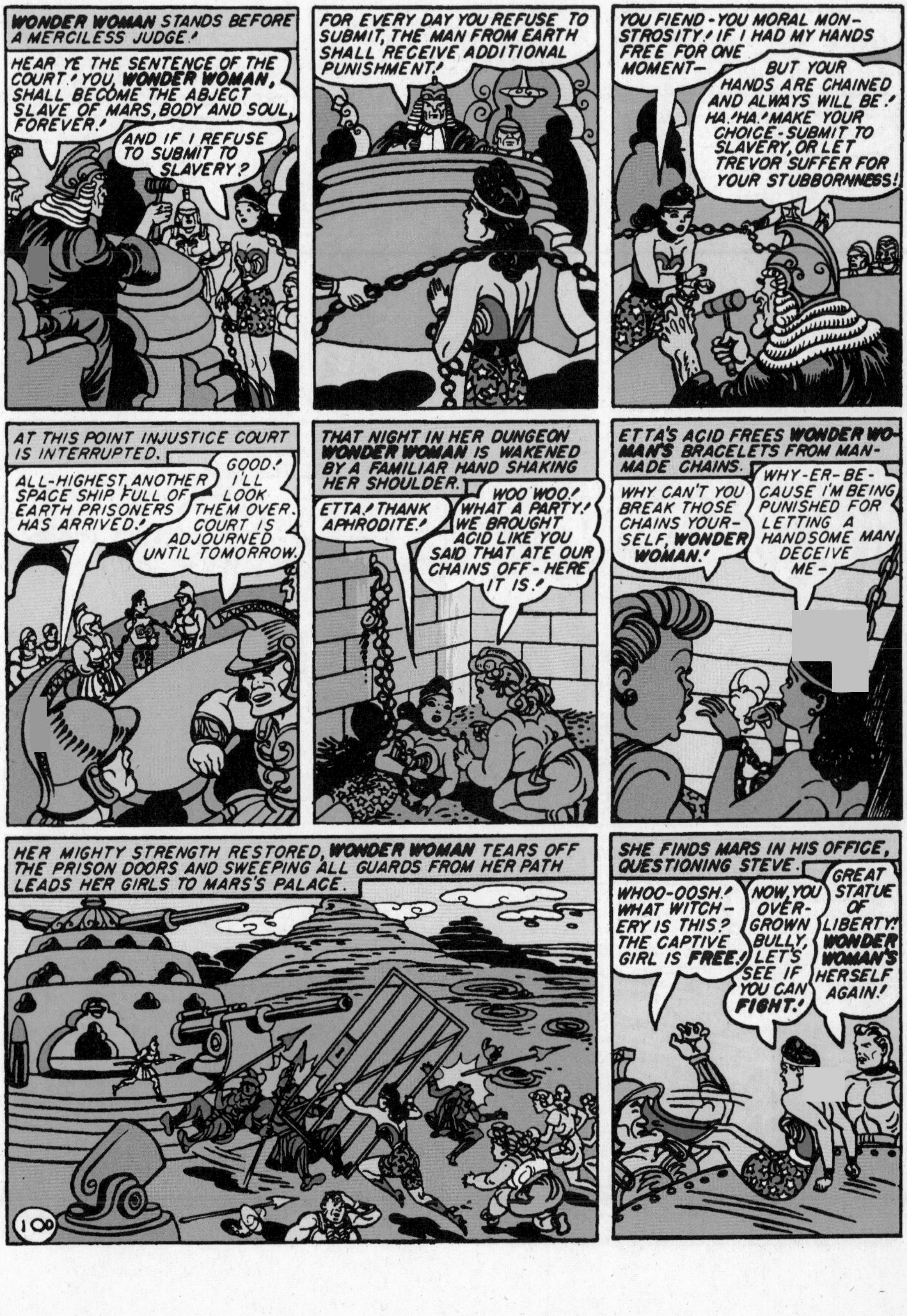
WONDER WOMAN STANDS BEFORE A MERCILESS JUDGE!
HEAR YE THE SENTENCE OF THE COURT! YOU, WONDER WOMAN, SHALL BECOME THE ABJECT SLAVE OF MARS, BODY AND SOUL, FOREVER!
AND IF I REFUSE TO SUBMIT TO SLAVERY?
FOR EVERY DAY YOU REFUSE TO SUBMIT, THE MAN FROM EARTH SHALL RECEIVE ADDITIONAL PUNISHMENT!
YOU FIEND - YOU MORAL MONSTROSITY! IF I HAD MY HANDS FREE FOR ONE MOMENT—
BUT YOUR HANDS ARE CHAINED AND ALWAYS WILL BE! HA! HA! MAKE YOUR CHOICE - SUBMIT TO SLAVERY, OR LET TREVOR SUFFER FOR YOUR STUBBORNNESS!
AT THIS POINT INJUSTICE COURT IS INTERRUPTED.
ALL-HIGHEST, ANOTHER SPACE SHIP FULL OF EARTH PRISONERS HAS ARRIVED!
GOOD! I'LL LOOK THEM OVER. COURT IS ADJOURNED UNTIL TOMORROW.
THAT NIGHT IN HER DUNGEON WONDER WOMAN IS WAKENED BY A FAMILIAR HAND SHAKING HER SHOULDER.
ETTA! THANK APHRODITE!
WOO WOO! WHAT A PARTY! WE BROUGHT ACID LIKE YOU SAID THAT ATE OUR CHAINS OFF - HERE IT IS!
ETTA'S ACID FREES WONDER WOMAN'S BRACELETS FROM MAN-MADE CHAINS.
WHY CAN'T YOU BREAK THOSE CHAINS YOURSELF, WONDER WOMAN!
WHY-ER-BECAUSE I'M BEING PUNISHED FOR LETTING A HANDSOME MAN DECEIVE ME—
HER MIGHTY STRENGTH RESTORED, WONDER WOMAN TEARS OFF THE PRISON DOORS AND SWEEPING ALL GUARDS FROM HER PATH LEADS HER GIRLS TO MARS'S PALACE.
100
SHE FINDS MARS IN HIS OFFICE, QUESTIONING STEVE.
WHOO-OOSH! WHAT WITCHERY IS THIS? THE CAPTIVE GIRL IS FREE!
NOW, YOU OVERGROWN BULLY, LET'S SEE IF YOU CAN FIGHT!
GREAT STATUE OF LIBERTY! WONDER WOMAN'S HERSELF AGAIN!

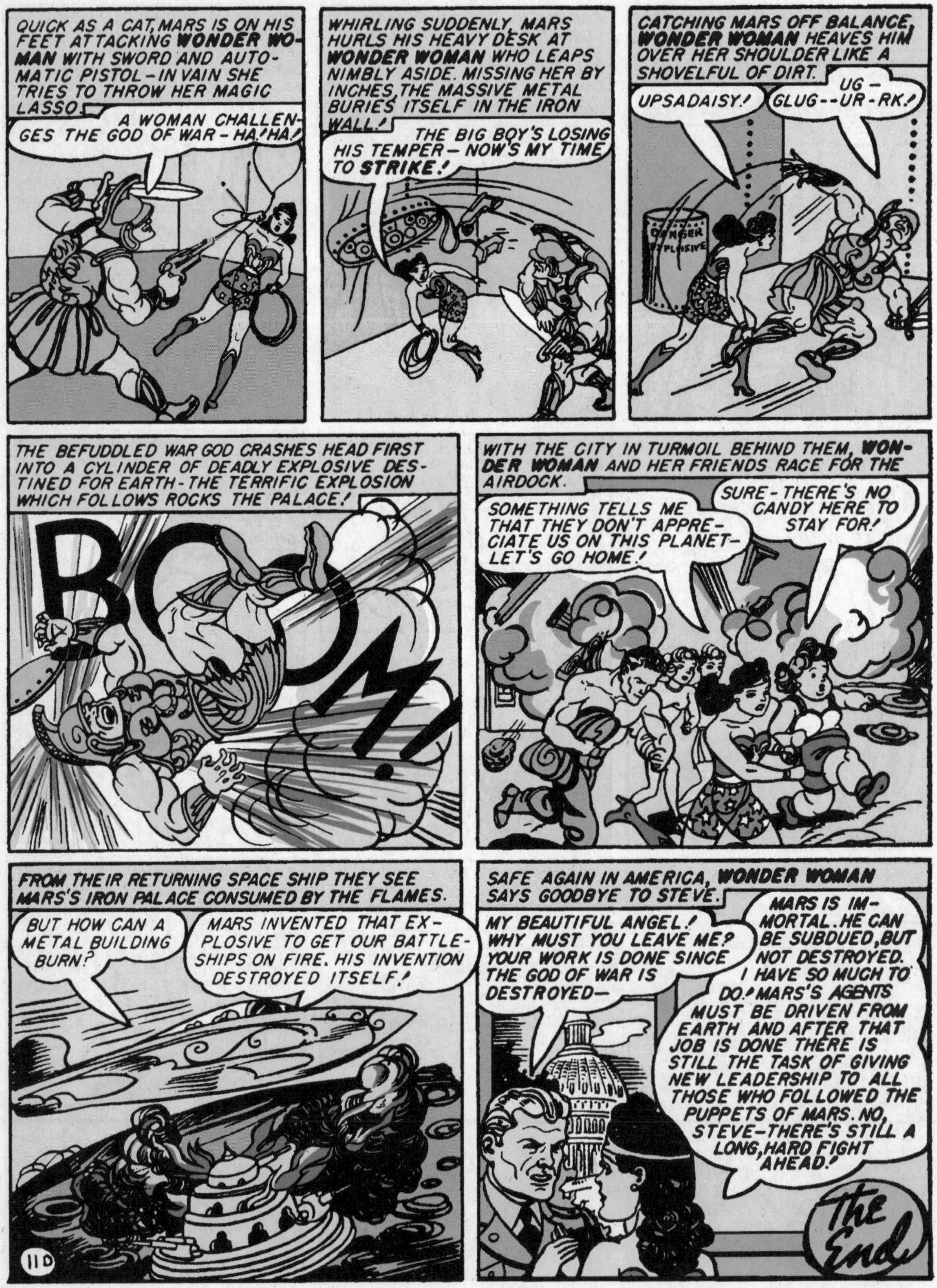
QUICK AS A CAT, MARS IS ON HIS FEET ATTACKING WONDER WOMAN WITH SWORD AND AUTOMATIC PISTOL—IN VAIN SHE TRIES TO THROW HER MAGIC LASSO.
A WOMAN CHALLENGES THE GOD OF WAR—HA! HA!
WHIRLING SUDDENLY, MARS HURLS HIS HEAVY DESK AT WONDER WOMAN WHO LEAPS NIMBLY ASIDE. MISSING HER BY INCHES, THE MASSIVE METAL BURIES ITSELF IN THE IRON WALL!
THE BIG BOY'S LOSING HIS TEMPER—NOW'S MY TIME TO STRIKE!
CATCHING MARS OFF BALANCE, WONDER WOMAN HEAVES HIM OVER HER SHOULDER LIKE A SHOVELFUL OF DIRT.
UPSADAISY!
UG—GLUG--UR-RK!
DANGER EXPLOSIVE
THE BEFUDDLED WAR GOD CRASHES HEAD FIRST INTO A CYLINDER OF DEADLY EXPLOSIVE DESTINED FOR EARTH—THE TERRIFIC EXPLOSION WHICH FOLLOWS ROCKS THE PALACE!
BOOM!
WITH THE CITY IN TURMOIL BEHIND THEM, WONDER WOMAN AND HER FRIENDS RACE FOR THE AIRDOCK.
SOMETHING TELLS ME THAT THEY DON'T APPRECIATE US ON THIS PLANET—LET'S GO HOME!
SURE—THERE'S NO CANDY HERE TO STAY FOR!
FROM THEIR RETURNING SPACE SHIP THEY SEE MARS'S IRON PALACE CONSUMED BY THE FLAMES.
BUT HOW CAN A METAL BUILDING BURN?
MARS INVENTED THAT EXPLOSIVE TO GET OUR BATTLESHIPS ON FIRE. HIS INVENTION DESTROYED ITSELF!
110
SAFE AGAIN IN AMERICA, WONDER WOMAN SAYS GOODBYE TO STEVE.
MY BEAUTIFUL ANGEL! WHY MUST YOU LEAVE ME? YOUR WORK IS DONE SINCE THE GOD OF WAR IS DESTROYED—
MARS IS IMMORTAL. HE CAN BE SUBDUED, BUT NOT DESTROYED. I HAVE SO MUCH TO DO! MARS'S AGENTS MUST BE DRIVEN FROM EARTH AND AFTER THAT JOB IS DONE THERE IS STILL THE TASK OF GIVING NEW LEADERSHIP TO ALL THOSE WHO FOLLOWED THE PUPPETS OF MARS. NO, STEVE—THERE'S STILL A LONG, HARD FIGHT AHEAD!
The End

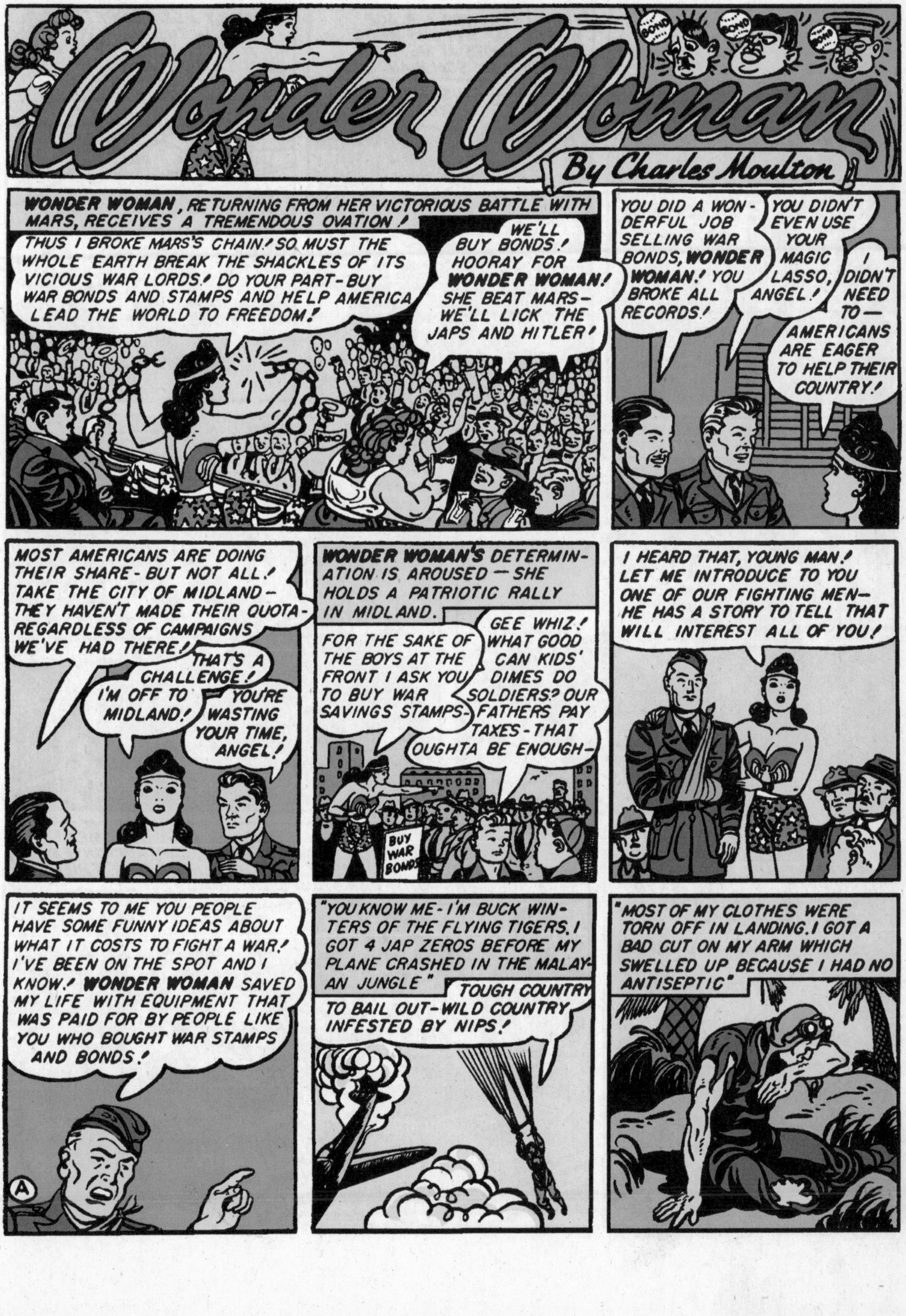
Wonder Woman
By Charles Moulton
BOND
BOND
BOND
WONDER WOMAN, RETURNING FROM HER VICTORIOUS BATTLE WITH MARS, RECEIVES A TREMENDOUS OVATION!
THUS I BROKE MARS'S CHAIN! SO MUST THE WHOLE EARTH BREAK THE SHACKLES OF ITS VICIOUS WAR LORDS! DO YOUR PART- BUY WAR BONDS AND STAMPS AND HELP AMERICA LEAD THE WORLD TO FREEDOM!
WE'LL BUY BONDS! HOORAY FOR WONDER WOMAN! SHE BEAT MARS- WE'LL LICK THE JAPS AND HITLER!
YOU DID A WONDERFUL JOB SELLING WAR BONDS, WONDER WOMAN! YOU BROKE ALL RECORDS!
YOU DIDN'T EVEN USE YOUR MAGIC LASSO, ANGEL!
I DIDN'T NEED TO— AMERICANS ARE EAGER TO HELP THEIR COUNTRY!
MOST AMERICANS ARE DOING THEIR SHARE- BUT NOT ALL! TAKE THE CITY OF MIDLAND- THEY HAVEN'T MADE THEIR QUOTA- REGARDLESS OF CAMPAIGNS WE'VE HAD THERE!
THAT'S A CHALLENGE! I'M OFF TO MIDLAND!
YOU'RE WASTING YOUR TIME, ANGEL!
WONDER WOMAN'S DETERMINATION IS AROUSED — SHE HOLDS A PATRIOTIC RALLY IN MIDLAND.
FOR THE SAKE OF THE BOYS AT THE FRONT I ASK YOU TO BUY WAR SAVINGS STAMPS-
GEE WHIZ! WHAT GOOD CAN KIDS' DIMES DO SOLDIERS? OUR FATHERS PAY TAXES- THAT OUGHTA BE ENOUGH-
BUY WAR BONDS
I HEARD THAT, YOUNG MAN! LET ME INTRODUCE TO YOU ONE OF OUR FIGHTING MEN- HE HAS A STORY TO TELL THAT WILL INTEREST ALL OF YOU!
IT SEEMS TO ME YOU PEOPLE HAVE SOME FUNNY IDEAS ABOUT WHAT IT COSTS TO FIGHT A WAR! I'VE BEEN ON THE SPOT AND I KNOW! WONDER WOMAN SAVED MY LIFE WITH EQUIPMENT THAT WAS PAID FOR BY PEOPLE LIKE YOU WHO BOUGHT WAR STAMPS AND BONDS!
A
"YOU KNOW ME- I'M BUCK WINTERS OF THE FLYING TIGERS. I GOT 4 JAP ZEROS BEFORE MY PLANE CRASHED IN THE MALAYAN JUNGLE"
TOUGH COUNTRY TO BAIL OUT- WILD COUNTRY INFESTED BY NIPS!
"MOST OF MY CLOTHES WERE TORN OFF IN LANDING. I GOT A BAD CUT ON MY ARM WHICH SWELLED UP BECAUSE I HAD NO ANTISEPTIC"

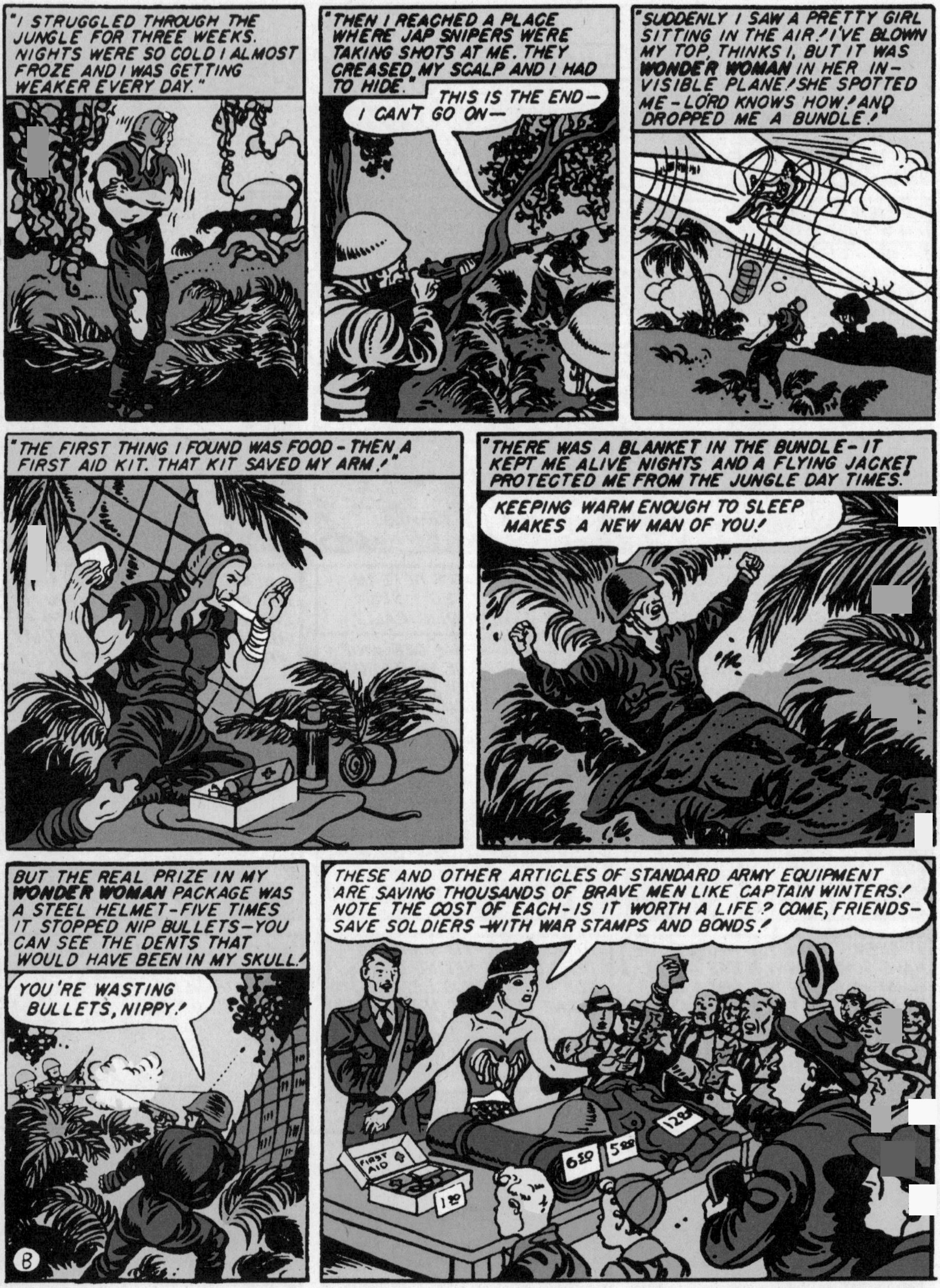
"I STRUGGLED THROUGH THE JUNGLE FOR THREE WEEKS. NIGHTS WERE SO COLD I ALMOST FROZE AND I WAS GETTING WEAKER EVERY DAY."
"THEN I REACHED A PLACE WHERE JAP SNIPERS WERE TAKING SHOTS AT ME. THEY CREASED MY SCALP AND I HAD TO HIDE."
THIS IS THE END— I CAN'T GO ON—
"SUDDENLY I SAW A PRETTY GIRL SITTING IN THE AIR! I'VE BLOWN MY TOP, THINKS I, BUT IT WAS WONDER WOMAN IN HER INVISIBLE PLANE! SHE SPOTTED ME - LORD KNOWS HOW! AND DROPPED ME A BUNDLE!"
"THE FIRST THING I FOUND WAS FOOD - THEN A FIRST AID KIT. THAT KIT SAVED MY ARM!"
"THERE WAS A BLANKET IN THE BUNDLE - IT KEPT ME ALIVE NIGHTS AND A FLYING JACKET PROTECTED ME FROM THE JUNGLE DAY TIMES."
KEEPING WARM ENOUGH TO SLEEP MAKES A NEW MAN OF YOU!
BUT THE REAL PRIZE IN MY WONDER WOMAN PACKAGE WAS A STEEL HELMET - FIVE TIMES IT STOPPED NIP BULLETS—YOU CAN SEE THE DENTS THAT WOULD HAVE BEEN IN MY SKULL!
YOU'RE WASTING BULLETS, NIPPY!
B
THESE AND OTHER ARTICLES OF STANDARD ARMY EQUIPMENT ARE SAVING THOUSANDS OF BRAVE MEN LIKE CAPTAIN WINTERS! NOTE THE COST OF EACH - IS IT WORTH A LIFE? COME, FRIENDS - SAVE SOLDIERS —WITH WAR STAMPS AND BONDS!
FIRST AID
1.80
6.50
5.00
1.25

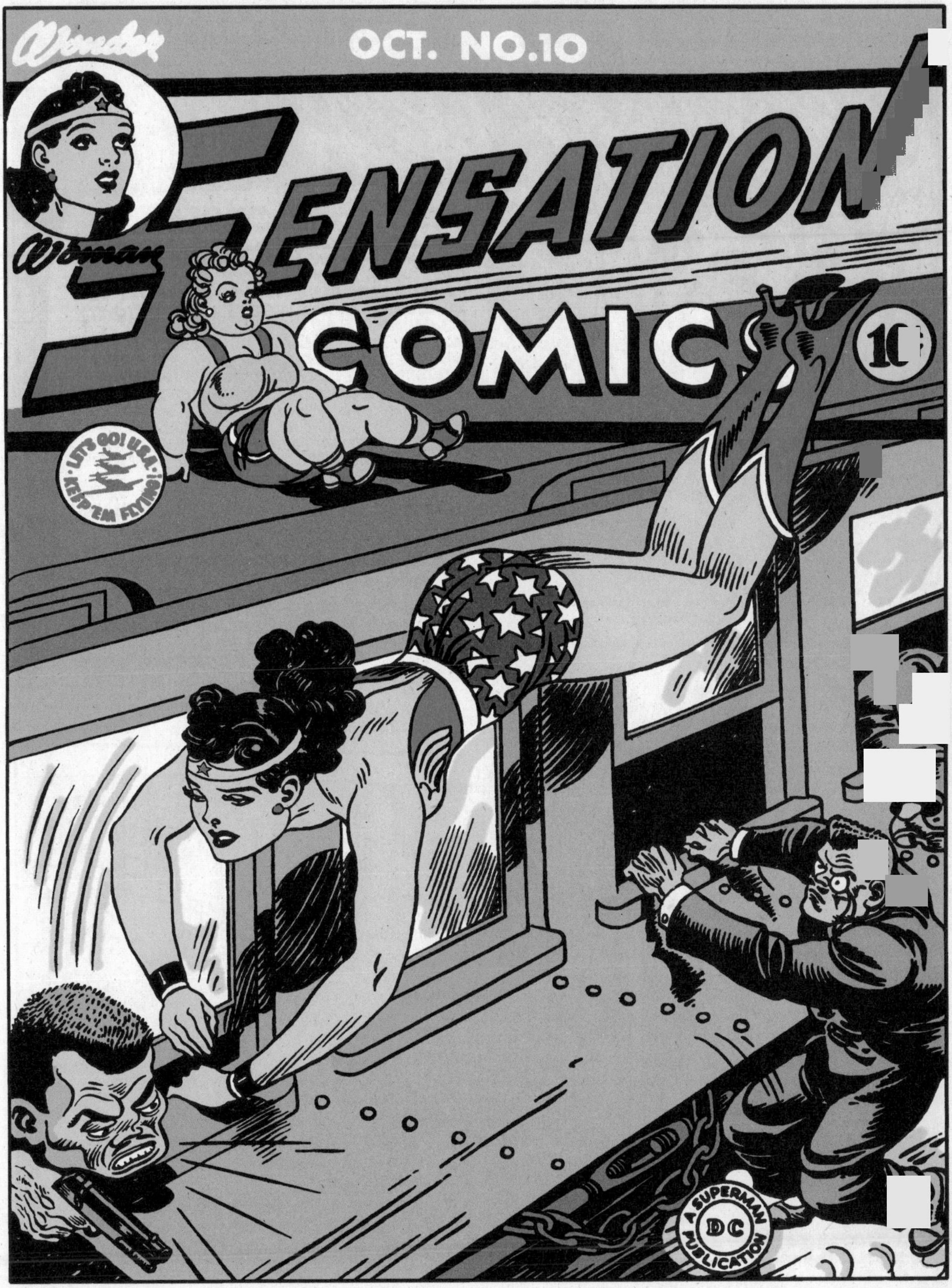
Wonder Woman
OCT. NO.10
SENSATION
COMICS
10
LET'S GO! U.S.A. KEEP 'EM FLYING!
A SUPERMAN DC PUBLICATION

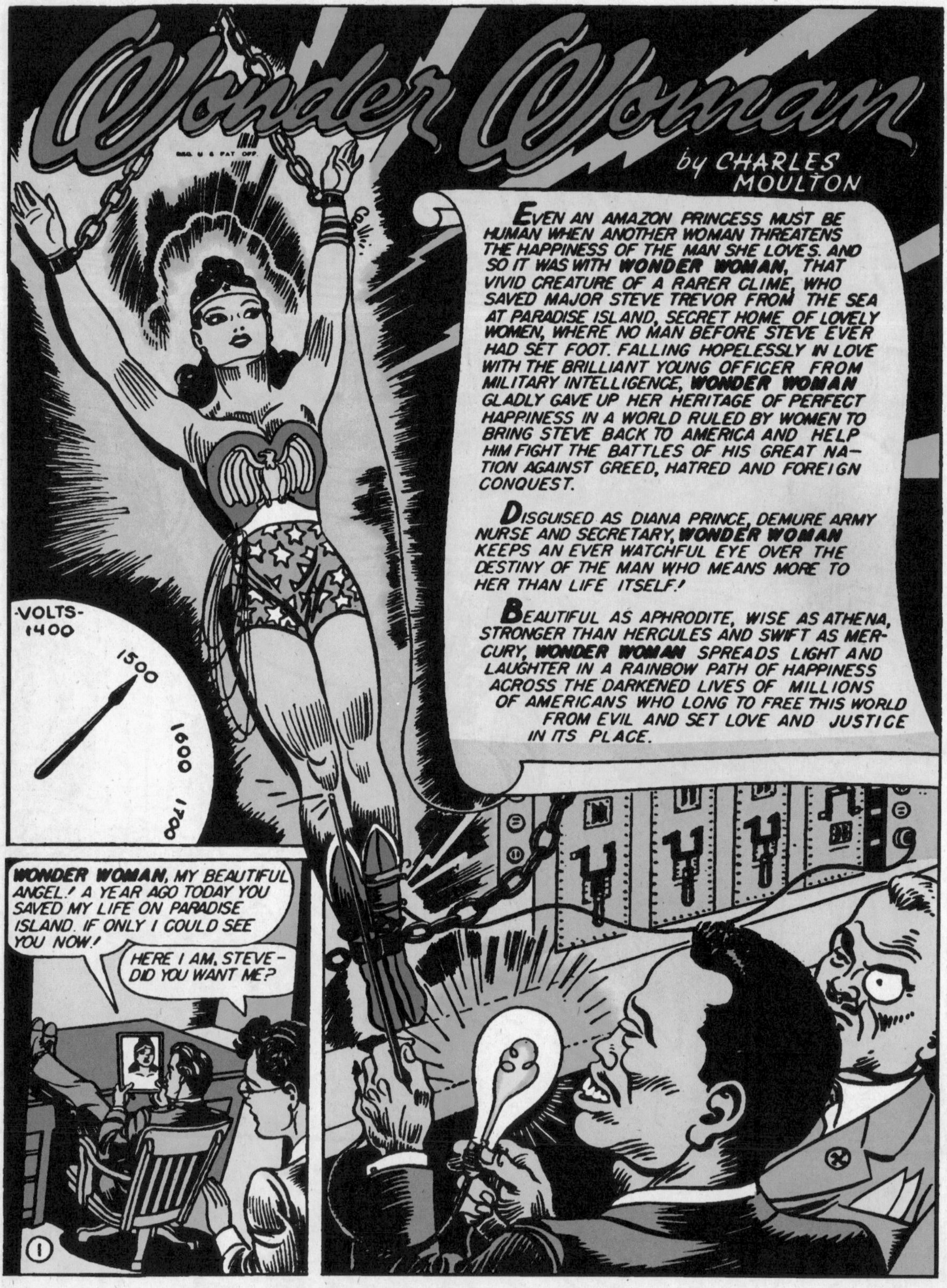
Wonder Woman
REG. U.S. PAT. OFF.
by CHARLES MOULTON
EVEN AN AMAZON PRINCESS MUST BE HUMAN WHEN ANOTHER WOMAN THREATENS THE HAPPINESS OF THE MAN SHE LOVES. AND SO IT WAS WITH WONDER WOMAN, THAT VIVID CREATURE OF A RARER CLIME, WHO SAVED MAJOR STEVE TREVOR FROM THE SEA AT PARADISE ISLAND, SECRET HOME OF LOVELY WOMEN, WHERE NO MAN BEFORE STEVE EVER HAD SET FOOT. FALLING HOPELESSLY IN LOVE WITH THE BRILLIANT YOUNG OFFICER FROM MILITARY INTELLIGENCE, WONDER WOMAN GLADLY GAVE UP HER HERITAGE OF PERFECT HAPPINESS IN A WORLD RULED BY WOMEN TO BRING STEVE BACK TO AMERICA AND HELP HIM FIGHT THE BATTLES OF HIS GREAT NATION AGAINST GREED, HATRED AND FOREIGN CONQUEST.
DISGUISED AS DIANA PRINCE, DEMURE ARMY NURSE AND SECRETARY, WONDER WOMAN KEEPS AN EVER WATCHFUL EYE OVER THE DESTINY OF THE MAN WHO MEANS MORE TO HER THAN LIFE ITSELF!
BEAUTIFUL AS APHRODITE, WISE AS ATHENA, STRONGER THAN HERCULES AND SWIFT AS MERCURY, WONDER WOMAN SPREADS LIGHT AND LAUGHTER IN A RAINBOW PATH OF HAPPINESS ACROSS THE DARKENED LIVES OF MILLIONS OF AMERICANS WHO LONG TO FREE THIS WORLD FROM EVIL AND SET LOVE AND JUSTICE IN ITS PLACE.
-VOLTS-
1400
1500
1600
1700
WONDER WOMAN, MY BEAUTIFUL ANGEL! A YEAR AGO TODAY YOU SAVED MY LIFE ON PARADISE ISLAND. IF ONLY I COULD SEE YOU NOW!
HERE I AM, STEVE- DID YOU WANT ME?
1

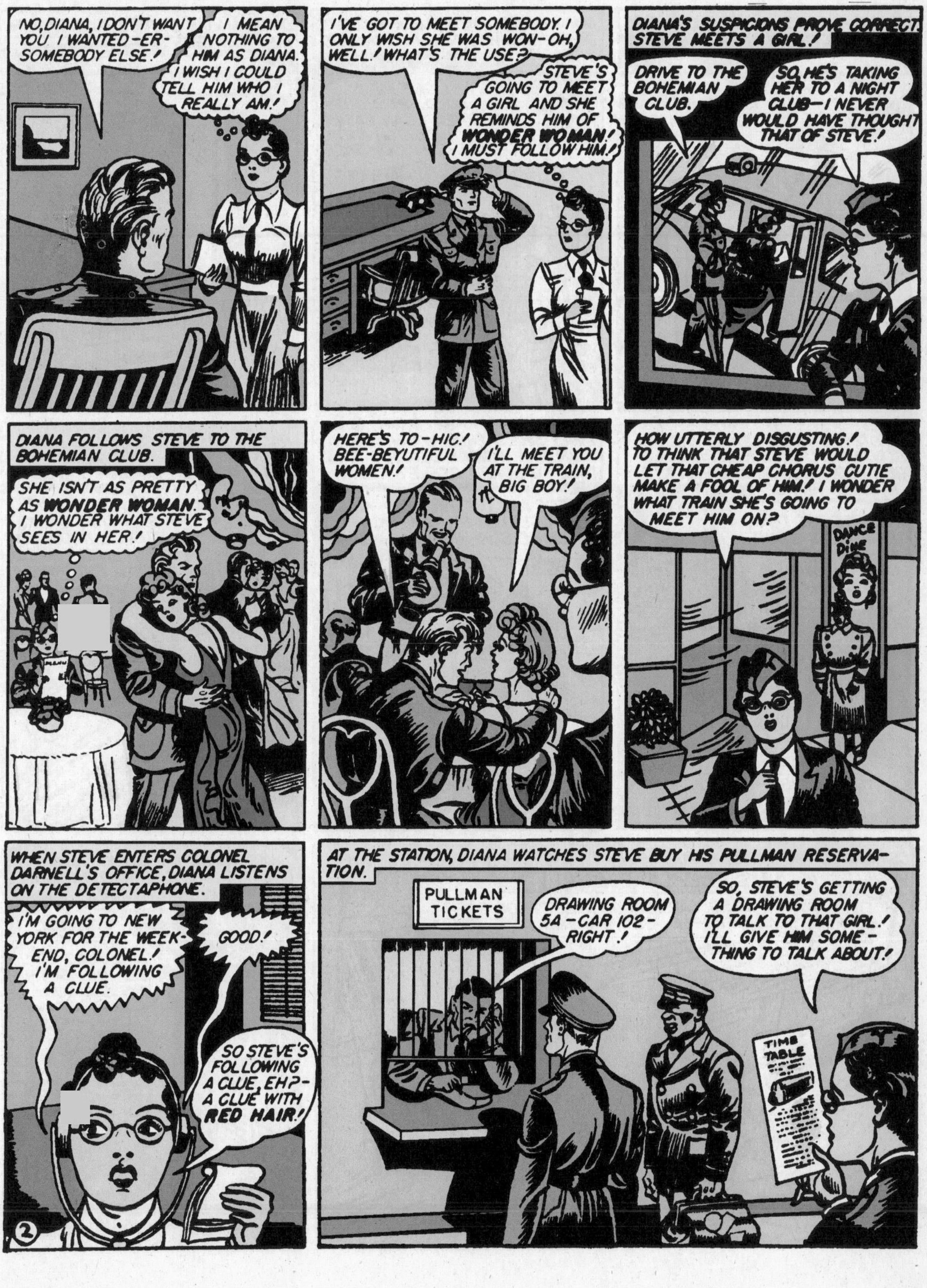

NO, DIANA, I DON'T WANT YOU. I WANTED -ER- SOMEBODY ELSE!
I MEAN NOTHING TO HIM AS DIANA. I WISH I COULD TELL HIM WHO I REALLY AM!
I'VE GOT TO MEET SOMEBODY. I ONLY WISH SHE WAS WON-OH, WELL! WHAT'S THE USE?
STEVE'S GOING TO MEET A GIRL AND SHE REMINDS HIM OF WONDER WOMAN! I MUST FOLLOW HIM!
DIANA'S SUSPICIONS PROVE CORRECT: STEVE MEETS A GIRL!
DRIVE TO THE BOHEMIAN CLUB.
SO, HE'S TAKING HER TO A NIGHT CLUB-I NEVER WOULD HAVE THOUGHT THAT OF STEVE!
DIANA FOLLOWS STEVE TO THE BOHEMIAN CLUB.
SHE ISN'T AS PRETTY AS WONDER WOMAN. I WONDER WHAT STEVE SEES IN HER!
HERE'S TO-HIC! BEE-BEYUTIFUL WOMEN!
I'LL MEET YOU AT THE TRAIN, BIG BOY!
HOW UTTERLY DISGUSTING! TO THINK THAT STEVE WOULD LET THAT CHEAP CHORUS CUTIE MAKE A FOOL OF HIM! I WONDER WHAT TRAIN SHE'S GOING TO MEET HIM ON?
DANCE DINE
WHEN STEVE ENTERS COLONEL DARNELL'S OFFICE, DIANA LISTENS ON THE DETECTAPHONE.
I'M GOING TO NEW YORK FOR THE WEEK-END, COLONEL! I'M FOLLOWING A CLUE.
GOOD!
SO STEVE'S FOLLOWING A CLUE, EH? - A CLUE WITH RED HAIR!
2
AT THE STATION, DIANA WATCHES STEVE BUY HIS PULLMAN RESERVATION.
PULLMAN TICKETS
DRAWING ROOM 5A-CAR 102-RIGHT!
SO, STEVE'S GETTING A DRAWING ROOM TO TALK TO THAT GIRL! I'LL GIVE HIM SOMETHING TO TALK ABOUT!
TIME TABLE

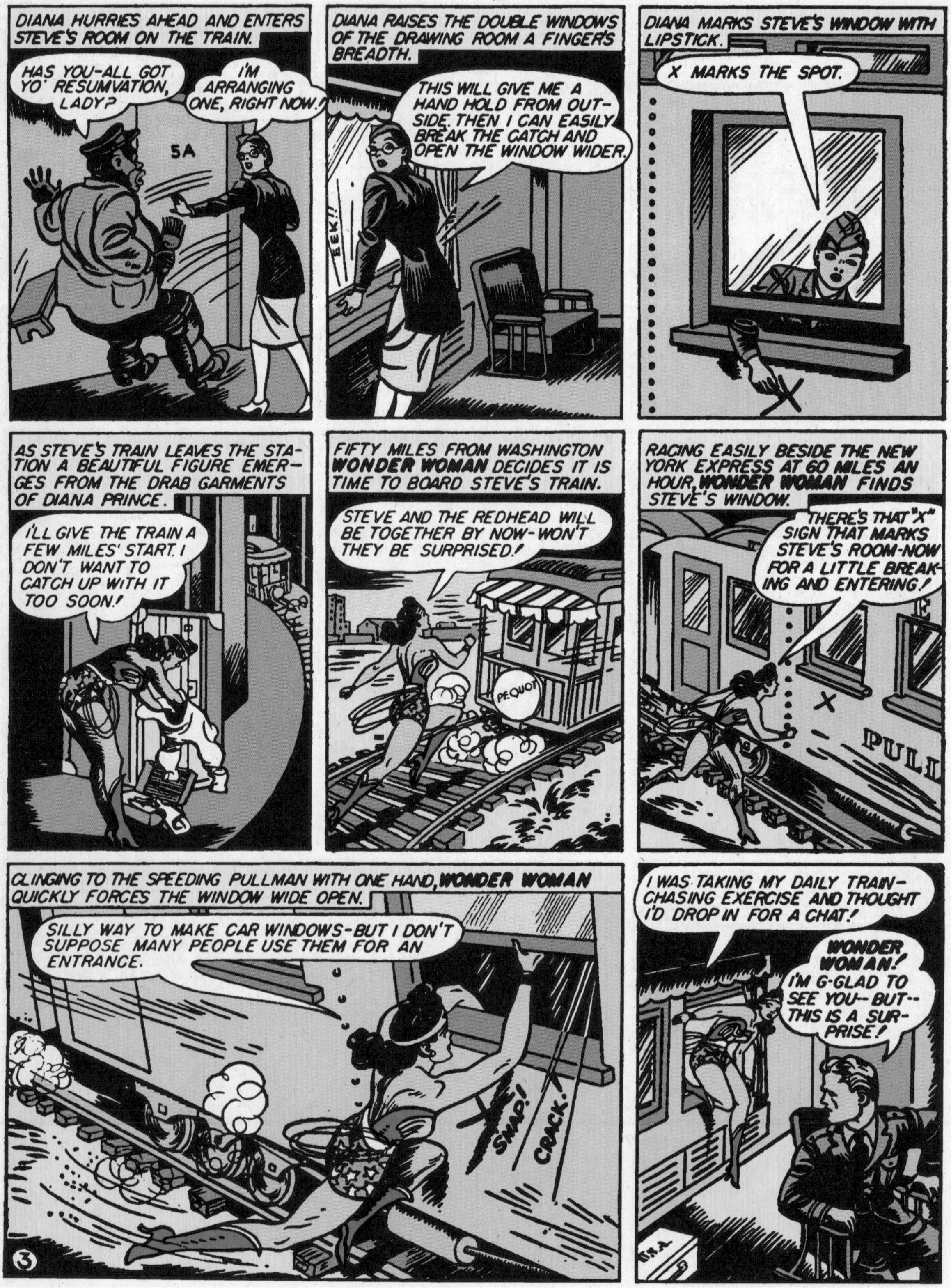
DIANA HURRIES AHEAD AND ENTERS STEVE'S ROOM ON THE TRAIN.
HAS YOU-ALL GOT YO' RESUMVATION, LADY?
I'M ARRANGING ONE, RIGHT NOW!
5A
DIANA RAISES THE DOUBLE WINDOWS OF THE DRAWING ROOM A FINGER'S BREADTH.
THIS WILL GIVE ME A HAND HOLD FROM OUTSIDE. THEN I CAN EASILY BREAK THE CATCH AND OPEN THE WINDOW WIDER.
EEK!!
DIANA MARKS STEVE'S WINDOW WITH LIPSTICK.
X MARKS THE SPOT.
AS STEVE'S TRAIN LEAVES THE STATION A BEAUTIFUL FIGURE EMERGES FROM THE DRAB GARMENTS OF DIANA PRINCE.
I'LL GIVE THE TRAIN A FEW MILES' START. I DON'T WANT TO CATCH UP WITH IT TOO SOON!
FIFTY MILES FROM WASHINGTON **WONDER WOMAN** DECIDES IT IS TIME TO BOARD STEVE'S TRAIN.
STEVE AND THE REDHEAD WILL BE TOGETHER BY NOW-WON'T THEY BE SURPRISED!
PEQUOT
RACING EASILY BESIDE THE NEW YORK EXPRESS AT 60 MILES AN HOUR, **WONDER WOMAN** FINDS STEVE'S WINDOW.
THERE'S THAT "X" SIGN THAT MARKS STEVE'S ROOM-NOW FOR A LITTLE BREAKING AND ENTERING!
X
PULL
CLINGING TO THE SPEEDING PULLMAN WITH ONE HAND, **WONDER WOMAN** QUICKLY FORCES THE WINDOW WIDE OPEN.
SILLY WAY TO MAKE CAR WINDOWS-BUT I DON'T SUPPOSE MANY PEOPLE USE THEM FOR AN ENTRANCE.
SNAP!
CRACK!
3
I WAS TAKING MY DAILY TRAIN-CHASING EXERCISE AND THOUGHT I'D DROP IN FOR A CHAT!
WONDER WOMAN! I'M G-GLAD TO SEE YOU-- BUT-- THIS IS A SURPRISE!

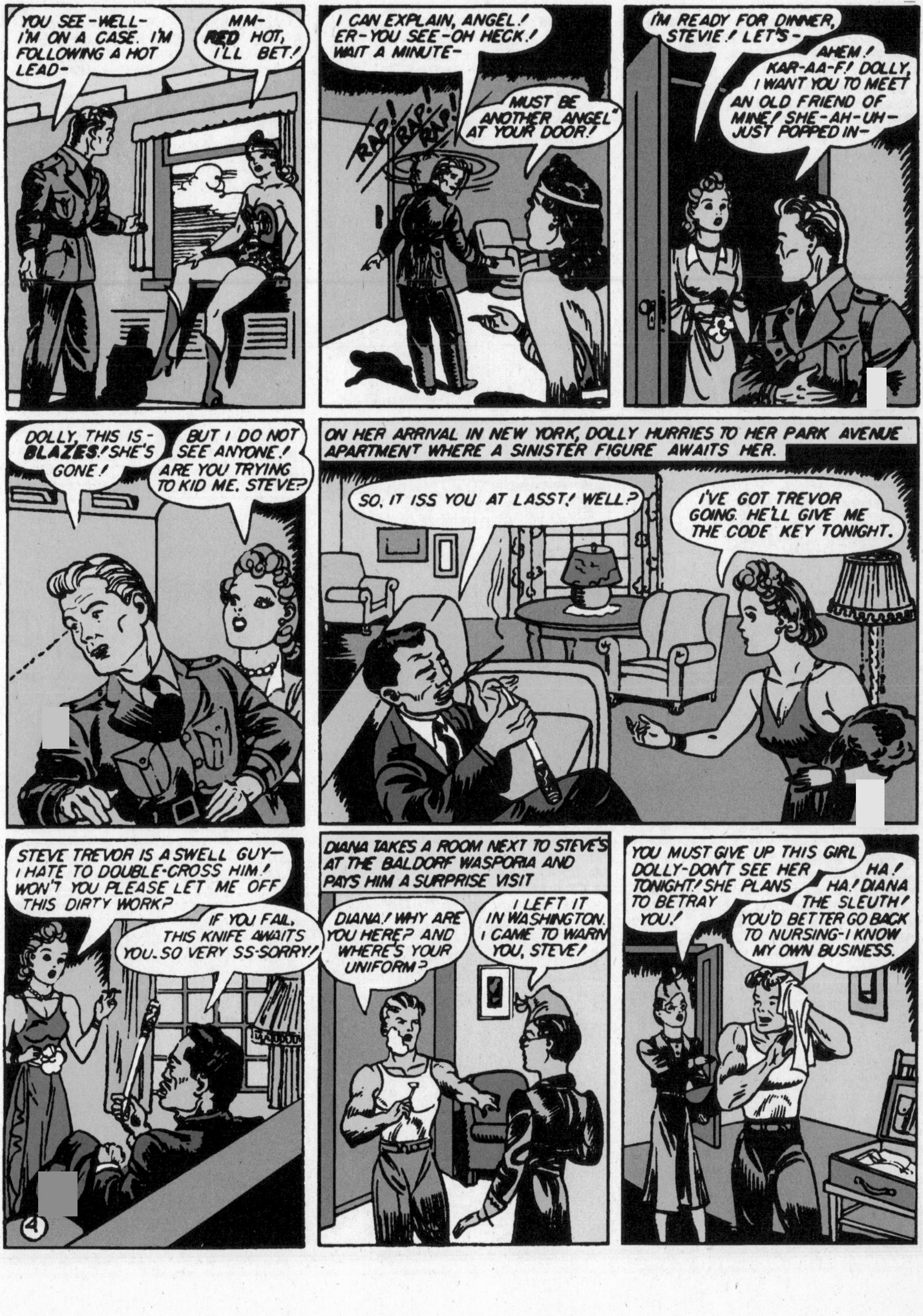

YOU SEE-WELL- I'M ON A CASE. I'M FOLLOWING A HOT LEAD-
MM- RED HOT, I'LL BET!
I CAN EXPLAIN, ANGEL! ER-YOU SEE-OH HECK! WAIT A MINUTE-
RAP! RAP! RAP!
MUST BE ANOTHER "ANGEL" AT YOUR DOOR!
I'M READY FOR DINNER, STEVIE! LET'S-
AHEM! KAR-AA-F! DOLLY, I WANT YOU TO MEET AN OLD FRIEND OF MINE! SHE-AH-UH- JUST POPPED IN-
DOLLY, THIS IS- BLAZES! SHE'S GONE!
BUT I DO NOT SEE ANYONE! ARE YOU TRYING TO KID ME, STEVE?
ON HER ARRIVAL IN NEW YORK, DOLLY HURRIES TO HER PARK AVENUE APARTMENT WHERE A SINISTER FIGURE AWAITS HER.
SO, IT ISS YOU AT LASST! WELL?
I'VE GOT TREVOR GOING. HE'LL GIVE ME THE CODE KEY TONIGHT.
STEVE TREVOR IS A SWELL GUY- I HATE TO DOUBLE-CROSS HIM! WON'T YOU PLEASE LET ME OFF THIS DIRTY WORK?
IF YOU FAIL, THIS KNIFE AWAITS YOU-SO VERY SS-SORRY!
4
DIANA TAKES A ROOM NEXT TO STEVE'S AT THE BALDORF WASPORIA AND PAYS HIM A SURPRISE VISIT
DIANA! WHY ARE YOU HERE? AND WHERE'S YOUR UNIFORM?
I LEFT IT IN WASHINGTON. I CAME TO WARN YOU, STEVE!
YOU MUST GIVE UP THIS GIRL DOLLY-DON'T SEE HER TONIGHT! SHE PLANS TO BETRAY YOU!
HA! HA! DIANA THE SLEUTH! YOU'D BETTER GO BACK TO NURSING-I KNOW MY OWN BUSINESS.

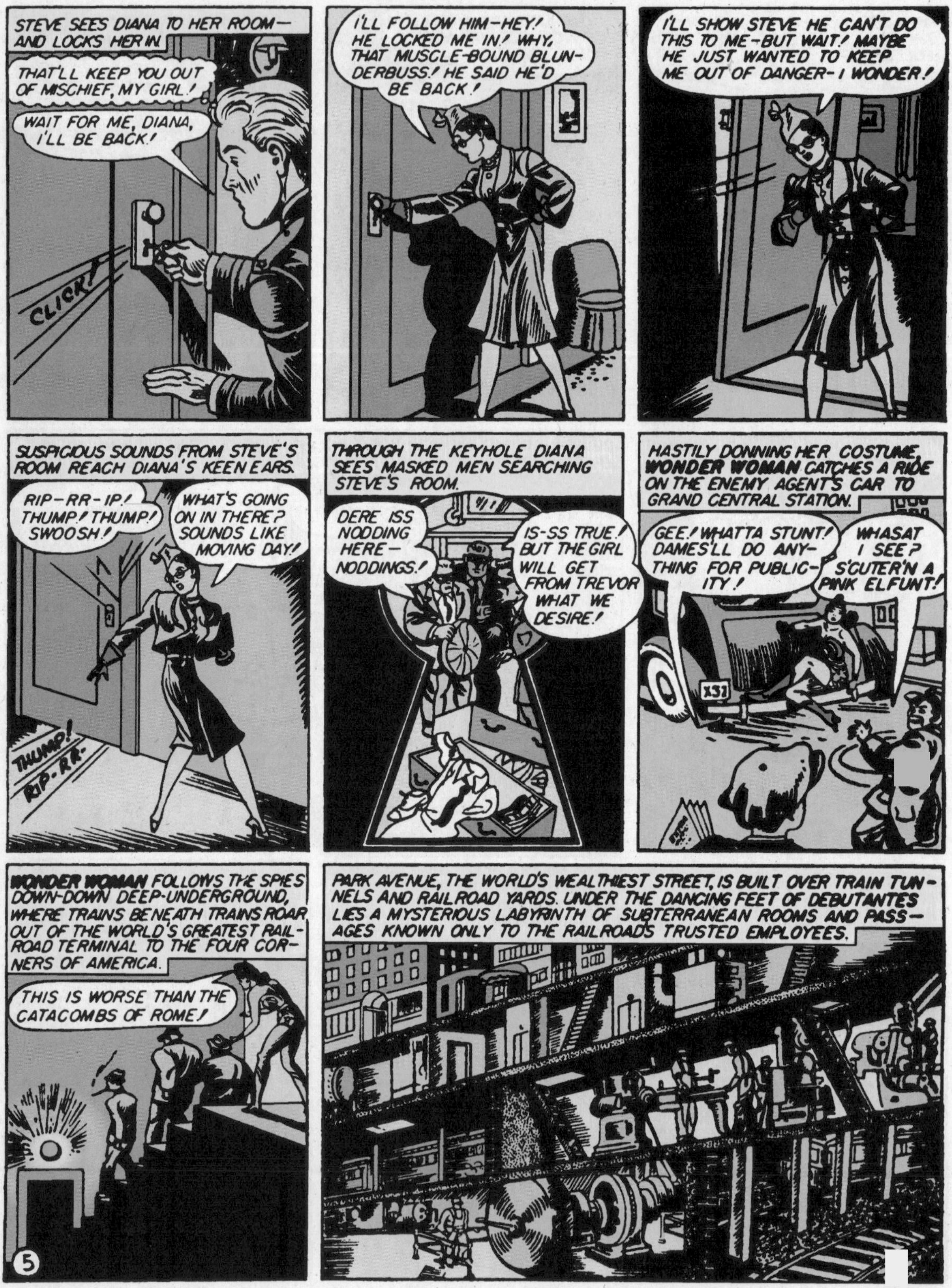

STEVE SEES DIANA TO HER ROOM—AND LOCKS HER IN.
THAT'LL KEEP YOU OUT OF MISCHIEF, MY GIRL!
WAIT FOR ME, DIANA, I'LL BE BACK!
CLICK!
I'LL FOLLOW HIM—HEY! HE LOCKED ME IN! WHY, THAT MUSCLE-BOUND BLUNDERBUSS! HE SAID HE'D BE BACK!
I'LL SHOW STEVE HE CAN'T DO THIS TO ME—BUT WAIT! MAYBE HE JUST WANTED TO KEEP ME OUT OF DANGER—I WONDER!
SUSPICIOUS SOUNDS FROM STEVE'S ROOM REACH DIANA'S KEEN EARS.
RIP-RR-IP! THUMP! THUMP! SWOOSH!
WHAT'S GOING ON IN THERE? SOUNDS LIKE MOVING DAY!
THUMP! RIP-RR.
THROUGH THE KEYHOLE DIANA SEES MASKED MEN SEARCHING STEVE'S ROOM.
DERE ISS NODDING HERE—NODDINGS!
IS-SS TRUE! BUT THE GIRL WILL GET FROM TREVOR WHAT WE DESIRE!
HASTILY DONNING HER COSTUME, WONDER WOMAN CATCHES A RIDE ON THE ENEMY AGENT'S CAR TO GRAND CENTRAL STATION.
GEE! WHATTA STUNT! DAMES'LL DO ANYTHING FOR PUBLICITY!
WHASAT I SEE? S'CUTER'N A PINK ELFUNT!
X37
WONDER WOMAN FOLLOWS THE SPIES DOWN-DOWN DEEP-UNDERGROUND, WHERE TRAINS BENEATH TRAINS ROAR OUT OF THE WORLD'S GREATEST RAILROAD TERMINAL TO THE FOUR CORNERS OF AMERICA.
THIS IS WORSE THAN THE CATACOMBS OF ROME!
5
PARK AVENUE, THE WORLD'S WEALTHIEST STREET, IS BUILT OVER TRAIN TUNNELS AND RAILROAD YARDS. UNDER THE DANCING FEET OF DEBUTANTES LIES A MYSTERIOUS LABYRINTH OF SUBTERRANEAN ROOMS AND PASSAGES KNOWN ONLY TO THE RAILROAD'S TRUSTED EMPLOYEES.

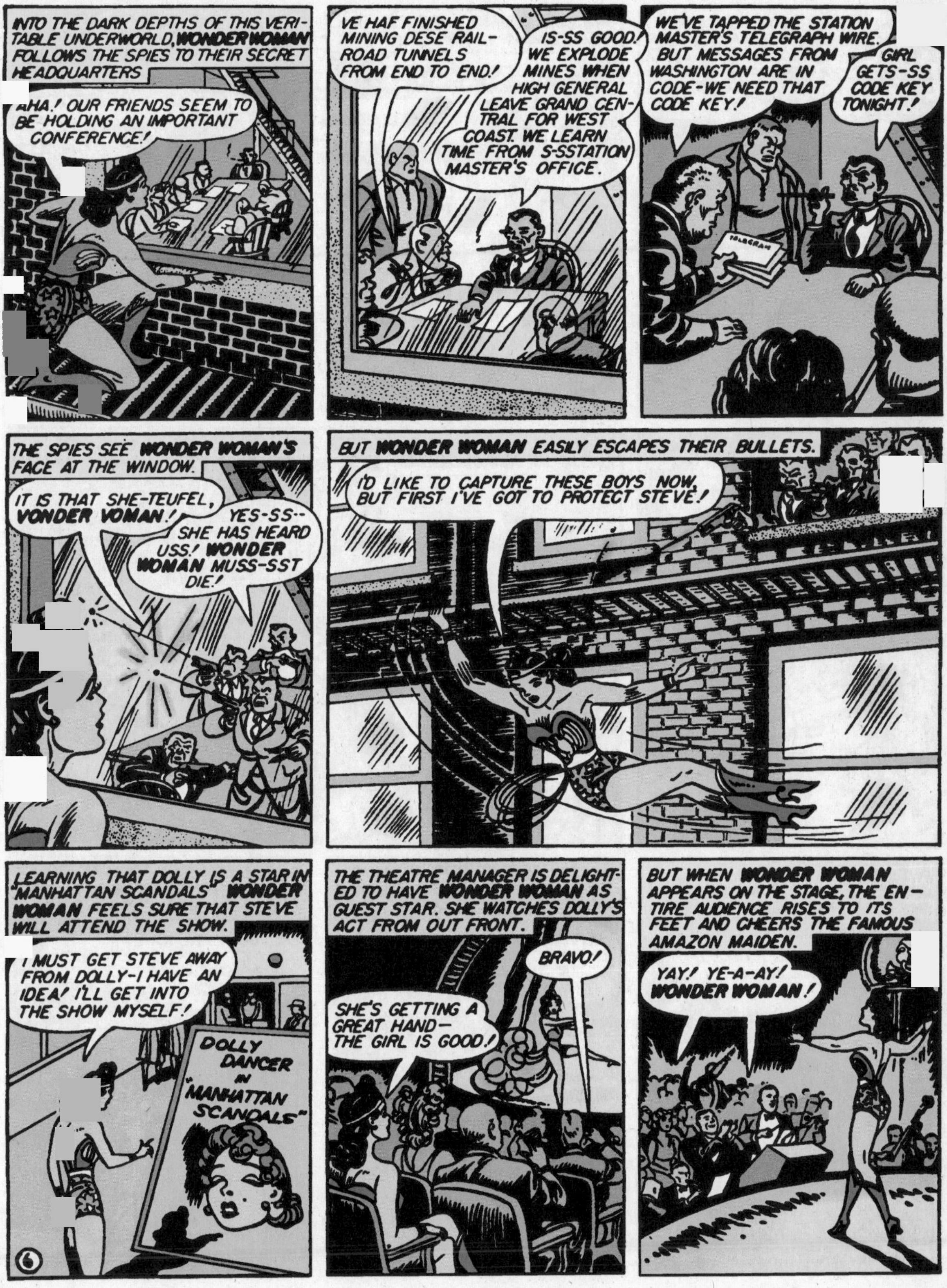
INTO THE DARK DEPTHS OF THIS VERITABLE UNDERWORLD, WONDER WOMAN FOLLOWS THE SPIES TO THEIR SECRET HEADQUARTERS
AHA! OUR FRIENDS SEEM TO BE HOLDING AN IMPORTANT CONFERENCE!
VE HAF FINISHED MINING DESE RAIL-ROAD TUNNELS FROM END TO END!
IS-SS GOOD! WE EXPLODE MINES WHEN HIGH GENERAL LEAVE GRAND CENTRAL FOR WEST COAST. WE LEARN TIME FROM S-SSTATION MASTER'S OFFICE.
WE'VE TAPPED THE STATION MASTER'S TELEGRAPH WIRE. BUT MESSAGES FROM WASHINGTON ARE IN CODE-WE NEED THAT CODE KEY!
GIRL GETS-SS CODE KEY TONIGHT!
THE SPIES SEE WONDER WOMAN'S FACE AT THE WINDOW.
IT IS THAT SHE-TEUFEL, VONDER VOMAN!
YES-SS-- SHE HAS HEARD USS! WONDER WOMAN MUSS-SST DIE!
BUT WONDER WOMAN EASILY ESCAPES THEIR BULLETS.
I'D LIKE TO CAPTURE THESE BOYS NOW, BUT FIRST I'VE GOT TO PROTECT STEVE!
LEARNING THAT DOLLY IS A STAR IN "MANHATTAN SCANDALS" WONDER WOMAN FEELS SURE THAT STEVE WILL ATTEND THE SHOW.
I MUST GET STEVE AWAY FROM DOLLY-I HAVE AN IDEA! I'LL GET INTO THE SHOW MYSELF!
DOLLY DANCER IN "MANHATTAN SCANDALS"
6
THE THEATRE MANAGER IS DELIGHTED TO HAVE WONDER WOMAN AS GUEST STAR. SHE WATCHES DOLLY'S ACT FROM OUT FRONT.
BRAVO!
SHE'S GETTING A GREAT HAND— THE GIRL IS GOOD!
BUT WHEN WONDER WOMAN APPEARS ON THE STAGE, THE ENTIRE AUDIENCE RISES TO ITS FEET AND CHEERS THE FAMOUS AMAZON MAIDEN.
YAY! YE-A-AY! WONDER WOMAN!

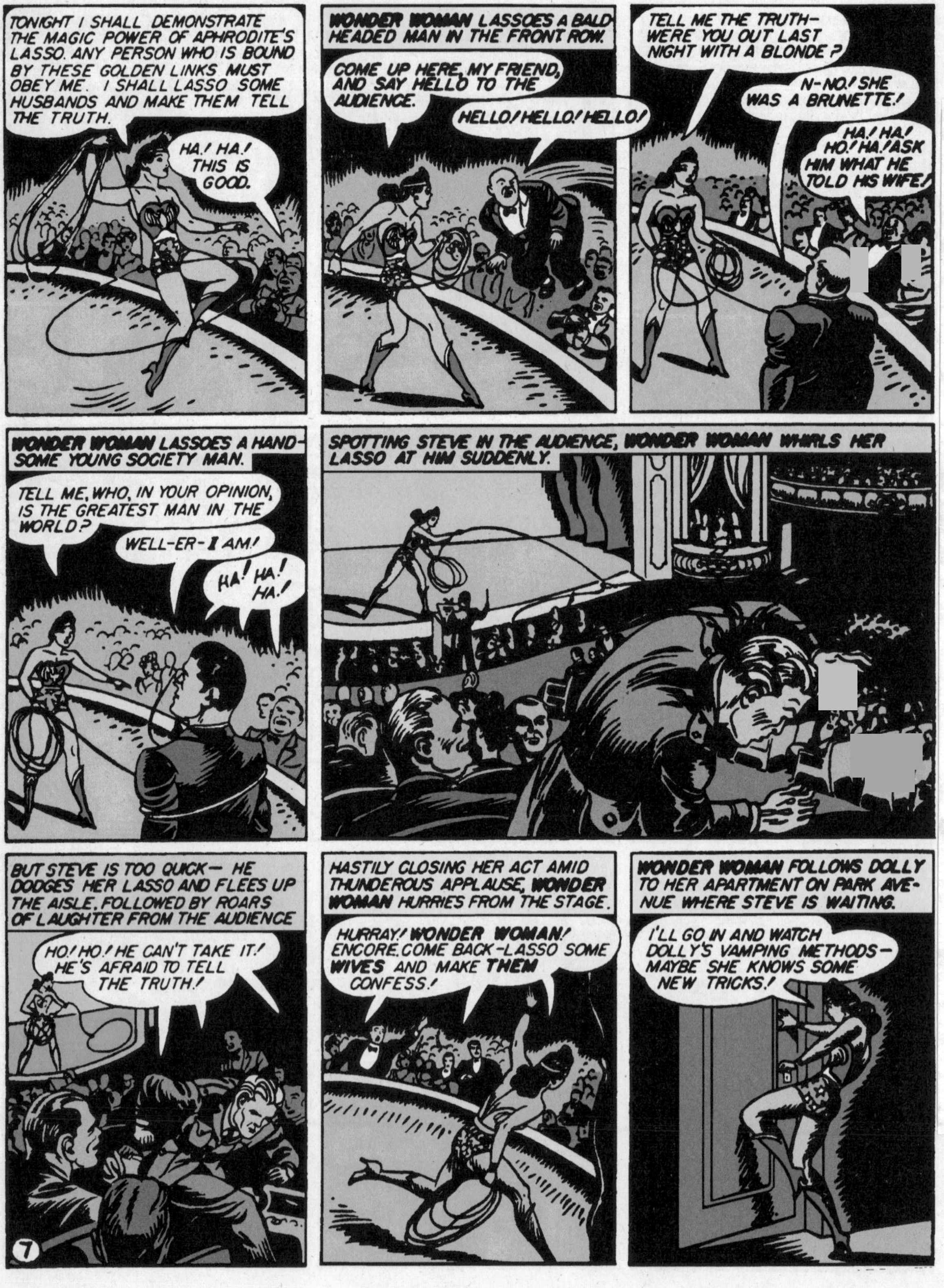
TONIGHT I SHALL DEMONSTRATE THE MAGIC POWER OF APHRODITE'S LASSO. ANY PERSON WHO IS BOUND BY THESE GOLDEN LINKS MUST OBEY ME. I SHALL LASSO SOME HUSBANDS AND MAKE THEM TELL THE TRUTH.
HA! HA! THIS IS GOOD.
WONDER WOMAN LASSOES A BALD HEADED MAN IN THE FRONT ROW.
COME UP HERE, MY FRIEND, AND SAY HELLO TO THE AUDIENCE.
HELLO! HELLO! HELLO!
TELL ME THE TRUTH— WERE YOU OUT LAST NIGHT WITH A BLONDE?
N-NO! SHE WAS A BRUNETTE!
HA! HA! HO! HA! ASK HIM WHAT HE TOLD HIS WIFE!
WONDER WOMAN LASSOES A HANDSOME YOUNG SOCIETY MAN.
TELL ME, WHO, IN YOUR OPINION, IS THE GREATEST MAN IN THE WORLD?
WELL-ER-I AM!
HA! HA! HA!
SPOTTING STEVE IN THE AUDIENCE, WONDER WOMAN WHIRLS HER LASSO AT HIM SUDDENLY.
BUT STEVE IS TOO QUICK— HE DODGES HER LASSO AND FLEES UP THE AISLE, FOLLOWED BY ROARS OF LAUGHTER FROM THE AUDIENCE
HO! HO! HE CAN'T TAKE IT! HE'S AFRAID TO TELL THE TRUTH!
7
HASTILY CLOSING HER ACT AMID THUNDEROUS APPLAUSE, WONDER WOMAN HURRIES FROM THE STAGE.
HURRAY! WONDER WOMAN! ENCORE, COME BACK-LASSO SOME WIVES AND MAKE THEM CONFESS!
WONDER WOMAN FOLLOWS DOLLY TO HER APARTMENT ON PARK AVENUE WHERE STEVE IS WAITING.
I'LL GO IN AND WATCH DOLLY'S VAMPING METHODS— MAYBE SHE KNOWS SOME NEW TRICKS!

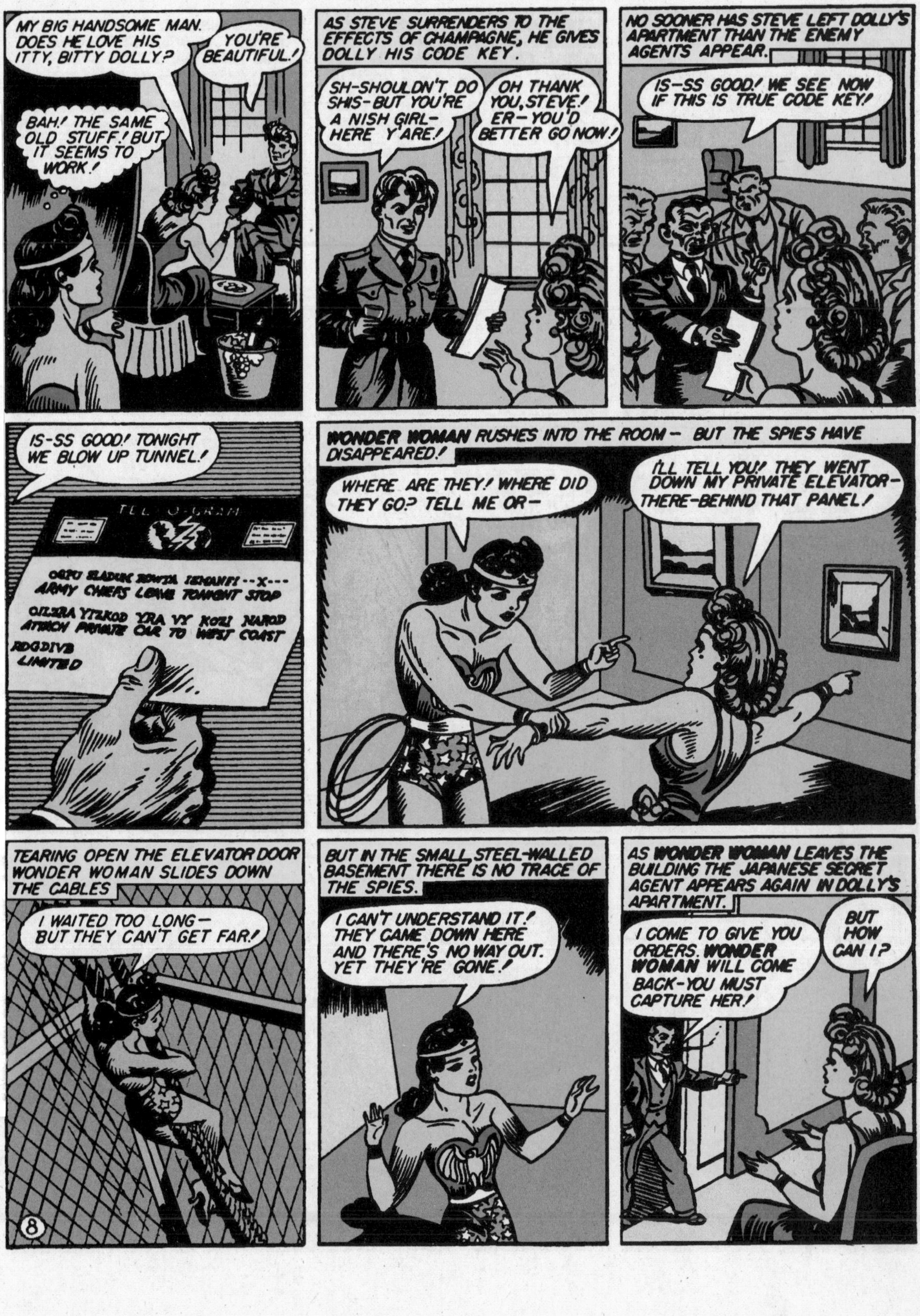

MY BIG HANDSOME MAN. DOES HE LOVE HIS ITTY, BITTY DOLLY?
YOU'RE BEAUTIFUL!
BAH! THE SAME OLD STUFF! BUT IT SEEMS TO WORK!
AS STEVE SURRENDERS TO THE EFFECTS OF CHAMPAGNE, HE GIVES DOLLY HIS CODE KEY.
SH-SHOULDN'T DO SHIS- BUT YOU'RE A NISH GIRL- HERE Y'ARE!
OH THANK YOU, STEVE! ER-YOU'D BETTER GO NOW!
NO SOONER HAS STEVE LEFT DOLLY'S APARTMENT THAN THE ENEMY AGENTS APPEAR.
IS-SS GOOD! WE SEE NOW IF THIS IS TRUE CODE KEY!
IS-SS GOOD! TONIGHT WE BLOW UP TUNNEL!
ARMY CHIEFS LEAVE TONIGHT STOP
ATTACH PRIVATE CAR TO WEST COAST
LIMITED
WONDER WOMAN RUSHES INTO THE ROOM - BUT THE SPIES HAVE DISAPPEARED!
WHERE ARE THEY! WHERE DID THEY GO? TELL ME OR-
I'LL TELL YOU! THEY WENT DOWN MY PRIVATE ELEVATOR- THERE-BEHIND THAT PANEL!
TEARING OPEN THE ELEVATOR DOOR WONDER WOMAN SLIDES DOWN THE CABLES
I WAITED TOO LONG- BUT THEY CAN'T GET FAR!
8
BUT IN THE SMALL, STEEL-WALLED BASEMENT THERE IS NO TRACE OF THE SPIES.
I CAN'T UNDERSTAND IT! THEY CAME DOWN HERE AND THERE'S NO WAY OUT. YET THEY'RE GONE!
AS WONDER WOMAN LEAVES THE BUILDING THE JAPANESE SECRET AGENT APPEARS AGAIN IN DOLLY'S APARTMENT.
I COME TO GIVE YOU ORDERS. WONDER WOMAN WILL COME BACK-YOU MUST CAPTURE HER!
BUT HOW CAN I?

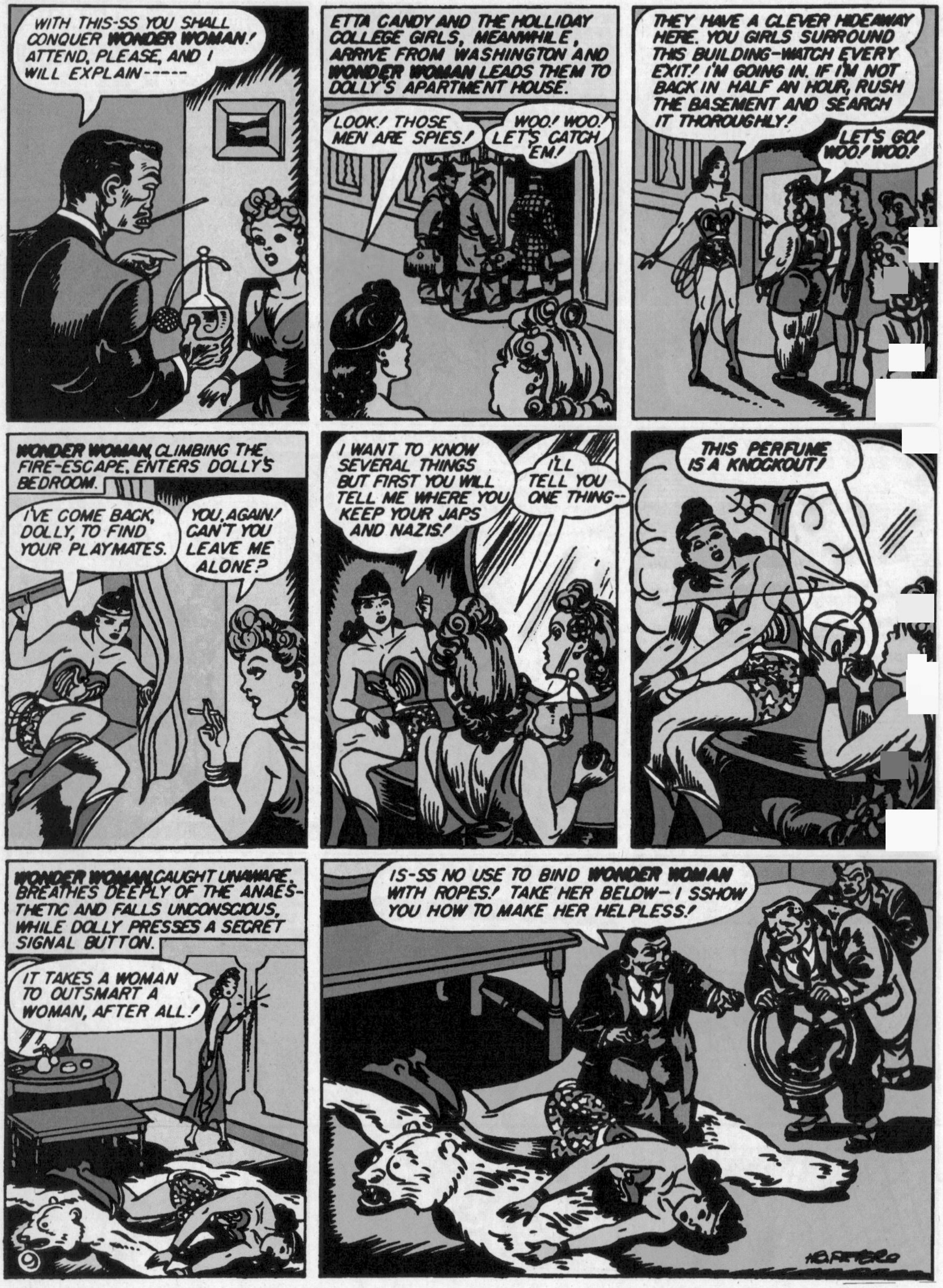
WITH THIS-SS YOU SHALL CONQUER WONDER WOMAN! ATTEND, PLEASE, AND I WILL EXPLAIN-----
ETTA CANDY AND THE HOLLIDAY COLLEGE GIRLS, MEANWHILE, ARRIVE FROM WASHINGTON AND WONDER WOMAN LEADS THEM TO DOLLY'S APARTMENT HOUSE.
LOOK! THOSE MEN ARE SPIES!
WOO! WOO! LET'S CATCH 'EM!
THEY HAVE A CLEVER HIDEAWAY HERE. YOU GIRLS SURROUND THIS BUILDING-WATCH EVERY EXIT! I'M GOING IN. IF I'M NOT BACK IN HALF AN HOUR, RUSH THE BASEMENT AND SEARCH IT THOROUGHLY!
LET'S GO! WOO! WOO!
WONDER WOMAN, CLIMBING THE FIRE-ESCAPE, ENTERS DOLLY'S BEDROOM.
I'VE COME BACK, DOLLY, TO FIND YOUR PLAYMATES.
YOU, AGAIN! CAN'T YOU LEAVE ME ALONE?
I WANT TO KNOW SEVERAL THINGS BUT FIRST YOU WILL TELL ME WHERE YOU KEEP YOUR JAPS AND NAZIS!
I'LL TELL YOU ONE THING--
THIS PERFUME IS A KNOCKOUT!
WONDER WOMAN CAUGHT UNAWARE, BREATHES DEEPLY OF THE ANAESTHETIC AND FALLS UNCONSCIOUS, WHILE DOLLY PRESSES A SECRET SIGNAL BUTTON.
IT TAKES A WOMAN TO OUTSMART A WOMAN, AFTER ALL!
IS-SS NO USE TO BIND WONDER WOMAN WITH ROPES! TAKE HER BELOW- I SSHOW YOU HOW TO MAKE HER HELPLESS!
H.G. PETER

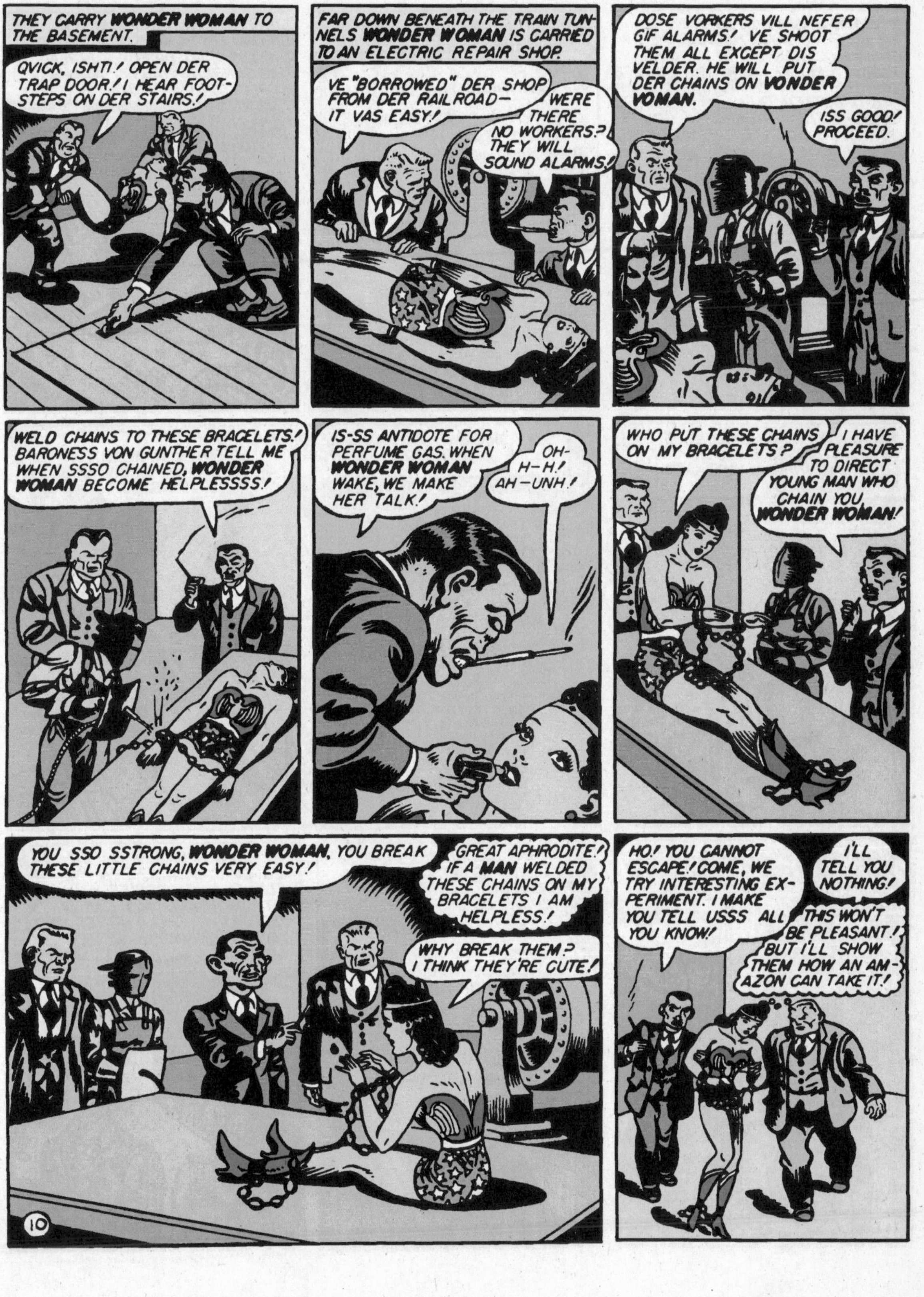
THEY CARRY WONDER WOMAN TO THE BASEMENT.
QVICK, ISHTI! OPEN DER TRAP DOOR! I HEAR FOOT-STEPS ON DER STAIRS!
FAR DOWN BENEATH THE TRAIN TUNNELS WONDER WOMAN IS CARRIED TO AN ELECTRIC REPAIR SHOP.
VE "BORROWED" DER SHOP FROM DER RAILROAD— IT VAS EASY!
WERE THERE NO WORKERS? THEY WILL SOUND ALARMS!
DOSE VORKERS VILL NEFER GIF ALARMS! VE SHOOT THEM ALL EXCEPT DIS VELDER. HE WILL PUT DER CHAINS ON VONDER VOMAN.
ISS GOOD! PROCEED.
WELD CHAINS TO THESE BRACELETS! BARONESS VON GUNTHER TELL ME WHEN SSSO CHAINED, WONDER WOMAN BECOME HELPLESSSS!
IS-SS ANTIDOTE FOR PERFUME GAS. WHEN WONDER WOMAN WAKE, WE MAKE HER TALK!
OH-H-H! AH—UNH!
WHO PUT THESE CHAINS ON MY BRACELETS?
I HAVE PLEASURE TO DIRECT YOUNG MAN WHO CHAIN YOU, WONDER WOMAN!
YOU SSO SSTRONG, WONDER WOMAN, YOU BREAK THESE LITTLE CHAINS VERY EASY!
GREAT APHRODITE! IF A MAN WELDED THESE CHAINS ON MY BRACELETS I AM HELPLESS!
WHY BREAK THEM? I THINK THEY'RE CUTE!
10
HO! YOU CANNOT ESCAPE! COME, WE TRY INTERESTING EXPERIMENT. I MAKE YOU TELL USSS ALL YOU KNOW!
I'LL TELL YOU NOTHING!
THIS WON'T BE PLEASANT! BUT I'LL SHOW THEM HOW AN AMAZON CAN TAKE IT!

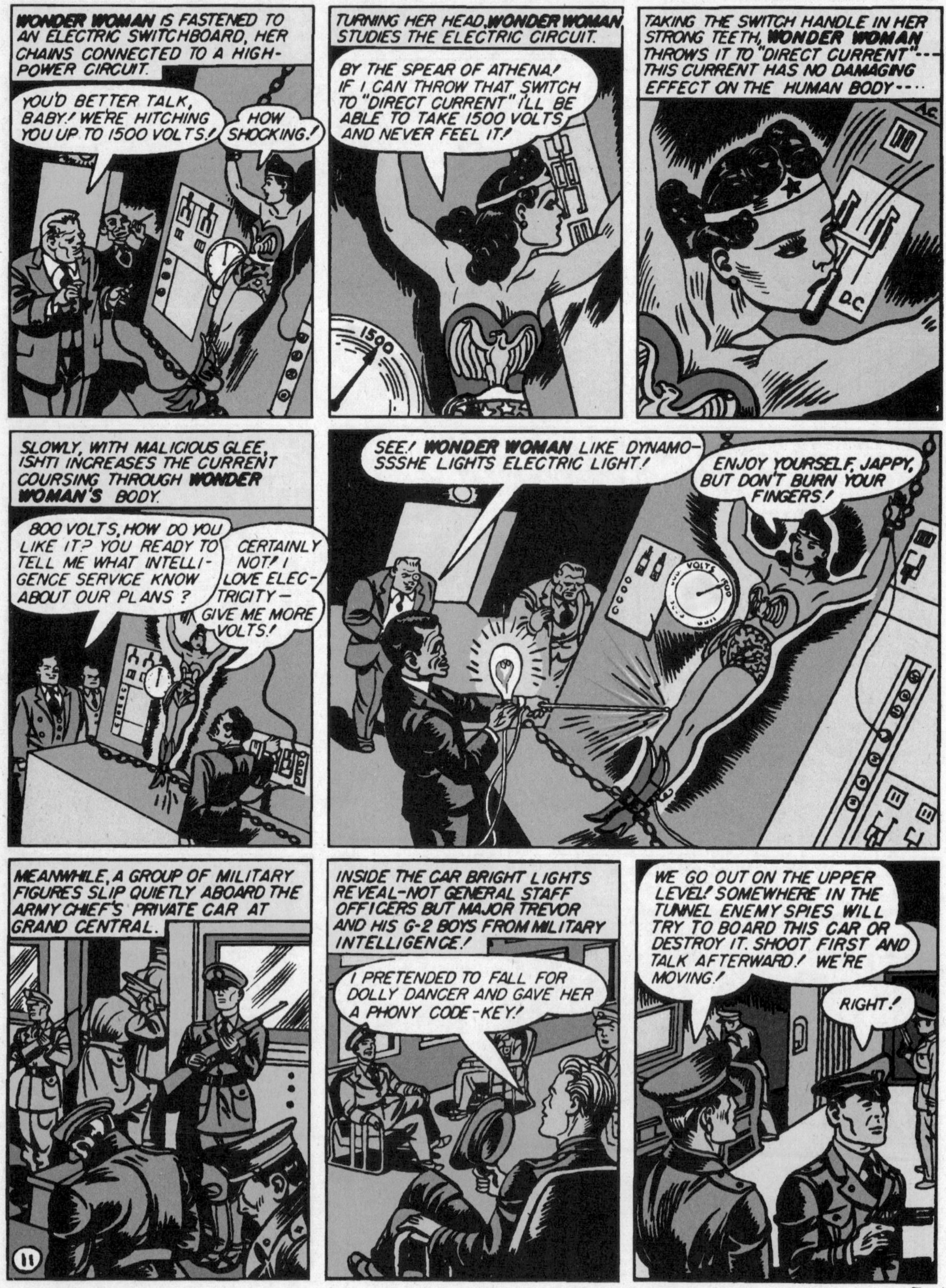

WONDER WOMAN IS FASTENED TO AN ELECTRIC SWITCHBOARD, HER CHAINS CONNECTED TO A HIGH-POWER CIRCUIT.
YOU'D BETTER TALK, BABY! WE'RE HITCHING YOU UP TO 1500 VOLTS!
HOW SHOCKING!
TURNING HER HEAD, WONDER WOMAN STUDIES THE ELECTRIC CIRCUIT.
BY THE SPEAR OF ATHENA! IF I CAN THROW THAT SWITCH TO "DIRECT CURRENT" I'LL BE ABLE TO TAKE 1500 VOLTS AND NEVER FEEL IT!
1500
TAKING THE SWITCH HANDLE IN HER STRONG TEETH, WONDER WOMAN THROWS IT TO "DIRECT CURRENT"--- THIS CURRENT HAS NO DAMAGING EFFECT ON THE HUMAN BODY---
A.C.
D.C.
SLOWLY, WITH MALICIOUS GLEE, ISHTI INCREASES THE CURRENT COURSING THROUGH WONDER WOMAN'S BODY.
800 VOLTS, HOW DO YOU LIKE IT? YOU READY TO TELL ME WHAT INTELLIGENCE SERVICE KNOW ABOUT OUR PLANS?
CERTAINLY NOT! I LOVE ELECTRICITY— GIVE ME MORE VOLTS!
SEE! WONDER WOMAN LIKE DYNAMO— SSSHE LIGHTS ELECTRIC LIGHT!
ENJOY YOURSELF, JAPPY, BUT DON'T BURN YOUR FINGERS!
VOLTS
MEANWHILE, A GROUP OF MILITARY FIGURES SLIP QUIETLY ABOARD THE ARMY CHIEF'S PRIVATE CAR AT GRAND CENTRAL.
11
INSIDE THE CAR BRIGHT LIGHTS REVEAL-NOT GENERAL STAFF OFFICERS BUT MAJOR TREVOR AND HIS G-2 BOYS FROM MILITARY INTELLIGENCE!
I PRETENDED TO FALL FOR DOLLY DANCER AND GAVE HER A PHONY CODE-KEY!
WE GO OUT ON THE UPPER LEVEL! SOMEWHERE IN THE TUNNEL ENEMY SPIES WILL TRY TO BOARD THIS CAR OR DESTROY IT. SHOOT FIRST AND TALK AFTERWARD! WE'RE MOVING!
RIGHT!

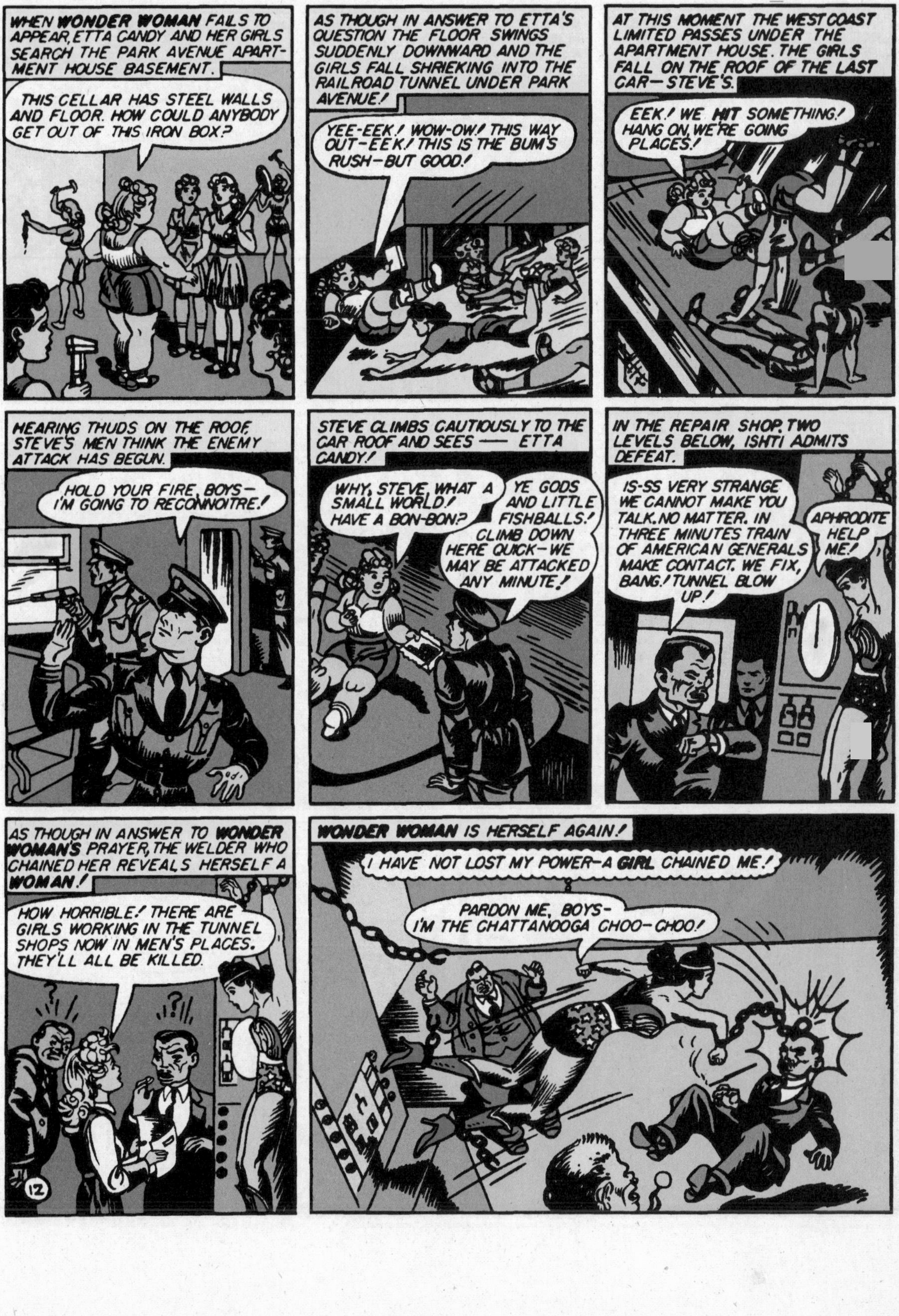

WHEN WONDER WOMAN FAILS TO APPEAR, ETTA CANDY AND HER GIRLS SEARCH THE PARK AVENUE APARTMENT HOUSE BASEMENT.
THIS CELLAR HAS STEEL WALLS AND FLOOR. HOW COULD ANYBODY GET OUT OF THIS IRON BOX?
AS THOUGH IN ANSWER TO ETTA'S QUESTION THE FLOOR SWINGS SUDDENLY DOWNWARD AND THE GIRLS FALL SHRIEKING INTO THE RAILROAD TUNNEL UNDER PARK AVENUE!
YEE-EEK! WOW-OW! THIS WAY OUT-EEK! THIS IS THE BUM'S RUSH-BUT GOOD!
AT THIS MOMENT THE WEST COAST LIMITED PASSES UNDER THE APARTMENT HOUSE. THE GIRLS FALL ON THE ROOF OF THE LAST CAR-STEVE'S.
EEK! WE HIT SOMETHING! HANG ON, WE'RE GOING PLACES!
HEARING THUDS ON THE ROOF, STEVE'S MEN THINK THE ENEMY ATTACK HAS BEGUN.
HOLD YOUR FIRE, BOYS-I'M GOING TO RECONNOITRE!
STEVE CLIMBS CAUTIOUSLY TO THE CAR ROOF AND SEES — ETTA CANDY!
WHY, STEVE, WHAT A SMALL WORLD! HAVE A BON-BON?
YE GODS AND LITTLE FISHBALLS! CLIMB DOWN HERE QUICK-WE MAY BE ATTACKED ANY MINUTE!
IN THE REPAIR SHOP, TWO LEVELS BELOW, ISHTI ADMITS DEFEAT.
IS-SS VERY STRANGE WE CANNOT MAKE YOU TALK. NO MATTER. IN THREE MINUTES TRAIN OF AMERICAN GENERALS MAKE CONTACT. WE FIX, BANG! TUNNEL BLOW UP!
APHRODITE HELP ME!
AS THOUGH IN ANSWER TO WONDER WOMAN'S PRAYER, THE WELDER WHO CHAINED HER REVEALS HERSELF A WOMAN!
HOW HORRIBLE! THERE ARE GIRLS WORKING IN THE TUNNEL SHOPS NOW IN MEN'S PLACES. THEY'LL ALL BE KILLED.
12
WONDER WOMAN IS HERSELF AGAIN!
I HAVE NOT LOST MY POWER-A GIRL CHAINED ME!
PARDON ME, BOYS-I'M THE CHATTANOOGA CHOO-CHOO!

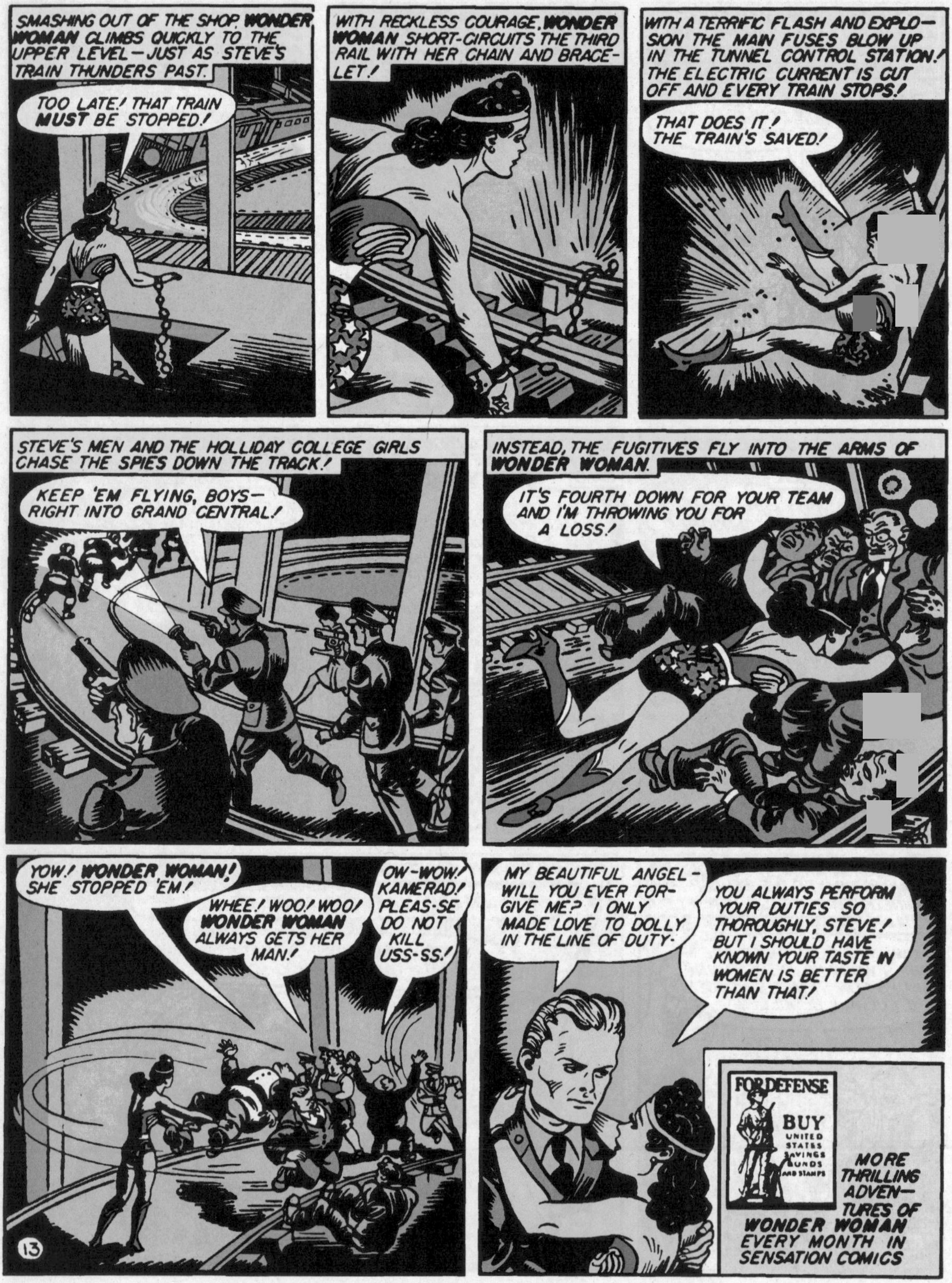
SMASHING OUT OF THE SHOP, WONDER WOMAN CLIMBS QUICKLY TO THE UPPER LEVEL—JUST AS STEVE'S TRAIN THUNDERS PAST.
TOO LATE! THAT TRAIN MUST BE STOPPED!
WITH RECKLESS COURAGE, WONDER WOMAN SHORT-CIRCUITS THE THIRD RAIL WITH HER CHAIN AND BRACELET!
WITH A TERRIFIC FLASH AND EXPLOSION THE MAIN FUSES BLOW UP IN THE TUNNEL CONTROL STATION! THE ELECTRIC CURRENT IS CUT OFF AND EVERY TRAIN STOPS!
THAT DOES IT! THE TRAIN'S SAVED!
STEVE'S MEN AND THE HOLLIDAY COLLEGE GIRLS CHASE THE SPIES DOWN THE TRACK!
KEEP 'EM FLYING, BOYS—RIGHT INTO GRAND CENTRAL!
INSTEAD, THE FUGITIVES FLY INTO THE ARMS OF WONDER WOMAN.
IT'S FOURTH DOWN FOR YOUR TEAM AND I'M THROWING YOU FOR A LOSS!
YOW! WONDER WOMAN! SHE STOPPED 'EM!
WHEE! WOO! WOO! WONDER WOMAN ALWAYS GETS HER MAN!
OW-WOW! KAMERAD! PLEAS-SE DO NOT KILL USS-SS!
13
MY BEAUTIFUL ANGEL—WILL YOU EVER FORGIVE ME? I ONLY MADE LOVE TO DOLLY IN THE LINE OF DUTY.
YOU ALWAYS PERFORM YOUR DUTIES SO THOROUGHLY, STEVE! BUT I SHOULD HAVE KNOWN YOUR TASTE IN WOMEN IS BETTER THAN THAT!
FOR DEFENSE
BUY UNITED STATES SAVINGS BONDS AND STAMPS
MORE THRILLING ADVENTURES OF WONDER WOMAN EVERY MONTH IN SENSATION COMICS

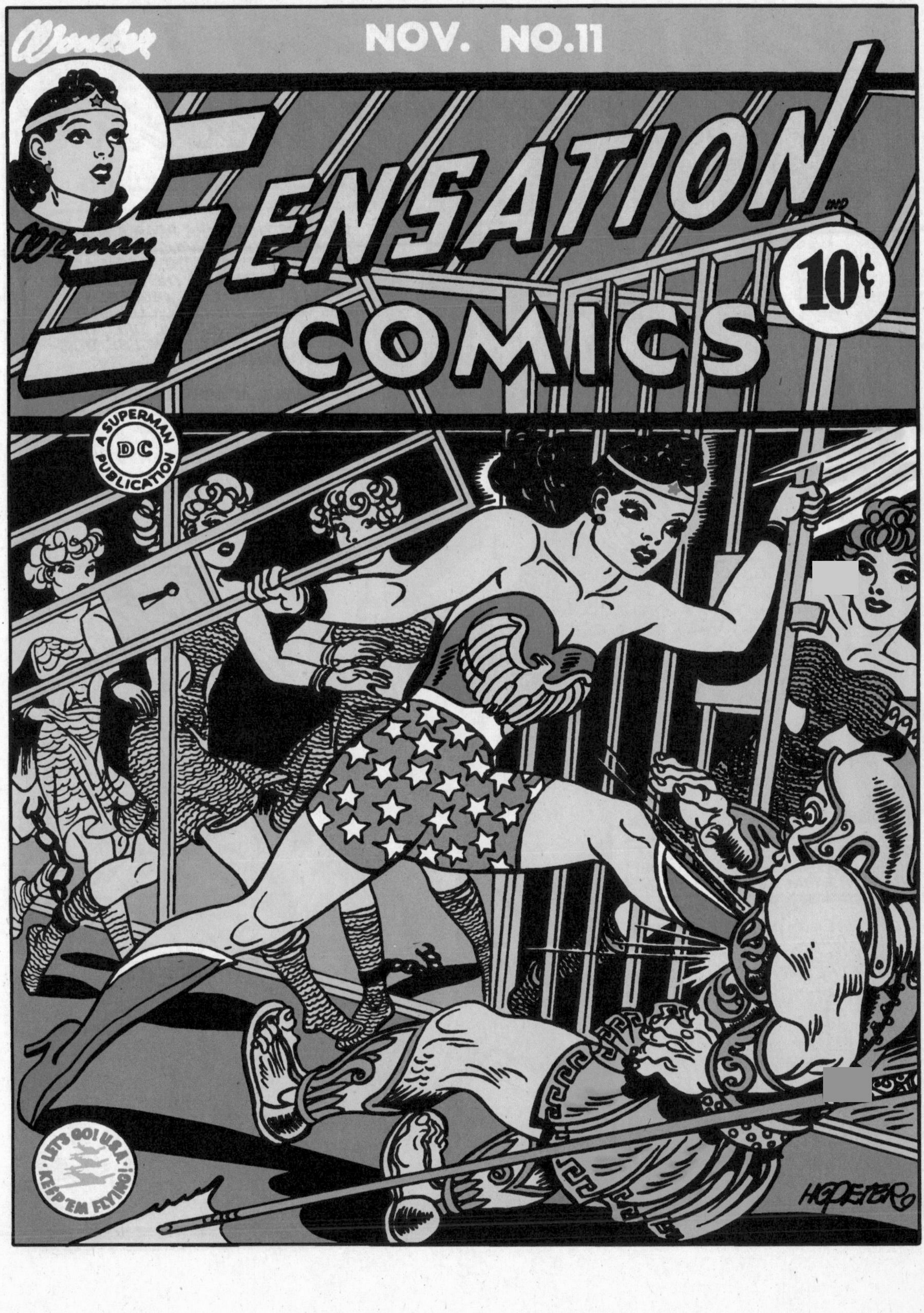

Wonder Woman
NOV. NO.11
SENSATION
COMICS
10¢
A SUPERMAN DC PUBLICATION
LET'S GO! U.S.A. KEEP 'EM FLYING!
HGPETER

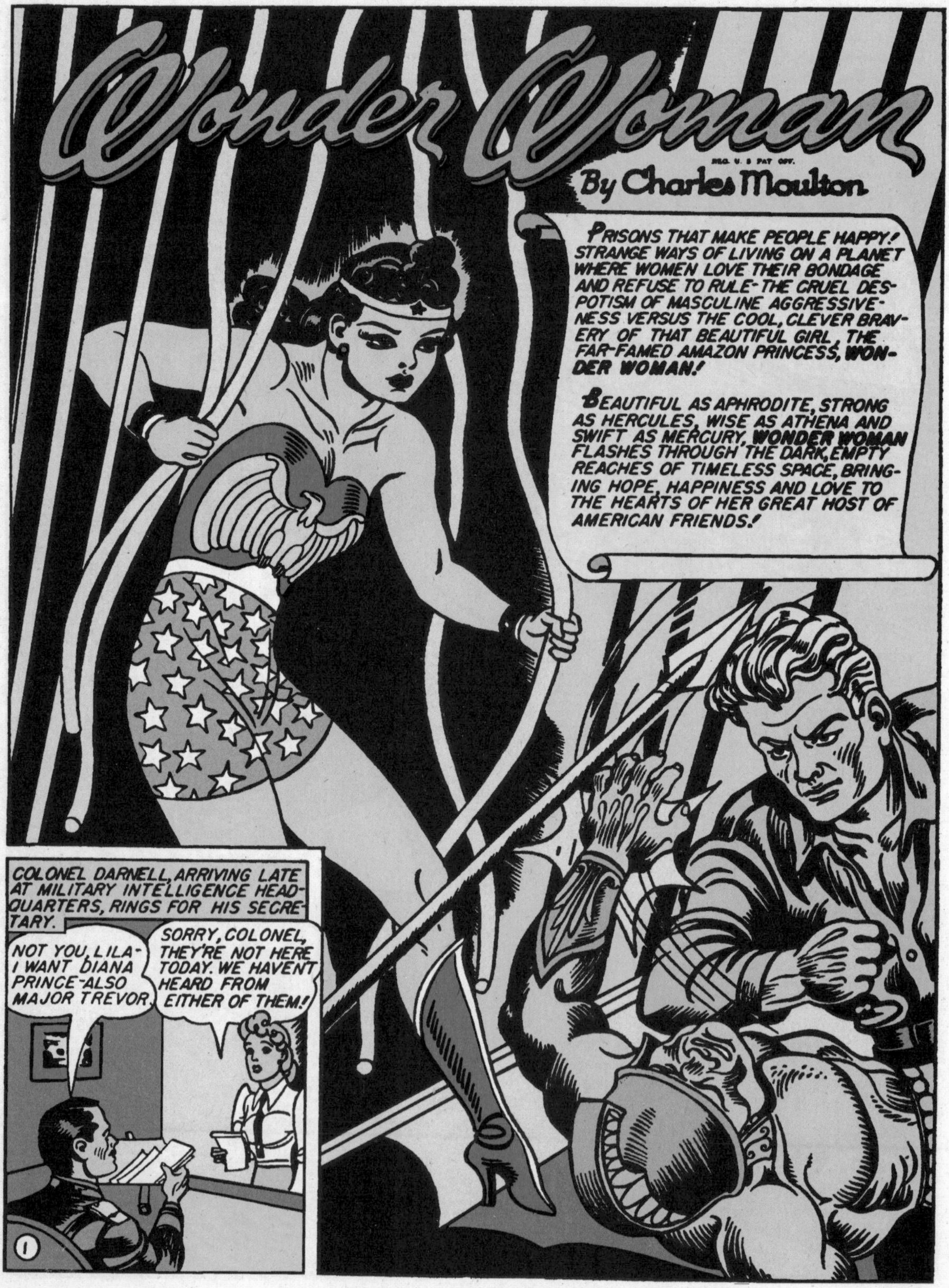
Wonder Woman
REG. U. S. PAT. OFF.
By Charles Moulton
PRISONS THAT MAKE PEOPLE HAPPY! STRANGE WAYS OF LIVING ON A PLANET WHERE WOMEN LOVE THEIR BONDAGE AND REFUSE TO RULE- THE CRUEL DESPOTISM OF MASCULINE AGGRESSIVENESS VERSUS THE COOL, CLEVER BRAVERY OF THAT BEAUTIFUL GIRL, THE FAR-FAMED AMAZON PRINCESS, WONDER WOMAN!
BEAUTIFUL AS APHRODITE, STRONG AS HERCULES, WISE AS ATHENA AND SWIFT AS MERCURY, WONDER WOMAN FLASHES THROUGH THE DARK, EMPTY REACHES OF TIMELESS SPACE, BRINGING HOPE, HAPPINESS AND LOVE TO THE HEARTS OF HER GREAT HOST OF AMERICAN FRIENDS!
COLONEL DARNELL, ARRIVING LATE AT MILITARY INTELLIGENCE HEADQUARTERS, RINGS FOR HIS SECRETARY.
NOT YOU, LILA- I WANT DIANA PRINCE-ALSO MAJOR TREVOR.
SORRY, COLONEL, THEY'RE NOT HERE TODAY. WE HAVEN'T HEARD FROM EITHER OF THEM!
1

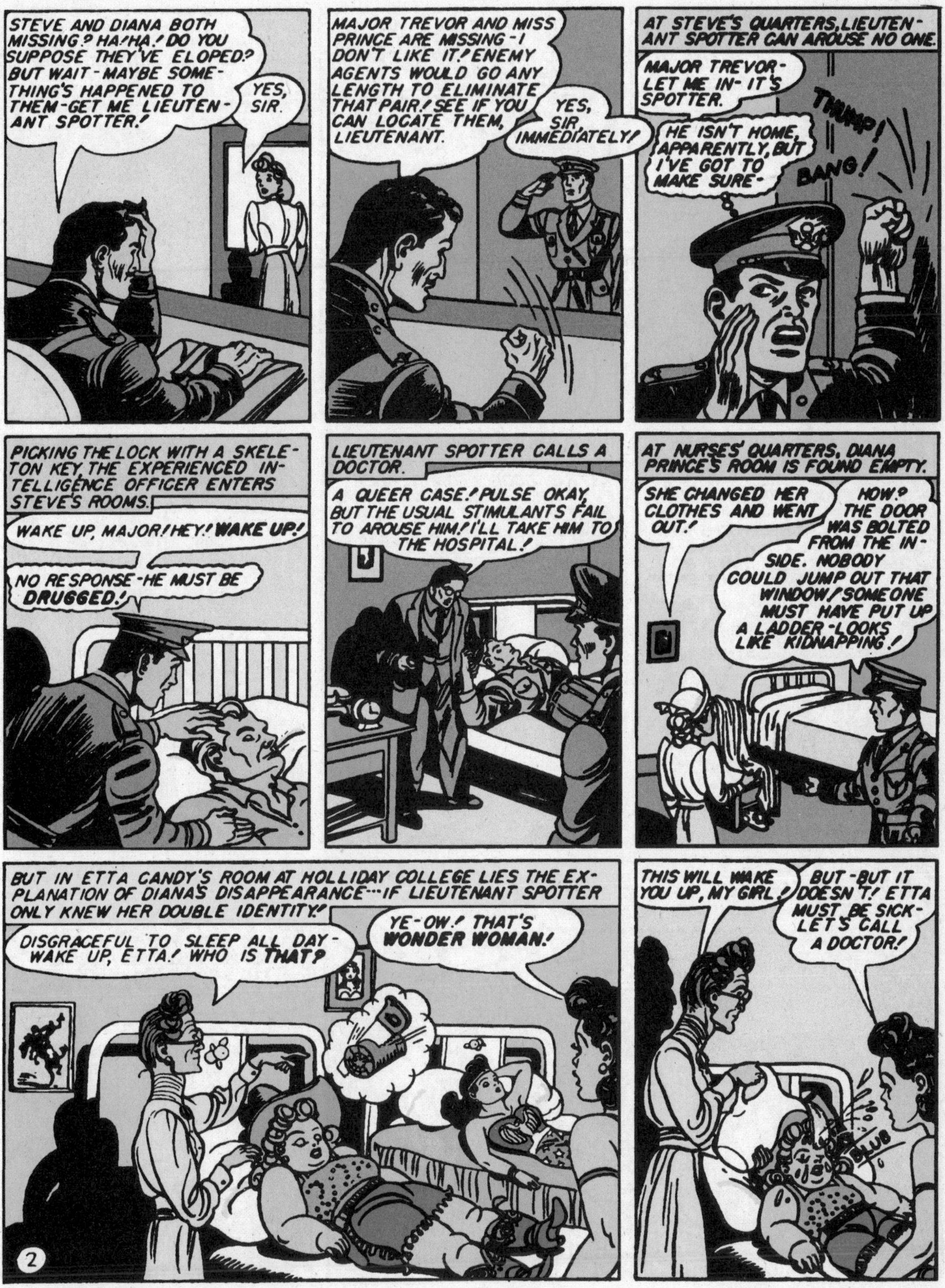
STEVE AND DIANA BOTH MISSING? HA! HA! DO YOU SUPPOSE THEY'VE ELOPED? BUT WAIT - MAYBE SOMETHING'S HAPPENED TO THEM - GET ME LIEUTENANT SPOTTER!
YES, SIR.
MAJOR TREVOR AND MISS PRINCE ARE MISSING - I DON'T LIKE IT! ENEMY AGENTS WOULD GO ANY LENGTH TO ELIMINATE THAT PAIR! SEE IF YOU CAN LOCATE THEM, LIEUTENANT.
YES, SIR, IMMEDIATELY!
AT STEVE'S QUARTERS, LIEUTENANT SPOTTER CAN AROUSE NO ONE.
MAJOR TREVOR - LET ME IN - IT'S SPOTTER.
HE ISN'T HOME, APPARENTLY, BUT I'VE GOT TO MAKE SURE-
THUMP!
BANG!
PICKING THE LOCK WITH A SKELETON KEY, THE EXPERIENCED INTELLIGENCE OFFICER ENTERS STEVE'S ROOMS.
WAKE UP, MAJOR! HEY! WAKE UP!
NO RESPONSE - HE MUST BE DRUGGED!
LIEUTENANT SPOTTER CALLS A DOCTOR.
A QUEER CASE! PULSE OKAY, BUT THE USUAL STIMULANTS FAIL TO AROUSE HIM! I'LL TAKE HIM TO THE HOSPITAL!
AT NURSES' QUARTERS, DIANA PRINCE'S ROOM IS FOUND EMPTY.
SHE CHANGED HER CLOTHES AND WENT OUT!
HOW? THE DOOR WAS BOLTED FROM THE INSIDE. NOBODY COULD JUMP OUT THAT WINDOW! SOMEONE MUST HAVE PUT UP A LADDER - LOOKS LIKE KIDNAPPING!
BUT IN ETTA CANDY'S ROOM AT HOLLIDAY COLLEGE LIES THE EXPLANATION OF DIANA'S DISAPPEARANCE --- IF LIEUTENANT SPOTTER ONLY KNEW HER DOUBLE IDENTITY!
DISGRACEFUL TO SLEEP ALL DAY - WAKE UP, ETTA! WHO IS THAT?
YE-OW! THAT'S WONDER WOMAN!
THIS WILL WAKE YOU UP, MY GIRL!
BUT - BUT IT DOESN'T! ETTA MUST BE SICK - LET'S CALL A DOCTOR!
BLUB
2

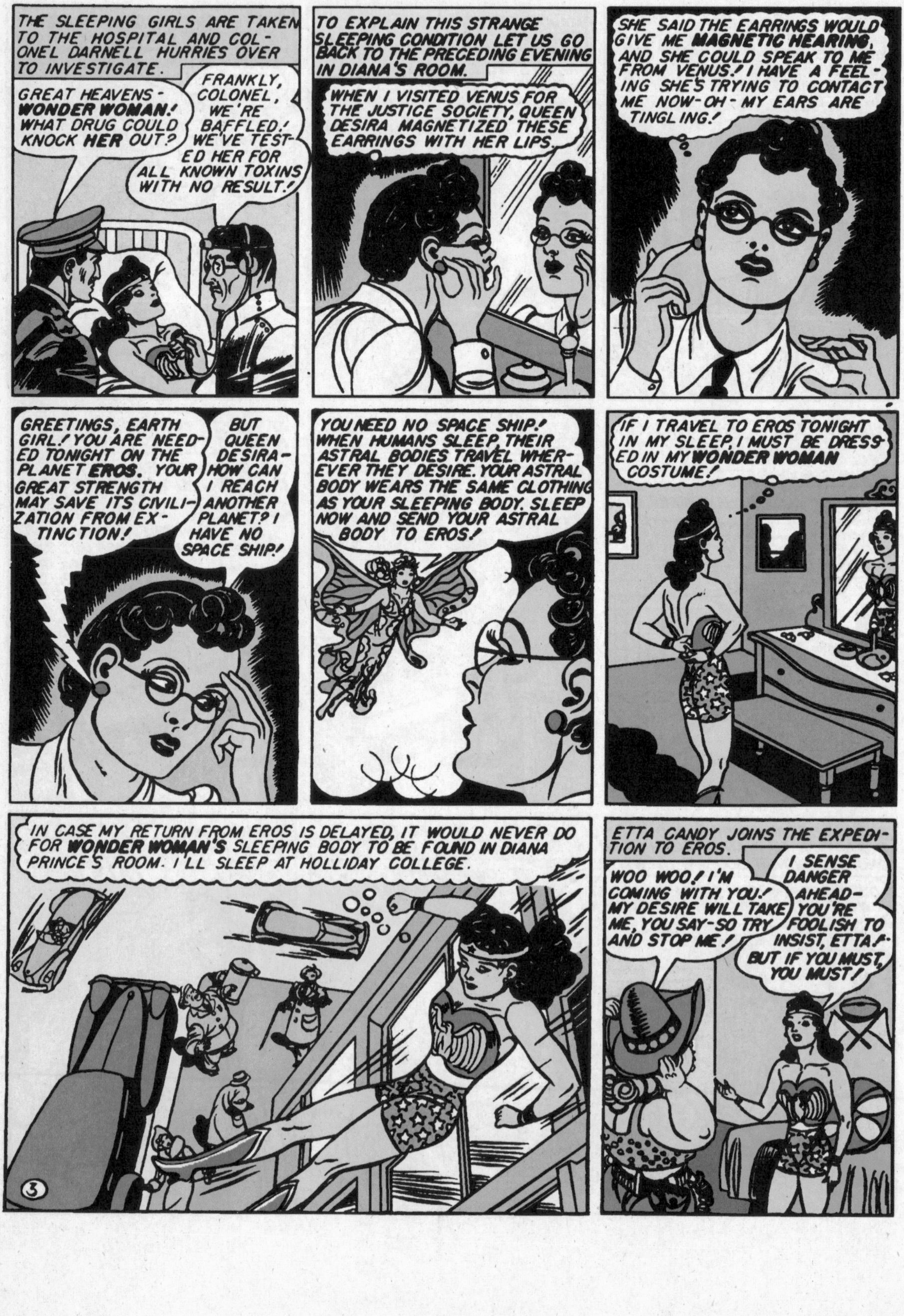
THE SLEEPING GIRLS ARE TAKEN TO THE HOSPITAL AND COLONEL DARNELL HURRIES OVER TO INVESTIGATE.
GREAT HEAVENS - WONDER WOMAN! WHAT DRUG COULD KNOCK HER OUT?
FRANKLY, COLONEL, WE'RE BAFFLED! WE'VE TESTED HER FOR ALL KNOWN TOXINS WITH NO RESULT!
TO EXPLAIN THIS STRANGE SLEEPING CONDITION LET US GO BACK TO THE PRECEDING EVENING IN DIANA'S ROOM.
WHEN I VISITED VENUS FOR THE JUSTICE SOCIETY, QUEEN DESIRA MAGNETIZED THESE EARRINGS WITH HER LIPS.
SHE SAID THE EARRINGS WOULD GIVE ME MAGNETIC HEARING, AND SHE COULD SPEAK TO ME FROM VENUS! I HAVE A FEELING SHE'S TRYING TO CONTACT ME NOW-OH- MY EARS ARE TINGLING!
GREETINGS, EARTH GIRL! YOU ARE NEEDED TONIGHT ON THE PLANET EROS. YOUR GREAT STRENGTH MAY SAVE ITS CIVILIZATION FROM EXTINCTION!
BUT QUEEN DESIRA- HOW CAN I REACH ANOTHER PLANET? I HAVE NO SPACE SHIP!
YOU NEED NO SPACE SHIP! WHEN HUMANS SLEEP, THEIR ASTRAL BODIES TRAVEL WHEREVER THEY DESIRE. YOUR ASTRAL BODY WEARS THE SAME CLOTHING AS YOUR SLEEPING BODY. SLEEP NOW AND SEND YOUR ASTRAL BODY TO EROS!
IF I TRAVEL TO EROS TONIGHT IN MY SLEEP, I MUST BE DRESSED IN MY WONDER WOMAN COSTUME!
IN CASE MY RETURN FROM EROS IS DELAYED, IT WOULD NEVER DO FOR WONDER WOMAN'S SLEEPING BODY TO BE FOUND IN DIANA PRINCE'S ROOM. I'LL SLEEP AT HOLLIDAY COLLEGE.
3
ETTA CANDY JOINS THE EXPEDITION TO EROS.
WOO WOO! I'M COMING WITH YOU! MY DESIRE WILL TAKE ME, YOU SAY-SO TRY AND STOP ME!
I SENSE DANGER AHEAD- YOU'RE FOOLISH TO INSIST, ETTA! BUT IF YOU MUST, YOU MUST!

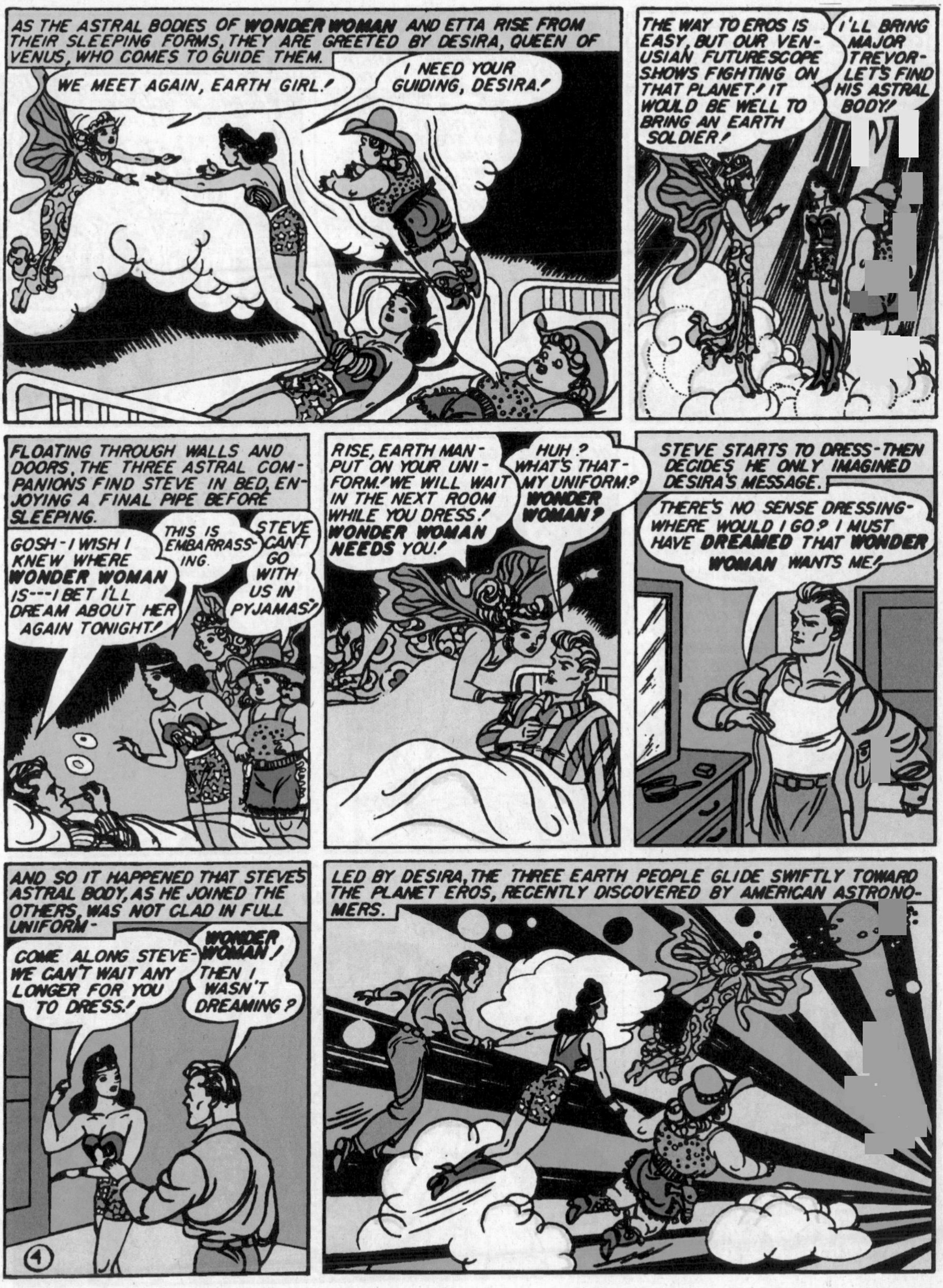
AS THE ASTRAL BODIES OF WONDER WOMAN AND ETTA RISE FROM THEIR SLEEPING FORMS, THEY ARE GREETED BY DESIRA, QUEEN OF VENUS, WHO COMES TO GUIDE THEM.
WE MEET AGAIN, EARTH GIRL!
I NEED YOUR GUIDING, DESIRA!
THE WAY TO EROS IS EASY, BUT OUR VENUSIAN FUTURESCOPE SHOWS FIGHTING ON THAT PLANET! IT WOULD BE WELL TO BRING AN EARTH SOLDIER!
I'LL BRING MAJOR TREVOR-LET'S FIND HIS ASTRAL BODY!
FLOATING THROUGH WALLS AND DOORS, THE THREE ASTRAL COMPANIONS FIND STEVE IN BED, ENJOYING A FINAL PIPE BEFORE SLEEPING.
GOSH-I WISH I KNEW WHERE WONDER WOMAN IS---I BET I'LL DREAM ABOUT HER AGAIN TONIGHT!
THIS IS EMBARRASSING.
STEVE CAN'T GO WITH US IN PYJAMAS!
RISE, EARTH MAN-PUT ON YOUR UNIFORM! WE WILL WAIT IN THE NEXT ROOM WHILE YOU DRESS! WONDER WOMAN NEEDS YOU!
HUH? WHAT'S THAT-MY UNIFORM? WONDER WOMAN?
STEVE STARTS TO DRESS-THEN DECIDES HE ONLY IMAGINED DESIRA'S MESSAGE.
THERE'S NO SENSE DRESSING-WHERE WOULD I GO? I MUST HAVE DREAMED THAT WONDER WOMAN WANTS ME!
AND SO IT HAPPENED THAT STEVE'S ASTRAL BODY, AS HE JOINED THE OTHERS, WAS NOT CLAD IN FULL UNIFORM-
COME ALONG STEVE-WE CAN'T WAIT ANY LONGER FOR YOU TO DRESS!
WONDER WOMAN! THEN I WASN'T DREAMING?
4
LED BY DESIRA, THE THREE EARTH PEOPLE GLIDE SWIFTLY TOWARD THE PLANET EROS, RECENTLY DISCOVERED BY AMERICAN ASTRONOMERS.

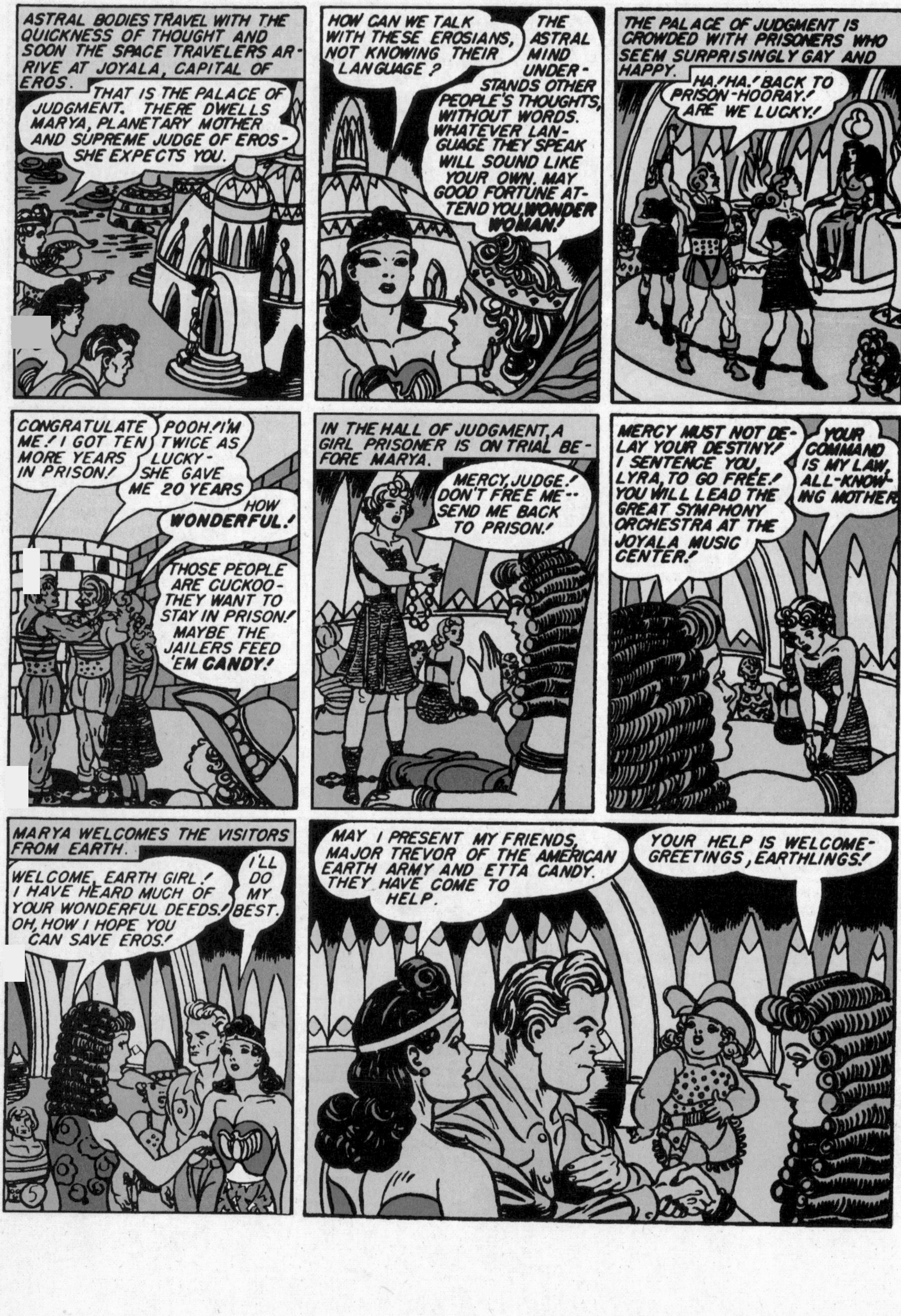

ASTRAL BODIES TRAVEL WITH THE QUICKNESS OF THOUGHT AND SOON THE SPACE TRAVELERS ARRIVE AT JOYALA, CAPITAL OF EROS.
THAT IS THE PALACE OF JUDGMENT. THERE DWELLS MARYA, PLANETARY MOTHER AND SUPREME JUDGE OF EROS-SHE EXPECTS YOU.
HOW CAN WE TALK WITH THESE EROSIANS, NOT KNOWING THEIR LANGUAGE?
THE ASTRAL MIND UNDERSTANDS OTHER PEOPLE'S THOUGHTS, WITHOUT WORDS. WHATEVER LANGUAGE THEY SPEAK WILL SOUND LIKE YOUR OWN. MAY GOOD FORTUNE ATTEND YOU, WONDER WOMAN!
THE PALACE OF JUDGMENT IS CROWDED WITH PRISONERS WHO SEEM SURPRISINGLY GAY AND HAPPY.
HA! HA! BACK TO PRISON-HOORAY! ARE WE LUCKY!
CONGRATULATE ME! I GOT TEN MORE YEARS IN PRISON!
POOH! I'M TWICE AS LUCKY-SHE GAVE ME 20 YEARS
HOW WONDERFUL!
THOSE PEOPLE ARE CUCKOO-THEY WANT TO STAY IN PRISON! MAYBE THE JAILERS FEED 'EM CANDY!
IN THE HALL OF JUDGMENT, A GIRL PRISONER IS ON TRIAL BEFORE MARYA.
MERCY, JUDGE! DON'T FREE ME--SEND ME BACK TO PRISON!
MERCY MUST NOT DELAY YOUR DESTINY! I SENTENCE YOU, LYRA, TO GO FREE! YOU WILL LEAD THE GREAT SYMPHONY ORCHESTRA AT THE JOYALA MUSIC CENTER!
YOUR COMMAND IS MY LAW, ALL-KNOWING MOTHER!
MARYA WELCOMES THE VISITORS FROM EARTH.
WELCOME, EARTH GIRL! I HAVE HEARD MUCH OF YOUR WONDERFUL DEEDS! OH, HOW I HOPE YOU CAN SAVE EROS!
I'LL DO MY BEST.
5
MAY I PRESENT MY FRIENDS, MAJOR TREVOR OF THE AMERICAN EARTH ARMY AND ETTA CANDY. THEY HAVE COME TO HELP.
YOUR HELP IS WELCOME-GREETINGS, EARTHLINGS!

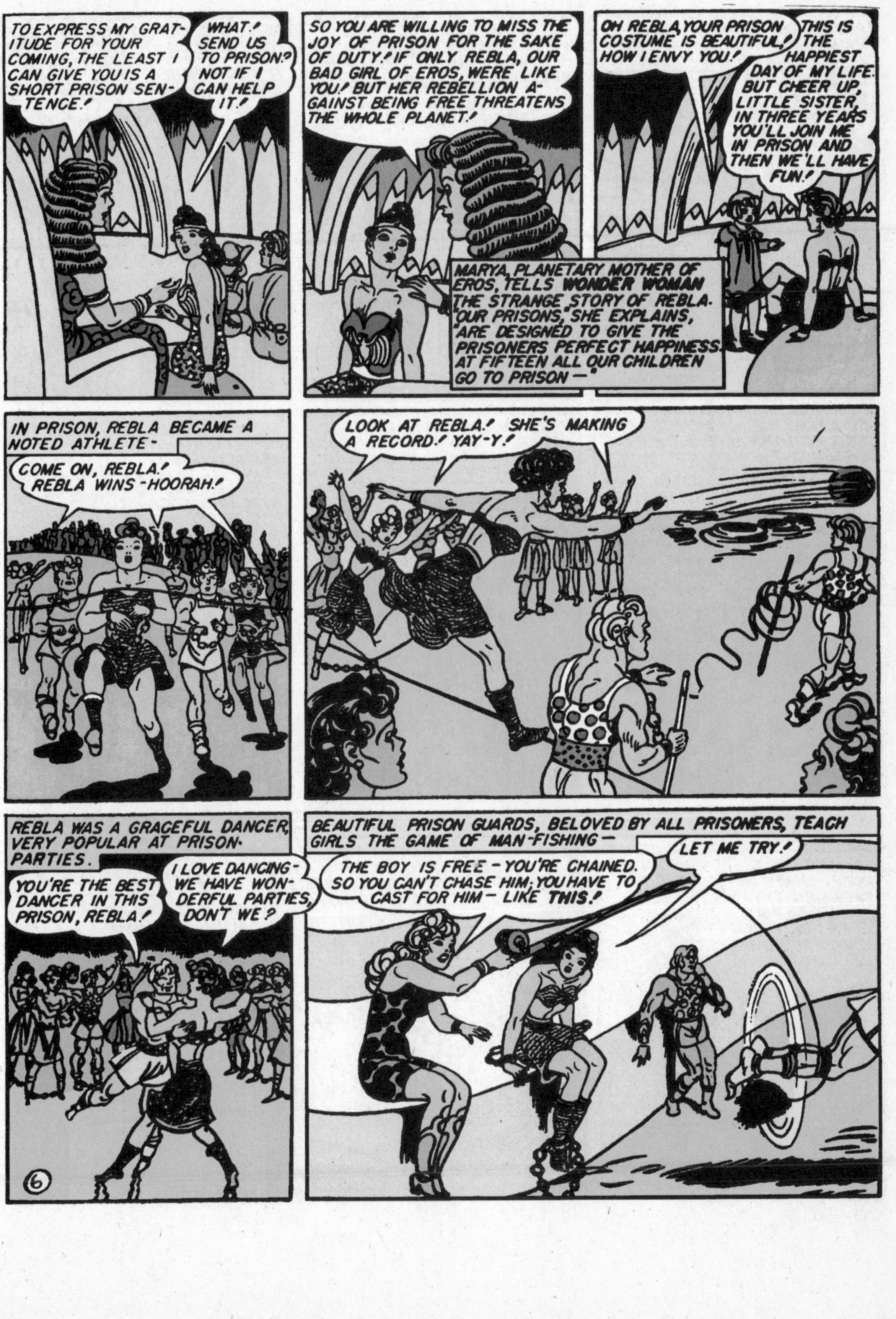
TO EXPRESS MY GRATITUDE FOR YOUR COMING, THE LEAST I CAN GIVE YOU IS A SHORT PRISON SENTENCE!
WHAT! SEND US TO PRISON? NOT IF I CAN HELP IT!
SO YOU ARE WILLING TO MISS THE JOY OF PRISON FOR THE SAKE OF DUTY! IF ONLY REBLA, OUR BAD GIRL OF EROS, WERE LIKE YOU! BUT HER REBELLION AGAINST BEING FREE THREATENS THE WHOLE PLANET!
MARYA, PLANETARY MOTHER OF EROS, TELLS WONDER WOMAN THE STRANGE STORY OF REBLA. "OUR PRISONS," SHE EXPLAINS, "ARE DESIGNED TO GIVE THE PRISONERS PERFECT HAPPINESS. AT FIFTEEN ALL OUR CHILDREN GO TO PRISON —"
OH REBLA, YOUR PRISON COSTUME IS BEAUTIFUL! HOW I ENVY YOU!
THIS IS THE HAPPIEST DAY OF MY LIFE. BUT CHEER UP, LITTLE SISTER, IN THREE YEARS YOU'LL JOIN ME IN PRISON AND THEN WE'LL HAVE FUN!
IN PRISON, REBLA BECAME A NOTED ATHLETE -
COME ON, REBLA! REBLA WINS - HOORAH!
LOOK AT REBLA! SHE'S MAKING A RECORD! YAY-Y!
REBLA WAS A GRACEFUL DANCER, VERY POPULAR AT PRISON PARTIES.
YOU'RE THE BEST DANCER IN THIS PRISON, REBLA!
I LOVE DANCING - WE HAVE WONDERFUL PARTIES, DON'T WE?
6
BEAUTIFUL PRISON GUARDS, BELOVED BY ALL PRISONERS, TEACH GIRLS THE GAME OF MAN-FISHING —
THE BOY IS FREE - YOU'RE CHAINED. SO YOU CAN'T CHASE HIM; YOU HAVE TO CAST FOR HIM - LIKE THIS!
LET ME TRY!

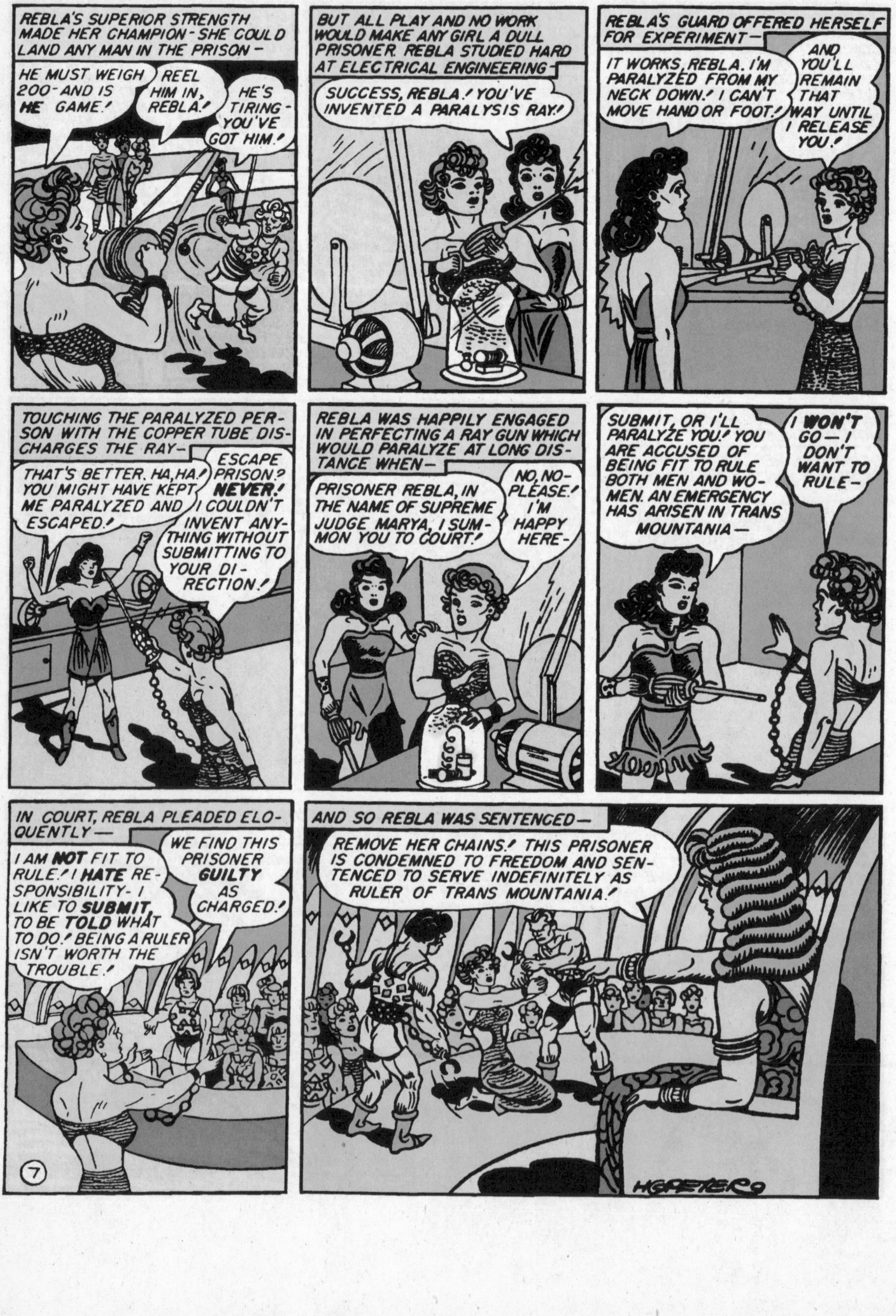
REBLA'S SUPERIOR STRENGTH MADE HER CHAMPION - SHE COULD LAND ANY MAN IN THE PRISON -
HE MUST WEIGH 200 - AND IS HE GAME!
REEL HIM IN, REBLA!
HE'S TIRING - YOU'VE GOT HIM!
BUT ALL PLAY AND NO WORK WOULD MAKE ANY GIRL A DULL PRISONER. REBLA STUDIED HARD AT ELECTRICAL ENGINEERING -
SUCCESS, REBLA! YOU'VE INVENTED A PARALYSIS RAY!
REBLA'S GUARD OFFERED HERSELF FOR EXPERIMENT -
IT WORKS, REBLA. I'M PARALYZED FROM MY NECK DOWN! I CAN'T MOVE HAND OR FOOT!
AND YOU'LL REMAIN THAT WAY UNTIL I RELEASE YOU!
TOUCHING THE PARALYZED PERSON WITH THE COPPER TUBE DISCHARGES THE RAY -
THAT'S BETTER. HA, HA! YOU MIGHT HAVE KEPT ME PARALYZED AND ESCAPED!
ESCAPE PRISON? NEVER! I COULDN'T INVENT ANYTHING WITHOUT SUBMITTING TO YOUR DIRECTION!
REBLA WAS HAPPILY ENGAGED IN PERFECTING A RAY GUN WHICH WOULD PARALYZE AT LONG DISTANCE WHEN -
PRISONER REBLA, IN THE NAME OF SUPREME JUDGE MARYA, I SUMMON YOU TO COURT!
NO, NO - PLEASE! I'M HAPPY HERE -
SUBMIT, OR I'LL PARALYZE YOU! YOU ARE ACCUSED OF BEING FIT TO RULE BOTH MEN AND WOMEN. AN EMERGENCY HAS ARISEN IN TRANS MOUNTANIA -
I WON'T GO - I DON'T WANT TO RULE -
IN COURT, REBLA PLEADED ELOQUENTLY —
I AM NOT FIT TO RULE! I HATE RESPONSIBILITY - I LIKE TO SUBMIT, TO BE TOLD WHAT TO DO! BEING A RULER ISN'T WORTH THE TROUBLE!
WE FIND THIS PRISONER GUILTY AS CHARGED!
AND SO REBLA WAS SENTENCED —
REMOVE HER CHAINS! THIS PRISONER IS CONDEMNED TO FREEDOM AND SENTENCED TO SERVE INDEFINITELY AS RULER OF TRANS MOUNTANIA!
7
H.G. PETER

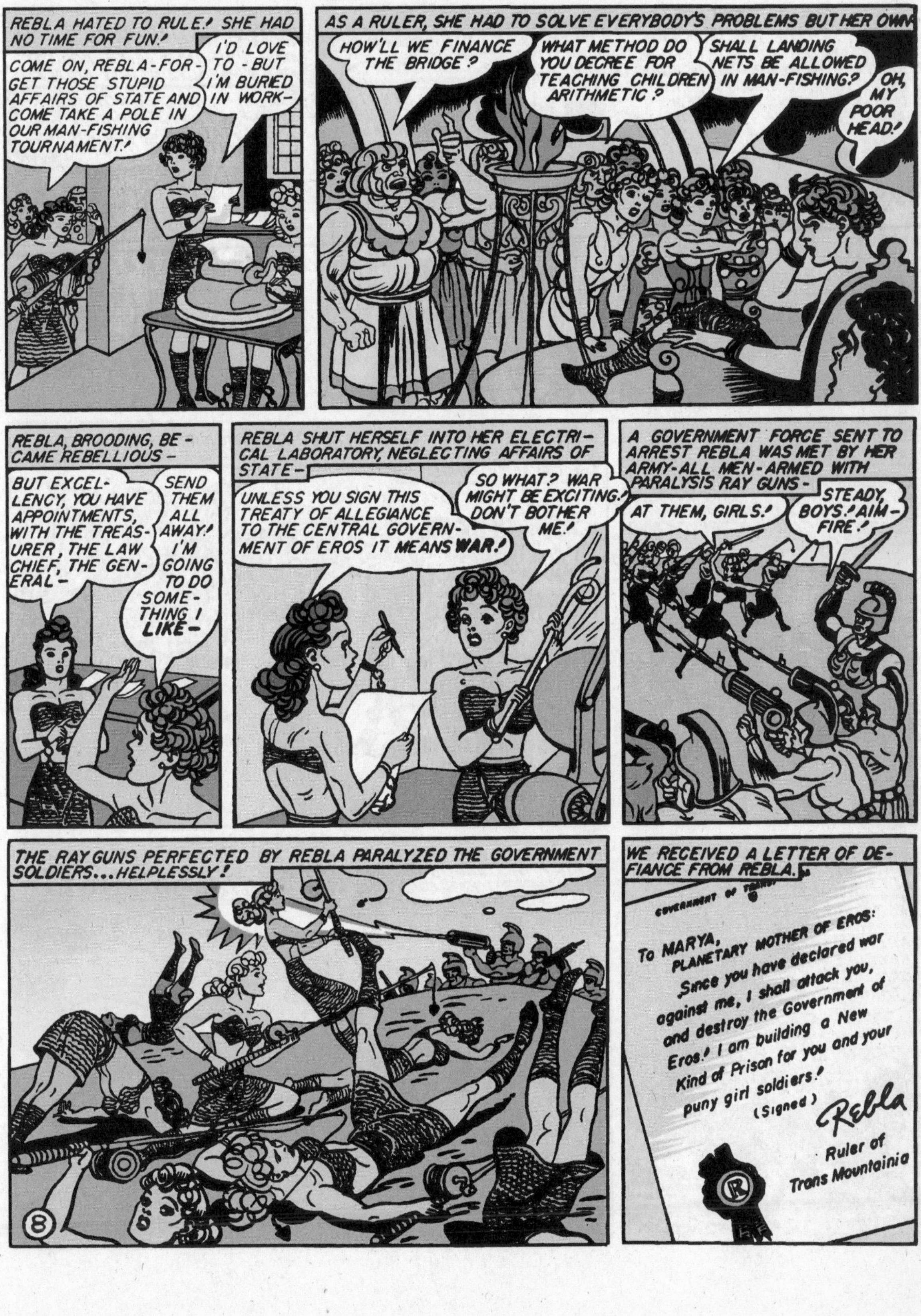
REBLA HATED TO RULE! SHE HAD NO TIME FOR FUN!
COME ON, REBLA-FORGET THOSE STUPID AFFAIRS OF STATE AND COME TAKE A POLE IN OUR MAN-FISHING TOURNAMENT!
I'D LOVE TO-BUT I'M BURIED IN WORK-
AS A RULER, SHE HAD TO SOLVE EVERYBODY'S PROBLEMS BUT HER OWN
HOW'LL WE FINANCE THE BRIDGE?
WHAT METHOD DO YOU DECREE FOR TEACHING CHILDREN ARITHMETIC?
SHALL LANDING NETS BE ALLOWED IN MAN-FISHING?
OH, MY POOR HEAD!
REBLA, BROODING, BECAME REBELLIOUS-
BUT EXCELLENCY, YOU HAVE APPOINTMENTS, WITH THE TREASURER, THE LAW CHIEF, THE GENERAL-
SEND THEM ALL AWAY! I'M GOING TO DO SOMETHING I LIKE-
REBLA SHUT HERSELF INTO HER ELECTRICAL LABORATORY, NEGLECTING AFFAIRS OF STATE-
UNLESS YOU SIGN THIS TREATY OF ALLEGIANCE TO THE CENTRAL GOVERNMENT OF EROS IT MEANS WAR!
SO WHAT? WAR MIGHT BE EXCITING! DON'T BOTHER ME!
A GOVERNMENT FORCE SENT TO ARREST REBLA WAS MET BY HER ARMY-ALL MEN-ARMED WITH PARALYSIS RAY GUNS-
AT THEM, GIRLS!
STEADY, BOYS! AIM-FIRE!
THE RAY GUNS PERFECTED BY REBLA PARALYZED THE GOVERNMENT SOLDIERS...HELPLESSLY!
8
WE RECEIVED A LETTER OF DEFIANCE FROM REBLA.
To MARYA, PLANETARY MOTHER OF EROS:
Since you have declared war against me, I shall attack you, and destroy the Government of Eros! I am building a New Kind of Prison for you and your puny girl soldiers!
(Signed) Rebla
Ruler of Trans Mountainia

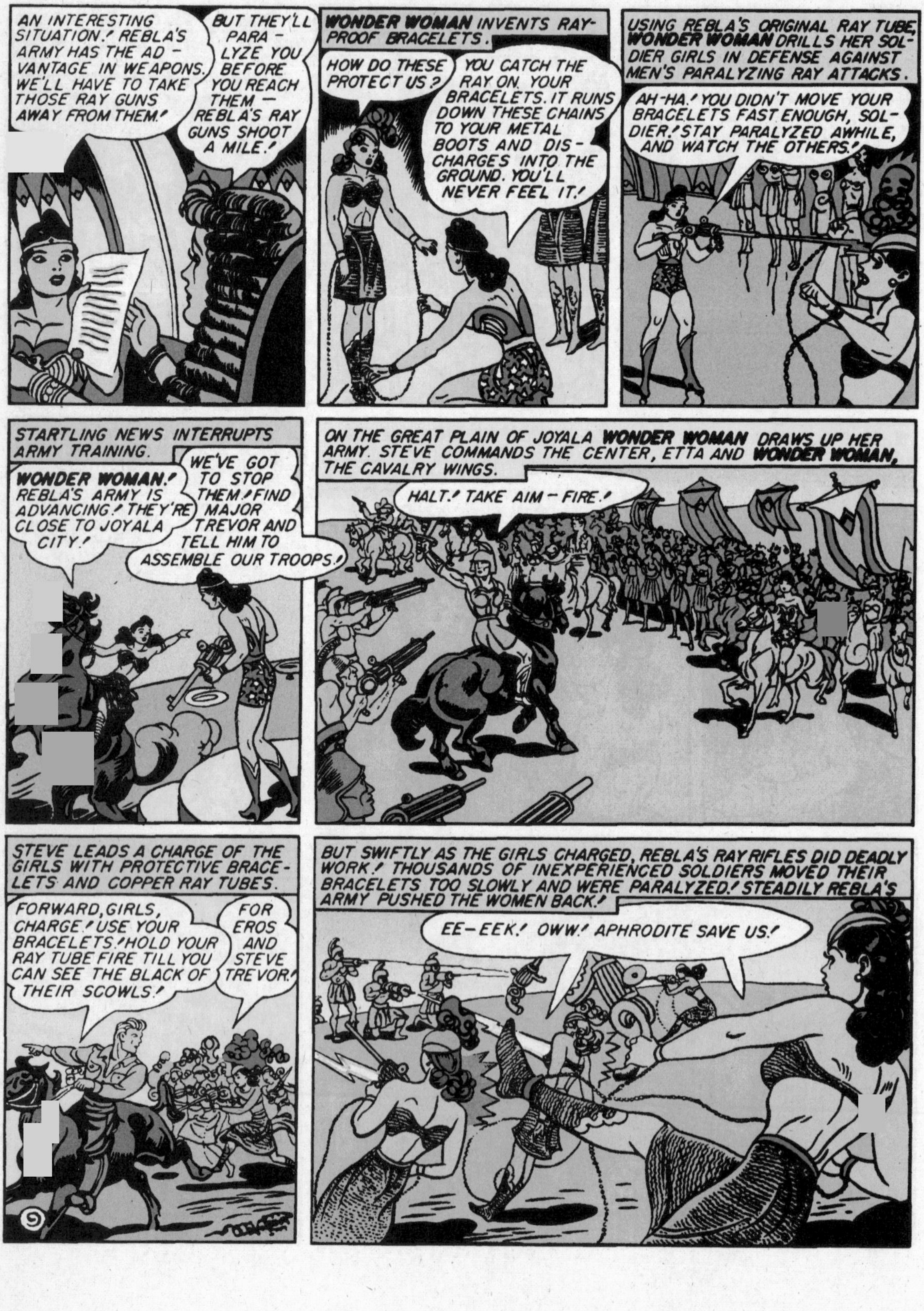
AN INTERESTING SITUATION! REBLA'S ARMY HAS THE AD- VANTAGE IN WEAPONS. WE'LL HAVE TO TAKE THOSE RAY GUNS AWAY FROM THEM!
BUT THEY'LL PARA- LYZE YOU BEFORE YOU REACH THEM — REBLA'S RAY GUNS SHOOT A MILE!
WONDER WOMAN INVENTS RAY-PROOF BRACELETS.
HOW DO THESE PROTECT US?
YOU CATCH THE RAY ON YOUR BRACELETS. IT RUNS DOWN THESE CHAINS TO YOUR METAL BOOTS AND DIS- CHARGES INTO THE GROUND. YOU'LL NEVER FEEL IT!
USING REBLA'S ORIGINAL RAY TUBE, WONDER WOMAN DRILLS HER SOL- DIER GIRLS IN DEFENSE AGAINST MEN'S PARALYZING RAY ATTACKS.
AH-HA! YOU DIDN'T MOVE YOUR BRACELETS FAST ENOUGH, SOL- DIER! STAY PARALYZED AWHILE, AND WATCH THE OTHERS!
STARTLING NEWS INTERRUPTS ARMY TRAINING.
WONDER WOMAN! REBLA'S ARMY IS ADVANCING! THEY'RE CLOSE TO JOYALA CITY!
WE'VE GOT TO STOP THEM! FIND MAJOR TREVOR AND TELL HIM TO ASSEMBLE OUR TROOPS!
ON THE GREAT PLAIN OF JOYALA WONDER WOMAN DRAWS UP HER ARMY. STEVE COMMANDS THE CENTER, ETTA AND WONDER WOMAN, THE CAVALRY WINGS.
HALT! TAKE AIM — FIRE!
STEVE LEADS A CHARGE OF THE GIRLS WITH PROTECTIVE BRACE- LETS AND COPPER RAY TUBES.
FORWARD, GIRLS, CHARGE! USE YOUR BRACELETS! HOLD YOUR RAY TUBE FIRE TILL YOU CAN SEE THE BLACK OF THEIR SCOWLS!
FOR EROS AND STEVE TREVOR!
9
BUT SWIFTLY AS THE GIRLS CHARGED, REBLA'S RAY RIFLES DID DEADLY WORK! THOUSANDS OF INEXPERIENCED SOLDIERS MOVED THEIR BRACELETS TOO SLOWLY AND WERE PARALYZED! STEADILY REBLA'S ARMY PUSHED THE WOMEN BACK!
EE-EEK! OWW! APHRODITE SAVE US!

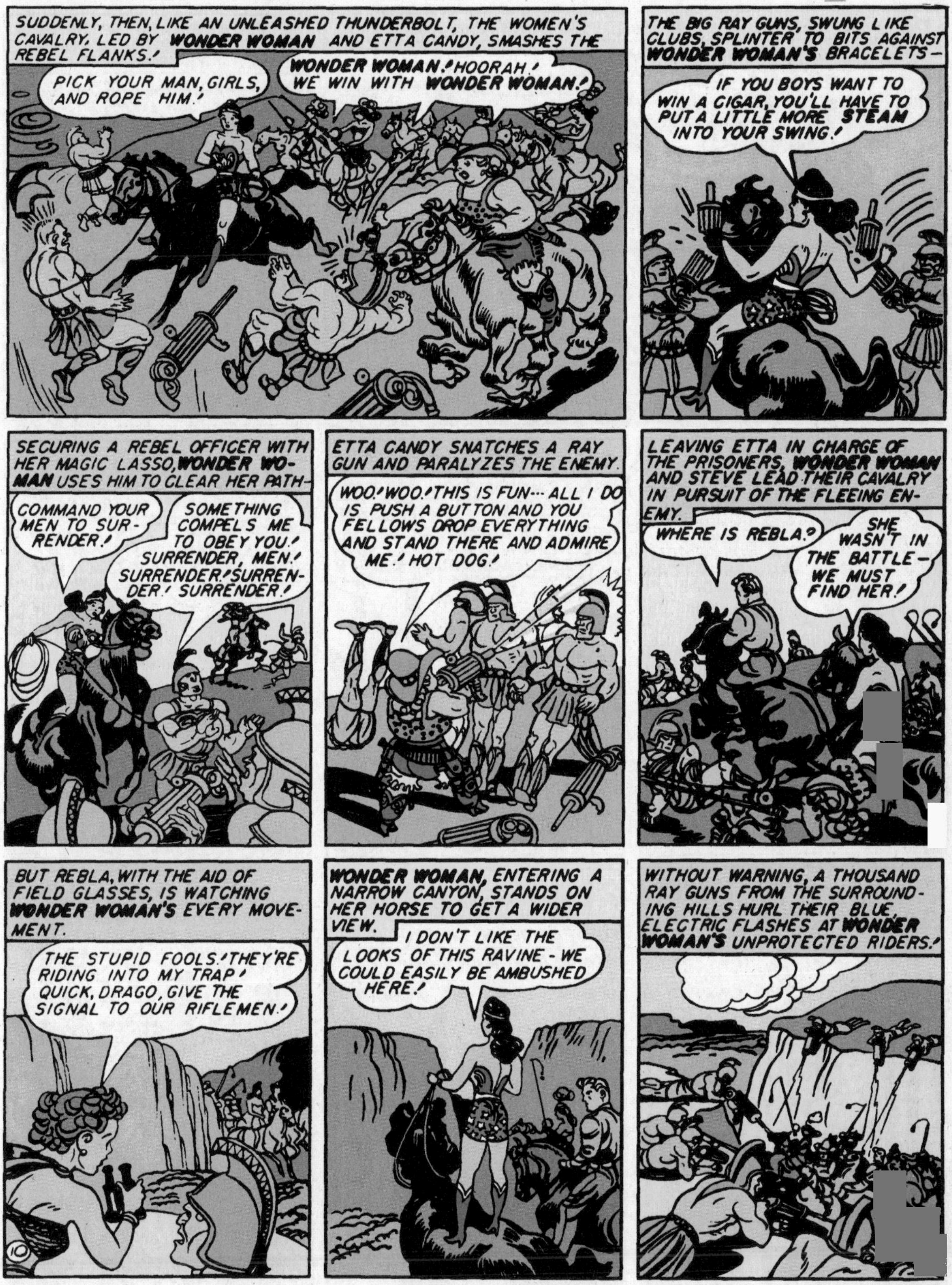
SUDDENLY, THEN, LIKE AN UNLEASHED THUNDERBOLT, THE WOMEN'S CAVALRY, LED BY WONDER WOMAN AND ETTA CANDY, SMASHES THE REBEL FLANKS.!
PICK YOUR MAN, GIRLS, AND ROPE HIM.!
WONDER WOMAN.! HOORAH.! WE WIN WITH WONDER WOMAN.!
THE BIG RAY GUNS, SWUNG LIKE CLUBS, SPLINTER TO BITS AGAINST WONDER WOMAN'S BRACELETS—
IF YOU BOYS WANT TO WIN A CIGAR, YOU'LL HAVE TO PUT A LITTLE MORE STEAM INTO YOUR SWING.!
SECURING A REBEL OFFICER WITH HER MAGIC LASSO, WONDER WOMAN USES HIM TO CLEAR HER PATH—
COMMAND YOUR MEN TO SURRENDER.!
SOMETHING COMPELS ME TO OBEY YOU.! SURRENDER, MEN.! SURRENDER.! SURRENDER.! SURRENDER.!
ETTA CANDY SNATCHES A RAY GUN AND PARALYZES THE ENEMY.
WOO.! WOO.! THIS IS FUN--- ALL I DO IS PUSH A BUTTON AND YOU FELLOWS DROP EVERYTHING AND STAND THERE AND ADMIRE ME.! HOT DOG.!
LEAVING ETTA IN CHARGE OF THE PRISONERS, WONDER WOMAN AND STEVE LEAD THEIR CAVALRY IN PURSUIT OF THE FLEEING ENEMY.
WHERE IS REBLA.?
SHE WASN'T IN THE BATTLE— WE MUST FIND HER.!
BUT REBLA, WITH THE AID OF FIELD GLASSES, IS WATCHING WONDER WOMAN'S EVERY MOVEMENT.
THE STUPID FOOLS.! THEY'RE RIDING INTO MY TRAP.! QUICK, DRAGO, GIVE THE SIGNAL TO OUR RIFLEMEN.!
10
WONDER WOMAN, ENTERING A NARROW CANYON, STANDS ON HER HORSE TO GET A WIDER VIEW.
I DON'T LIKE THE LOOKS OF THIS RAVINE - WE COULD EASILY BE AMBUSHED HERE.!
WITHOUT WARNING, A THOUSAND RAY GUNS FROM THE SURROUNDING HILLS HURL THEIR BLUE, ELECTRIC FLASHES AT WONDER WOMAN'S UNPROTECTED RIDERS.!

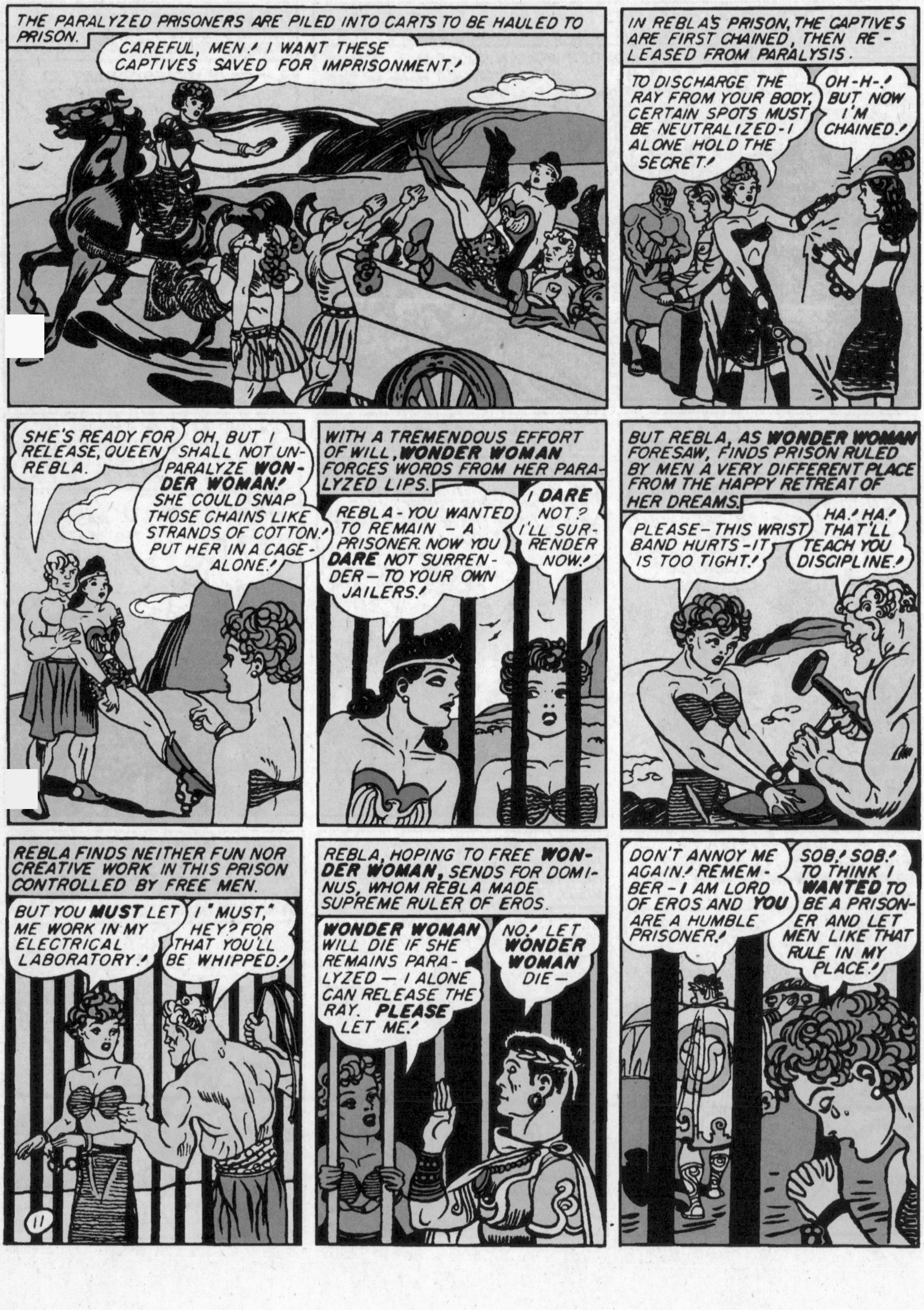
THE PARALYZED PRISONERS ARE PILED INTO CARTS TO BE HAULED TO PRISON.
CAREFUL, MEN! I WANT THESE CAPTIVES SAVED FOR IMPRISONMENT!
IN REBLA'S PRISON, THE CAPTIVES ARE FIRST CHAINED, THEN RE-LEASED FROM PARALYSIS.
TO DISCHARGE THE RAY FROM YOUR BODY, CERTAIN SPOTS MUST BE NEUTRALIZED - I ALONE HOLD THE SECRET!
OH-H-! BUT NOW I'M CHAINED!
SHE'S READY FOR RELEASE, QUEEN REBLA.
OH, BUT I SHALL NOT UN-PARALYZE WON-DER WOMAN! SHE COULD SNAP THOSE CHAINS LIKE STRANDS OF COTTON! PUT HER IN A CAGE-ALONE!
WITH A TREMENDOUS EFFORT OF WILL, WONDER WOMAN FORCES WORDS FROM HER PARA-LYZED LIPS.
REBLA - YOU WANTED TO REMAIN - A PRISONER. NOW YOU DARE NOT SURREN-DER - TO YOUR OWN JAILERS!
I DARE NOT? I'LL SUR-RENDER NOW!
BUT REBLA, AS WONDER WOMAN FORESAW, FINDS PRISON RULED BY MEN A VERY DIFFERENT PLACE FROM THE HAPPY RETREAT OF HER DREAMS.
PLEASE - THIS WRIST BAND HURTS - IT IS TOO TIGHT!
HA! HA! THAT'LL TEACH YOU DISCIPLINE!
REBLA FINDS NEITHER FUN NOR CREATIVE WORK IN THIS PRISON CONTROLLED BY FREE MEN.
BUT YOU MUST LET ME WORK IN MY ELECTRICAL LABORATORY!
I "MUST," HEY? FOR THAT YOU'LL BE WHIPPED!
11
REBLA, HOPING TO FREE WON-DER WOMAN, SENDS FOR DOMI-NUS, WHOM REBLA MADE SUPREME RULER OF EROS.
WONDER WOMAN WILL DIE IF SHE REMAINS PARA-LYZED - I ALONE CAN RELEASE THE RAY. PLEASE LET ME!
NO! LET WONDER WOMAN DIE -
DON'T ANNOY ME AGAIN! REMEM-BER - I AM LORD OF EROS AND YOU ARE A HUMBLE PRISONER!
SOB! SOB! TO THINK I WANTED TO BE A PRISON-ER AND LET MEN LIKE THAT RULE IN MY PLACE!

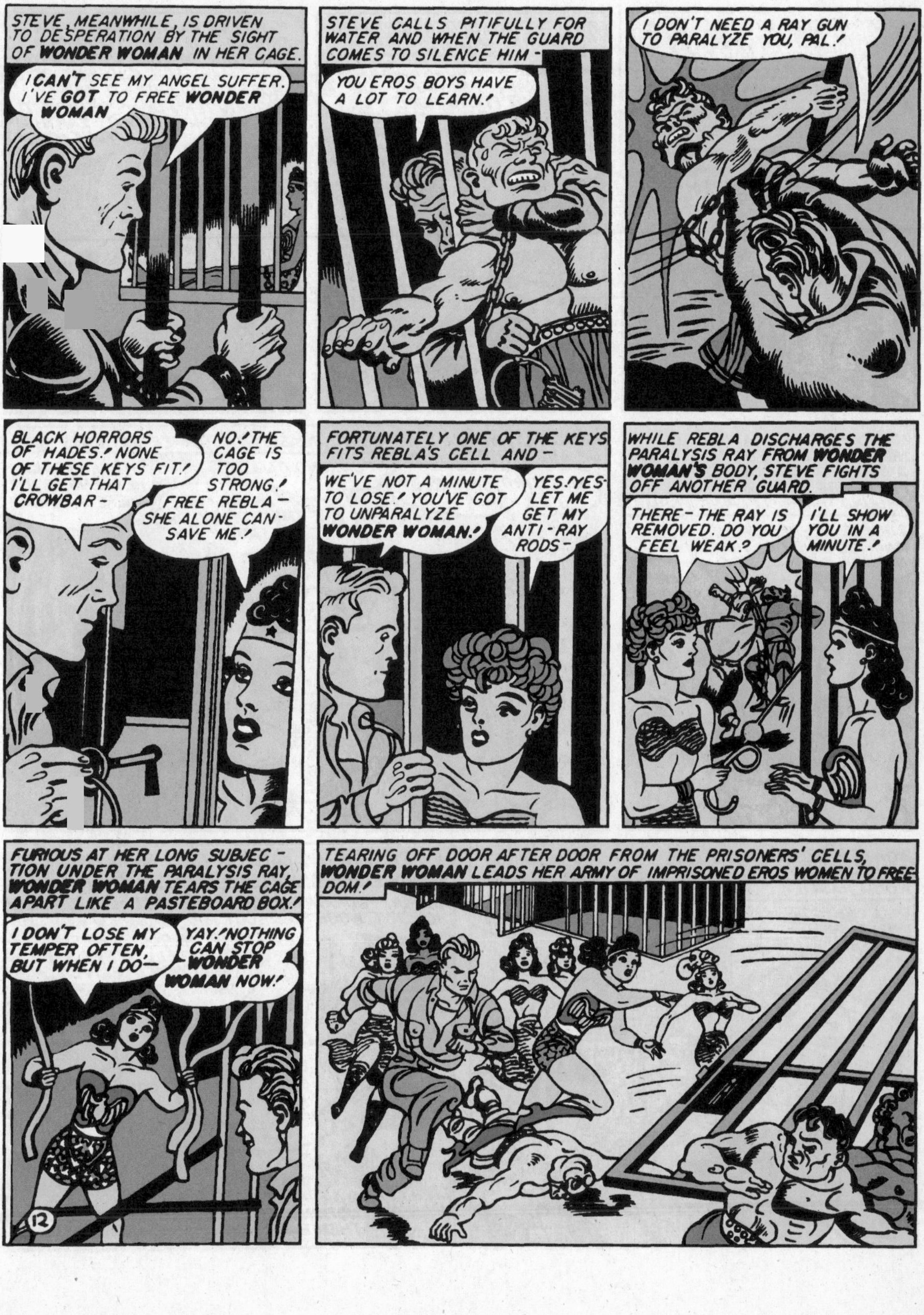
STEVE, MEANWHILE, IS DRIVEN TO DESPERATION BY THE SIGHT OF WONDER WOMAN IN HER CAGE.
I CAN'T SEE MY ANGEL SUFFER. I'VE GOT TO FREE WONDER WOMAN
STEVE CALLS PITIFULLY FOR WATER AND WHEN THE GUARD COMES TO SILENCE HIM-
YOU EROS BOYS HAVE A LOT TO LEARN.!
I DON'T NEED A RAY GUN TO PARALYZE YOU, PAL.!
BLACK HORRORS OF HADES.! NONE OF THESE KEYS FIT.! I'LL GET THAT CROWBAR-
NO.! THE CAGE IS TOO STRONG.! FREE REBLA- SHE ALONE CAN SAVE ME.!
FORTUNATELY ONE OF THE KEYS FITS REBLA'S CELL AND-
WE'VE NOT A MINUTE TO LOSE.! YOU'VE GOT TO UNPARALYZE WONDER WOMAN.!
YES.! YES- LET ME GET MY ANTI-RAY RODS-
WHILE REBLA DISCHARGES THE PARALYSIS RAY FROM WONDER WOMAN'S BODY, STEVE FIGHTS OFF ANOTHER GUARD.
THERE- THE RAY IS REMOVED. DO YOU FEEL WEAK?
I'LL SHOW YOU IN A MINUTE.!
FURIOUS AT HER LONG SUBJECTION UNDER THE PARALYSIS RAY, WONDER WOMAN TEARS THE CAGE APART LIKE A PASTEBOARD BOX.!
I DON'T LOSE MY TEMPER OFTEN, BUT WHEN I DO-
YAY.! NOTHING CAN STOP WONDER WOMAN NOW.!
12
TEARING OFF DOOR AFTER DOOR FROM THE PRISONERS' CELLS, WONDER WOMAN LEADS HER ARMY OF IMPRISONED EROS WOMEN TO FREEDOM.!

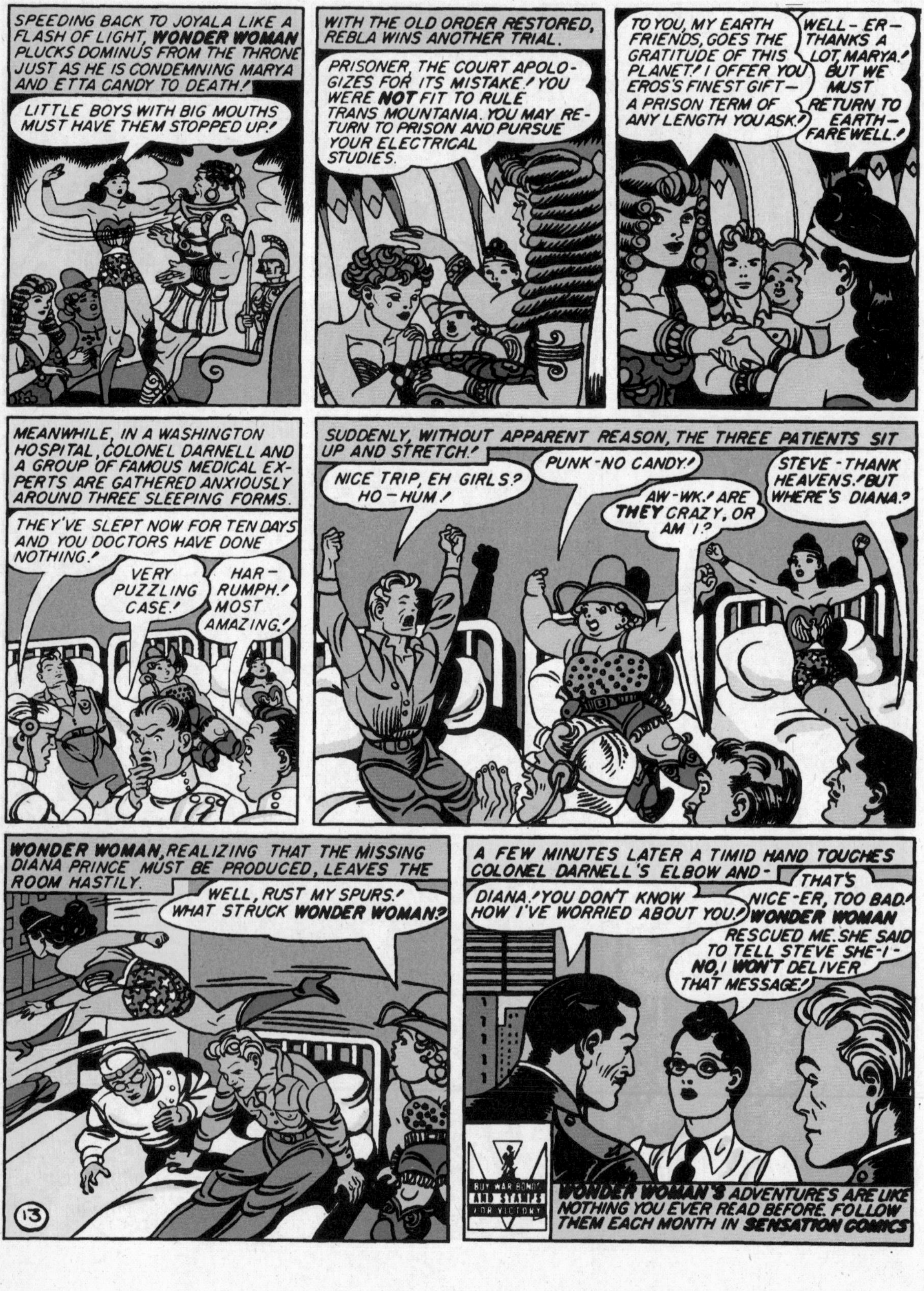

SPEEDING BACK TO JOYALA LIKE A FLASH OF LIGHT, WONDER WOMAN PLUCKS DOMINUS FROM THE THRONE JUST AS HE IS CONDEMNING MARYA AND ETTA CANDY TO DEATH!
LITTLE BOYS WITH BIG MOUTHS MUST HAVE THEM STOPPED UP!
WITH THE OLD ORDER RESTORED, REBLA WINS ANOTHER TRIAL.
PRISONER, THE COURT APOLOGIZES FOR ITS MISTAKE! YOU WERE NOT FIT TO RULE TRANS MOUNTANIA. YOU MAY RETURN TO PRISON AND PURSUE YOUR ELECTRICAL STUDIES.
TO YOU, MY EARTH FRIENDS, GOES THE GRATITUDE OF THIS PLANET! I OFFER YOU EROS'S FINEST GIFT— A PRISON TERM OF ANY LENGTH YOU ASK!
WELL- ER— THANKS A LOT, MARYA! BUT WE MUST RETURN TO EARTH— FAREWELL!
MEANWHILE, IN A WASHINGTON HOSPITAL, COLONEL DARNELL AND A GROUP OF FAMOUS MEDICAL EXPERTS ARE GATHERED ANXIOUSLY AROUND THREE SLEEPING FORMS.
THEY'VE SLEPT NOW FOR TEN DAYS AND YOU DOCTORS HAVE DONE NOTHING!
VERY PUZZLING CASE!
HAR-RUMPH! MOST AMAZING!
SUDDENLY, WITHOUT APPARENT REASON, THE THREE PATIENTS SIT UP AND STRETCH!
NICE TRIP, EH GIRLS? HO-HUM!
PUNK-NO CANDY!
AW-WK! ARE THEY CRAZY, OR AM I?
STEVE-THANK HEAVENS! BUT WHERE'S DIANA?
WONDER WOMAN, REALIZING THAT THE MISSING DIANA PRINCE MUST BE PRODUCED, LEAVES THE ROOM HASTILY.
WELL, RUST MY SPURS! WHAT STRUCK WONDER WOMAN?
13
A FEW MINUTES LATER A TIMID HAND TOUCHES COLONEL DARNELL'S ELBOW AND—
DIANA! YOU DON'T KNOW HOW I'VE WORRIED ABOUT YOU!
THAT'S NICE-ER, TOO BAD! WONDER WOMAN RESCUED ME. SHE SAID TO TELL STEVE SHE-I- NO, I WON'T DELIVER THAT MESSAGE!
BUY WAR BONDS AND STAMPS FOR VICTORY
WONDER WOMAN'S ADVENTURES ARE LIKE NOTHING YOU EVER READ BEFORE. FOLLOW THEM EACH MONTH IN SENSATION COMICS

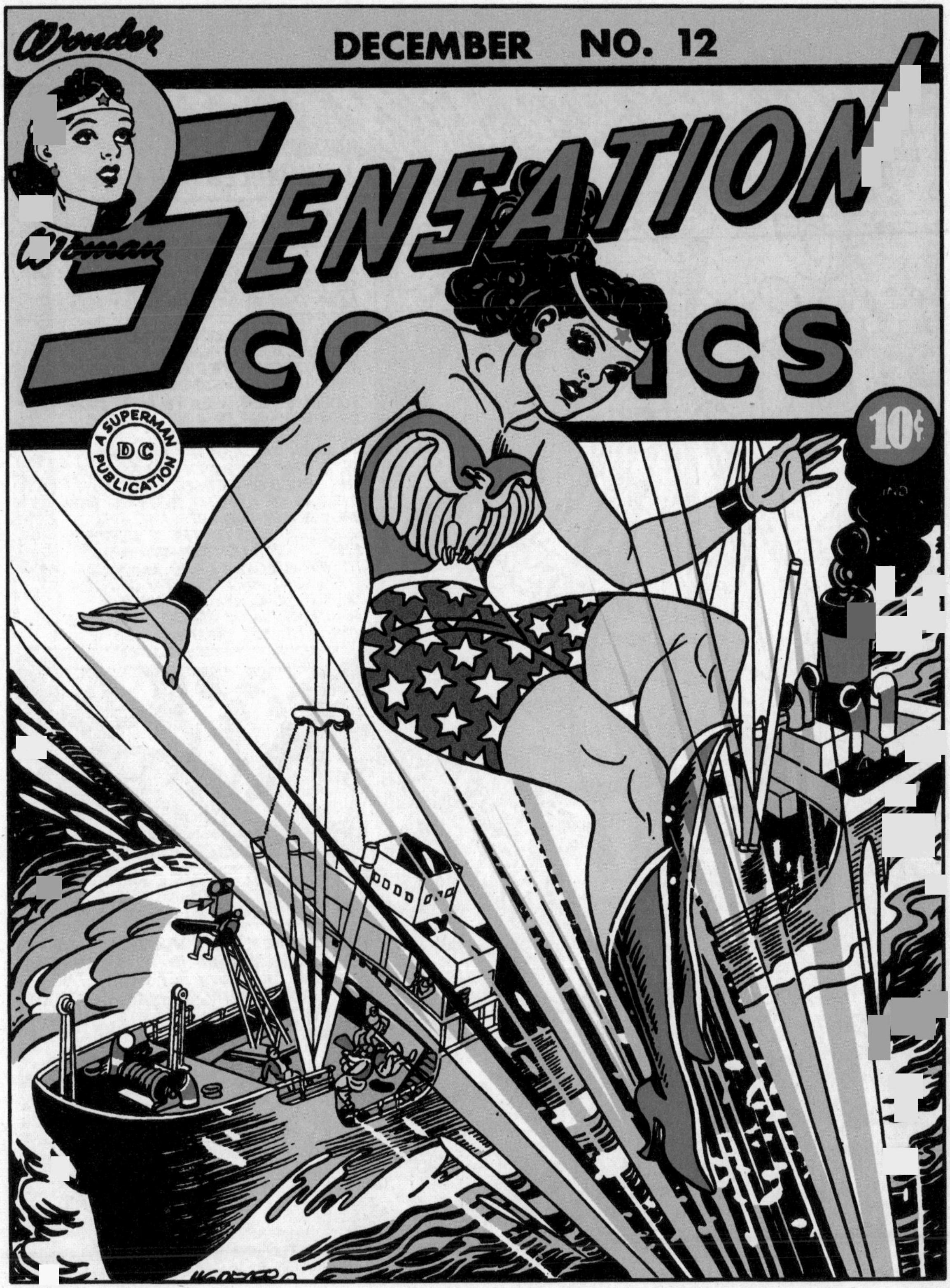
Wonder Woman
DECEMBER NO. 12
SENSATION COMICS
10¢
A SUPERMAN DC PUBLICATION

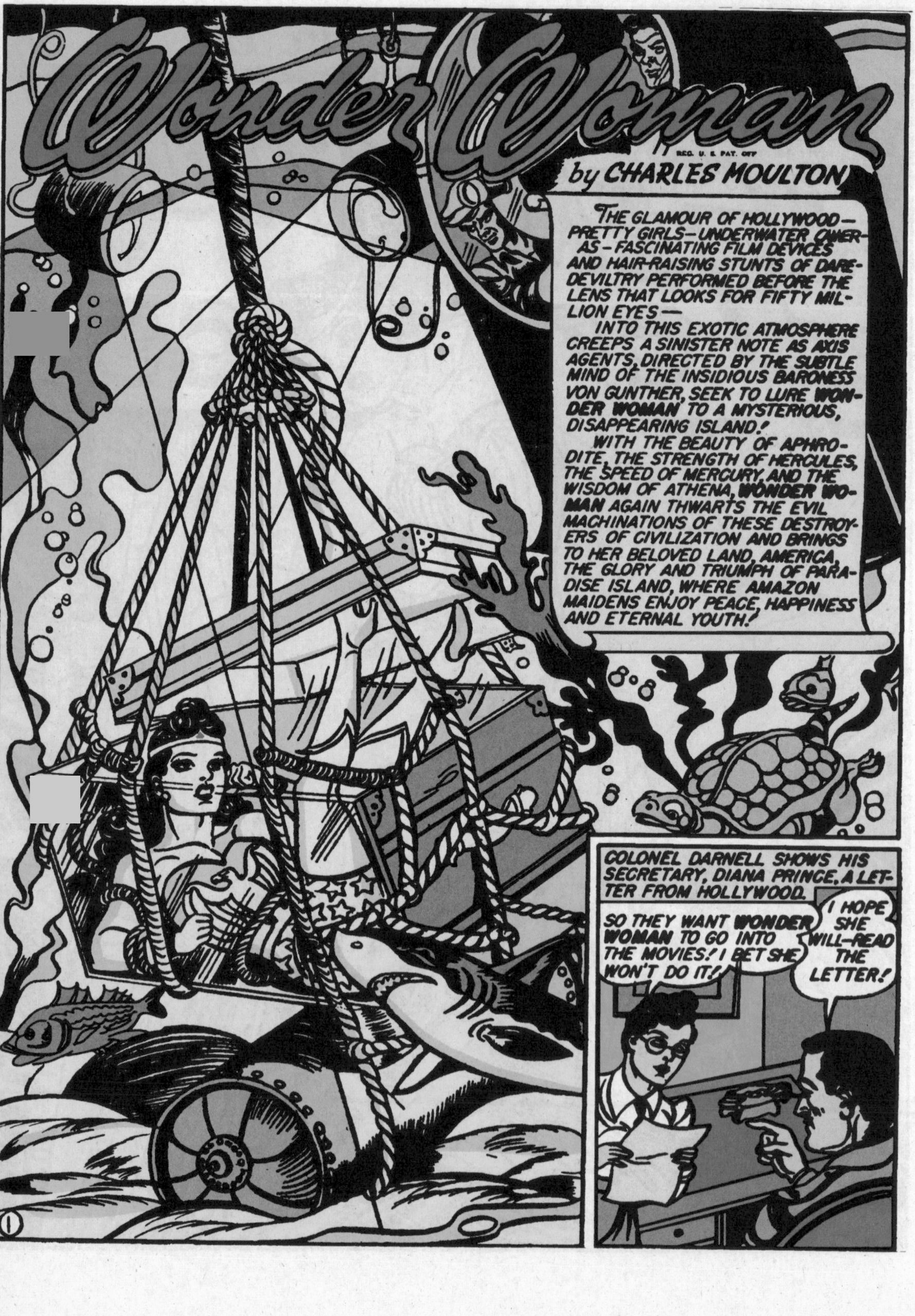
Wonder Woman
REG. U. S. PAT. OFF.
by CHARLES MOULTON
THE GLAMOUR OF HOLLYWOOD—PRETTY GIRLS—UNDERWATER CAMER-AS—FASCINATING FILM DEVICES AND HAIR-RAISING STUNTS OF DARE-DEVILTRY PERFORMED BEFORE THE LENS THAT LOOKS FOR FIFTY MIL-LION EYES—
INTO THIS EXOTIC ATMOSPHERE CREEPS A SINISTER NOTE AS AXIS AGENTS, DIRECTED BY THE SUBTLE MIND OF THE INSIDIOUS BARONESS VON GUNTHER, SEEK TO LURE WONDER WOMAN TO A MYSTERIOUS, DISAPPEARING ISLAND!
WITH THE BEAUTY OF APHRO-DITE, THE STRENGTH OF HERCULES, THE SPEED OF MERCURY, AND THE WISDOM OF ATHENA, WONDER WO-MAN AGAIN THWARTS THE EVIL MACHINATIONS OF THESE DESTROY-ERS OF CIVILIZATION AND BRINGS TO HER BELOVED LAND, AMERICA, THE GLORY AND TRIUMPH OF PARA-DISE ISLAND, WHERE AMAZON MAIDENS ENJOY PEACE, HAPPINESS AND ETERNAL YOUTH!
1
COLONEL DARNELL SHOWS HIS SECRETARY, DIANA PRINCE, A LET-TER FROM HOLLYWOOD.
SO THEY WANT WONDER WOMAN TO GO INTO THE MOVIES! I BET SHE WON'T DO IT!
I HOPE SHE WILL—READ THE LETTER!

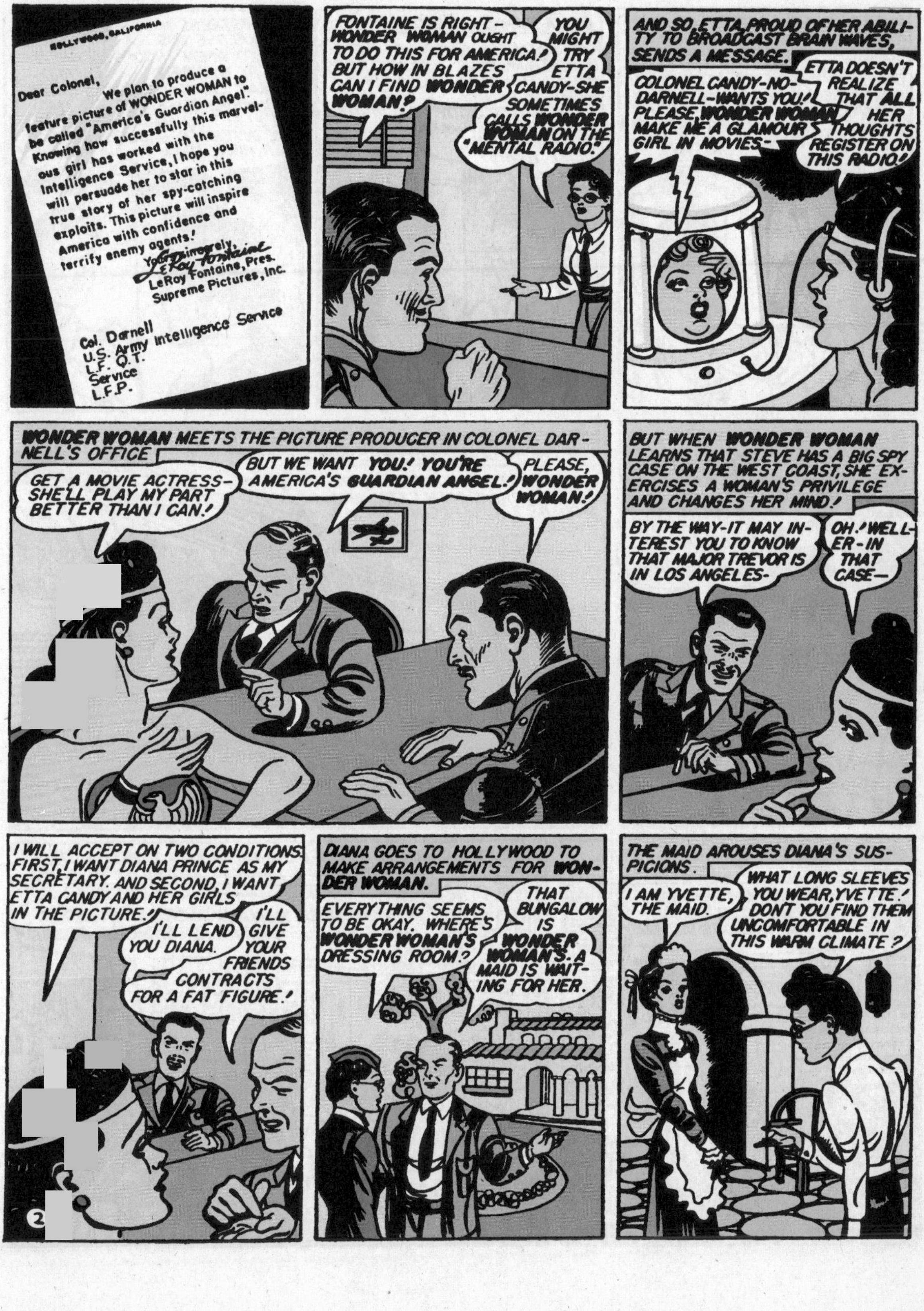
HOLLYWOOD, CALIFORNIA
Dear Colonel,
We plan to produce a feature picture of WONDER WOMAN to be called "America's Guardian Angel." Knowing how successfully this marvelous girl has worked with the Intelligence Service, I hope you will persuade her to star in this true story of her spy-catching exploits. This picture will inspire America with confidence and terrify enemy agents!
Yours sincerely,
LeRoy Fontaine
LeRoy Fontaine, Pres.
Supreme Pictures, Inc.
Col. Darnell
U.S. Army Intelligence Service
L.F. Q.T.
Service
L.F.P.
FONTAINE IS RIGHT – WONDER WOMAN OUGHT TO DO THIS FOR AMERICA! BUT HOW IN BLAZES CAN I FIND WONDER WOMAN?
YOU MIGHT TRY ETTA CANDY–SHE SOMETIMES CALLS WONDER WOMAN ON THE "MENTAL RADIO."
AND SO, ETTA, PROUD OF HER ABILITY TO BROADCAST BRAIN WAVES, SENDS A MESSAGE.
COLONEL CANDY–NO–DARNELL–WANTS YOU! PLEASE, WONDER WOMAN, MAKE ME A GLAMOUR GIRL IN MOVIES–
ETTA DOESN'T REALIZE THAT ALL HER THOUGHTS REGISTER ON THIS RADIO!
WONDER WOMAN MEETS THE PICTURE PRODUCER IN COLONEL DARNELL'S OFFICE
GET A MOVIE ACTRESS–SHE'LL PLAY MY PART BETTER THAN I CAN!
BUT WE WANT YOU! YOU'RE AMERICA'S GUARDIAN ANGEL!
PLEASE, WONDER WOMAN!
BUT WHEN WONDER WOMAN LEARNS THAT STEVE HAS A BIG SPY CASE ON THE WEST COAST, SHE EXERCISES A WOMAN'S PRIVILEGE AND CHANGES HER MIND!
BY THE WAY–IT MAY INTEREST YOU TO KNOW THAT MAJOR TREVOR IS IN LOS ANGELES–
OH! WELL–ER–IN THAT CASE–
I WILL ACCEPT ON TWO CONDITIONS. FIRST, I WANT DIANA PRINCE AS MY SECRETARY. AND SECOND, I WANT ETTA CANDY AND HER GIRLS IN THE PICTURE!
I'LL LEND YOU DIANA.
I'LL GIVE YOUR FRIENDS CONTRACTS FOR A FAT FIGURE!
2
DIANA GOES TO HOLLYWOOD TO MAKE ARRANGEMENTS FOR WONDER WOMAN.
EVERYTHING SEEMS TO BE OKAY. WHERE'S WONDER WOMAN'S DRESSING ROOM?
THAT BUNGALOW IS WONDER WOMAN'S. A MAID IS WAITING FOR HER.
THE MAID AROUSES DIANA'S SUSPICIONS.
I AM YVETTE, THE MAID.
WHAT LONG SLEEVES YOU WEAR, YVETTE! DONT YOU FIND THEM UNCOMFORTABLE IN THIS WARM CLIMATE?

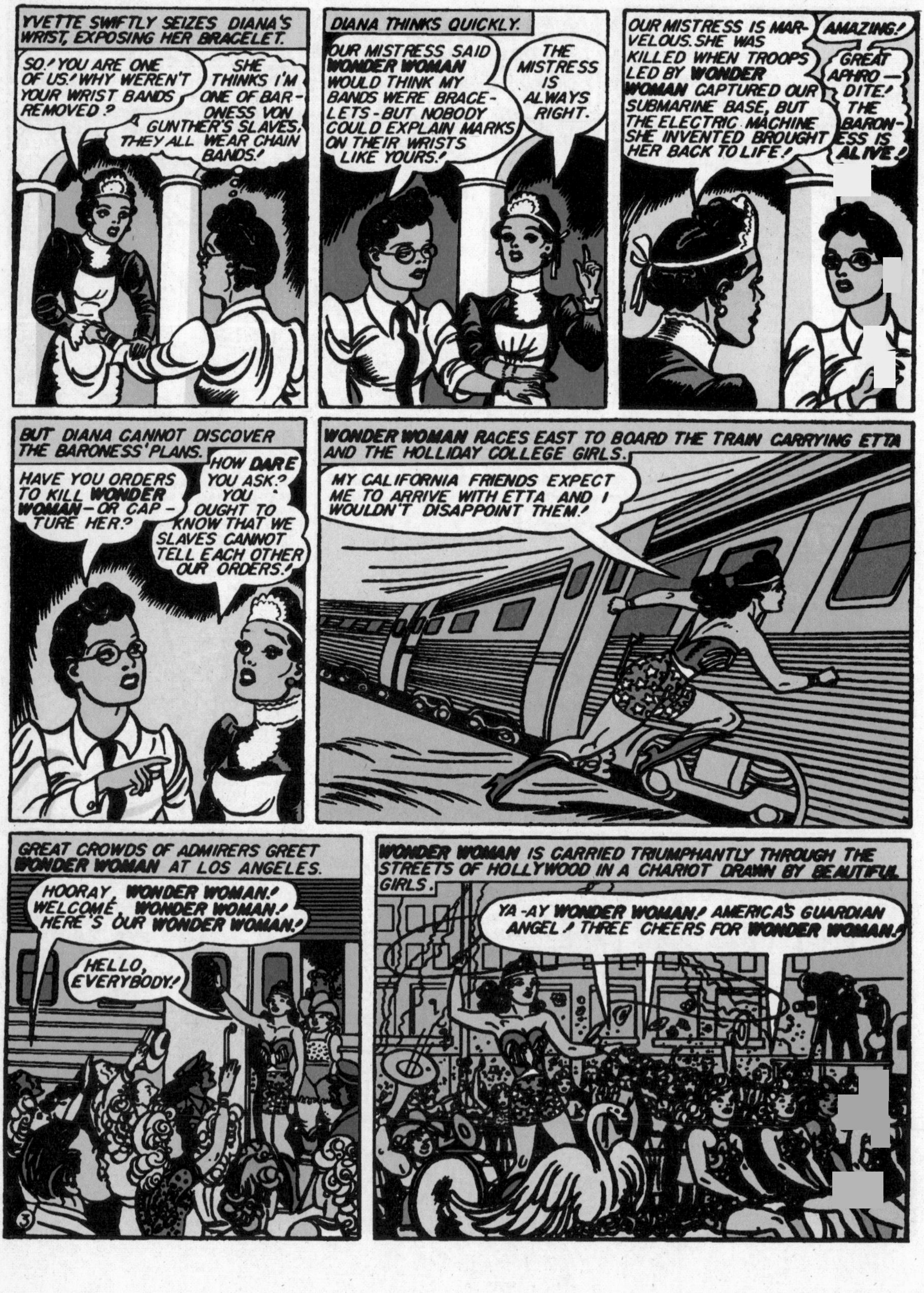
YVETTE SWIFTLY SEIZES DIANA'S WRIST, EXPOSING HER BRACELET.
SO! YOU ARE ONE OF US! WHY WEREN'T YOUR WRIST BANDS REMOVED?
SHE THINKS I'M ONE OF BARONESS VON GUNTHER'S SLAVES. THEY ALL WEAR CHAIN BANDS!
DIANA THINKS QUICKLY.
OUR MISTRESS SAID WONDER WOMAN WOULD THINK MY BANDS WERE BRACELETS - BUT NOBODY COULD EXPLAIN MARKS ON THEIR WRISTS LIKE YOURS!
THE MISTRESS IS ALWAYS RIGHT.
OUR MISTRESS IS MARVELOUS. SHE WAS KILLED WHEN TROOPS LED BY WONDER WOMAN CAPTURED OUR SUBMARINE BASE, BUT THE ELECTRIC MACHINE SHE INVENTED BROUGHT HER BACK TO LIFE!
AMAZING!
GREAT APHRODITE! THE BARONESS IS ALIVE!
BUT DIANA CANNOT DISCOVER THE BARONESS' PLANS.
HAVE YOU ORDERS TO KILL WONDER WOMAN—OR CAPTURE HER?
HOW DARE YOU ASK? YOU OUGHT TO KNOW THAT WE SLAVES CANNOT TELL EACH OTHER OUR ORDERS!
WONDER WOMAN RACES EAST TO BOARD THE TRAIN CARRYING ETTA AND THE HOLLIDAY COLLEGE GIRLS.
MY CALIFORNIA FRIENDS EXPECT ME TO ARRIVE WITH ETTA AND I WOULDN'T DISAPPOINT THEM!
GREAT CROWDS OF ADMIRERS GREET WONDER WOMAN AT LOS ANGELES.
HOORAY, WONDER WOMAN! WELCOME, WONDER WOMAN! HERE'S OUR WONDER WOMAN!
HELLO, EVERYBODY!
3
WONDER WOMAN IS CARRIED TRIUMPHANTLY THROUGH THE STREETS OF HOLLYWOOD IN A CHARIOT DRAWN BY BEAUTIFUL GIRLS.
YA-AY WONDER WOMAN! AMERICA'S GUARDIAN ANGEL! THREE CHEERS FOR WONDER WOMAN!

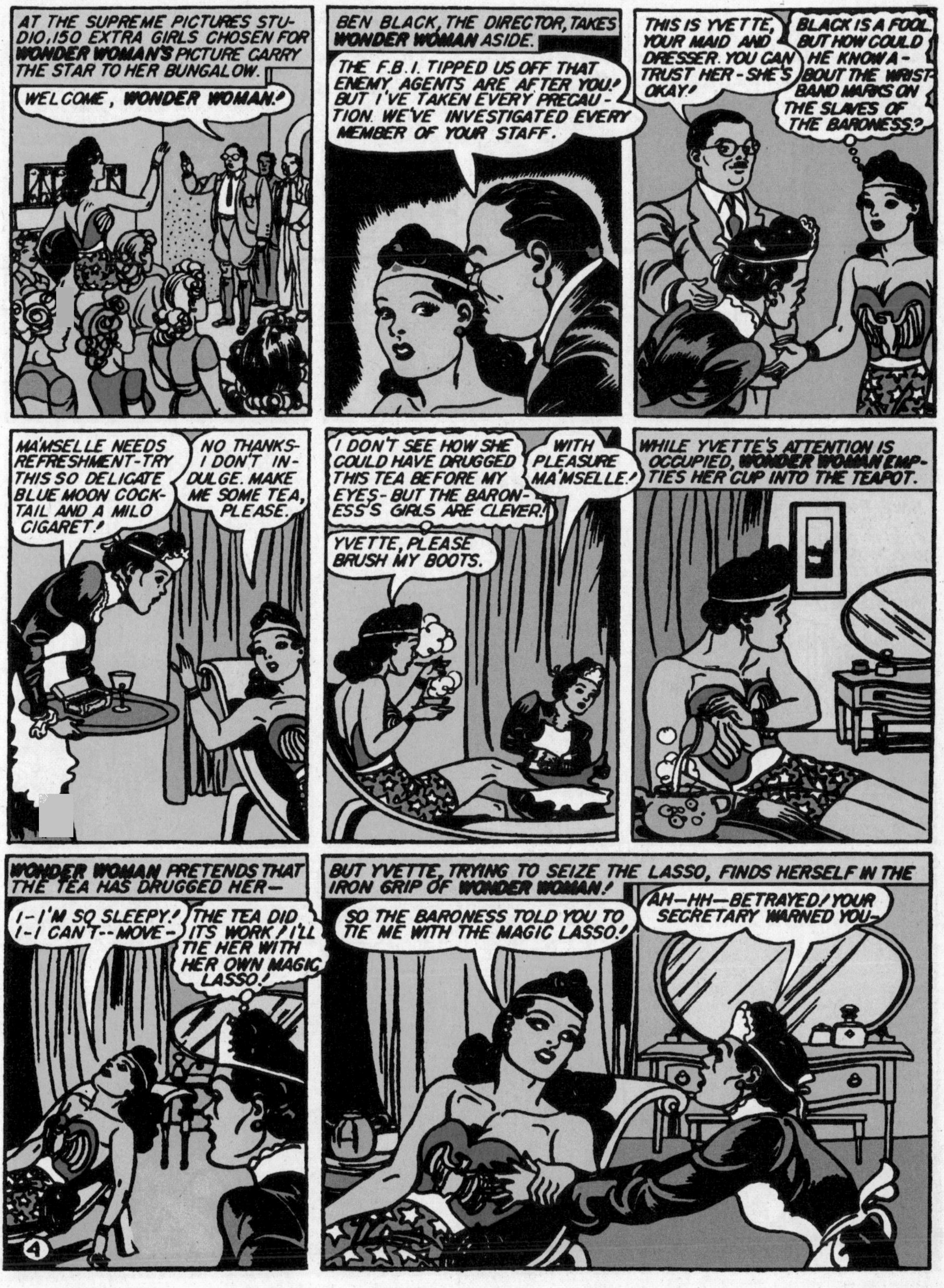
AT THE SUPREME PICTURES STUDIO, 150 EXTRA GIRLS CHOSEN FOR WONDER WOMAN'S PICTURE CARRY THE STAR TO HER BUNGALOW.
WELCOME, WONDER WOMAN!
BEN BLACK, THE DIRECTOR, TAKES WONDER WOMAN ASIDE.
THE F.B.I. TIPPED US OFF THAT ENEMY AGENTS ARE AFTER YOU! BUT I'VE TAKEN EVERY PRECAUTION. WE'VE INVESTIGATED EVERY MEMBER OF YOUR STAFF.
THIS IS YVETTE, YOUR MAID AND DRESSER. YOU CAN TRUST HER - SHE'S OKAY!
BLACK IS A FOOL. BUT HOW COULD HE KNOW ABOUT THE WRIST-BAND MARKS ON THE SLAVES OF THE BARONESS?
MA'MSELLE NEEDS REFRESHMENT-TRY THIS SO DELICATE BLUE MOON COCKTAIL AND A MILO CIGARET!
NO THANKS-I DON'T INDULGE. MAKE ME SOME TEA, PLEASE.
I DON'T SEE HOW SHE COULD HAVE DRUGGED THIS TEA BEFORE MY EYES- BUT THE BARONESS'S GIRLS ARE CLEVER!
WITH PLEASURE MA'MSELLE!
YVETTE, PLEASE BRUSH MY BOOTS.
WHILE YVETTE'S ATTENTION IS OCCUPIED, WONDER WOMAN EMPTIES HER CUP INTO THE TEAPOT.
WONDER WOMAN PRETENDS THAT THE TEA HAS DRUGGED HER—
I-I'M SO SLEEPY! I-I CAN'T--MOVE-
THE TEA DID ITS WORK! I'LL TIE HER WITH HER OWN MAGIC LASSO!
4
BUT YVETTE, TRYING TO SEIZE THE LASSO, FINDS HERSELF IN THE IRON GRIP OF WONDER WOMAN!
SO THE BARONESS TOLD YOU TO TIE ME WITH THE MAGIC LASSO!
AH—HH—BETRAYED! YOUR SECRETARY WARNED YOU-

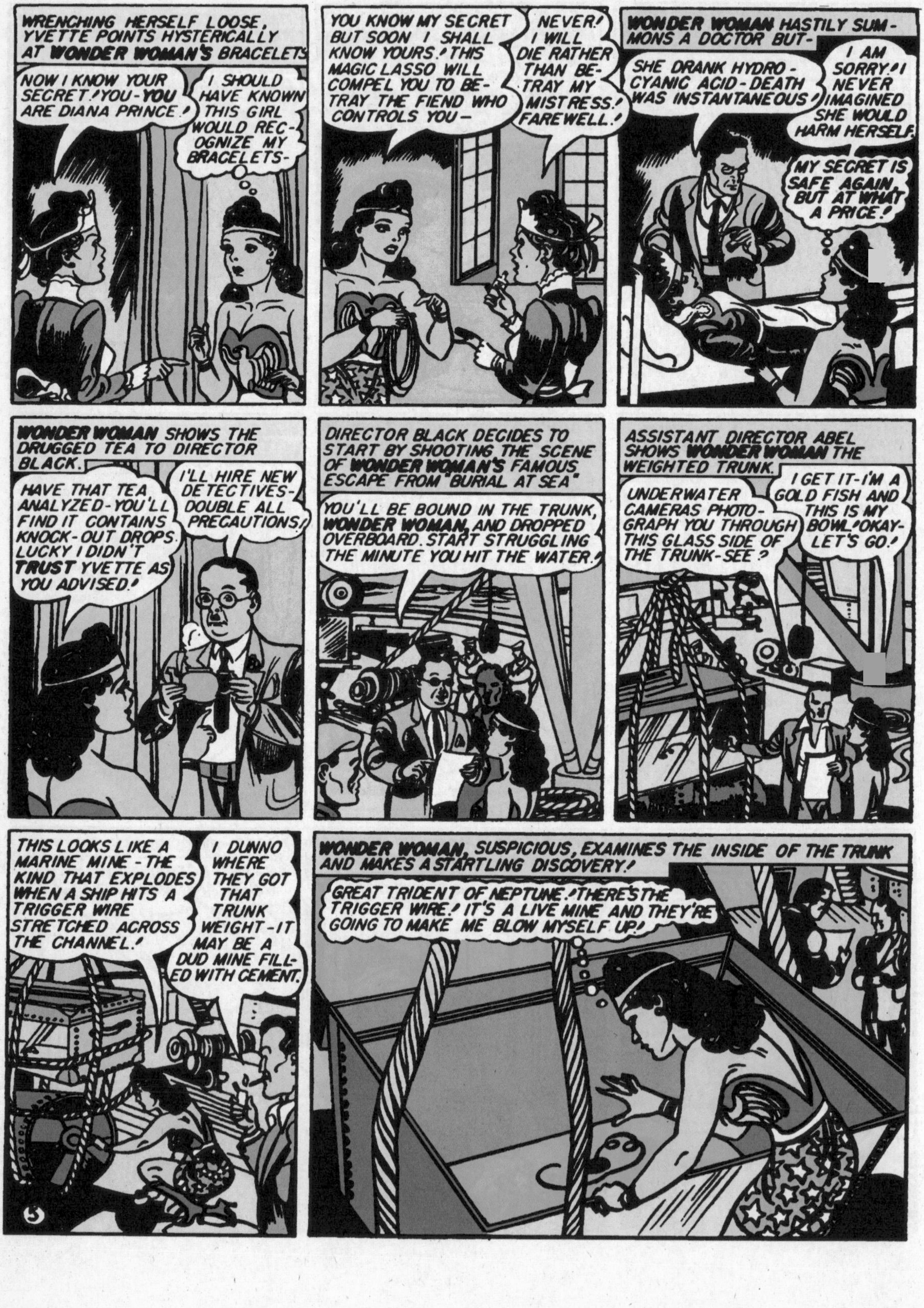
WRENCHING HERSELF LOOSE, YVETTE POINTS HYSTERICALLY AT WONDER WOMAN'S BRACELETS
NOW I KNOW YOUR SECRET! YOU-YOU ARE DIANA PRINCE!
I SHOULD HAVE KNOWN THIS GIRL WOULD RECOGNIZE MY BRACELETS-
YOU KNOW MY SECRET BUT SOON I SHALL KNOW YOURS! THIS MAGIC LASSO WILL COMPEL YOU TO BETRAY THE FIEND WHO CONTROLS YOU—
NEVER! I WILL DIE RATHER THAN BETRAY MY MISTRESS! FAREWELL!
WONDER WOMAN HASTILY SUMMONS A DOCTOR BUT-
SHE DRANK HYDRO-CYANIC ACID-DEATH WAS INSTANTANEOUS!
I AM SORRY! I NEVER IMAGINED SHE WOULD HARM HERSELF.
MY SECRET IS SAFE AGAIN, BUT AT WHAT A PRICE!
WONDER WOMAN SHOWS THE DRUGGED TEA TO DIRECTOR BLACK.
HAVE THAT TEA ANALYZED-YOU'LL FIND IT CONTAINS KNOCK-OUT DROPS. LUCKY I DIDN'T TRUST YVETTE AS YOU ADVISED!
I'LL HIRE NEW DETECTIVES-DOUBLE ALL PRECAUTIONS!
DIRECTOR BLACK DECIDES TO START BY SHOOTING THE SCENE OF WONDER WOMAN'S FAMOUS ESCAPE FROM "BURIAL AT SEA"
YOU'LL BE BOUND IN THE TRUNK, WONDER WOMAN, AND DROPPED OVERBOARD. START STRUGGLING THE MINUTE YOU HIT THE WATER!
ASSISTANT DIRECTOR ABEL SHOWS WONDER WOMAN THE WEIGHTED TRUNK.
UNDERWATER CAMERAS PHOTOGRAPH YOU THROUGH THIS GLASS SIDE OF THE TRUNK-SEE?
I GET IT-I'M A GOLD FISH AND THIS IS MY BOWL! OKAY-LET'S GO!
THIS LOOKS LIKE A MARINE MINE-THE KIND THAT EXPLODES WHEN A SHIP HITS A TRIGGER WIRE STRETCHED ACROSS THE CHANNEL!
I DUNNO WHERE THEY GOT THAT TRUNK WEIGHT-IT MAY BE A DUD MINE FILLED WITH CEMENT.
5
WONDER WOMAN, SUSPICIOUS, EXAMINES THE INSIDE OF THE TRUNK AND MAKES A STARTLING DISCOVERY!
GREAT TRIDENT OF NEPTUNE! THERE'S THE TRIGGER WIRE! IT'S A LIVE MINE AND THEY'RE GOING TO MAKE ME BLOW MYSELF UP!

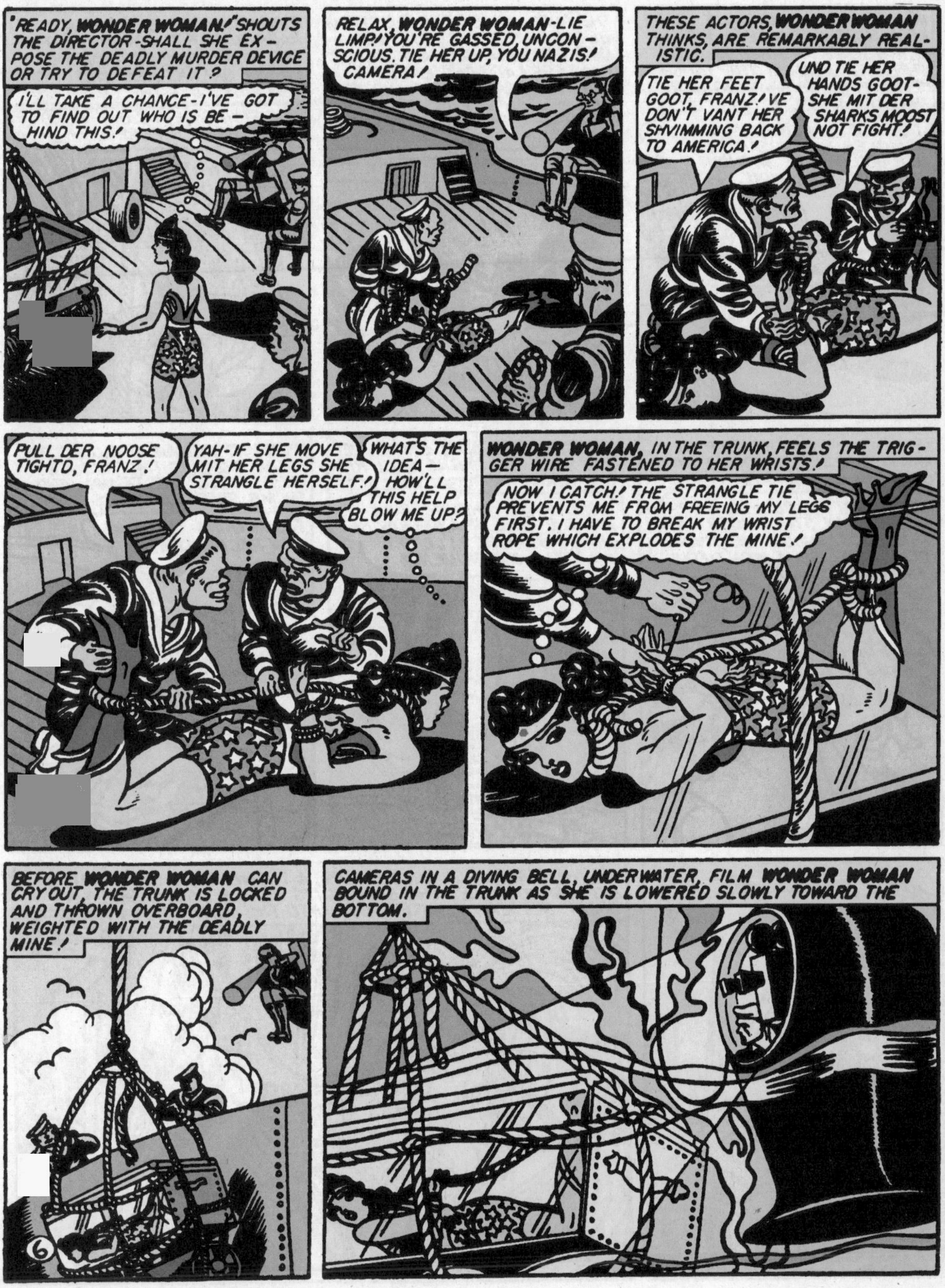
"READY, WONDER WOMAN!" SHOUTS THE DIRECTOR-SHALL SHE EX-POSE THE DEADLY MURDER DEVICE OR TRY TO DEFEAT IT?
I'LL TAKE A CHANCE-I'VE GOT TO FIND OUT WHO IS BE-HIND THIS!
RELAX, WONDER WOMAN-LIE LIMP! YOU'RE GASSED, UNCON-SCIOUS. TIE HER UP, YOU NAZIS! CAMERA!
THESE ACTORS, WONDER WOMAN THINKS, ARE REMARKABLY REAL-ISTIC.
TIE HER FEET GOOT, FRANZ! VE DON'T VANT HER SHVIMMING BACK TO AMERICA!
UND TIE HER HANDS GOOT-SHE MIT DER SHARKS MOOST NOT FIGHT!
PULL DER NOOSE TIGHTD, FRANZ!
YAH-IF SHE MOVE MIT HER LEGS SHE STRANGLE HERSELF!
WHAT'S THE IDEA-HOW'LL THIS HELP BLOW ME UP?
WONDER WOMAN, IN THE TRUNK, FEELS THE TRIG-GER WIRE FASTENED TO HER WRISTS!
NOW I CATCH! THE STRANGLE TIE PREVENTS ME FROM FREEING MY LEGS FIRST. I HAVE TO BREAK MY WRIST ROPE WHICH EXPLODES THE MINE!
BEFORE WONDER WOMAN CAN CRY OUT, THE TRUNK IS LOCKED AND THROWN OVERBOARD, WEIGHTED WITH THE DEADLY MINE!
6
CAMERAS IN A DIVING BELL, UNDERWATER, FILM WONDER WOMAN BOUND IN THE TRUNK AS SHE IS LOWERED SLOWLY TOWARD THE BOTTOM.

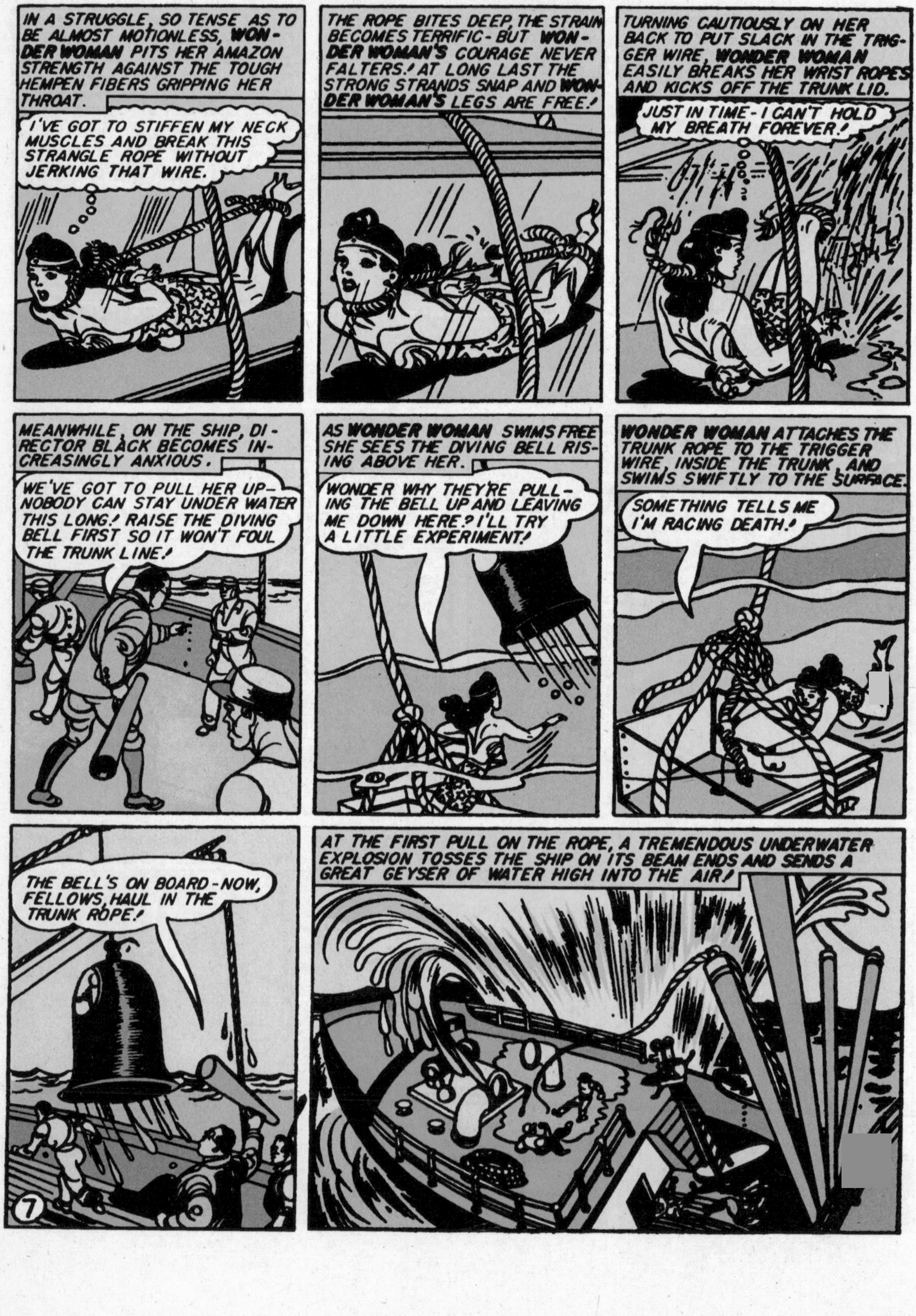

IN A STRUGGLE, SO TENSE AS TO BE ALMOST MOTIONLESS, WONDER WOMAN PITS HER AMAZON STRENGTH AGAINST THE TOUGH HEMPEN FIBERS GRIPPING HER THROAT.
I'VE GOT TO STIFFEN MY NECK MUSCLES AND BREAK THIS STRANGLE ROPE WITHOUT JERKING THAT WIRE.
THE ROPE BITES DEEP, THE STRAIN BECOMES TERRIFIC - BUT WONDER WOMAN'S COURAGE NEVER FALTERS! AT LONG LAST THE STRONG STRANDS SNAP AND WONDER WOMAN'S LEGS ARE FREE!
TURNING CAUTIOUSLY ON HER BACK TO PUT SLACK IN THE TRIGGER WIRE, WONDER WOMAN EASILY BREAKS HER WRIST ROPES AND KICKS OFF THE TRUNK LID.
JUST IN TIME - I CAN'T HOLD MY BREATH FOREVER!
MEANWHILE, ON THE SHIP, DIRECTOR BLACK BECOMES INCREASINGLY ANXIOUS.
WE'VE GOT TO PULL HER UP - NOBODY CAN STAY UNDER WATER THIS LONG! RAISE THE DIVING BELL FIRST SO IT WON'T FOUL THE TRUNK LINE!
AS WONDER WOMAN SWIMS FREE SHE SEES THE DIVING BELL RISING ABOVE HER.
WONDER WHY THEY'RE PULLING THE BELL UP AND LEAVING ME DOWN HERE? I'LL TRY A LITTLE EXPERIMENT!
WONDER WOMAN ATTACHES THE TRUNK ROPE TO THE TRIGGER WIRE, INSIDE THE TRUNK, AND SWIMS SWIFTLY TO THE SURFACE.
SOMETHING TELLS ME I'M RACING DEATH!
THE BELL'S ON BOARD - NOW, FELLOWS, HAUL IN THE TRUNK ROPE!
7
AT THE FIRST PULL ON THE ROPE, A TREMENDOUS UNDERWATER EXPLOSION TOSSES THE SHIP ON ITS BEAM ENDS AND SENDS A GREAT GEYSER OF WATER HIGH INTO THE AIR!

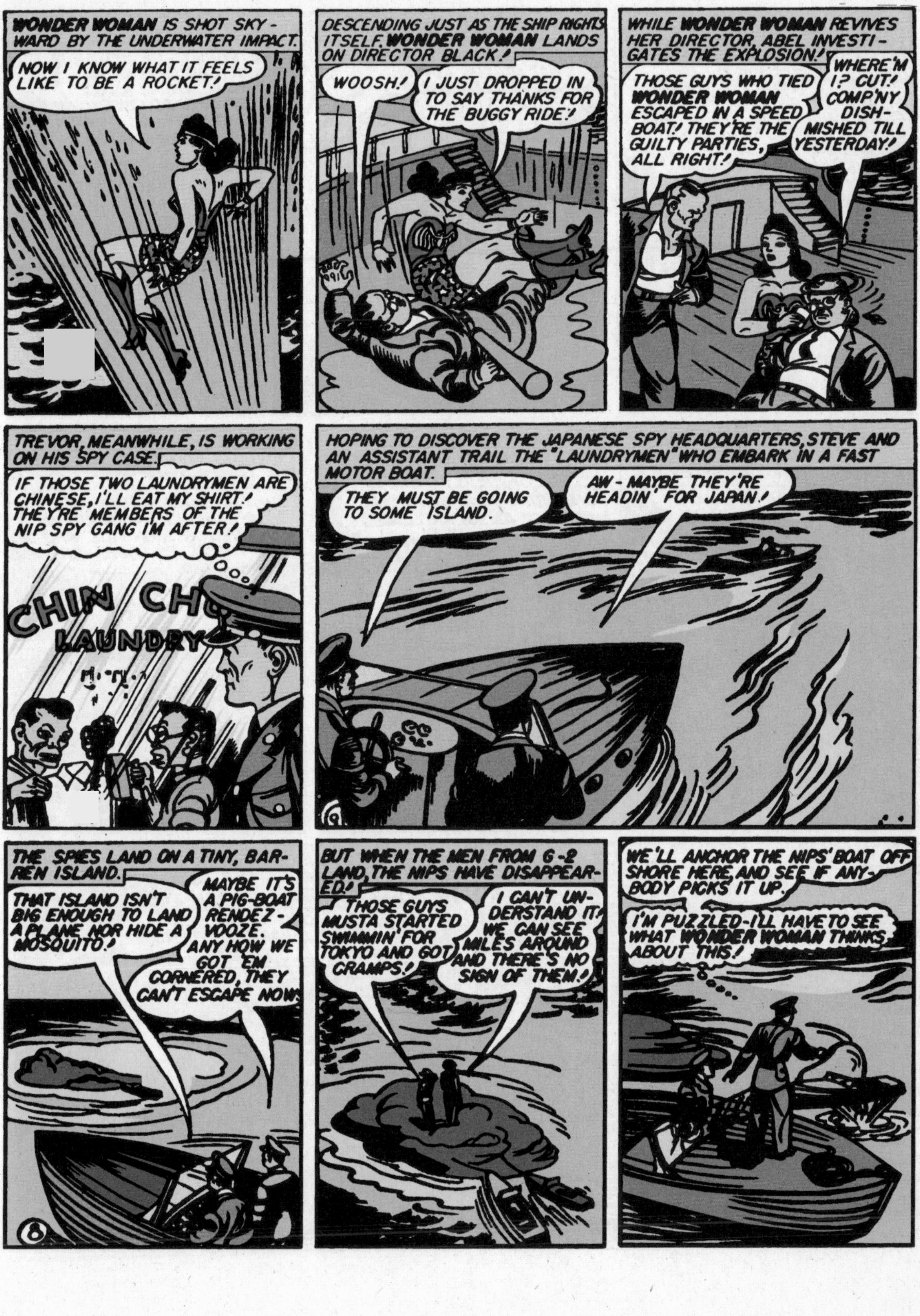

WONDER WOMAN IS SHOT SKYWARD BY THE UNDERWATER IMPACT.
NOW I KNOW WHAT IT FEELS LIKE TO BE A ROCKET!
DESCENDING JUST AS THE SHIP RIGHTS ITSELF, WONDER WOMAN LANDS ON DIRECTOR BLACK!
WOOSH!
I JUST DROPPED IN TO SAY THANKS FOR THE BUGGY RIDE!
WHILE WONDER WOMAN REVIVES HER DIRECTOR, ABEL INVESTIGATES THE EXPLOSION!
THOSE GUYS WHO TIED WONDER WOMAN ESCAPED IN A SPEED BOAT! THEY'RE THE GUILTY PARTIES, ALL RIGHT!
WHERE'M I? CUT! COMP'NY DISHMISHED TILL YESTERDAY!
TREVOR, MEANWHILE, IS WORKING ON HIS SPY CASE.
IF THOSE TWO LAUNDRYMEN ARE CHINESE, I'LL EAT MY SHIRT! THEY'RE MEMBERS OF THE NIP SPY GANG I'M AFTER!
CHIN CH
LAUNDRY
HOPING TO DISCOVER THE JAPANESE SPY HEADQUARTERS, STEVE AND AN ASSISTANT TRAIL THE "LAUNDRYMEN" WHO EMBARK IN A FAST MOTOR BOAT.
THEY MUST BE GOING TO SOME ISLAND.
AW- MAYBE THEY'RE HEADIN' FOR JAPAN!
THE SPIES LAND ON A TINY, BARREN ISLAND.
THAT ISLAND ISN'T BIG ENOUGH TO LAND A PLANE NOR HIDE A MOSQUITO!
MAYBE IT'S A PIG-BOAT RENDEZVOOZE. ANY HOW WE GOT 'EM CORNERED, THEY CAN'T ESCAPE NOW!
BUT WHEN THE MEN FROM G-2 LAND, THE NIPS HAVE DISAPPEARED!
THOSE GUYS MUSTA STARTED SWIMMIN' FOR TOKYO AND GOT CRAMPS!
I CAN'T UNDERSTAND IT! WE CAN SEE MILES AROUND AND THERE'S NO SIGN OF THEM!
WE'LL ANCHOR THE NIPS' BOAT OFF SHORE HERE, AND SEE IF ANYBODY PICKS IT UP.
I'M PUZZLED-I'LL HAVE TO SEE WHAT WONDER WOMAN THINKS ABOUT THIS!

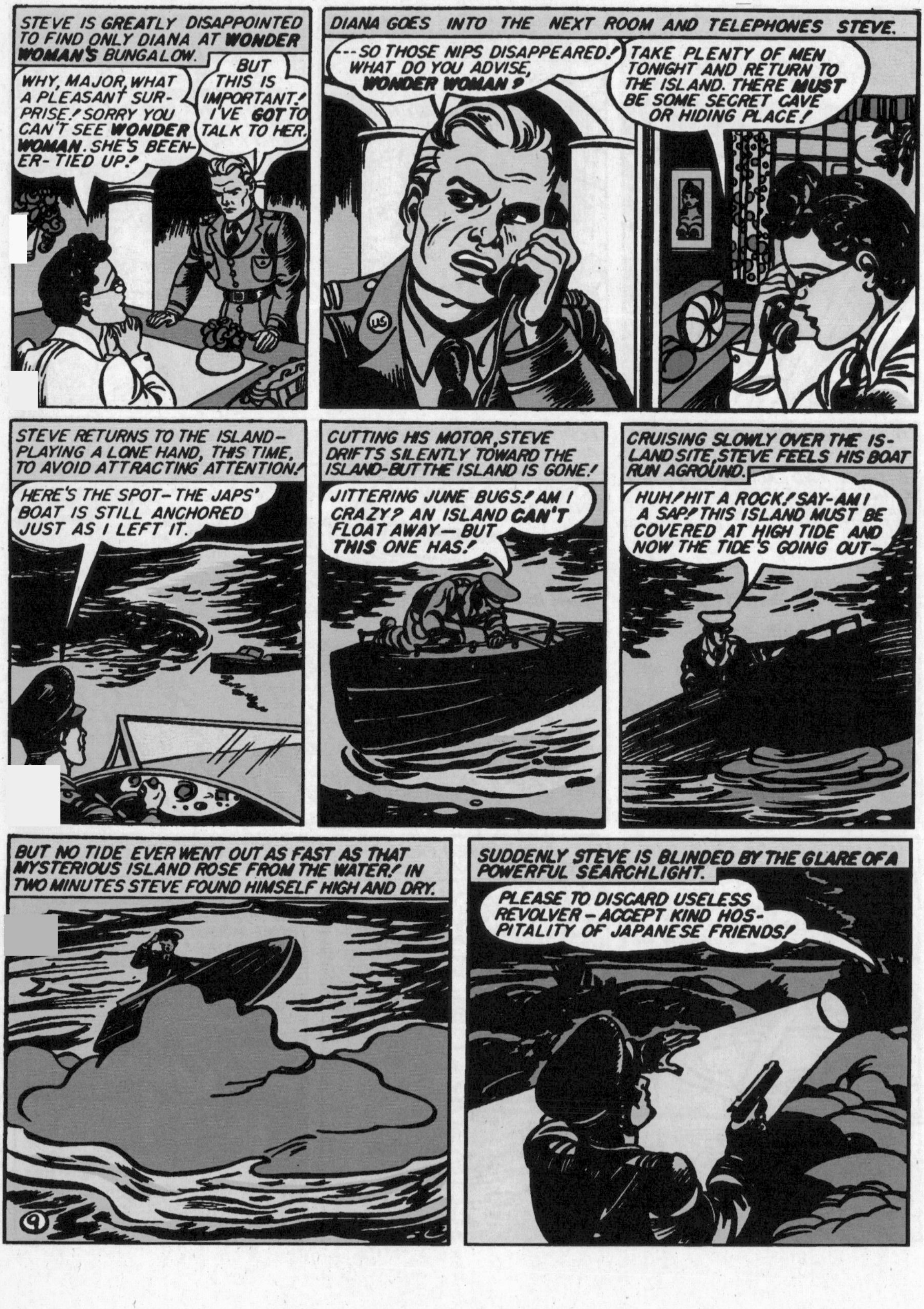
STEVE IS GREATLY DISAPPOINTED TO FIND ONLY DIANA AT WONDER WOMAN'S BUNGALOW.
WHY, MAJOR, WHAT A PLEASANT SURPRISE! SORRY YOU CAN'T SEE WONDER WOMAN. SHE'S BEEN-ER-TIED UP!
BUT THIS IS IMPORTANT! I'VE GOT TO TALK TO HER.
DIANA GOES INTO THE NEXT ROOM AND TELEPHONES STEVE.
---SO THOSE NIPS DISAPPEARED! WHAT DO YOU ADVISE, WONDER WOMAN?
TAKE PLENTY OF MEN TONIGHT AND RETURN TO THE ISLAND. THERE MUST BE SOME SECRET CAVE OR HIDING PLACE!
STEVE RETURNS TO THE ISLAND-PLAYING A LONE HAND, THIS TIME, TO AVOID ATTRACTING ATTENTION!
HERE'S THE SPOT-THE JAPS' BOAT IS STILL ANCHORED JUST AS I LEFT IT.
CUTTING HIS MOTOR, STEVE DRIFTS SILENTLY TOWARD THE ISLAND-BUT THE ISLAND IS GONE!
JITTERING JUNE BUGS! AM I CRAZY? AN ISLAND CAN'T FLOAT AWAY—BUT THIS ONE HAS!
CRUISING SLOWLY OVER THE ISLAND SITE, STEVE FEELS HIS BOAT RUN AGROUND.
HUH! HIT A ROCK! SAY-AM I A SAP! THIS ISLAND MUST BE COVERED AT HIGH TIDE AND NOW THE TIDE'S GOING OUT-
BUT NO TIDE EVER WENT OUT AS FAST AS THAT MYSTERIOUS ISLAND ROSE FROM THE WATER! IN TWO MINUTES STEVE FOUND HIMSELF HIGH AND DRY.
9
SUDDENLY STEVE IS BLINDED BY THE GLARE OF A POWERFUL SEARCHLIGHT.
PLEASE TO DISCARD USELESS REVOLVER-ACCEPT KIND HOSPITALITY OF JAPANESE FRIENDS!

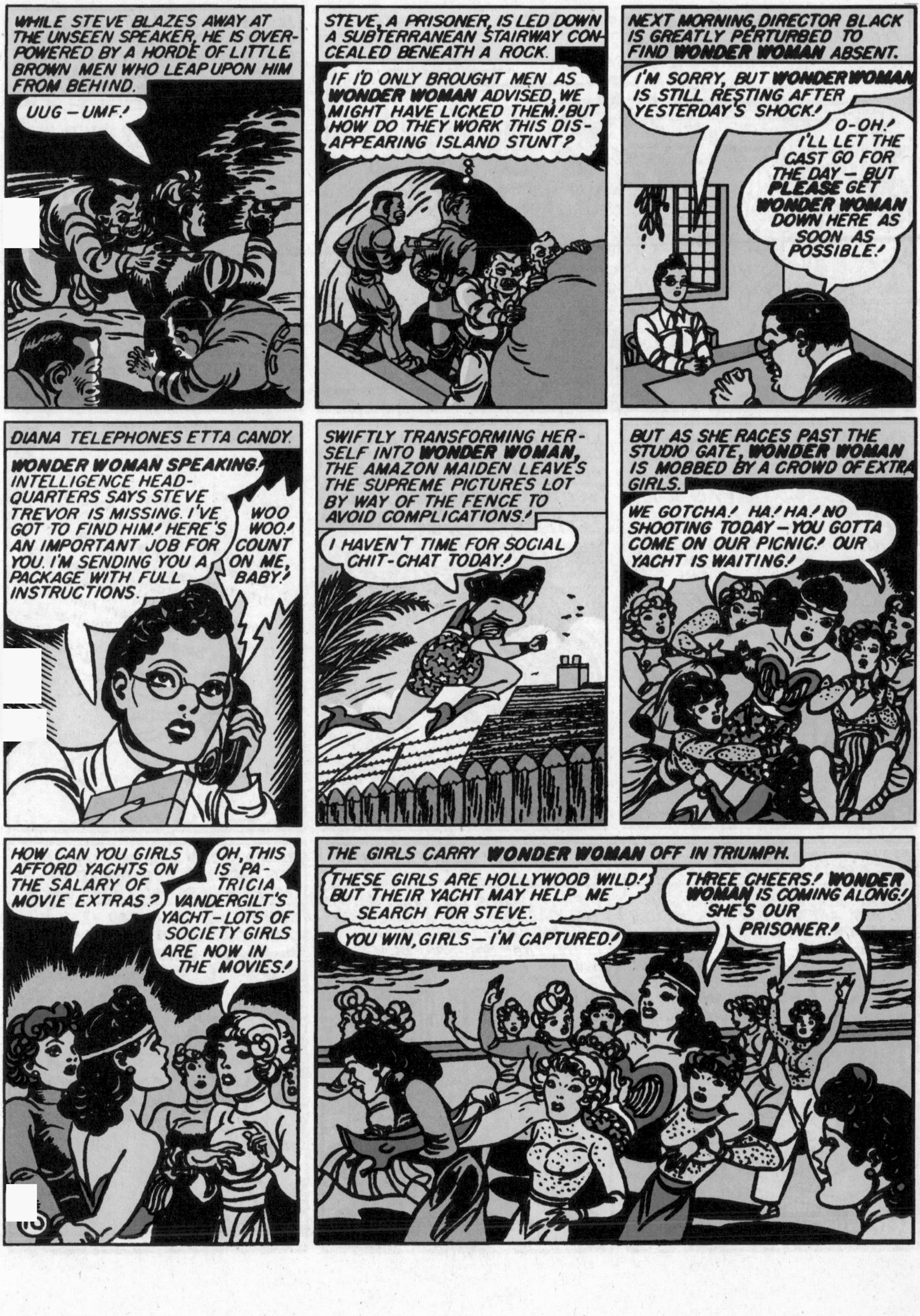
WHILE STEVE BLAZES AWAY AT THE UNSEEN SPEAKER, HE IS OVERPOWERED BY A HORDE OF LITTLE BROWN MEN WHO LEAP UPON HIM FROM BEHIND.
UUG — UMF!
STEVE, A PRISONER, IS LED DOWN A SUBTERRANEAN STAIRWAY CONCEALED BENEATH A ROCK.
IF I'D ONLY BROUGHT MEN AS WONDER WOMAN ADVISED, WE MIGHT HAVE LICKED THEM! BUT HOW DO THEY WORK THIS DISAPPEARING ISLAND STUNT?
NEXT MORNING, DIRECTOR BLACK IS GREATLY PERTURBED TO FIND WONDER WOMAN ABSENT.
I'M SORRY, BUT WONDER WOMAN IS STILL RESTING AFTER YESTERDAY'S SHOCK!
O-OH! I'LL LET THE CAST GO FOR THE DAY — BUT PLEASE GET WONDER WOMAN DOWN HERE AS SOON AS POSSIBLE!
DIANA TELEPHONES ETTA CANDY.
WONDER WOMAN SPEAKING! INTELLIGENCE HEADQUARTERS SAYS STEVE TREVOR IS MISSING. I'VE GOT TO FIND HIM! HERE'S AN IMPORTANT JOB FOR YOU. I'M SENDING YOU A PACKAGE WITH FULL INSTRUCTIONS.
WOO WOO! COUNT ON ME, BABY!
SWIFTLY TRANSFORMING HERSELF INTO WONDER WOMAN, THE AMAZON MAIDEN LEAVES THE SUPREME PICTURES LOT BY WAY OF THE FENCE TO AVOID COMPLICATIONS!
I HAVEN'T TIME FOR SOCIAL CHIT-CHAT TODAY!
BUT AS SHE RACES PAST THE STUDIO GATE, WONDER WOMAN IS MOBBED BY A CROWD OF EXTRA GIRLS.
WE GOTCHA! HA! HA! NO SHOOTING TODAY — YOU GOTTA COME ON OUR PICNIC! OUR YACHT IS WAITING!
HOW CAN YOU GIRLS AFFORD YACHTS ON THE SALARY OF MOVIE EXTRAS?
OH, THIS IS PATRICIA VANDERGILT'S YACHT — LOTS OF SOCIETY GIRLS ARE NOW IN THE MOVIES!
THE GIRLS CARRY WONDER WOMAN OFF IN TRIUMPH.
THESE GIRLS ARE HOLLYWOOD WILD! BUT THEIR YACHT MAY HELP ME SEARCH FOR STEVE.
YOU WIN, GIRLS — I'M CAPTURED!
THREE CHEERS! WONDER WOMAN IS COMING ALONG! SHE'S OUR PRISONER!

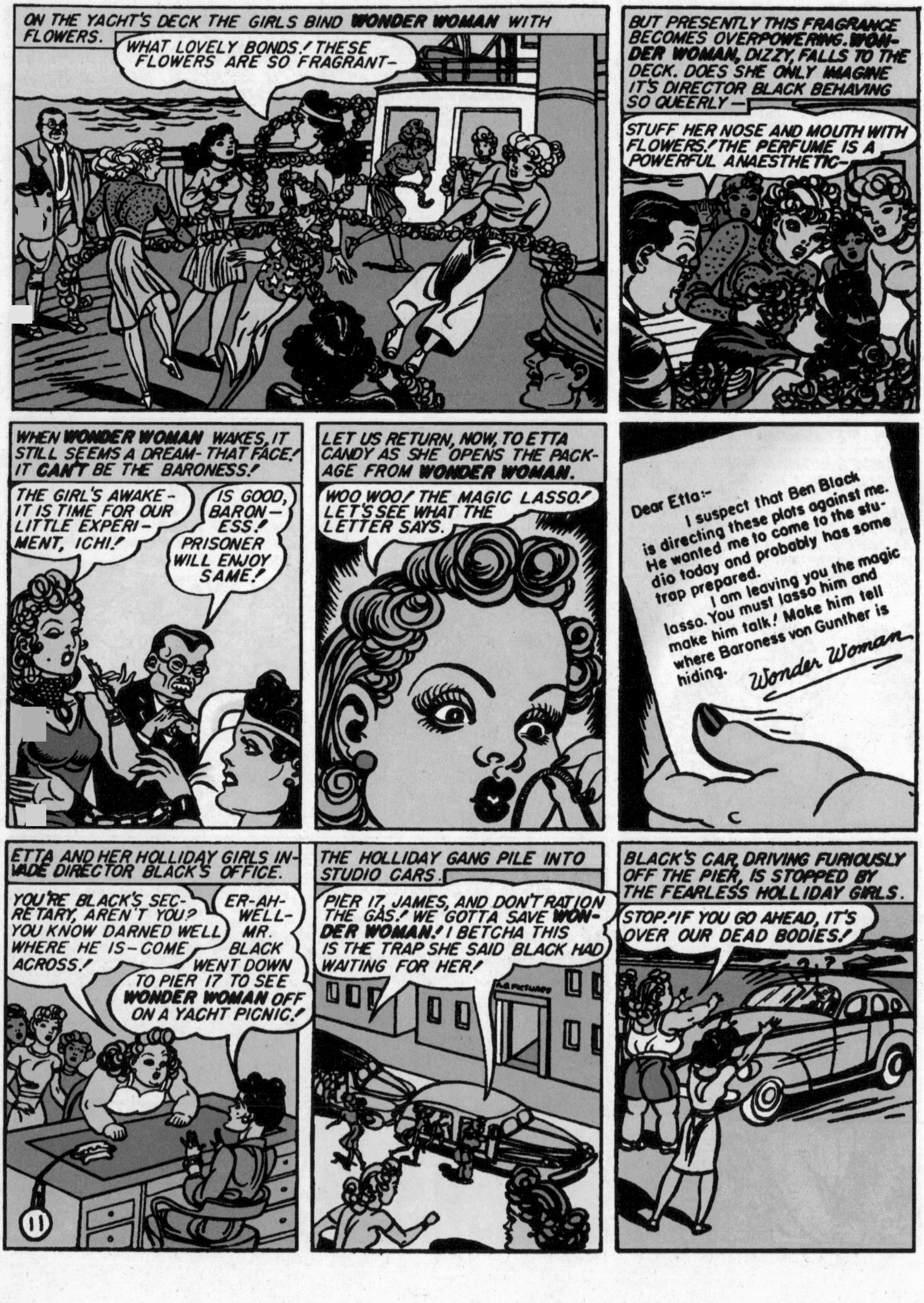
ON THE YACHT'S DECK THE GIRLS BIND WONDER WOMAN WITH FLOWERS.
WHAT LOVELY BONDS! THESE FLOWERS ARE SO FRAGRANT-
BUT PRESENTLY THIS FRAGRANCE BECOMES OVERPOWERING. WONDER WOMAN, DIZZY, FALLS TO THE DECK. DOES SHE ONLY IMAGINE IT'S DIRECTOR BLACK BEHAVING SO QUEERLY-
STUFF HER NOSE AND MOUTH WITH FLOWERS! THE PERFUME IS A POWERFUL ANAESTHETIC-
WHEN WONDER WOMAN WAKES, IT STILL SEEMS A DREAM-THAT FACE! IT CAN'T BE THE BARONESS!
THE GIRL'S AWAKE- IT IS TIME FOR OUR LITTLE EXPERIMENT, ICHI!
IS GOOD, BARON-ESS! PRISONER WILL ENJOY SAME!
LET US RETURN, NOW, TO ETTA CANDY AS SHE OPENS THE PACKAGE FROM WONDER WOMAN.
WOO WOO! THE MAGIC LASSO! LET'S SEE WHAT THE LETTER SAYS.
Dear Etta:-
I suspect that Ben Black is directing these plots against me. He wanted me to come to the studio today and probably has some trap prepared.
I am leaving you the magic lasso. You must lasso him and make him talk! Make him tell where Baroness von Gunther is hiding.
Wonder Woman
ETTA AND HER HOLLIDAY GIRLS INVADE DIRECTOR BLACK'S OFFICE.
YOU'RE BLACK'S SECRETARY, AREN'T YOU? YOU KNOW DARNED WELL WHERE HE IS-COME ACROSS!
ER-AH-WELL-MR. BLACK WENT DOWN TO PIER 17 TO SEE WONDER WOMAN OFF ON A YACHT PICNIC!
11
THE HOLLIDAY GANG PILE INTO STUDIO CARS.
PIER 17, JAMES, AND DON'T RATION THE GAS! WE GOTTA SAVE WONDER WOMAN! I BETCHA THIS IS THE TRAP SHE SAID BLACK HAD WAITING FOR HER!
BLACK'S CAR, DRIVING FURIOUSLY OFF THE PIER, IS STOPPED BY THE FEARLESS HOLLIDAY GIRLS.
STOP! IF YOU GO AHEAD, IT'S OVER OUR DEAD BODIES!
?.?

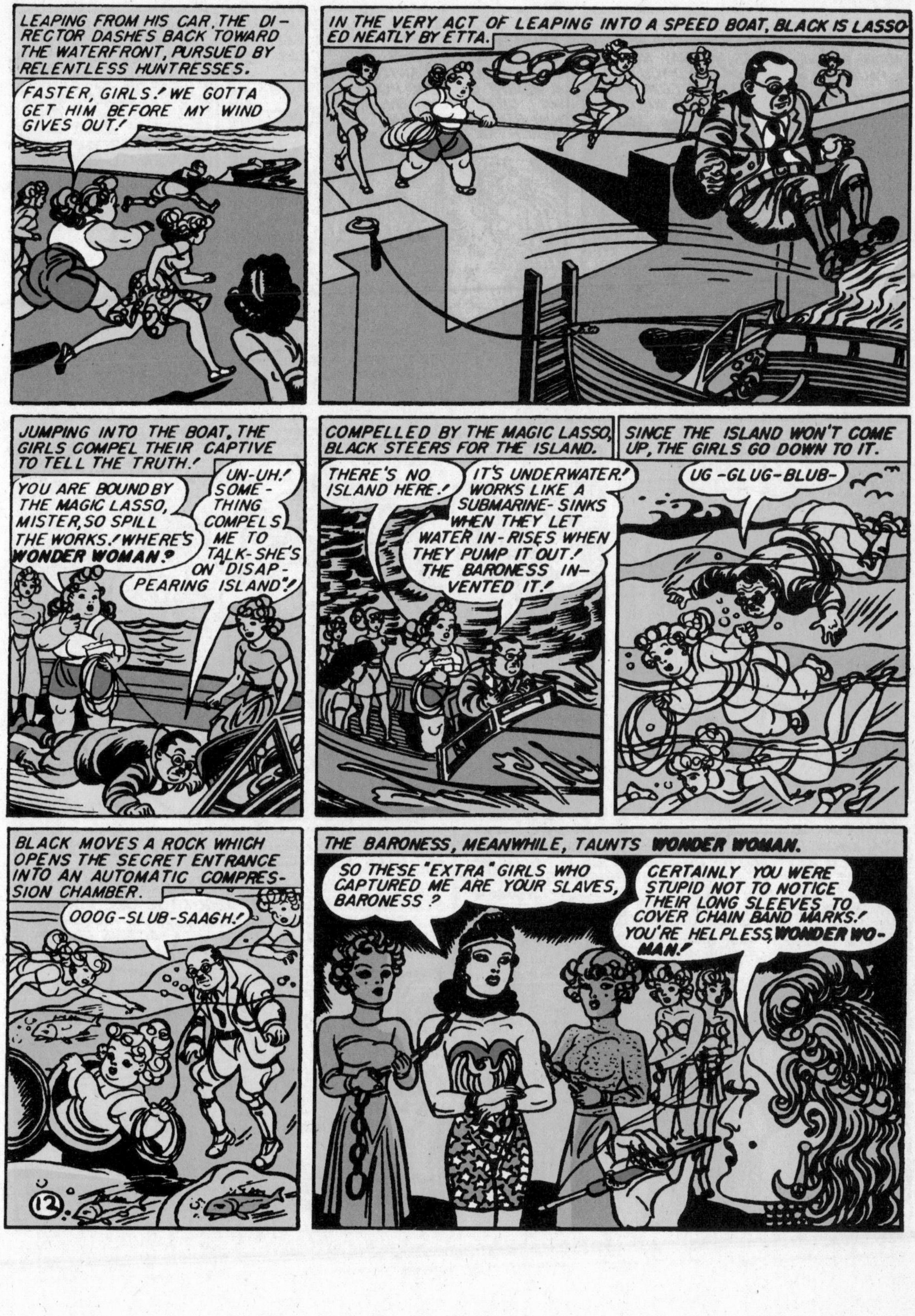
LEAPING FROM HIS CAR, THE DIRECTOR DASHES BACK TOWARD THE WATERFRONT, PURSUED BY RELENTLESS HUNTRESSES.
FASTER, GIRLS! WE GOTTA GET HIM BEFORE MY WIND GIVES OUT!
IN THE VERY ACT OF LEAPING INTO A SPEED BOAT, BLACK IS LASSOED NEATLY BY ETTA.
JUMPING INTO THE BOAT, THE GIRLS COMPEL THEIR CAPTIVE TO TELL THE TRUTH!
YOU ARE BOUND BY THE MAGIC LASSO, MISTER, SO SPILL THE WORKS! WHERE'S WONDER WOMAN?
UN-UH! SOMETHING COMPELS ME TO TALK-SHE'S ON "DISAPPEARING ISLAND"!
COMPELLED BY THE MAGIC LASSO, BLACK STEERS FOR THE ISLAND.
THERE'S NO ISLAND HERE!
IT'S UNDERWATER! WORKS LIKE A SUBMARINE- SINKS WHEN THEY LET WATER IN- RISES WHEN THEY PUMP IT OUT! THE BARONESS INVENTED IT!
SINCE THE ISLAND WON'T COME UP, THE GIRLS GO DOWN TO IT.
UG-GLUG-BLUB-
BLACK MOVES A ROCK WHICH OPENS THE SECRET ENTRANCE INTO AN AUTOMATIC COMPRESSION CHAMBER.
OOOG-SLUB-SAAGH!
12
THE BARONESS, MEANWHILE, TAUNTS WONDER WOMAN.
SO THESE "EXTRA" GIRLS WHO CAPTURED ME ARE YOUR SLAVES, BARONESS?
CERTAINLY YOU WERE STUPID NOT TO NOTICE THEIR LONG SLEEVES TO COVER CHAIN BAND MARKS! YOU'RE HELPLESS, WONDER WOMAN!

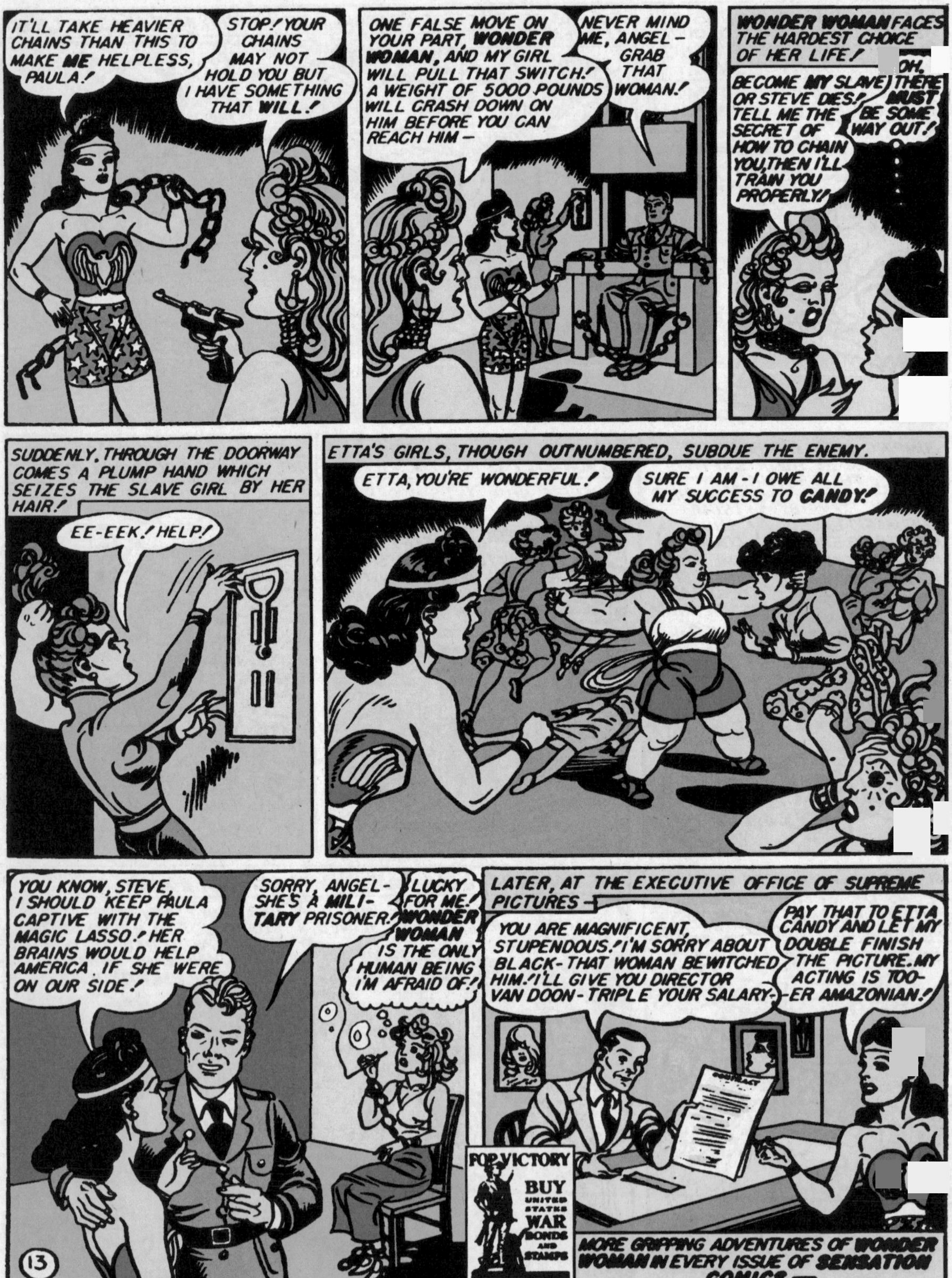
IT'LL TAKE HEAVIER CHAINS THAN THIS TO MAKE ME HELPLESS, PAULA!
STOP! YOUR CHAINS MAY NOT HOLD YOU BUT I HAVE SOMETHING THAT WILL!
ONE FALSE MOVE ON YOUR PART, WONDER WOMAN, AND MY GIRL WILL PULL THAT SWITCH! A WEIGHT OF 5000 POUNDS WILL CRASH DOWN ON HIM BEFORE YOU CAN REACH HIM—
NEVER MIND ME, ANGEL—GRAB THAT WOMAN!
WONDER WOMAN FACES THE HARDEST CHOICE OF HER LIFE!
BECOME MY SLAVE OR STEVE DIES! TELL ME THE SECRET OF HOW TO CHAIN YOU, THEN I'LL TRAIN YOU PROPERLY!
OH, THERE MUST BE SOME WAY OUT!
SUDDENLY, THROUGH THE DOORWAY COMES A PLUMP HAND WHICH SEIZES THE SLAVE GIRL BY HER HAIR!
EE-EEK! HELP!
ETTA'S GIRLS, THOUGH OUTNUMBERED, SUBDUE THE ENEMY.
ETTA, YOU'RE WONDERFUL!
SURE I AM—I OWE ALL MY SUCCESS TO CANDY!
YOU KNOW, STEVE, I SHOULD KEEP PAULA CAPTIVE WITH THE MAGIC LASSO! HER BRAINS WOULD HELP AMERICA IF SHE WERE ON OUR SIDE!
SORRY, ANGEL—SHE'S A MILITARY PRISONER!
LUCKY FOR ME! WONDER WOMAN IS THE ONLY HUMAN BEING I'M AFRAID OF!
LATER, AT THE EXECUTIVE OFFICE OF SUPREME PICTURES—
YOU ARE MAGNIFICENT, STUPENDOUS! I'M SORRY ABOUT BLACK—THAT WOMAN BEWITCHED HIM! I'LL GIVE YOU DIRECTOR VAN DOON—TRIPLE YOUR SALARY—
PAY THAT TO ETTA CANDY AND LET MY DOUBLE FINISH THE PICTURE. MY ACTING IS TOO-ER AMAZONIAN!
FOR VICTORY
BUY UNITED STATES WAR BONDS AND STAMPS
MORE GRIPPING ADVENTURES OF WONDER WOMAN IN EVERY ISSUE OF SENSATION COMICS—
13

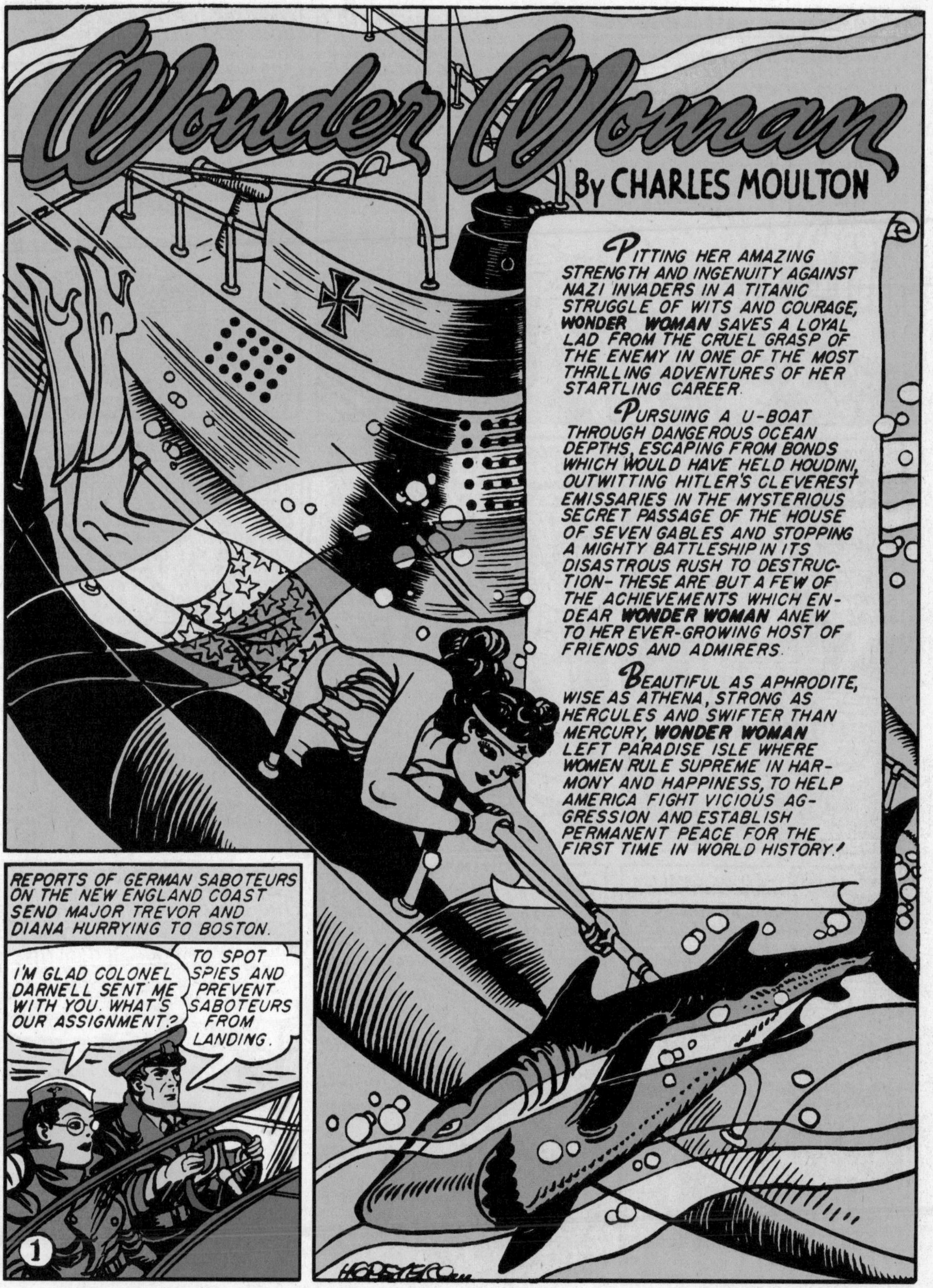
Wonder Woman
By CHARLES MOULTON
PITTING HER AMAZING STRENGTH AND INGENUITY AGAINST NAZI INVADERS IN A TITANIC STRUGGLE OF WITS AND COURAGE, WONDER WOMAN SAVES A LOYAL LAD FROM THE CRUEL GRASP OF THE ENEMY IN ONE OF THE MOST THRILLING ADVENTURES OF HER STARTLING CAREER.
PURSUING A U-BOAT THROUGH DANGEROUS OCEAN DEPTHS, ESCAPING FROM BONDS WHICH WOULD HAVE HELD HOUDINI, OUTWITTING HITLER'S CLEVEREST EMISSARIES IN THE MYSTERIOUS SECRET PASSAGE OF THE HOUSE OF SEVEN GABLES AND STOPPING A MIGHTY BATTLESHIP IN ITS DISASTROUS RUSH TO DESTRUCTION- THESE ARE BUT A FEW OF THE ACHIEVEMENTS WHICH ENDEAR WONDER WOMAN ANEW TO HER EVER-GROWING HOST OF FRIENDS AND ADMIRERS.
BEAUTIFUL AS APHRODITE, WISE AS ATHENA, STRONG AS HERCULES AND SWIFTER THAN MERCURY, WONDER WOMAN LEFT PARADISE ISLE WHERE WOMEN RULE SUPREME IN HARMONY AND HAPPINESS, TO HELP AMERICA FIGHT VICIOUS AGGRESSION AND ESTABLISH PERMANENT PEACE FOR THE FIRST TIME IN WORLD HISTORY!
REPORTS OF GERMAN SABOTEURS ON THE NEW ENGLAND COAST SEND MAJOR TREVOR AND DIANA HURRYING TO BOSTON.
I'M GLAD COLONEL DARNELL SENT ME WITH YOU. WHAT'S OUR ASSIGNMENT?
TO SPOT SPIES AND PREVENT SABOTEURS FROM LANDING.
1

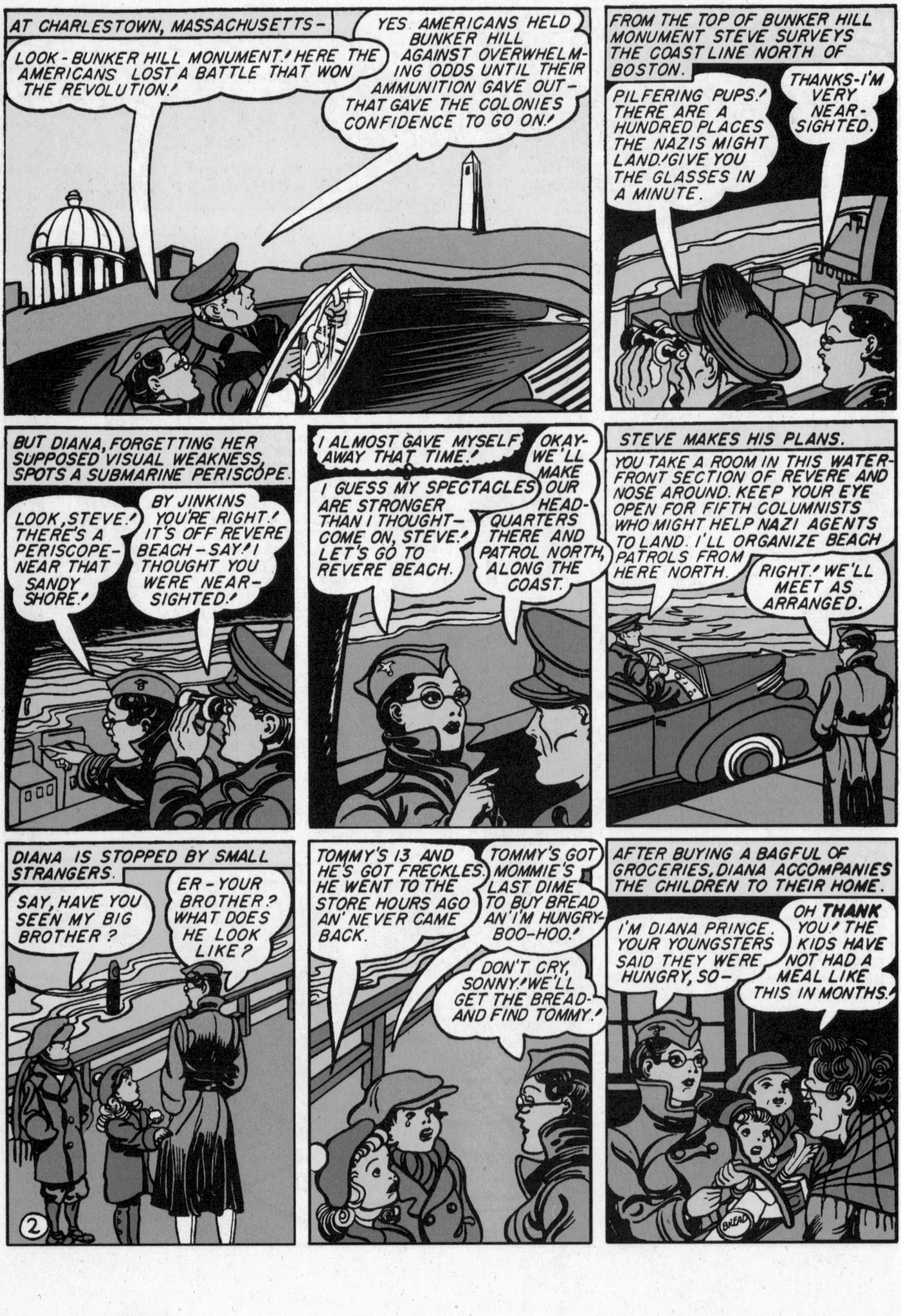
AT CHARLESTOWN, MASSACHUSETTS-
LOOK-BUNKER HILL MONUMENT! HERE THE AMERICANS LOST A BATTLE THAT WON THE REVOLUTION!
YES. AMERICANS HELD BUNKER HILL AGAINST OVERWHELMING ODDS UNTIL THEIR AMMUNITION GAVE OUT-THAT GAVE THE COLONIES CONFIDENCE TO GO ON!
FROM THE TOP OF BUNKER HILL MONUMENT STEVE SURVEYS THE COAST LINE NORTH OF BOSTON.
PILFERING PUPS! THERE ARE A HUNDRED PLACES THE NAZIS MIGHT LAND! GIVE YOU THE GLASSES IN A MINUTE.
THANKS-I'M VERY NEAR-SIGHTED.
BUT DIANA, FORGETTING HER SUPPOSED VISUAL WEAKNESS, SPOTS A SUBMARINE PERISCOPE.
LOOK, STEVE! THERE'S A PERISCOPE-NEAR THAT SANDY SHORE!
BY JINKINS YOU'RE RIGHT! IT'S OFF REVERE BEACH-SAY! I THOUGHT YOU WERE NEAR-SIGHTED!
I ALMOST GAVE MYSELF AWAY THAT TIME!
I GUESS MY SPECTACLES ARE STRONGER THAN I THOUGHT-COME ON, STEVE! LET'S GO TO REVERE BEACH.
OKAY-WE'LL MAKE OUR HEADQUARTERS THERE AND PATROL NORTH, ALONG THE COAST.
STEVE MAKES HIS PLANS.
YOU TAKE A ROOM IN THIS WATER-FRONT SECTION OF REVERE AND NOSE AROUND. KEEP YOUR EYE OPEN FOR FIFTH COLUMNISTS WHO MIGHT HELP NAZI AGENTS TO LAND. I'LL ORGANIZE BEACH PATROLS FROM HERE NORTH.
RIGHT! WE'LL MEET AS ARRANGED.
DIANA IS STOPPED BY SMALL STRANGERS.
SAY, HAVE YOU SEEN MY BIG BROTHER?
ER-YOUR BROTHER? WHAT DOES HE LOOK LIKE?
2
TOMMY'S 13 AND HE'S GOT FRECKLES. HE WENT TO THE STORE HOURS AGO AN' NEVER CAME BACK.
TOMMY'S GOT MOMMIE'S LAST DIME TO BUY BREAD AN' I'M HUNGRY-BOO-HOO!
DON'T CRY, SONNY! WE'LL GET THE BREAD-AND FIND TOMMY!
AFTER BUYING A BAGFUL OF GROCERIES, DIANA ACCOMPANIES THE CHILDREN TO THEIR HOME.
I'M DIANA PRINCE. YOUR YOUNGSTERS SAID THEY WERE HUNGRY, SO-
OH THANK YOU! THE KIDS HAVE NOT HAD A MEAL LIKE THIS IN MONTHS!
BREAD

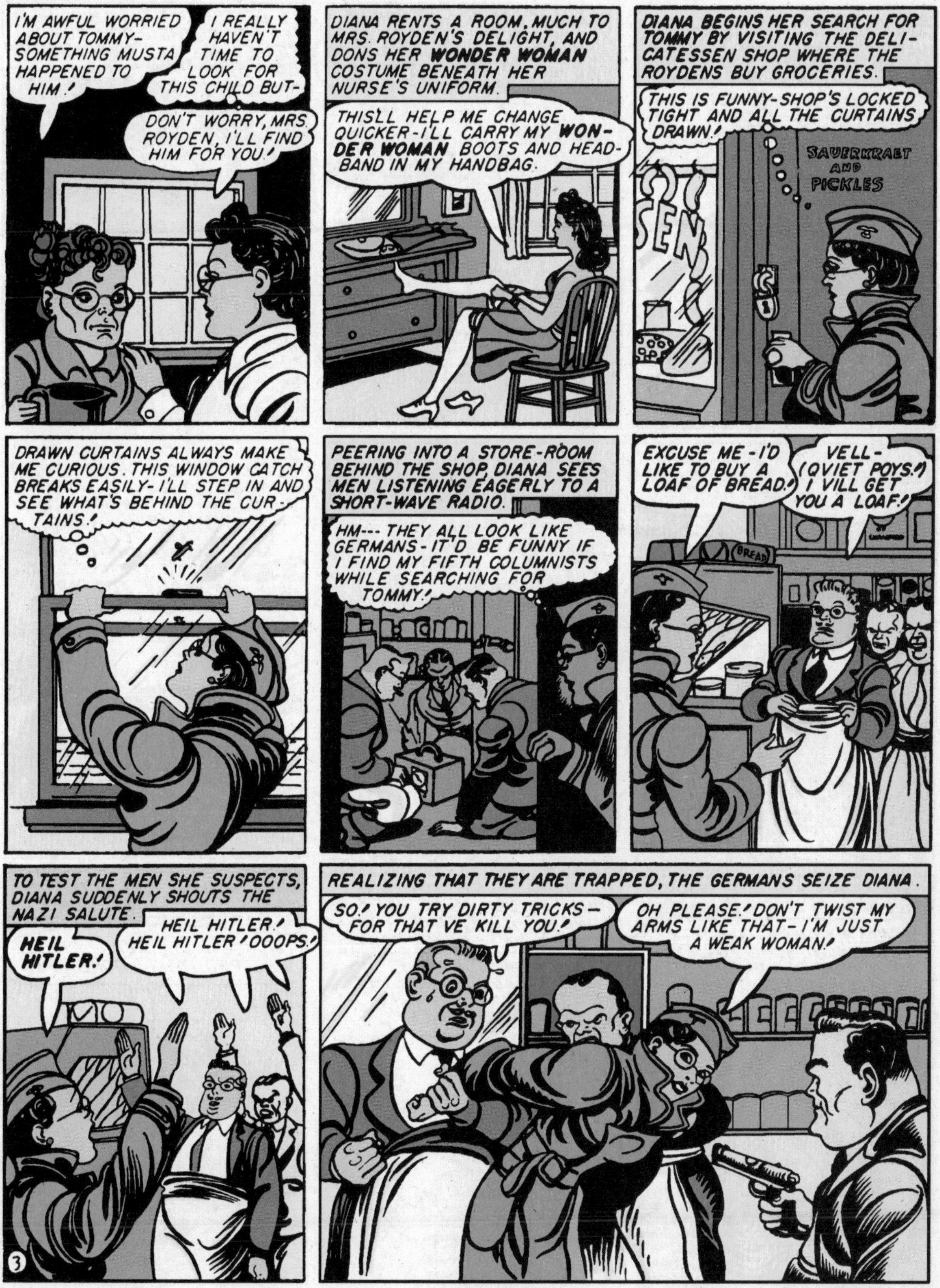
I'M AWFUL WORRIED ABOUT TOMMY- SOMETHING MUSTA HAPPENED TO HIM!
I REALLY HAVEN'T TIME TO LOOK FOR THIS CHILD BUT-
DON'T WORRY, MRS. ROYDEN, I'LL FIND HIM FOR YOU!
DIANA RENTS A ROOM, MUCH TO MRS. ROYDEN'S DELIGHT, AND DONS HER WONDER WOMAN COSTUME BENEATH HER NURSE'S UNIFORM.
THIS'LL HELP ME CHANGE QUICKER-I'LL CARRY MY WONDER WOMAN BOOTS AND HEADBAND IN MY HANDBAG.
DIANA BEGINS HER SEARCH FOR TOMMY BY VISITING THE DELICATESSEN SHOP WHERE THE ROYDENS BUY GROCERIES.
THIS IS FUNNY-SHOP'S LOCKED TIGHT AND ALL THE CURTAINS DRAWN!
SAUERKRAUT AND PICKLES
DRAWN CURTAINS ALWAYS MAKE ME CURIOUS. THIS WINDOW CATCH BREAKS EASILY- I'LL STEP IN AND SEE WHAT'S BEHIND THE CURTAINS!
PEERING INTO A STORE-ROOM BEHIND THE SHOP, DIANA SEES MEN LISTENING EAGERLY TO A SHORT-WAVE RADIO.
HM--- THEY ALL LOOK LIKE GERMANS - IT'D BE FUNNY IF I FIND MY FIFTH COLUMNISTS WHILE SEARCHING FOR TOMMY!
EXCUSE ME - I'D LIKE TO BUY A LOAF OF BREAD!
VELL- (QVIET POYS!) I VILL GET YOU A LOAF!
BREAD
TO TEST THE MEN SHE SUSPECTS, DIANA SUDDENLY SHOUTS THE NAZI SALUTE.
HEIL HITLER!
HEIL HITLER! HEIL HITLER! OOOPS!
REALIZING THAT THEY ARE TRAPPED, THE GERMANS SEIZE DIANA.
SO! YOU TRY DIRTY TRICKS— FOR THAT VE KILL YOU!
OH PLEASE! DON'T TWIST MY ARMS LIKE THAT - I'M JUST A WEAK WOMAN!
3

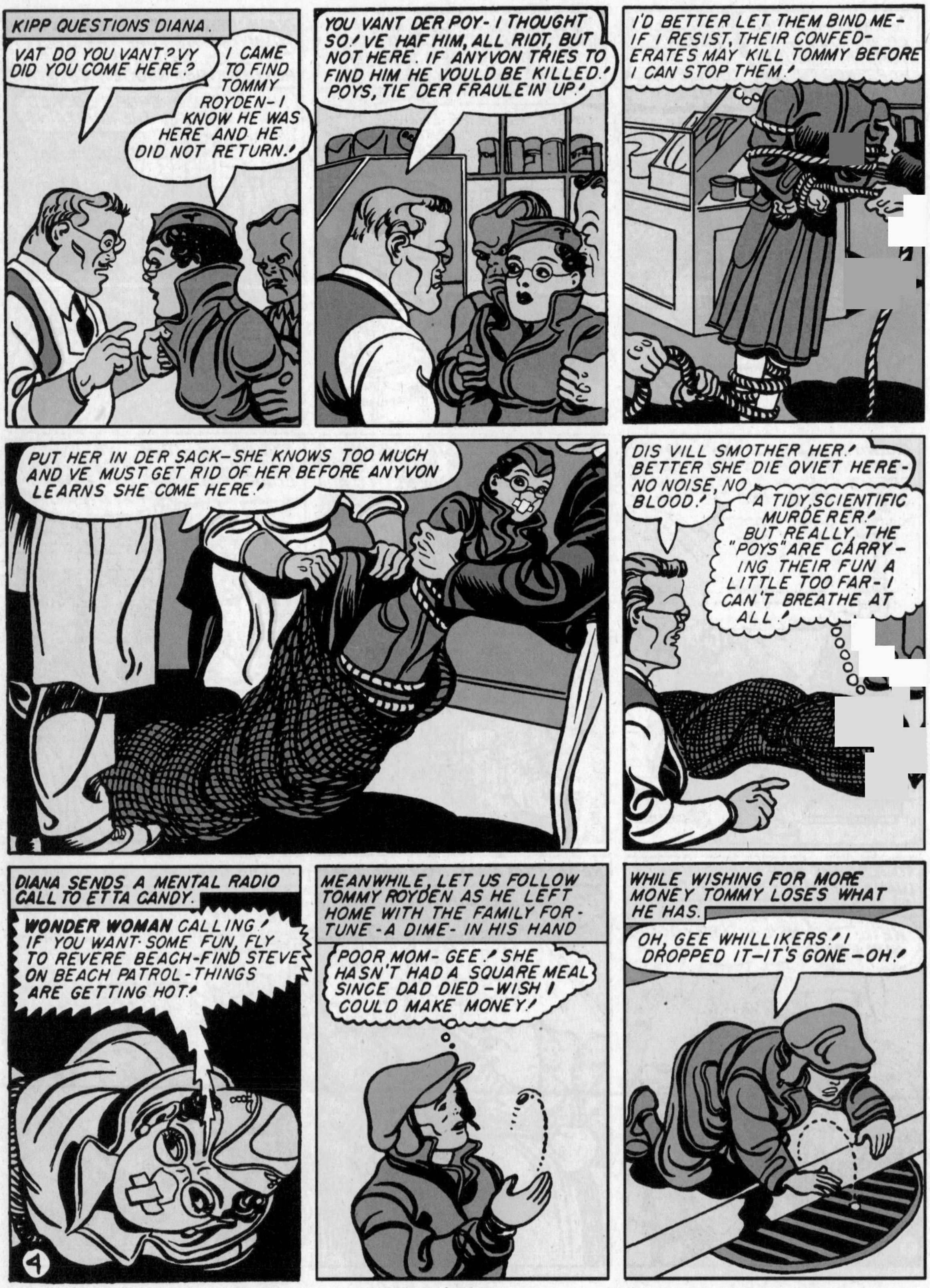

KIPP QUESTIONS DIANA.
VAT DO YOU VANT? VY DID YOU COME HERE?
I CAME TO FIND TOMMY ROYDEN- I KNOW HE WAS HERE AND HE DID NOT RETURN!
YOU VANT DER POY- I THOUGHT SO! VE HAF HIM, ALL RIDT, BUT NOT HERE. IF ANYVON TRIES TO FIND HIM HE VOULD BE KILLED! POYS, TIE DER FRAULEIN UP!
I'D BETTER LET THEM BIND ME- IF I RESIST, THEIR CONFED- ERATES MAY KILL TOMMY BEFORE I CAN STOP THEM!
PUT HER IN DER SACK-SHE KNOWS TOO MUCH AND VE MUST GET RID OF HER BEFORE ANYVON LEARNS SHE COME HERE!
DIS VILL SMOTHER HER! BETTER SHE DIE QVIET HERE- NO NOISE, NO BLOOD!
A TIDY, SCIENTIFIC MURDERER! BUT REALLY, THE "POYS" ARE CARRY- ING THEIR FUN A LITTLE TOO FAR- I CAN'T BREATHE AT ALL!
DIANA SENDS A MENTAL RADIO CALL TO ETTA CANDY.
WONDER WOMAN CALLING! IF YOU WANT SOME FUN, FLY TO REVERE BEACH-FIND STEVE ON BEACH PATROL-THINGS ARE GETTING HOT!
4
MEANWHILE, LET US FOLLOW TOMMY ROYDEN AS HE LEFT HOME WITH THE FAMILY FOR- TUNE -A DIME- IN HIS HAND
POOR MOM- GEE! SHE HASN'T HAD A SQUARE MEAL SINCE DAD DIED -WISH I COULD MAKE MONEY!
WHILE WISHING FOR MORE MONEY TOMMY LOSES WHAT HE HAS.
OH, GEE WHILLIKERS! I DROPPED IT-IT'S GONE-OH!

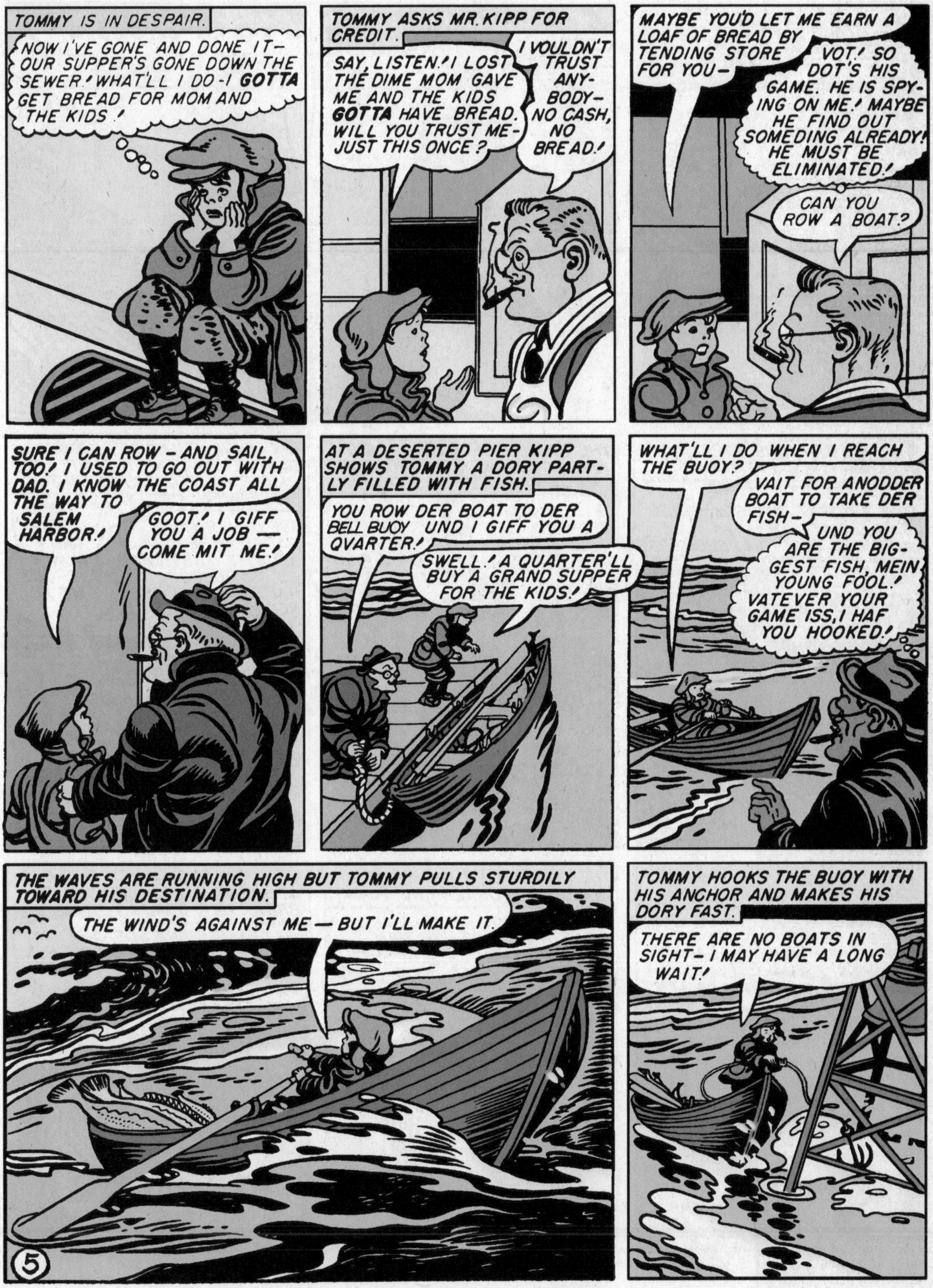
TOMMY IS IN DESPAIR.
NOW I'VE GONE AND DONE IT- OUR SUPPER'S GONE DOWN THE SEWER! WHAT'LL I DO-I GOTTA GET BREAD FOR MOM AND THE KIDS!
TOMMY ASKS MR. KIPP FOR CREDIT.
SAY, LISTEN! I LOST THE DIME MOM GAVE ME AND THE KIDS GOTTA HAVE BREAD. WILL YOU TRUST ME- JUST THIS ONCE?
I VOULDN'T TRUST ANY-BODY- NO CASH, NO BREAD!
MAYBE YOU'D LET ME EARN A LOAF OF BREAD BY TENDING STORE FOR YOU-
VOT! SO DOT'S HIS GAME. HE IS SPY-ING ON ME! MAYBE HE FIND OUT SOMEDING ALREADY! HE MUST BE ELIMINATED!
CAN YOU ROW A BOAT?
SURE I CAN ROW - AND SAIL, TOO! I USED TO GO OUT WITH DAD. I KNOW THE COAST ALL THE WAY TO SALEM HARBOR!
GOOT! I GIFF YOU A JOB — COME MIT ME!
AT A DESERTED PIER KIPP SHOWS TOMMY A DORY PARTLY FILLED WITH FISH.
YOU ROW DER BOAT TO DER BELL BUOY UND I GIFF YOU A QVARTER!
SWELL! A QUARTER'LL BUY A GRAND SUPPER FOR THE KIDS!
WHAT'LL I DO WHEN I REACH THE BUOY?
VAIT FOR ANODDER BOAT TO TAKE DER FISH-
UND YOU ARE THE BIG-GEST FISH, MEIN YOUNG FOOL! VATEVER YOUR GAME ISS, I HAF YOU HOOKED!
THE WAVES ARE RUNNING HIGH BUT TOMMY PULLS STURDILY TOWARD HIS DESTINATION.
THE WIND'S AGAINST ME — BUT I'LL MAKE IT.
5
TOMMY HOOKS THE BUOY WITH HIS ANCHOR AND MAKES HIS DORY FAST.
THERE ARE NO BOATS IN SIGHT- I MAY HAVE A LONG WAIT!

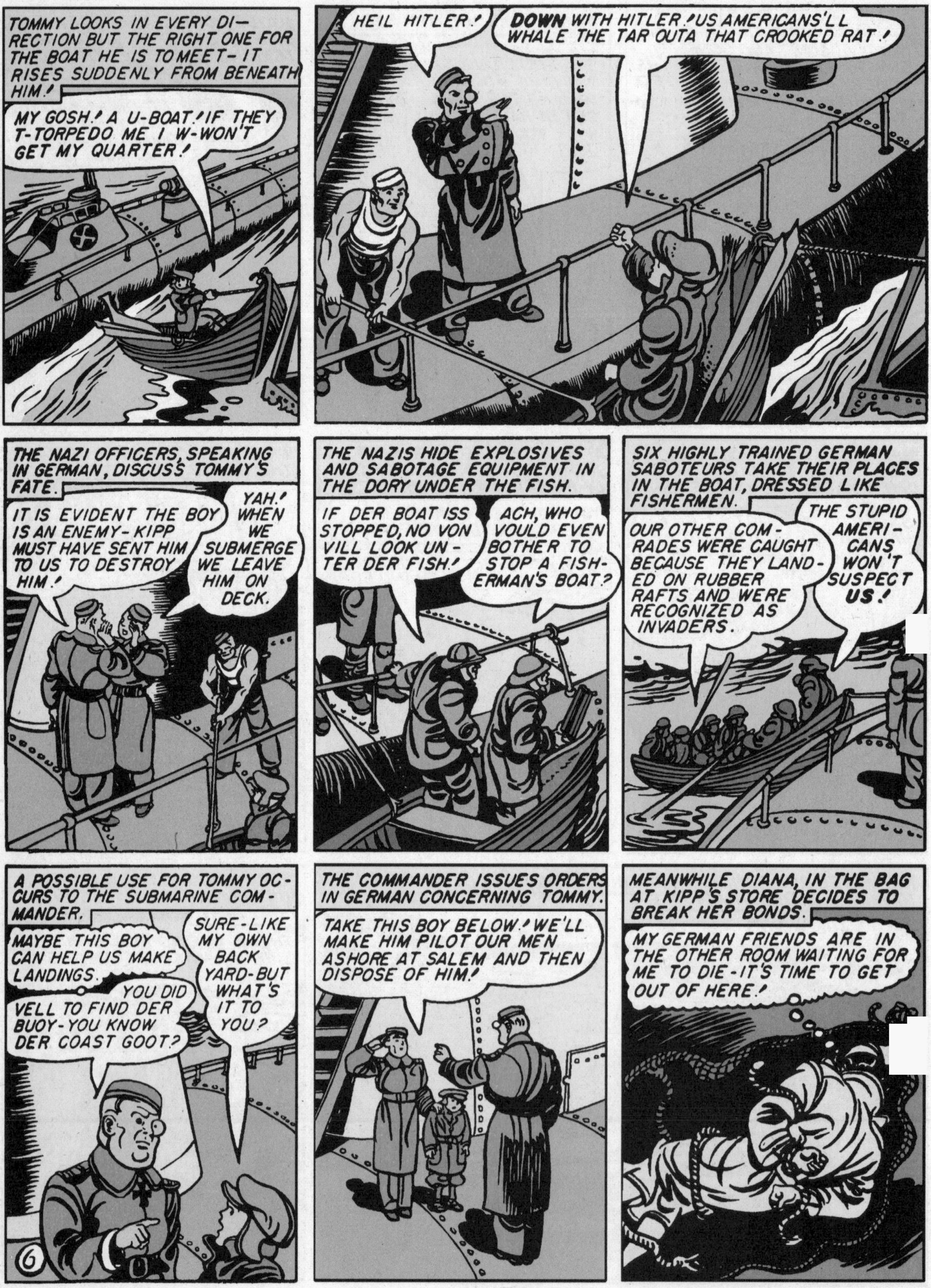
TOMMY LOOKS IN EVERY DIRECTION BUT THE RIGHT ONE FOR THE BOAT HE IS TO MEET- IT RISES SUDDENLY FROM BENEATH HIM!
MY GOSH! A U-BOAT! IF THEY T-TORPEDO ME I W-WON'T GET MY QUARTER!
HEIL HITLER!
DOWN WITH HITLER! US AMERICANS'LL WHALE THE TAR OUTA THAT CROOKED RAT!
THE NAZI OFFICERS, SPEAKING IN GERMAN, DISCUSS TOMMY'S FATE.
IT IS EVIDENT THE BOY IS AN ENEMY- KIPP MUST HAVE SENT HIM TO US TO DESTROY HIM!
YAH! WHEN WE SUBMERGE WE LEAVE HIM ON DECK.
THE NAZIS HIDE EXPLOSIVES AND SABOTAGE EQUIPMENT IN THE DORY UNDER THE FISH.
IF DER BOAT ISS STOPPED, NO VON VILL LOOK UNTER DER FISH!
ACH, WHO VOULD EVEN BOTHER TO STOP A FISHERMAN'S BOAT?
SIX HIGHLY TRAINED GERMAN SABOTEURS TAKE THEIR PLACES IN THE BOAT, DRESSED LIKE FISHERMEN.
OUR OTHER COMRADES WERE CAUGHT BECAUSE THEY LANDED ON RUBBER RAFTS AND WERE RECOGNIZED AS INVADERS.
THE STUPID AMERICANS WON'T SUSPECT US!
A POSSIBLE USE FOR TOMMY OCCURS TO THE SUBMARINE COMMANDER.
MAYBE THIS BOY CAN HELP US MAKE LANDINGS.
YOU DID VELL TO FIND DER BUOY-YOU KNOW DER COAST GOOT?
SURE-LIKE MY OWN BACK YARD-BUT WHAT'S IT TO YOU?
6
THE COMMANDER ISSUES ORDERS IN GERMAN CONCERNING TOMMY.
TAKE THIS BOY BELOW! WE'LL MAKE HIM PILOT OUR MEN ASHORE AT SALEM AND THEN DISPOSE OF HIM!
MEANWHILE DIANA, IN THE BAG AT KIPP'S STORE DECIDES TO BREAK HER BONDS.
MY GERMAN FRIENDS ARE IN THE OTHER ROOM WAITING FOR ME TO DIE-IT'S TIME TO GET OUT OF HERE!

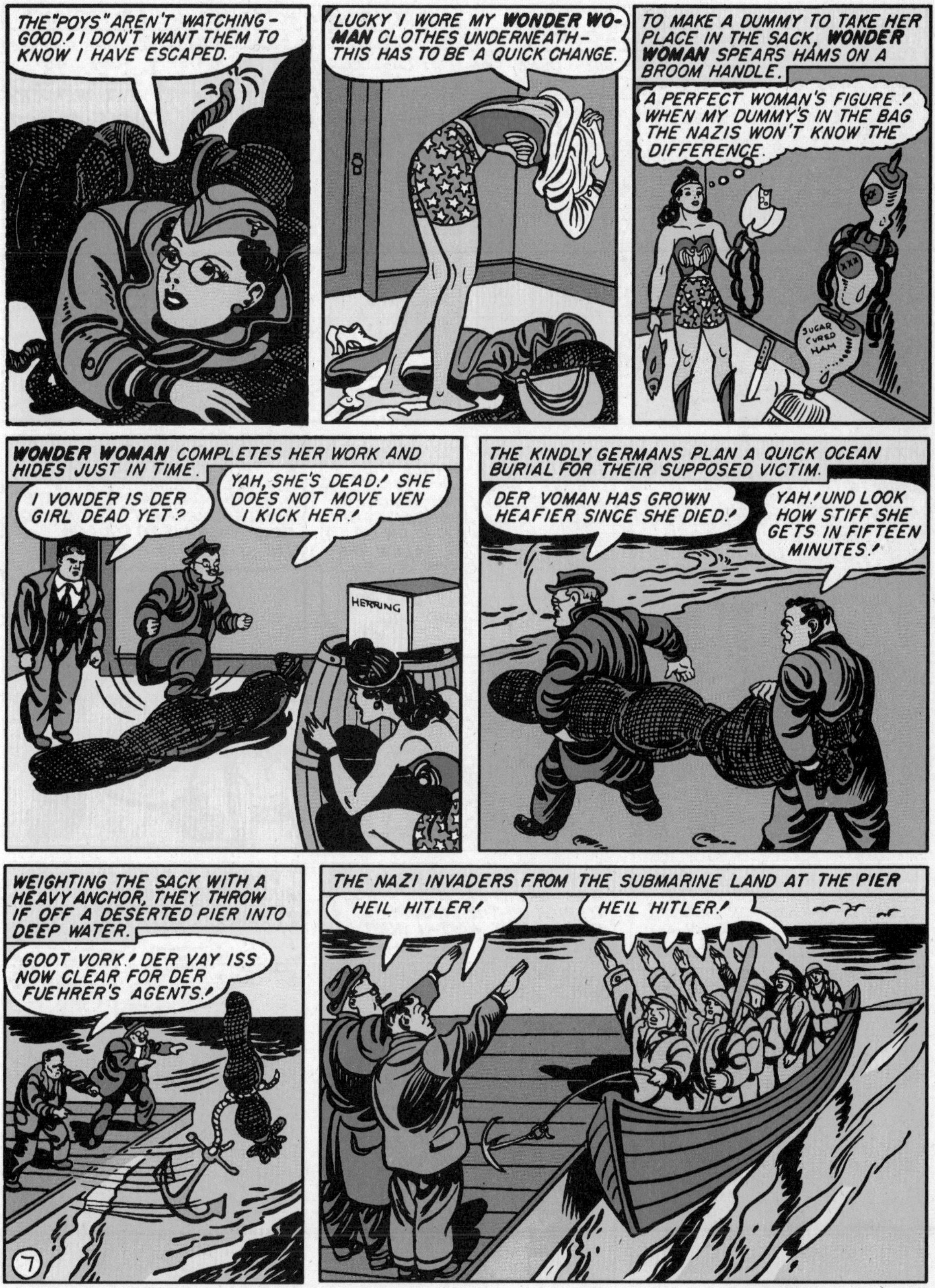

THE "POYS" AREN'T WATCHING - GOOD! I DON'T WANT THEM TO KNOW I HAVE ESCAPED.
LUCKY I WORE MY **WONDER WOMAN** CLOTHES UNDERNEATH - THIS HAS TO BE A QUICK CHANGE.
TO MAKE A DUMMY TO TAKE HER PLACE IN THE SACK, **WONDER WOMAN** SPEARS HAMS ON A BROOM HANDLE.
A PERFECT WOMAN'S FIGURE! WHEN MY DUMMY'S IN THE BAG THE NAZIS WON'T KNOW THE DIFFERENCE.
SUGAR CURED HAM
WONDER WOMAN COMPLETES HER WORK AND HIDES JUST IN TIME.
I VONDER IS DER GIRL DEAD YET?
YAH, SHE'S DEAD! SHE DOES NOT MOVE VEN I KICK HER!
HERRING
THE KINDLY GERMANS PLAN A QUICK OCEAN BURIAL FOR THEIR SUPPOSED VICTIM.
DER VOMAN HAS GROWN HEAFIER SINCE SHE DIED!
YAH! UND LOOK HOW STIFF SHE GETS IN FIFTEEN MINUTES!
WEIGHTING THE SACK WITH A HEAVY ANCHOR, THEY THROW IF OFF A DESERTED PIER INTO DEEP WATER.
GOOT VORK! DER VAY ISS NOW CLEAR FOR DER FUEHRER'S AGENTS!
7
THE NAZI INVADERS FROM THE SUBMARINE LAND AT THE PIER
HEIL HITLER!
HEIL HITLER!

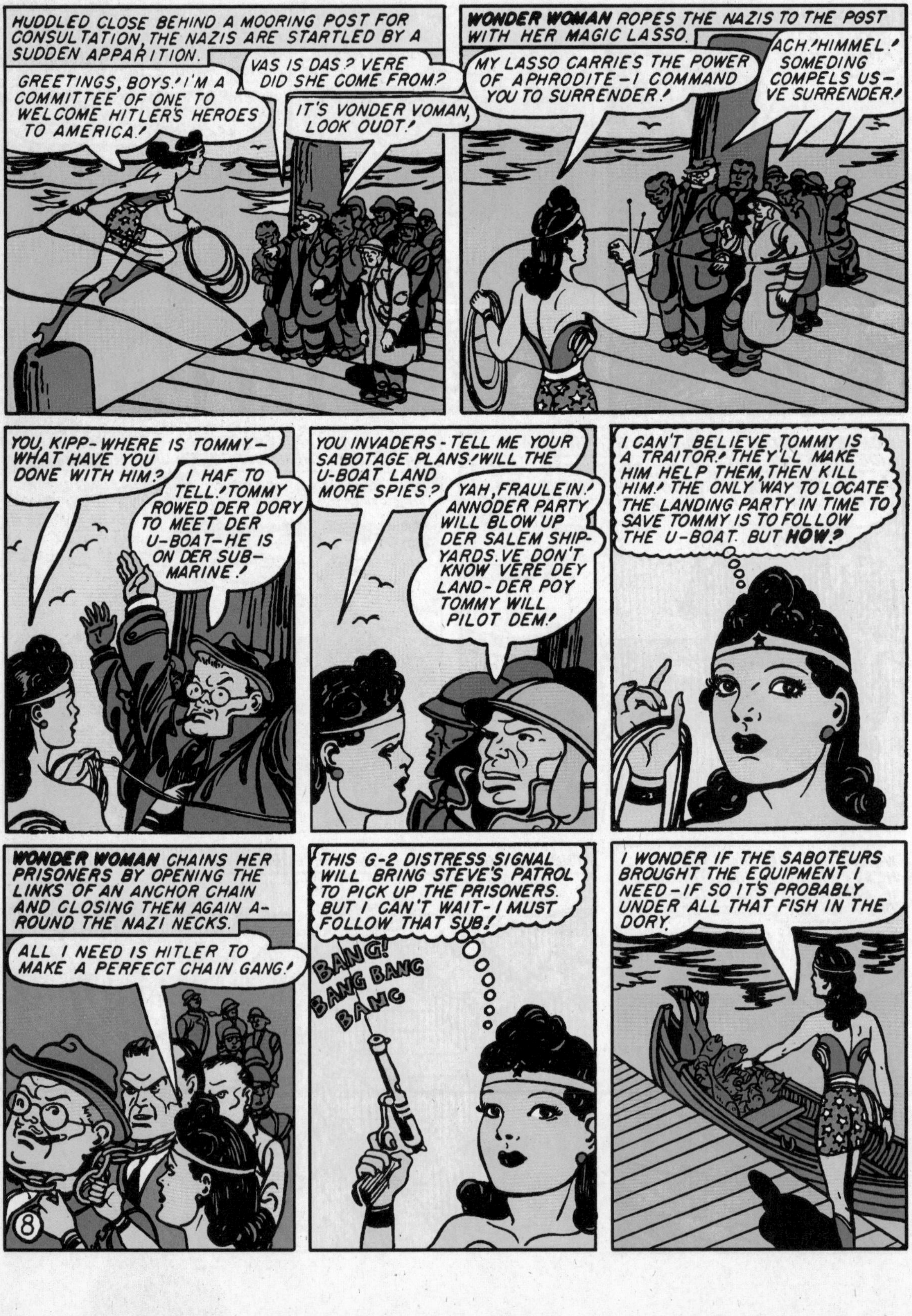

HUDDLED CLOSE BEHIND A MOORING POST FOR CONSULTATION, THE NAZIS ARE STARTLED BY A SUDDEN APPARITION.
GREETINGS, BOYS! I'M A COMMITTEE OF ONE TO WELCOME HITLER'S HEROES TO AMERICA!
VAS IS DAS? VERE DID SHE COME FROM?
IT'S VONDER VOMAN, LOOK OUDT!
WONDER WOMAN ROPES THE NAZIS TO THE POST WITH HER MAGIC LASSO.
MY LASSO CARRIES THE POWER OF APHRODITE – I COMMAND YOU TO SURRENDER!
ACH! HIMMEL! SOMEDING COMPELS US – VE SURRENDER!
YOU, KIPP – WHERE IS TOMMY – WHAT HAVE YOU DONE WITH HIM?
I HAF TO TELL! TOMMY ROWED DER DORY TO MEET DER U-BOAT – HE IS ON DER SUBMARINE!
YOU INVADERS – TELL ME YOUR SABOTAGE PLANS! WILL THE U-BOAT LAND MORE SPIES?
YAH, FRAULEIN! ANNODER PARTY WILL BLOW UP DER SALEM SHIPYARDS. VE DON'T KNOW VERE DEY LAND – DER POY TOMMY WILL PILOT DEM!
I CAN'T BELIEVE TOMMY IS A TRAITOR! THEY'LL MAKE HIM HELP THEM, THEN KILL HIM! THE ONLY WAY TO LOCATE THE LANDING PARTY IN TIME TO SAVE TOMMY IS TO FOLLOW THE U-BOAT. BUT HOW?
WONDER WOMAN CHAINS HER PRISONERS BY OPENING THE LINKS OF AN ANCHOR CHAIN AND CLOSING THEM AGAIN AROUND THE NAZI NECKS.
ALL I NEED IS HITLER TO MAKE A PERFECT CHAIN GANG!
8
THIS G-2 DISTRESS SIGNAL WILL BRING STEVE'S PATROL TO PICK UP THE PRISONERS. BUT I CAN'T WAIT – I MUST FOLLOW THAT SUB!
BANG! BANG BANG BANG
I WONDER IF THE SABOTEURS BROUGHT THE EQUIPMENT I NEED – IF SO IT'S PROBABLY UNDER ALL THAT FISH IN THE DORY.

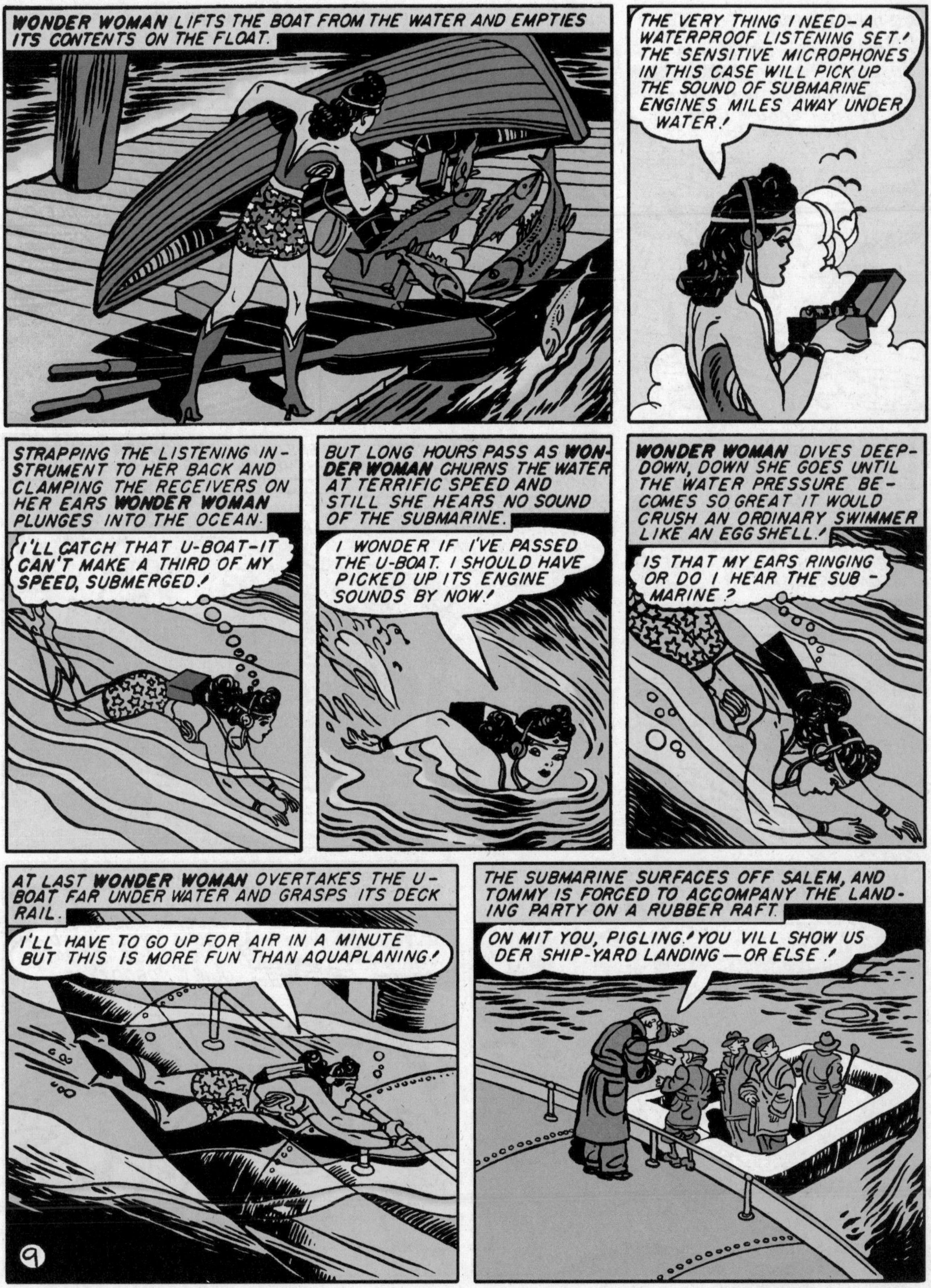
WONDER WOMAN LIFTS THE BOAT FROM THE WATER AND EMPTIES ITS CONTENTS ON THE FLOAT.
THE VERY THING I NEED– A WATERPROOF LISTENING SET! THE SENSITIVE MICROPHONES IN THIS CASE WILL PICK UP THE SOUND OF SUBMARINE ENGINES MILES AWAY UNDER WATER!
STRAPPING THE LISTENING INSTRUMENT TO HER BACK AND CLAMPING THE RECEIVERS ON HER EARS WONDER WOMAN PLUNGES INTO THE OCEAN.
I'LL CATCH THAT U-BOAT–IT CAN'T MAKE A THIRD OF MY SPEED, SUBMERGED!
BUT LONG HOURS PASS AS WONDER WOMAN CHURNS THE WATER AT TERRIFIC SPEED AND STILL SHE HEARS NO SOUND OF THE SUBMARINE.
I WONDER IF I'VE PASSED THE U-BOAT. I SHOULD HAVE PICKED UP ITS ENGINE SOUNDS BY NOW!
WONDER WOMAN DIVES DEEP–DOWN, DOWN SHE GOES UNTIL THE WATER PRESSURE BECOMES SO GREAT IT WOULD CRUSH AN ORDINARY SWIMMER LIKE AN EGG SHELL!
IS THAT MY EARS RINGING OR DO I HEAR THE SUBMARINE?
AT LAST WONDER WOMAN OVERTAKES THE U-BOAT FAR UNDER WATER AND GRASPS ITS DECK RAIL.
I'LL HAVE TO GO UP FOR AIR IN A MINUTE BUT THIS IS MORE FUN THAN AQUAPLANING!
9
THE SUBMARINE SURFACES OFF SALEM, AND TOMMY IS FORCED TO ACCOMPANY THE LANDING PARTY ON A RUBBER RAFT.
ON MIT YOU, PIGLING! YOU VILL SHOW US DER SHIP-YARD LANDING — OR ELSE!

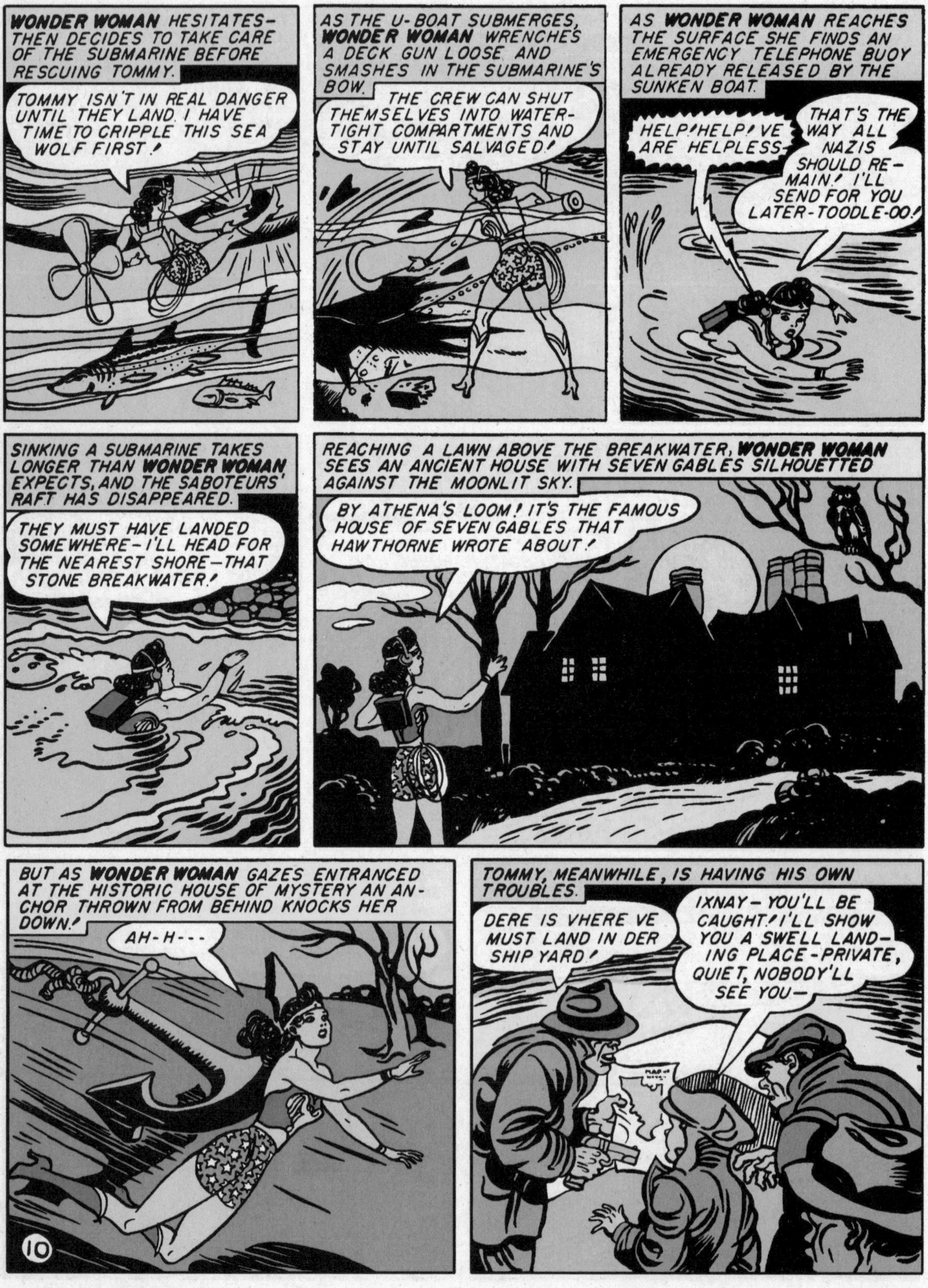
WONDER WOMAN HESITATES—THEN DECIDES TO TAKE CARE OF THE SUBMARINE BEFORE RESCUING TOMMY.
TOMMY ISN'T IN REAL DANGER UNTIL THEY LAND. I HAVE TIME TO CRIPPLE THIS SEA WOLF FIRST!
AS THE U-BOAT SUBMERGES, WONDER WOMAN WRENCHES A DECK GUN LOOSE AND SMASHES IN THE SUBMARINE'S BOW.
THE CREW CAN SHUT THEMSELVES INTO WATER-TIGHT COMPARTMENTS AND STAY UNTIL SALVAGED!
AS WONDER WOMAN REACHES THE SURFACE SHE FINDS AN EMERGENCY TELEPHONE BUOY ALREADY RELEASED BY THE SUNKEN BOAT.
HELP! HELP! VE ARE HELPLESS—
THAT'S THE WAY ALL NAZIS SHOULD REMAIN! I'LL SEND FOR YOU LATER-TOODLE-OO!
SINKING A SUBMARINE TAKES LONGER THAN WONDER WOMAN EXPECTS, AND THE SABOTEURS' RAFT HAS DISAPPEARED.
THEY MUST HAVE LANDED SOMEWHERE—I'LL HEAD FOR THE NEAREST SHORE—THAT STONE BREAKWATER!
REACHING A LAWN ABOVE THE BREAKWATER, WONDER WOMAN SEES AN ANCIENT HOUSE WITH SEVEN GABLES SILHOUETTED AGAINST THE MOONLIT SKY.
BY ATHENA'S LOOM! IT'S THE FAMOUS HOUSE OF SEVEN GABLES THAT HAWTHORNE WROTE ABOUT!
BUT AS WONDER WOMAN GAZES ENTRANCED AT THE HISTORIC HOUSE OF MYSTERY AN ANCHOR THROWN FROM BEHIND KNOCKS HER DOWN!
AH-H---
10
TOMMY, MEANWHILE, IS HAVING HIS OWN TROUBLES.
DERE IS VHERE VE MUST LAND IN DER SHIP YARD!
IXNAY—YOU'LL BE CAUGHT! I'LL SHOW YOU A SWELL LANDING PLACE-PRIVATE, QUIET, NOBODY'LL SEE YOU—

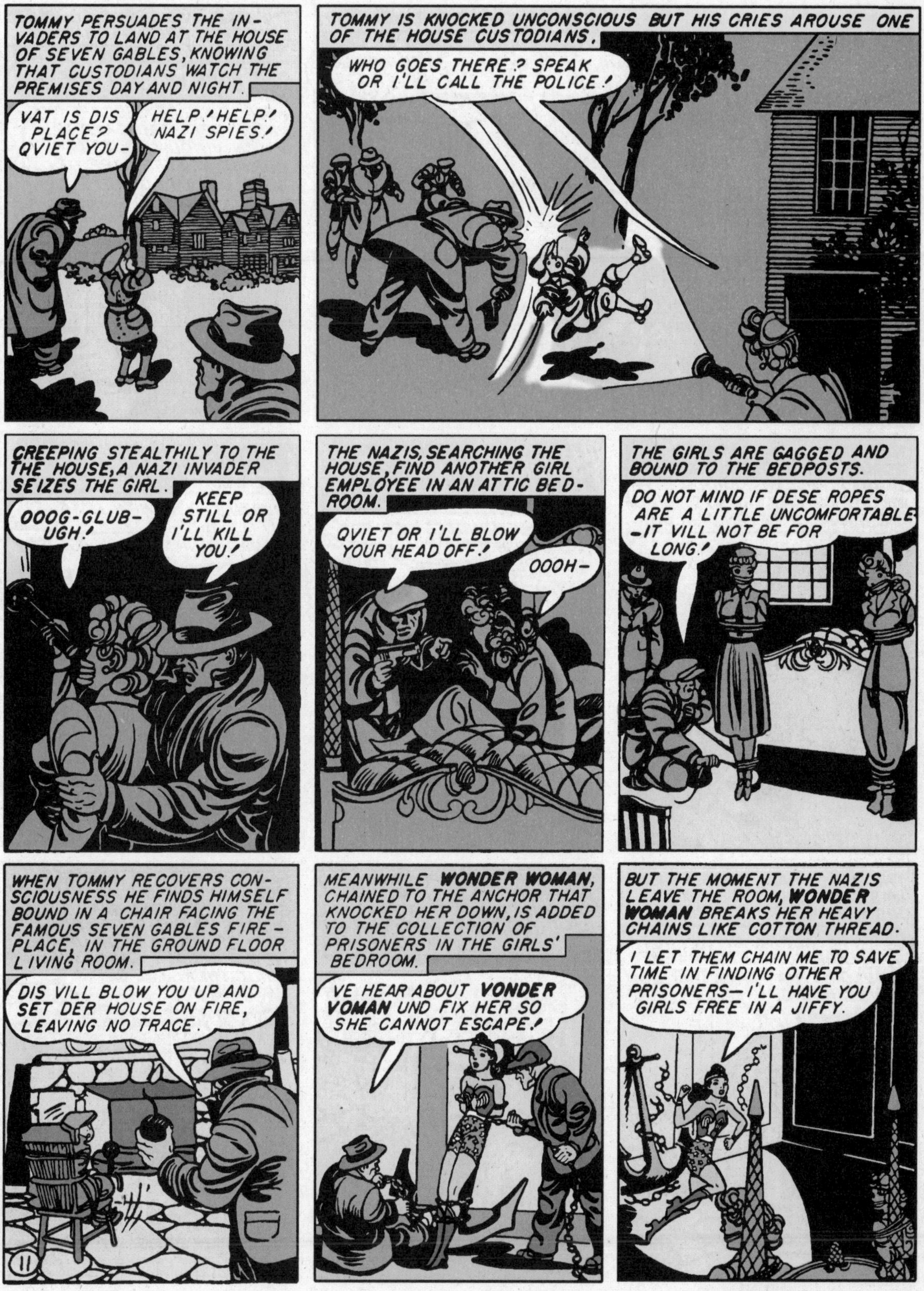
TOMMY PERSUADES THE INVADERS TO LAND AT THE HOUSE OF SEVEN GABLES, KNOWING THAT CUSTODIANS WATCH THE PREMISES DAY AND NIGHT.
VAT IS DIS PLACE? QVIET YOU-
HELP! HELP! NAZI SPIES!
TOMMY IS KNOCKED UNCONSCIOUS BUT HIS CRIES AROUSE ONE OF THE HOUSE CUSTODIANS.
WHO GOES THERE? SPEAK OR I'LL CALL THE POLICE!
CREEPING STEALTHILY TO THE THE HOUSE, A NAZI INVADER SEIZES THE GIRL.
OOOG-GLUB-UGH!
KEEP STILL OR I'LL KILL YOU!
THE NAZIS, SEARCHING THE HOUSE, FIND ANOTHER GIRL EMPLOYEE IN AN ATTIC BEDROOM.
QVIET OR I'LL BLOW YOUR HEAD OFF!
OOOH-
THE GIRLS ARE GAGGED AND BOUND TO THE BEDPOSTS.
DO NOT MIND IF DESE ROPES ARE A LITTLE UNCOMFORTABLE -IT VILL NOT BE FOR LONG!
WHEN TOMMY RECOVERS CONSCIOUSNESS HE FINDS HIMSELF BOUND IN A CHAIR FACING THE FAMOUS SEVEN GABLES FIRE-PLACE, IN THE GROUND FLOOR LIVING ROOM.
DIS VILL BLOW YOU UP AND SET DER HOUSE ON FIRE, LEAVING NO TRACE.
11
MEANWHILE WONDER WOMAN, CHAINED TO THE ANCHOR THAT KNOCKED HER DOWN, IS ADDED TO THE COLLECTION OF PRISONERS IN THE GIRLS' BEDROOM.
VE HEAR ABOUT VONDER VOMAN UND FIX HER SO SHE CANNOT ESCAPE!
BUT THE MOMENT THE NAZIS LEAVE THE ROOM, WONDER WOMAN BREAKS HER HEAVY CHAINS LIKE COTTON THREAD.
I LET THEM CHAIN ME TO SAVE TIME IN FINDING OTHER PRISONERS—I'LL HAVE YOU GIRLS FREE IN A JIFFY.

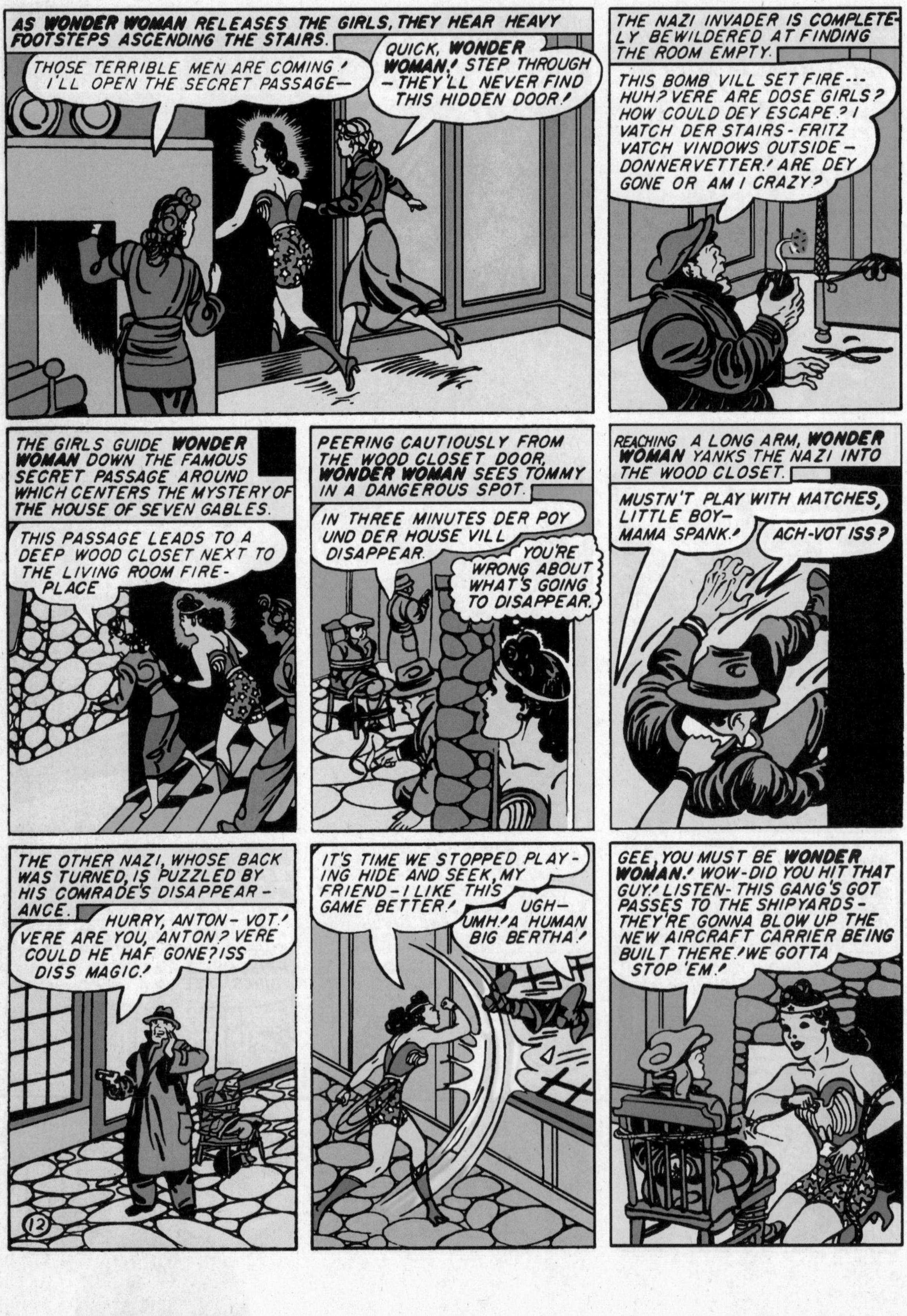
AS WONDER WOMAN RELEASES THE GIRLS, THEY HEAR HEAVY FOOTSTEPS ASCENDING THE STAIRS.
THOSE TERRIBLE MEN ARE COMING! I'LL OPEN THE SECRET PASSAGE—
QUICK, WONDER WOMAN! STEP THROUGH —THEY'LL NEVER FIND THIS HIDDEN DOOR!
THE NAZI INVADER IS COMPLETELY BEWILDERED AT FINDING THE ROOM EMPTY.
THIS BOMB VILL SET FIRE--- HUH? VERE ARE DOSE GIRLS? HOW COULD DEY ESCAPE? I VATCH DER STAIRS - FRITZ VATCH VINDOWS OUTSIDE — DONNERVETTER! ARE DEY GONE OR AM I CRAZY?
THE GIRLS GUIDE WONDER WOMAN DOWN THE FAMOUS SECRET PASSAGE AROUND WHICH CENTERS THE MYSTERY OF THE HOUSE OF SEVEN GABLES.
THIS PASSAGE LEADS TO A DEEP WOOD CLOSET NEXT TO THE LIVING ROOM FIRE-PLACE
PEERING CAUTIOUSLY FROM THE WOOD CLOSET DOOR, WONDER WOMAN SEES TOMMY IN A DANGEROUS SPOT.
IN THREE MINUTES DER POY UND DER HOUSE VILL DISAPPEAR.
YOU'RE WRONG ABOUT WHAT'S GOING TO DISAPPEAR.
REACHING A LONG ARM, WONDER WOMAN YANKS THE NAZI INTO THE WOOD CLOSET.
MUSTN'T PLAY WITH MATCHES, LITTLE BOY— MAMA SPANK!
ACH-VOT ISS?
THE OTHER NAZI, WHOSE BACK WAS TURNED, IS PUZZLED BY HIS COMRADE'S DISAPPEARANCE.
HURRY, ANTON- VOT! VERE ARE YOU, ANTON? VERE COULD HE HAF GONE? ISS DISS MAGIC!
12
IT'S TIME WE STOPPED PLAYING HIDE AND SEEK, MY FRIEND—I LIKE THIS GAME BETTER!
UGH— UMH! A HUMAN BIG BERTHA!
GEE, YOU MUST BE WONDER WOMAN! WOW-DID YOU HIT THAT GUY! LISTEN- THIS GANG'S GOT PASSES TO THE SHIPYARDS - THEY'RE GONNA BLOW UP THE NEW AIRCRAFT CARRIER BEING BUILT THERE! WE GOTTA STOP 'EM!

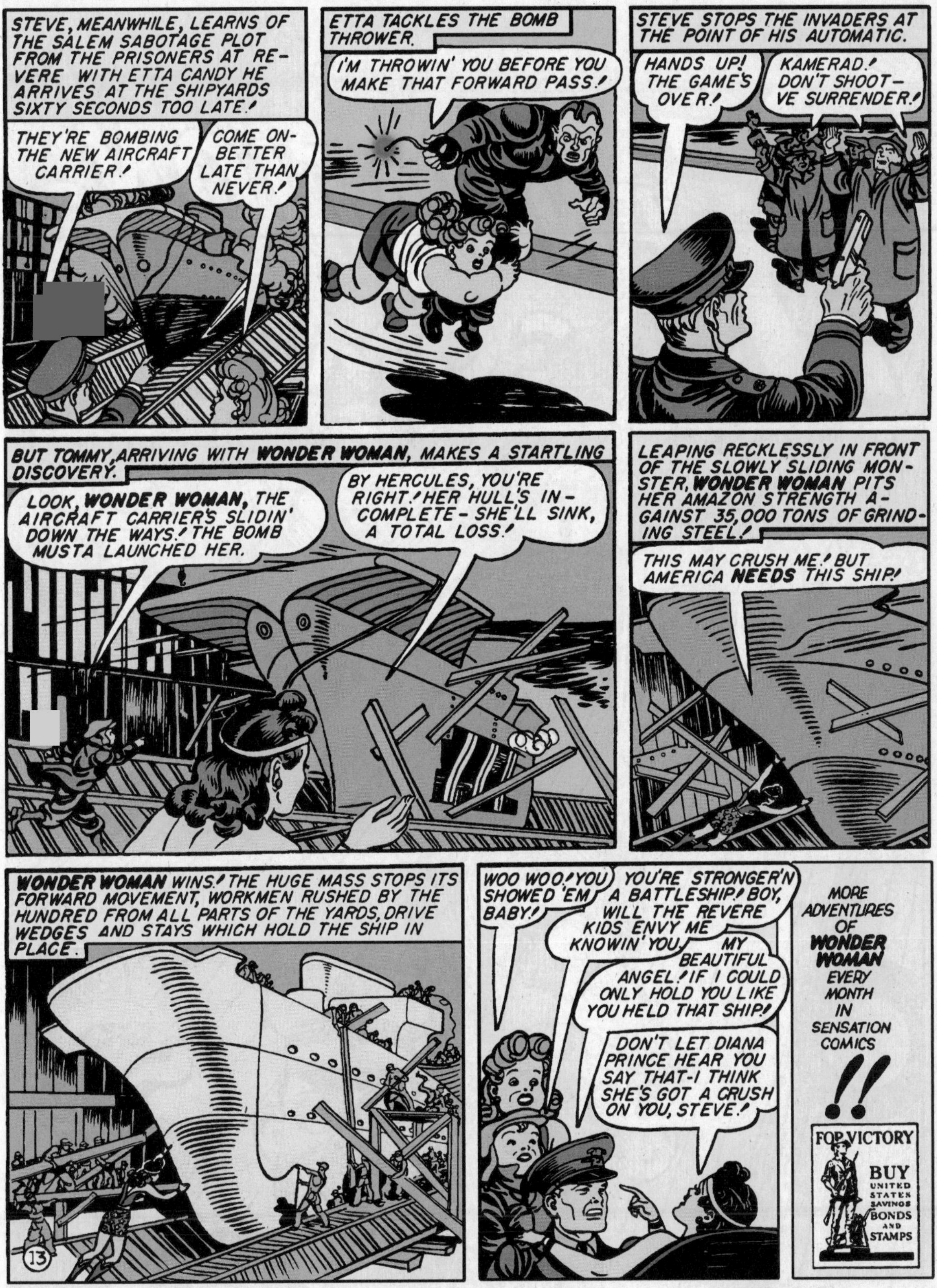

STEVE, MEANWHILE, LEARNS OF THE SALEM SABOTAGE PLOT FROM THE PRISONERS AT REVERE WITH ETTA CANDY HE ARRIVES AT THE SHIPYARDS SIXTY SECONDS TOO LATE!
THEY'RE BOMBING THE NEW AIRCRAFT CARRIER!
COME ON- BETTER LATE THAN NEVER!
ETTA TACKLES THE BOMB THROWER.
I'M THROWIN' YOU BEFORE YOU MAKE THAT FORWARD PASS!
STEVE STOPS THE INVADERS AT THE POINT OF HIS AUTOMATIC.
HANDS UP! THE GAME'S OVER!
KAMERAD! DON'T SHOOT- VE SURRENDER!
BUT TOMMY, ARRIVING WITH WONDER WOMAN, MAKES A STARTLING DISCOVERY.
LOOK, WONDER WOMAN, THE AIRCRAFT CARRIER'S SLIDIN' DOWN THE WAYS! THE BOMB MUSTA LAUNCHED HER.
BY HERCULES, YOU'RE RIGHT! HER HULL'S INCOMPLETE - SHE'LL SINK, A TOTAL LOSS!
LEAPING RECKLESSLY IN FRONT OF THE SLOWLY SLIDING MONSTER, WONDER WOMAN PITS HER AMAZON STRENGTH AGAINST 35,000 TONS OF GRINDING STEEL!
THIS MAY CRUSH ME! BUT AMERICA NEEDS THIS SHIP!
WONDER WOMAN WINS! THE HUGE MASS STOPS ITS FORWARD MOVEMENT, WORKMEN RUSHED BY THE HUNDRED FROM ALL PARTS OF THE YARDS, DRIVE WEDGES AND STAYS WHICH HOLD THE SHIP IN PLACE.
13
WOO WOO! YOU SHOWED 'EM BABY!
YOU'RE STRONGER'N A BATTLESHIP! BOY, WILL THE REVERE KIDS ENVY ME KNOWIN' YOU!
MY BEAUTIFUL ANGEL! IF I COULD ONLY HOLD YOU LIKE YOU HELD THAT SHIP!
DON'T LET DIANA PRINCE HEAR YOU SAY THAT-I THINK SHE'S GOT A CRUSH ON YOU, STEVE!
MORE ADVENTURES OF WONDER WOMAN EVERY MONTH IN SENSATION COMICS
!!
FOR VICTORY
BUY UNITED STATES SAVINGS BONDS AND STAMPS

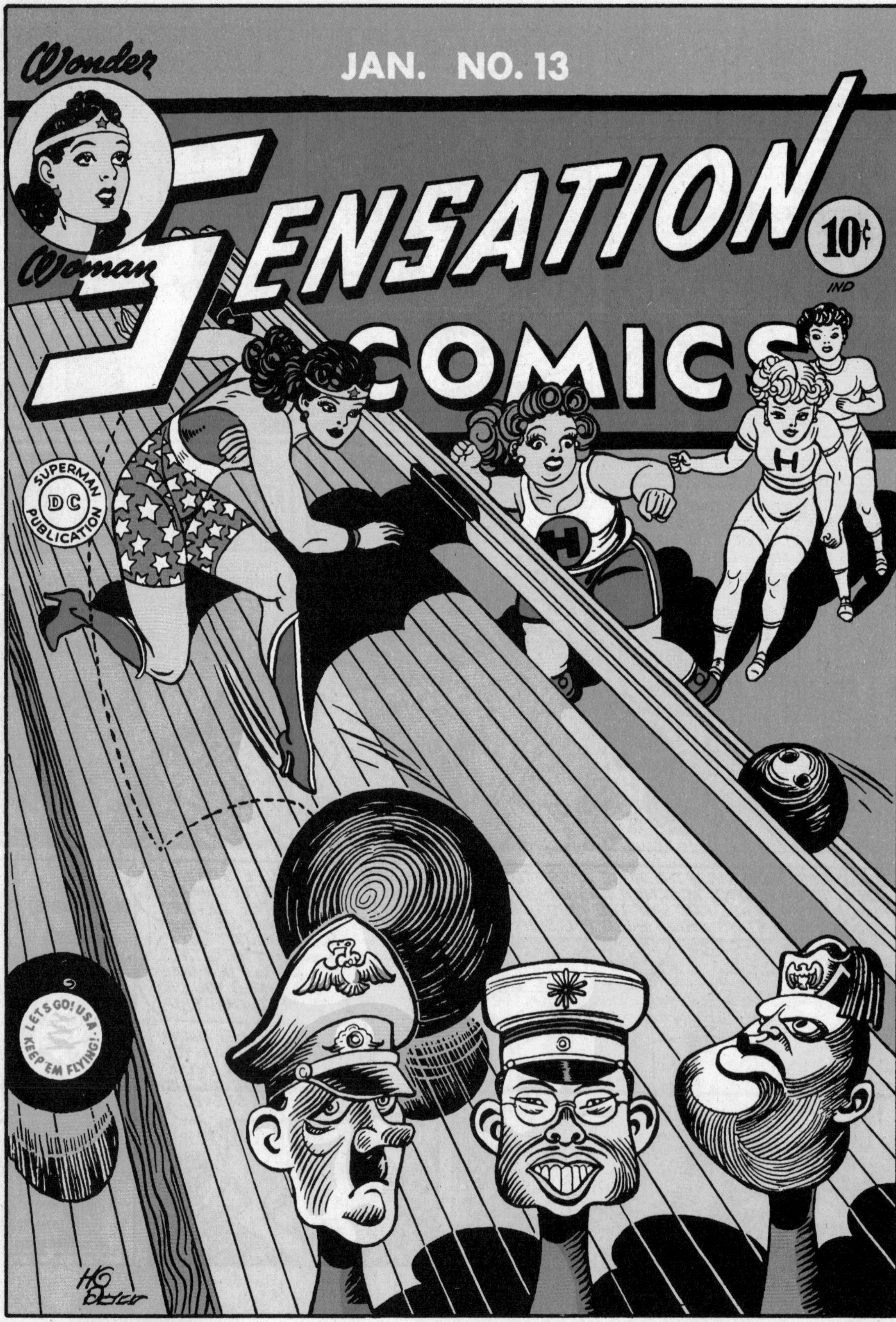
Wonder Woman
JAN. NO. 13
SENSATION COMICS
10¢
IND
SUPERMAN DC PUBLICATION
LET'S GO! U.S.A. KEEP 'EM FLYING!
H
H

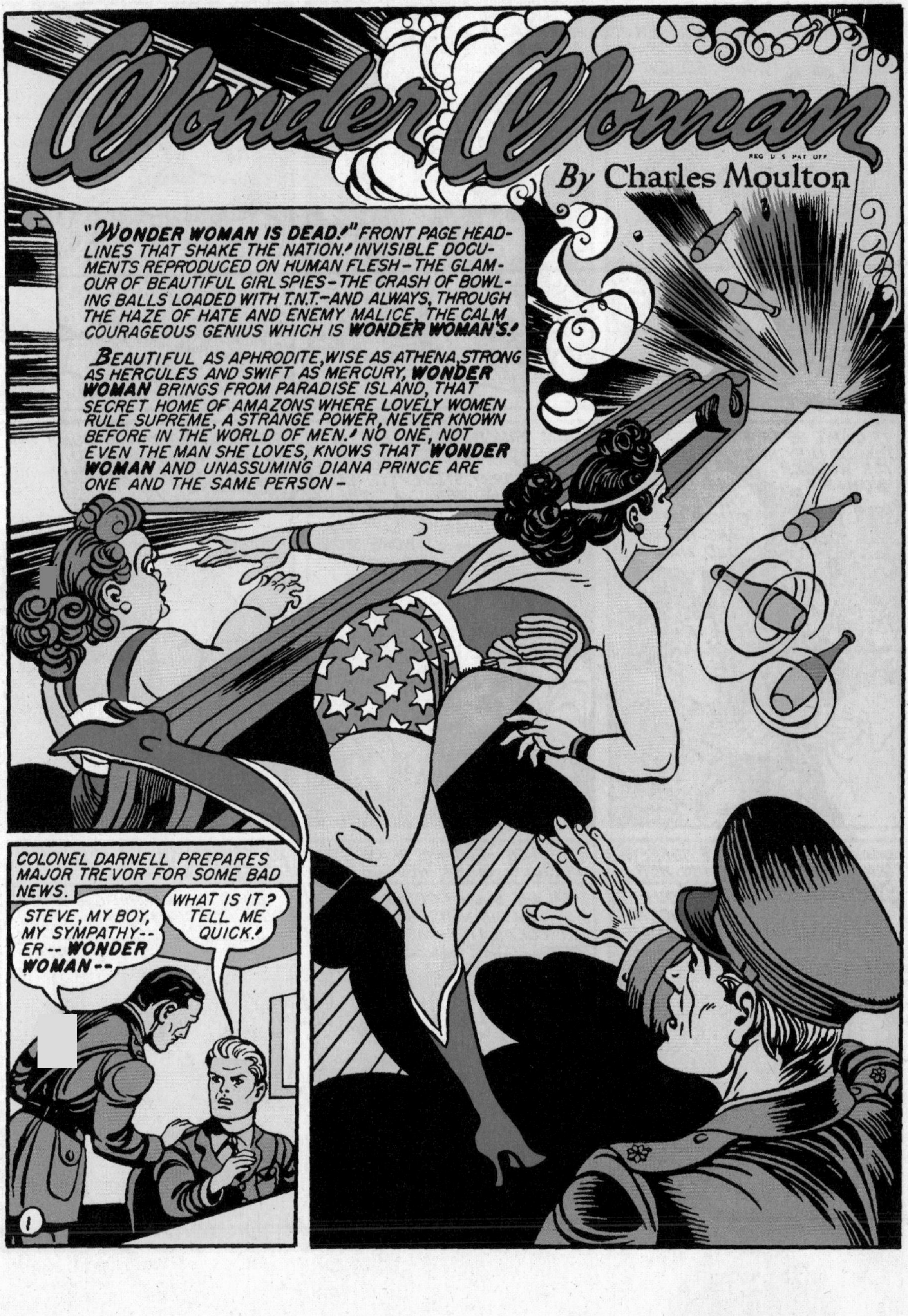
Wonder Woman
REG U S PAT OFF
By Charles Moulton
"WONDER WOMAN IS DEAD!" FRONT PAGE HEADLINES THAT SHAKE THE NATION! INVISIBLE DOCUMENTS REPRODUCED ON HUMAN FLESH - THE GLAMOUR OF BEAUTIFUL GIRL SPIES - THE CRASH OF BOWLING BALLS LOADED WITH T.N.T.- AND ALWAYS, THROUGH THE HAZE OF HATE AND ENEMY MALICE, THE CALM COURAGEOUS GENIUS WHICH IS WONDER WOMAN'S!
BEAUTIFUL AS APHRODITE, WISE AS ATHENA, STRONG AS HERCULES AND SWIFT AS MERCURY, WONDER WOMAN BRINGS FROM PARADISE ISLAND, THAT SECRET HOME OF AMAZONS WHERE LOVELY WOMEN RULE SUPREME, A STRANGE POWER, NEVER KNOWN BEFORE IN THE WORLD OF MEN! NO ONE, NOT EVEN THE MAN SHE LOVES, KNOWS THAT WONDER WOMAN AND UNASSUMING DIANA PRINCE ARE ONE AND THE SAME PERSON -
COLONEL DARNELL PREPARES MAJOR TREVOR FOR SOME BAD NEWS.
STEVE, MY BOY, MY SYMPATHY-- ER -- WONDER WOMAN --
WHAT IS IT? TELL ME QUICK!
1

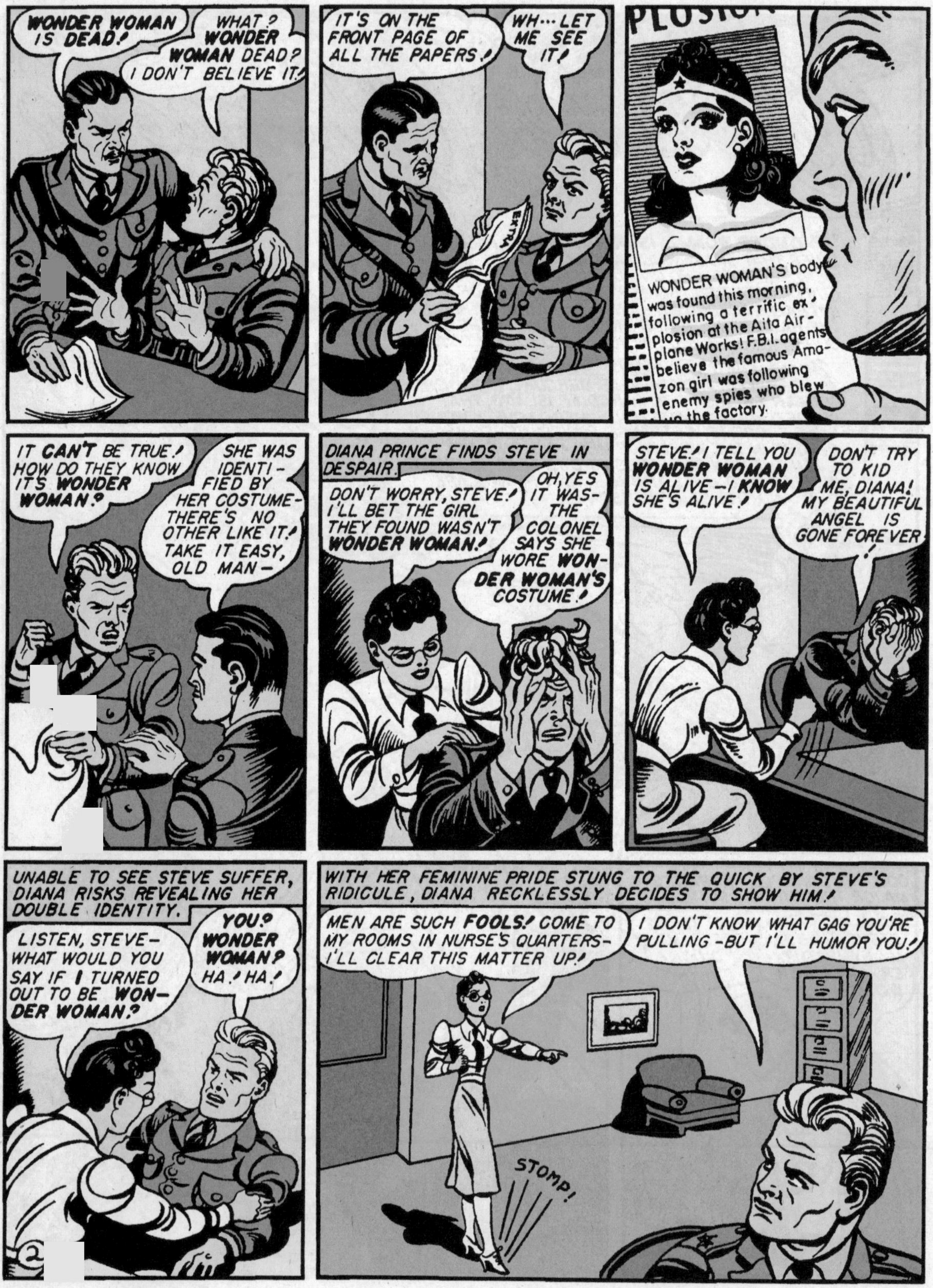
WONDER WOMAN IS DEAD!
WHAT? WONDER WOMAN DEAD? I DON'T BELIEVE IT!
IT'S ON THE FRONT PAGE OF ALL THE PAPERS!
WH... LET ME SEE IT!
EXTRA
PLOSION
WONDER WOMAN'S body was found this morning, following a terrific explosion at the Aita Airplane Works! F.B.I. agents believe the famous Amazon girl was following enemy spies who blew up the factory.
IT CAN'T BE TRUE! HOW DO THEY KNOW IT'S WONDER WOMAN?
SHE WAS IDENTIFIED BY HER COSTUME-THERE'S NO OTHER LIKE IT! TAKE IT EASY, OLD MAN-
DIANA PRINCE FINDS STEVE IN DESPAIR.
DON'T WORRY, STEVE! I'LL BET THE GIRL THEY FOUND WASN'T WONDER WOMAN!
OH, YES IT WAS-THE COLONEL SAYS SHE WORE WONDER WOMAN'S COSTUME!
STEVE! I TELL YOU WONDER WOMAN IS ALIVE-I KNOW SHE'S ALIVE!
DON'T TRY TO KID ME, DIANA! MY BEAUTIFUL ANGEL IS GONE FOREVER!
UNABLE TO SEE STEVE SUFFER, DIANA RISKS REVEALING HER DOUBLE IDENTITY.
LISTEN, STEVE-WHAT WOULD YOU SAY IF I TURNED OUT TO BE WONDER WOMAN?
YOU? WONDER WOMAN? HA! HA!
2
WITH HER FEMININE PRIDE STUNG TO THE QUICK BY STEVE'S RIDICULE, DIANA RECKLESSLY DECIDES TO SHOW HIM!
MEN ARE SUCH FOOLS! COME TO MY ROOMS IN NURSE'S QUARTERS-I'LL CLEAR THIS MATTER UP!
I DON'T KNOW WHAT GAG YOU'RE PULLING-BUT I'LL HUMOR YOU!
STOMP!

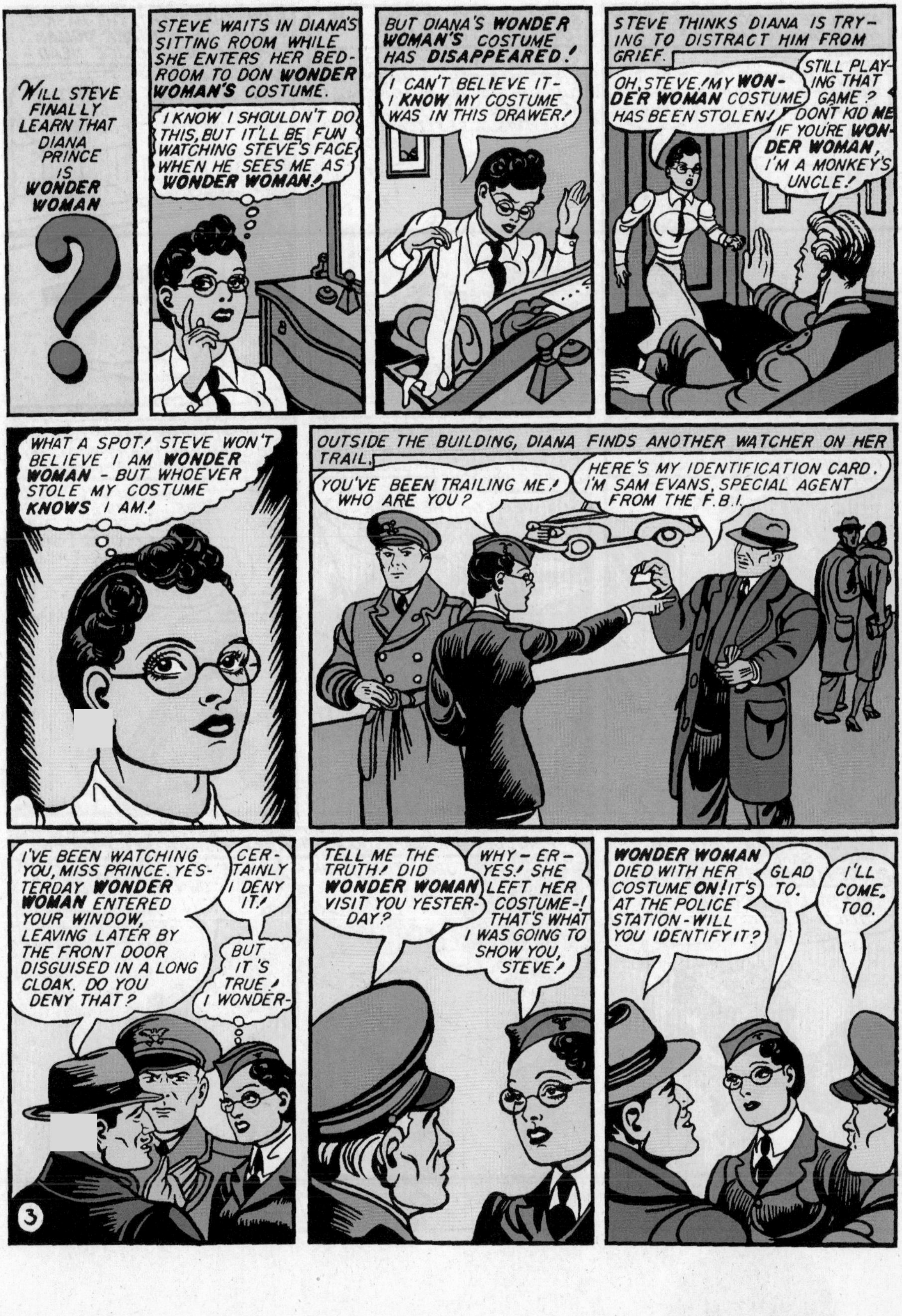
WILL STEVE FINALLY LEARN THAT DIANA PRINCE IS WONDER WOMAN ?
STEVE WAITS IN DIANA'S SITTING ROOM WHILE SHE ENTERS HER BED-ROOM TO DON WONDER WOMAN'S COSTUME.
I KNOW I SHOULDN'T DO THIS, BUT IT'LL BE FUN WATCHING STEVE'S FACE WHEN HE SEES ME AS WONDER WOMAN!
BUT DIANA'S WONDER WOMAN'S COSTUME HAS DISAPPEARED!
I CAN'T BELIEVE IT- I KNOW MY COSTUME WAS IN THIS DRAWER!
STEVE THINKS DIANA IS TRY-ING TO DISTRACT HIM FROM GRIEF.
OH, STEVE! MY WON-DER WOMAN COSTUME HAS BEEN STOLEN!
STILL PLAY-ING THAT GAME? DON'T KID ME! IF YOU'RE WON-DER WOMAN, I'M A MONKEY'S UNCLE!
WHAT A SPOT! STEVE WON'T BELIEVE I AM WONDER WOMAN - BUT WHOEVER STOLE MY COSTUME KNOWS I AM!
OUTSIDE THE BUILDING, DIANA FINDS ANOTHER WATCHER ON HER TRAIL.
YOU'VE BEEN TRAILING ME! WHO ARE YOU?
HERE'S MY IDENTIFICATION CARD. I'M SAM EVANS, SPECIAL AGENT FROM THE F.B.I.
I'VE BEEN WATCHING YOU, MISS PRINCE. YES-TERDAY WONDER WOMAN ENTERED YOUR WINDOW, LEAVING LATER BY THE FRONT DOOR DISGUISED IN A LONG CLOAK. DO YOU DENY THAT?
CER-TAINLY I DENY IT!
BUT IT'S TRUE! I WONDER-
TELL ME THE TRUTH! DID WONDER WOMAN VISIT YOU YESTER-DAY?
WHY - ER - YES! SHE LEFT HER COSTUME-! THAT'S WHAT I WAS GOING TO SHOW YOU, STEVE!
WONDER WOMAN DIED WITH HER COSTUME ON! IT'S AT THE POLICE STATION - WILL YOU IDENTIFY IT?
GLAD TO.
I'LL COME, TOO.
3

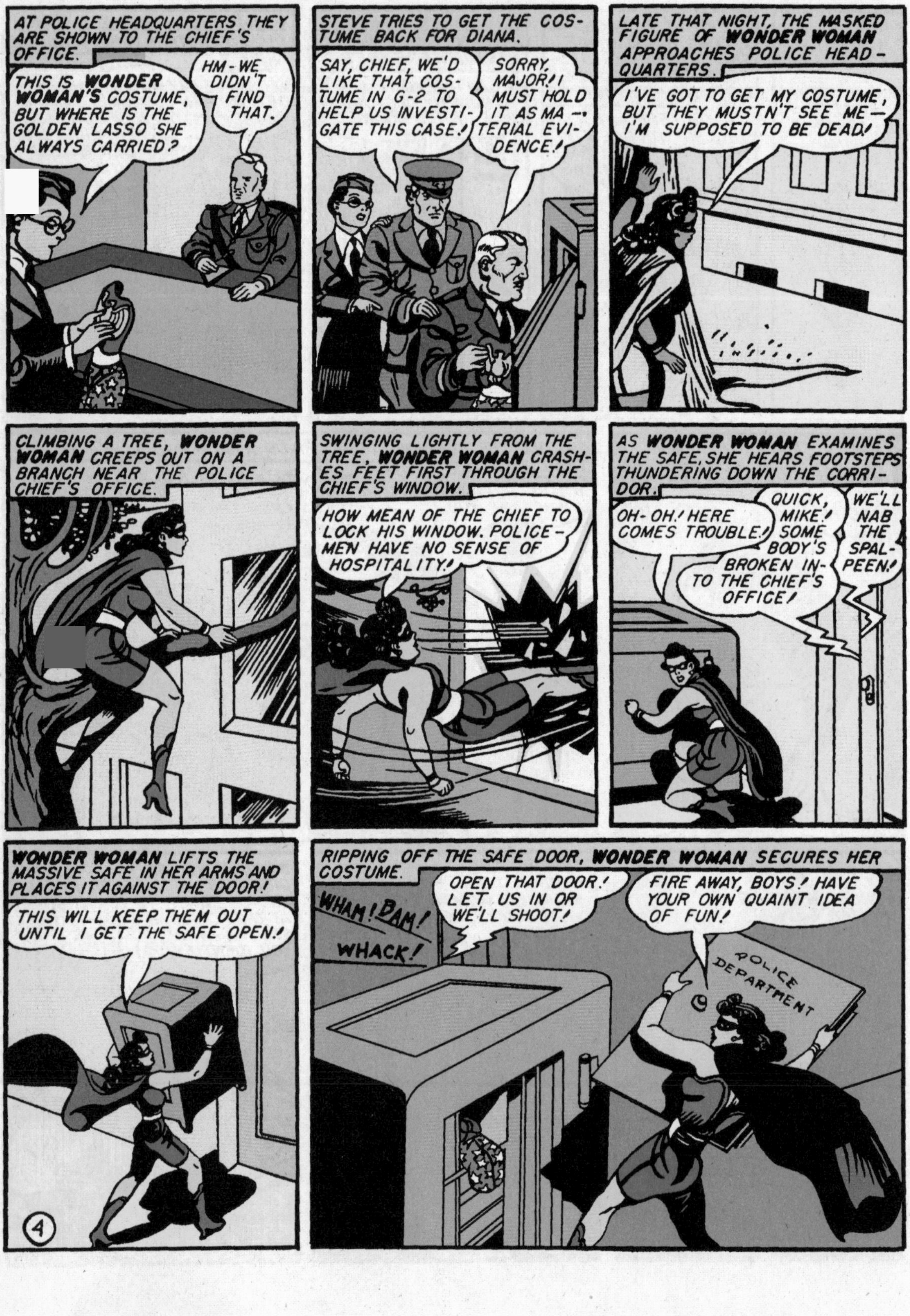
AT POLICE HEADQUARTERS THEY ARE SHOWN TO THE CHIEF'S OFFICE.
THIS IS WONDER WOMAN'S COSTUME, BUT WHERE IS THE GOLDEN LASSO SHE ALWAYS CARRIED?
HM-WE DIDN'T FIND THAT.
STEVE TRIES TO GET THE COSTUME BACK FOR DIANA.
SAY, CHIEF, WE'D LIKE THAT COSTUME IN G-2 TO HELP US INVESTIGATE THIS CASE!
SORRY, MAJOR! I MUST HOLD IT AS MATERIAL EVIDENCE!
LATE THAT NIGHT, THE MASKED FIGURE OF WONDER WOMAN APPROACHES POLICE HEADQUARTERS.
I'VE GOT TO GET MY COSTUME, BUT THEY MUSTN'T SEE ME— I'M SUPPOSED TO BE DEAD!
CLIMBING A TREE, WONDER WOMAN CREEPS OUT ON A BRANCH NEAR THE POLICE CHIEF'S OFFICE.
SWINGING LIGHTLY FROM THE TREE, WONDER WOMAN CRASHES FEET FIRST THROUGH THE CHIEF'S WINDOW.
HOW MEAN OF THE CHIEF TO LOCK HIS WINDOW. POLICEMEN HAVE NO SENSE OF HOSPITALITY!
AS WONDER WOMAN EXAMINES THE SAFE, SHE HEARS FOOTSTEPS THUNDERING DOWN THE CORRIDOR.
OH-OH! HERE COMES TROUBLE!
QUICK, MIKE! SOME BODY'S BROKEN INTO THE CHIEF'S OFFICE!
WE'LL NAB THE SPALPEEN!
WONDER WOMAN LIFTS THE MASSIVE SAFE IN HER ARMS AND PLACES IT AGAINST THE DOOR!
THIS WILL KEEP THEM OUT UNTIL I GET THE SAFE OPEN!
4
RIPPING OFF THE SAFE DOOR, WONDER WOMAN SECURES HER COSTUME.
WHAM! BAM!
WHACK!
OPEN THAT DOOR! LET US IN OR WE'LL SHOOT!
FIRE AWAY, BOYS! HAVE YOUR OWN QUAINT IDEA OF FUN!
POLICE DEPARTMENT

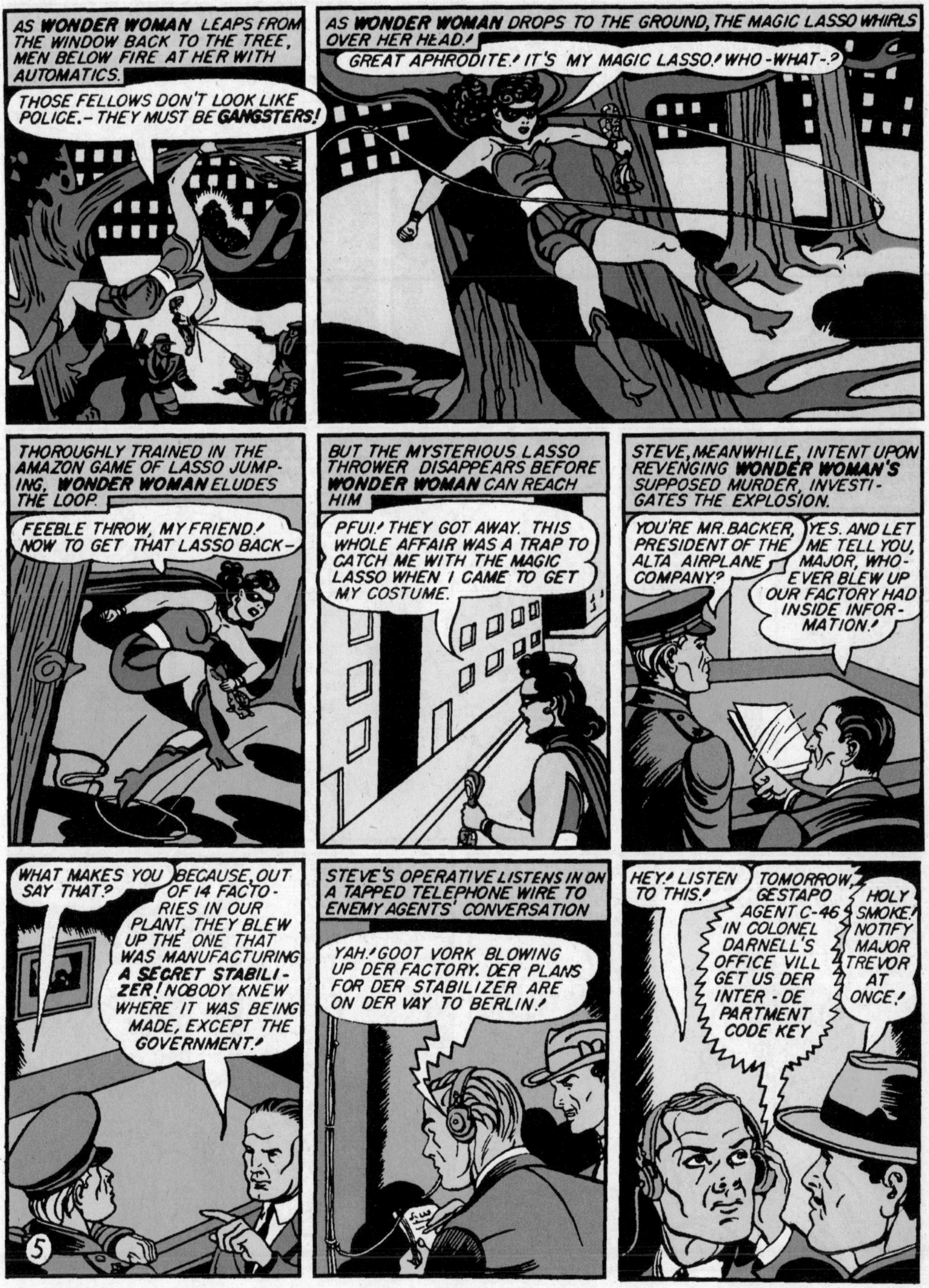
AS WONDER WOMAN LEAPS FROM THE WINDOW BACK TO THE TREE, MEN BELOW FIRE AT HER WITH AUTOMATICS.
THOSE FELLOWS DON'T LOOK LIKE POLICE.- THEY MUST BE GANGSTERS!
AS WONDER WOMAN DROPS TO THE GROUND, THE MAGIC LASSO WHIRLS OVER HER HEAD!
GREAT APHRODITE! IT'S MY MAGIC LASSO! WHO -WHAT-.?
THOROUGHLY TRAINED IN THE AMAZON GAME OF LASSO JUMPING, WONDER WOMAN ELUDES THE LOOP.
FEEBLE THROW, MY FRIEND! NOW TO GET THAT LASSO BACK-
BUT THE MYSTERIOUS LASSO THROWER DISAPPEARS BEFORE WONDER WOMAN CAN REACH HIM
PFUI! THEY GOT AWAY. THIS WHOLE AFFAIR WAS A TRAP TO CATCH ME WITH THE MAGIC LASSO WHEN I CAME TO GET MY COSTUME.
STEVE, MEANWHILE, INTENT UPON REVENGING WONDER WOMAN'S SUPPOSED MURDER, INVESTIGATES THE EXPLOSION.
YOU'RE MR. BACKER, PRESIDENT OF THE ALTA AIRPLANE COMPANY?
YES. AND LET ME TELL YOU, MAJOR, WHOEVER BLEW UP OUR FACTORY HAD INSIDE INFORMATION!
WHAT MAKES YOU SAY THAT?
BECAUSE, OUT OF 14 FACTORIES IN OUR PLANT, THEY BLEW UP THE ONE THAT WAS MANUFACTURING A SECRET STABILIZER! NOBODY KNEW WHERE IT WAS BEING MADE, EXCEPT THE GOVERNMENT!
5
STEVE'S OPERATIVE LISTENS IN ON A TAPPED TELEPHONE WIRE TO ENEMY AGENTS' CONVERSATION
YAH! GOOT VORK BLOWING UP DER FACTORY. DER PLANS FOR DER STABILIZER ARE ON DER VAY TO BERLIN!
HEY! LISTEN TO THIS!
TOMORROW, GESTAPO AGENT C-46 IN COLONEL DARNELL'S OFFICE VILL GET US DER INTER-DEPARTMENT CODE KEY
HOLY SMOKE! NOTIFY MAJOR TREVOR AT ONCE!

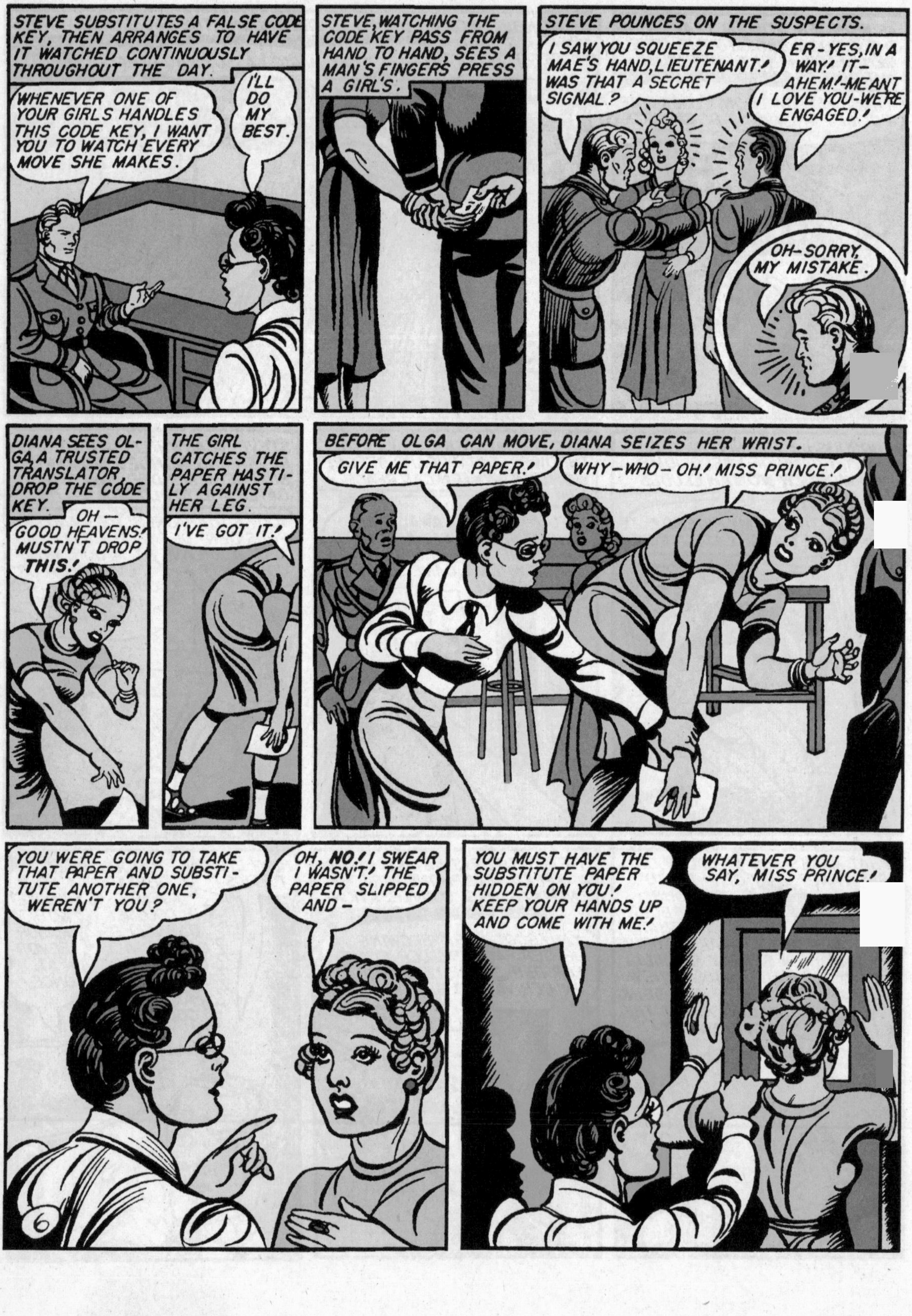
STEVE SUBSTITUTES A FALSE CODE KEY, THEN ARRANGES TO HAVE IT WATCHED CONTINUOUSLY THROUGHOUT THE DAY.
WHENEVER ONE OF YOUR GIRLS HANDLES THIS CODE KEY, I WANT YOU TO WATCH EVERY MOVE SHE MAKES.
I'LL DO MY BEST.
STEVE, WATCHING THE CODE KEY PASS FROM HAND TO HAND, SEES A MAN'S FINGERS PRESS A GIRL'S.
STEVE POUNCES ON THE SUSPECTS.
I SAW YOU SQUEEZE MAE'S HAND, LIEUTENANT! WAS THAT A SECRET SIGNAL?
ER-YES, IN A WAY! IT-AHEM!-MEANT I LOVE YOU-WE'RE ENGAGED!
OH-SORRY, MY MISTAKE.
DIANA SEES OLGA, A TRUSTED TRANSLATOR, DROP THE CODE KEY.
OH- GOOD HEAVENS! MUSTN'T DROP THIS!
THE GIRL CATCHES THE PAPER HASTILY AGAINST HER LEG.
I'VE GOT IT!
BEFORE OLGA CAN MOVE, DIANA SEIZES HER WRIST.
GIVE ME THAT PAPER!
WHY-WHO-OH! MISS PRINCE!
YOU WERE GOING TO TAKE THAT PAPER AND SUBSTITUTE ANOTHER ONE, WEREN'T YOU?
OH, NO! I SWEAR I WASN'T! THE PAPER SLIPPED AND-
YOU MUST HAVE THE SUBSTITUTE PAPER HIDDEN ON YOU! KEEP YOUR HANDS UP AND COME WITH ME!
WHATEVER YOU SAY, MISS PRINCE!
6

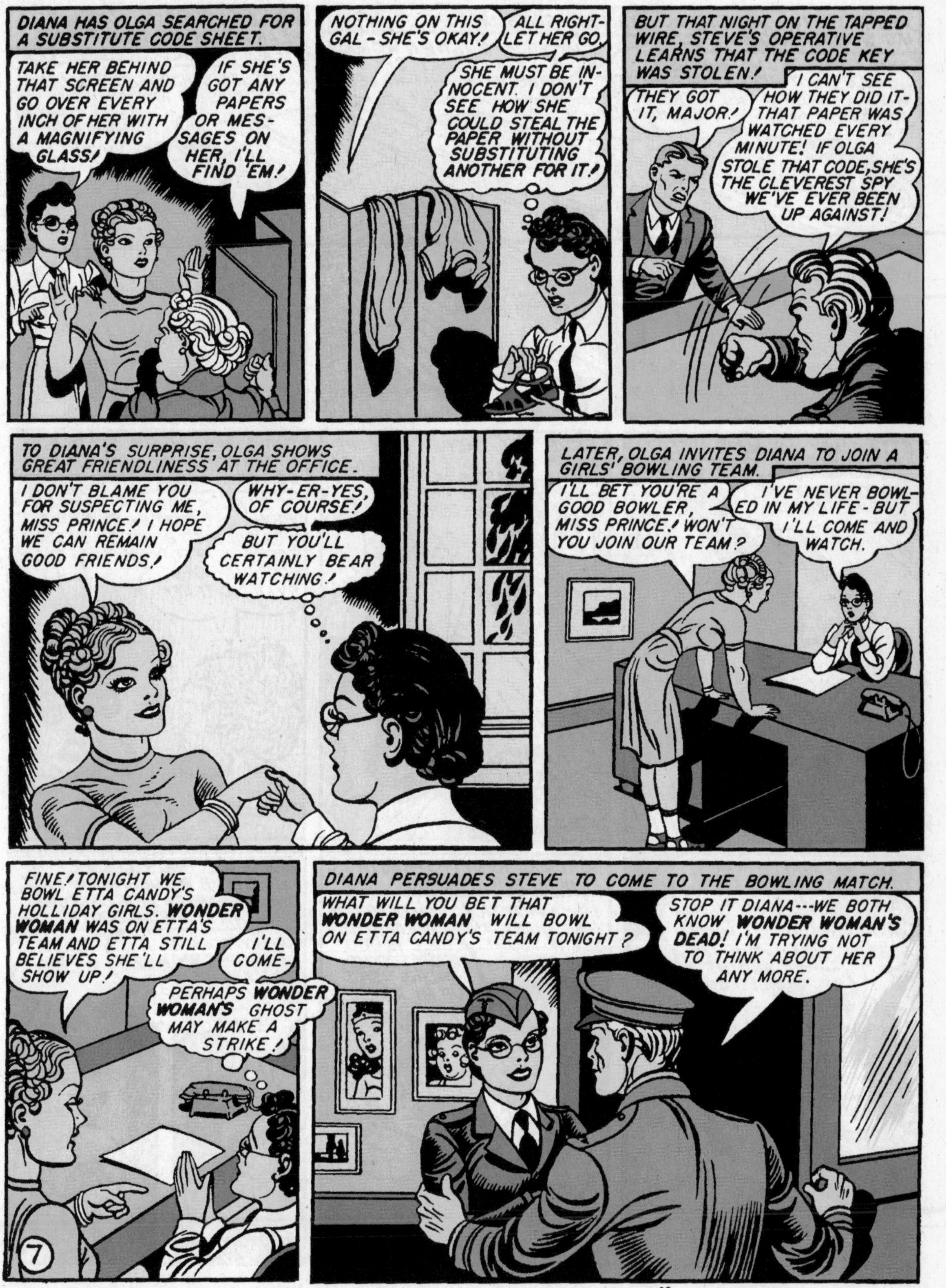

DIANA HAS OLGA SEARCHED FOR A SUBSTITUTE CODE SHEET.
TAKE HER BEHIND THAT SCREEN AND GO OVER EVERY INCH OF HER WITH A MAGNIFYING GLASS!
IF SHE'S GOT ANY PAPERS OR MESSAGES ON HER, I'LL FIND 'EM!
NOTHING ON THIS GAL - SHE'S OKAY!
ALL RIGHT- LET HER GO.
SHE MUST BE INNOCENT. I DON'T SEE HOW SHE COULD STEAL THE PAPER WITHOUT SUBSTITUTING ANOTHER FOR IT!
BUT THAT NIGHT ON THE TAPPED WIRE, STEVE'S OPERATIVE LEARNS THAT THE CODE KEY WAS STOLEN!
THEY GOT IT, MAJOR!
I CAN'T SEE HOW THEY DID IT- THAT PAPER WAS WATCHED EVERY MINUTE! IF OLGA STOLE THAT CODE, SHE'S THE CLEVEREST SPY WE'VE EVER BEEN UP AGAINST!
TO DIANA'S SURPRISE, OLGA SHOWS GREAT FRIENDLINESS AT THE OFFICE.
I DON'T BLAME YOU FOR SUSPECTING ME, MISS PRINCE! I HOPE WE CAN REMAIN GOOD FRIENDS!
WHY-ER-YES, OF COURSE!
BUT YOU'LL CERTAINLY BEAR WATCHING!
LATER, OLGA INVITES DIANA TO JOIN A GIRLS' BOWLING TEAM.
I'LL BET YOU'RE A GOOD BOWLER, MISS PRINCE! WON'T YOU JOIN OUR TEAM?
I'VE NEVER BOWLED IN MY LIFE - BUT I'LL COME AND WATCH.
FINE! TONIGHT WE BOWL ETTA CANDY'S HOLLIDAY GIRLS. WONDER WOMAN WAS ON ETTA'S TEAM AND ETTA STILL BELIEVES SHE'LL SHOW UP!
I'LL COME-
PERHAPS WONDER WOMAN'S GHOST MAY MAKE A STRIKE!
7
DIANA PERSUADES STEVE TO COME TO THE BOWLING MATCH.
WHAT WILL YOU BET THAT WONDER WOMAN WILL BOWL ON ETTA CANDY'S TEAM TONIGHT?
STOP IT DIANA---WE BOTH KNOW WONDER WOMAN'S DEAD! I'M TRYING NOT TO THINK ABOUT HER ANY MORE.

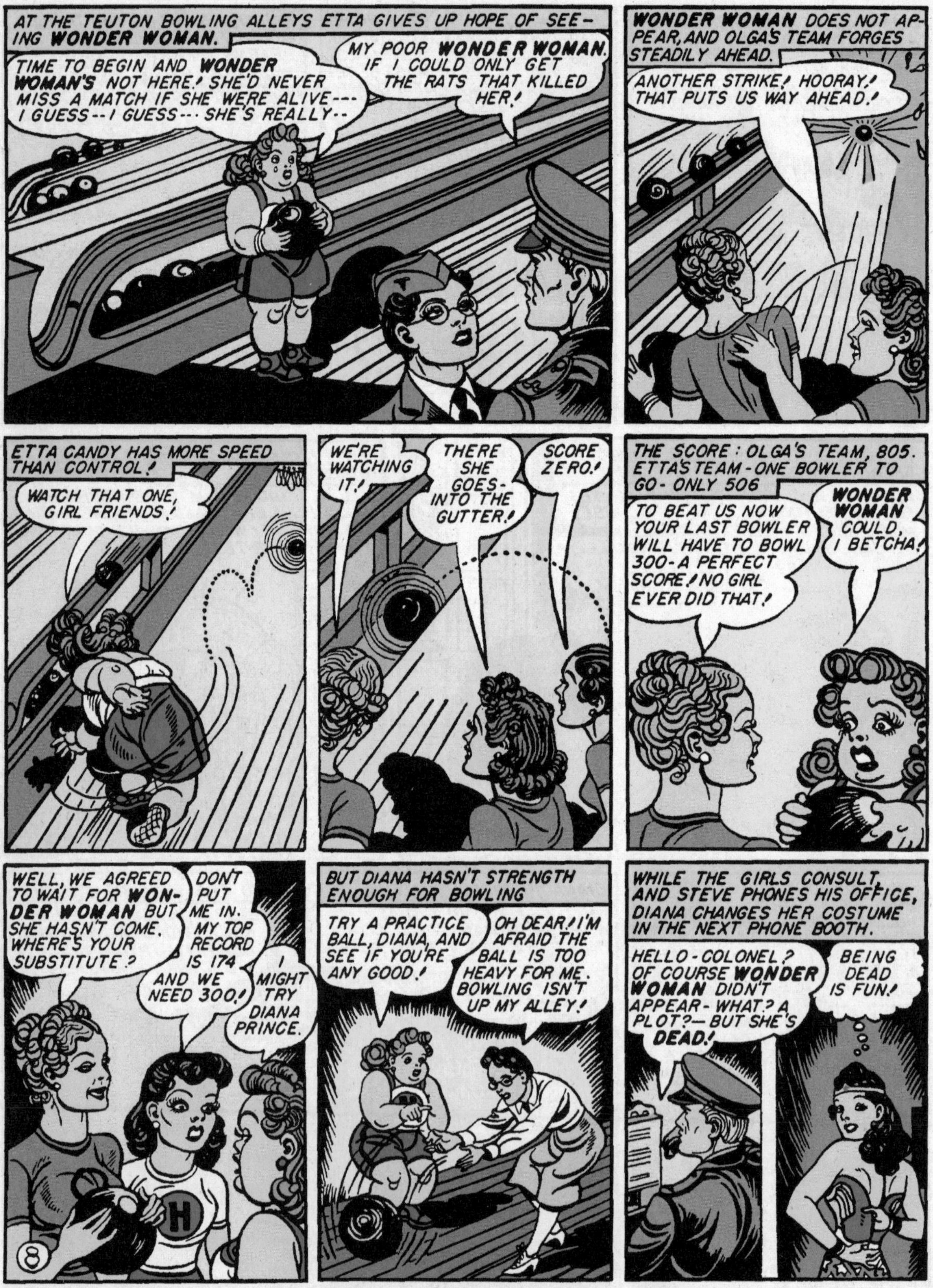
AT THE TEUTON BOWLING ALLEYS ETTA GIVES UP HOPE OF SEEING WONDER WOMAN.
TIME TO BEGIN AND WONDER WOMAN'S NOT HERE! SHE'D NEVER MISS A MATCH IF SHE WERE ALIVE--- I GUESS--I GUESS--- SHE'S REALLY--
MY POOR WONDER WOMAN. IF I COULD ONLY GET THE RATS THAT KILLED HER!
WONDER WOMAN DOES NOT APPEAR, AND OLGA'S TEAM FORGES STEADILY AHEAD.
ANOTHER STRIKE! HOORAY! THAT PUTS US WAY AHEAD!
ETTA CANDY HAS MORE SPEED THAN CONTROL!
WATCH THAT ONE, GIRL FRIENDS!
WE'RE WATCHING IT!
THERE SHE GOES-INTO THE GUTTER!
SCORE ZERO!
THE SCORE: OLGA'S TEAM, 805. ETTA'S TEAM-ONE BOWLER TO GO-ONLY 506
TO BEAT US NOW YOUR LAST BOWLER WILL HAVE TO BOWL 300-A PERFECT SCORE! NO GIRL EVER DID THAT!
WONDER WOMAN COULD, I BETCHA!
WELL, WE AGREED TO WAIT FOR WONDER WOMAN BUT SHE HASN'T COME. WHERE'S YOUR SUBSTITUTE?
DON'T PUT ME IN. MY TOP RECORD IS 174
AND WE NEED 300!
I MIGHT TRY DIANA PRINCE.
8
BUT DIANA HASN'T STRENGTH ENOUGH FOR BOWLING
TRY A PRACTICE BALL, DIANA, AND SEE IF YOU'RE ANY GOOD!
OH DEAR! I'M AFRAID THE BALL IS TOO HEAVY FOR ME. BOWLING ISN'T UP MY ALLEY!
WHILE THE GIRLS CONSULT, AND STEVE PHONES HIS OFFICE, DIANA CHANGES HER COSTUME IN THE NEXT PHONE BOOTH.
HELLO-COLONEL? OF COURSE WONDER WOMAN DIDN'T APPEAR- WHAT? A PLOT?— BUT SHE'S DEAD!
BEING DEAD IS FUN!

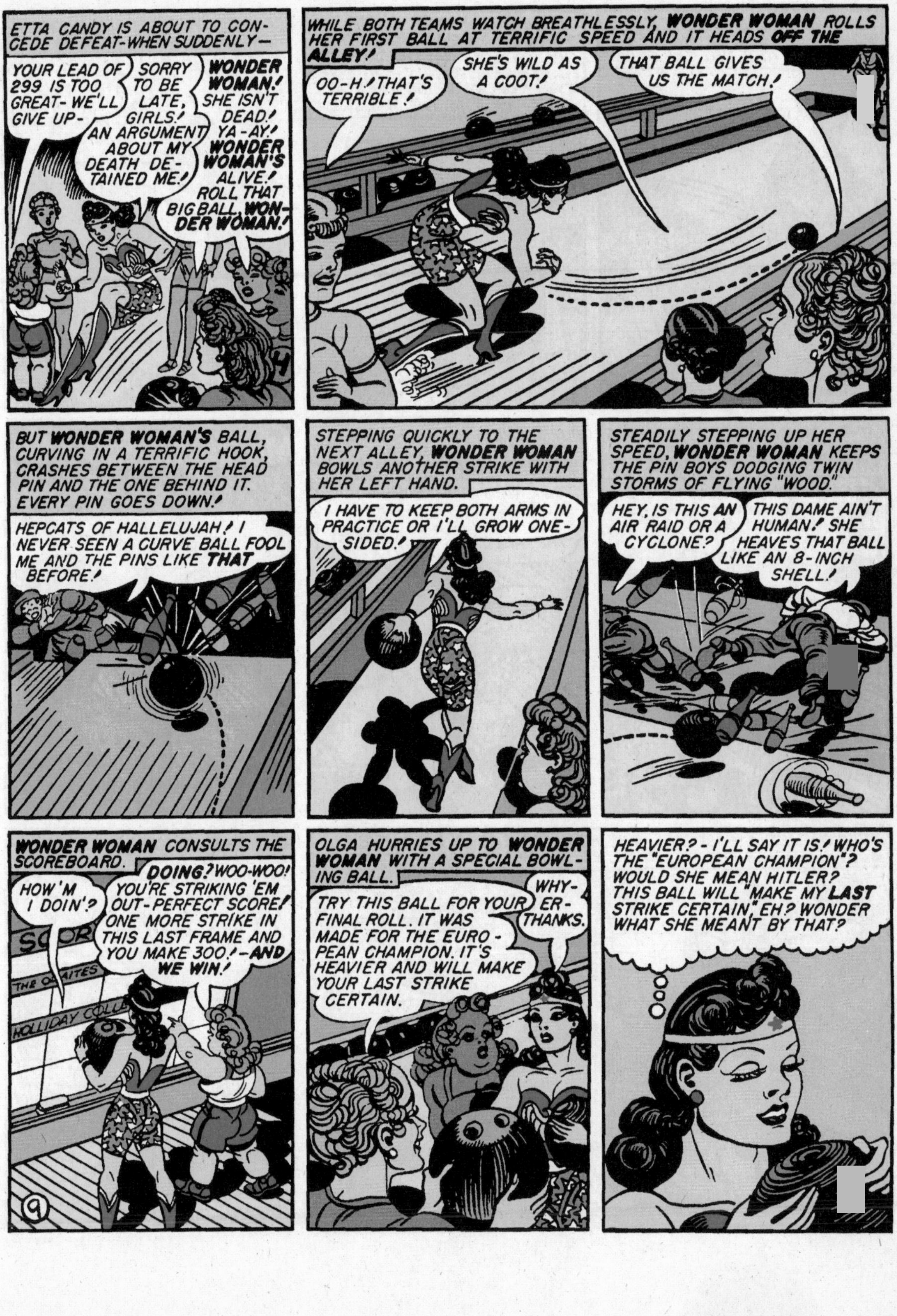

ETTA CANDY IS ABOUT TO CONCEDE DEFEAT-WHEN SUDDENLY—
YOUR LEAD OF 299 IS TOO GREAT- WE'LL GIVE UP-
SORRY TO BE LATE, GIRLS! AN ARGUMENT ABOUT MY DEATH DETAINED ME!
WONDER WOMAN! SHE ISN'T DEAD! YA-AY! WONDER WOMAN'S ALIVE!
ROLL THAT BIG BALL, WONDER WOMAN!
WHILE BOTH TEAMS WATCH BREATHLESSLY, WONDER WOMAN ROLLS HER FIRST BALL AT TERRIFIC SPEED AND IT HEADS OFF THE ALLEY!
OO-H! THAT'S TERRIBLE!
SHE'S WILD AS A COOT!
THAT BALL GIVES US THE MATCH!
BUT WONDER WOMAN'S BALL, CURVING IN A TERRIFIC HOOK, CRASHES BETWEEN THE HEAD PIN AND THE ONE BEHIND IT. EVERY PIN GOES DOWN!
HEPCATS OF HALLELUJAH! I NEVER SEEN A CURVE BALL FOOL ME AND THE PINS LIKE THAT BEFORE!
STEPPING QUICKLY TO THE NEXT ALLEY, WONDER WOMAN BOWLS ANOTHER STRIKE WITH HER LEFT HAND.
I HAVE TO KEEP BOTH ARMS IN PRACTICE OR I'LL GROW ONE-SIDED!
STEADILY STEPPING UP HER SPEED, WONDER WOMAN KEEPS THE PIN BOYS DODGING TWIN STORMS OF FLYING "WOOD."
HEY, IS THIS AN AIR RAID OR A CYCLONE?
THIS DAME AIN'T HUMAN! SHE HEAVES THAT BALL LIKE AN 8-INCH SHELL!
WONDER WOMAN CONSULTS THE SCOREBOARD.
HOW'M I DOIN'?
DOING? WOO-WOO! YOU'RE STRIKING 'EM OUT-PERFECT SCORE! ONE MORE STRIKE IN THIS LAST FRAME AND YOU MAKE 300! -AND WE WIN!
SCOR
THE
HOLLIDAY COLL
9
OLGA HURRIES UP TO WONDER WOMAN WITH A SPECIAL BOWLING BALL.
TRY THIS BALL FOR YOUR FINAL ROLL. IT WAS MADE FOR THE EUROPEAN CHAMPION. IT'S HEAVIER AND WILL MAKE YOUR LAST STRIKE CERTAIN.
WHY- ER- THANKS.
HEAVIER? - I'LL SAY IT IS! WHO'S THE "EUROPEAN CHAMPION"? WOULD SHE MEAN HITLER? THIS BALL WILL "MAKE MY LAST STRIKE CERTAIN," EH? WONDER WHAT SHE MEANT BY THAT?

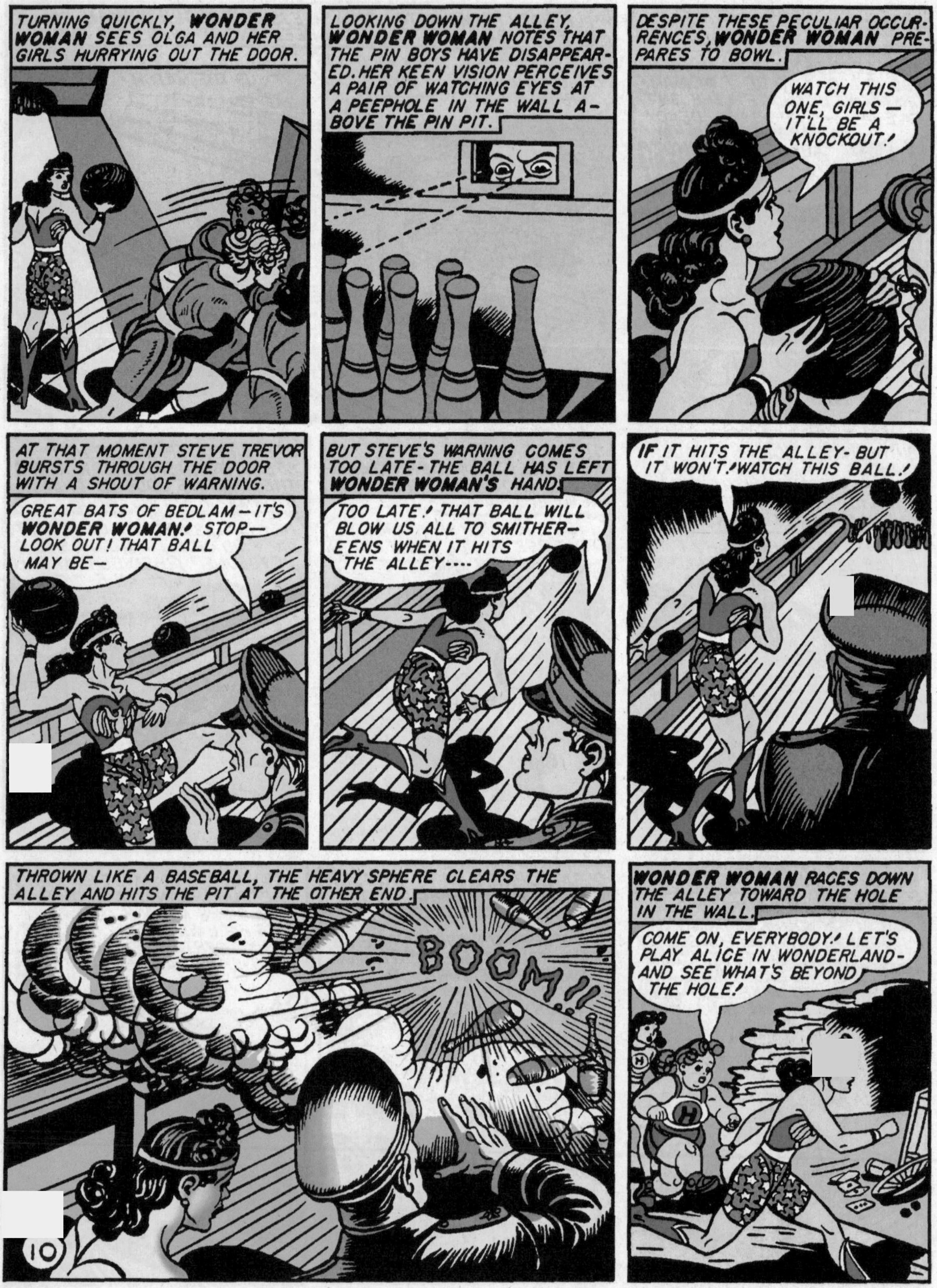
TURNING QUICKLY, WONDER WOMAN SEES OLGA AND HER GIRLS HURRYING OUT THE DOOR.
LOOKING DOWN THE ALLEY, WONDER WOMAN NOTES THAT THE PIN BOYS HAVE DISAPPEARED. HER KEEN VISION PERCEIVES A PAIR OF WATCHING EYES AT A PEEPHOLE IN THE WALL ABOVE THE PIN PIT.
DESPITE THESE PECULIAR OCCURRENCES, WONDER WOMAN PREPARES TO BOWL.
WATCH THIS ONE, GIRLS — IT'LL BE A KNOCKOUT!
AT THAT MOMENT STEVE TREVOR BURSTS THROUGH THE DOOR WITH A SHOUT OF WARNING.
GREAT BATS OF BEDLAM — IT'S WONDER WOMAN! STOP — LOOK OUT! THAT BALL MAY BE—
BUT STEVE'S WARNING COMES TOO LATE - THE BALL HAS LEFT WONDER WOMAN'S HANDS
TOO LATE! THAT BALL WILL BLOW US ALL TO SMITHEREENS WHEN IT HITS THE ALLEY----
IF IT HITS THE ALLEY- BUT IT WON'T! WATCH THIS BALL!
THROWN LIKE A BASEBALL, THE HEAVY SPHERE CLEARS THE ALLEY AND HITS THE PIT AT THE OTHER END.
BOOM!!
10
WONDER WOMAN RACES DOWN THE ALLEY TOWARD THE HOLE IN THE WALL.
COME ON, EVERYBODY! LET'S PLAY ALICE IN WONDERLAND - AND SEE WHAT'S BEYOND THE HOLE!

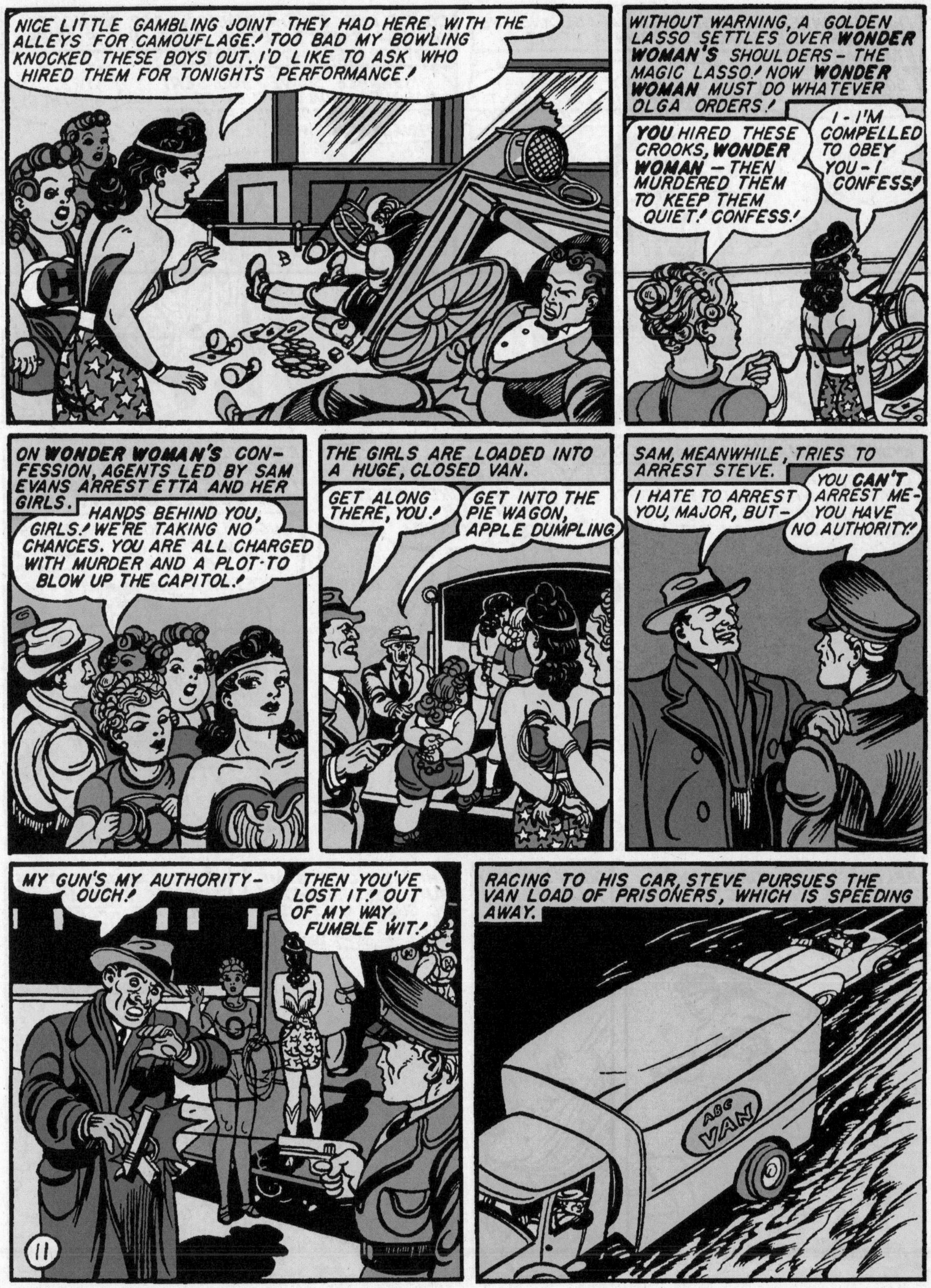
NICE LITTLE GAMBLING JOINT THEY HAD HERE, WITH THE ALLEYS FOR CAMOUFLAGE! TOO BAD MY BOWLING KNOCKED THESE BOYS OUT. I'D LIKE TO ASK WHO HIRED THEM FOR TONIGHT'S PERFORMANCE!
WITHOUT WARNING, A GOLDEN LASSO SETTLES OVER WONDER WOMAN'S SHOULDERS - THE MAGIC LASSO! NOW WONDER WOMAN MUST DO WHATEVER OLGA ORDERS!
YOU HIRED THESE CROOKS, WONDER WOMAN - THEN MURDERED THEM TO KEEP THEM QUIET! CONFESS!
I - I'M COMPELLED TO OBEY YOU - I CONFESS!
ON WONDER WOMAN'S CONFESSION, AGENTS LED BY SAM EVANS ARREST ETTA AND HER GIRLS.
HANDS BEHIND YOU, GIRLS! WE'RE TAKING NO CHANCES. YOU ARE ALL CHARGED WITH MURDER AND A PLOT TO BLOW UP THE CAPITOL!
THE GIRLS ARE LOADED INTO A HUGE, CLOSED VAN.
GET ALONG THERE, YOU!
GET INTO THE PIE WAGON, APPLE DUMPLING.
SAM, MEANWHILE, TRIES TO ARREST STEVE.
I HATE TO ARREST YOU, MAJOR, BUT-
YOU CAN'T ARREST ME- YOU HAVE NO AUTHORITY!
MY GUN'S MY AUTHORITY- OUCH!
THEN YOU'VE LOST IT! OUT OF MY WAY, FUMBLE WIT!
11
RACING TO HIS CAR, STEVE PURSUES THE VAN LOAD OF PRISONERS, WHICH IS SPEEDING AWAY.
ABC VAN

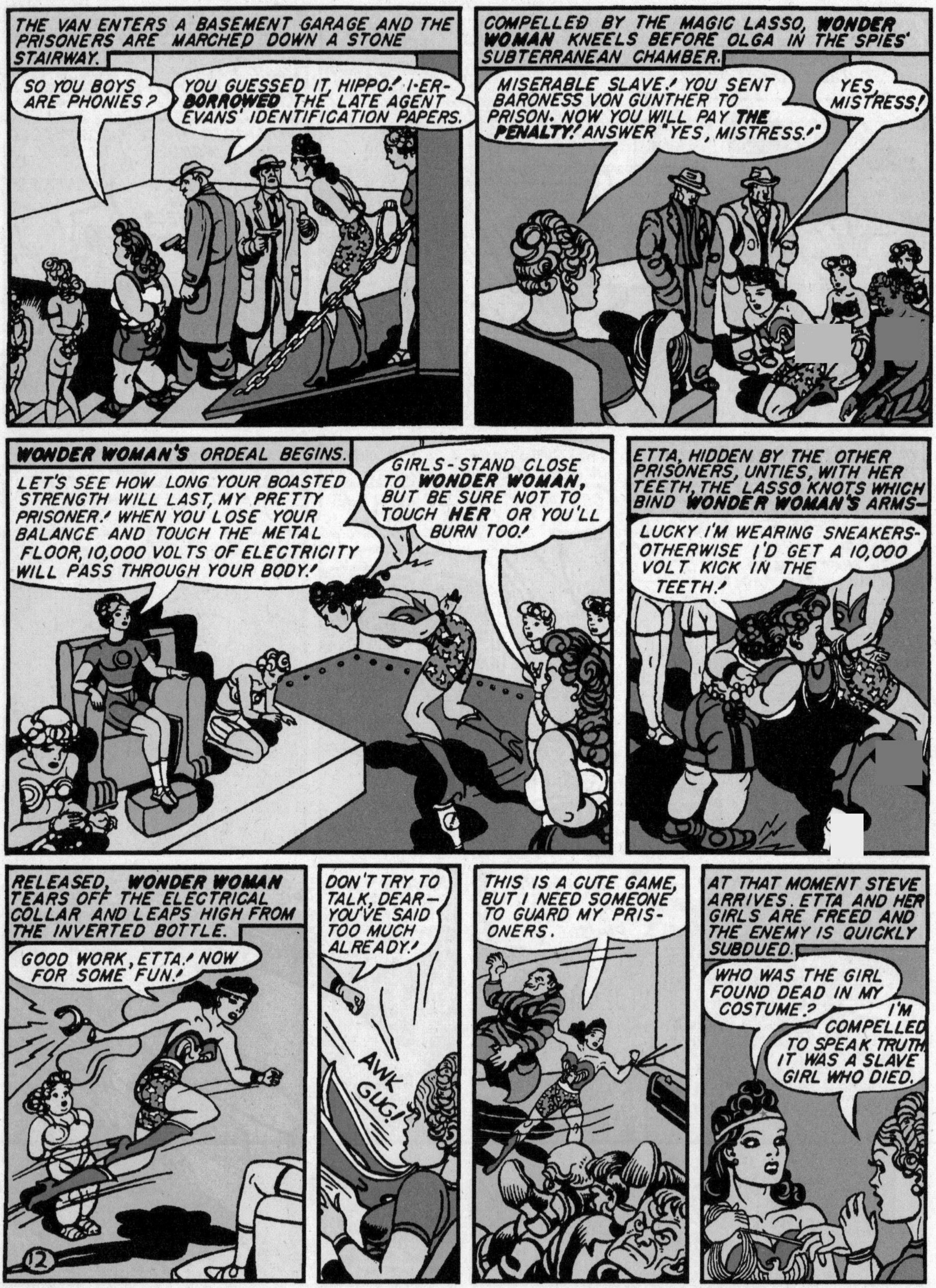
THE VAN ENTERS A BASEMENT GARAGE AND THE PRISONERS ARE MARCHED DOWN A STONE STAIRWAY.
SO YOU BOYS ARE PHONIES?
YOU GUESSED IT, HIPPO! I-ER-BORROWED THE LATE AGENT EVANS' IDENTIFICATION PAPERS.
COMPELLED BY THE MAGIC LASSO, WONDER WOMAN KNEELS BEFORE OLGA IN THE SPIES' SUBTERRANEAN CHAMBER.
MISERABLE SLAVE! YOU SENT BARONESS VON GUNTHER TO PRISON. NOW YOU WILL PAY THE PENALTY! ANSWER "YES, MISTRESS!"
YES, MISTRESS!
WONDER WOMAN'S ORDEAL BEGINS.
LET'S SEE HOW LONG YOUR BOASTED STRENGTH WILL LAST, MY PRETTY PRISONER! WHEN YOU LOSE YOUR BALANCE AND TOUCH THE METAL FLOOR, 10,000 VOLTS OF ELECTRICITY WILL PASS THROUGH YOUR BODY!
GIRLS - STAND CLOSE TO WONDER WOMAN, BUT BE SURE NOT TO TOUCH HER OR YOU'LL BURN TOO!
ETTA, HIDDEN BY THE OTHER PRISONERS, UNTIES, WITH HER TEETH, THE LASSO KNOTS WHICH BIND WONDER WOMAN'S ARMS-
LUCKY I'M WEARING SNEAKERS-OTHERWISE I'D GET A 10,000 VOLT KICK IN THE TEETH!
RELEASED, WONDER WOMAN TEARS OFF THE ELECTRICAL COLLAR AND LEAPS HIGH FROM THE INVERTED BOTTLE.
GOOD WORK, ETTA! NOW FOR SOME FUN!
12
DON'T TRY TO TALK, DEAR-YOU'VE SAID TOO MUCH ALREADY!
AWK GUG!
THIS IS A CUTE GAME, BUT I NEED SOMEONE TO GUARD MY PRIS-ONERS.
AT THAT MOMENT STEVE ARRIVES. ETTA AND HER GIRLS ARE FREED AND THE ENEMY IS QUICKLY SUBDUED.
WHO WAS THE GIRL FOUND DEAD IN MY COSTUME?
I'M COMPELLED TO SPEAK TRUTH IT WAS A SLAVE GIRL WHO DIED.

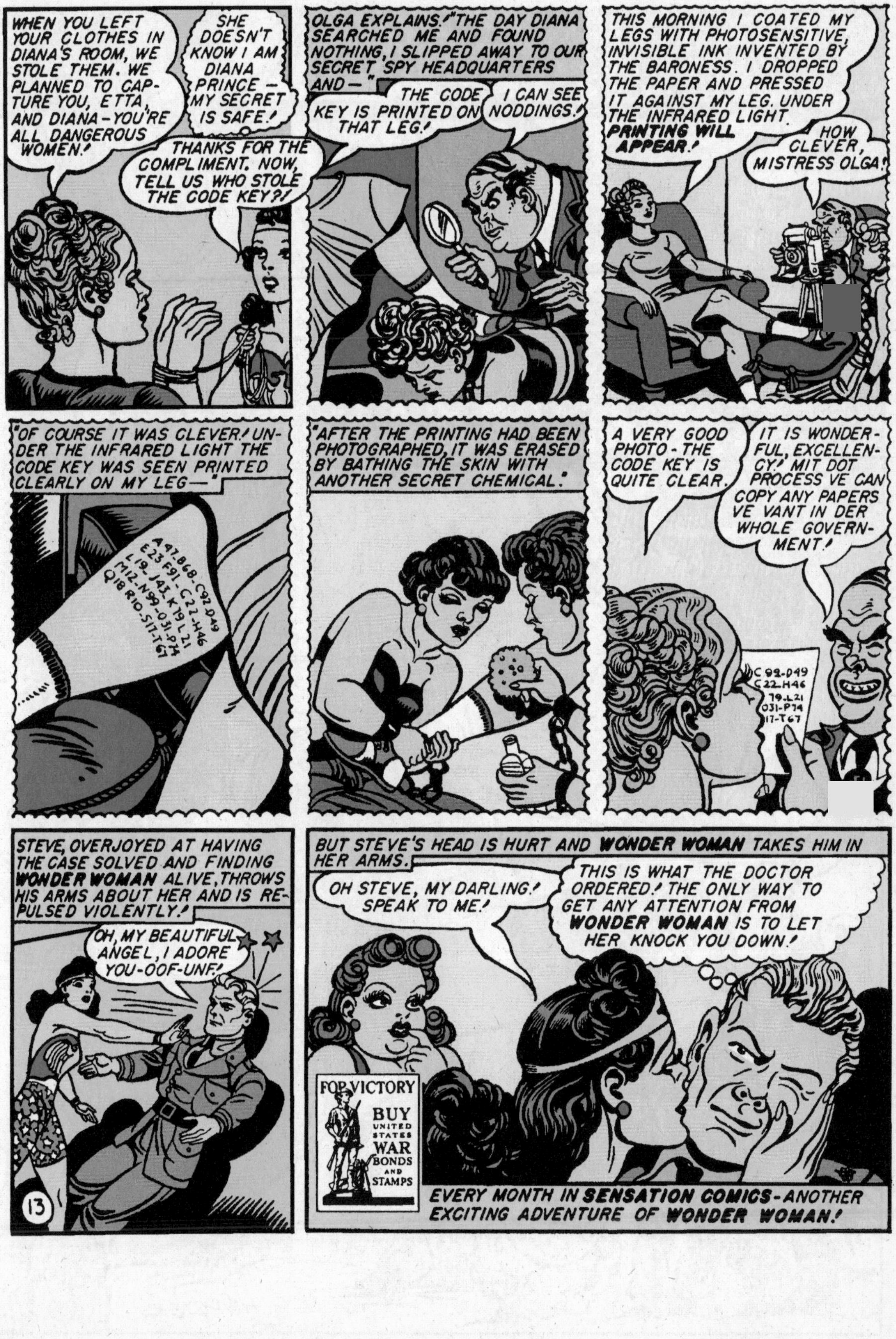
WHEN YOU LEFT YOUR CLOTHES IN DIANA'S ROOM, WE STOLE THEM. WE PLANNED TO CAPTURE YOU, ETTA, AND DIANA—YOU'RE ALL DANGEROUS WOMEN!
SHE DOESN'T KNOW I AM DIANA PRINCE—MY SECRET IS SAFE!
THANKS FOR THE COMPLIMENT. NOW, TELL US WHO STOLE THE CODE KEY?!
OLGA EXPLAINS: "THE DAY DIANA SEARCHED ME AND FOUND NOTHING, I SLIPPED AWAY TO OUR SECRET SPY HEADQUARTERS AND—"
THE CODE KEY IS PRINTED ON THAT LEG!
I CAN SEE NODDINGS!
THIS MORNING I COATED MY LEGS WITH PHOTOSENSITIVE, INVISIBLE INK INVENTED BY THE BARONESS. I DROPPED THE PAPER AND PRESSED IT AGAINST MY LEG. UNDER THE INFRARED LIGHT, PRINTING WILL APPEAR!
HOW CLEVER, MISTRESS OLGA!
"OF COURSE IT WAS CLEVER! UNDER THE INFRARED LIGHT THE CODE KEY WAS SEEN PRINTED CLEARLY ON MY LEG—"
"AFTER THE PRINTING HAD BEEN PHOTOGRAPHED, IT WAS ERASED BY BATHING THE SKIN WITH ANOTHER SECRET CHEMICAL."
A VERY GOOD PHOTO - THE CODE KEY IS QUITE CLEAR.
IT IS WONDERFUL, EXCELLENCY! MIT DOT PROCESS VE CAN COPY ANY PAPERS VE VANT IN DER WHOLE GOVERNMENT!
STEVE, OVERJOYED AT HAVING THE CASE SOLVED AND FINDING WONDER WOMAN ALIVE, THROWS HIS ARMS ABOUT HER AND IS REPULSED VIOLENTLY!
OH, MY BEAUTIFUL ANGEL, I ADORE YOU-OOF-UNF!
13
BUT STEVE'S HEAD IS HURT AND WONDER WOMAN TAKES HIM IN HER ARMS.
OH STEVE, MY DARLING! SPEAK TO ME!
THIS IS WHAT THE DOCTOR ORDERED! THE ONLY WAY TO GET ANY ATTENTION FROM WONDER WOMAN IS TO LET HER KNOCK YOU DOWN!
FOR VICTORY BUY UNITED STATES WAR BONDS AND STAMPS
EVERY MONTH IN SENSATION COMICS - ANOTHER EXCITING ADVENTURE OF WONDER WOMAN!

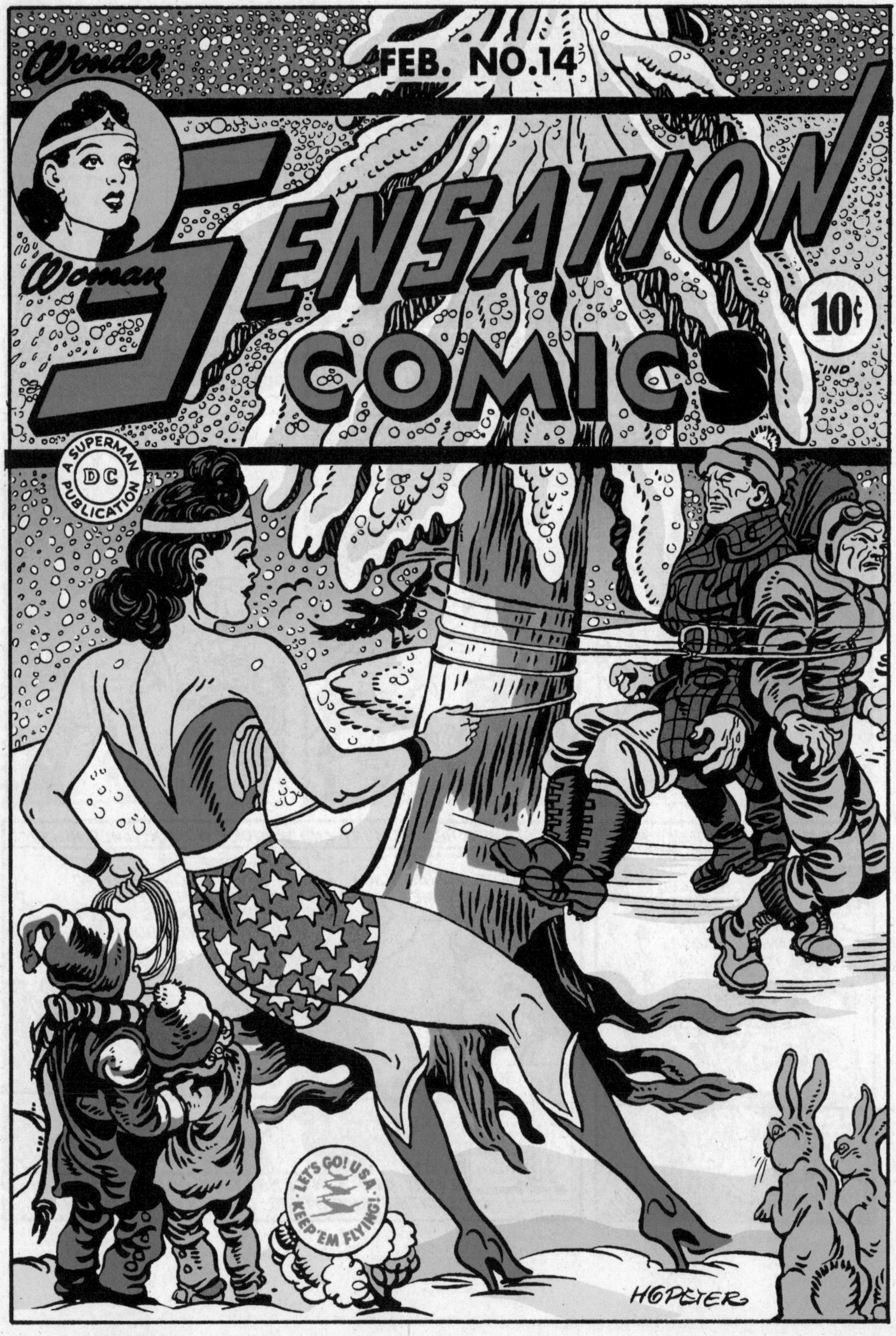
Wonder Woman
FEB. NO.14
SENSATION COMICS
10¢
IND
A SUPERMAN DC PUBLICATION
LET'S GO! U.S.A. KEEP 'EM FLYING!
HGPETER

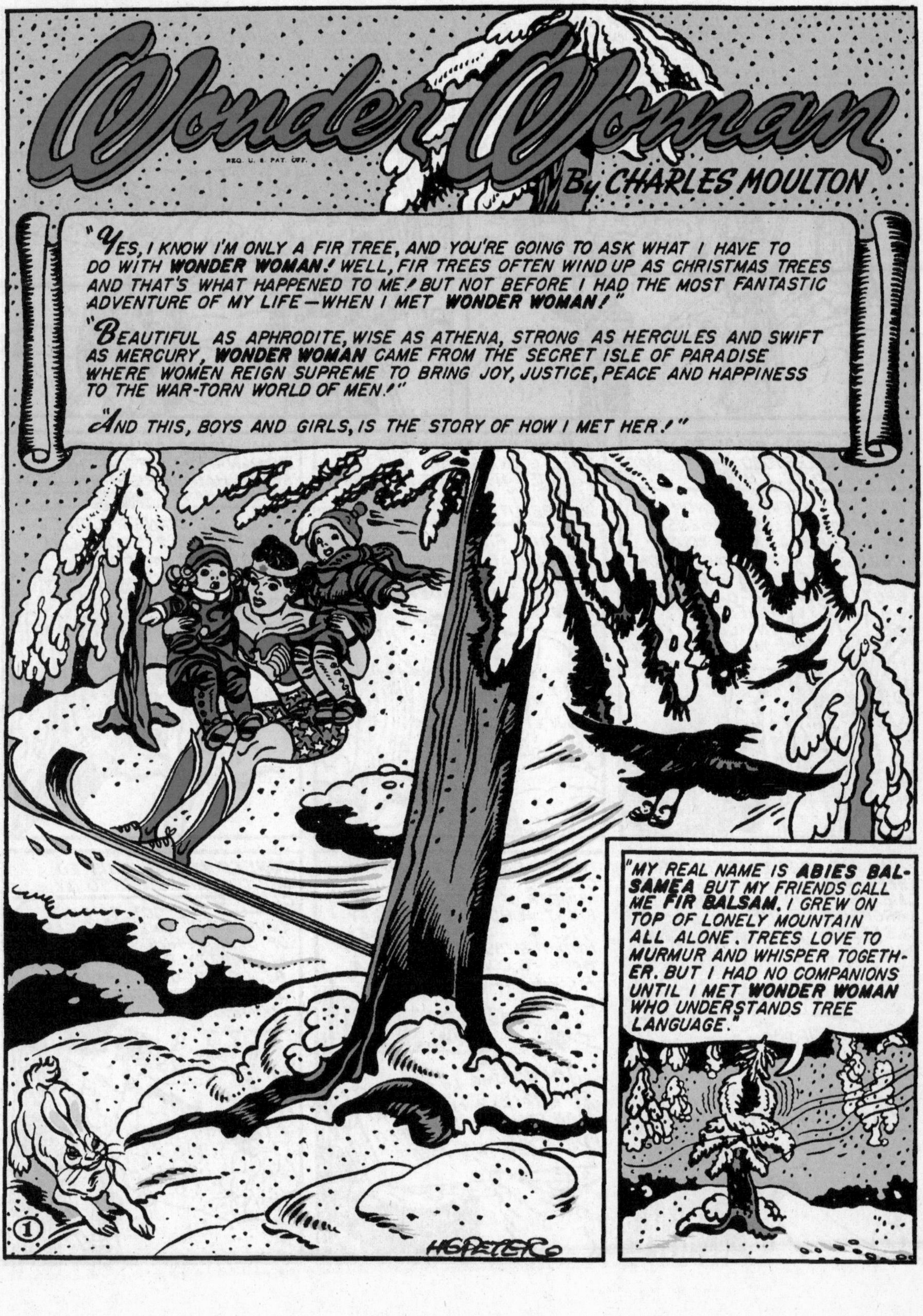
Wonder Woman
REG. U. S. PAT. OFF.
By CHARLES MOULTON
"YES, I KNOW I'M ONLY A FIR TREE, AND YOU'RE GOING TO ASK WHAT I HAVE TO DO WITH WONDER WOMAN! WELL, FIR TREES OFTEN WIND UP AS CHRISTMAS TREES AND THAT'S WHAT HAPPENED TO ME! BUT NOT BEFORE I HAD THE MOST FANTASTIC ADVENTURE OF MY LIFE—WHEN I MET WONDER WOMAN!"
"BEAUTIFUL AS APHRODITE, WISE AS ATHENA, STRONG AS HERCULES AND SWIFT AS MERCURY, WONDER WOMAN CAME FROM THE SECRET ISLE OF PARADISE WHERE WOMEN REIGN SUPREME TO BRING JOY, JUSTICE, PEACE AND HAPPINESS TO THE WAR-TORN WORLD OF MEN!"
"AND THIS, BOYS AND GIRLS, IS THE STORY OF HOW I MET HER!"
1
HGPETER
"MY REAL NAME IS ABIES BALSAMEA BUT MY FRIENDS CALL ME FIR BALSAM. I GREW ON TOP OF LONELY MOUNTAIN ALL ALONE. TREES LOVE TO MURMUR AND WHISPER TOGETHER. BUT I HAD NO COMPANIONS UNTIL I MET WONDER WOMAN WHO UNDERSTANDS TREE LANGUAGE."

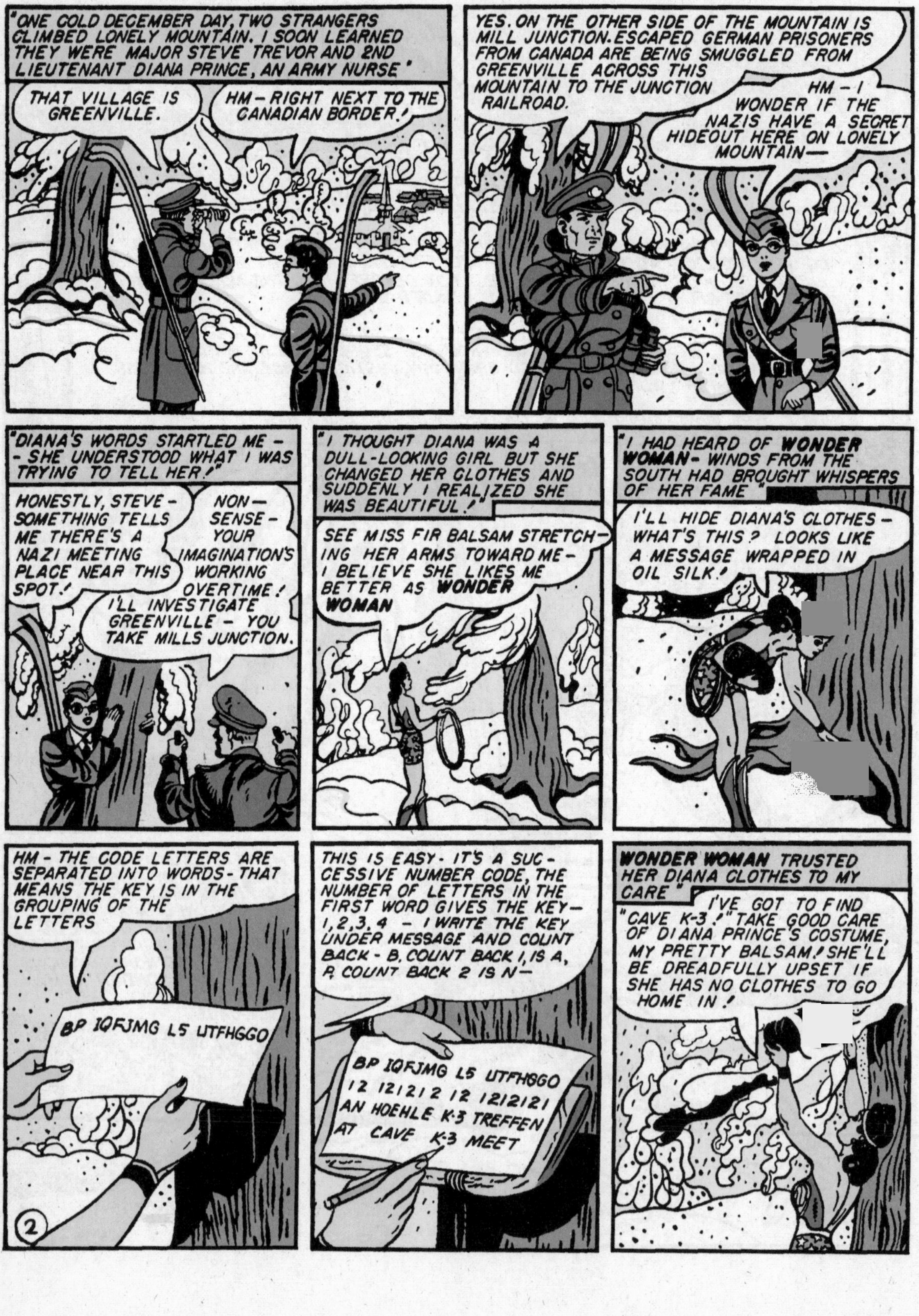
"ONE COLD DECEMBER DAY, TWO STRANGERS CLIMBED LONELY MOUNTAIN. I SOON LEARNED THEY WERE MAJOR STEVE TREVOR AND 2ND LIEUTENANT DIANA PRINCE, AN ARMY NURSE"
THAT VILLAGE IS GREENVILLE.
HM—RIGHT NEXT TO THE CANADIAN BORDER!
YES. ON THE OTHER SIDE OF THE MOUNTAIN IS MILL JUNCTION. ESCAPED GERMAN PRISONERS FROM CANADA ARE BEING SMUGGLED FROM GREENVILLE ACROSS THIS MOUNTAIN TO THE JUNCTION RAILROAD.
HM—I WONDER IF THE NAZIS HAVE A SECRET HIDEOUT HERE ON LONELY MOUNTAIN—
"DIANA'S WORDS STARTLED ME—SHE UNDERSTOOD WHAT I WAS TRYING TO TELL HER!"
HONESTLY, STEVE—SOMETHING TELLS ME THERE'S A NAZI MEETING PLACE NEAR THIS SPOT!
NON-SENSE—YOUR IMAGINATION'S WORKING OVERTIME! I'LL INVESTIGATE GREENVILLE—YOU TAKE MILLS JUNCTION.
"I THOUGHT DIANA WAS A DULL-LOOKING GIRL BUT SHE CHANGED HER CLOTHES AND SUDDENLY I REALIZED SHE WAS BEAUTIFUL!"
SEE MISS FIR BALSAM STRETCHING HER ARMS TOWARD ME—I BELIEVE SHE LIKES ME BETTER AS WONDER WOMAN
"I HAD HEARD OF WONDER WOMAN—WINDS FROM THE SOUTH HAD BROUGHT WHISPERS OF HER FAME"
I'LL HIDE DIANA'S CLOTHES—WHAT'S THIS? LOOKS LIKE A MESSAGE WRAPPED IN OIL SILK!
HM—THE CODE LETTERS ARE SEPARATED INTO WORDS—THAT MEANS THE KEY IS IN THE GROUPING OF THE LETTERS
BP IQFJMG L5 UTFHGGO
2
THIS IS EASY—IT'S A SUCCESSIVE NUMBER CODE, THE NUMBER OF LETTERS IN THE FIRST WORD GIVES THE KEY—1, 2, 3, 4—I WRITE THE KEY UNDER MESSAGE AND COUNT BACK—B, COUNT BACK 1, IS A, P, COUNT BACK 2 IS N—
BP IQFJMG L5 UTFHGGO
12 121212 12 1212121
AN HOEHLE K-3 TREFFEN
AT CAVE K-3 MEET
WONDER WOMAN TRUSTED HER DIANA CLOTHES TO MY CARE"
I'VE GOT TO FIND "CAVE K-3!" TAKE GOOD CARE OF DIANA PRINCE'S COSTUME, MY PRETTY BALSAM! SHE'LL BE DREADFULLY UPSET IF SHE HAS NO CLOTHES TO GO HOME IN!

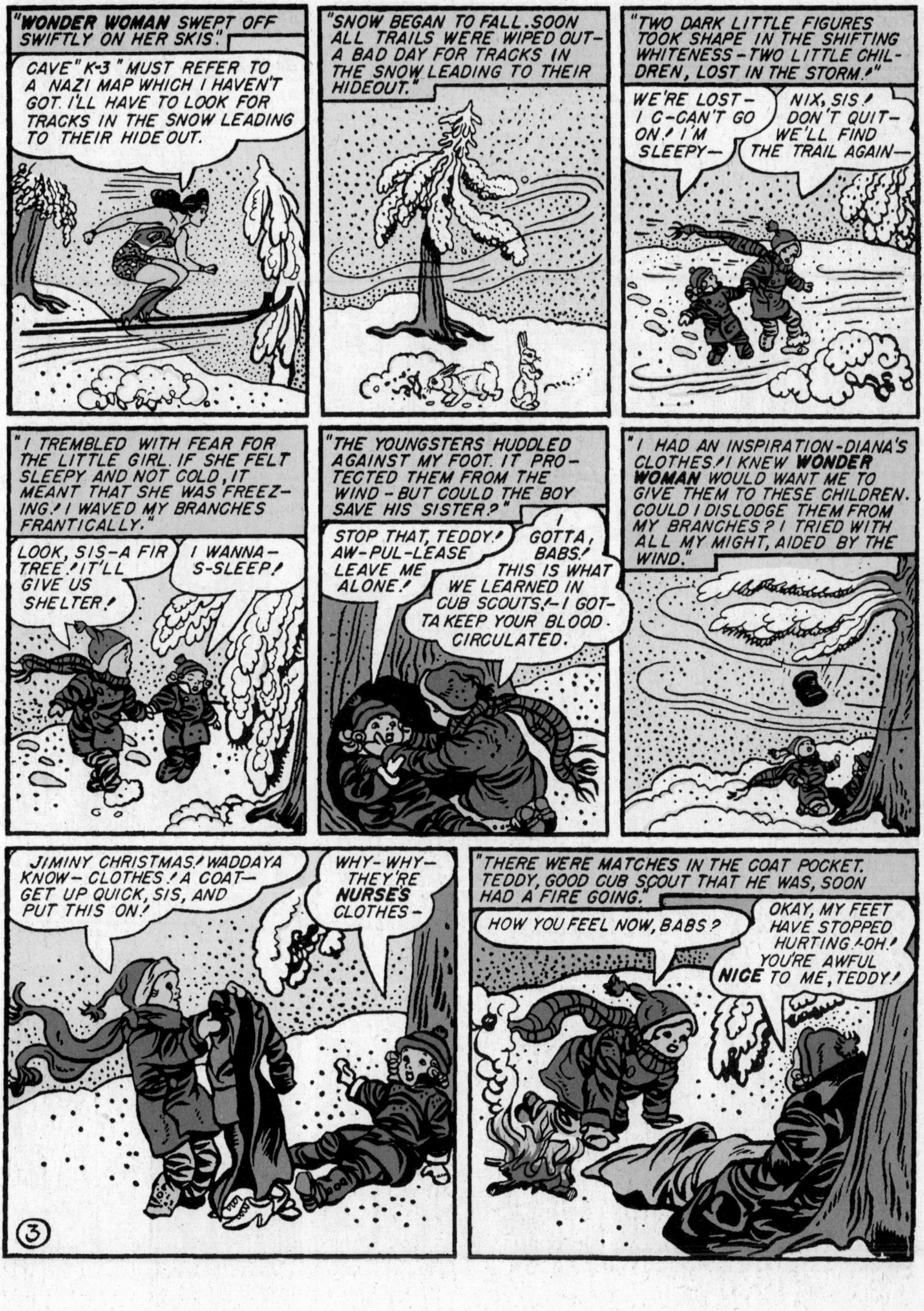
"WONDER WOMAN SWEPT OFF SWIFTLY ON HER SKIS."
CAVE "K-3" MUST REFER TO A NAZI MAP WHICH I HAVEN'T GOT. I'LL HAVE TO LOOK FOR TRACKS IN THE SNOW LEADING TO THEIR HIDE OUT.
"SNOW BEGAN TO FALL. SOON ALL TRAILS WERE WIPED OUT- A BAD DAY FOR TRACKS IN THE SNOW LEADING TO THEIR HIDEOUT."
"TWO DARK LITTLE FIGURES TOOK SHAPE IN THE SHIFTING WHITENESS - TWO LITTLE CHILDREN, LOST IN THE STORM!"
WE'RE LOST- I C-CAN'T GO ON! I'M SLEEPY—
NIX, SIS! DON'T QUIT- WE'LL FIND THE TRAIL AGAIN—
"I TREMBLED WITH FEAR FOR THE LITTLE GIRL. IF SHE FELT SLEEPY AND NOT COLD, IT MEANT THAT SHE WAS FREEZING! I WAVED MY BRANCHES FRANTICALLY."
LOOK, SIS-A FIR TREE! IT'LL GIVE US SHELTER!
I WANNA- S-SLEEP!
"THE YOUNGSTERS HUDDLED AGAINST MY FOOT. IT PROTECTED THEM FROM THE WIND - BUT COULD THE BOY SAVE HIS SISTER?"
STOP THAT, TEDDY! AW-PUL-LEASE LEAVE ME ALONE!
I GOTTA, BABS! THIS IS WHAT WE LEARNED IN CUB SCOUTS!-I GOTTA KEEP YOUR BLOOD CIRCULATED.
"I HAD AN INSPIRATION-DIANA'S CLOTHES! I KNEW WONDER WOMAN WOULD WANT ME TO GIVE THEM TO THESE CHILDREN. COULD I DISLODGE THEM FROM MY BRANCHES? I TRIED WITH ALL MY MIGHT, AIDED BY THE WIND."
JIMINY CHRISTMAS! WADDAYA KNOW- CLOTHES! A COAT- GET UP QUICK, SIS, AND PUT THIS ON!
WHY- WHY- THEY'RE NURSE'S CLOTHES-
3
"THERE WERE MATCHES IN THE COAT POCKET. TEDDY, GOOD CUB SCOUT THAT HE WAS, SOON HAD A FIRE GOING."
HOW YOU FEEL NOW, BABS?
OKAY, MY FEET HAVE STOPPED HURTING! -OH! YOU'RE AWFUL NICE TO ME, TEDDY!

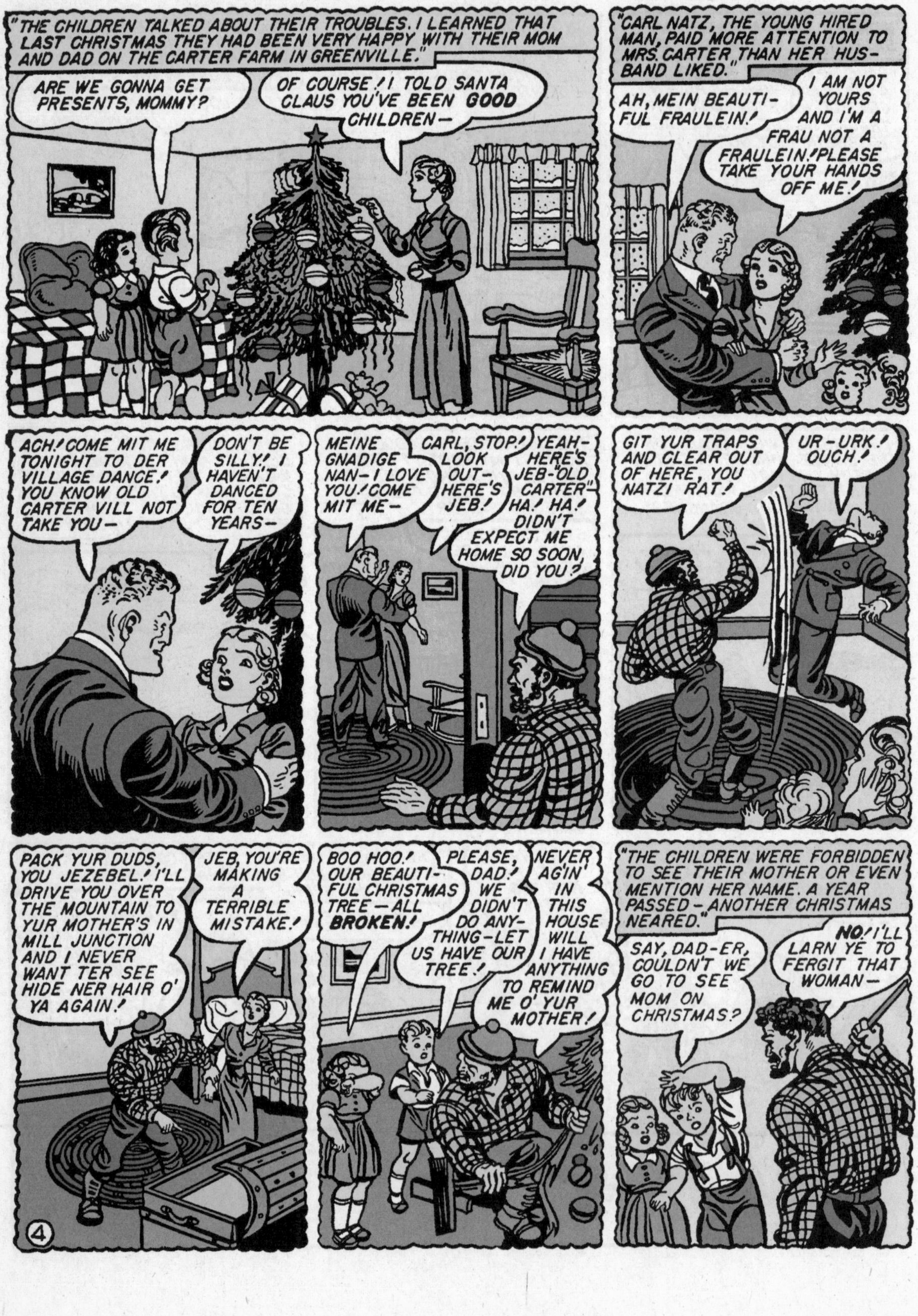
"THE CHILDREN TALKED ABOUT THEIR TROUBLES. I LEARNED THAT LAST CHRISTMAS THEY HAD BEEN VERY HAPPY WITH THEIR MOM AND DAD ON THE CARTER FARM IN GREENVILLE."
ARE WE GONNA GET PRESENTS, MOMMY?
OF COURSE! I TOLD SANTA CLAUS YOU'VE BEEN GOOD CHILDREN—
"CARL NATZ, THE YOUNG HIRED MAN, PAID MORE ATTENTION TO MRS. CARTER THAN HER HUSBAND LIKED."
AH, MEIN BEAUTIFUL FRAULEIN!
I AM NOT YOURS AND I'M A FRAU NOT A FRAULEIN! PLEASE TAKE YOUR HANDS OFF ME!
ACH! COME MIT ME TONIGHT TO DER VILLAGE DANCE! YOU KNOW OLD CARTER VILL NOT TAKE YOU—
DON'T BE SILLY! I HAVEN'T DANCED FOR TEN YEARS—
MEINE GNADIGE NAN—I LOVE YOU! COME MIT ME—
CARL, STOP! LOOK OUT—HERE'S JEB!
YEAH—HERE'S JEB—"OLD CARTER"—HA! HA! DIDN'T EXPECT ME HOME SO SOON, DID YOU?
GIT YUR TRAPS AND CLEAR OUT OF HERE, YOU NATZI RAT!
UR-URK! OUCH!
PACK YUR DUDS, YOU JEZEBEL! I'LL DRIVE YOU OVER THE MOUNTAIN TO YUR MOTHER'S IN MILL JUNCTION AND I NEVER WANT TER SEE HIDE NER HAIR O' YA AGAIN!
JEB, YOU'RE MAKING A TERRIBLE MISTAKE!
4
BOO HOO! OUR BEAUTIFUL CHRISTMAS TREE—ALL BROKEN!
PLEASE, DAD! WE DIDN'T DO ANYTHING—LET US HAVE OUR TREE!
NEVER AG'IN' IN THIS HOUSE WILL I HAVE ANYTHING TO REMIND ME O' YUR MOTHER!
"THE CHILDREN WERE FORBIDDEN TO SEE THEIR MOTHER OR EVEN MENTION HER NAME. A YEAR PASSED—ANOTHER CHRISTMAS NEARED."
SAY, DAD—ER, COULDN'T WE GO TO SEE MOM ON CHRISTMAS?
NO! I'LL LARN YE TO FERGIT THAT WOMAN—

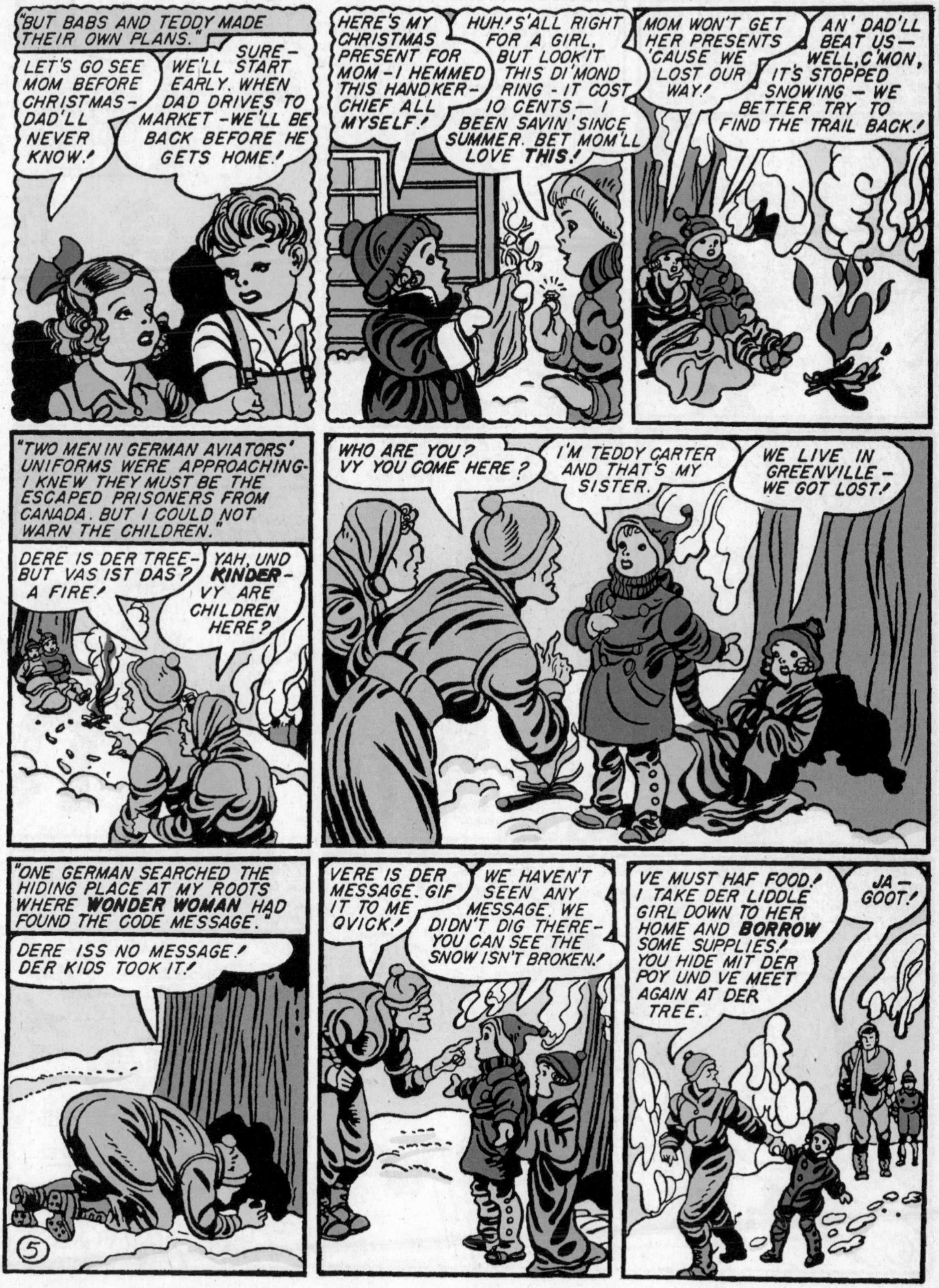
"BUT BABS AND TEDDY MADE THEIR OWN PLANS."
LET'S GO SEE MOM BEFORE CHRISTMAS- DAD'LL NEVER KNOW!
SURE- WE'LL START EARLY. WHEN DAD DRIVES TO MARKET -WE'LL BE BACK BEFORE HE GETS HOME!
HERE'S MY CHRISTMAS PRESENT FOR MOM - I HEMMED THIS HANDKER-CHIEF ALL MYSELF!
HUH! S'ALL RIGHT FOR A GIRL, BUT LOOKIT THIS DI'MOND RING - IT COST 10 CENTS - I BEEN SAVIN' SINCE SUMMER. BET MOM'LL LOVE THIS!
MOM WON'T GET HER PRESENTS 'CAUSE WE LOST OUR WAY!
AN' DAD'LL BEAT US- WELL, C'MON, IT'S STOPPED SNOWING - WE BETTER TRY TO FIND THE TRAIL BACK!
"TWO MEN IN GERMAN AVIATORS' UNIFORMS WERE APPROACHING- I KNEW THEY MUST BE THE ESCAPED PRISONERS FROM CANADA. BUT I COULD NOT WARN THE CHILDREN."
DERE IS DER TREE- BUT VAS IST DAS? A FIRE!
YAH, UND KINDER- VY ARE CHILDREN HERE?
WHO ARE YOU? VY YOU COME HERE?
I'M TEDDY CARTER AND THAT'S MY SISTER.
WE LIVE IN GREENVILLE - WE GOT LOST!
"ONE GERMAN SEARCHED THE HIDING PLACE AT MY ROOTS WHERE WONDER WOMAN HAD FOUND THE CODE MESSAGE."
DERE ISS NO MESSAGE! DER KIDS TOOK IT!
5
VERE IS DER MESSAGE. GIF IT TO ME QVICK!
WE HAVEN'T SEEN ANY MESSAGE. WE DIDN'T DIG THERE- YOU CAN SEE THE SNOW ISN'T BROKEN!
VE MUST HAF FOOD! I TAKE DER LIDDLE GIRL DOWN TO HER HOME AND BORROW SOME SUPPLIES! YOU HIDE MIT DER POY UND VE MEET AGAIN AT DER TREE.
JA- GOOT!

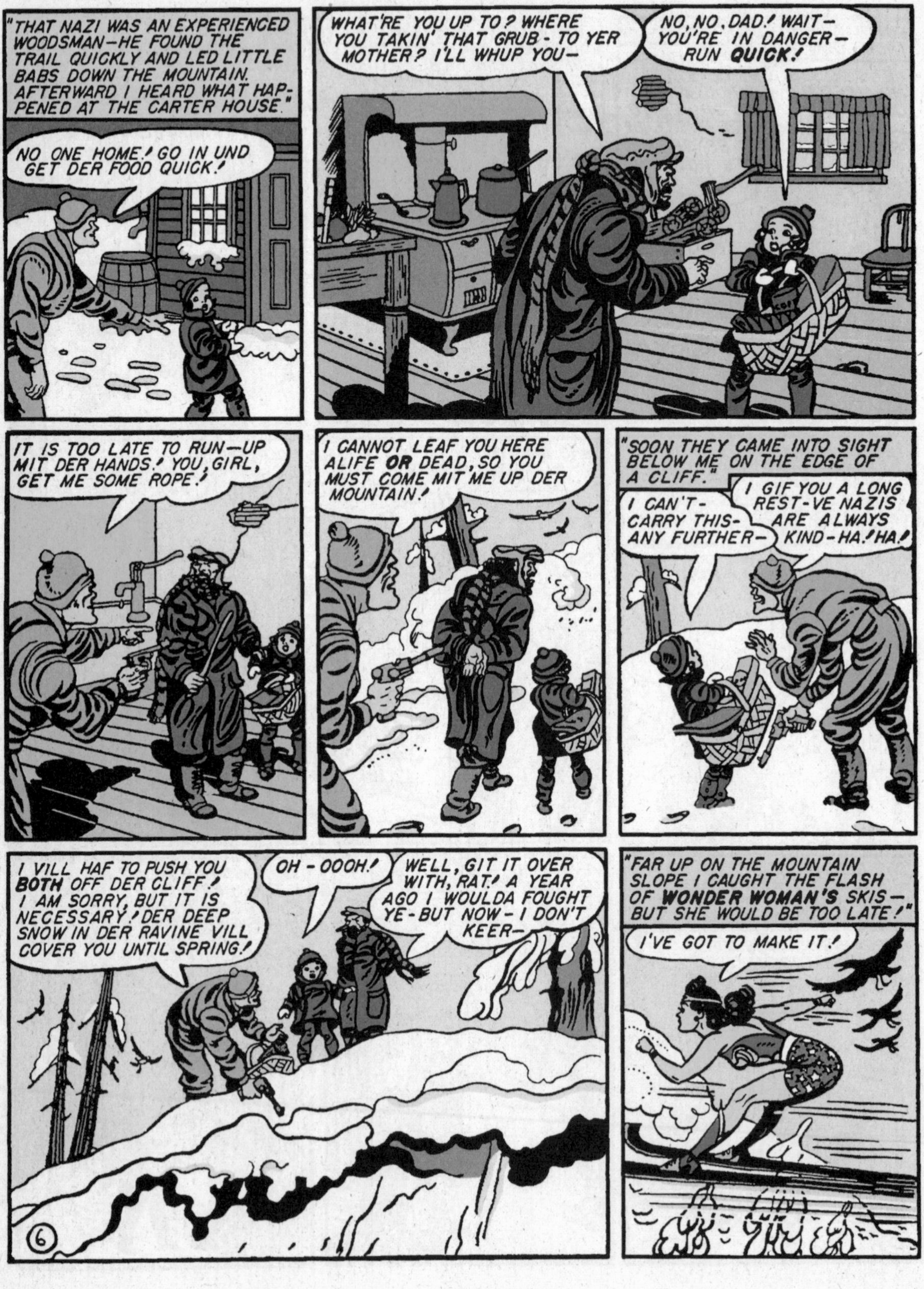
"THAT NAZI WAS AN EXPERIENCED WOODSMAN—HE FOUND THE TRAIL QUICKLY AND LED LITTLE BABS DOWN THE MOUNTAIN. AFTERWARD I HEARD WHAT HAPPENED AT THE CARTER HOUSE."
NO ONE HOME! GO IN UND GET DER FOOD QUICK!
WHAT'RE YOU UP TO? WHERE YOU TAKIN' THAT GRUB - TO YER MOTHER? I'LL WHUP YOU—
NO, NO, DAD! WAIT—YOU'RE IN DANGER—RUN **QUICK!**
IT IS TOO LATE TO RUN—UP MIT DER HANDS! YOU, GIRL, GET ME SOME ROPE!
I CANNOT LEAF YOU HERE ALIFE **OR** DEAD, SO YOU MUST COME MIT ME UP DER MOUNTAIN!
"SOON THEY CAME INTO SIGHT BELOW ME ON THE EDGE OF A CLIFF."
I CAN'T- CARRY THIS- ANY FURTHER-
I GIF YOU A LONG REST-VE NAZIS ARE ALWAYS KIND-HA! HA!
I VILL HAF TO PUSH YOU **BOTH** OFF DER CLIFF! I AM SORRY, BUT IT IS NECESSARY! DER DEEP SNOW IN DER RAVINE VILL COVER YOU UNTIL SPRING!
OH - OOOH!
WELL, GIT IT OVER WITH, RAT! A YEAR AGO I WOULDA FOUGHT YE-BUT NOW - I DON'T KEER—
6
"FAR UP ON THE MOUNTAIN SLOPE I CAUGHT THE FLASH OF **WONDER WOMAN'S** SKIS—BUT SHE WOULD BE TOO LATE!"
I'VE GOT TO MAKE IT!

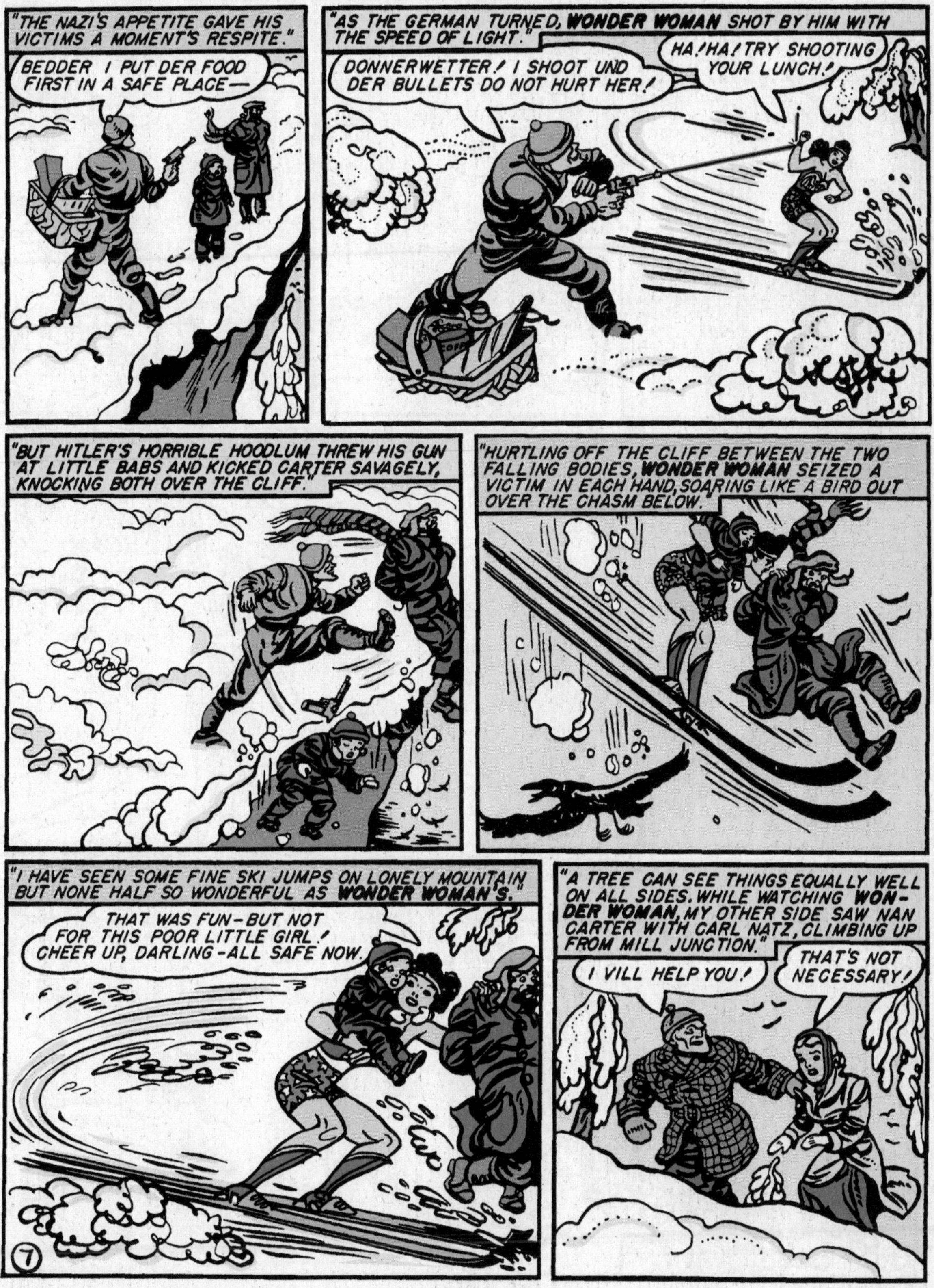
"THE NAZI'S APPETITE GAVE HIS VICTIMS A MOMENT'S RESPITE."
BEDDER I PUT DER FOOD FIRST IN A SAFE PLACE—
"AS THE GERMAN TURNED, WONDER WOMAN SHOT BY HIM WITH THE SPEED OF LIGHT."
DONNERWETTER! I SHOOT UND DER BULLETS DO NOT HURT HER!
HA! HA! TRY SHOOTING YOUR LUNCH!
"BUT HITLER'S HORRIBLE HOODLUM THREW HIS GUN AT LITTLE BABS AND KICKED CARTER SAVAGELY, KNOCKING BOTH OVER THE CLIFF."
"HURTLING OFF THE CLIFF BETWEEN THE TWO FALLING BODIES, WONDER WOMAN SEIZED A VICTIM IN EACH HAND, SOARING LIKE A BIRD OUT OVER THE CHASM BELOW."
"I HAVE SEEN SOME FINE SKI JUMPS ON LONELY MOUNTAIN BUT NONE HALF SO WONDERFUL AS WONDER WOMAN'S."
THAT WAS FUN—BUT NOT FOR THIS POOR LITTLE GIRL! CHEER UP, DARLING—ALL SAFE NOW.
7
"A TREE CAN SEE THINGS EQUALLY WELL ON ALL SIDES. WHILE WATCHING WONDER WOMAN, MY OTHER SIDE SAW NAN CARTER WITH CARL NATZ, CLIMBING UP FROM MILL JUNCTION."
I VILL HELP YOU!
THAT'S NOT NECESSARY!

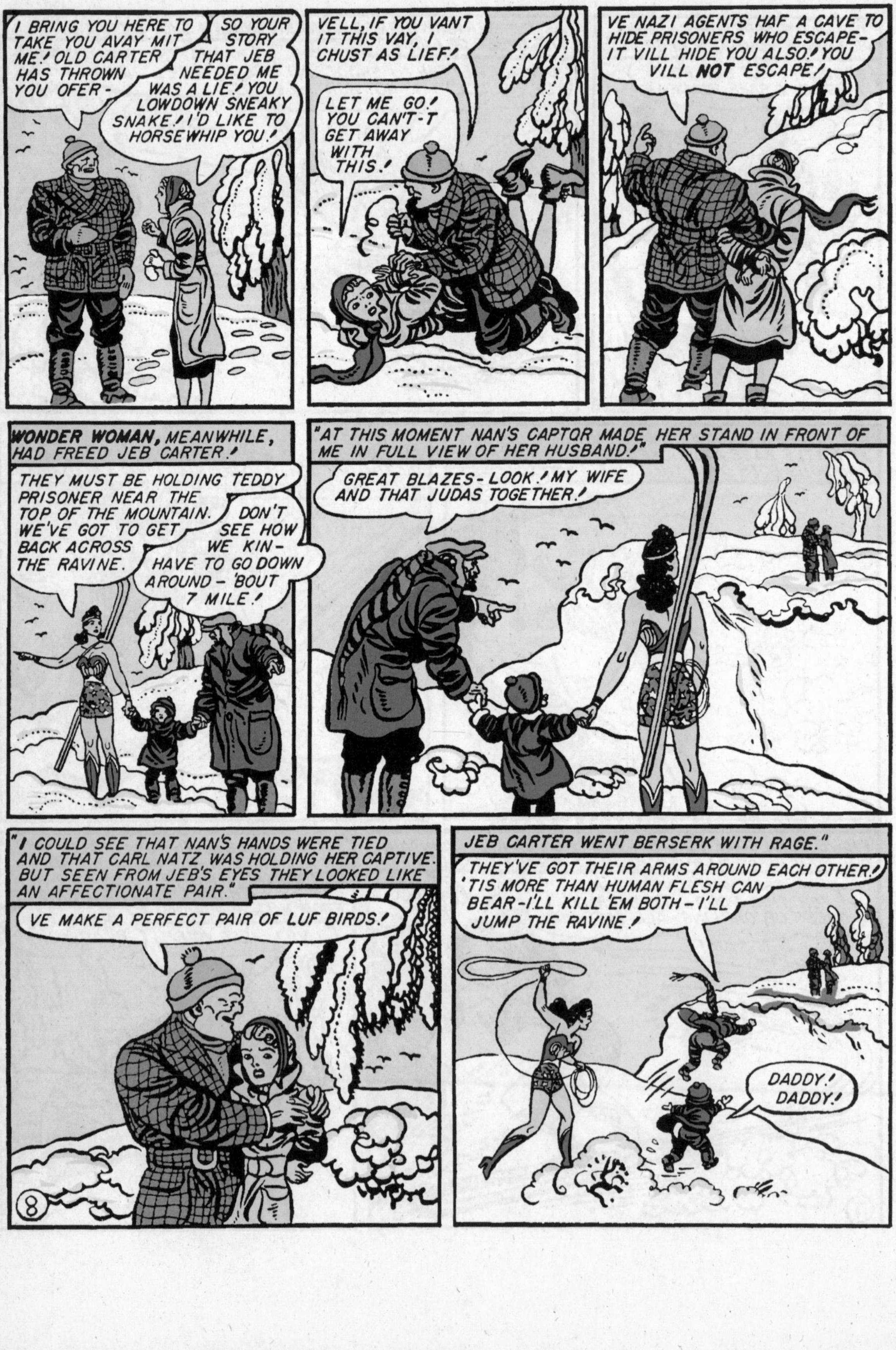
I BRING YOU HERE TO TAKE YOU AVAY MIT ME.! OLD CARTER HAS THROWN YOU OFER-
SO YOUR STORY THAT JEB NEEDED ME WAS A LIE! YOU LOWDOWN SNEAKY SNAKE! I'D LIKE TO HORSEWHIP YOU!
VELL, IF YOU VANT IT THIS VAY, I CHUST AS LIEF!
LET ME GO! YOU CAN'T-T GET AWAY WITH THIS!
VE NAZI AGENTS HAF A CAVE TO HIDE PRISONERS WHO ESCAPE-IT VILL HIDE YOU ALSO! YOU VILL NOT ESCAPE!
WONDER WOMAN, MEANWHILE, HAD FREED JEB CARTER!
THEY MUST BE HOLDING TEDDY PRISONER NEAR THE TOP OF THE MOUNTAIN. WE'VE GOT TO GET BACK ACROSS THE RAVINE.
DON'T SEE HOW WE KIN-HAVE TO GO DOWN AROUND - 'BOUT 7 MILE!
"AT THIS MOMENT NAN'S CAPTOR MADE HER STAND IN FRONT OF ME IN FULL VIEW OF HER HUSBAND!"
GREAT BLAZES- LOOK! MY WIFE AND THAT JUDAS TOGETHER!
"I COULD SEE THAT NAN'S HANDS WERE TIED AND THAT CARL NATZ WAS HOLDING HER CAPTIVE. BUT SEEN FROM JEB'S EYES THEY LOOKED LIKE AN AFFECTIONATE PAIR."
VE MAKE A PERFECT PAIR OF LUF BIRDS!
8
JEB CARTER WENT BERSERK WITH RAGE."
THEY'VE GOT THEIR ARMS AROUND EACH OTHER! 'TIS MORE THAN HUMAN FLESH CAN BEAR-I'LL KILL 'EM BOTH-I'LL JUMP THE RAVINE!
DADDY! DADDY!

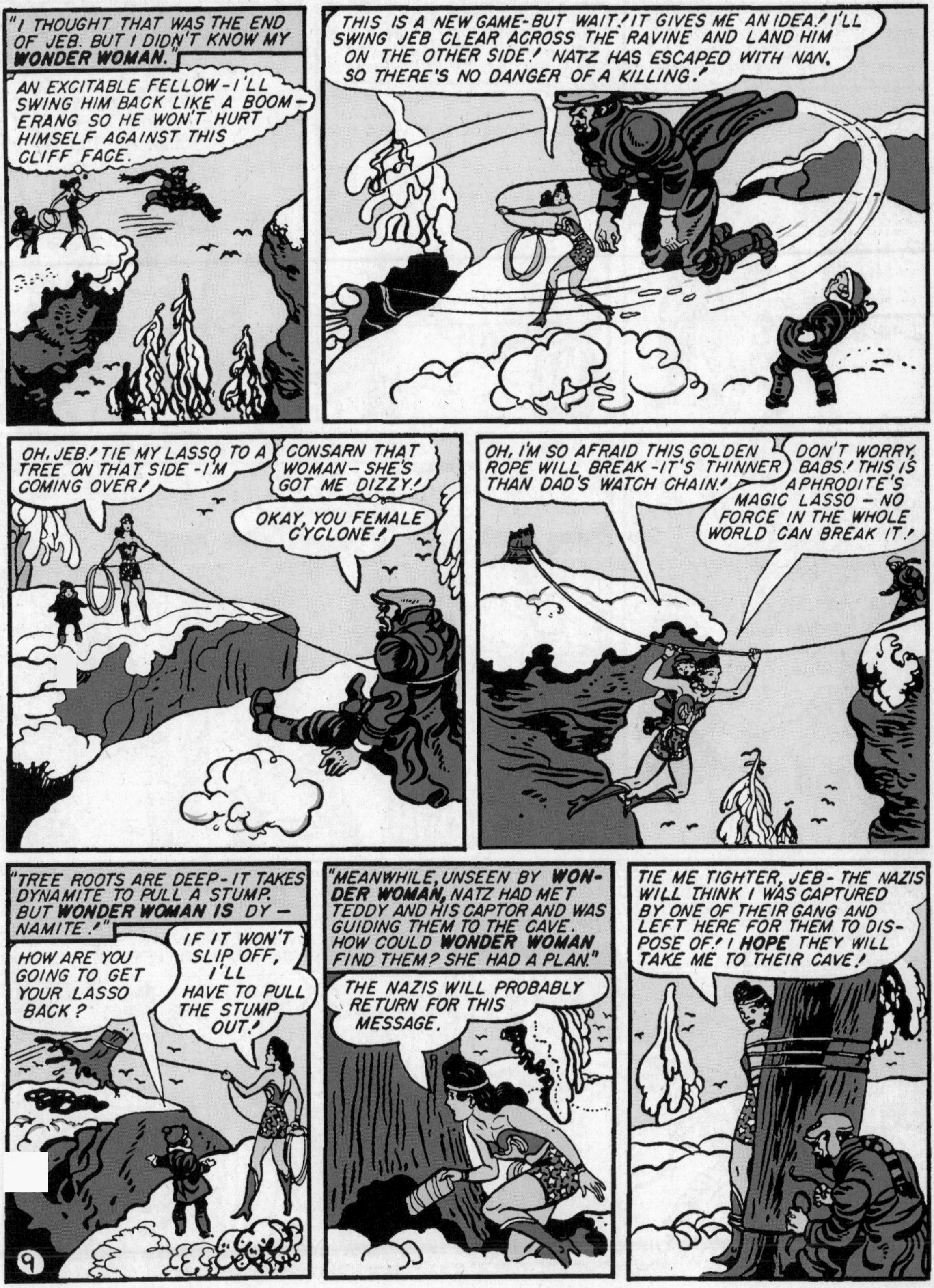
"I THOUGHT THAT WAS THE END OF JEB. BUT I DIDN'T KNOW MY WONDER WOMAN."
AN EXCITABLE FELLOW-I'LL SWING HIM BACK LIKE A BOOMERANG SO HE WON'T HURT HIMSELF AGAINST THIS CLIFF FACE.
THIS IS A NEW GAME-BUT WAIT! IT GIVES ME AN IDEA! I'LL SWING JEB CLEAR ACROSS THE RAVINE AND LAND HIM ON THE OTHER SIDE! NATZ HAS ESCAPED WITH NAN, SO THERE'S NO DANGER OF A KILLING!"
OH, JEB! TIE MY LASSO TO A TREE ON THAT SIDE -I'M COMING OVER!
CONSARN THAT WOMAN- SHE'S GOT ME DIZZY!
OKAY, YOU FEMALE CYCLONE!
OH, I'M SO AFRAID THIS GOLDEN ROPE WILL BREAK -IT'S THINNER THAN DAD'S WATCH CHAIN!
DON'T WORRY, BABS! THIS IS APHRODITE'S MAGIC LASSO - NO FORCE IN THE WHOLE WORLD CAN BREAK IT!
"TREE ROOTS ARE DEEP- IT TAKES DYNAMITE TO PULL A STUMP. BUT WONDER WOMAN IS DYNAMITE!"
HOW ARE YOU GOING TO GET YOUR LASSO BACK?
IF IT WON'T SLIP OFF, I'LL HAVE TO PULL THE STUMP OUT!
9
"MEANWHILE, UNSEEN BY WONDER WOMAN, NATZ HAD MET TEDDY AND HIS CAPTOR AND WAS GUIDING THEM TO THE CAVE. HOW COULD WONDER WOMAN FIND THEM? SHE HAD A PLAN."
THE NAZIS WILL PROBABLY RETURN FOR THIS MESSAGE.
TIE ME TIGHTER, JEB- THE NAZIS WILL THINK I WAS CAPTURED BY ONE OF THEIR GANG AND LEFT HERE FOR THEM TO DISPOSE OF! I HOPE THEY WILL TAKE ME TO THEIR CAVE!

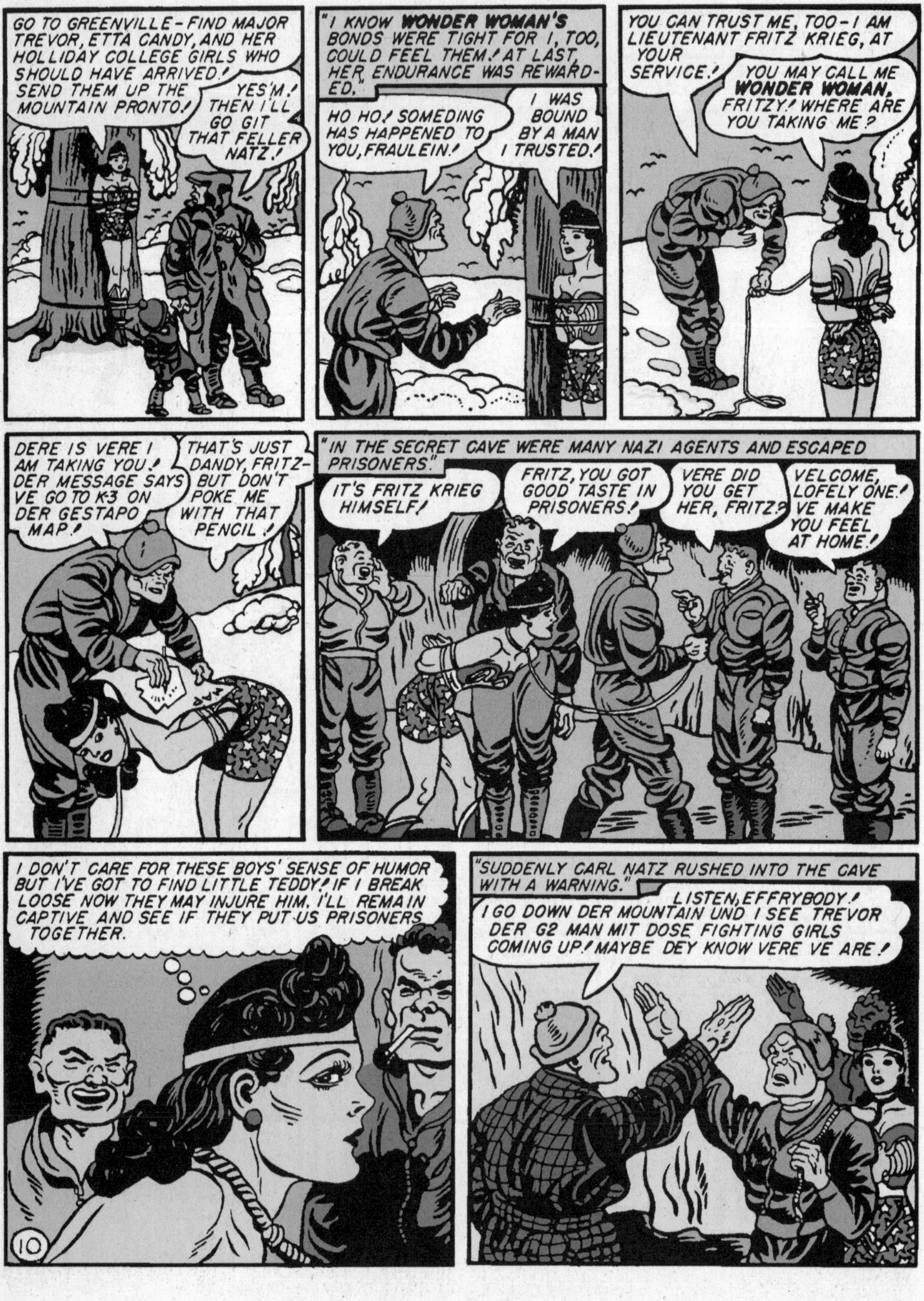
GO TO GREENVILLE - FIND MAJOR TREVOR, ETTA CANDY, AND HER HOLLIDAY COLLEGE GIRLS WHO SHOULD HAVE ARRIVED! SEND THEM UP THE MOUNTAIN PRONTO!
YES'M! THEN I'LL GO GIT THAT FELLER NATZ!
"I KNOW WONDER WOMAN'S BONDS WERE TIGHT FOR I, TOO, COULD FEEL THEM! AT LAST, HER ENDURANCE WAS REWARDED."
HO HO! SOMEDING HAS HAPPENED TO YOU, FRAULEIN!
I WAS BOUND BY A MAN I TRUSTED!
YOU CAN TRUST ME, TOO - I AM LIEUTENANT FRITZ KRIEG, AT YOUR SERVICE!
YOU MAY CALL ME WONDER WOMAN, FRITZY! WHERE ARE YOU TAKING ME?
DERE IS VERE I AM TAKING YOU! DER MESSAGE SAYS VE GO TO K-3 ON DER GESTAPO MAP!
THAT'S JUST DANDY, FRITZ- BUT DON'T POKE ME WITH THAT PENCIL!
MAP
"IN THE SECRET CAVE WERE MANY NAZI AGENTS AND ESCAPED PRISONERS."
IT'S FRITZ KRIEG HIMSELF!
FRITZ, YOU GOT GOOD TASTE IN PRISONERS!
VERE DID YOU GET HER, FRITZ?
VELCOME, LOFELY ONE! VE MAKE YOU FEEL AT HOME!
I DON'T CARE FOR THESE BOYS' SENSE OF HUMOR BUT I'VE GOT TO FIND LITTLE TEDDY! IF I BREAK LOOSE NOW THEY MAY INJURE HIM. I'LL REMAIN CAPTIVE AND SEE IF THEY PUT US PRISONERS TOGETHER.
10
"SUDDENLY CARL NATZ RUSHED INTO THE CAVE WITH A WARNING."
LISTEN, EFFRYBODY! I GO DOWN DER MOUNTAIN UND I SEE TREVOR DER G2 MAN MIT DOSE FIGHTING GIRLS COMING UP! MAYBE DEY KNOW VERE VE ARE!

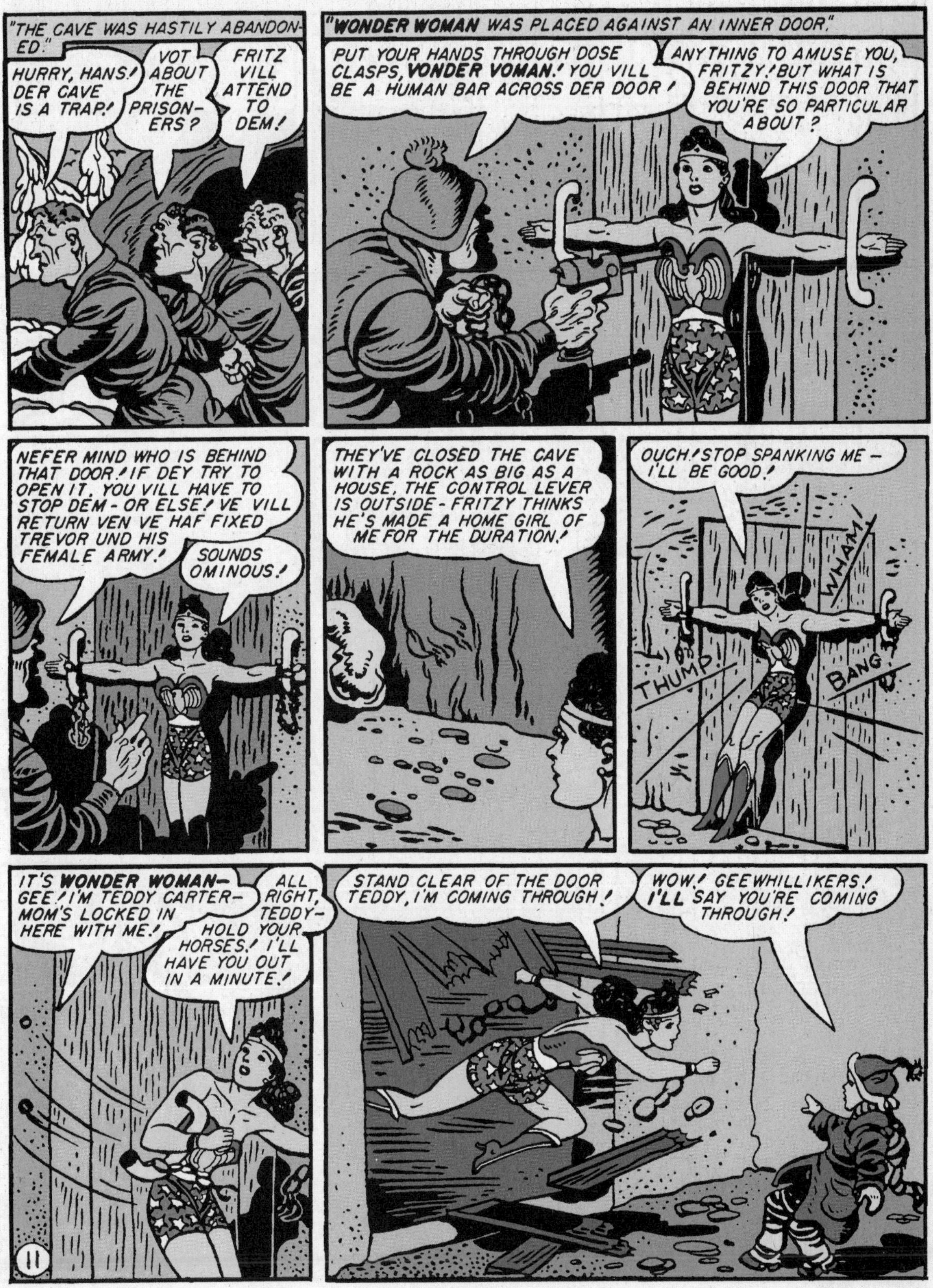
"THE CAVE WAS HASTILY ABANDONED."
HURRY, HANS! DER CAVE IS A TRAP!
VOT ABOUT THE PRISONERS?
FRITZ VILL ATTEND TO DEM!
"WONDER WOMAN WAS PLACED AGAINST AN INNER DOOR."
PUT YOUR HANDS THROUGH DOSE CLASPS, VONDER VOMAN! YOU VILL BE A HUMAN BAR ACROSS DER DOOR!
ANYTHING TO AMUSE YOU, FRITZY! BUT WHAT IS BEHIND THIS DOOR THAT YOU'RE SO PARTICULAR ABOUT?
NEFER MIND WHO IS BEHIND THAT DOOR! IF DEY TRY TO OPEN IT, YOU VILL HAVE TO STOP DEM - OR ELSE! VE VILL RETURN VEN VE HAF FIXED TREVOR UND HIS FEMALE ARMY!
SOUNDS OMINOUS!
THEY'VE CLOSED THE CAVE WITH A ROCK AS BIG AS A HOUSE. THE CONTROL LEVER IS OUTSIDE - FRITZY THINKS HE'S MADE A HOME GIRL OF ME FOR THE DURATION!
OUCH! STOP SPANKING ME - I'LL BE GOOD!
WHAM!
THUMP!
BANG!
IT'S WONDER WOMAN- GEE! I'M TEDDY CARTER- MOM'S LOCKED IN HERE WITH ME!
ALL RIGHT, TEDDY- HOLD YOUR HORSES! I'LL HAVE YOU OUT IN A MINUTE!
11
STAND CLEAR OF THE DOOR TEDDY, I'M COMING THROUGH!
WOW! GEEWHILLIKERS! I'LL SAY YOU'RE COMING THROUGH!

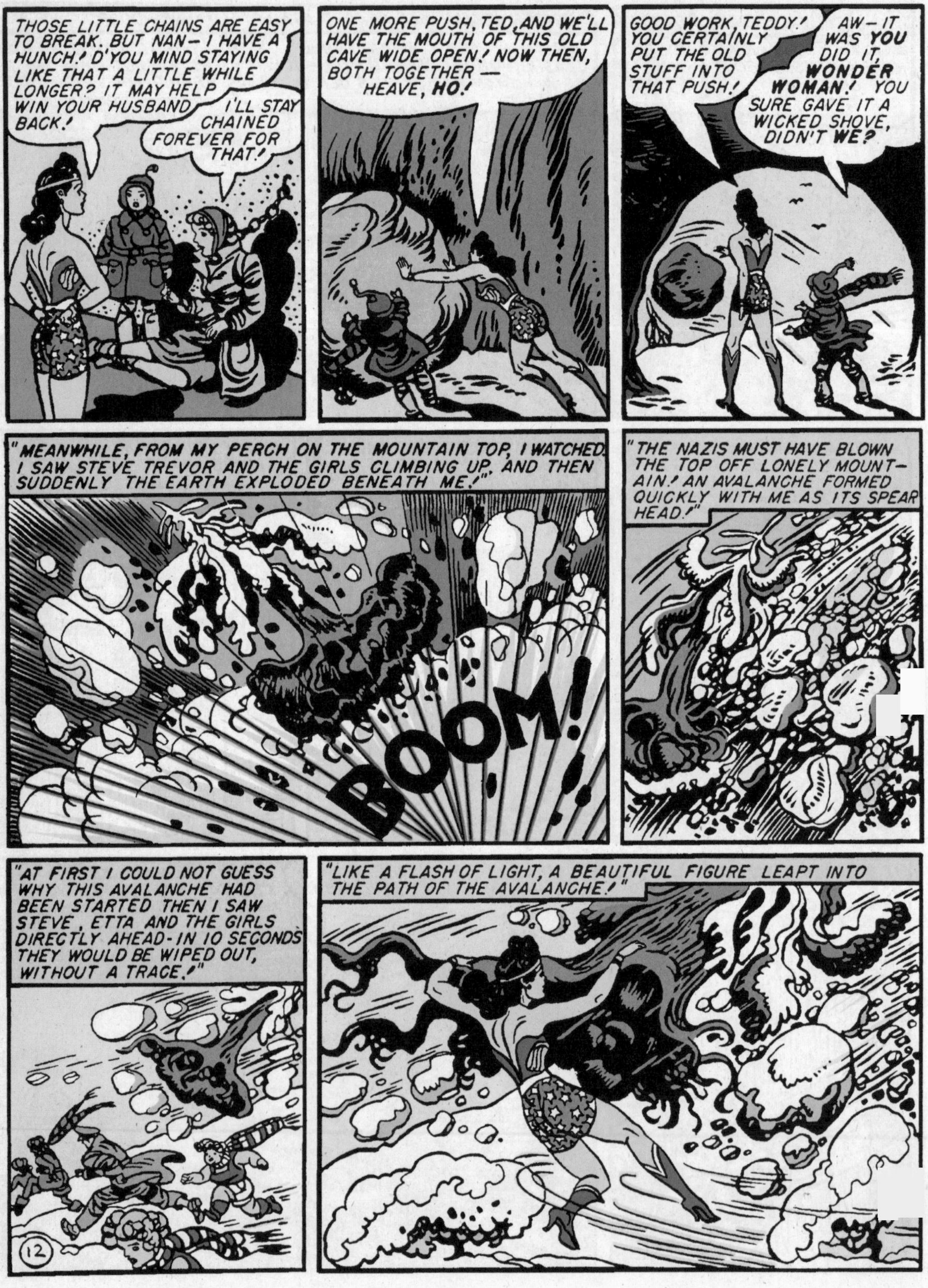

THOSE LITTLE CHAINS ARE EASY TO BREAK. BUT NAN— I HAVE A HUNCH! D'YOU MIND STAYING LIKE THAT A LITTLE WHILE LONGER? IT MAY HELP WIN YOUR HUSBAND BACK!
I'LL STAY CHAINED FOREVER FOR THAT!
ONE MORE PUSH, TED, AND WE'LL HAVE THE MOUTH OF THIS OLD CAVE WIDE OPEN! NOW THEN, BOTH TOGETHER — HEAVE, HO!
GOOD WORK, TEDDY! YOU CERTAINLY PUT THE OLD STUFF INTO THAT PUSH!
AW— IT WAS YOU DID IT, WONDER WOMAN! YOU SURE GAVE IT A WICKED SHOVE, DIDN'T WE?
"MEANWHILE, FROM MY PERCH ON THE MOUNTAIN TOP, I WATCHED. I SAW STEVE TREVOR AND THE GIRLS CLIMBING UP, AND THEN SUDDENLY THE EARTH EXPLODED BENEATH ME!"
BOOM!
"THE NAZIS MUST HAVE BLOWN THE TOP OFF LONELY MOUNTAIN! AN AVALANCHE FORMED QUICKLY WITH ME AS ITS SPEAR HEAD!"
"AT FIRST I COULD NOT GUESS WHY THIS AVALANCHE HAD BEEN STARTED THEN I SAW STEVE, ETTA AND THE GIRLS DIRECTLY AHEAD- IN 10 SECONDS THEY WOULD BE WIPED OUT, WITHOUT A TRACE!"
12
"LIKE A FLASH OF LIGHT, A BEAUTIFUL FIGURE LEAPT INTO THE PATH OF THE AVALANCHE!"

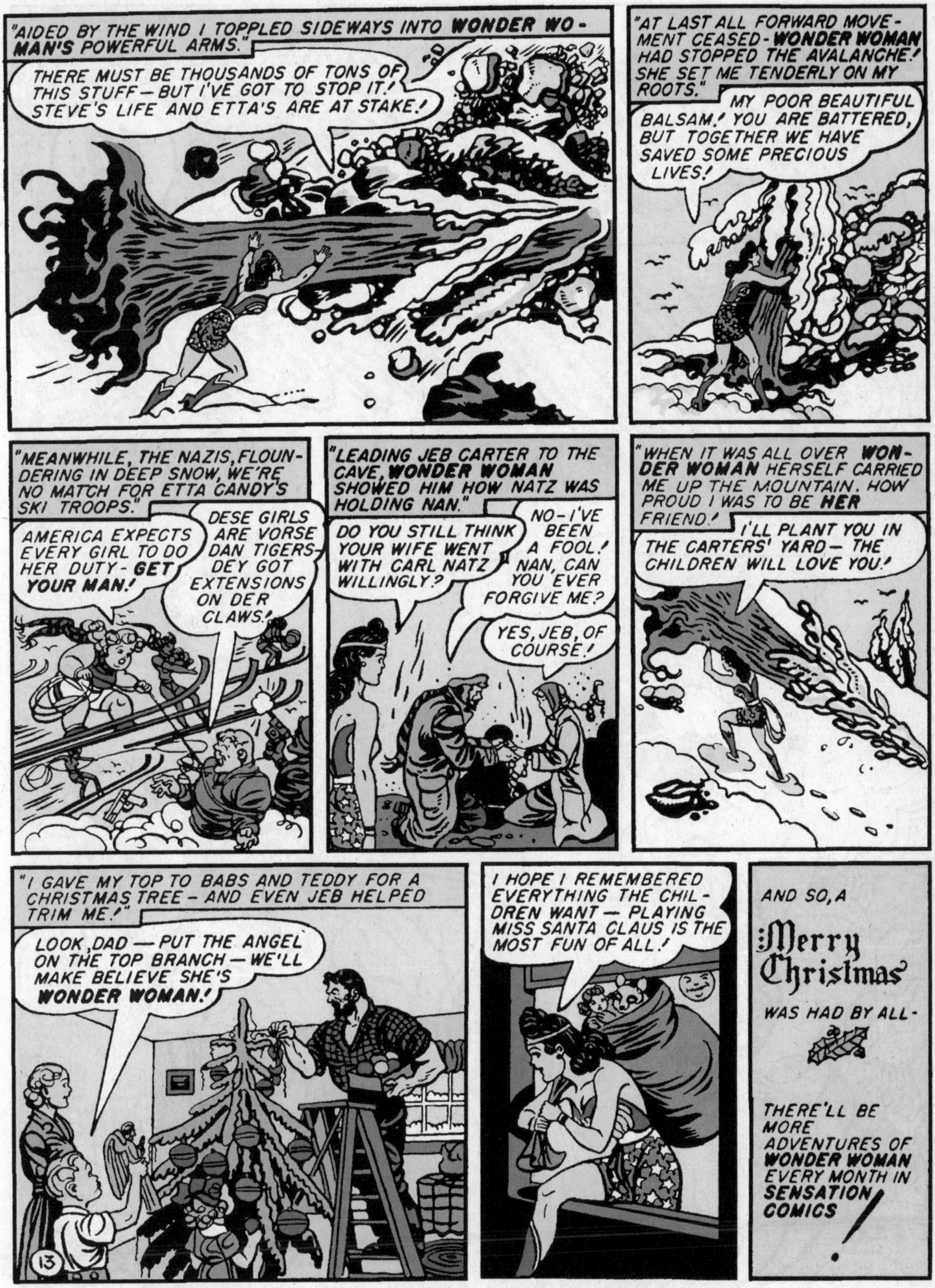

"AIDED BY THE WIND I TOPPLED SIDEWAYS INTO **WONDER WOMAN'S** POWERFUL ARMS."
THERE MUST BE THOUSANDS OF TONS OF THIS STUFF—BUT I'VE GOT TO STOP IT! STEVE'S LIFE AND ETTA'S ARE AT STAKE!
"AT LAST ALL FORWARD MOVEMENT CEASED-**WONDER WOMAN** HAD STOPPED THE AVALANCHE! SHE SET ME TENDERLY ON MY ROOTS."
MY POOR BEAUTIFUL BALSAM! YOU ARE BATTERED, BUT TOGETHER WE HAVE SAVED SOME PRECIOUS LIVES!
"MEANWHILE, THE NAZIS, FLOUNDERING IN DEEP SNOW, WE'RE NO MATCH FOR ETTA CANDY'S SKI TROOPS."
AMERICA EXPECTS EVERY GIRL TO DO HER DUTY-**GET YOUR MAN!**
DESE GIRLS ARE VORSE DAN TIGERS-DEY GOT EXTENSIONS ON DER CLAWS!
"LEADING JEB CARTER TO THE CAVE, **WONDER WOMAN** SHOWED HIM HOW NATZ WAS HOLDING NAN."
DO YOU STILL THINK YOUR WIFE WENT WITH CARL NATZ WILLINGLY?
NO-I'VE BEEN A FOOL! NAN, CAN YOU EVER FORGIVE ME?
YES, JEB, OF COURSE!
"WHEN IT WAS ALL OVER **WONDER WOMAN** HERSELF CARRIED ME UP THE MOUNTAIN. HOW PROUD I WAS TO BE **HER** FRIEND!"
I'LL PLANT YOU IN THE CARTERS' YARD—THE CHILDREN WILL LOVE YOU!
"I GAVE MY TOP TO BABS AND TEDDY FOR A CHRISTMAS TREE—AND EVEN JEB HELPED TRIM ME!"
LOOK, DAD—PUT THE ANGEL ON THE TOP BRANCH—WE'LL MAKE BELIEVE SHE'S **WONDER WOMAN!**
13
I HOPE I REMEMBERED EVERYTHING THE CHILDREN WANT—PLAYING MISS SANTA CLAUS IS THE MOST FUN OF ALL!
AND SO, A
Merry Christmas
WAS HAD BY ALL-
THERE'LL BE MORE ADVENTURES OF **WONDER WOMAN** EVERY MONTH IN **SENSATION COMICS**!

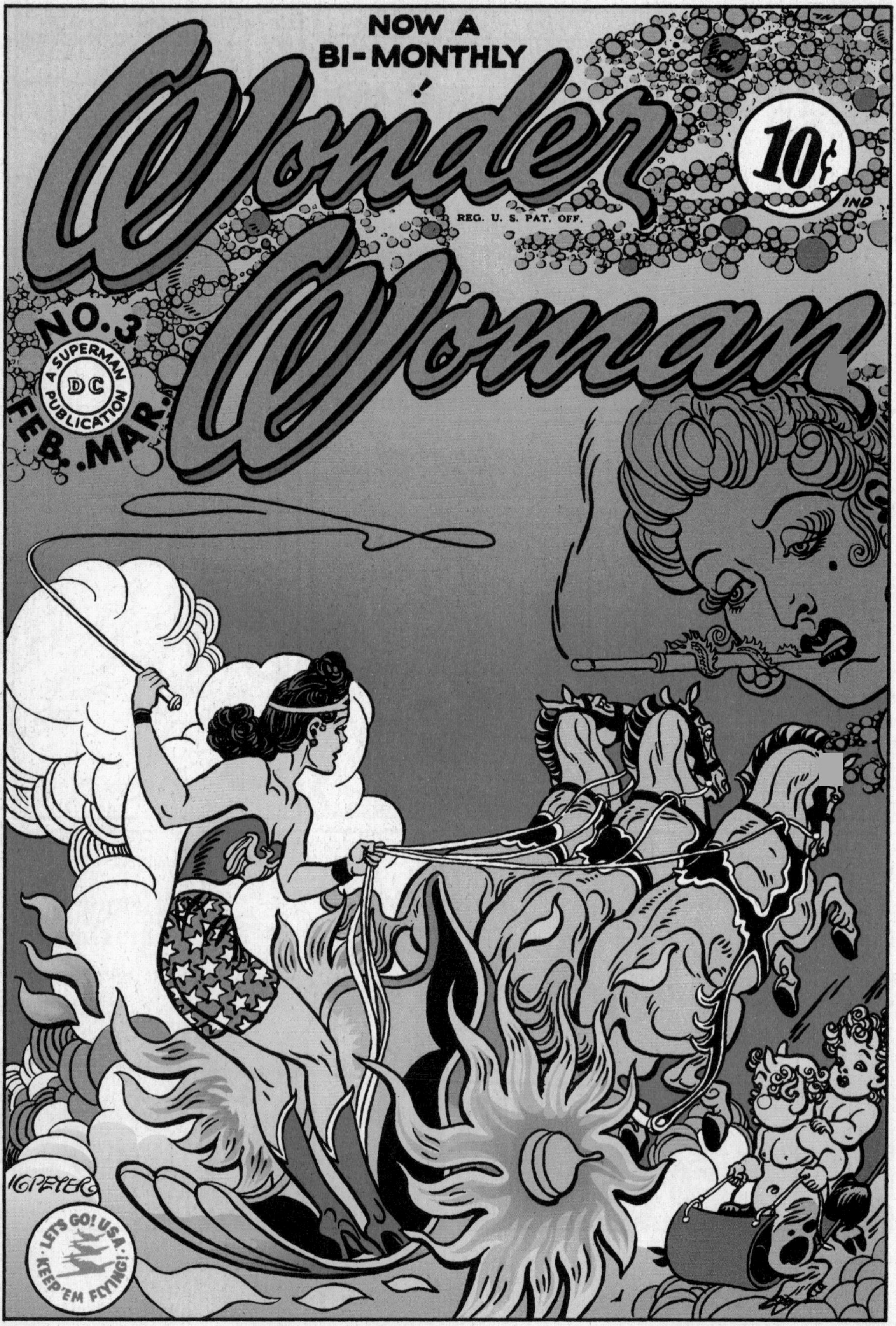
NOW A
BI-MONTHLY
Wonder Woman
REG. U. S. PAT. OFF.
10¢
IND
NO. 3
A SUPERMAN PUBLICATION
DC
FEB.-MAR.
LET'S GO! U.S.A.
KEEP 'EM FLYING!

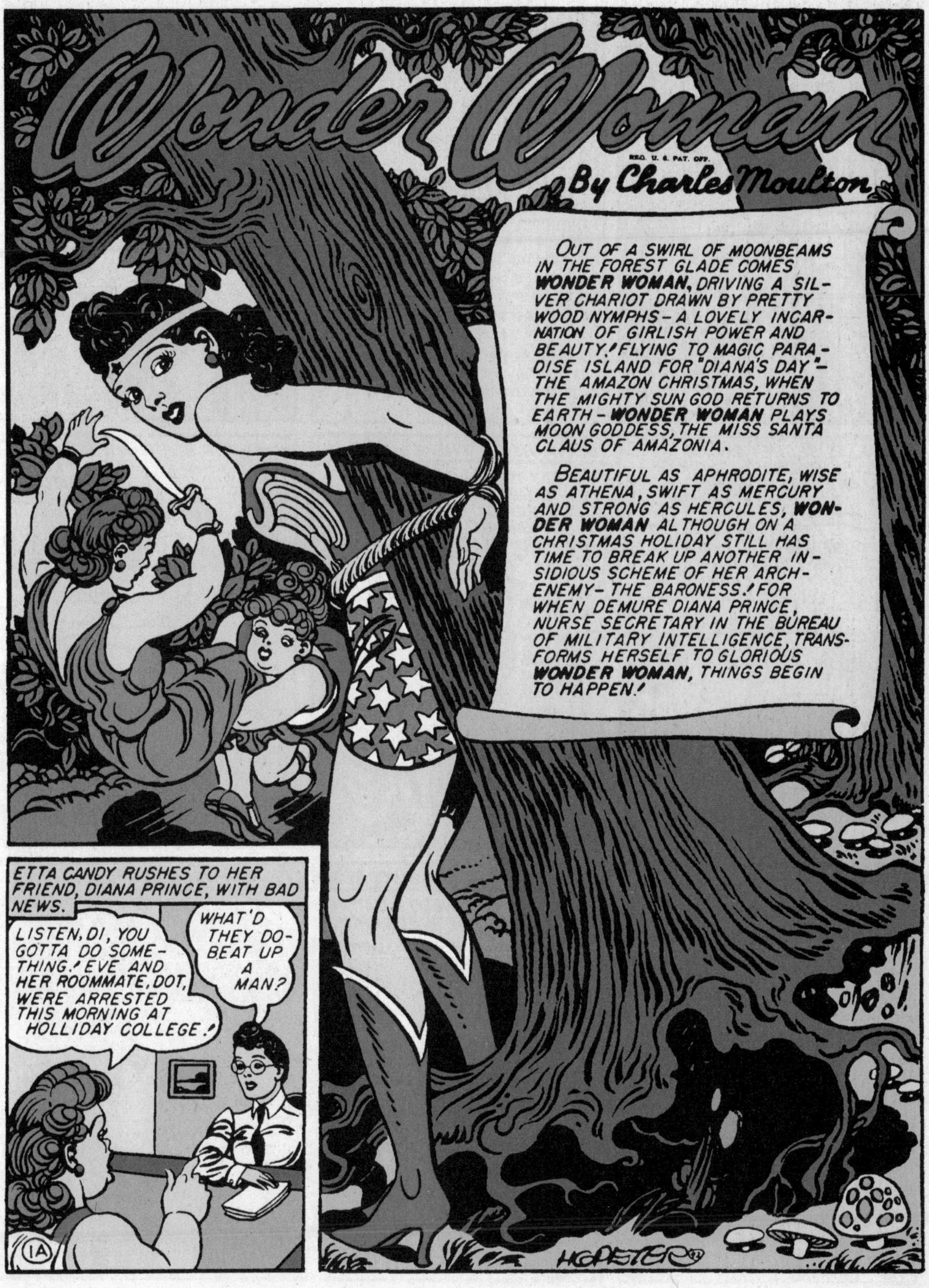
Wonder Woman
REG. U. S. PAT. OFF.
By Charles Moulton
OUT OF A SWIRL OF MOONBEAMS IN THE FOREST GLADE COMES WONDER WOMAN, DRIVING A SILVER CHARIOT DRAWN BY PRETTY WOOD NYMPHS - A LOVELY INCARNATION OF GIRLISH POWER AND BEAUTY! FLYING TO MAGIC PARADISE ISLAND FOR "DIANA'S DAY" - THE AMAZON CHRISTMAS, WHEN THE MIGHTY SUN GOD RETURNS TO EARTH - WONDER WOMAN PLAYS MOON GODDESS, THE MISS SANTA CLAUS OF AMAZONIA.
BEAUTIFUL AS APHRODITE, WISE AS ATHENA, SWIFT AS MERCURY AND STRONG AS HERCULES, WONDER WOMAN ALTHOUGH ON A CHRISTMAS HOLIDAY STILL HAS TIME TO BREAK UP ANOTHER INSIDIOUS SCHEME OF HER ARCHENEMY - THE BARONESS! FOR WHEN DEMURE DIANA PRINCE, NURSE SECRETARY IN THE BUREAU OF MILITARY INTELLIGENCE, TRANSFORMS HERSELF TO GLORIOUS WONDER WOMAN, THINGS BEGIN TO HAPPEN!
ETTA CANDY RUSHES TO HER FRIEND, DIANA PRINCE, WITH BAD NEWS.
LISTEN, DI, YOU GOTTA DO SOMETHING! EVE AND HER ROOMMATE, DOT, WERE ARRESTED THIS MORNING AT HOLLIDAY COLLEGE!
WHAT'D THEY DO - BEAT UP A MAN?
1A
HGPETER

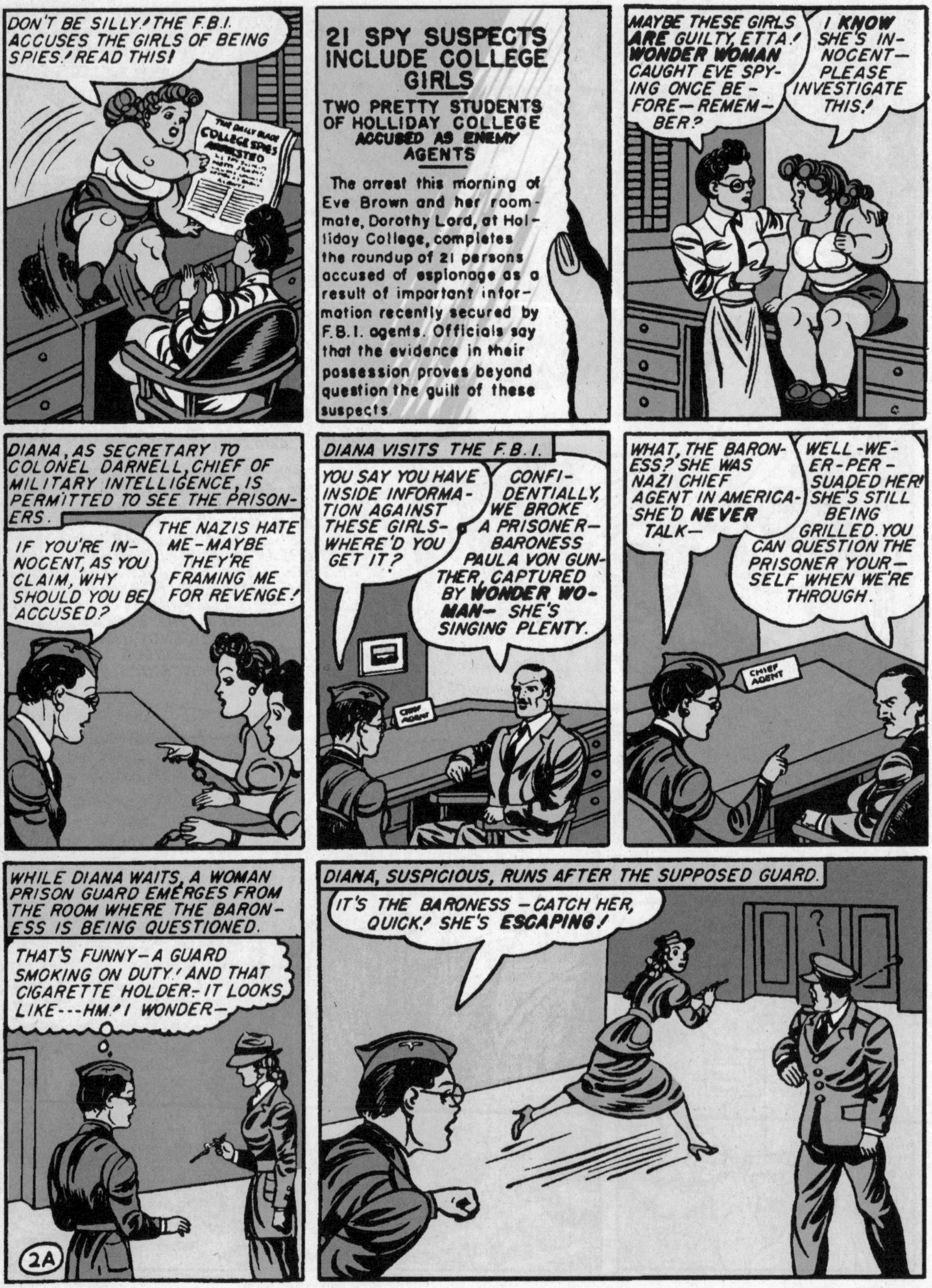

DON'T BE SILLY! THE F.B.I. ACCUSES THE GIRLS OF BEING SPIES! READ THIS!
21 SPY SUSPECTS INCLUDE COLLEGE GIRLS
TWO PRETTY STUDENTS OF HOLLIDAY COLLEGE ACCUSED AS ENEMY AGENTS
The arrest this morning of Eve Brown and her roommate, Dorothy Lord, at Holliday College, completes the roundup of 21 persons accused of espionage as a result of important information recently secured by F.B.I. agents. Officials say that the evidence in their possession proves beyond question the guilt of these suspects.
MAYBE THESE GIRLS ARE GUILTY, ETTA! WONDER WOMAN CAUGHT EVE SPYING ONCE BEFORE—REMEMBER?
I KNOW SHE'S INNOCENT—PLEASE INVESTIGATE THIS!
DIANA, AS SECRETARY TO COLONEL DARNELL, CHIEF OF MILITARY INTELLIGENCE, IS PERMITTED TO SEE THE PRISONERS.
IF YOU'RE INNOCENT, AS YOU CLAIM, WHY SHOULD YOU BE ACCUSED?
THE NAZIS HATE ME—MAYBE THEY'RE FRAMING ME FOR REVENGE!
DIANA VISITS THE F.B.I.
YOU SAY YOU HAVE INSIDE INFORMATION AGAINST THESE GIRLS—WHERE'D YOU GET IT?
CONFIDENTIALLY, WE BROKE A PRISONER—BARONESS PAULA VON GUNTHER, CAPTURED BY WONDER WOMAN—SHE'S SINGING PLENTY.
WHAT, THE BARONESS? SHE WAS NAZI CHIEF AGENT IN AMERICA—SHE'D NEVER TALK—
WELL-WE-ER-PERSUADED HER! SHE'S STILL BEING GRILLED. YOU CAN QUESTION THE PRISONER YOURSELF WHEN WE'RE THROUGH.
CHIEF AGENT
WHILE DIANA WAITS, A WOMAN PRISON GUARD EMERGES FROM THE ROOM WHERE THE BARONESS IS BEING QUESTIONED.
THAT'S FUNNY—A GUARD SMOKING ON DUTY! AND THAT CIGARETTE HOLDER—IT LOOKS LIKE---HM! I WONDER—
2A
DIANA, SUSPICIOUS, RUNS AFTER THE SUPPOSED GUARD.
IT'S THE BARONESS—CATCH HER, QUICK! SHE'S ESCAPING!
?

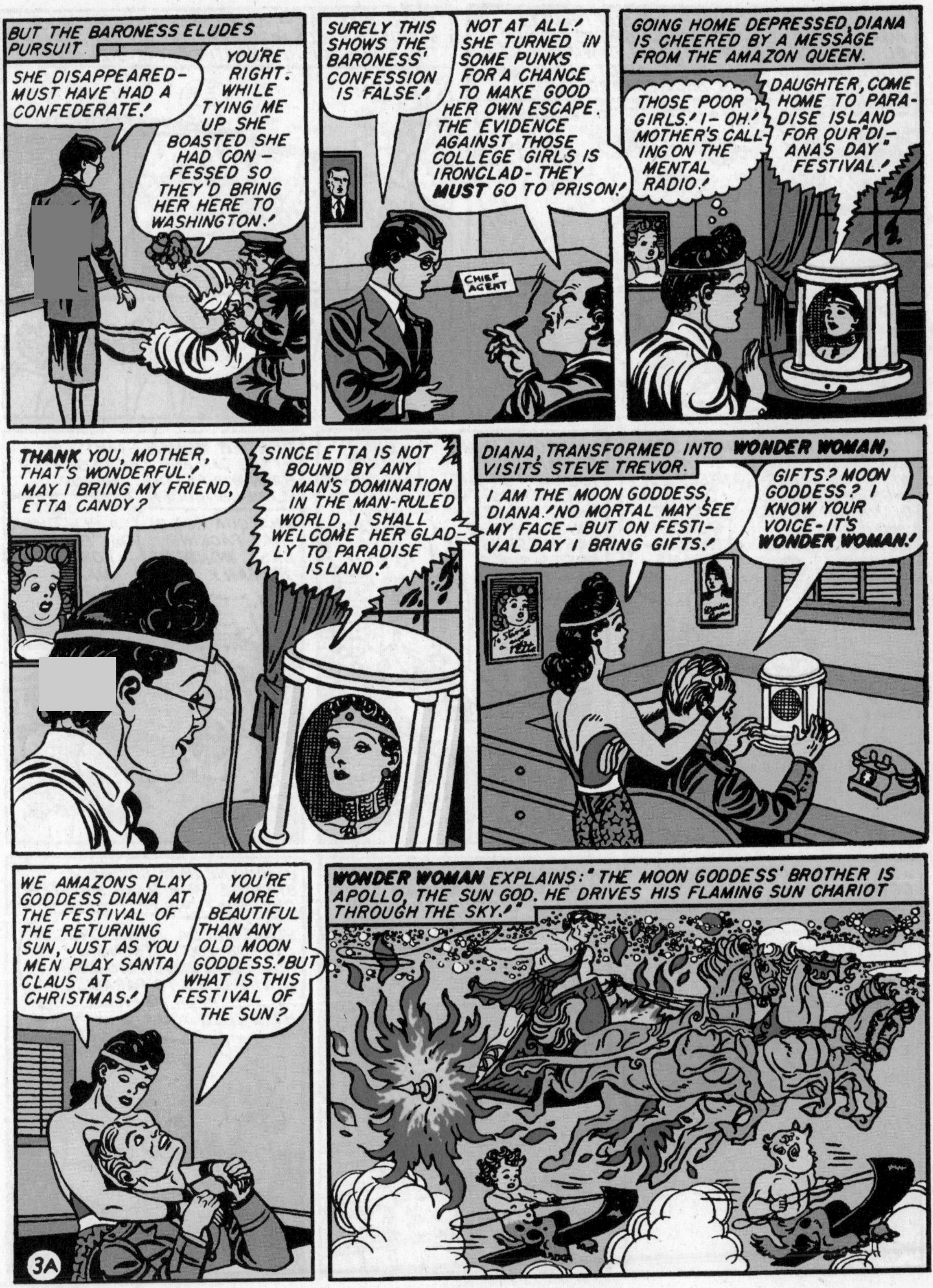

BUT THE BARONESS ELUDES PURSUIT
SHE DISAPPEARED- MUST HAVE HAD A CONFEDERATE!
YOU'RE RIGHT. WHILE TYING ME UP SHE BOASTED SHE HAD CON-FESSED SO THEY'D BRING HER HERE TO WASHINGTON!
SURELY THIS SHOWS THE BARONESS' CONFESSION IS FALSE!
NOT AT ALL! SHE TURNED IN SOME PUNKS FOR A CHANCE TO MAKE GOOD HER OWN ESCAPE. THE EVIDENCE AGAINST THOSE COLLEGE GIRLS IS IRONCLAD- THEY **MUST** GO TO PRISON!
CHIEF AGENT
GOING HOME DEPRESSED, DIANA IS CHEERED BY A MESSAGE FROM THE AMAZON QUEEN.
THOSE POOR GIRLS! I- OH! MOTHER'S CALL-ING ON THE MENTAL RADIO!
DAUGHTER, COME HOME TO PARA-DISE ISLAND FOR OUR "DI-ANA'S DAY" FESTIVAL!
THANK YOU, MOTHER, THAT'S WONDERFUL! MAY I BRING MY FRIEND, ETTA CANDY?
SINCE ETTA IS NOT BOUND BY ANY MAN'S DOMINATION IN THE MAN-RULED WORLD, I SHALL WELCOME HER GLAD-LY TO PARADISE ISLAND!
DIANA, TRANSFORMED INTO **WONDER WOMAN,** VISITS STEVE TREVOR.
I AM THE MOON GODDESS, DIANA! NO MORTAL MAY SEE MY FACE- BUT ON FESTI-VAL DAY I BRING GIFTS!
GIFTS? MOON GODDESS? I KNOW YOUR VOICE- IT'S **WONDER WOMAN!**
WE AMAZONS PLAY GODDESS DIANA AT THE FESTIVAL OF THE RETURNING SUN, JUST AS YOU MEN PLAY SANTA CLAUS AT CHRISTMAS!
YOU'RE MORE BEAUTIFUL THAN ANY OLD MOON GODDESS! BUT WHAT IS THIS FESTIVAL OF THE SUN?
WONDER WOMAN EXPLAINS: "THE MOON GODDESS' BROTHER IS APOLLO, THE SUN GOD. HE DRIVES HIS FLAMING SUN CHARIOT THROUGH THE SKY!"
3A

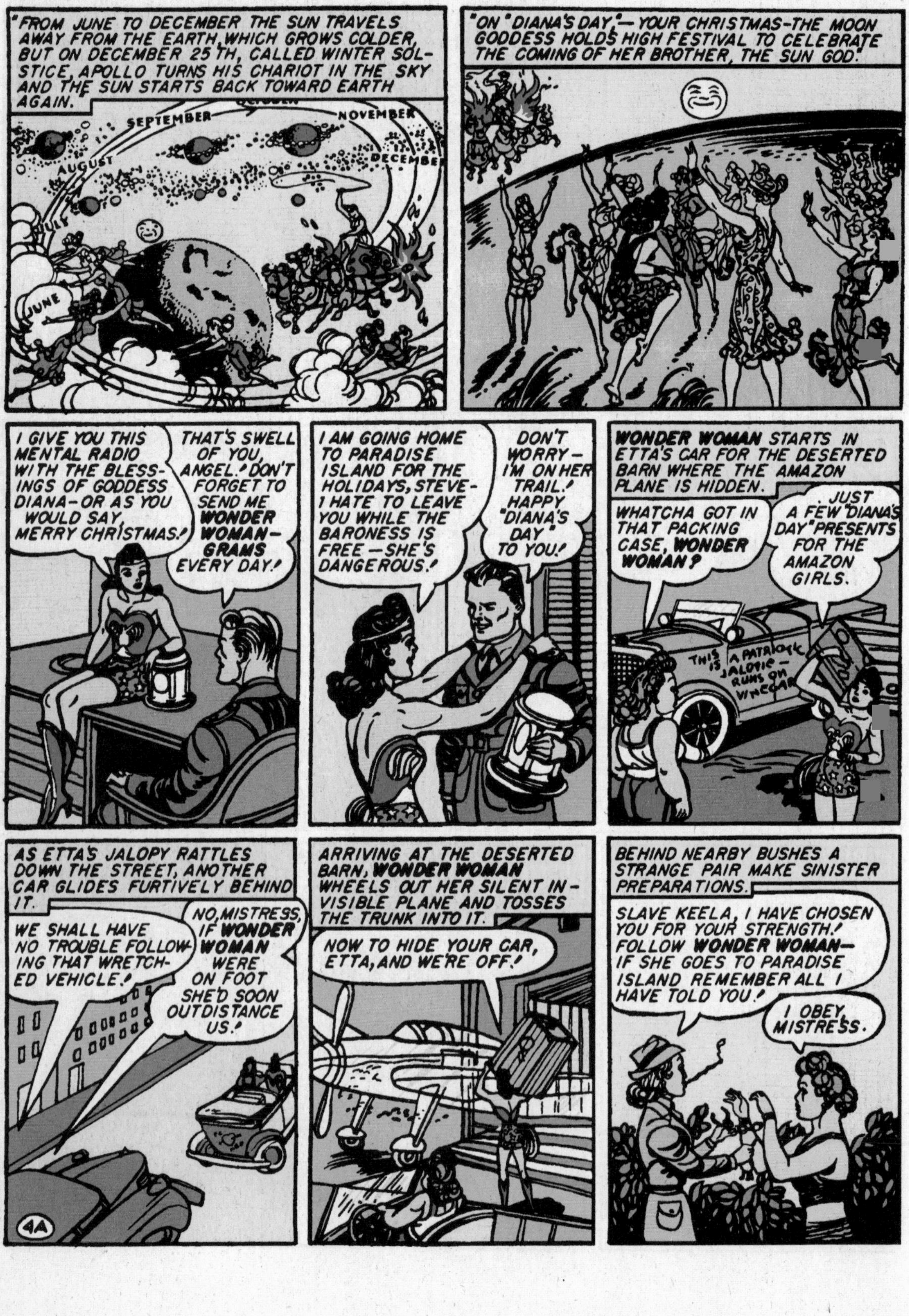
"FROM JUNE TO DECEMBER THE SUN TRAVELS AWAY FROM THE EARTH WHICH GROWS COLDER, BUT ON DECEMBER 25TH, CALLED WINTER SOLSTICE, APOLLO TURNS HIS CHARIOT IN THE SKY AND THE SUN STARTS BACK TOWARD EARTH AGAIN.
SEPTEMBER
NOVEMBER
AUGUST
DECEMBER
JULY
JUNE
"ON "DIANA'S DAY"— YOUR CHRISTMAS-THE MOON GODDESS HOLDS HIGH FESTIVAL TO CELEBRATE THE COMING OF HER BROTHER, THE SUN GOD."
I GIVE YOU THIS MENTAL RADIO WITH THE BLESSINGS OF GODDESS DIANA—OR AS YOU WOULD SAY, MERRY CHRISTMAS!
THAT'S SWELL OF YOU, ANGEL! DON'T FORGET TO SEND ME WONDER WOMAN-GRAMS EVERY DAY!
I AM GOING HOME TO PARADISE ISLAND FOR THE HOLIDAYS, STEVE—I HATE TO LEAVE YOU WHILE THE BARONESS IS FREE—SHE'S DANGEROUS!
DON'T WORRY—I'M ON HER TRAIL! HAPPY "DIANA'S DAY" TO YOU!
WONDER WOMAN STARTS IN ETTA'S CAR FOR THE DESERTED BARN WHERE THE AMAZON PLANE IS HIDDEN.
WHATCHA GOT IN THAT PACKING CASE, WONDER WOMAN?
JUST A FEW "DIANA'S DAY" PRESENTS FOR THE AMAZON GIRLS.
AS ETTA'S JALOPY RATTLES DOWN THE STREET, ANOTHER CAR GLIDES FURTIVELY BEHIND IT.
WE SHALL HAVE NO TROUBLE FOLLOWING THAT WRETCHED VEHICLE!
NO, MISTRESS, IF WONDER WOMAN WERE ON FOOT SHE'D SOON OUTDISTANCE US!
4A
ARRIVING AT THE DESERTED BARN, WONDER WOMAN WHEELS OUT HER SILENT INVISIBLE PLANE AND TOSSES THE TRUNK INTO IT.
NOW TO HIDE YOUR CAR, ETTA, AND WE'RE OFF!
BEHIND NEARBY BUSHES A STRANGE PAIR MAKE SINISTER PREPARATIONS.
SLAVE KEELA, I HAVE CHOSEN YOU FOR YOUR STRENGTH! FOLLOW WONDER WOMAN—IF SHE GOES TO PARADISE ISLAND REMEMBER ALL I HAVE TOLD YOU!
I OBEY, MISTRESS.

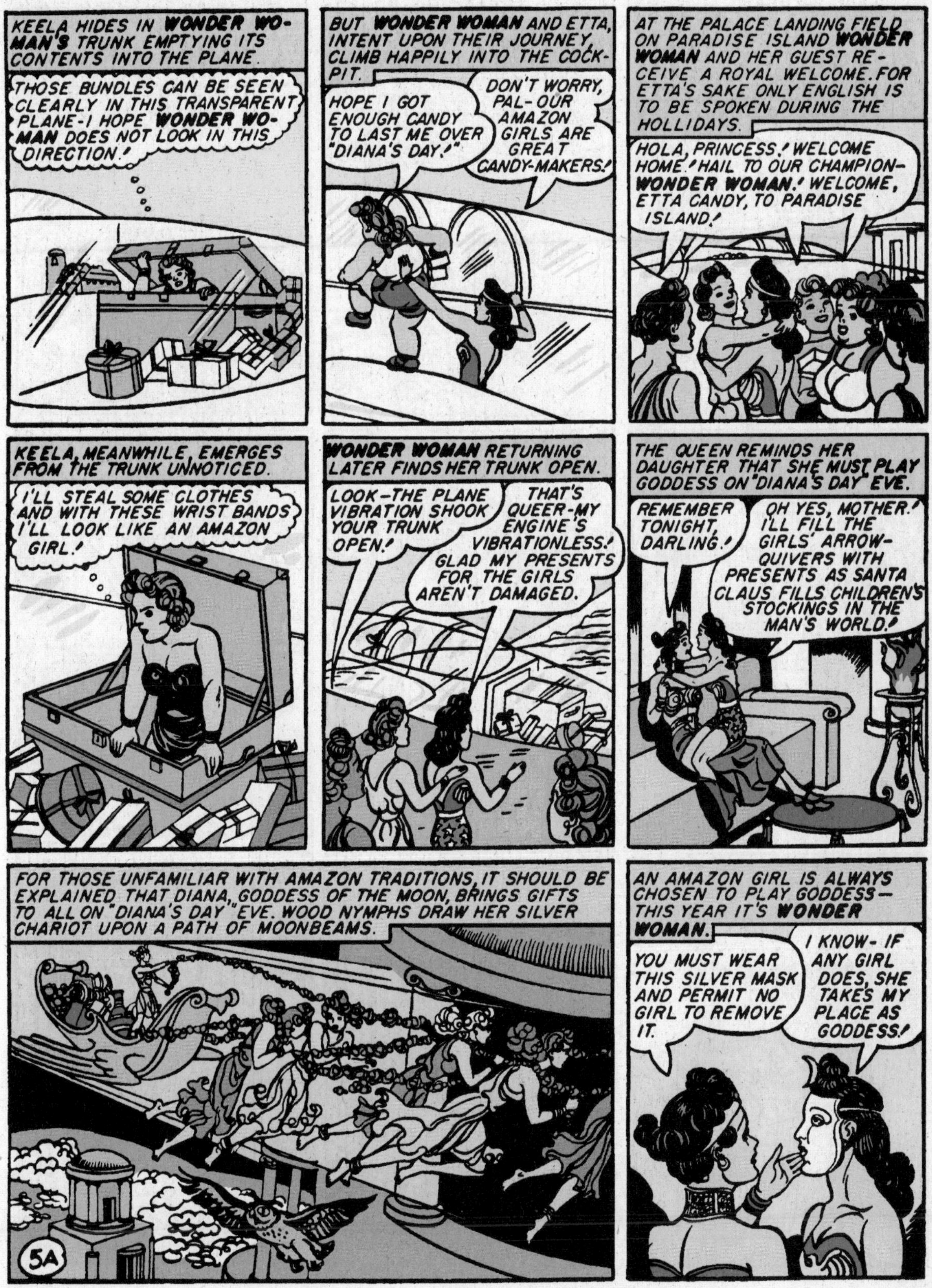

KEELA HIDES IN WONDER WOMAN'S TRUNK EMPTYING ITS CONTENTS INTO THE PLANE.
THOSE BUNDLES CAN BE SEEN CLEARLY IN THIS TRANSPARENT PLANE-I HOPE WONDER WOMAN DOES NOT LOOK IN THIS DIRECTION!
BUT WONDER WOMAN AND ETTA, INTENT UPON THEIR JOURNEY, CLIMB HAPPILY INTO THE COCKPIT.
HOPE I GOT ENOUGH CANDY TO LAST ME OVER "DIANA'S DAY!"
DON'T WORRY, PAL-OUR AMAZON GIRLS ARE GREAT CANDY-MAKERS!
AT THE PALACE LANDING FIELD ON PARADISE ISLAND WONDER WOMAN AND HER GUEST RECEIVE A ROYAL WELCOME. FOR ETTA'S SAKE ONLY ENGLISH IS TO BE SPOKEN DURING THE HOLLIDAYS.
HOLA, PRINCESS! WELCOME HOME! HAIL TO OUR CHAMPION-WONDER WOMAN! WELCOME, ETTA CANDY, TO PARADISE ISLAND!
KEELA, MEANWHILE, EMERGES FROM THE TRUNK UNNOTICED.
I'LL STEAL SOME CLOTHES AND WITH THESE WRIST BANDS I'LL LOOK LIKE AN AMAZON GIRL!
WONDER WOMAN RETURNING LATER FINDS HER TRUNK OPEN.
LOOK-THE PLANE VIBRATION SHOOK YOUR TRUNK OPEN!
THAT'S QUEER-MY ENGINE'S VIBRATIONLESS! GLAD MY PRESENTS FOR THE GIRLS AREN'T DAMAGED.
THE QUEEN REMINDS HER DAUGHTER THAT SHE MUST PLAY GODDESS ON "DIANA'S DAY" EVE.
REMEMBER TONIGHT, DARLING!
OH YES, MOTHER! I'LL FILL THE GIRLS' ARROW-QUIVERS WITH PRESENTS AS SANTA CLAUS FILLS CHILDREN'S STOCKINGS IN THE MAN'S WORLD!
FOR THOSE UNFAMILIAR WITH AMAZON TRADITIONS, IT SHOULD BE EXPLAINED THAT DIANA, GODDESS OF THE MOON, BRINGS GIFTS TO ALL ON "DIANA'S DAY" EVE. WOOD NYMPHS DRAW HER SILVER CHARIOT UPON A PATH OF MOONBEAMS.
5A
AN AMAZON GIRL IS ALWAYS CHOSEN TO PLAY GODDESS—THIS YEAR IT'S WONDER WOMAN.
YOU MUST WEAR THIS SILVER MASK AND PERMIT NO GIRL TO REMOVE IT.
I KNOW- IF ANY GIRL DOES, SHE TAKES MY PLACE AS GODDESS!

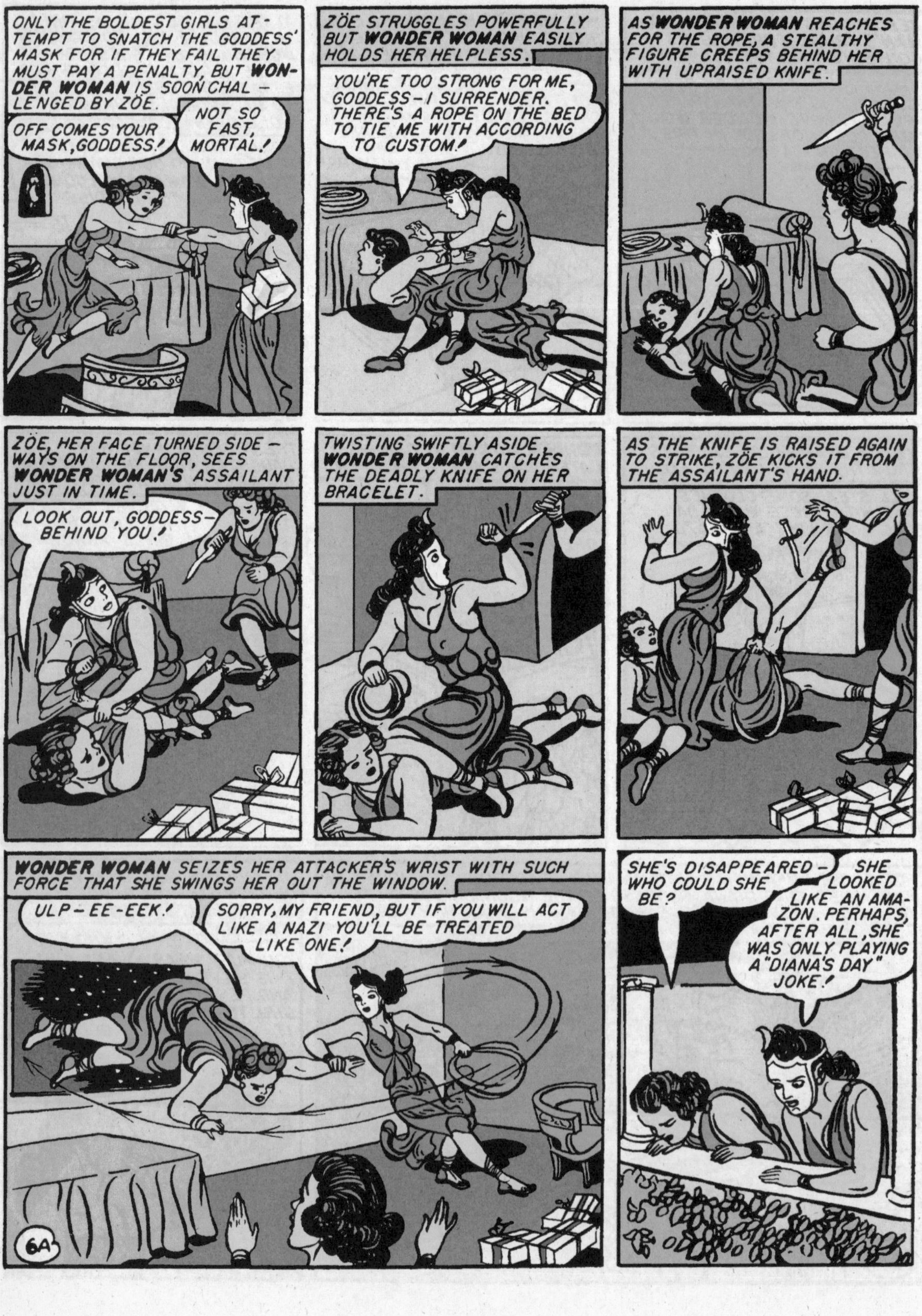

ONLY THE BOLDEST GIRLS ATTEMPT TO SNATCH THE GODDESS' MASK FOR IF THEY FAIL THEY MUST PAY A PENALTY, BUT WONDER WOMAN IS SOON CHALLENGED BY ZÖE.
OFF COMES YOUR MASK, GODDESS!
NOT SO FAST, MORTAL!
ZÖE STRUGGLES POWERFULLY BUT WONDER WOMAN EASILY HOLDS HER HELPLESS.
YOU'RE TOO STRONG FOR ME, GODDESS—I SURRENDER. THERE'S A ROPE ON THE BED TO TIE ME WITH ACCORDING TO CUSTOM!
AS WONDER WOMAN REACHES FOR THE ROPE, A STEALTHY FIGURE CREEPS BEHIND HER WITH UPRAISED KNIFE.
ZÖE, HER FACE TURNED SIDEWAYS ON THE FLOOR, SEES WONDER WOMAN'S ASSAILANT JUST IN TIME.
LOOK OUT, GODDESS—BEHIND YOU!
TWISTING SWIFTLY ASIDE, WONDER WOMAN CATCHES THE DEADLY KNIFE ON HER BRACELET.
AS THE KNIFE IS RAISED AGAIN TO STRIKE, ZÖE KICKS IT FROM THE ASSAILANT'S HAND.
WONDER WOMAN SEIZES HER ATTACKER'S WRIST WITH SUCH FORCE THAT SHE SWINGS HER OUT THE WINDOW.
ULP-EE-EEK!
SORRY, MY FRIEND, BUT IF YOU WILL ACT LIKE A NAZI YOU'LL BE TREATED LIKE ONE!
6A
SHE'S DISAPPEARED—WHO COULD SHE BE?
SHE LOOKED LIKE AN AMAZON. PERHAPS, AFTER ALL, SHE WAS ONLY PLAYING A "DIANA'S DAY" JOKE!

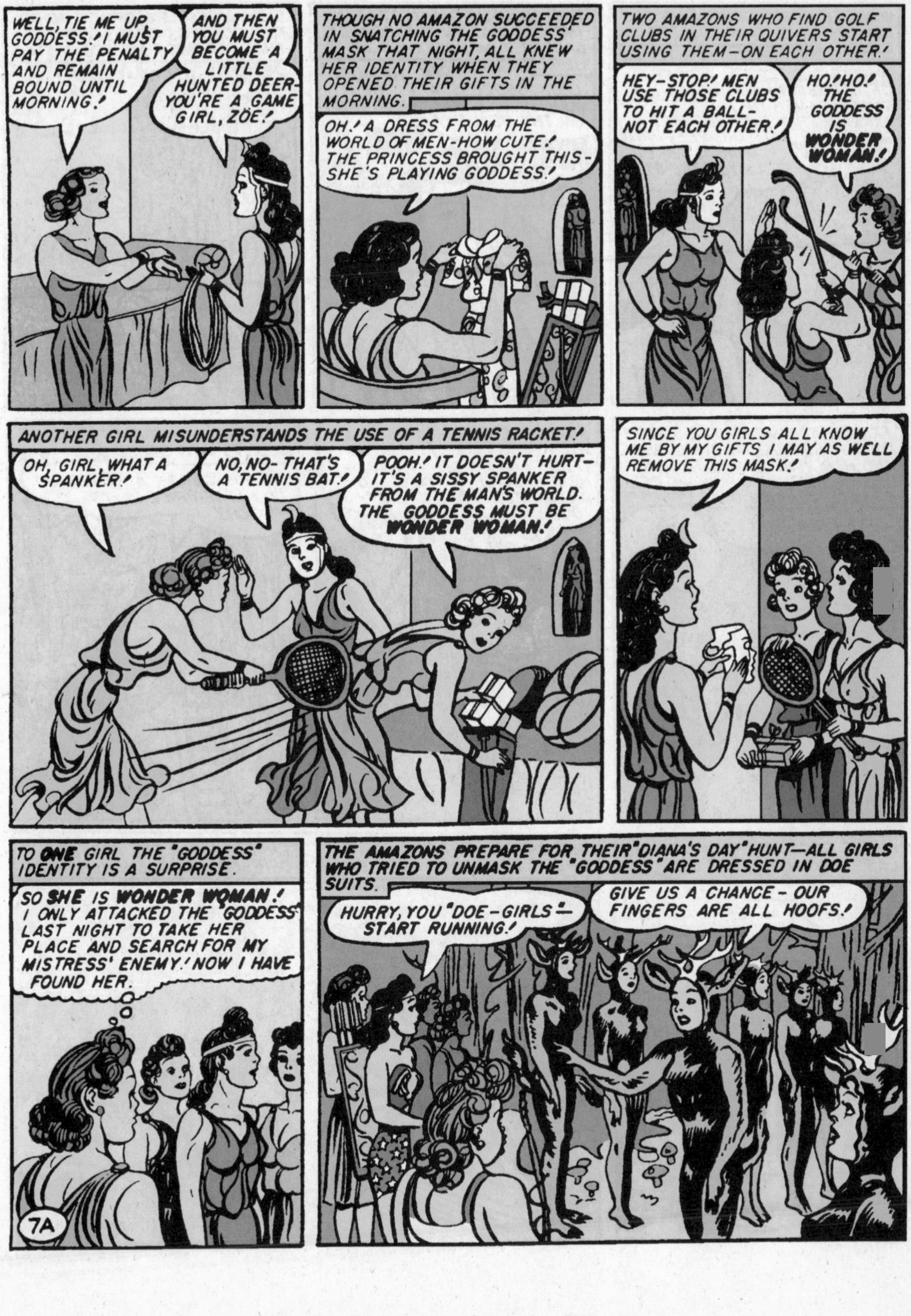
WELL, TIE ME UP, GODDESS! I MUST PAY THE PENALTY AND REMAIN BOUND UNTIL MORNING!
AND THEN YOU MUST BECOME A LITTLE HUNTED DEER-YOU'RE A GAME GIRL, ZÖE!
THOUGH NO AMAZON SUCCEEDED IN SNATCHING THE GODDESS' MASK THAT NIGHT, ALL KNEW HER IDENTITY WHEN THEY OPENED THEIR GIFTS IN THE MORNING.
OH! A DRESS FROM THE WORLD OF MEN-HOW CUTE! THE PRINCESS BROUGHT THIS-SHE'S PLAYING GODDESS!
TWO AMAZONS WHO FIND GOLF CLUBS IN THEIR QUIVERS START USING THEM-ON EACH OTHER!
HEY-STOP! MEN USE THOSE CLUBS TO HIT A BALL-NOT EACH OTHER!
HO! HO! THE GODDESS IS WONDER WOMAN!
ANOTHER GIRL MISUNDERSTANDS THE USE OF A TENNIS RACKET!
OH, GIRL, WHAT A SPANKER!
NO, NO- THAT'S A TENNIS BAT!
POOH! IT DOESN'T HURT-IT'S A SISSY SPANKER FROM THE MAN'S WORLD. THE GODDESS MUST BE WONDER WOMAN!
SINCE YOU GIRLS ALL KNOW ME BY MY GIFTS I MAY AS WELL REMOVE THIS MASK!
TO ONE GIRL THE "GODDESS" IDENTITY IS A SURPRISE.
SO SHE IS WONDER WOMAN! I ONLY ATTACKED THE "GODDESS" LAST NIGHT TO TAKE HER PLACE AND SEARCH FOR MY MISTRESS' ENEMY! NOW I HAVE FOUND HER.
7A
THE AMAZONS PREPARE FOR THEIR "DIANA'S DAY" HUNT—ALL GIRLS WHO TRIED TO UNMASK THE "GODDESS" ARE DRESSED IN DOE SUITS.
HURRY, YOU "DOE-GIRLS"—START RUNNING!
GIVE US A CHANCE - OUR FINGERS ARE ALL HOOFS!

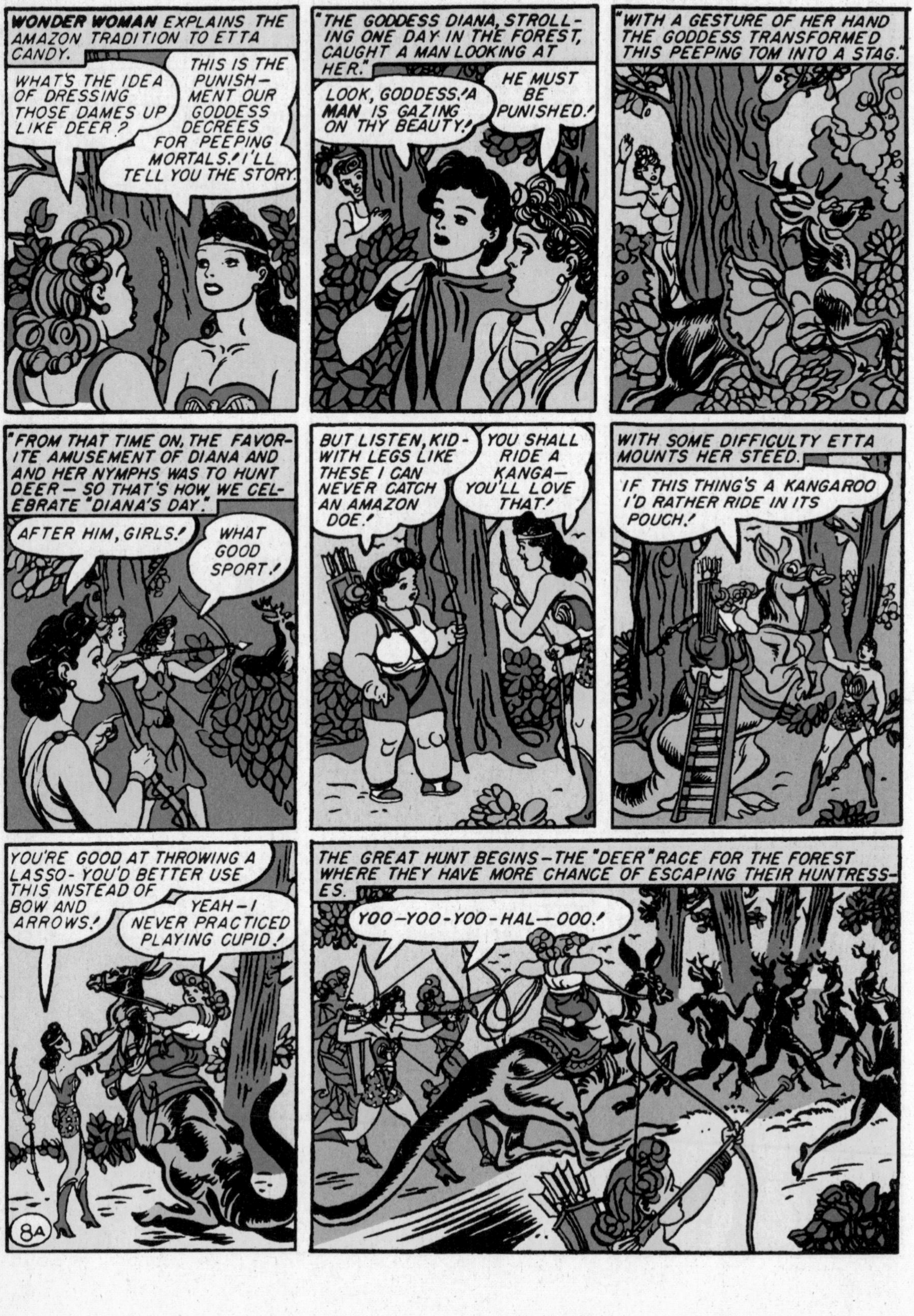
WONDER WOMAN EXPLAINS THE AMAZON TRADITION TO ETTA CANDY.
WHAT'S THE IDEA OF DRESSING THOSE DAMES UP LIKE DEER?
THIS IS THE PUNISH- MENT OUR GODDESS DECREES FOR PEEPING MORTALS! I'LL TELL YOU THE STORY.
"THE GODDESS DIANA, STROLL- ING ONE DAY IN THE FOREST, CAUGHT A MAN LOOKING AT HER."
LOOK, GODDESS! A MAN IS GAZING ON THY BEAUTY!
HE MUST BE PUNISHED!
"WITH A GESTURE OF HER HAND THE GODDESS TRANSFORMED THIS PEEPING TOM INTO A STAG."
"FROM THAT TIME ON, THE FAVOR- ITE AMUSEMENT OF DIANA AND AND HER NYMPHS WAS TO HUNT DEER — SO THAT'S HOW WE CEL- EBRATE "DIANA'S DAY."
AFTER HIM, GIRLS!
WHAT GOOD SPORT!
BUT LISTEN, KID- WITH LEGS LIKE THESE I CAN NEVER CATCH AN AMAZON DOE!
YOU SHALL RIDE A KANGA— YOU'LL LOVE THAT!
WITH SOME DIFFICULTY ETTA MOUNTS HER STEED.
IF THIS THING'S A KANGAROO I'D RATHER RIDE IN ITS POUCH!
YOU'RE GOOD AT THROWING A LASSO- YOU'D BETTER USE THIS INSTEAD OF BOW AND ARROWS!
YEAH—I NEVER PRACTICED PLAYING CUPID!
8A
THE GREAT HUNT BEGINS—THE "DEER" RACE FOR THE FOREST WHERE THEY HAVE MORE CHANCE OF ESCAPING THEIR HUNTRESS- ES.
YOO-YOO-YOO-HAL—OOO!

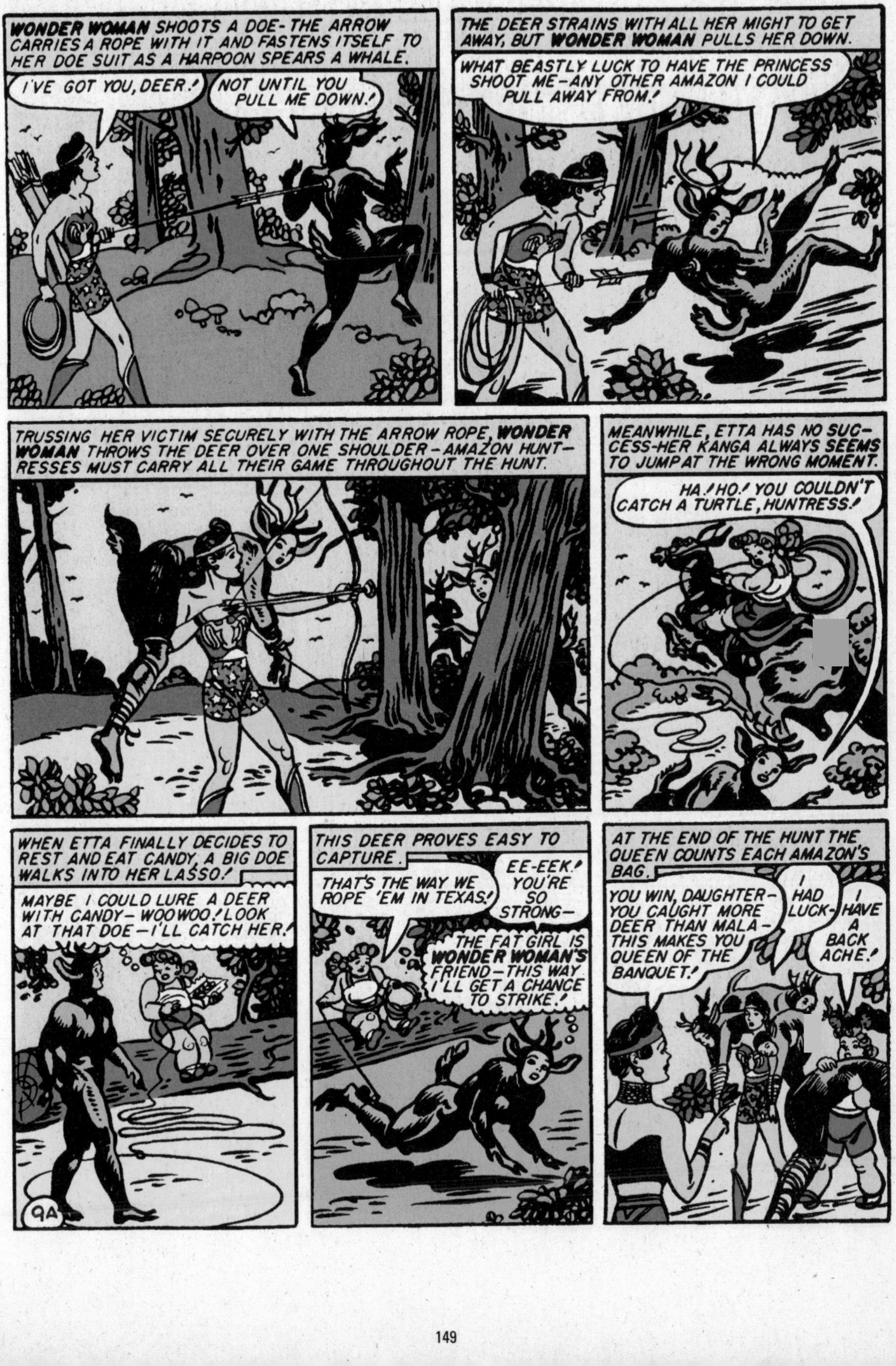
WONDER WOMAN SHOOTS A DOE- THE ARROW CARRIES A ROPE WITH IT AND FASTENS ITSELF TO HER DOE SUIT AS A HARPOON SPEARS A WHALE.
I'VE GOT YOU, DEER.!
NOT UNTIL YOU PULL ME DOWN.!
THE DEER STRAINS WITH ALL HER MIGHT TO GET AWAY, BUT WONDER WOMAN PULLS HER DOWN.
WHAT BEASTLY LUCK TO HAVE THE PRINCESS SHOOT ME-ANY OTHER AMAZON I COULD PULL AWAY FROM!
TRUSSING HER VICTIM SECURELY WITH THE ARROW ROPE, WONDER WOMAN THROWS THE DEER OVER ONE SHOULDER-AMAZON HUNT-RESSES MUST CARRY ALL THEIR GAME THROUGHOUT THE HUNT.
MEANWHILE, ETTA HAS NO SUC-CESS-HER KANGA ALWAYS SEEMS TO JUMP AT THE WRONG MOMENT.
HA! HO! YOU COULDN'T CATCH A TURTLE, HUNTRESS!
WHEN ETTA FINALLY DECIDES TO REST AND EAT CANDY, A BIG DOE WALKS INTO HER LASSO!
MAYBE I COULD LURE A DEER WITH CANDY- WOOWOO! LOOK AT THAT DOE-I'LL CATCH HER!
9A
THIS DEER PROVES EASY TO CAPTURE.
THAT'S THE WAY WE ROPE 'EM IN TEXAS!
EE-EEK! YOU'RE SO STRONG-
THE FAT GIRL IS WONDER WOMAN'S FRIEND-THIS WAY I'LL GET A CHANCE TO STRIKE!
AT THE END OF THE HUNT THE QUEEN COUNTS EACH AMAZON'S BAG.
YOU WIN, DAUGHTER-YOU CAUGHT MORE DEER THAN MALA-THIS MAKES YOU QUEEN OF THE BANQUET!
I HAD LUCK-
I HAVE A BACK ACHE!

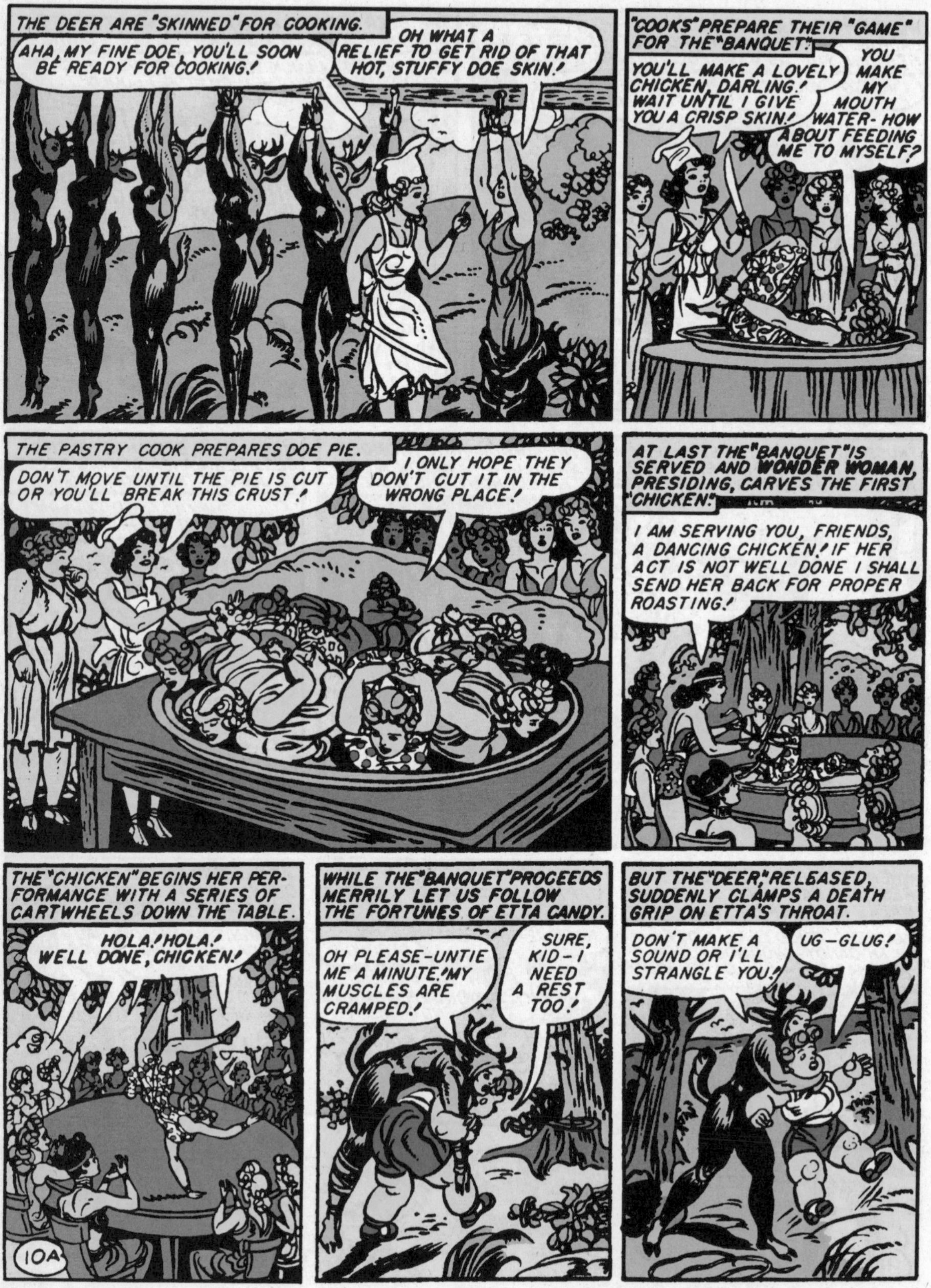

THE DEER ARE "SKINNED" FOR COOKING.
AHA, MY FINE DOE, YOU'LL SOON BE READY FOR COOKING!
OH WHAT A RELIEF TO GET RID OF THAT HOT, STUFFY DOE SKIN!
"COOKS" PREPARE THEIR "GAME" FOR THE "BANQUET."
YOU'LL MAKE A LOVELY CHICKEN, DARLING! WAIT UNTIL I GIVE YOU A CRISP SKIN!
YOU MAKE MY MOUTH WATER- HOW ABOUT FEEDING ME TO MYSELF?
THE PASTRY COOK PREPARES DOE PIE.
DON'T MOVE UNTIL THE PIE IS CUT OR YOU'LL BREAK THIS CRUST!
I ONLY HOPE THEY DON'T CUT IT IN THE WRONG PLACE!
AT LAST THE "BANQUET" IS SERVED AND WONDER WOMAN, PRESIDING, CARVES THE FIRST "CHICKEN."
I AM SERVING YOU, FRIENDS, A DANCING CHICKEN! IF HER ACT IS NOT WELL DONE I SHALL SEND HER BACK FOR PROPER ROASTING!
THE "CHICKEN" BEGINS HER PERFORMANCE WITH A SERIES OF CARTWHEELS DOWN THE TABLE.
HOLA! HOLA! WELL DONE, CHICKEN!
10A
WHILE THE "BANQUET" PROCEEDS MERRILY LET US FOLLOW THE FORTUNES OF ETTA CANDY.
OH PLEASE-UNTIE ME A MINUTE! MY MUSCLES ARE CRAMPED!
SURE, KID-I NEED A REST TOO!
BUT THE "DEER," RELEASED, SUDDENLY CLAMPS A DEATH GRIP ON ETTA'S THROAT.
DON'T MAKE A SOUND OR I'LL STRANGLE YOU!
UG-GLUG!

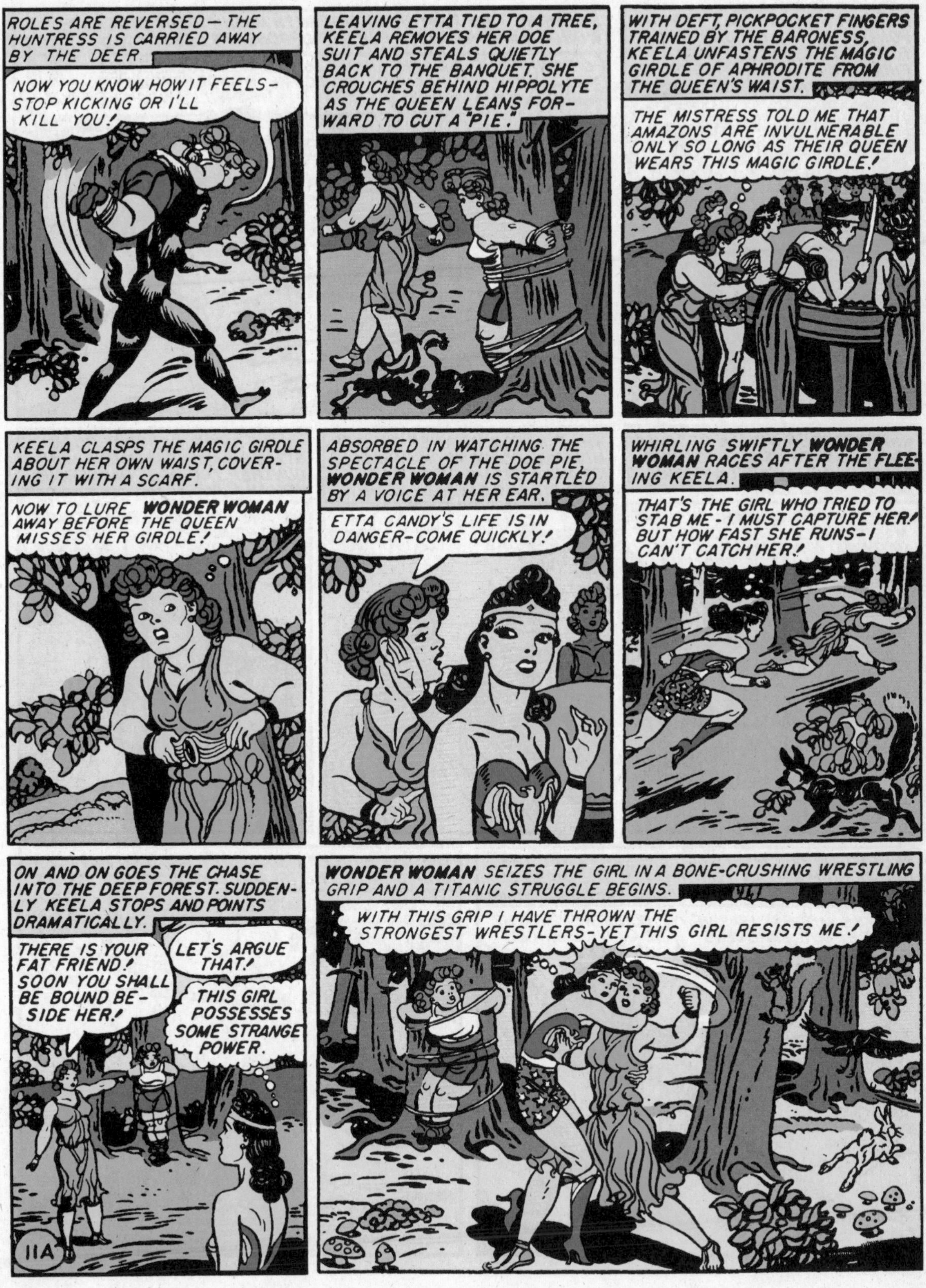
ROLES ARE REVERSED—THE HUNTRESS IS CARRIED AWAY BY THE DEER
NOW YOU KNOW HOW IT FEELS- STOP KICKING OR I'LL KILL YOU!
LEAVING ETTA TIED TO A TREE, KEELA REMOVES HER DOE SUIT AND STEALS QUIETLY BACK TO THE BANQUET. SHE CROUCHES BEHIND HIPPOLYTE AS THE QUEEN LEANS FORWARD TO CUT A "PIE."
WITH DEFT, PICKPOCKET FINGERS TRAINED BY THE BARONESS, KEELA UNFASTENS THE MAGIC GIRDLE OF APHRODITE FROM THE QUEEN'S WAIST.
THE MISTRESS TOLD ME THAT AMAZONS ARE INVULNERABLE ONLY SO LONG AS THEIR QUEEN WEARS THIS MAGIC GIRDLE!
KEELA CLASPS THE MAGIC GIRDLE ABOUT HER OWN WAIST, COVERING IT WITH A SCARF.
NOW TO LURE WONDER WOMAN AWAY BEFORE THE QUEEN MISSES HER GIRDLE!
ABSORBED IN WATCHING THE SPECTACLE OF THE DOE PIE, WONDER WOMAN IS STARTLED BY A VOICE AT HER EAR.
ETTA CANDY'S LIFE IS IN DANGER—COME QUICKLY!
WHIRLING SWIFTLY WONDER WOMAN RACES AFTER THE FLEEING KEELA.
THAT'S THE GIRL WHO TRIED TO STAB ME - I MUST CAPTURE HER! BUT HOW FAST SHE RUNS - I CAN'T CATCH HER!
ON AND ON GOES THE CHASE INTO THE DEEP FOREST. SUDDENLY KEELA STOPS AND POINTS DRAMATICALLY.
THERE IS YOUR FAT FRIEND! SOON YOU SHALL BE BOUND BESIDE HER!
LET'S ARGUE THAT!
THIS GIRL POSSESSES SOME STRANGE POWER.
11A
WONDER WOMAN SEIZES THE GIRL IN A BONE-CRUSHING WRESTLING GRIP AND A TITANIC STRUGGLE BEGINS.
WITH THIS GRIP I HAVE THROWN THE STRONGEST WRESTLERS-YET THIS GIRL RESISTS ME!

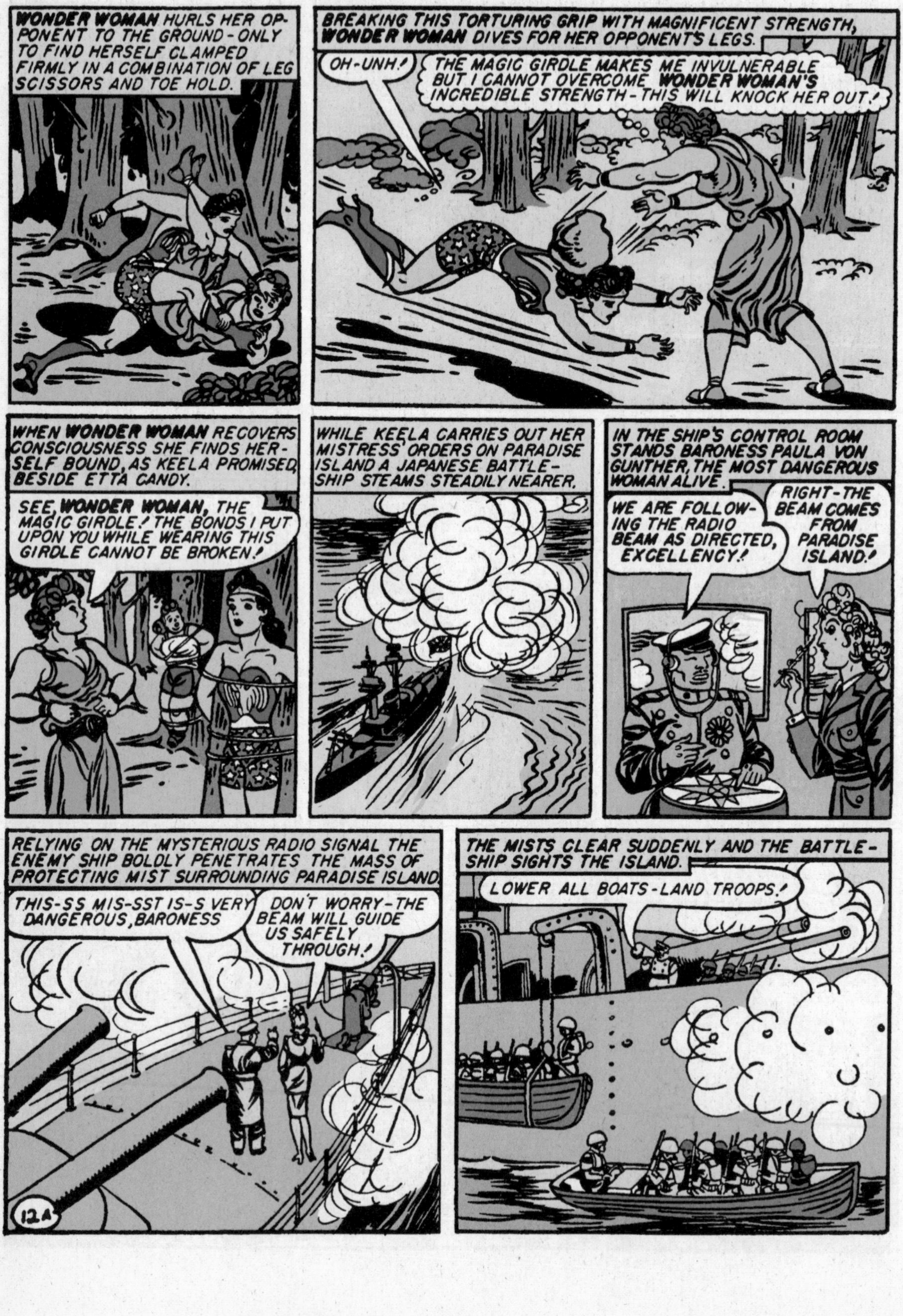
WONDER WOMAN HURLS HER OPPONENT TO THE GROUND - ONLY TO FIND HERSELF CLAMPED FIRMLY IN A COMBINATION OF LEG SCISSORS AND TOE HOLD.
BREAKING THIS TORTURING GRIP WITH MAGNIFICENT STRENGTH, WONDER WOMAN DIVES FOR HER OPPONENT'S LEGS.
OH-UNH!
THE MAGIC GIRDLE MAKES ME INVULNERABLE BUT I CANNOT OVERCOME WONDER WOMAN'S INCREDIBLE STRENGTH - THIS WILL KNOCK HER OUT!
WHEN WONDER WOMAN RECOVERS CONSCIOUSNESS SHE FINDS HERSELF BOUND, AS KEELA PROMISED, BESIDE ETTA CANDY.
SEE, WONDER WOMAN, THE MAGIC GIRDLE! THE BONDS I PUT UPON YOU WHILE WEARING THIS GIRDLE CANNOT BE BROKEN!
WHILE KEELA CARRIES OUT HER MISTRESS' ORDERS ON PARADISE ISLAND A JAPANESE BATTLESHIP STEAMS STEADILY NEARER.
IN THE SHIP'S CONTROL ROOM STANDS BARONESS PAULA VON GUNTHER, THE MOST DANGEROUS WOMAN ALIVE.
WE ARE FOLLOWING THE RADIO BEAM AS DIRECTED, EXCELLENCY!
RIGHT-THE BEAM COMES FROM PARADISE ISLAND!
RELYING ON THE MYSTERIOUS RADIO SIGNAL THE ENEMY SHIP BOLDLY PENETRATES THE MASS OF PROTECTING MIST SURROUNDING PARADISE ISLAND
THIS-SS MIS-SST IS-S VERY DANGEROUS, BARONESS
DON'T WORRY-THE BEAM WILL GUIDE US SAFELY THROUGH!
12A
THE MISTS CLEAR SUDDENLY AND THE BATTLESHIP SIGHTS THE ISLAND.
LOWER ALL BOATS-LAND TROOPS!

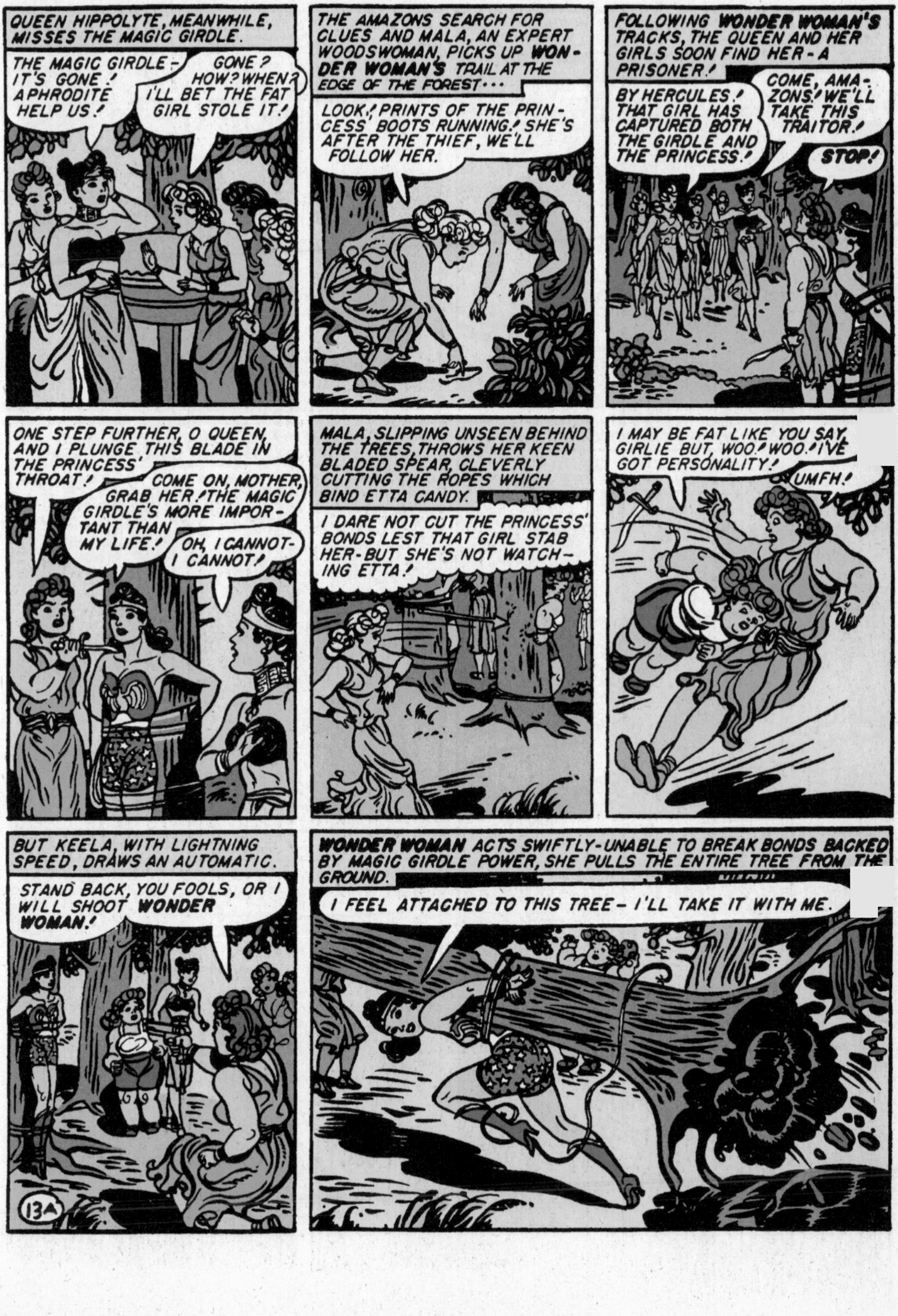

QUEEN HIPPOLYTE, MEANWHILE, MISSES THE MAGIC GIRDLE.
THE MAGIC GIRDLE - IT'S GONE! APHRODITE HELP US!
GONE? HOW? WHEN? I'LL BET THE FAT GIRL STOLE IT!
THE AMAZONS SEARCH FOR CLUES AND MALA, AN EXPERT WOODSWOMAN, PICKS UP WONDER WOMAN'S TRAIL AT THE EDGE OF THE FOREST...
LOOK! PRINTS OF THE PRINCESS' BOOTS RUNNING! SHE'S AFTER THE THIEF, WE'LL FOLLOW HER.
FOLLOWING WONDER WOMAN'S TRACKS, THE QUEEN AND HER GIRLS SOON FIND HER - A PRISONER!
BY HERCULES! THAT GIRL HAS CAPTURED BOTH THE GIRDLE AND THE PRINCESS!
COME, AMAZONS! WE'LL TAKE THIS TRAITOR!
STOP!
ONE STEP FURTHER, O QUEEN, AND I PLUNGE THIS BLADE IN THE PRINCESS' THROAT!
COME ON, MOTHER, GRAB HER! THE MAGIC GIRDLE'S MORE IMPORTANT THAN MY LIFE!
OH, I CANNOT - I CANNOT!
MALA, SLIPPING UNSEEN BEHIND THE TREES, THROWS HER KEEN BLADED SPEAR, CLEVERLY CUTTING THE ROPES WHICH BIND ETTA CANDY.
I DARE NOT CUT THE PRINCESS' BONDS LEST THAT GIRL STAB HER - BUT SHE'S NOT WATCHING ETTA!
I MAY BE FAT LIKE YOU SAY, GIRLIE BUT, WOO! WOO! I'VE GOT PERSONALITY!
UMFH!
BUT KEELA, WITH LIGHTNING SPEED, DRAWS AN AUTOMATIC.
STAND BACK, YOU FOOLS, OR I WILL SHOOT WONDER WOMAN!
13A
WONDER WOMAN ACTS SWIFTLY - UNABLE TO BREAK BONDS BACKED BY MAGIC GIRDLE POWER, SHE PULLS THE ENTIRE TREE FROM THE GROUND.
I FEEL ATTACHED TO THIS TREE - I'LL TAKE IT WITH ME.

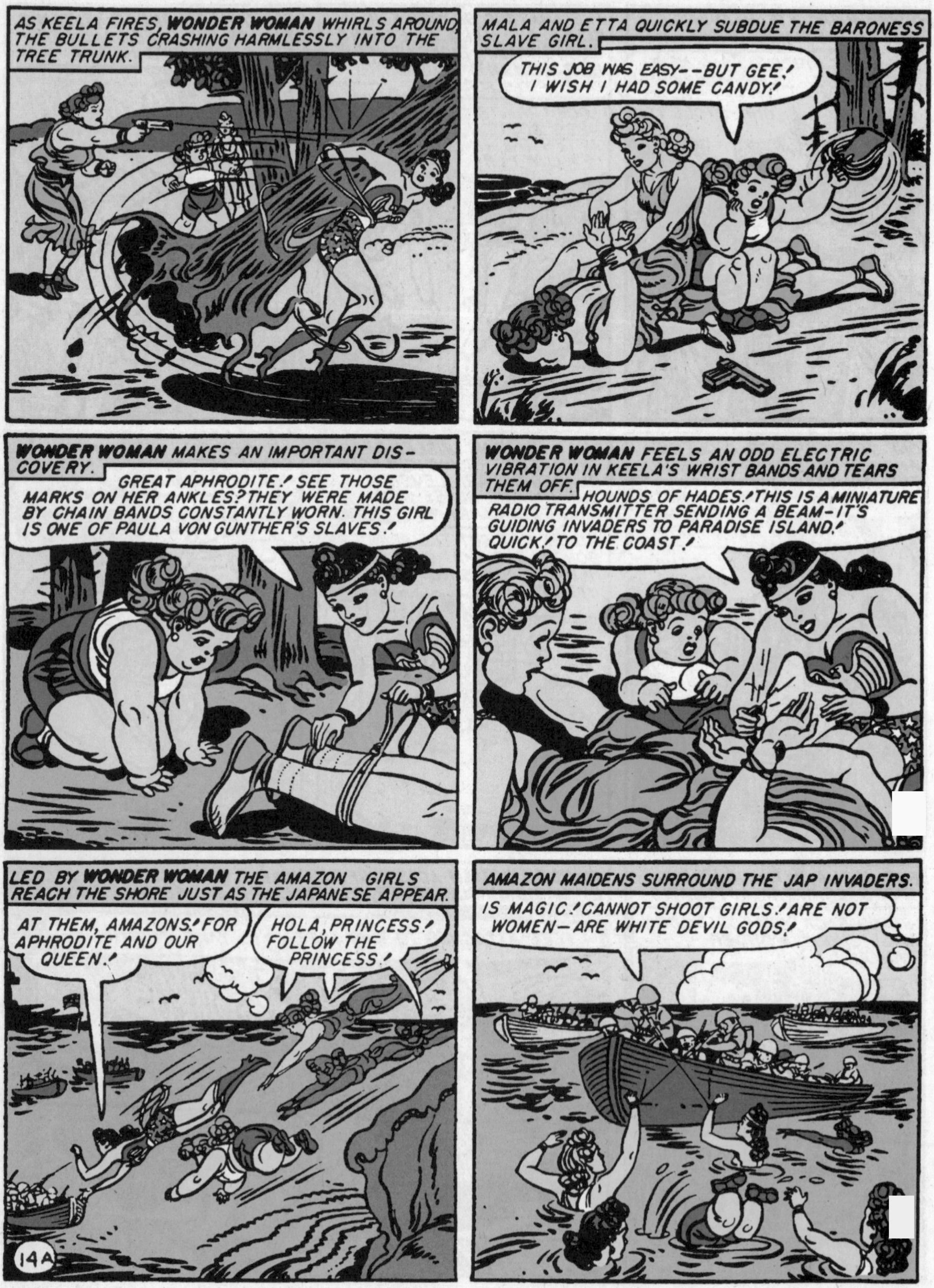

AS KEELA FIRES, WONDER WOMAN WHIRLS AROUND, THE BULLETS CRASHING HARMLESSLY INTO THE TREE TRUNK.
MALA AND ETTA QUICKLY SUBDUE THE BARONESS SLAVE GIRL.
THIS JOB WAS EASY--BUT GEE! I WISH I HAD SOME CANDY!
WONDER WOMAN MAKES AN IMPORTANT DISCOVERY.
GREAT APHRODITE! SEE THOSE MARKS ON HER ANKLES? THEY WERE MADE BY CHAIN BANDS CONSTANTLY WORN. THIS GIRL IS ONE OF PAULA VON GUNTHER'S SLAVES!
WONDER WOMAN FEELS AN ODD ELECTRIC VIBRATION IN KEELA'S WRIST BANDS AND TEARS THEM OFF.
HOUNDS OF HADES! THIS IS A MINIATURE RADIO TRANSMITTER SENDING A BEAM-IT'S GUIDING INVADERS TO PARADISE ISLAND! QUICK! TO THE COAST!
LED BY WONDER WOMAN THE AMAZON GIRLS REACH THE SHORE JUST AS THE JAPANESE APPEAR.
AT THEM, AMAZONS! FOR APHRODITE AND OUR QUEEN!
HOLA, PRINCESS! FOLLOW THE PRINCESS!
14A
AMAZON MAIDENS SURROUND THE JAP INVADERS.
IS MAGIC! CANNOT SHOOT GIRLS! ARE NOT WOMEN—ARE WHITE DEVIL GODS!

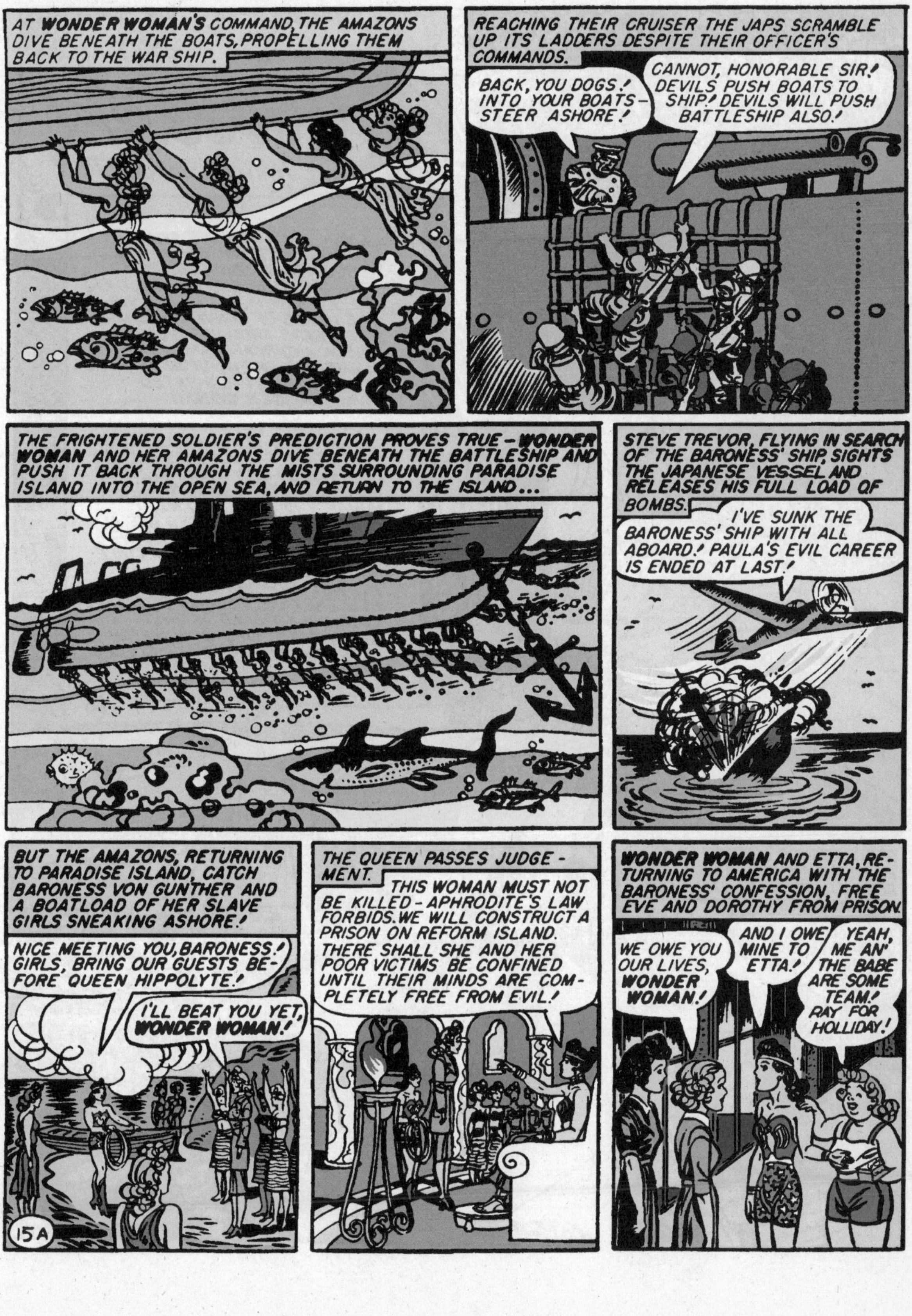

AT WONDER WOMAN'S COMMAND, THE AMAZONS DIVE BENEATH THE BOATS, PROPELLING THEM BACK TO THE WAR SHIP.
REACHING THEIR CRUISER THE JAPS SCRAMBLE UP ITS LADDERS DESPITE THEIR OFFICER'S COMMANDS.
BACK, YOU DOGS! INTO YOUR BOATS- STEER ASHORE!
CANNOT, HONORABLE SIR! DEVILS PUSH BOATS TO SHIP! DEVILS WILL PUSH BATTLESHIP ALSO!
THE FRIGHTENED SOLDIER'S PREDICTION PROVES TRUE - WONDER WOMAN AND HER AMAZONS DIVE BENEATH THE BATTLESHIP AND PUSH IT BACK THROUGH THE MISTS SURROUNDING PARADISE ISLAND INTO THE OPEN SEA, AND RETURN TO THE ISLAND...
STEVE TREVOR, FLYING IN SEARCH OF THE BARONESS' SHIP, SIGHTS THE JAPANESE VESSEL AND RELEASES HIS FULL LOAD OF BOMBS.
I'VE SUNK THE BARONESS' SHIP WITH ALL ABOARD! PAULA'S EVIL CAREER IS ENDED AT LAST!
BUT THE AMAZONS, RETURNING TO PARADISE ISLAND, CATCH BARONESS VON GUNTHER AND A BOATLOAD OF HER SLAVE GIRLS SNEAKING ASHORE!
NICE MEETING YOU, BARONESS! GIRLS, BRING OUR GUESTS BEFORE QUEEN HIPPOLYTE!
I'LL BEAT YOU YET, WONDER WOMAN!
15A
THE QUEEN PASSES JUDGEMENT.
THIS WOMAN MUST NOT BE KILLED - APHRODITE'S LAW FORBIDS. WE WILL CONSTRUCT A PRISON ON REFORM ISLAND. THERE SHALL SHE AND HER POOR VICTIMS BE CONFINED UNTIL THEIR MINDS ARE COMPLETELY FREE FROM EVIL!
WONDER WOMAN AND ETTA, RETURNING TO AMERICA WITH THE BARONESS' CONFESSION, FREE EVE AND DOROTHY FROM PRISON.
WE OWE YOU OUR LIVES, WONDER WOMAN!
AND I OWE MINE TO ETTA!
YEAH, ME AN' THE BABE ARE SOME TEAM! RAY FOR HOLLIDAY!

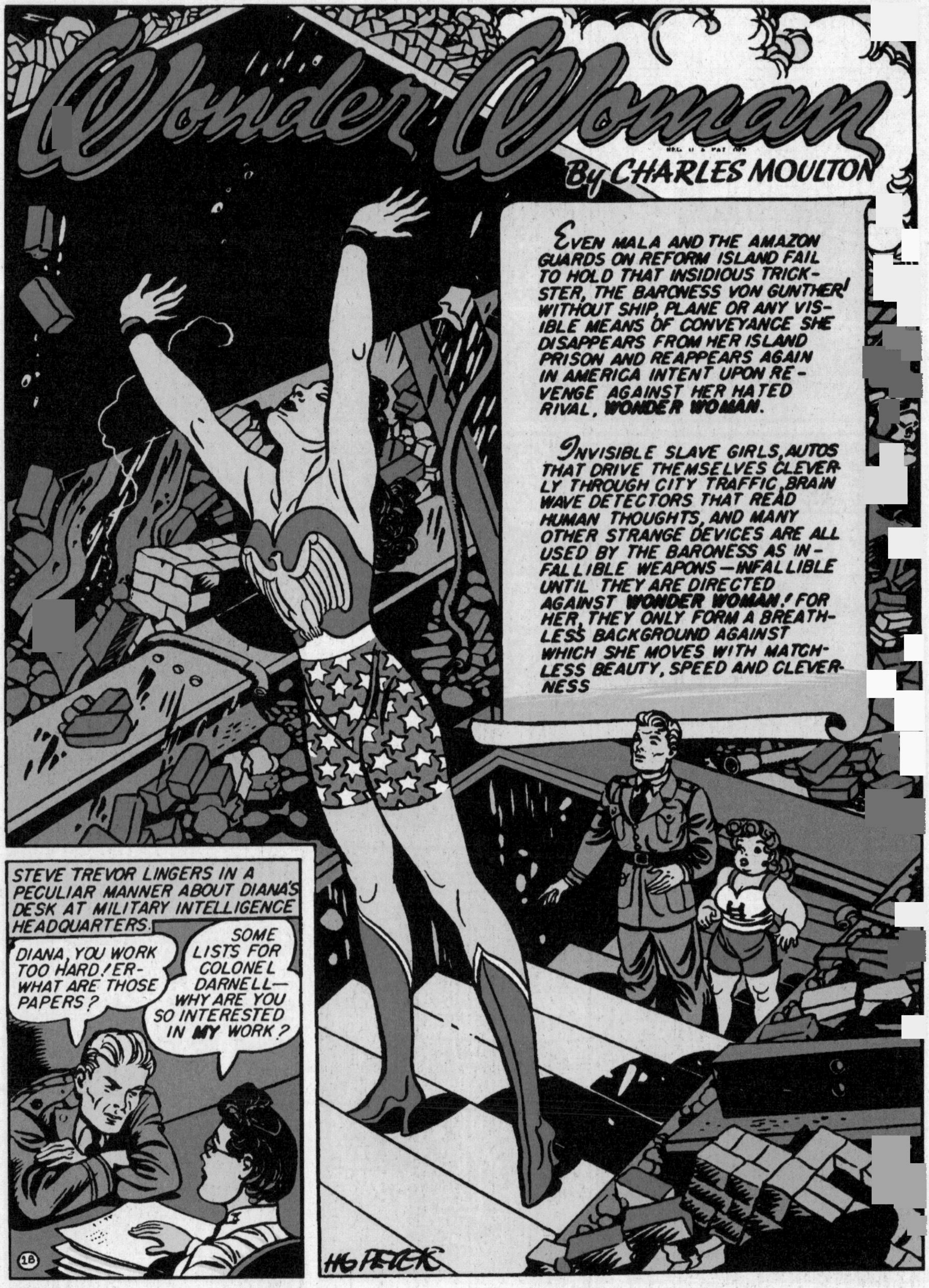

Wonder Woman
By CHARLES MOULTON
EVEN MALA AND THE AMAZON GUARDS ON REFORM ISLAND FAIL TO HOLD THAT INSIDIOUS TRICKSTER, THE BARONESS VON GUNTHER! WITHOUT SHIP, PLANE OR ANY VISIBLE MEANS OF CONVEYANCE SHE DISAPPEARS FROM HER ISLAND PRISON AND REAPPEARS AGAIN IN AMERICA INTENT UPON REVENGE AGAINST HER HATED RIVAL, WONDER WOMAN.
INVISIBLE SLAVE GIRLS, AUTOS THAT DRIVE THEMSELVES CLEVERLY THROUGH CITY TRAFFIC, BRAIN WAVE DETECTORS THAT READ HUMAN THOUGHTS, AND MANY OTHER STRANGE DEVICES ARE ALL USED BY THE BARONESS AS INFALLIBLE WEAPONS—INFALLIBLE UNTIL THEY ARE DIRECTED AGAINST WONDER WOMAN! FOR HER, THEY ONLY FORM A BREATHLESS BACKGROUND AGAINST WHICH SHE MOVES WITH MATCHLESS BEAUTY, SPEED AND CLEVERNESS
STEVE TREVOR LINGERS IN A PECULIAR MANNER ABOUT DIANA'S DESK AT MILITARY INTELLIGENCE HEADQUARTERS.
DIANA, YOU WORK TOO HARD! ER—WHAT ARE THOSE PAPERS?
SOME LISTS FOR COLONEL DARNELL—WHY ARE YOU SO INTERESTED IN MY WORK?
18
HG PETER

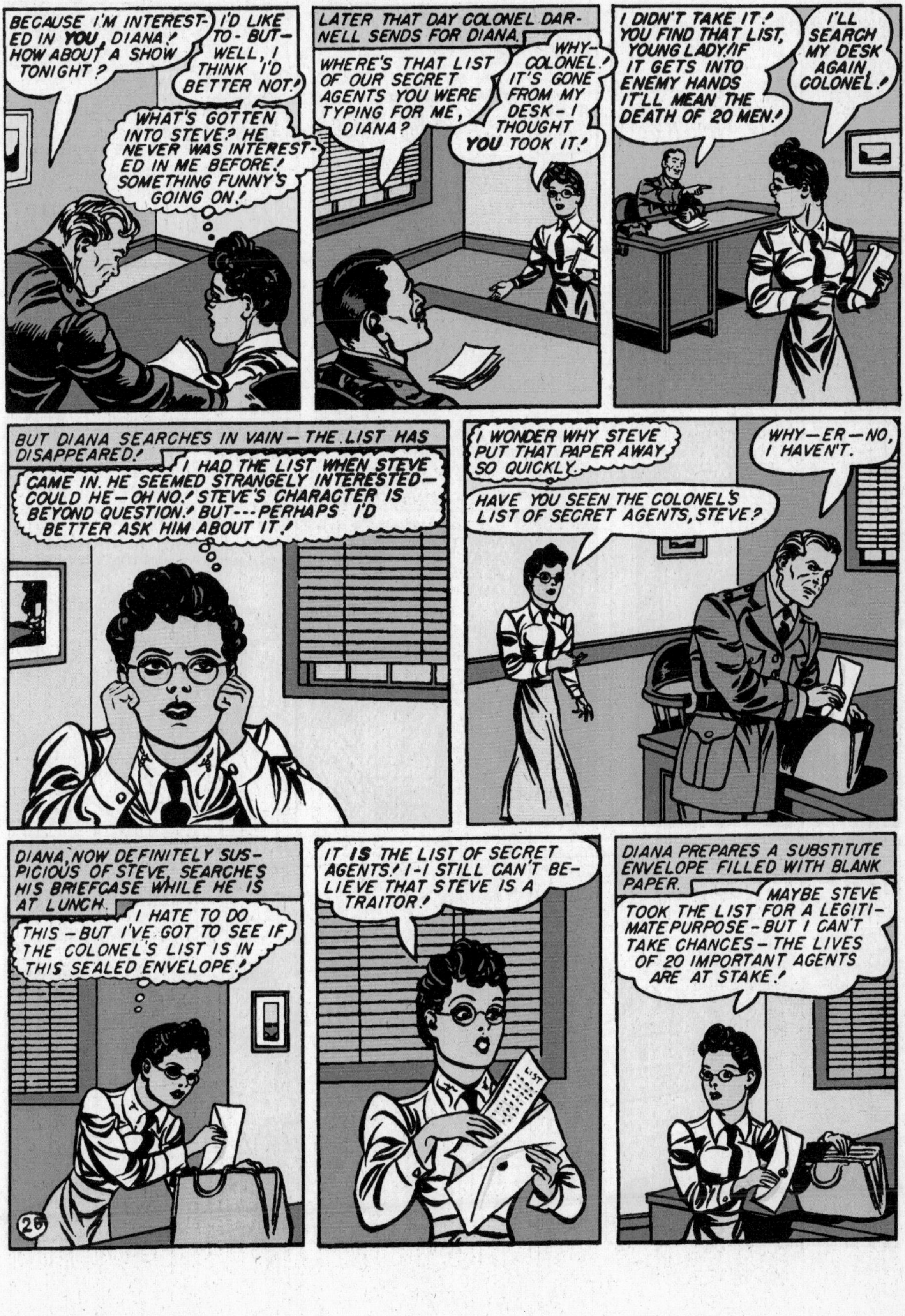

BECAUSE I'M INTERESTED IN **YOU**, DIANA! HOW ABOUT A SHOW TONIGHT?
I'D LIKE TO - BUT - WELL, I THINK I'D BETTER NOT!
WHAT'S GOTTEN INTO STEVE? HE NEVER WAS INTERESTED IN ME BEFORE! SOMETHING FUNNY'S GOING ON!
LATER THAT DAY COLONEL DARNELL SENDS FOR DIANA.
WHERE'S THAT LIST OF OUR SECRET AGENTS YOU WERE TYPING FOR ME, DIANA?
WHY - COLONEL! IT'S GONE FROM MY DESK - I THOUGHT **YOU** TOOK IT!
I DIDN'T TAKE IT! YOU FIND THAT LIST, YOUNG LADY! IF IT GETS INTO ENEMY HANDS IT'LL MEAN THE DEATH OF 20 MEN!
I'LL SEARCH MY DESK AGAIN, COLONEL!
BUT DIANA SEARCHES IN VAIN — THE LIST HAS DISAPPEARED!
I HAD THE LIST WHEN STEVE CAME IN. HE SEEMED STRANGELY INTERESTED — COULD HE — OH NO! STEVE'S CHARACTER IS BEYOND QUESTION! BUT --- PERHAPS I'D BETTER ASK HIM ABOUT IT!
I WONDER WHY STEVE PUT THAT PAPER AWAY SO QUICKLY.
HAVE YOU SEEN THE COLONEL'S LIST OF SECRET AGENTS, STEVE?
WHY — ER — NO, I HAVEN'T.
DIANA, NOW DEFINITELY SUSPICIOUS OF STEVE, SEARCHES HIS BRIEFCASE WHILE HE IS AT LUNCH.
I HATE TO DO THIS — BUT I'VE GOT TO SEE IF THE COLONEL'S LIST IS IN THIS SEALED ENVELOPE!
26
IT **IS** THE LIST OF SECRET AGENTS! I-I STILL CAN'T BELIEVE THAT STEVE IS A TRAITOR!
LIST
DIANA PREPARES A SUBSTITUTE ENVELOPE FILLED WITH BLANK PAPER.
MAYBE STEVE TOOK THE LIST FOR A LEGITIMATE PURPOSE — BUT I CAN'T TAKE CHANCES — THE LIVES OF 20 IMPORTANT AGENTS ARE AT STAKE!

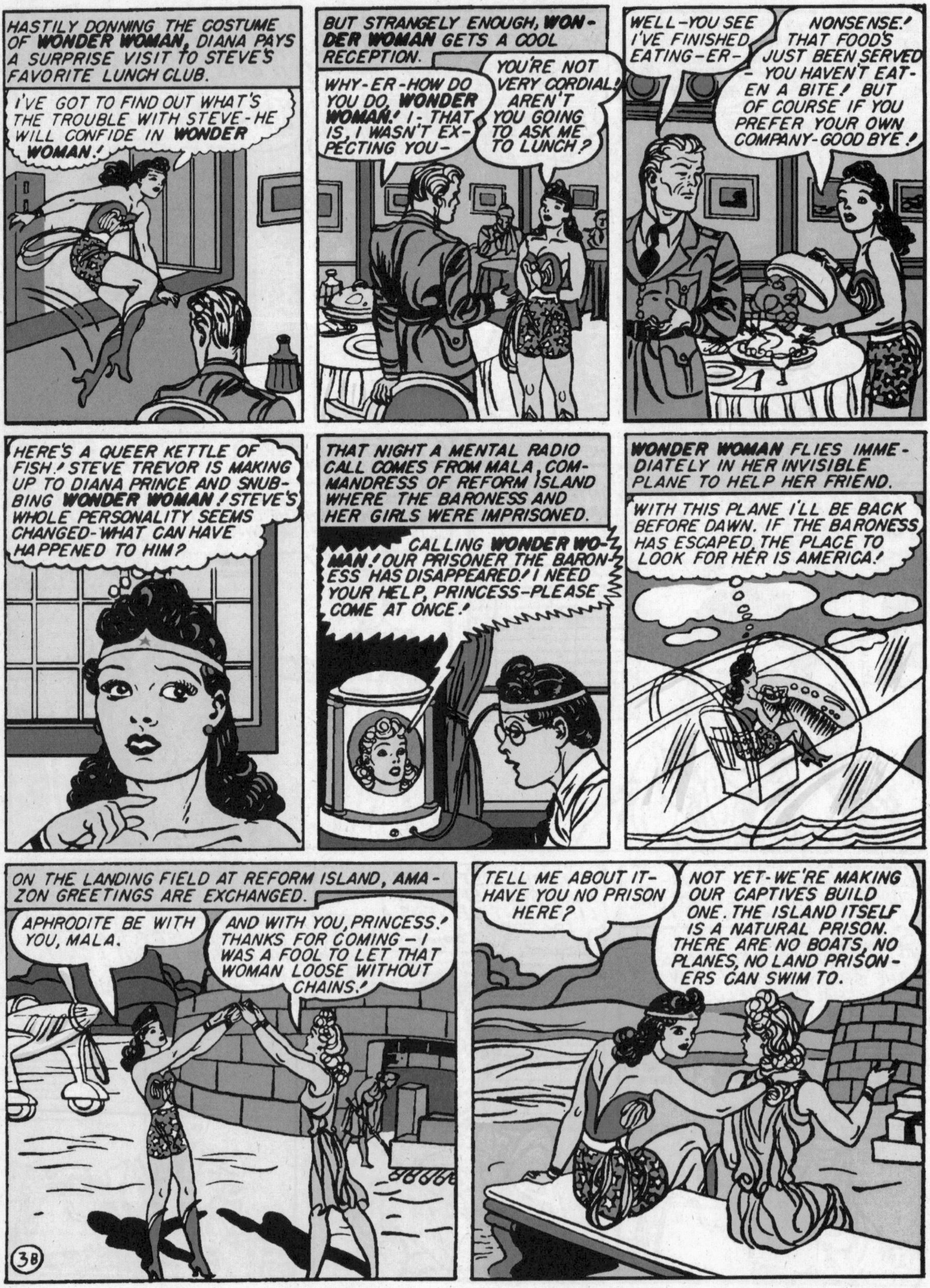
HASTILY DONNING THE COSTUME OF WONDER WOMAN, DIANA PAYS A SURPRISE VISIT TO STEVE'S FAVORITE LUNCH CLUB.
I'VE GOT TO FIND OUT WHAT'S THE TROUBLE WITH STEVE-HE WILL CONFIDE IN WONDER WOMAN!
BUT STRANGELY ENOUGH, WONDER WOMAN GETS A COOL RECEPTION.
WHY-ER-HOW DO YOU DO, WONDER WOMAN! I-THAT IS, I WASN'T EXPECTING YOU-
YOU'RE NOT VERY CORDIAL! AREN'T YOU GOING TO ASK ME TO LUNCH?
WELL-YOU SEE I'VE FINISHED EATING-ER-
NONSENSE! THAT FOOD'S JUST BEEN SERVED - YOU HAVEN'T EATEN A BITE! BUT OF COURSE IF YOU PREFER YOUR OWN COMPANY-GOOD BYE!
HERE'S A QUEER KETTLE OF FISH! STEVE TREVOR IS MAKING UP TO DIANA PRINCE AND SNUBBING WONDER WOMAN! STEVE'S WHOLE PERSONALITY SEEMS CHANGED-WHAT CAN HAVE HAPPENED TO HIM?
THAT NIGHT A MENTAL RADIO CALL COMES FROM MALA, COMMANDRESS OF REFORM ISLAND WHERE THE BARONESS AND HER GIRLS WERE IMPRISONED.
CALLING WONDER WOMAN! OUR PRISONER THE BARONESS HAS DISAPPEARED! I NEED YOUR HELP, PRINCESS-PLEASE COME AT ONCE!
WONDER WOMAN FLIES IMMEDIATELY IN HER INVISIBLE PLANE TO HELP HER FRIEND.
WITH THIS PLANE I'LL BE BACK BEFORE DAWN. IF THE BARONESS HAS ESCAPED, THE PLACE TO LOOK FOR HER IS AMERICA!
ON THE LANDING FIELD AT REFORM ISLAND, AMAZON GREETINGS ARE EXCHANGED.
APHRODITE BE WITH YOU, MALA.
AND WITH YOU, PRINCESS! THANKS FOR COMING - I WAS A FOOL TO LET THAT WOMAN LOOSE WITHOUT CHAINS!
3B
TELL ME ABOUT IT-HAVE YOU NO PRISON HERE?
NOT YET-WE'RE MAKING OUR CAPTIVES BUILD ONE. THE ISLAND ITSELF IS A NATURAL PRISON. THERE ARE NO BOATS, NO PLANES, NO LAND PRISONERS CAN SWIM TO.

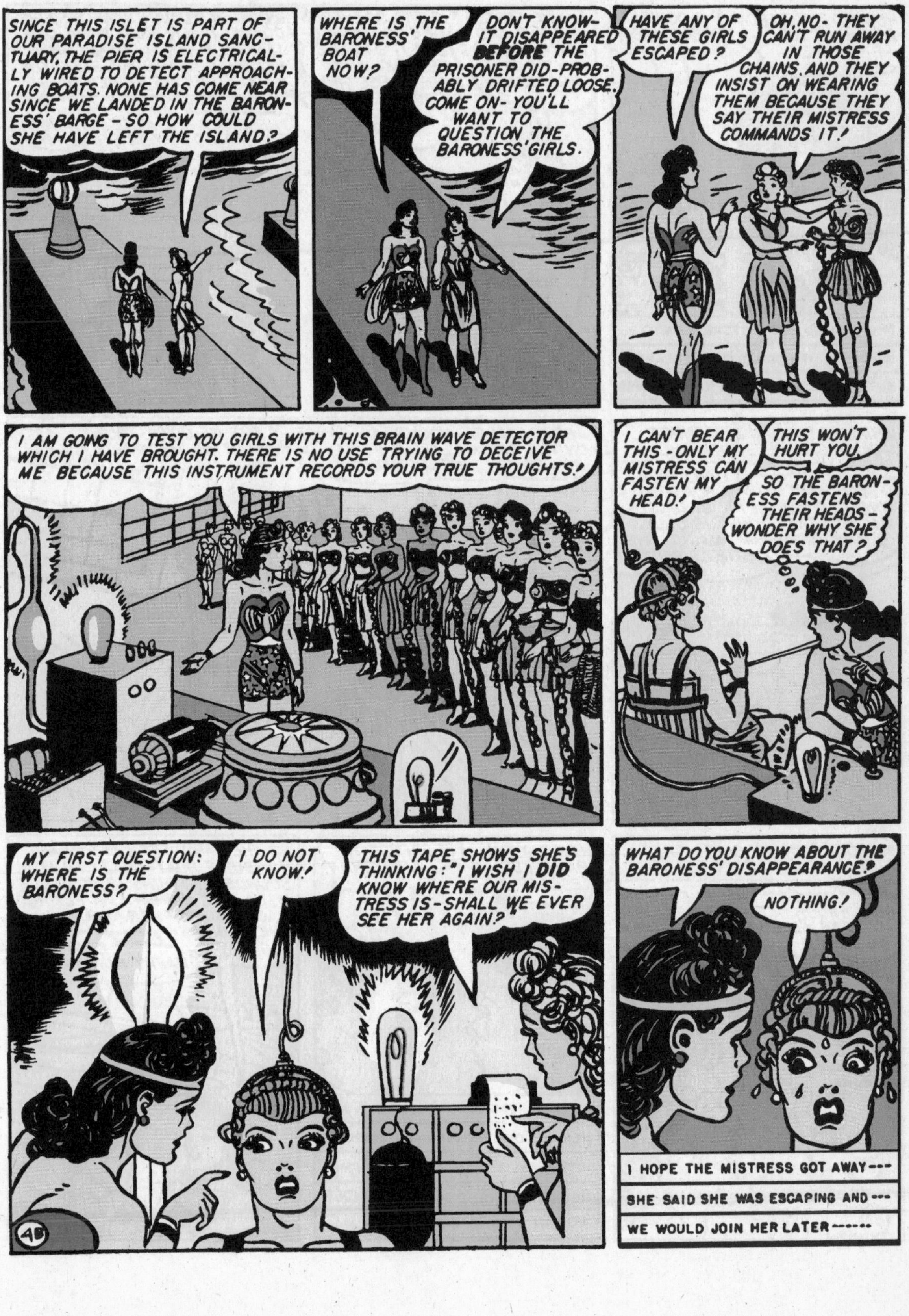
SINCE THIS ISLET IS PART OF OUR PARADISE ISLAND SANCTUARY, THE PIER IS ELECTRICALLY WIRED TO DETECT APPROACHING BOATS. NONE HAS COME NEAR SINCE WE LANDED IN THE BARONESS' BARGE - SO HOW COULD SHE HAVE LEFT THE ISLAND?
WHERE IS THE BARONESS' BOAT NOW?
DON'T KNOW- IT DISAPPEARED BEFORE THE PRISONER DID-PROBABLY DRIFTED LOOSE. COME ON- YOU'LL WANT TO QUESTION THE BARONESS' GIRLS.
HAVE ANY OF THESE GIRLS ESCAPED?
OH, NO- THEY CAN'T RUN AWAY IN THOSE CHAINS. AND THEY INSIST ON WEARING THEM BECAUSE THEY SAY THEIR MISTRESS COMMANDS IT!
I AM GOING TO TEST YOU GIRLS WITH THIS BRAIN WAVE DETECTOR WHICH I HAVE BROUGHT. THERE IS NO USE TRYING TO DECEIVE ME BECAUSE THIS INSTRUMENT RECORDS YOUR TRUE THOUGHTS!
I CAN'T BEAR THIS - ONLY MY MISTRESS CAN FASTEN MY HEAD!
THIS WON'T HURT YOU.
SO THE BARONESS FASTENS THEIR HEADS - WONDER WHY SHE DOES THAT?
MY FIRST QUESTION: WHERE IS THE BARONESS?
I DO NOT KNOW!
THIS TAPE SHOWS SHE'S THINKING: "I WISH I DID KNOW WHERE OUR MISTRESS IS - SHALL WE EVER SEE HER AGAIN?"
WHAT DO YOU KNOW ABOUT THE BARONESS' DISAPPEARANCE?
NOTHING!
I HOPE THE MISTRESS GOT AWAY---
SHE SAID SHE WAS ESCAPING AND ---
WE WOULD JOIN HER LATER------

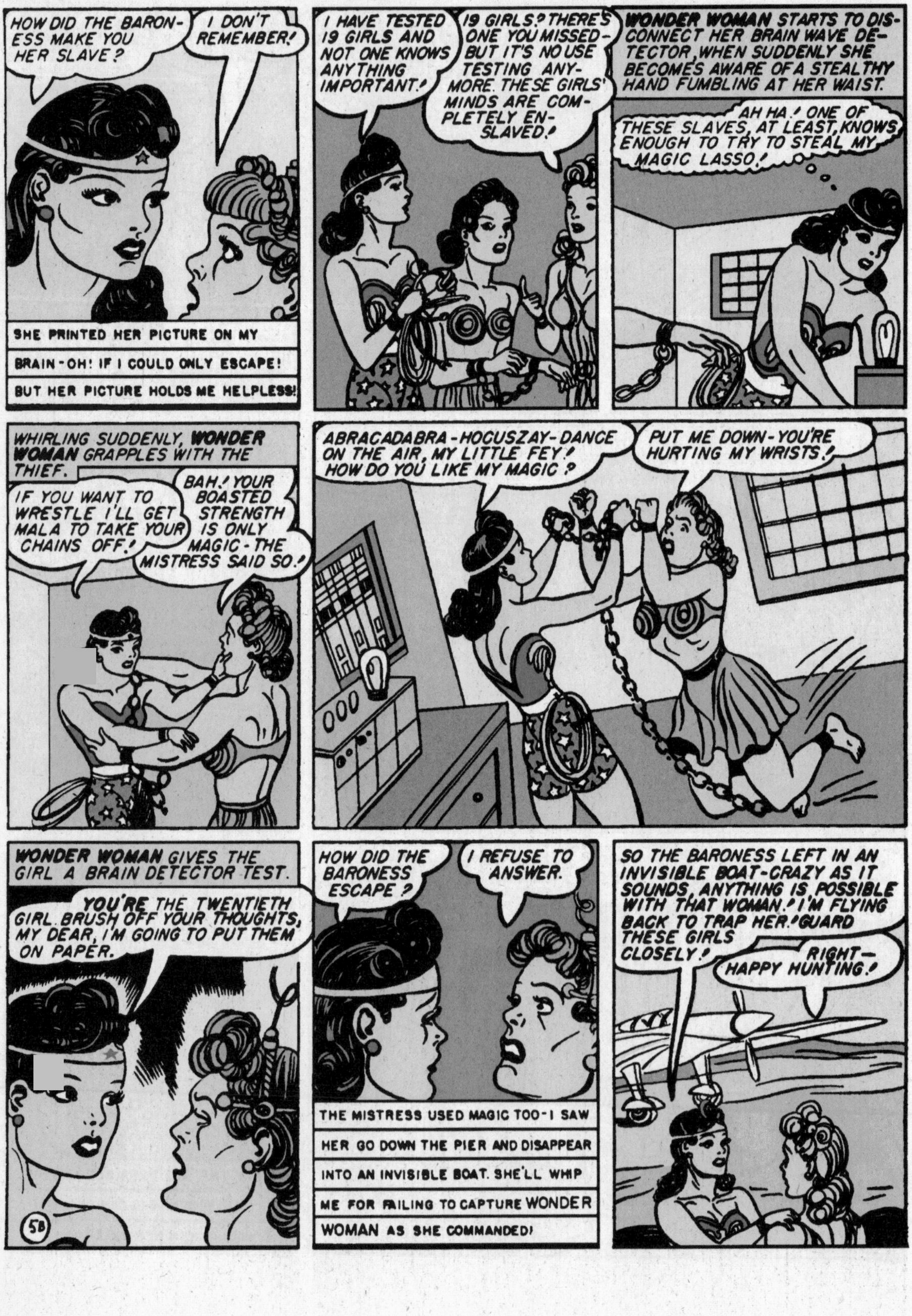

HOW DID THE BARONESS MAKE YOU HER SLAVE?
I DON'T REMEMBER!
SHE PRINTED HER PICTURE ON MY
BRAIN-OH! IF I COULD ONLY ESCAPE!
BUT HER PICTURE HOLDS ME HELPLESS!
I HAVE TESTED 19 GIRLS AND NOT ONE KNOWS ANYTHING IMPORTANT!
19 GIRLS? THERE'S ONE YOU MISSED-BUT IT'S NO USE TESTING ANYMORE. THESE GIRLS' MINDS ARE COMPLETELY ENSLAVED!
WONDER WOMAN STARTS TO DISCONNECT HER BRAIN WAVE DETECTOR, WHEN SUDDENLY SHE BECOMES AWARE OF A STEALTHY HAND FUMBLING AT HER WAIST.
AH HA! ONE OF THESE SLAVES, AT LEAST, KNOWS ENOUGH TO TRY TO STEAL MY MAGIC LASSO!
WHIRLING SUDDENLY, WONDER WOMAN GRAPPLES WITH THE THIEF.
IF YOU WANT TO WRESTLE I'LL GET MALA TO TAKE YOUR CHAINS OFF!
BAH! YOUR BOASTED STRENGTH IS ONLY MAGIC-THE MISTRESS SAID SO!
ABRACADABRA-HOCUSZAY-DANCE ON THE AIR, MY LITTLE FEY! HOW DO YOU LIKE MY MAGIC?
PUT ME DOWN-YOU'RE HURTING MY WRISTS!
WONDER WOMAN GIVES THE GIRL A BRAIN DETECTOR TEST.
YOU'RE THE TWENTIETH GIRL. BRUSH OFF YOUR THOUGHTS, MY DEAR, I'M GOING TO PUT THEM ON PAPER.
58
HOW DID THE BARONESS ESCAPE?
I REFUSE TO ANSWER.
THE MISTRESS USED MAGIC TOO-I SAW
HER GO DOWN THE PIER AND DISAPPEAR
INTO AN INVISIBLE BOAT. SHE'LL WHIP
ME FOR FAILING TO CAPTURE WONDER
WOMAN AS SHE COMMANDED!
SO THE BARONESS LEFT IN AN INVISIBLE BOAT-CRAZY AS IT SOUNDS, ANYTHING IS POSSIBLE WITH THAT WOMAN! I'M FLYING BACK TO TRAP HER! GUARD THESE GIRLS CLOSELY!
RIGHT—HAPPY HUNTING!

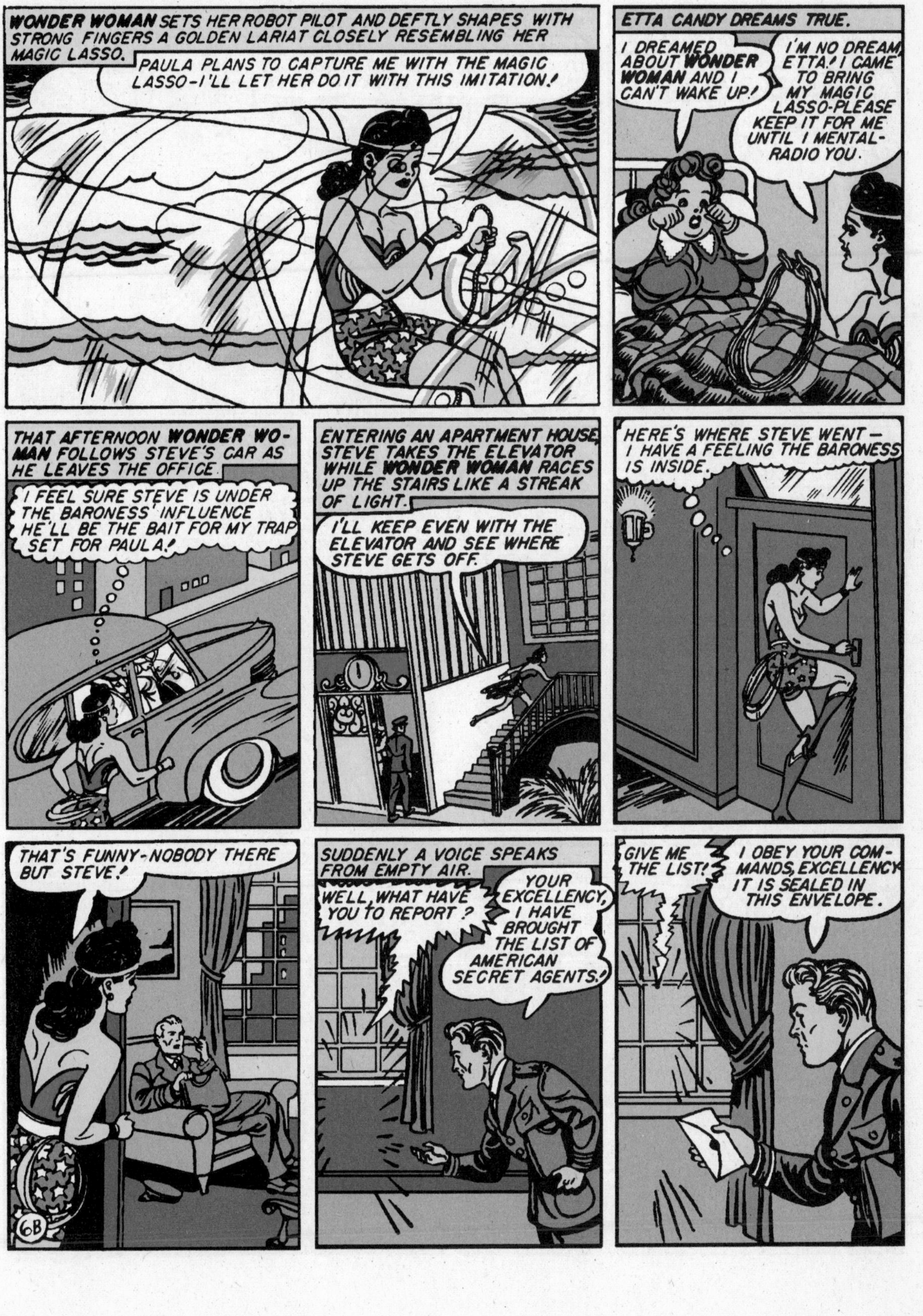
WONDER WOMAN SETS HER ROBOT PILOT AND DEFTLY SHAPES WITH STRONG FINGERS A GOLDEN LARIAT CLOSELY RESEMBLING HER MAGIC LASSO.
PAULA PLANS TO CAPTURE ME WITH THE MAGIC LASSO-I'LL LET HER DO IT WITH THIS IMITATION!
ETTA CANDY DREAMS TRUE.
I DREAMED ABOUT WONDER WOMAN AND I CAN'T WAKE UP!
I'M NO DREAM, ETTA! I CAME TO BRING MY MAGIC LASSO-PLEASE KEEP IT FOR ME UNTIL I MENTAL-RADIO YOU.
THAT AFTERNOON WONDER WOMAN FOLLOWS STEVE'S CAR AS HE LEAVES THE OFFICE.
I FEEL SURE STEVE IS UNDER THE BARONESS' INFLUENCE HE'LL BE THE BAIT FOR MY TRAP SET FOR PAULA!
ENTERING AN APARTMENT HOUSE, STEVE TAKES THE ELEVATOR WHILE WONDER WOMAN RACES UP THE STAIRS LIKE A STREAK OF LIGHT.
I'LL KEEP EVEN WITH THE ELEVATOR AND SEE WHERE STEVE GETS OFF.
HERE'S WHERE STEVE WENT — I HAVE A FEELING THE BARONESS IS INSIDE.
THAT'S FUNNY-NOBODY THERE BUT STEVE!
6B
SUDDENLY A VOICE SPEAKS FROM EMPTY AIR.
WELL, WHAT HAVE YOU TO REPORT ?
YOUR EXCELLENCY, I HAVE BROUGHT THE LIST OF AMERICAN SECRET AGENTS!
GIVE ME THE LIST!
I OBEY YOUR COMMANDS, EXCELLENCY IT IS SEALED IN THIS ENVELOPE.

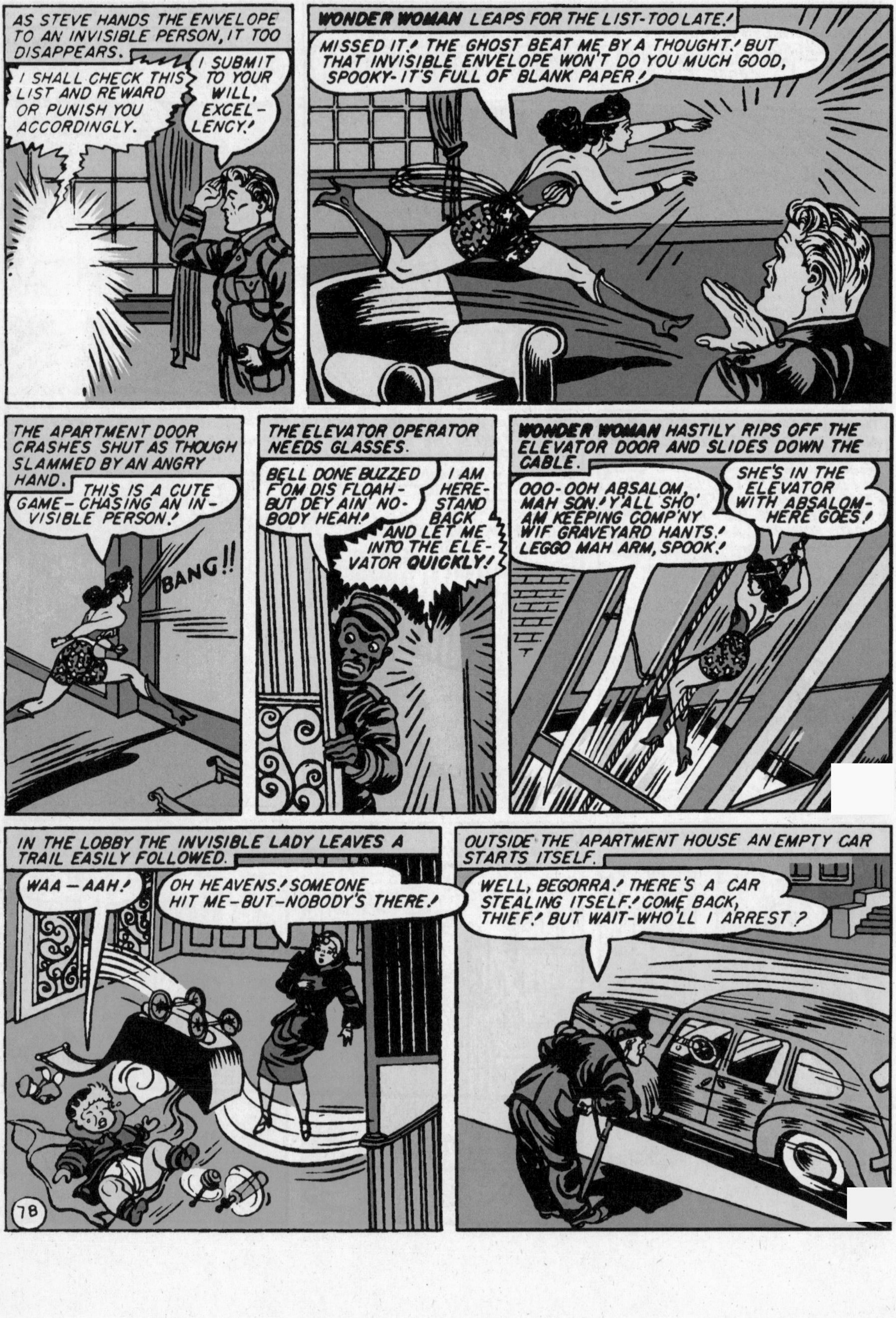
AS STEVE HANDS THE ENVELOPE TO AN INVISIBLE PERSON, IT TOO DISAPPEARS.
I SHALL CHECK THIS LIST AND REWARD OR PUNISH YOU ACCORDINGLY.
I SUBMIT TO YOUR WILL, EXCEL-LENCY!
WONDER WOMAN LEAPS FOR THE LIST-TOO LATE!
MISSED IT! THE GHOST BEAT ME BY A THOUGHT! BUT THAT INVISIBLE ENVELOPE WON'T DO YOU MUCH GOOD, SPOOKY-IT'S FULL OF BLANK PAPER!
THE APARTMENT DOOR CRASHES SHUT AS THOUGH SLAMMED BY AN ANGRY HAND.
THIS IS A CUTE GAME-CHASING AN IN-VISIBLE PERSON!
BANG!!
THE ELEVATOR OPERATOR NEEDS GLASSES.
BELL DONE BUZZED F'OM DIS FLOAH-BUT DEY AIN' NO-BODY HEAH!
I AM HERE-STAND BACK AND LET ME INTO THE ELE-VATOR QUICKLY!
WONDER WOMAN HASTILY RIPS OFF THE ELEVATOR DOOR AND SLIDES DOWN THE CABLE.
OOO-OOH ABSALOM, MAH SON! Y'ALL SHO' AM KEEPING COMP'NY WIF GRAVEYARD HANTS! LEGGO MAH ARM, SPOOK!
SHE'S IN THE ELEVATOR WITH ABSALOM-HERE GOES!
IN THE LOBBY THE INVISIBLE LADY LEAVES A TRAIL EASILY FOLLOWED.
WAA-AAH!
OH HEAVENS! SOMEONE HIT ME-BUT-NOBODY'S THERE!
7B
OUTSIDE THE APARTMENT HOUSE AN EMPTY CAR STARTS ITSELF.
WELL, BEGORRA! THERE'S A CAR STEALING ITSELF! COME BACK, THIEF! BUT WAIT-WHO'LL I ARREST?

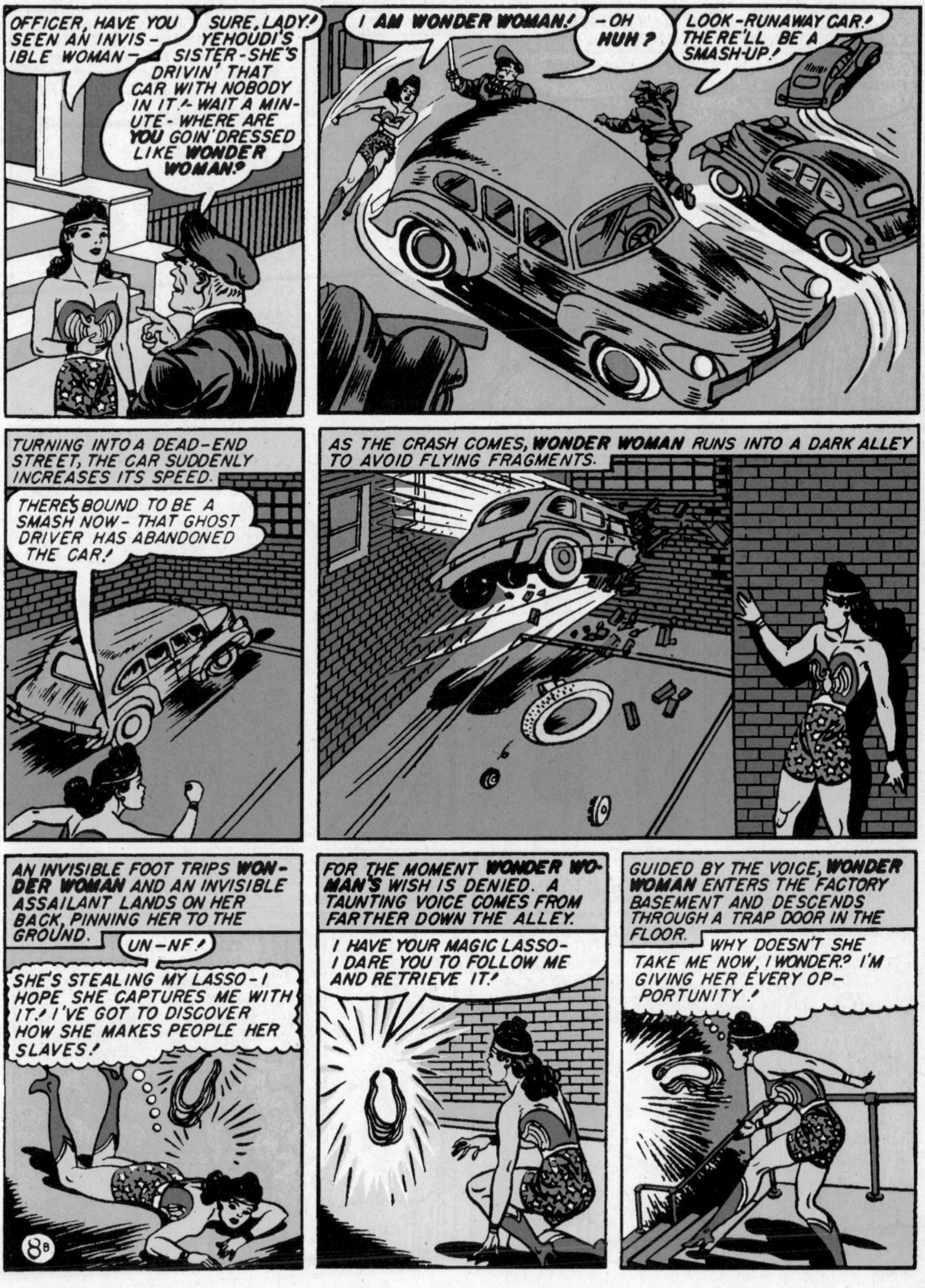

OFFICER, HAVE YOU SEEN AN INVISIBLE WOMAN—
SURE, LADY! YEHOUDI'S SISTER—SHE'S DRIVIN' THAT CAR WITH NOBODY IN IT!—WAIT A MINUTE—WHERE ARE YOU GOIN' DRESSED LIKE WONDER WOMAN?
I AM WONDER WOMAN!
—OH HUH?
LOOK—RUNAWAY CAR! THERE'LL BE A SMASH-UP!
TURNING INTO A DEAD-END STREET, THE CAR SUDDENLY INCREASES ITS SPEED.
THERE'S BOUND TO BE A SMASH NOW—THAT GHOST DRIVER HAS ABANDONED THE CAR!
AS THE CRASH COMES, WONDER WOMAN RUNS INTO A DARK ALLEY TO AVOID FLYING FRAGMENTS.
AN INVISIBLE FOOT TRIPS WONDER WOMAN AND AN INVISIBLE ASSAILANT LANDS ON HER BACK, PINNING HER TO THE GROUND.
UN—NF!
SHE'S STEALING MY LASSO—I HOPE SHE CAPTURES ME WITH IT! I'VE GOT TO DISCOVER HOW SHE MAKES PEOPLE HER SLAVES!
8B
FOR THE MOMENT WONDER WOMAN'S WISH IS DENIED. A TAUNTING VOICE COMES FROM FARTHER DOWN THE ALLEY.
I HAVE YOUR MAGIC LASSO—I DARE YOU TO FOLLOW ME AND RETRIEVE IT!
GUIDED BY THE VOICE, WONDER WOMAN ENTERS THE FACTORY BASEMENT AND DESCENDS THROUGH A TRAP DOOR IN THE FLOOR.
WHY DOESN'T SHE TAKE ME NOW, I WONDER? I'M GIVING HER EVERY OPPORTUNITY!

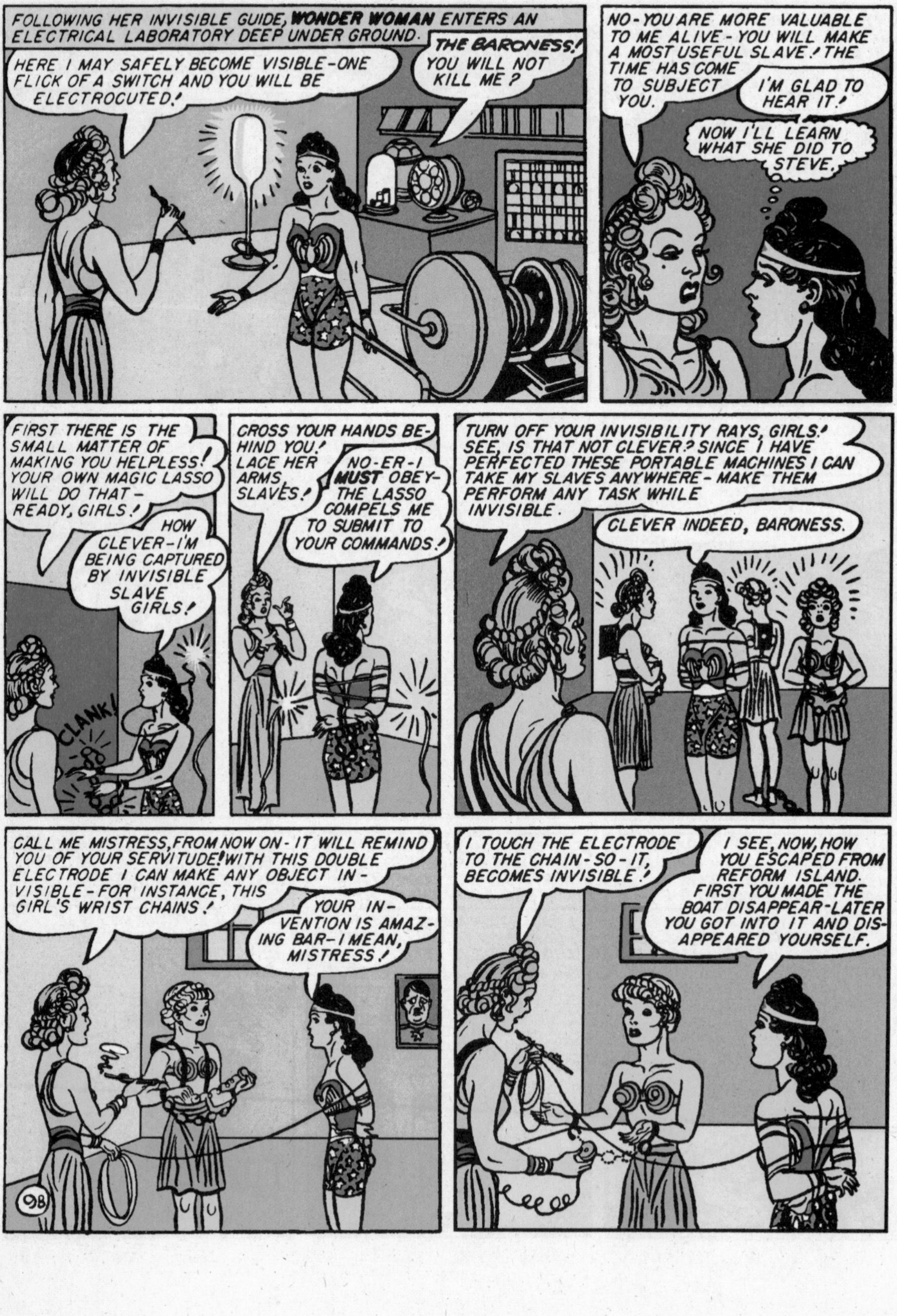
FOLLOWING HER INVISIBLE GUIDE, WONDER WOMAN ENTERS AN ELECTRICAL LABORATORY DEEP UNDER GROUND.
HERE I MAY SAFELY BECOME VISIBLE-ONE FLICK OF A SWITCH AND YOU WILL BE ELECTROCUTED!
THE BARONESS! YOU WILL NOT KILL ME?
NO-YOU ARE MORE VALUABLE TO ME ALIVE-YOU WILL MAKE A MOST USEFUL SLAVE! THE TIME HAS COME TO SUBJECT YOU.
I'M GLAD TO HEAR IT!
NOW I'LL LEARN WHAT SHE DID TO STEVE.
FIRST THERE IS THE SMALL MATTER OF MAKING YOU HELPLESS! YOUR OWN MAGIC LASSO WILL DO THAT-READY, GIRLS!
HOW CLEVER-I'M BEING CAPTURED BY INVISIBLE SLAVE GIRLS!
CLANK!
CROSS YOUR HANDS BEHIND YOU! LACE HER ARMS, SLAVES!
NO-ER-I MUST OBEY-THE LASSO COMPELS ME TO SUBMIT TO YOUR COMMANDS!
TURN OFF YOUR INVISIBILITY RAYS, GIRLS! SEE, IS THAT NOT CLEVER? SINCE I HAVE PERFECTED THESE PORTABLE MACHINES I CAN TAKE MY SLAVES ANYWHERE-MAKE THEM PERFORM ANY TASK WHILE INVISIBLE.
CLEVER INDEED, BARONESS.
CALL ME MISTRESS, FROM NOW ON-IT WILL REMIND YOU OF YOUR SERVITUDE! WITH THIS DOUBLE ELECTRODE I CAN MAKE ANY OBJECT INVISIBLE-FOR INSTANCE, THIS GIRL'S WRIST CHAINS!
YOUR INVENTION IS AMAZING BAR-I MEAN, MISTRESS!
9B
I TOUCH THE ELECTRODE TO THE CHAIN-SO-IT BECOMES INVISIBLE!
I SEE, NOW, HOW YOU ESCAPED FROM REFORM ISLAND. FIRST YOU MADE THE BOAT DISAPPEAR-LATER YOU GOT INTO IT AND DISAPPEARED YOURSELF.

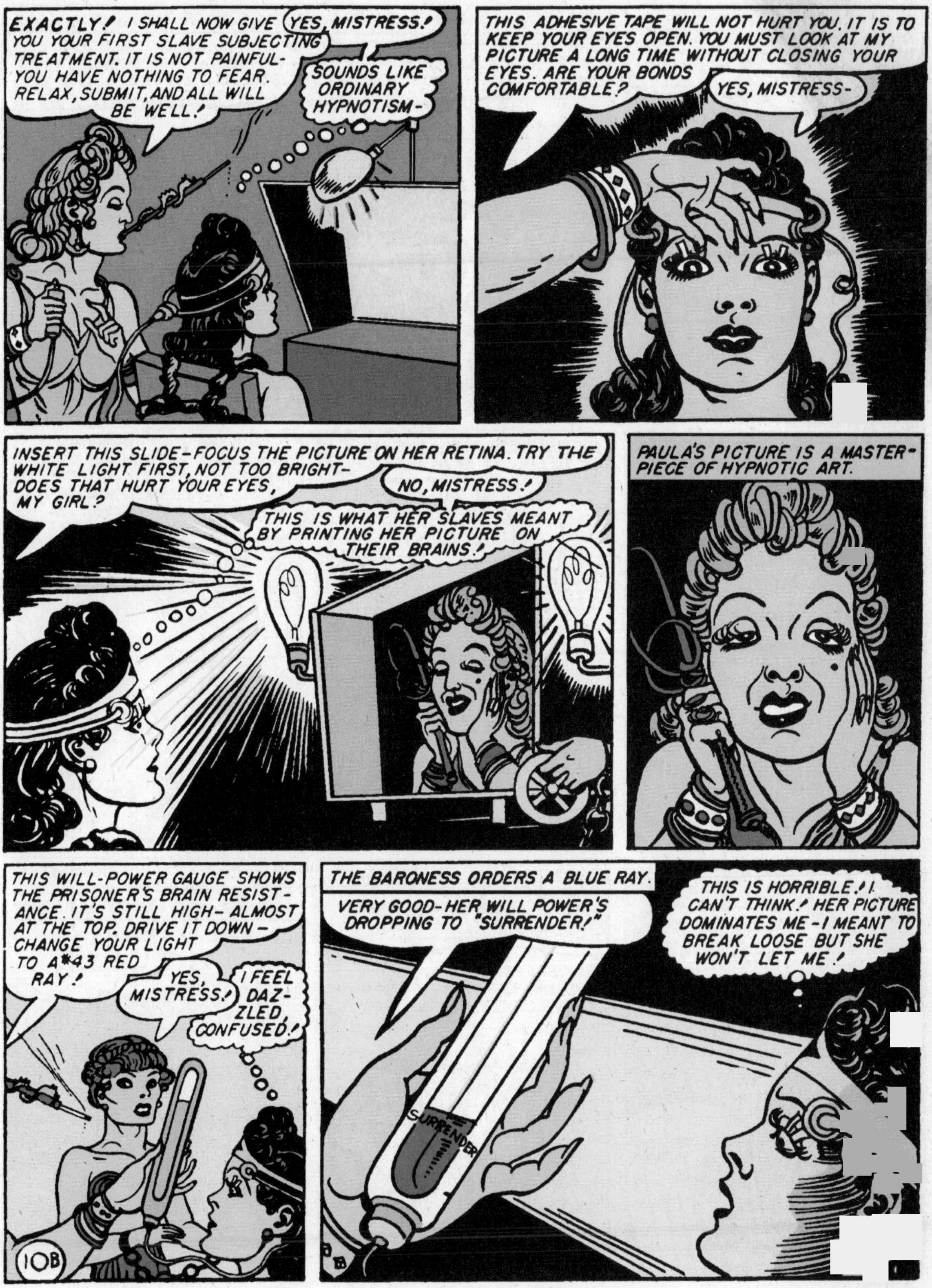
EXACTLY! I SHALL NOW GIVE YOU YOUR FIRST SLAVE SUBJECTING TREATMENT. IT IS NOT PAINFUL- YOU HAVE NOTHING TO FEAR. RELAX, SUBMIT, AND ALL WILL BE WELL!
YES, MISTRESS!
SOUNDS LIKE ORDINARY HYPNOTISM-
THIS ADHESIVE TAPE WILL NOT HURT YOU. IT IS TO KEEP YOUR EYES OPEN. YOU MUST LOOK AT MY PICTURE A LONG TIME WITHOUT CLOSING YOUR EYES. ARE YOUR BONDS COMFORTABLE?
YES, MISTRESS-
INSERT THIS SLIDE-FOCUS THE PICTURE ON HER RETINA. TRY THE WHITE LIGHT FIRST, NOT TOO BRIGHT- DOES THAT HURT YOUR EYES, MY GIRL?
NO, MISTRESS!
THIS IS WHAT HER SLAVES MEANT BY PRINTING HER PICTURE ON THEIR BRAINS!
PAULA'S PICTURE IS A MASTER-PIECE OF HYPNOTIC ART.
THIS WILL-POWER GAUGE SHOWS THE PRISONER'S BRAIN RESISTANCE. IT'S STILL HIGH- ALMOST AT THE TOP. DRIVE IT DOWN - CHANGE YOUR LIGHT TO A #43 RED RAY!
YES, MISTRESS!
I FEEL DAZZLED, CONFUSED!
10B
THE BARONESS ORDERS A BLUE RAY.
VERY GOOD-HER WILL POWER'S DROPPING TO "SURRENDER!"
SURRENDER
THIS IS HORRIBLE! I CAN'T THINK! HER PICTURE DOMINATES ME-I MEANT TO BREAK LOOSE BUT SHE WON'T LET ME!

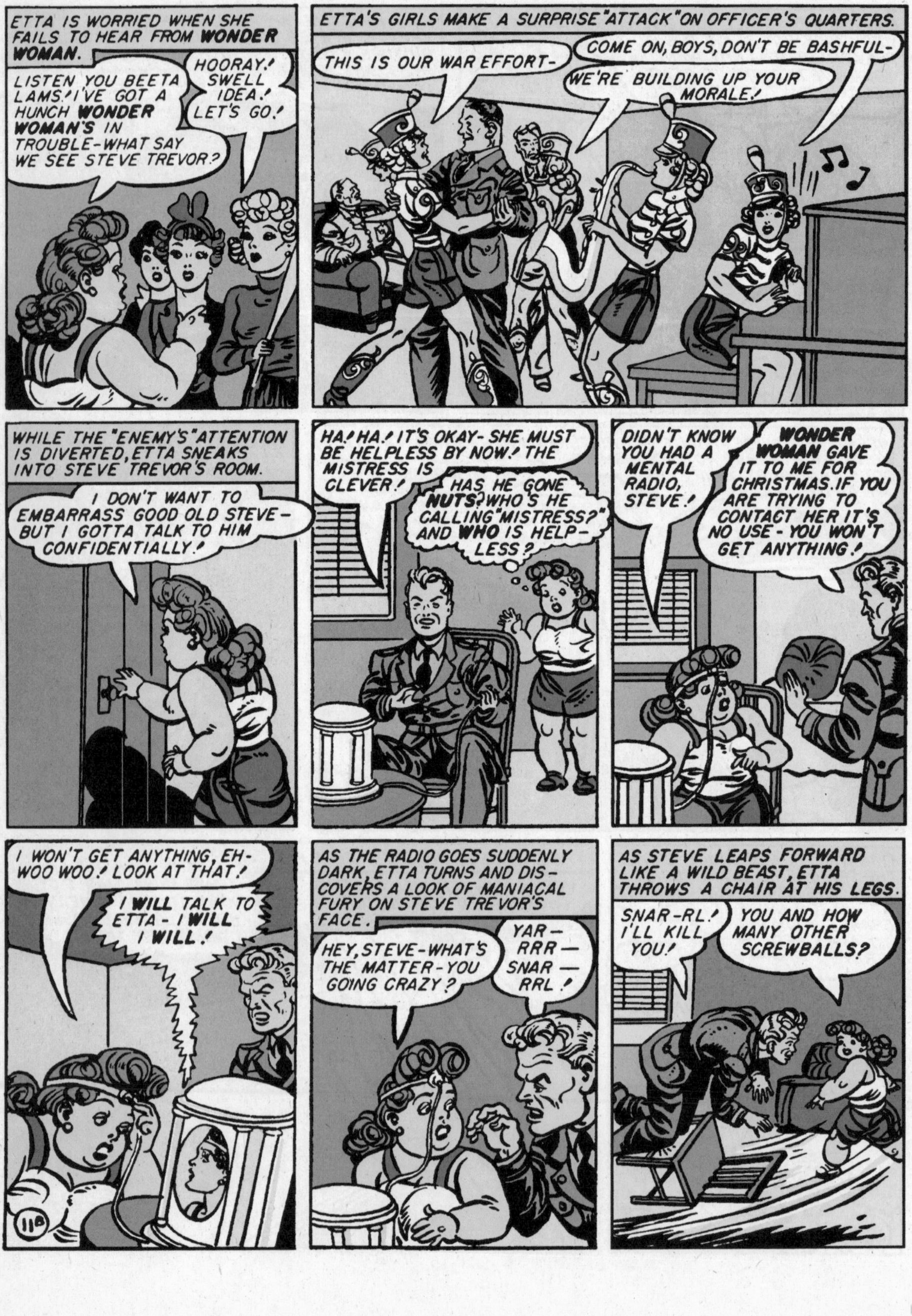
ETTA IS WORRIED WHEN SHE FAILS TO HEAR FROM WONDER WOMAN.
LISTEN YOU BEETA LAMS! I'VE GOT A HUNCH WONDER WOMAN'S IN TROUBLE-WHAT SAY WE SEE STEVE TREVOR?
HOORAY! SWELL IDEA! LET'S GO!
ETTA'S GIRLS MAKE A SURPRISE "ATTACK" ON OFFICER'S QUARTERS.
THIS IS OUR WAR EFFORT-
COME ON, BOYS, DON'T BE BASHFUL-
WE'RE BUILDING UP YOUR MORALE!
WHILE THE "ENEMY'S" ATTENTION IS DIVERTED, ETTA SNEAKS INTO STEVE TREVOR'S ROOM.
I DON'T WANT TO EMBARRASS GOOD OLD STEVE-BUT I GOTTA TALK TO HIM CONFIDENTIALLY!
HA! HA! IT'S OKAY- SHE MUST BE HELPLESS BY NOW! THE MISTRESS IS CLEVER!
HAS HE GONE NUTS? WHO'S HE CALLING "MISTRESS?" AND WHO IS HELP-LESS?
DIDN'T KNOW YOU HAD A MENTAL RADIO, STEVE!
WONDER WOMAN GAVE IT TO ME FOR CHRISTMAS. IF YOU ARE TRYING TO CONTACT HER IT'S NO USE - YOU WON'T GET ANYTHING!
I WON'T GET ANYTHING, EH- WOO WOO! LOOK AT THAT!
I WILL TALK TO ETTA - I WILL I WILL!
AS THE RADIO GOES SUDDENLY DARK, ETTA TURNS AND DIS-COVERS A LOOK OF MANIACAL FURY ON STEVE TREVOR'S FACE.
HEY, STEVE-WHAT'S THE MATTER-YOU GOING CRAZY?
YAR- RRR- SNAR- RRL!
AS STEVE LEAPS FORWARD LIKE A WILD BEAST, ETTA THROWS A CHAIR AT HIS LEGS.
SNAR-RL! I'LL KILL YOU!
YOU AND HOW MANY OTHER SCREWBALLS?

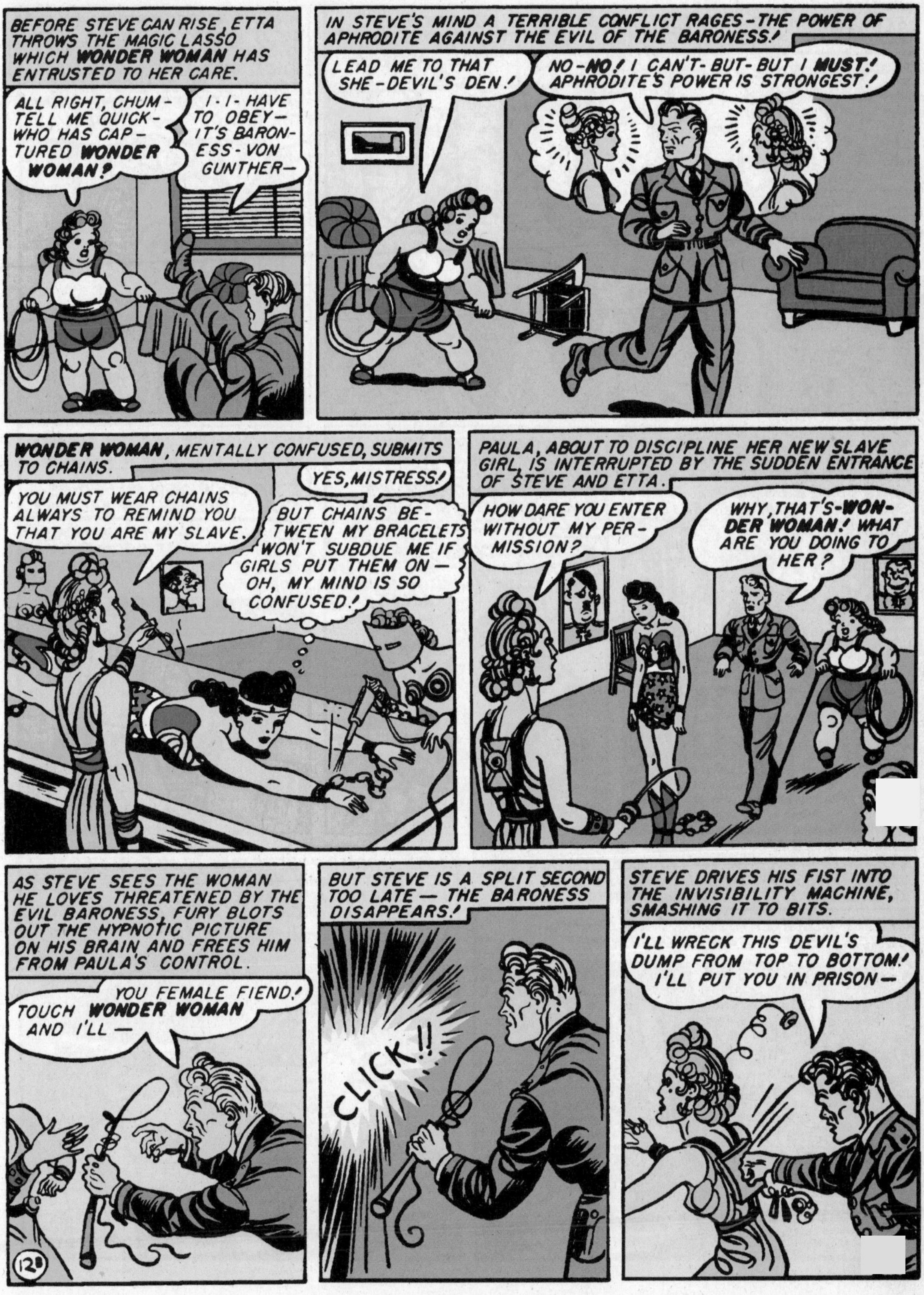
BEFORE STEVE CAN RISE, ETTA THROWS THE MAGIC LASSO WHICH **WONDER WOMAN** HAS ENTRUSTED TO HER CARE.
ALL RIGHT, CHUM - TELL ME QUICK - WHO HAS CAPTURED **WONDER WOMAN?**
I - I - HAVE TO OBEY - IT'S BARONESS - VON GUNTHER -
IN STEVE'S MIND A TERRIBLE CONFLICT RAGES - THE POWER OF APHRODITE AGAINST THE EVIL OF THE BARONESS!
LEAD ME TO THAT SHE-DEVIL'S DEN!
NO - **NO!** I CAN'T - BUT - BUT I **MUST!** APHRODITE'S POWER IS STRONGEST!
WONDER WOMAN, MENTALLY CONFUSED, SUBMITS TO CHAINS.
YOU MUST WEAR CHAINS ALWAYS TO REMIND YOU THAT YOU ARE MY SLAVE.
YES, MISTRESS!
BUT CHAINS BETWEEN MY BRACELETS WON'T SUBDUE ME IF GIRLS PUT THEM ON - OH, MY MIND IS SO CONFUSED!
PAULA, ABOUT TO DISCIPLINE HER NEW SLAVE GIRL, IS INTERRUPTED BY THE SUDDEN ENTRANCE OF STEVE AND ETTA.
HOW DARE YOU ENTER WITHOUT MY PERMISSION?
WHY, THAT'S - **WONDER WOMAN!** WHAT ARE YOU DOING TO HER?
AS STEVE SEES THE WOMAN HE LOVES THREATENED BY THE EVIL BARONESS, FURY BLOTS OUT THE HYPNOTIC PICTURE ON HIS BRAIN AND FREES HIM FROM PAULA'S CONTROL.
YOU FEMALE FIEND! TOUCH **WONDER WOMAN** AND I'LL -
12B
BUT STEVE IS A SPLIT SECOND TOO LATE - THE BARONESS DISAPPEARS!
CLICK!!
STEVE DRIVES HIS FIST INTO THE INVISIBILITY MACHINE, SMASHING IT TO BITS.
I'LL WRECK THIS DEVIL'S DUMP FROM TOP TO BOTTOM! I'LL PUT YOU IN PRISON -

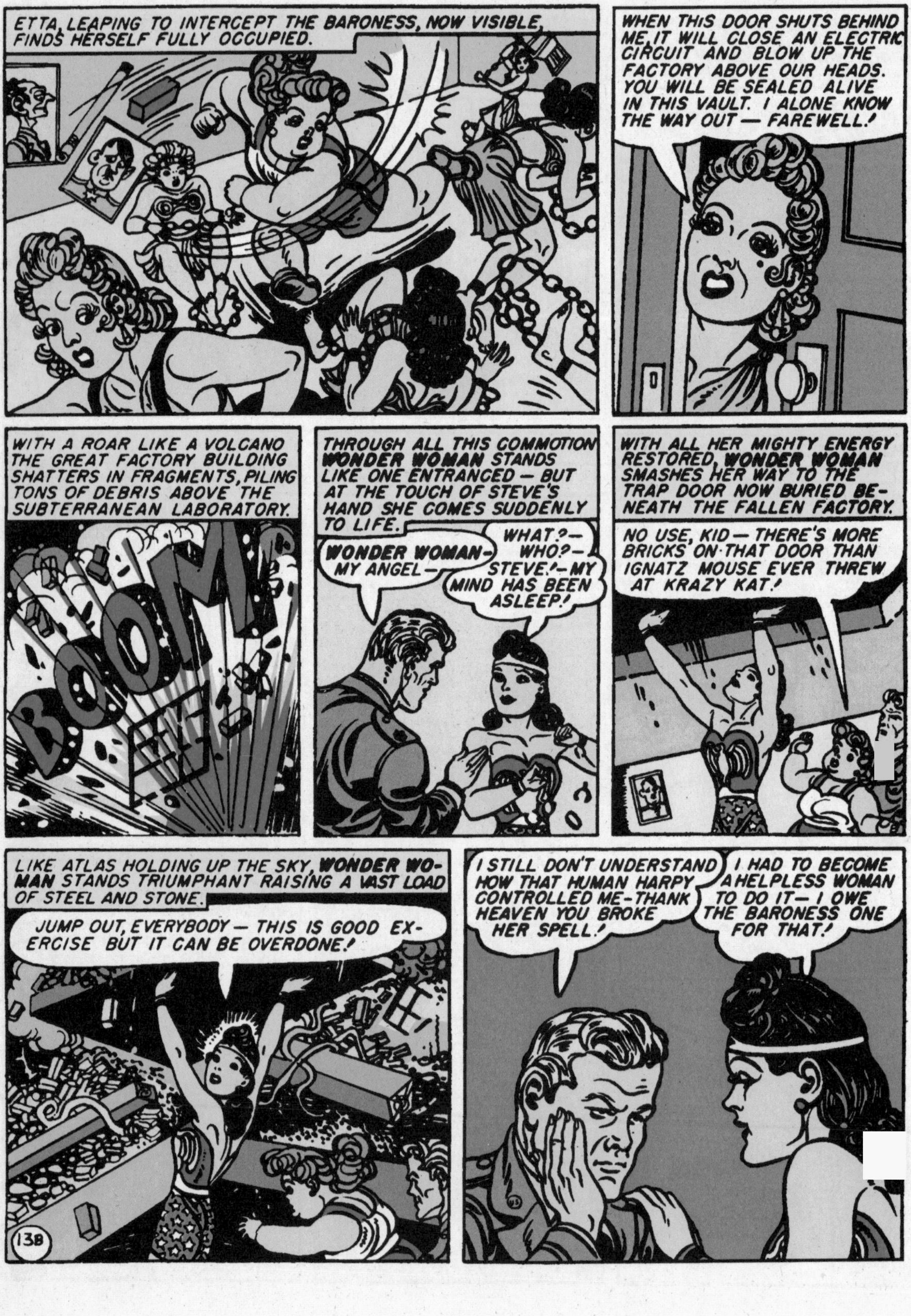

ETTA, LEAPING TO INTERCEPT THE BARONESS, NOW VISIBLE, FINDS HERSELF FULLY OCCUPIED.
WHEN THIS DOOR SHUTS BEHIND ME, IT WILL CLOSE AN ELECTRIC CIRCUIT AND BLOW UP THE FACTORY ABOVE OUR HEADS. YOU WILL BE SEALED ALIVE IN THIS VAULT. I ALONE KNOW THE WAY OUT — FAREWELL!
WITH A ROAR LIKE A VOLCANO THE GREAT FACTORY BUILDING SHATTERS IN FRAGMENTS, PILING TONS OF DEBRIS ABOVE THE SUBTERRANEAN LABORATORY.
BOOM
THROUGH ALL THIS COMMOTION WONDER WOMAN STANDS LIKE ONE ENTRANCED — BUT AT THE TOUCH OF STEVE'S HAND SHE COMES SUDDENLY TO LIFE.
WONDER WOMAN- MY ANGEL—
WHAT?— WHO?— STEVE!—MY MIND HAS BEEN ASLEEP!
WITH ALL HER MIGHTY ENERGY RESTORED, WONDER WOMAN SMASHES HER WAY TO THE TRAP DOOR NOW BURIED BENEATH THE FALLEN FACTORY.
NO USE, KID— THERE'S MORE BRICKS ON THAT DOOR THAN IGNATZ MOUSE EVER THREW AT KRAZY KAT!
LIKE ATLAS HOLDING UP THE SKY, WONDER WOMAN STANDS TRIUMPHANT RAISING A VAST LOAD OF STEEL AND STONE.
JUMP OUT, EVERYBODY — THIS IS GOOD EXERCISE BUT IT CAN BE OVERDONE!
13B
I STILL DON'T UNDERSTAND HOW THAT HUMAN HARPY CONTROLLED ME-THANK HEAVEN YOU BROKE HER SPELL!
I HAD TO BECOME A HELPLESS WOMAN TO DO IT— I OWE THE BARONESS ONE FOR THAT!

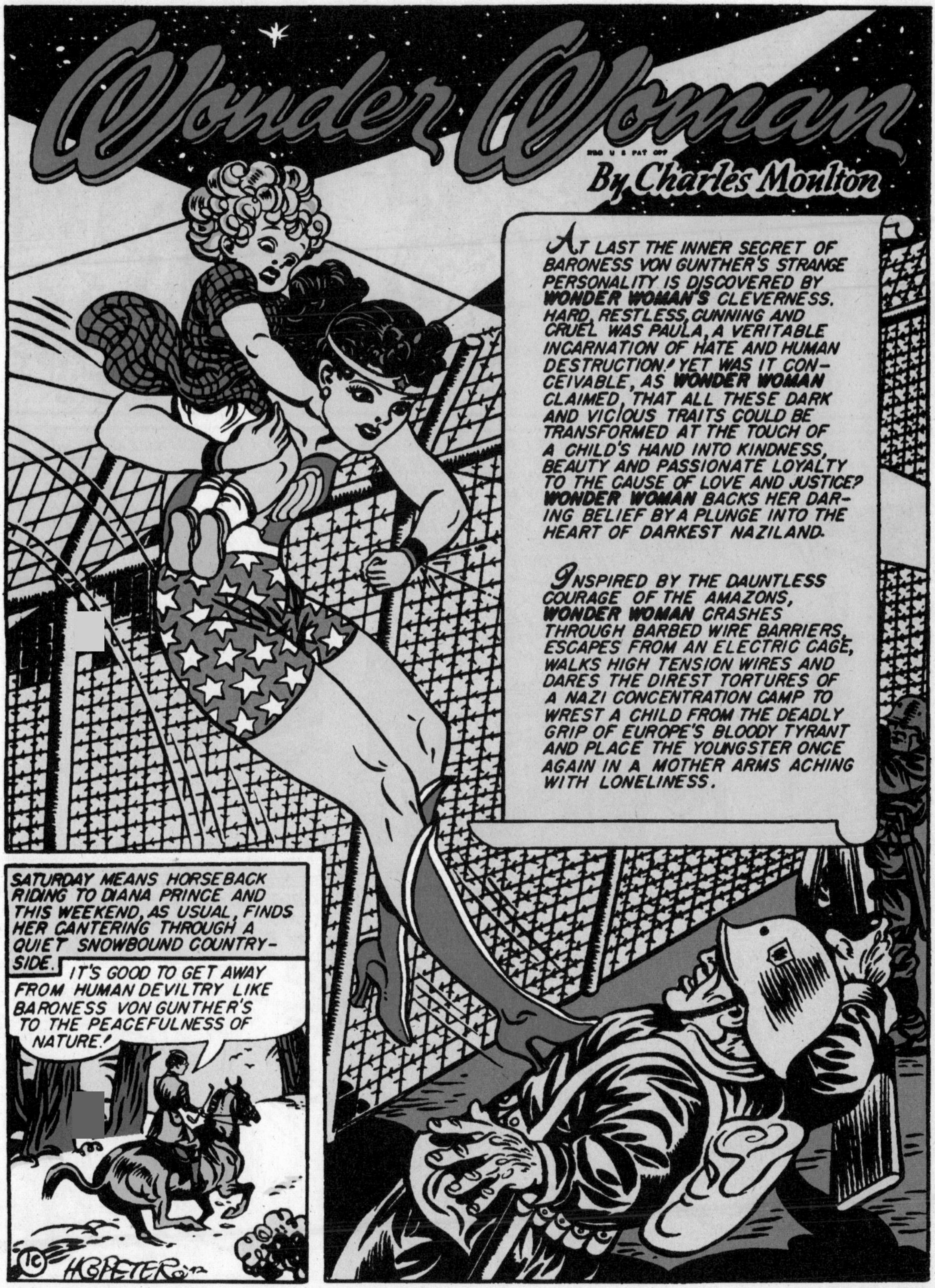
Wonder Woman
REG. U. S. PAT. OFF.
By Charles Moulton
AT LAST THE INNER SECRET OF BARONESS VON GUNTHER'S STRANGE PERSONALITY IS DISCOVERED BY WONDER WOMAN'S CLEVERNESS. HARD, RESTLESS, CUNNING AND CRUEL WAS PAULA, A VERITABLE INCARNATION OF HATE AND HUMAN DESTRUCTION! YET WAS IT CONCEIVABLE, AS WONDER WOMAN CLAIMED, THAT ALL THESE DARK AND VICIOUS TRAITS COULD BE TRANSFORMED AT THE TOUCH OF A CHILD'S HAND INTO KINDNESS, BEAUTY AND PASSIONATE LOYALTY TO THE CAUSE OF LOVE AND JUSTICE? WONDER WOMAN BACKS HER DARING BELIEF BY A PLUNGE INTO THE HEART OF DARKEST NAZILAND.
INSPIRED BY THE DAUNTLESS COURAGE OF THE AMAZONS, WONDER WOMAN CRASHES THROUGH BARBED WIRE BARRIERS, ESCAPES FROM AN ELECTRIC CAGE, WALKS HIGH TENSION WIRES AND DARES THE DIREST TORTURES OF A NAZI CONCENTRATION CAMP TO WREST A CHILD FROM THE DEADLY GRIP OF EUROPE'S BLOODY TYRANT AND PLACE THE YOUNGSTER ONCE AGAIN IN A MOTHER ARMS ACHING WITH LONELINESS.
SATURDAY MEANS HORSEBACK RIDING TO DIANA PRINCE AND THIS WEEKEND, AS USUAL, FINDS HER CANTERING THROUGH A QUIET SNOWBOUND COUNTRYSIDE.
IT'S GOOD TO GET AWAY FROM HUMAN DEVILTRY LIKE BARONESS VON GUNTHER'S TO THE PEACEFULNESS OF NATURE!
HGPETER

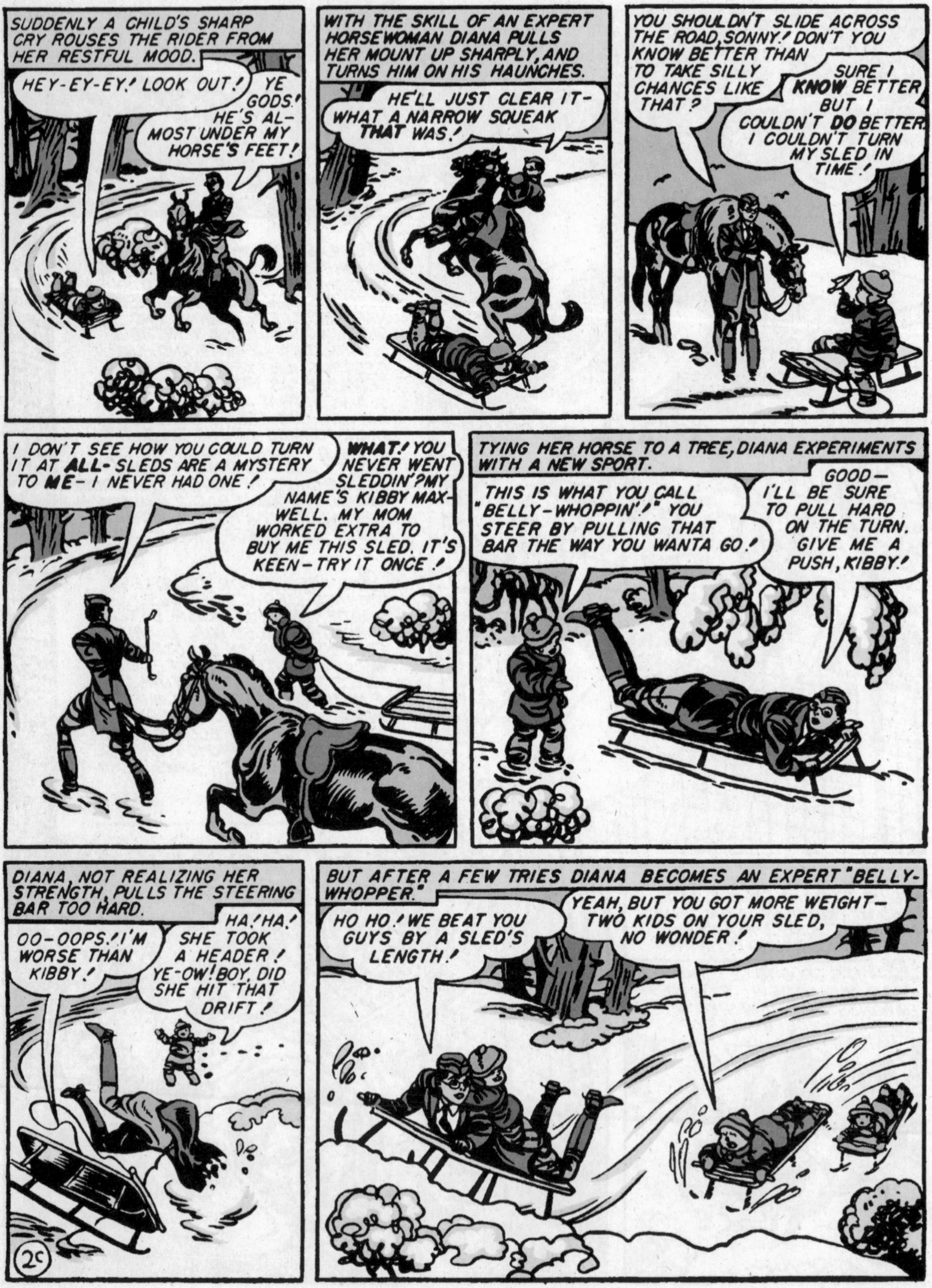
SUDDENLY A CHILD'S SHARP CRY ROUSES THE RIDER FROM HER RESTFUL MOOD.
HEY-EY-EY! LOOK OUT!
YE GODS! HE'S ALMOST UNDER MY HORSE'S FEET!
WITH THE SKILL OF AN EXPERT HORSEWOMAN DIANA PULLS HER MOUNT UP SHARPLY, AND TURNS HIM ON HIS HAUNCHES.
HE'LL JUST CLEAR IT-WHAT A NARROW SQUEAK THAT WAS!
YOU SHOULDN'T SLIDE ACROSS THE ROAD, SONNY! DON'T YOU KNOW BETTER THAN TO TAKE SILLY CHANCES LIKE THAT?
SURE I KNOW BETTER BUT I COULDN'T DO BETTER. I COULDN'T TURN MY SLED IN TIME!
I DON'T SEE HOW YOU COULD TURN IT AT ALL- SLEDS ARE A MYSTERY TO ME- I NEVER HAD ONE!
WHAT! YOU NEVER WENT SLEDDIN'? MY NAME'S KIBBY MAXWELL. MY MOM WORKED EXTRA TO BUY ME THIS SLED. IT'S KEEN-TRY IT ONCE!
TYING HER HORSE TO A TREE, DIANA EXPERIMENTS WITH A NEW SPORT.
THIS IS WHAT YOU CALL "BELLY-WHOPPIN'!" YOU STEER BY PULLING THAT BAR THE WAY YOU WANTA GO!
GOOD- I'LL BE SURE TO PULL HARD ON THE TURN. GIVE ME A PUSH, KIBBY!
DIANA, NOT REALIZING HER STRENGTH, PULLS THE STEERING BAR TOO HARD.
OO-OOPS! I'M WORSE THAN KIBBY!
HA! HA! SHE TOOK A HEADER! YE-OW! BOY, DID SHE HIT THAT DRIFT!
2c
BUT AFTER A FEW TRIES DIANA BECOMES AN EXPERT "BELLY-WHOPPER."
HO HO! WE BEAT YOU GUYS BY A SLED'S LENGTH!
YEAH, BUT YOU GOT MORE WEIGHT- TWO KIDS ON YOUR SLED, NO WONDER!

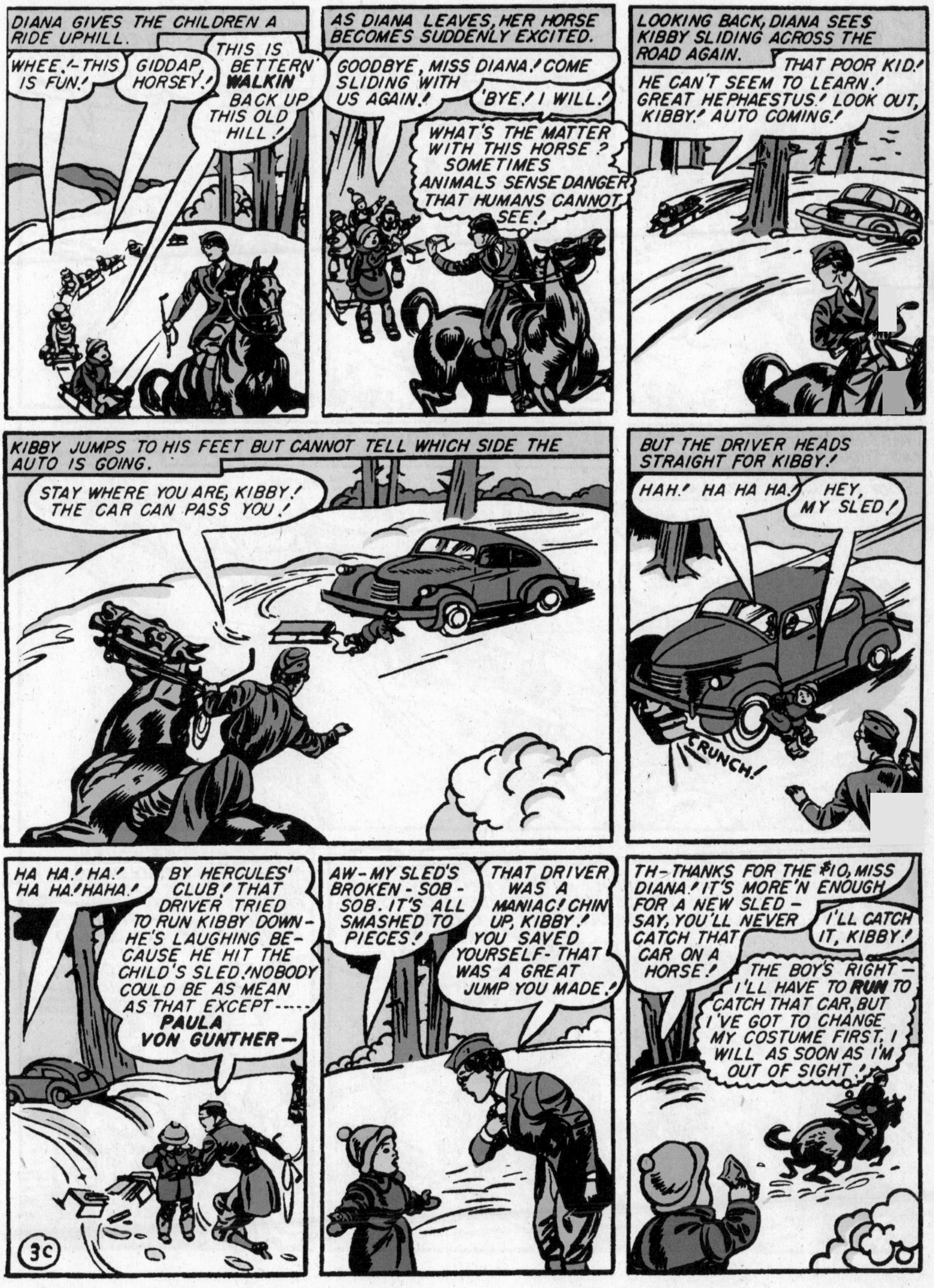

DIANA GIVES THE CHILDREN A RIDE UPHILL.
WHEE!–THIS IS FUN!
GIDDAP, HORSEY!
THIS IS BETTER'N WALKIN BACK UP THIS OLD HILL!
AS DIANA LEAVES, HER HORSE BECOMES SUDDENLY EXCITED.
GOODBYE, MISS DIANA! COME SLIDING WITH US AGAIN!
'BYE! I WILL!
WHAT'S THE MATTER WITH THIS HORSE? SOMETIMES ANIMALS SENSE DANGER THAT HUMANS CANNOT SEE!
LOOKING BACK, DIANA SEES KIBBY SLIDING ACROSS THE ROAD AGAIN.
THAT POOR KID! HE CAN'T SEEM TO LEARN! GREAT HEPHAESTUS! LOOK OUT, KIBBY! AUTO COMING!
KIBBY JUMPS TO HIS FEET BUT CANNOT TELL WHICH SIDE THE AUTO IS GOING.
STAY WHERE YOU ARE, KIBBY! THE CAR CAN PASS YOU!
BUT THE DRIVER HEADS STRAIGHT FOR KIBBY!
HAH! HA HA HA!
HEY, MY SLED!
CRUNCH!
HA HA! HA! HA HA! HAHA!
BY HERCULES' CLUB! THAT DRIVER TRIED TO RUN KIBBY DOWN–HE'S LAUGHING BECAUSE HE HIT THE CHILD'S SLED! NOBODY COULD BE AS MEAN AS THAT EXCEPT----- PAULA VON GUNTHER–
3C
AW–MY SLED'S BROKEN–SOB–SOB. IT'S ALL SMASHED TO PIECES!
THAT DRIVER WAS A MANIAC! CHIN UP, KIBBY! YOU SAVED YOURSELF–THAT WAS A GREAT JUMP YOU MADE!
TH–THANKS FOR THE $10, MISS DIANA! IT'S MORE'N ENOUGH FOR A NEW SLED–SAY, YOU'LL NEVER CATCH THAT CAR ON A HORSE!
I'LL CATCH IT, KIBBY!
THE BOY'S RIGHT–I'LL HAVE TO RUN TO CATCH THAT CAR, BUT I'VE GOT TO CHANGE MY COSTUME FIRST. I WILL AS SOON AS I'M OUT OF SIGHT!

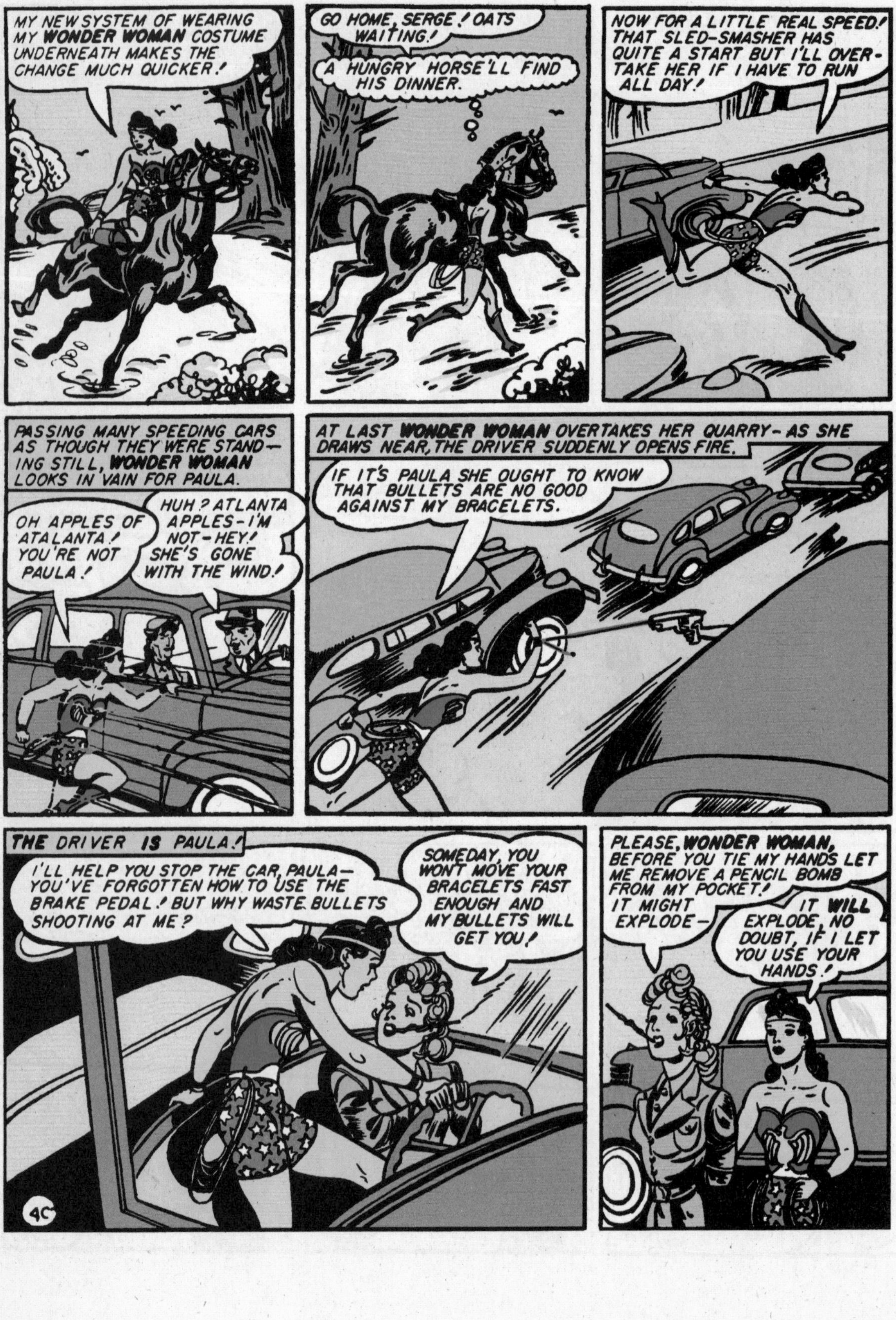

MY NEW SYSTEM OF WEARING MY WONDER WOMAN COSTUME UNDERNEATH MAKES THE CHANGE MUCH QUICKER!
GO HOME, SERGE! OATS WAITING!
A HUNGRY HORSE'LL FIND HIS DINNER.
NOW FOR A LITTLE REAL SPEED! THAT SLED-SMASHER HAS QUITE A START BUT I'LL OVER-TAKE HER IF I HAVE TO RUN ALL DAY!
PASSING MANY SPEEDING CARS AS THOUGH THEY WERE STAND-ING STILL, WONDER WOMAN LOOKS IN VAIN FOR PAULA.
OH APPLES OF ATALANTA! YOU'RE NOT PAULA!
HUH? ATLANTA APPLES-I'M NOT-HEY! SHE'S GONE WITH THE WIND!
AT LAST WONDER WOMAN OVERTAKES HER QUARRY-AS SHE DRAWS NEAR, THE DRIVER SUDDENLY OPENS FIRE.
IF IT'S PAULA SHE OUGHT TO KNOW THAT BULLETS ARE NO GOOD AGAINST MY BRACELETS.
THE DRIVER IS PAULA!
I'LL HELP YOU STOP THE CAR, PAULA-YOU'VE FORGOTTEN HOW TO USE THE BRAKE PEDAL! BUT WHY WASTE BULLETS SHOOTING AT ME?
SOMEDAY, YOU WON'T MOVE YOUR BRACELETS FAST ENOUGH AND MY BULLETS WILL GET YOU!
4C
PLEASE, WONDER WOMAN, BEFORE YOU TIE MY HANDS LET ME REMOVE A PENCIL BOMB FROM MY POCKET! IT MIGHT EXPLODE-
IT WILL EXPLODE, NO DOUBT, IF I LET YOU USE YOUR HANDS!

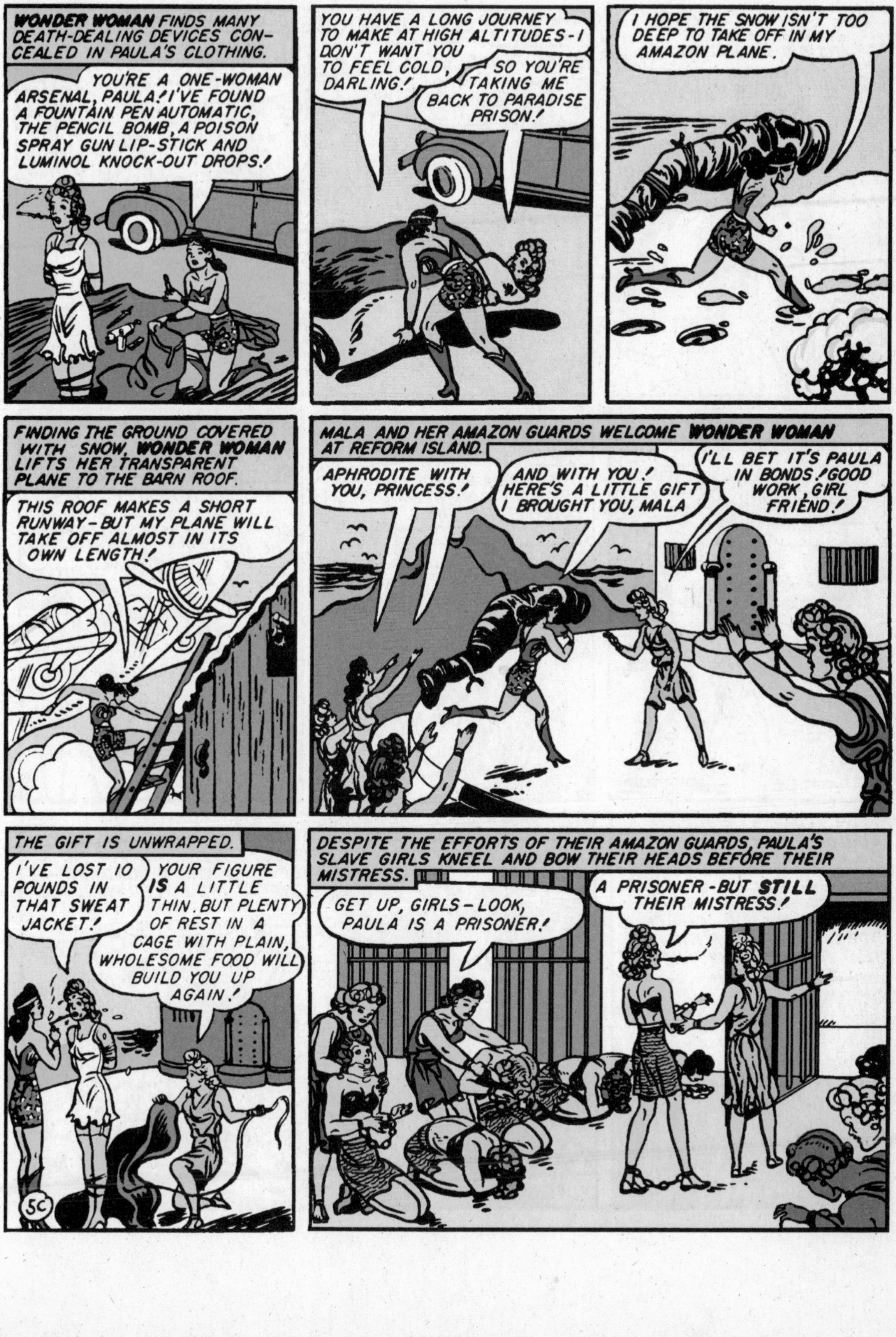
WONDER WOMAN FINDS MANY DEATH-DEALING DEVICES CONCEALED IN PAULA'S CLOTHING.
YOU'RE A ONE-WOMAN ARSENAL, PAULA! I'VE FOUND A FOUNTAIN PEN AUTOMATIC, THE PENCIL BOMB, A POISON SPRAY GUN LIP-STICK AND LUMINOL KNOCK-OUT DROPS!
YOU HAVE A LONG JOURNEY TO MAKE AT HIGH ALTITUDES - I DON'T WANT YOU TO FEEL COLD, DARLING!
SO YOU'RE TAKING ME BACK TO PARADISE PRISON!
I HOPE THE SNOW ISN'T TOO DEEP TO TAKE OFF IN MY AMAZON PLANE.
FINDING THE GROUND COVERED WITH SNOW, WONDER WOMAN LIFTS HER TRANSPARENT PLANE TO THE BARN ROOF.
THIS ROOF MAKES A SHORT RUNWAY - BUT MY PLANE WILL TAKE OFF ALMOST IN ITS OWN LENGTH!
MALA AND HER AMAZON GUARDS WELCOME WONDER WOMAN AT REFORM ISLAND.
APHRODITE WITH YOU, PRINCESS!
AND WITH YOU! HERE'S A LITTLE GIFT I BROUGHT YOU, MALA
I'LL BET IT'S PAULA IN BONDS! GOOD WORK, GIRL FRIEND!
THE GIFT IS UNWRAPPED.
I'VE LOST 10 POUNDS IN THAT SWEAT JACKET!
YOUR FIGURE IS A LITTLE THIN. BUT PLENTY OF REST IN A CAGE WITH PLAIN, WHOLESOME FOOD WILL BUILD YOU UP AGAIN!
5C
DESPITE THE EFFORTS OF THEIR AMAZON GUARDS, PAULA'S SLAVE GIRLS KNEEL AND BOW THEIR HEADS BEFORE THEIR MISTRESS.
GET UP, GIRLS - LOOK, PAULA IS A PRISONER!
A PRISONER - BUT STILL THEIR MISTRESS!

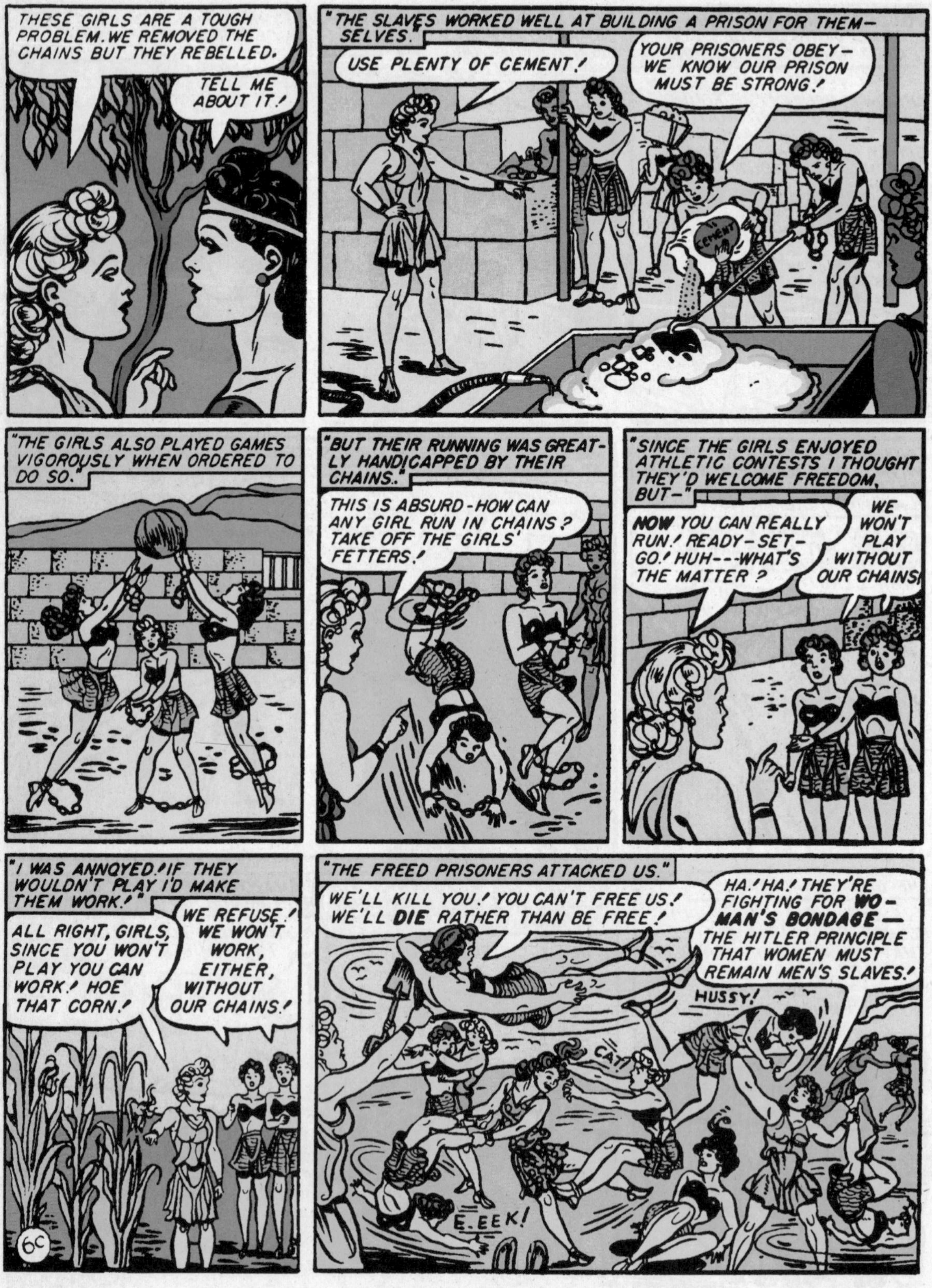
THESE GIRLS ARE A TOUGH PROBLEM. WE REMOVED THE CHAINS BUT THEY REBELLED.
TELL ME ABOUT IT!
"THE SLAVES WORKED WELL AT BUILDING A PRISON FOR THEMSELVES."
USE PLENTY OF CEMENT!
YOUR PRISONERS OBEY— WE KNOW OUR PRISON MUST BE STRONG!
CEMENT
"THE GIRLS ALSO PLAYED GAMES VIGOROUSLY WHEN ORDERED TO DO SO."
"BUT THEIR RUNNING WAS GREATLY HANDICAPPED BY THEIR CHAINS."
THIS IS ABSURD-HOW CAN ANY GIRL RUN IN CHAINS? TAKE OFF THE GIRLS' FETTERS!
"SINCE THE GIRLS ENJOYED ATHLETIC CONTESTS I THOUGHT THEY'D WELCOME FREEDOM, BUT—"
NOW YOU CAN REALLY RUN! READY-SET-GO! HUH---WHAT'S THE MATTER?
WE WON'T PLAY WITHOUT OUR CHAINS!
"I WAS ANNOYED! IF THEY WOULDN'T PLAY I'D MAKE THEM WORK!"
ALL RIGHT, GIRLS, SINCE YOU WON'T PLAY YOU CAN WORK! HOE THAT CORN!
WE REFUSE! WE WON'T WORK, EITHER, WITHOUT OUR CHAINS!
6C
"THE FREED PRISONERS ATTACKED US."
WE'LL KILL YOU! YOU CAN'T FREE US! WE'LL DIE RATHER THAN BE FREE!
HA! HA! THEY'RE FIGHTING FOR WOMAN'S BONDAGE — THE HITLER PRINCIPLE THAT WOMEN MUST REMAIN MEN'S SLAVES!
HUSSY!
CAT!
E-EEK!

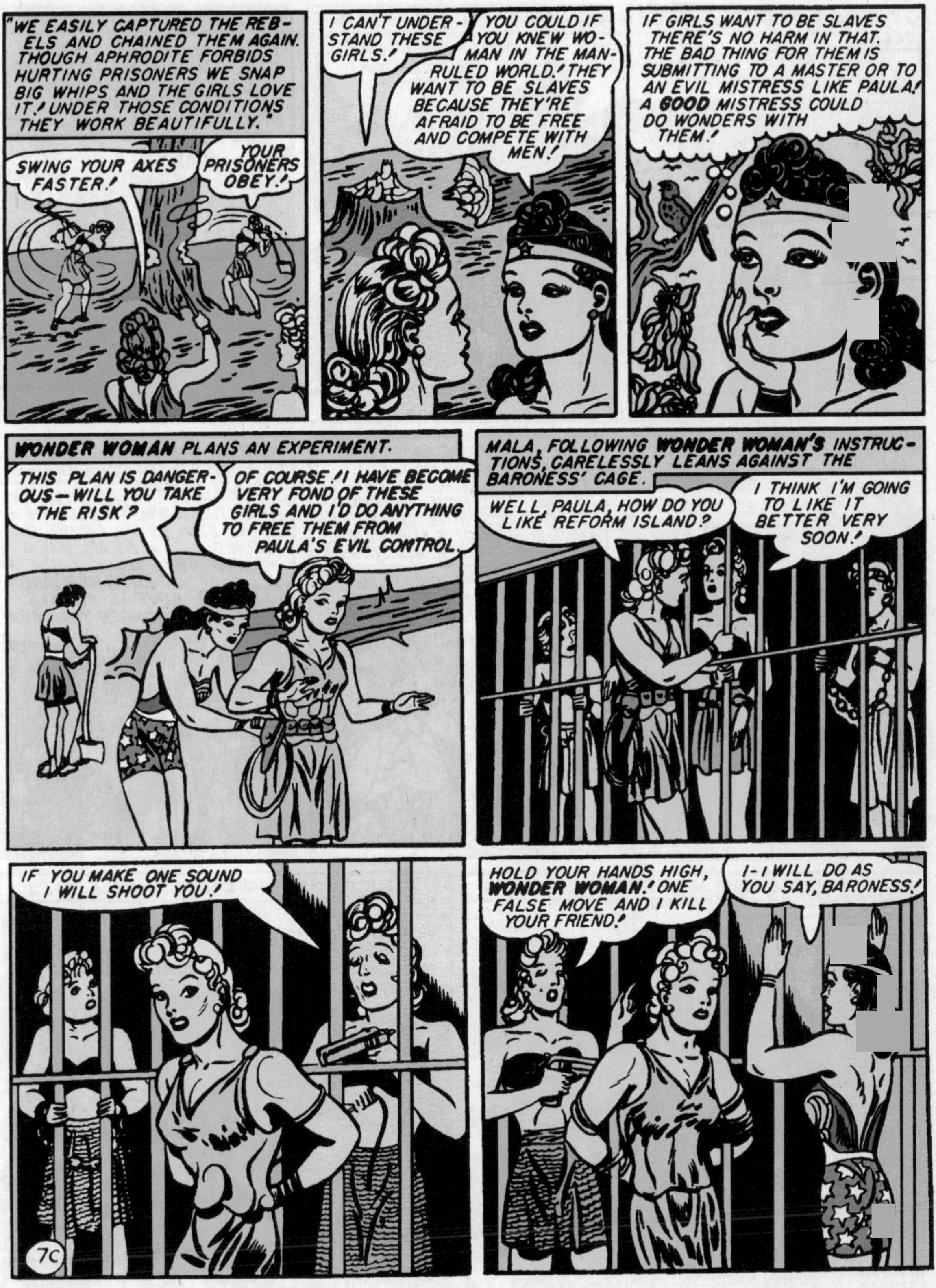
"WE EASILY CAPTURED THE REBELS AND CHAINED THEM AGAIN. THOUGH APHRODITE FORBIDS HURTING PRISONERS WE SNAP BIG WHIPS AND THE GIRLS LOVE IT! UNDER THOSE CONDITIONS THEY WORK BEAUTIFULLY."
SWING YOUR AXES FASTER!
YOUR PRISONERS OBEY!
I CAN'T UNDERSTAND THESE GIRLS!
YOU COULD IF YOU KNEW WOMAN IN THE MAN-RULED WORLD! THEY WANT TO BE SLAVES BECAUSE THEY'RE AFRAID TO BE FREE AND COMPETE WITH MEN!
IF GIRLS WANT TO BE SLAVES THERE'S NO HARM IN THAT. THE BAD THING FOR THEM IS SUBMITTING TO A MASTER OR TO AN EVIL MISTRESS LIKE PAULA! A GOOD MISTRESS COULD DO WONDERS WITH THEM!
WONDER WOMAN PLANS AN EXPERIMENT.
THIS PLAN IS DANGEROUS—WILL YOU TAKE THE RISK?
OF COURSE! I HAVE BECOME VERY FOND OF THESE GIRLS AND I'D DO ANYTHING TO FREE THEM FROM PAULA'S EVIL CONTROL.
MALA, FOLLOWING WONDER WOMAN'S INSTRUCTIONS, CARELESSLY LEANS AGAINST THE BARONESS' CAGE.
WELL, PAULA, HOW DO YOU LIKE REFORM ISLAND?
I THINK I'M GOING TO LIKE IT BETTER VERY SOON!
IF YOU MAKE ONE SOUND I WILL SHOOT YOU!
7C
HOLD YOUR HANDS HIGH, WONDER WOMAN! ONE FALSE MOVE AND I KILL YOUR FRIEND!
I-I WILL DO AS YOU SAY, BARONESS!

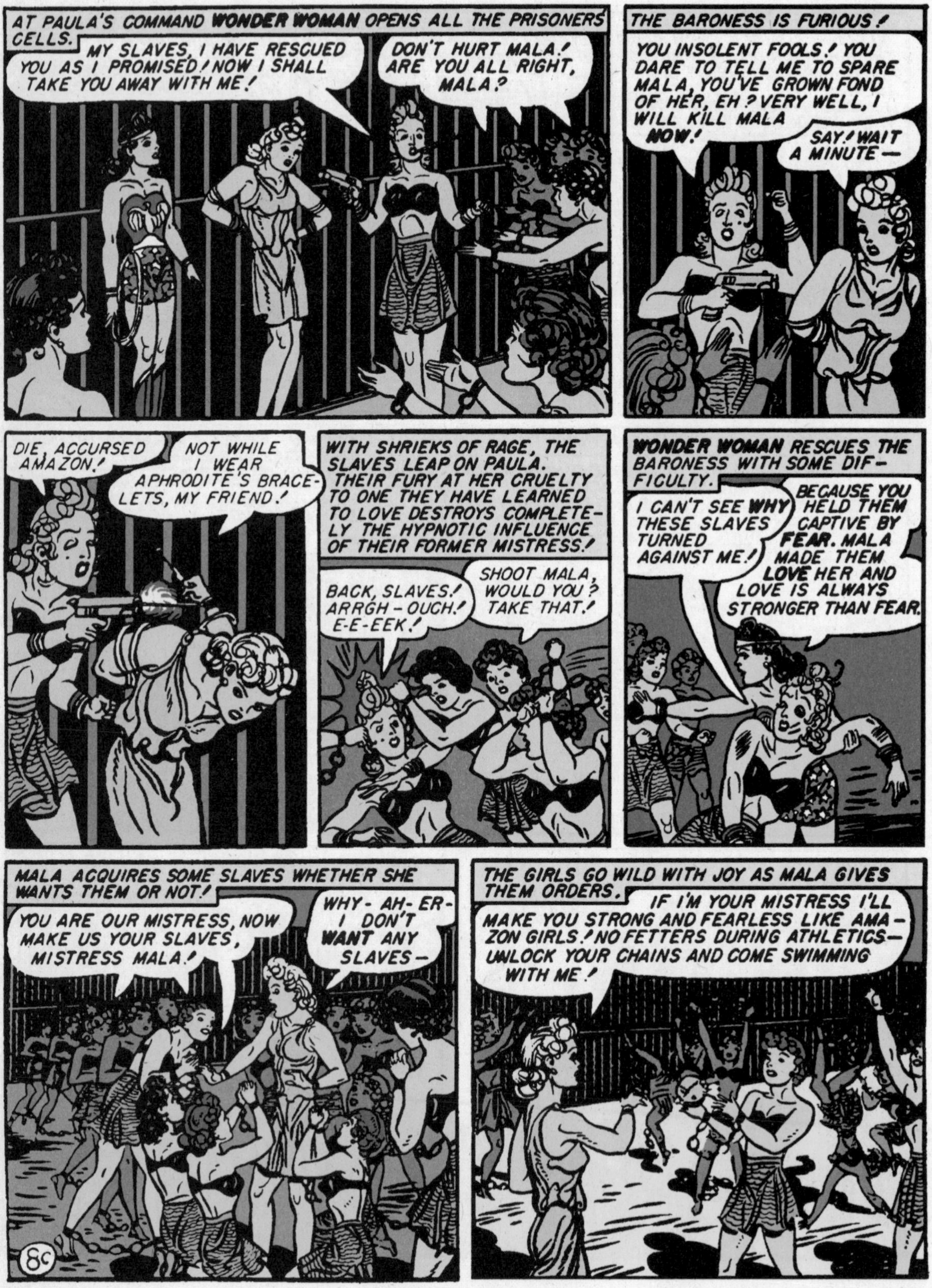
AT PAULA'S COMMAND WONDER WOMAN OPENS ALL THE PRISONERS CELLS.
MY SLAVES, I HAVE RESCUED YOU AS I PROMISED! NOW I SHALL TAKE YOU AWAY WITH ME!
DON'T HURT MALA! ARE YOU ALL RIGHT, MALA?
THE BARONESS IS FURIOUS!
YOU INSOLENT FOOLS! YOU DARE TO TELL ME TO SPARE MALA, YOU'VE GROWN FOND OF HER, EH? VERY WELL, I WILL KILL MALA NOW!
SAY! WAIT A MINUTE—
DIE, ACCURSED AMAZON!
NOT WHILE I WEAR APHRODITE'S BRACELETS, MY FRIEND!
WITH SHRIEKS OF RAGE, THE SLAVES LEAP ON PAULA. THEIR FURY AT HER CRUELTY TO ONE THEY HAVE LEARNED TO LOVE DESTROYS COMPLETELY THE HYPNOTIC INFLUENCE OF THEIR FORMER MISTRESS!
BACK, SLAVES! ARRGH—OUCH! E-E-EEK!
SHOOT MALA, WOULD YOU? TAKE THAT!
WONDER WOMAN RESCUES THE BARONESS WITH SOME DIFFICULTY.
I CAN'T SEE WHY THESE SLAVES TURNED AGAINST ME!
BECAUSE YOU HELD THEM CAPTIVE BY FEAR. MALA MADE THEM LOVE HER AND LOVE IS ALWAYS STRONGER THAN FEAR.
MALA ACQUIRES SOME SLAVES WHETHER SHE WANTS THEM OR NOT!
YOU ARE OUR MISTRESS, NOW MAKE US YOUR SLAVES, MISTRESS MALA!
WHY- AH- ER- I DON'T WANT ANY SLAVES—
8c
THE GIRLS GO WILD WITH JOY AS MALA GIVES THEM ORDERS.
IF I'M YOUR MISTRESS I'LL MAKE YOU STRONG AND FEARLESS LIKE AMAZON GIRLS! NO FETTERS DURING ATHLETICS—UNLOCK YOUR CHAINS AND COME SWIMMING WITH ME!

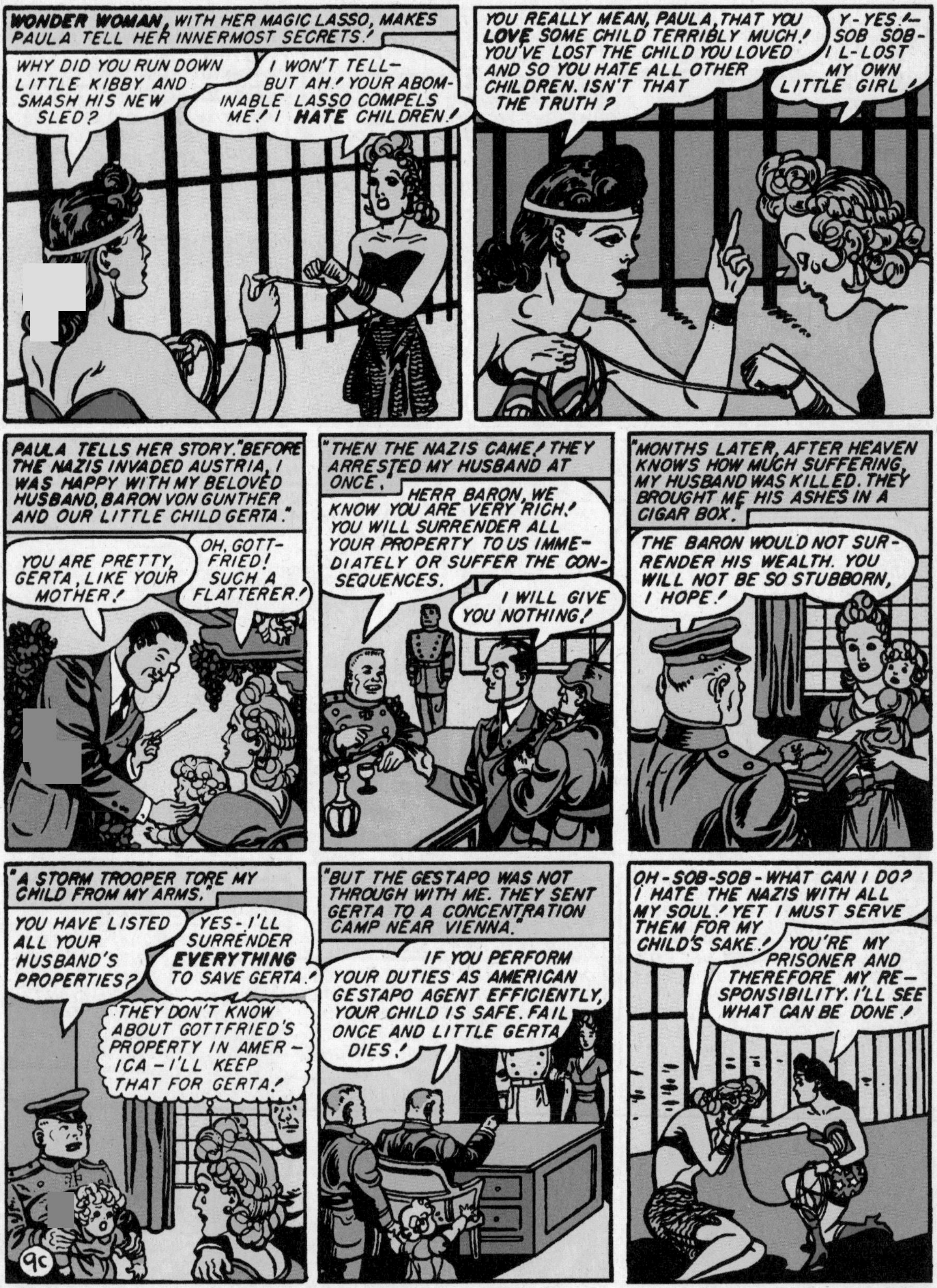
WONDER WOMAN, WITH HER MAGIC LASSO, MAKES PAULA TELL HER INNERMOST SECRETS!
WHY DID YOU RUN DOWN LITTLE KIBBY AND SMASH HIS NEW SLED?
I WON'T TELL– BUT AH! YOUR ABOMINABLE LASSO COMPELS ME! I HATE CHILDREN!
YOU REALLY MEAN, PAULA, THAT YOU LOVE SOME CHILD TERRIBLY MUCH! YOU'VE LOST THE CHILD YOU LOVED AND SO YOU HATE ALL OTHER CHILDREN. ISN'T THAT THE TRUTH?
Y-YES!–SOB SOB– I L-LOST MY OWN LITTLE GIRL!
PAULA TELLS HER STORY. "BEFORE THE NAZIS INVADED AUSTRIA, I WAS HAPPY WITH MY BELOVED HUSBAND, BARON VON GUNTHER AND OUR LITTLE CHILD GERTA."
YOU ARE PRETTY, GERTA, LIKE YOUR MOTHER!
OH, GOTTFRIED! SUCH A FLATTERER!
"THEN THE NAZIS CAME! THEY ARRESTED MY HUSBAND AT ONCE."
HERR BARON, WE KNOW YOU ARE VERY RICH! YOU WILL SURRENDER ALL YOUR PROPERTY TO US IMMEDIATELY OR SUFFER THE CONSEQUENCES.
I WILL GIVE YOU NOTHING!
"MONTHS LATER, AFTER HEAVEN KNOWS HOW MUCH SUFFERING, MY HUSBAND WAS KILLED. THEY BROUGHT ME HIS ASHES IN A CIGAR BOX."
THE BARON WOULD NOT SURRENDER HIS WEALTH. YOU WILL NOT BE SO STUBBORN, I HOPE!
"A STORM TROOPER TORE MY CHILD FROM MY ARMS."
YOU HAVE LISTED ALL YOUR HUSBAND'S PROPERTIES?
YES-I'LL SURRENDER EVERYTHING TO SAVE GERTA!
THEY DON'T KNOW ABOUT GOTTFRIED'S PROPERTY IN AMERICA–I'LL KEEP THAT FOR GERTA!
9c
"BUT THE GESTAPO WAS NOT THROUGH WITH ME. THEY SENT GERTA TO A CONCENTRATION CAMP NEAR VIENNA."
IF YOU PERFORM YOUR DUTIES AS AMERICAN GESTAPO AGENT EFFICIENTLY, YOUR CHILD IS SAFE. FAIL ONCE AND LITTLE GERTA DIES!
OH-SOB-SOB-WHAT CAN I DO? I HATE THE NAZIS WITH ALL MY SOUL! YET I MUST SERVE THEM FOR MY CHILD'S SAKE!
YOU'RE MY PRISONER AND THEREFORE MY RESPONSIBILITY. I'LL SEE WHAT CAN BE DONE!

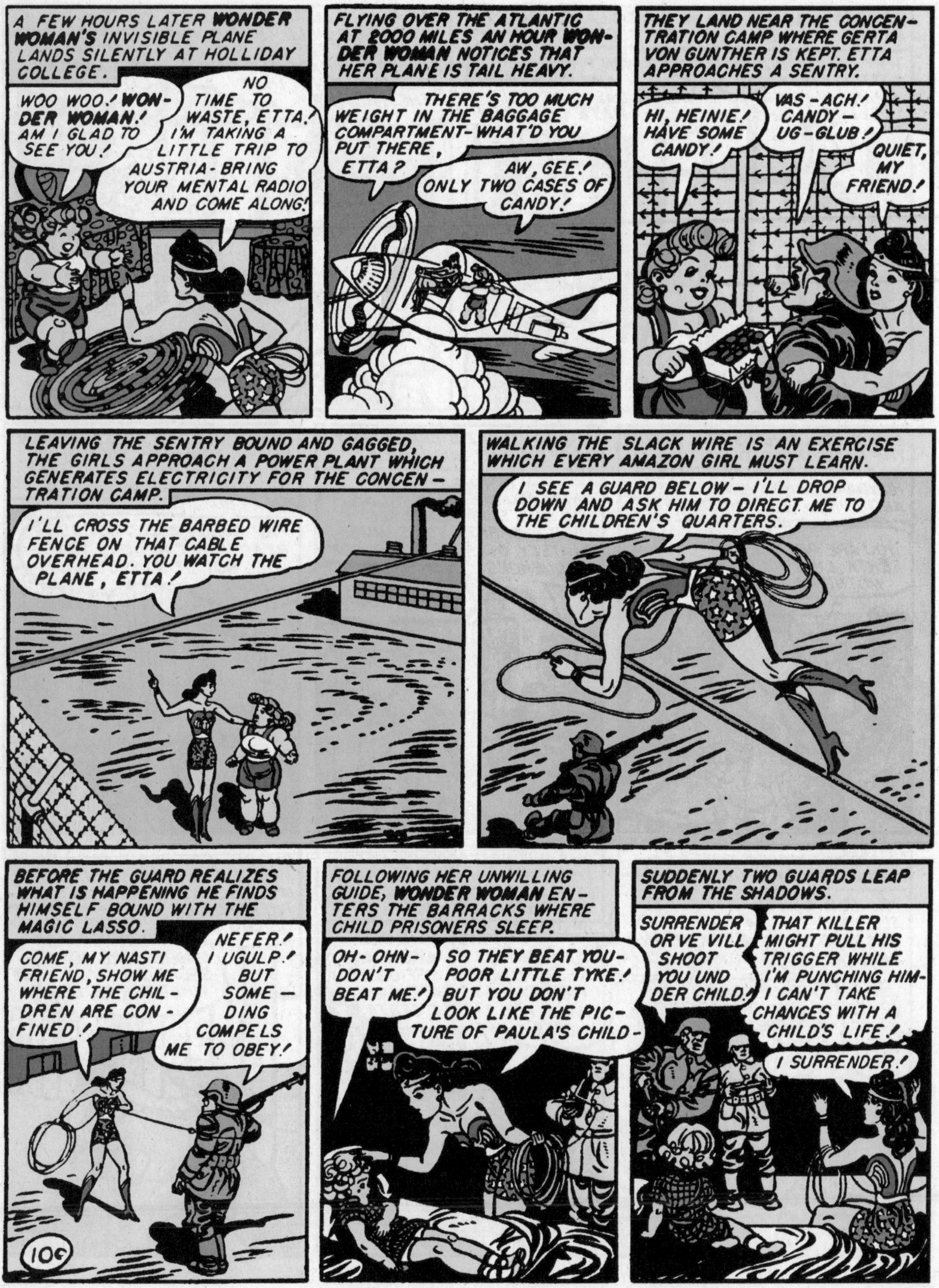
A FEW HOURS LATER WONDER WOMAN'S INVISIBLE PLANE LANDS SILENTLY AT HOLLIDAY COLLEGE.
WOO WOO! WONDER WOMAN! AM I GLAD TO SEE YOU!
NO TIME TO WASTE, ETTA! I'M TAKING A LITTLE TRIP TO AUSTRIA-BRING YOUR MENTAL RADIO AND COME ALONG!
FLYING OVER THE ATLANTIC AT 2000 MILES AN HOUR WONDER WOMAN NOTICES THAT HER PLANE IS TAIL HEAVY.
THERE'S TOO MUCH WEIGHT IN THE BAGGAGE COMPARTMENT- WHAT'D YOU PUT THERE, ETTA?
AW, GEE! ONLY TWO CASES OF CANDY!
THEY LAND NEAR THE CONCENTRATION CAMP WHERE GERTA VON GUNTHER IS KEPT. ETTA APPROACHES A SENTRY.
HI, HEINIE! HAVE SOME CANDY!
VAS-ACH! CANDY-UG-GLUB!
QUIET, MY FRIEND!
LEAVING THE SENTRY BOUND AND GAGGED, THE GIRLS APPROACH A POWER PLANT WHICH GENERATES ELECTRICITY FOR THE CONCENTRATION CAMP.
I'LL CROSS THE BARBED WIRE FENCE ON THAT CABLE OVERHEAD. YOU WATCH THE PLANE, ETTA!
WALKING THE SLACK WIRE IS AN EXERCISE WHICH EVERY AMAZON GIRL MUST LEARN.
I SEE A GUARD BELOW - I'LL DROP DOWN AND ASK HIM TO DIRECT ME TO THE CHILDREN'S QUARTERS.
BEFORE THE GUARD REALIZES WHAT IS HAPPENING HE FINDS HIMSELF BOUND WITH THE MAGIC LASSO.
COME, MY NASTI FRIEND, SHOW ME WHERE THE CHILDREN ARE CONFINED!
NEFER! I UGULP! BUT SOMEDING COMPELS ME TO OBEY!
10¢
FOLLOWING HER UNWILLING GUIDE, WONDER WOMAN ENTERS THE BARRACKS WHERE CHILD PRISONERS SLEEP.
OH-OHN-DON'T BEAT ME!
SO THEY BEAT YOU- POOR LITTLE TYKE! BUT YOU DON'T LOOK LIKE THE PICTURE OF PAULA'S CHILD-
SUDDENLY TWO GUARDS LEAP FROM THE SHADOWS.
SURRENDER OR VE VILL SHOOT YOU UND DER CHILD!
THAT KILLER MIGHT PULL HIS TRIGGER WHILE I'M PUNCHING HIM- I CAN'T TAKE CHANCES WITH A CHILD'S LIFE!
I SURRENDER!

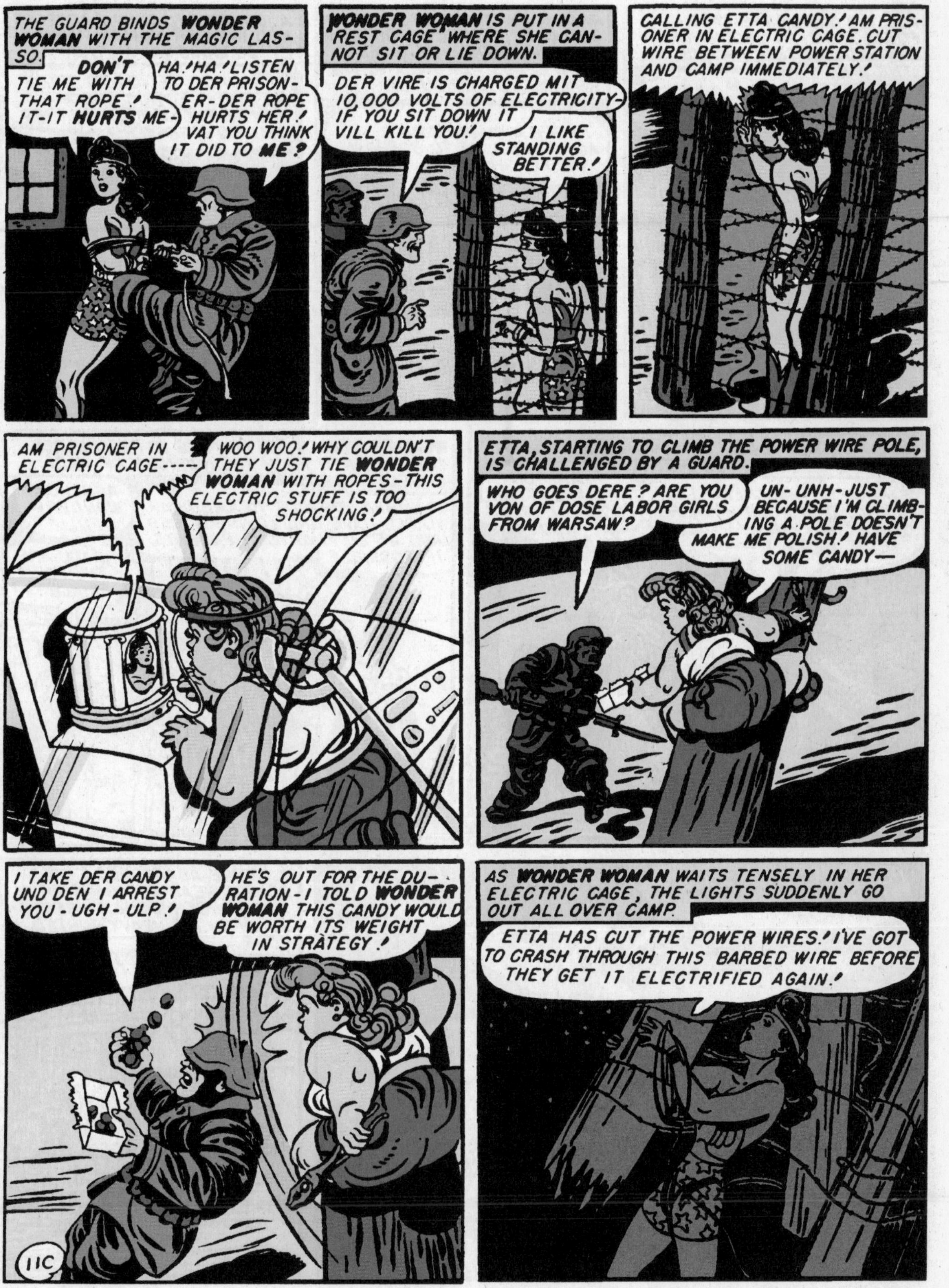
THE GUARD BINDS WONDER WOMAN WITH THE MAGIC LASSO.
DON'T TIE ME WITH THAT ROPE! IT-IT HURTS ME-
HA! HA! LISTEN TO DER PRISONER-DER ROPE HURTS HER! VAT YOU THINK IT DID TO ME?
WONDER WOMAN IS PUT IN A REST CAGE WHERE SHE CANNOT SIT OR LIE DOWN.
DER VIRE IS CHARGED MIT 10,000 VOLTS OF ELECTRICITY-IF YOU SIT DOWN IT VILL KILL YOU!
I LIKE STANDING BETTER!
CALLING ETTA CANDY! AM PRISONER IN ELECTRIC CAGE. CUT WIRE BETWEEN POWER STATION AND CAMP IMMEDIATELY!
AM PRISONER IN ELECTRIC CAGE----
WOO WOO! WHY COULDN'T THEY JUST TIE WONDER WOMAN WITH ROPES-THIS ELECTRIC STUFF IS TOO SHOCKING!
ETTA, STARTING TO CLIMB THE POWER WIRE POLE, IS CHALLENGED BY A GUARD.
WHO GOES DERE? ARE YOU VON OF DOSE LABOR GIRLS FROM WARSAW?
UN-UNH-JUST BECAUSE I'M CLIMBING A POLE DOESN'T MAKE ME POLISH! HAVE SOME CANDY—
I TAKE DER CANDY UND DEN I ARREST YOU-UGH-ULP!
HE'S OUT FOR THE DURATION-I TOLD WONDER WOMAN THIS CANDY WOULD BE WORTH ITS WEIGHT IN STRATEGY!
AS WONDER WOMAN WAITS TENSELY IN HER ELECTRIC CAGE, THE LIGHTS SUDDENLY GO OUT ALL OVER CAMP.
ETTA HAS CUT THE POWER WIRES! I'VE GOT TO CRASH THROUGH THIS BARBED WIRE BEFORE THEY GET IT ELECTRIFIED AGAIN!
11C

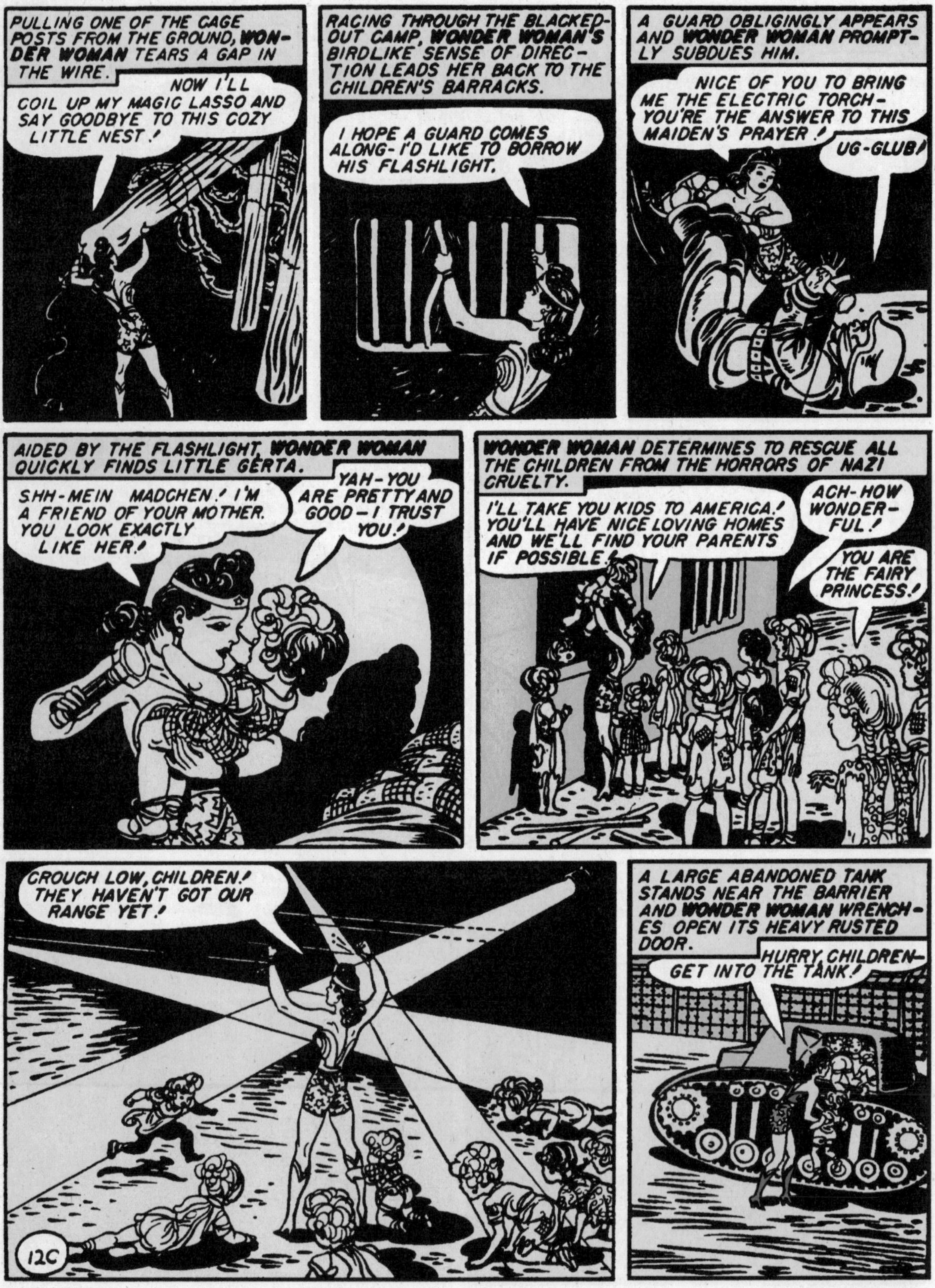
PULLING ONE OF THE CAGE POSTS FROM THE GROUND, WONDER WOMAN TEARS A GAP IN THE WIRE.
NOW I'LL COIL UP MY MAGIC LASSO AND SAY GOODBYE TO THIS COZY LITTLE NEST!
RACING THROUGH THE BLACKED-OUT CAMP, WONDER WOMAN'S BIRDLIKE SENSE OF DIRECTION LEADS HER BACK TO THE CHILDREN'S BARRACKS.
I HOPE A GUARD COMES ALONG- I'D LIKE TO BORROW HIS FLASHLIGHT.
A GUARD OBLIGINGLY APPEARS AND WONDER WOMAN PROMPTLY SUBDUES HIM.
NICE OF YOU TO BRING ME THE ELECTRIC TORCH- YOU'RE THE ANSWER TO THIS MAIDEN'S PRAYER!
UG-GLUB!
AIDED BY THE FLASHLIGHT, WONDER WOMAN QUICKLY FINDS LITTLE GERTA.
SHH-MEIN MADCHEN! I'M A FRIEND OF YOUR MOTHER. YOU LOOK EXACTLY LIKE HER!
YAH-YOU ARE PRETTY AND GOOD-I TRUST YOU!
WONDER WOMAN DETERMINES TO RESCUE ALL THE CHILDREN FROM THE HORRORS OF NAZI CRUELTY.
I'LL TAKE YOU KIDS TO AMERICA! YOU'LL HAVE NICE LOVING HOMES AND WE'LL FIND YOUR PARENTS IF POSSIBLE!
ACH-HOW WONDERFUL!
YOU ARE THE FAIRY PRINCESS!
CROUCH LOW, CHILDREN! THEY HAVEN'T GOT OUR RANGE YET!
12C
A LARGE ABANDONED TANK STANDS NEAR THE BARRIER AND WONDER WOMAN WRENCHES OPEN ITS HEAVY RUSTED DOOR.
HURRY, CHILDREN-GET INTO THE TANK!

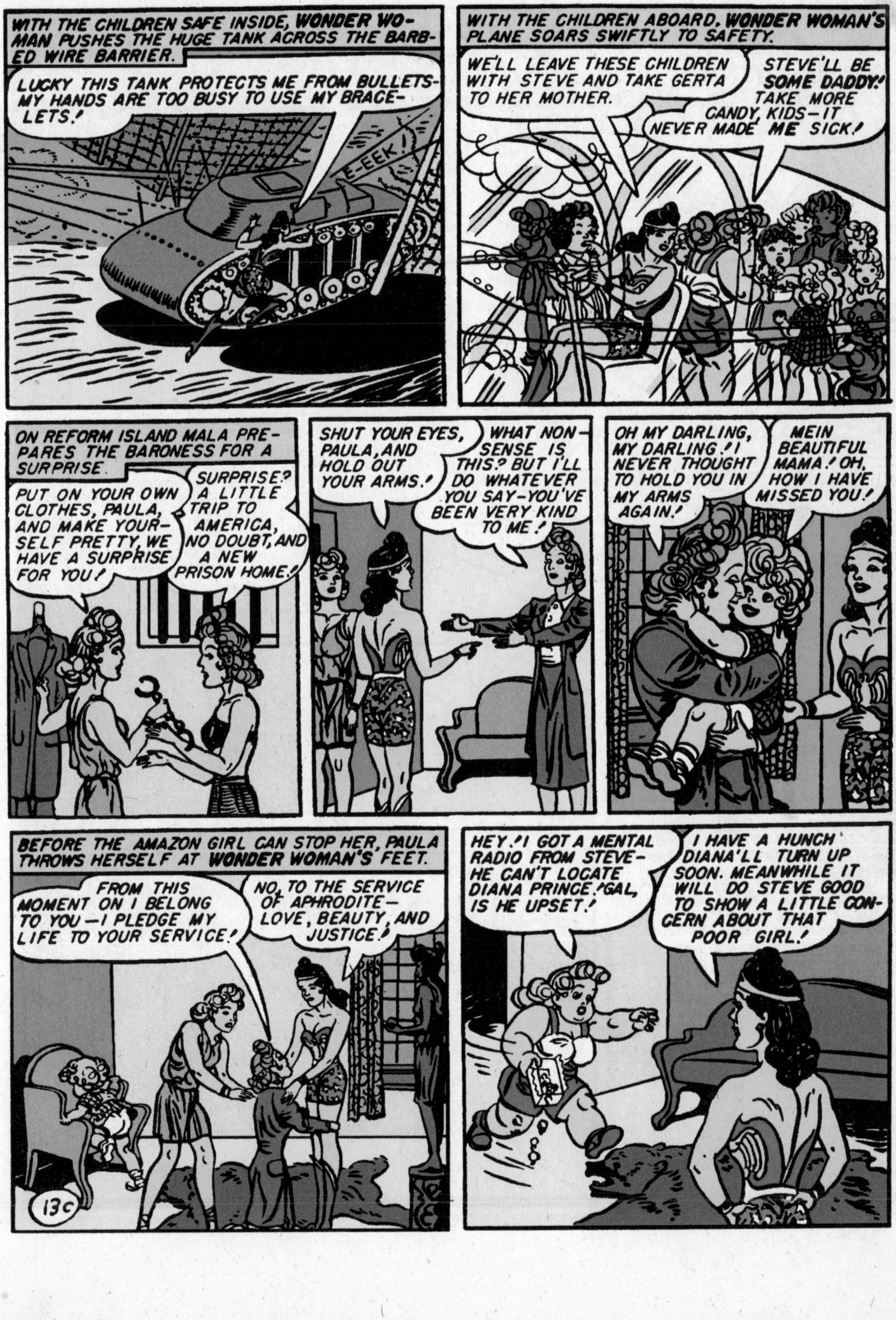
WITH THE CHILDREN SAFE INSIDE, WONDER WOMAN PUSHES THE HUGE TANK ACROSS THE BARBED WIRE BARRIER.
LUCKY THIS TANK PROTECTS ME FROM BULLETS-MY HANDS ARE TOO BUSY TO USE MY BRACELETS!
E-EEK!
WITH THE CHILDREN ABOARD, WONDER WOMAN'S PLANE SOARS SWIFTLY TO SAFETY.
WE'LL LEAVE THESE CHILDREN WITH STEVE AND TAKE GERTA TO HER MOTHER.
STEVE'LL BE SOME DADDY! TAKE MORE CANDY, KIDS—IT NEVER MADE ME SICK!
ON REFORM ISLAND MALA PREPARES THE BARONESS FOR A SURPRISE.
PUT ON YOUR OWN CLOTHES, PAULA, AND MAKE YOURSELF PRETTY, WE HAVE A SURPRISE FOR YOU!
SURPRISE? A LITTLE TRIP TO AMERICA, NO DOUBT, AND A NEW PRISON HOME!
SHUT YOUR EYES, PAULA, AND HOLD OUT YOUR ARMS!
WHAT NONSENSE IS THIS? BUT I'LL DO WHATEVER YOU SAY-YOU'VE BEEN VERY KIND TO ME!
OH MY DARLING, MY DARLING! I NEVER THOUGHT TO HOLD YOU IN MY ARMS AGAIN!
MEIN BEAUTIFUL MAMA! OH, HOW I HAVE MISSED YOU!
BEFORE THE AMAZON GIRL CAN STOP HER, PAULA THROWS HERSELF AT WONDER WOMAN'S FEET.
FROM THIS MOMENT ON I BELONG TO YOU—I PLEDGE MY LIFE TO YOUR SERVICE!
NO, TO THE SERVICE OF APHRODITE—LOVE, BEAUTY, AND JUSTICE!
13c
HEY! I GOT A MENTAL RADIO FROM STEVE-HE CAN'T LOCATE DIANA PRINCE! GAL, IS HE UPSET!
I HAVE A HUNCH DIANA'LL TURN UP SOON. MEANWHILE IT WILL DO STEVE GOOD TO SHOW A LITTLE CONCERN ABOUT THAT POOR GIRL!

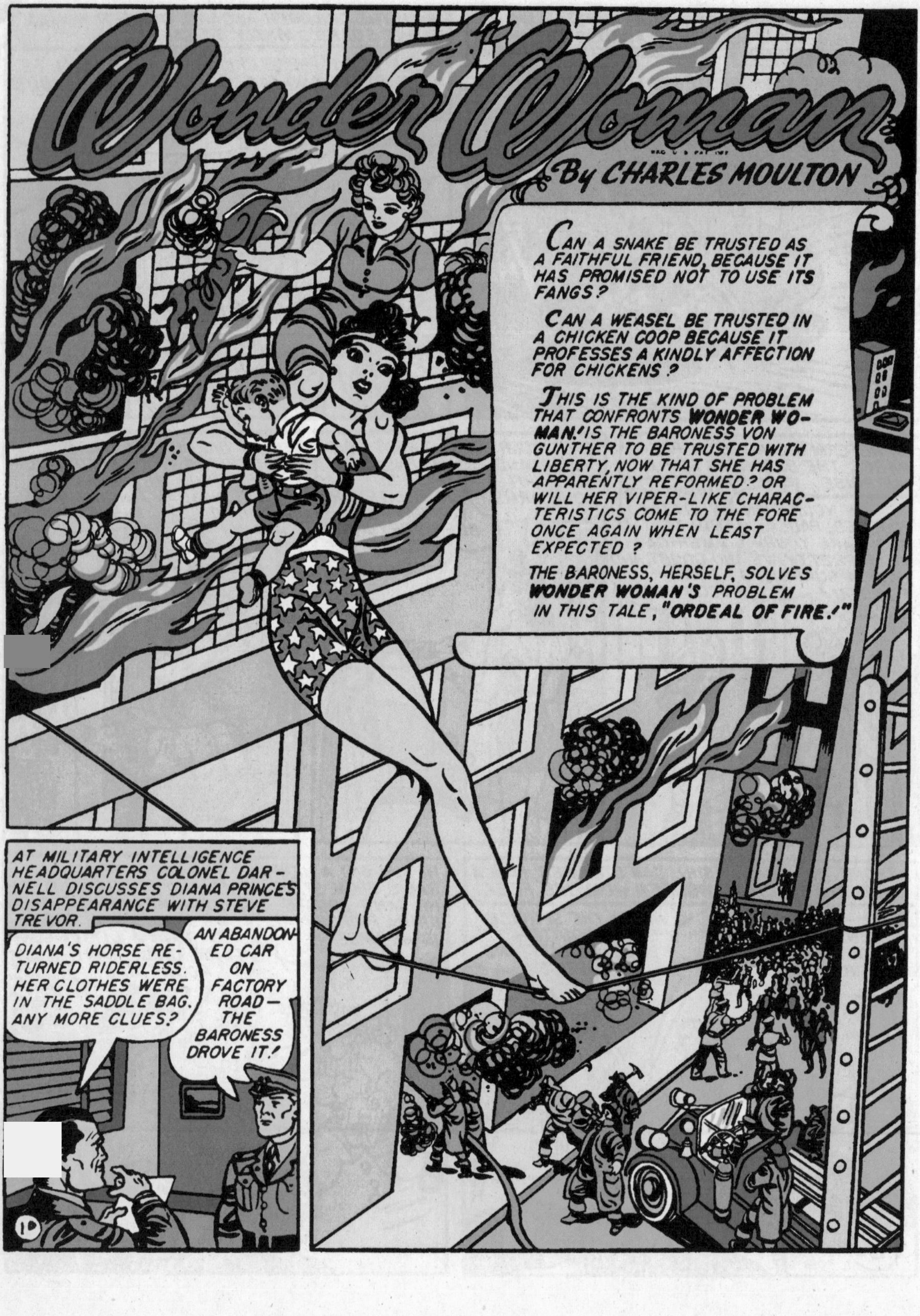
Wonder Woman
By CHARLES MOULTON
CAN A SNAKE BE TRUSTED AS A FAITHFUL FRIEND, BECAUSE IT HAS PROMISED NOT TO USE ITS FANGS?
CAN A WEASEL BE TRUSTED IN A CHICKEN COOP BECAUSE IT PROFESSES A KINDLY AFFECTION FOR CHICKENS?
THIS IS THE KIND OF PROBLEM THAT CONFRONTS WONDER WOMAN! IS THE BARONESS VON GUNTHER TO BE TRUSTED WITH LIBERTY, NOW THAT SHE HAS APPARENTLY REFORMED? OR WILL HER VIPER-LIKE CHARACTERISTICS COME TO THE FORE ONCE AGAIN WHEN LEAST EXPECTED?
THE BARONESS, HERSELF, SOLVES WONDER WOMAN'S PROBLEM IN THIS TALE, "ORDEAL OF FIRE!"
AT MILITARY INTELLIGENCE HEADQUARTERS COLONEL DARNELL DISCUSSES DIANA PRINCE'S DISAPPEARANCE WITH STEVE TREVOR.
DIANA'S HORSE RETURNED RIDERLESS. HER CLOTHES WERE IN THE SADDLE BAG. ANY MORE CLUES?
AN ABANDONED CAR ON FACTORY ROAD—THE BARONESS DROVE IT!
10

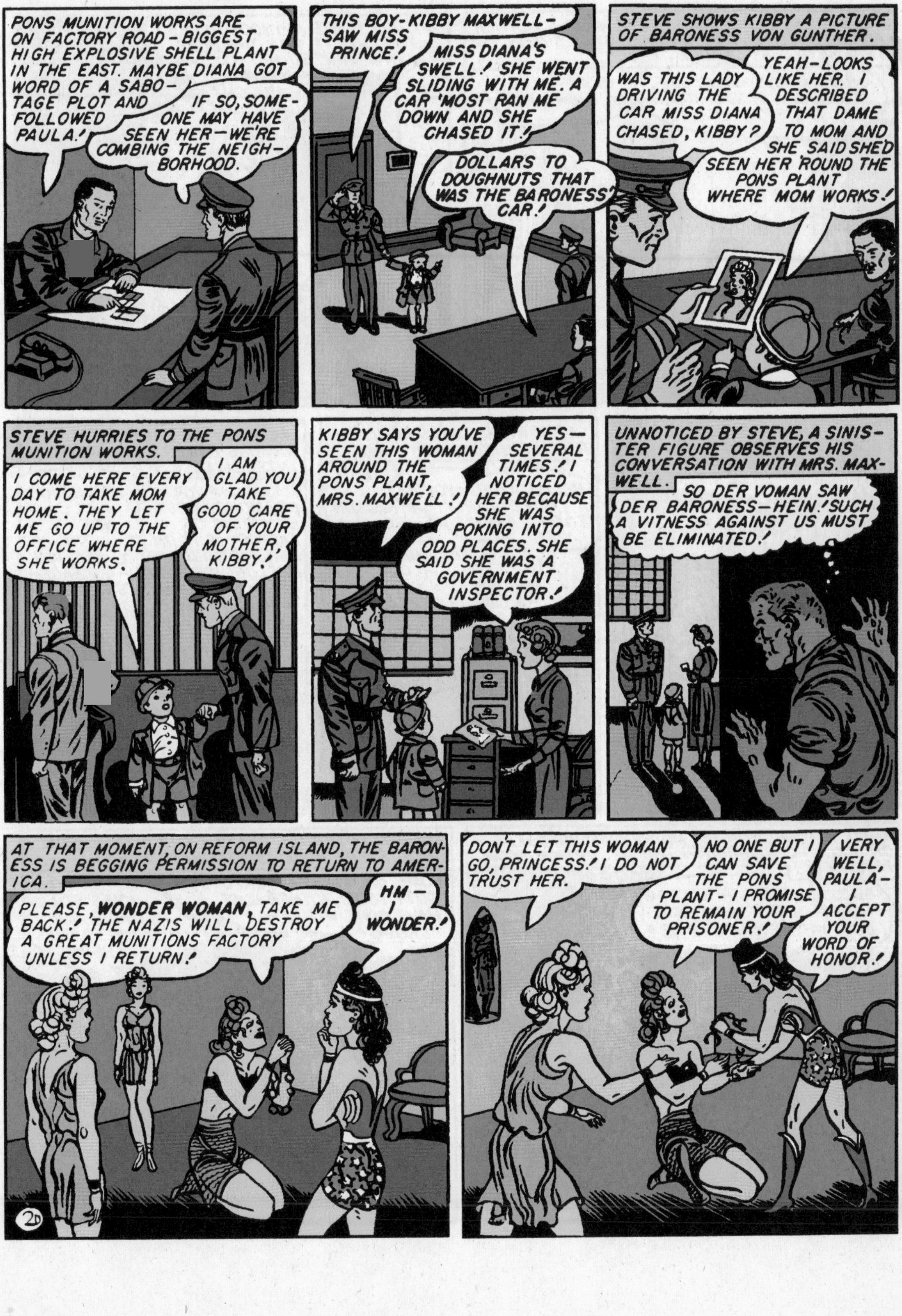
PONS MUNITION WORKS ARE ON FACTORY ROAD - BIGGEST HIGH EXPLOSIVE SHELL PLANT IN THE EAST. MAYBE DIANA GOT WORD OF A SABOTAGE PLOT AND FOLLOWED PAULA!
IF SO, SOMEONE MAY HAVE SEEN HER—WE'RE COMBING THE NEIGHBORHOOD.
THIS BOY-KIBBY MAXWELL-SAW MISS PRINCE!
MISS DIANA'S SWELL! SHE WENT SLIDING WITH ME. A CAR 'MOST RAN ME DOWN AND SHE CHASED IT!
DOLLARS TO DOUGHNUTS THAT WAS THE BARONESS' CAR!
STEVE SHOWS KIBBY A PICTURE OF BARONESS VON GUNTHER.
WAS THIS LADY DRIVING THE CAR MISS DIANA CHASED, KIBBY?
YEAH-LOOKS LIKE HER. I DESCRIBED THAT DAME TO MOM AND SHE SAID SHED SEEN HER 'ROUND THE PONS PLANT WHERE MOM WORKS!
STEVE HURRIES TO THE PONS MUNITION WORKS.
I COME HERE EVERY DAY TO TAKE MOM HOME. THEY LET ME GO UP TO THE OFFICE WHERE SHE WORKS.
I AM GLAD YOU TAKE GOOD CARE OF YOUR MOTHER, KIBBY!
KIBBY SAYS YOU'VE SEEN THIS WOMAN AROUND THE PONS PLANT, MRS. MAXWELL!
YES—SEVERAL TIMES! I NOTICED HER BECAUSE SHE WAS POKING INTO ODD PLACES. SHE SAID SHE WAS A GOVERNMENT INSPECTOR!
UNNOTICED BY STEVE, A SINISTER FIGURE OBSERVES HIS CONVERSATION WITH MRS. MAXWELL.
SO DER VOMAN SAW DER BARONESS—HEIN! SUCH A VITNESS AGAINST US MUST BE ELIMINATED!
AT THAT MOMENT, ON REFORM ISLAND, THE BARONESS IS BEGGING PERMISSION TO RETURN TO AMERICA.
PLEASE, WONDER WOMAN, TAKE ME BACK! THE NAZIS WILL DESTROY A GREAT MUNITIONS FACTORY UNLESS I RETURN!
HM—I WONDER!
20
DON'T LET THIS WOMAN GO, PRINCESS! I DO NOT TRUST HER.
NO ONE BUT I CAN SAVE THE PONS PLANT- I PROMISE TO REMAIN YOUR PRISONER!
VERY WELL, PAULA-I ACCEPT YOUR WORD OF HONOR!

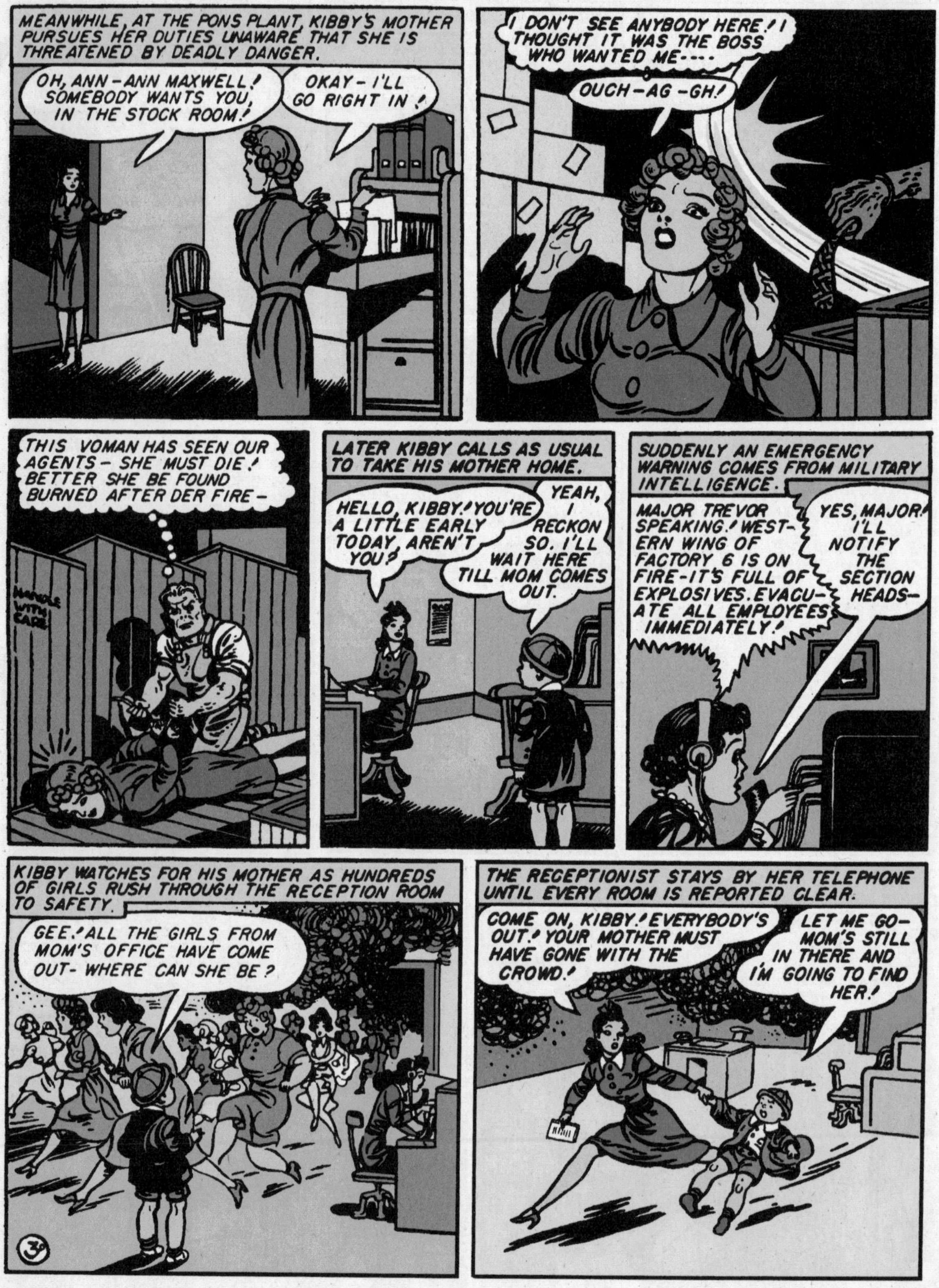
MEANWHILE, AT THE PONS PLANT, KIBBY'S MOTHER PURSUES HER DUTIES UNAWARE THAT SHE IS THREATENED BY DEADLY DANGER.
OH, ANN-ANN MAXWELL! SOMEBODY WANTS YOU, IN THE STOCK ROOM!
OKAY-I'LL GO RIGHT IN!
I DON'T SEE ANYBODY HERE! I THOUGHT IT WAS THE BOSS WHO WANTED ME----
OUCH-AG-GH!
THIS VOMAN HAS SEEN OUR AGENTS- SHE MUST DIE! BETTER SHE BE FOUND BURNED AFTER DER FIRE-
LATER KIBBY CALLS AS USUAL TO TAKE HIS MOTHER HOME.
HELLO, KIBBY! YOU'RE A LITTLE EARLY TODAY, AREN'T YOU?
YEAH, I RECKON SO. I'LL WAIT HERE TILL MOM COMES OUT.
SUDDENLY AN EMERGENCY WARNING COMES FROM MILITARY INTELLIGENCE.
MAJOR TREVOR SPEAKING! WESTERN WING OF FACTORY 6 IS ON FIRE-IT'S FULL OF EXPLOSIVES. EVACUATE ALL EMPLOYEES IMMEDIATELY!
YES, MAJOR! I'LL NOTIFY THE SECTION HEADS-
KIBBY WATCHES FOR HIS MOTHER AS HUNDREDS OF GIRLS RUSH THROUGH THE RECEPTION ROOM TO SAFETY.
GEE! ALL THE GIRLS FROM MOM'S OFFICE HAVE COME OUT- WHERE CAN SHE BE?
3
THE RECEPTIONIST STAYS BY HER TELEPHONE UNTIL EVERY ROOM IS REPORTED CLEAR.
COME ON, KIBBY! EVERYBODY'S OUT! YOUR MOTHER MUST HAVE GONE WITH THE CROWD!
LET ME GO- MOM'S STILL IN THERE AND I'M GOING TO FIND HER!

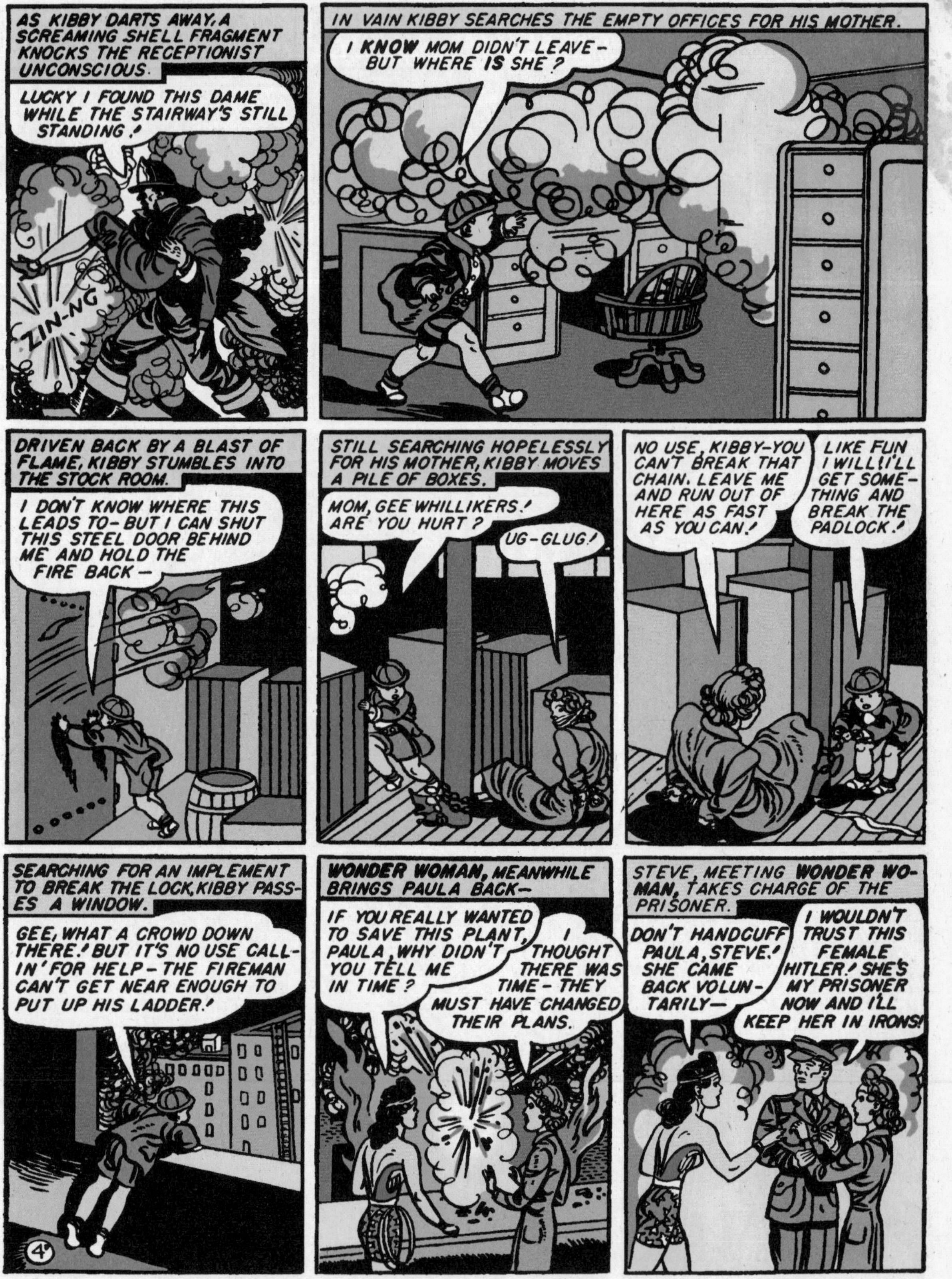
AS KIBBY DARTS AWAY, A SCREAMING SHELL FRAGMENT KNOCKS THE RECEPTIONIST UNCONSCIOUS.
LUCKY I FOUND THIS DAME WHILE THE STAIRWAY'S STILL STANDING!
ZIN-NG
IN VAIN KIBBY SEARCHES THE EMPTY OFFICES FOR HIS MOTHER.
I KNOW MOM DIDN'T LEAVE- BUT WHERE IS SHE?
DRIVEN BACK BY A BLAST OF FLAME, KIBBY STUMBLES INTO THE STOCK ROOM.
I DON'T KNOW WHERE THIS LEADS TO- BUT I CAN SHUT THIS STEEL DOOR BEHIND ME AND HOLD THE FIRE BACK-
STILL SEARCHING HOPELESSLY FOR HIS MOTHER, KIBBY MOVES A PILE OF BOXES.
MOM, GEE WHILLIKERS! ARE YOU HURT?
UG-GLUG!
NO USE, KIBBY-YOU CAN'T BREAK THAT CHAIN. LEAVE ME AND RUN OUT OF HERE AS FAST AS YOU CAN!
LIKE FUN I WILL! I'LL GET SOMETHING AND BREAK THE PADLOCK!
SEARCHING FOR AN IMPLEMENT TO BREAK THE LOCK, KIBBY PASSES A WINDOW.
GEE, WHAT A CROWD DOWN THERE! BUT IT'S NO USE CALLIN' FOR HELP-THE FIREMAN CAN'T GET NEAR ENOUGH TO PUT UP HIS LADDER!
4
WONDER WOMAN, MEANWHILE BRINGS PAULA BACK-
IF YOU REALLY WANTED TO SAVE THIS PLANT, PAULA, WHY DIDN'T YOU TELL ME IN TIME?
I THOUGHT THERE WAS TIME-THEY MUST HAVE CHANGED THEIR PLANS.
STEVE, MEETING WONDER WOMAN, TAKES CHARGE OF THE PRISONER.
DON'T HANDCUFF PAULA, STEVE! SHE CAME BACK VOLUNTARILY-
I WOULDN'T TRUST THIS FEMALE HITLER! SHE'S MY PRISONER NOW AND I'LL KEEP HER IN IRONS!

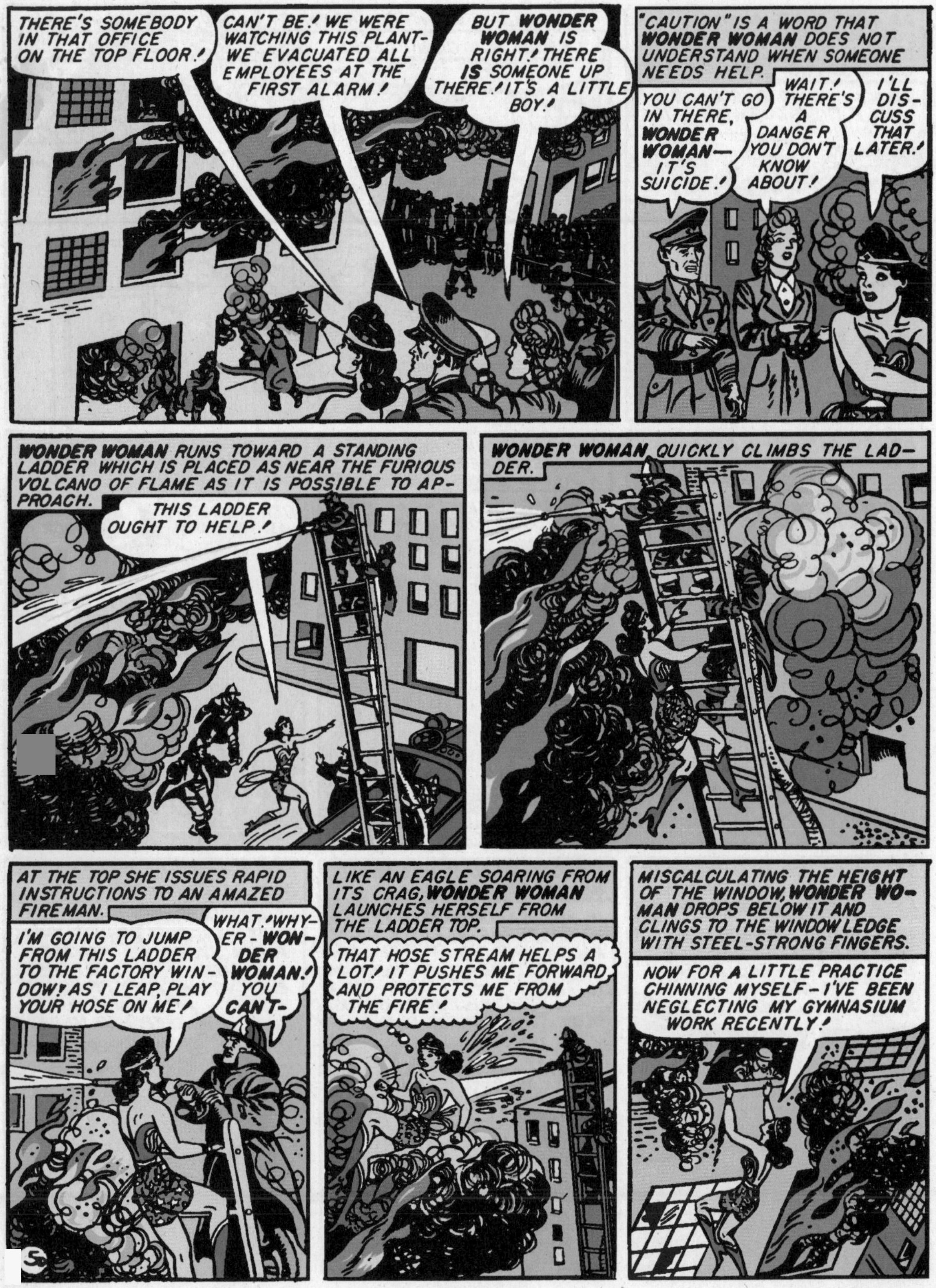

THERE'S SOMEBODY IN THAT OFFICE ON THE TOP FLOOR!
CAN'T BE! WE WERE WATCHING THIS PLANT- WE EVACUATED ALL EMPLOYEES AT THE FIRST ALARM!
BUT WONDER WOMAN IS RIGHT! THERE IS SOMEONE UP THERE! IT'S A LITTLE BOY!
"CAUTION" IS A WORD THAT WONDER WOMAN DOES NOT UNDERSTAND WHEN SOMEONE NEEDS HELP.
YOU CAN'T GO IN THERE, WONDER WOMAN— IT'S SUICIDE!
WAIT! THERE'S A DANGER YOU DON'T KNOW ABOUT!
I'LL DISCUSS THAT LATER!
WONDER WOMAN RUNS TOWARD A STANDING LADDER WHICH IS PLACED AS NEAR THE FURIOUS VOLCANO OF FLAME AS IT IS POSSIBLE TO APPROACH.
THIS LADDER OUGHT TO HELP!
WONDER WOMAN QUICKLY CLIMBS THE LADDER.
AT THE TOP SHE ISSUES RAPID INSTRUCTIONS TO AN AMAZED FIREMAN.
I'M GOING TO JUMP FROM THIS LADDER TO THE FACTORY WINDOW! AS I LEAP, PLAY YOUR HOSE ON ME!
WHAT! WHY-ER- WONDER WOMAN! YOU CAN'T-
LIKE AN EAGLE SOARING FROM ITS CRAG, WONDER WOMAN LAUNCHES HERSELF FROM THE LADDER TOP.
THAT HOSE STREAM HELPS A LOT! IT PUSHES ME FORWARD AND PROTECTS ME FROM THE FIRE!
MISCALCULATING THE HEIGHT OF THE WINDOW, WONDER WOMAN DROPS BELOW IT AND CLINGS TO THE WINDOW LEDGE WITH STEEL-STRONG FINGERS.
NOW FOR A LITTLE PRACTICE CHINNING MYSELF - I'VE BEEN NEGLECTING MY GYMNASIUM WORK RECENTLY!

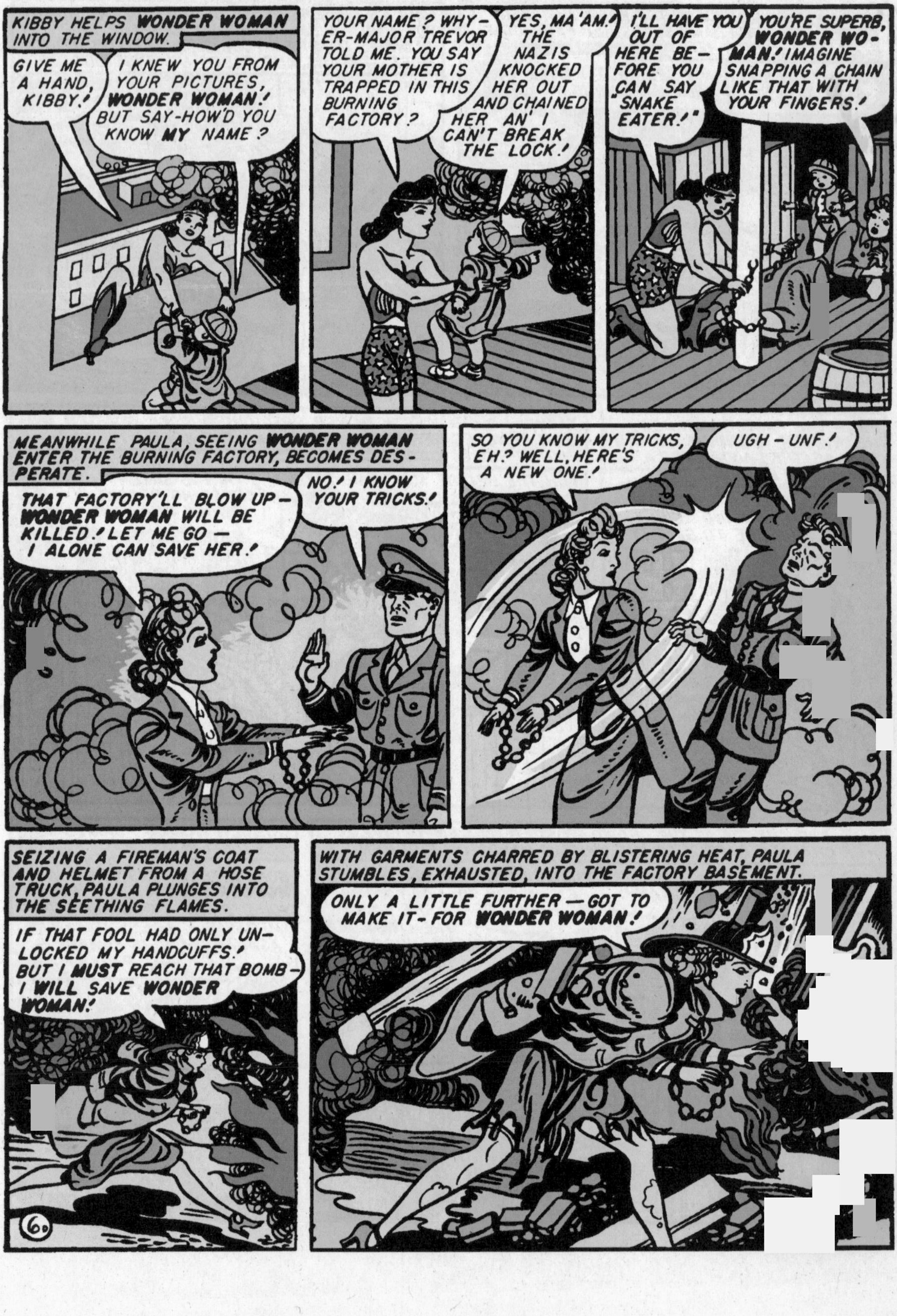
KIBBY HELPS WONDER WOMAN INTO THE WINDOW.
GIVE ME A HAND, KIBBY.!
I KNEW YOU FROM YOUR PICTURES, WONDER WOMAN.! BUT SAY-HOW'D YOU KNOW MY NAME?
YOUR NAME? WHY-ER-MAJOR TREVOR TOLD ME. YOU SAY YOUR MOTHER IS TRAPPED IN THIS BURNING FACTORY?
YES, MA'AM.! THE NAZIS KNOCKED HER OUT AND CHAINED HER AN' I CAN'T BREAK THE LOCK.!
I'LL HAVE YOU OUT OF HERE BEFORE YOU CAN SAY "SNAKE EATER.!"
YOU'RE SUPERB, WONDER WOMAN.! IMAGINE SNAPPING A CHAIN LIKE THAT WITH YOUR FINGERS.!
MEANWHILE PAULA, SEEING WONDER WOMAN ENTER THE BURNING FACTORY, BECOMES DESPERATE.
THAT FACTORY'LL BLOW UP— WONDER WOMAN WILL BE KILLED.! LET ME GO— I ALONE CAN SAVE HER.!
NO.! I KNOW YOUR TRICKS.!
SO YOU KNOW MY TRICKS, EH.? WELL, HERE'S A NEW ONE.!
UGH—UNF.!
SEIZING A FIREMAN'S COAT AND HELMET FROM A HOSE TRUCK, PAULA PLUNGES INTO THE SEETHING FLAMES.
IF THAT FOOL HAD ONLY UNLOCKED MY HANDCUFFS.! BUT I MUST REACH THAT BOMB— I WILL SAVE WONDER WOMAN.!
6
WITH GARMENTS CHARRED BY BLISTERING HEAT, PAULA STUMBLES, EXHAUSTED, INTO THE FACTORY BASEMENT.
ONLY A LITTLE FURTHER—GOT TO MAKE IT- FOR WONDER WOMAN.!

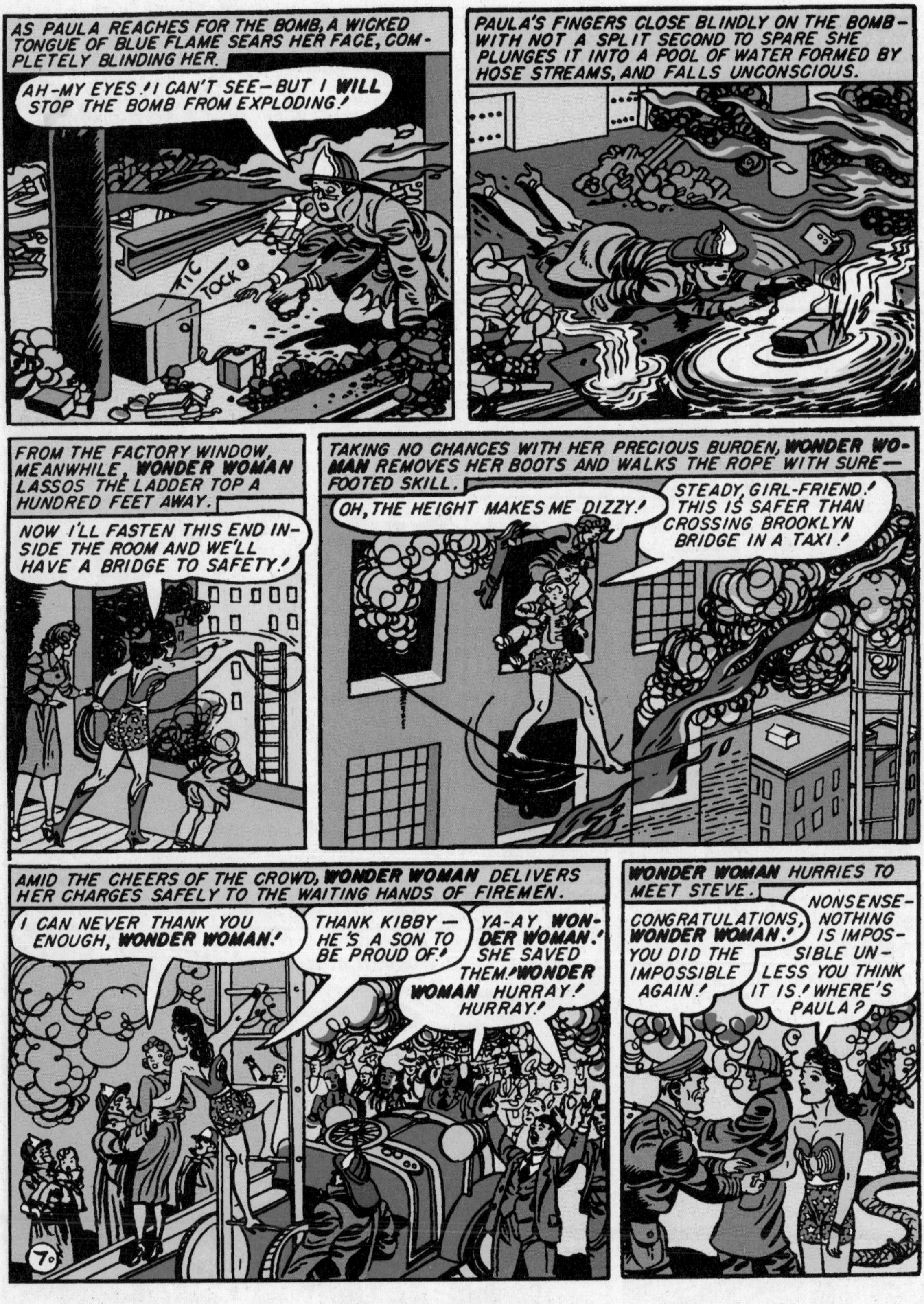
AS PAULA REACHES FOR THE BOMB, A WICKED TONGUE OF BLUE FLAME SEARS HER FACE, COMPLETELY BLINDING HER.
AH-MY EYES! I CAN'T SEE-BUT I WILL STOP THE BOMB FROM EXPLODING!
TIC
TOCK
PAULA'S FINGERS CLOSE BLINDLY ON THE BOMB-WITH NOT A SPLIT SECOND TO SPARE SHE PLUNGES IT INTO A POOL OF WATER FORMED BY HOSE STREAMS, AND FALLS UNCONSCIOUS.
FROM THE FACTORY WINDOW, MEANWHILE, WONDER WOMAN LASSOS THE LADDER TOP A HUNDRED FEET AWAY.
NOW I'LL FASTEN THIS END INSIDE THE ROOM AND WE'LL HAVE A BRIDGE TO SAFETY!
TAKING NO CHANCES WITH HER PRECIOUS BURDEN, WONDER WOMAN REMOVES HER BOOTS AND WALKS THE ROPE WITH SURE-FOOTED SKILL.
OH, THE HEIGHT MAKES ME DIZZY!
STEADY, GIRL-FRIEND! THIS IS SAFER THAN CROSSING BROOKLYN BRIDGE IN A TAXI!
AMID THE CHEERS OF THE CROWD, WONDER WOMAN DELIVERS HER CHARGES SAFELY TO THE WAITING HANDS OF FIREMEN.
I CAN NEVER THANK YOU ENOUGH, WONDER WOMAN!
THANK KIBBY-HE'S A SON TO BE PROUD OF!
YA-AY WONDER WOMAN! SHE SAVED THEM! WONDER WOMAN HURRAY! HURRAY!
7
WONDER WOMAN HURRIES TO MEET STEVE.
CONGRATULATIONS, WONDER WOMAN! YOU DID THE IMPOSSIBLE AGAIN!
NONSENSE-NOTHING IS IMPOSSIBLE UNLESS YOU THINK IT IS! WHERE'S PAULA?

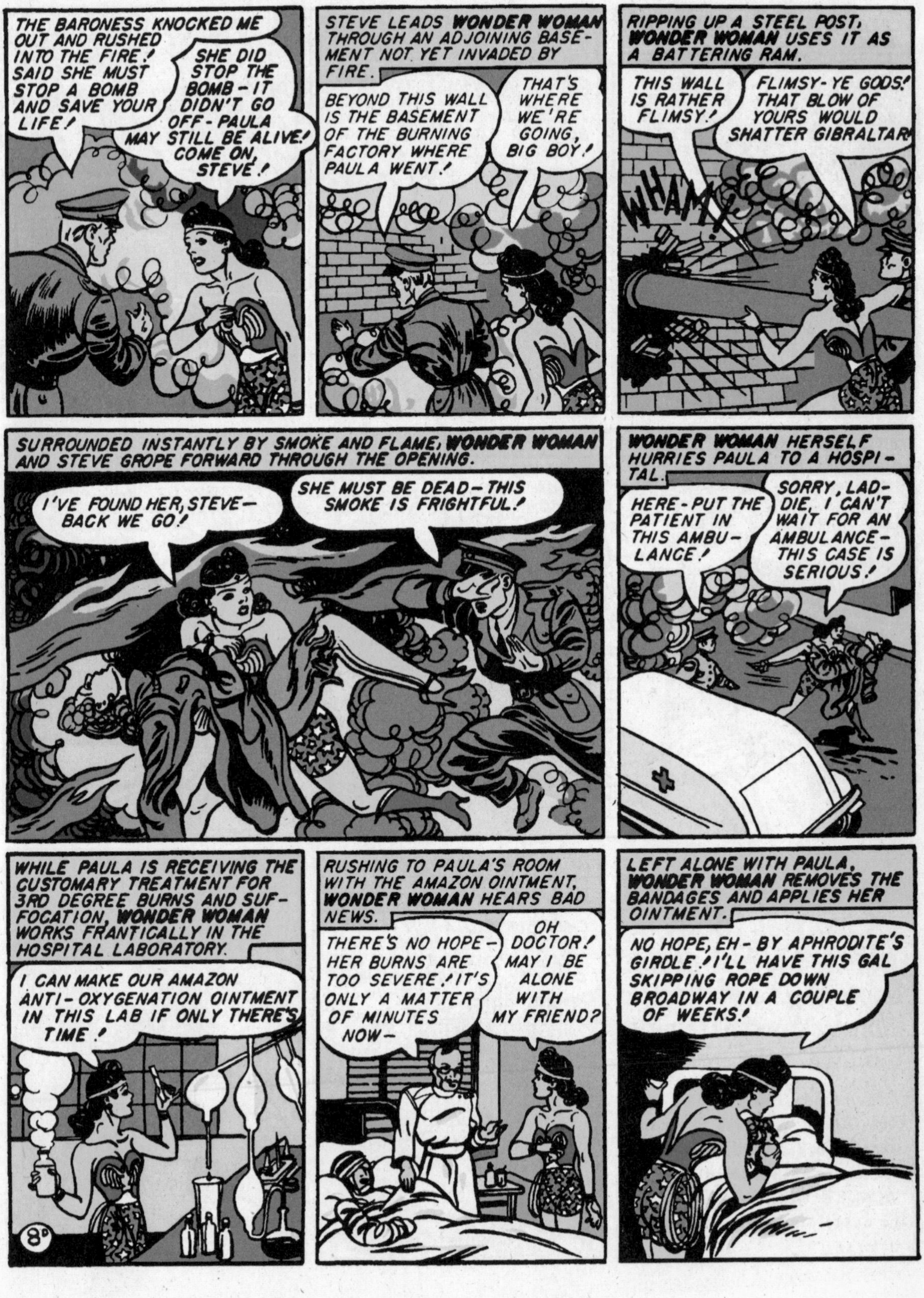
THE BARONESS KNOCKED ME OUT AND RUSHED INTO THE FIRE! SAID SHE MUST STOP A BOMB AND SAVE YOUR LIFE!
SHE DID STOP THE BOMB - IT DIDN'T GO OFF - PAULA MAY STILL BE ALIVE! COME ON, STEVE!
STEVE LEADS WONDER WOMAN THROUGH AN ADJOINING BASEMENT NOT YET INVADED BY FIRE.
BEYOND THIS WALL IS THE BASEMENT OF THE BURNING FACTORY WHERE PAULA WENT!
THAT'S WHERE WE'RE GOING, BIG BOY!
RIPPING UP A STEEL POST, WONDER WOMAN USES IT AS A BATTERING RAM.
THIS WALL IS RATHER FLIMSY!
FLIMSY - YE GODS! THAT BLOW OF YOURS WOULD SHATTER GIBRALTAR!
WHAM!
SURROUNDED INSTANTLY BY SMOKE AND FLAME, WONDER WOMAN AND STEVE GROPE FORWARD THROUGH THE OPENING.
SHE MUST BE DEAD - THIS SMOKE IS FRIGHTFUL!
I'VE FOUND HER, STEVE - BACK WE GO!
WONDER WOMAN HERSELF HURRIES PAULA TO A HOSPITAL.
HERE - PUT THE PATIENT IN THIS AMBULANCE!
SORRY, LADDIE, I CAN'T WAIT FOR AN AMBULANCE - THIS CASE IS SERIOUS!
WHILE PAULA IS RECEIVING THE CUSTOMARY TREATMENT FOR 3RD DEGREE BURNS AND SUFFOCATION, WONDER WOMAN WORKS FRANTICALLY IN THE HOSPITAL LABORATORY.
I CAN MAKE OUR AMAZON ANTI-OXYGENATION OINTMENT IN THIS LAB IF ONLY THERE'S TIME!
8D
RUSHING TO PAULA'S ROOM WITH THE AMAZON OINTMENT, WONDER WOMAN HEARS BAD NEWS.
THERE'S NO HOPE - HER BURNS ARE TOO SEVERE! IT'S ONLY A MATTER OF MINUTES NOW -
OH DOCTOR! MAY I BE ALONE WITH MY FRIEND?
LEFT ALONE WITH PAULA, WONDER WOMAN REMOVES THE BANDAGES AND APPLIES HER OINTMENT.
NO HOPE, EH - BY APHRODITE'S GIRDLE! I'LL HAVE THIS GAL SKIPPING ROPE DOWN BROADWAY IN A COUPLE OF WEEKS!

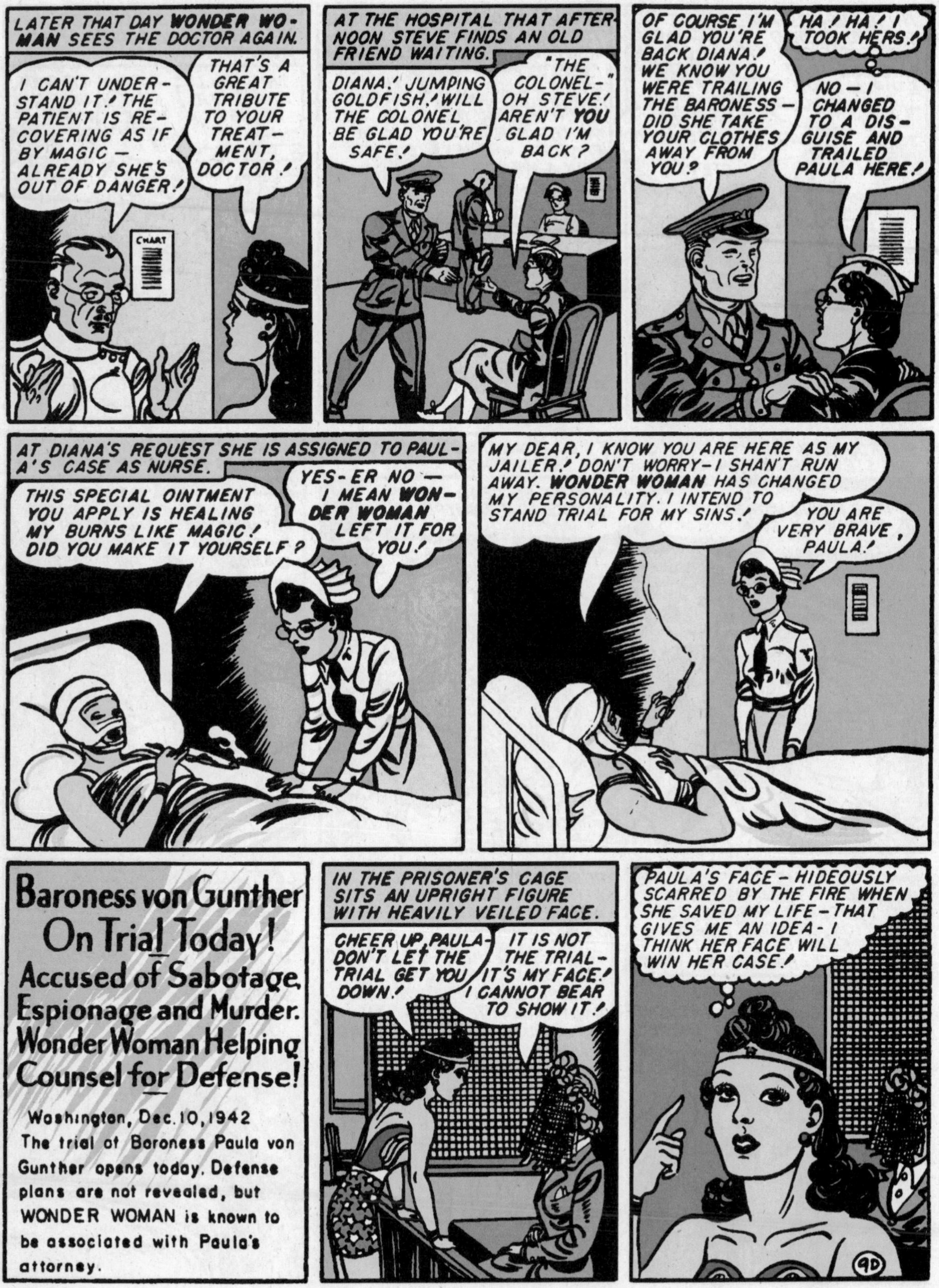

LATER THAT DAY WONDER WOMAN SEES THE DOCTOR AGAIN.
I CAN'T UNDERSTAND IT! THE PATIENT IS RECOVERING AS IF BY MAGIC — ALREADY SHE'S OUT OF DANGER!
THAT'S A GREAT TRIBUTE TO YOUR TREATMENT, DOCTOR!
CHART
AT THE HOSPITAL THAT AFTERNOON STEVE FINDS AN OLD FRIEND WAITING.
DIANA! JUMPING GOLDFISH! WILL THE COLONEL BE GLAD YOU'RE SAFE!
"THE COLONEL-" OH STEVE! AREN'T YOU GLAD I'M BACK?
OF COURSE I'M GLAD YOU'RE BACK DIANA! WE KNOW YOU WERE TRAILING THE BARONESS - DID SHE TAKE YOUR CLOTHES AWAY FROM YOU?
HA! HA! I TOOK HERS!
NO — I CHANGED TO A DISGUISE AND TRAILED PAULA HERE!
AT DIANA'S REQUEST SHE IS ASSIGNED TO PAULA'S CASE AS NURSE.
THIS SPECIAL OINTMENT YOU APPLY IS HEALING MY BURNS LIKE MAGIC! DID YOU MAKE IT YOURSELF?
YES- ER NO — I MEAN WONDER WOMAN LEFT IT FOR YOU!
MY DEAR, I KNOW YOU ARE HERE AS MY JAILER! DON'T WORRY- I SHAN'T RUN AWAY. WONDER WOMAN HAS CHANGED MY PERSONALITY. I INTEND TO STAND TRIAL FOR MY SINS!
YOU ARE VERY BRAVE, PAULA!
Baroness von Gunther On Trial Today! Accused of Sabotage, Espionage and Murder. Wonder Woman Helping Counsel for Defense!
Washington, Dec. 10, 1942
The trial of Baroness Paula von Gunther opens today. Defense plans are not revealed, but WONDER WOMAN is known to be associated with Paula's attorney.
IN THE PRISONER'S CAGE SITS AN UPRIGHT FIGURE WITH HEAVILY VEILED FACE.
CHEER UP, PAULA- DON'T LET THE TRIAL GET YOU DOWN!
IT IS NOT THE TRIAL- IT'S MY FACE! I CANNOT BEAR TO SHOW IT!
PAULA'S FACE - HIDEOUSLY SCARRED BY THE FIRE WHEN SHE SAVED MY LIFE - THAT GIVES ME AN IDEA - I THINK HER FACE WILL WIN HER CASE!
9D

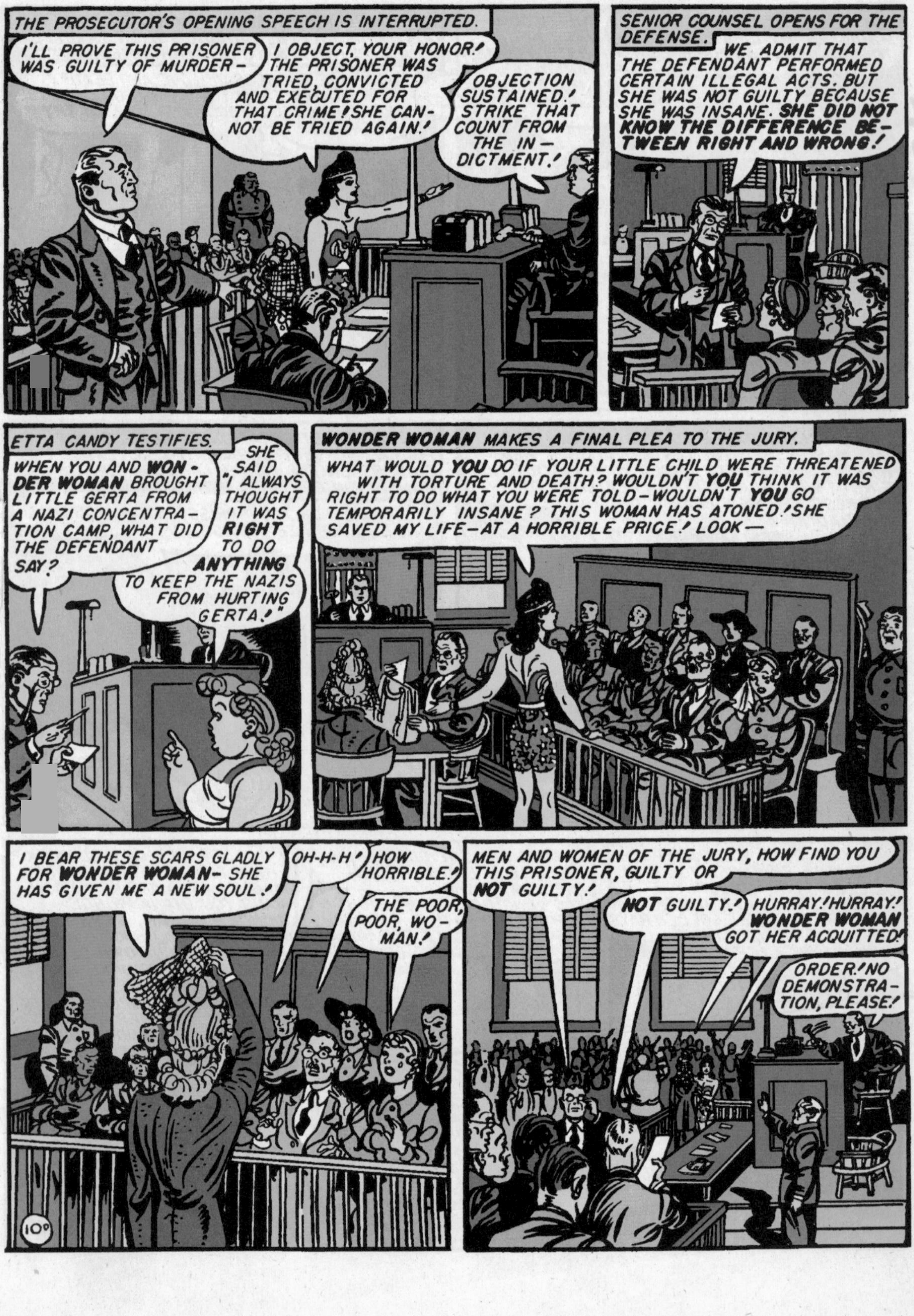
THE PROSECUTOR'S OPENING SPEECH IS INTERRUPTED.
I'LL PROVE THIS PRISONER WAS GUILTY OF MURDER-
I OBJECT, YOUR HONOR! THE PRISONER WAS TRIED, CONVICTED AND EXECUTED FOR THAT CRIME! SHE CANNOT BE TRIED AGAIN!
OBJECTION SUSTAINED! STRIKE THAT COUNT FROM THE INDICTMENT!
SENIOR COUNSEL OPENS FOR THE DEFENSE.
WE ADMIT THAT THE DEFENDANT PERFORMED CERTAIN ILLEGAL ACTS. BUT SHE WAS NOT GUILTY BECAUSE SHE WAS INSANE. SHE DID NOT KNOW THE DIFFERENCE BETWEEN RIGHT AND WRONG!
ETTA CANDY TESTIFIES.
WHEN YOU AND WONDER WOMAN BROUGHT LITTLE GERTA FROM A NAZI CONCENTRATION CAMP, WHAT DID THE DEFENDANT SAY?
SHE SAID "I ALWAYS THOUGHT IT WAS RIGHT TO DO ANYTHING TO KEEP THE NAZIS FROM HURTING GERTA!"
WONDER WOMAN MAKES A FINAL PLEA TO THE JURY.
WHAT WOULD YOU DO IF YOUR LITTLE CHILD WERE THREATENED WITH TORTURE AND DEATH? WOULDN'T YOU THINK IT WAS RIGHT TO DO WHAT YOU WERE TOLD-WOULDN'T YOU GO TEMPORARILY INSANE? THIS WOMAN HAS ATONED! SHE SAVED MY LIFE-AT A HORRIBLE PRICE! LOOK-
I BEAR THESE SCARS GLADLY FOR WONDER WOMAN- SHE HAS GIVEN ME A NEW SOUL!
OH-H-H!
HOW HORRIBLE!
THE POOR, POOR, WOMAN!
10
MEN AND WOMEN OF THE JURY, HOW FIND YOU THIS PRISONER, GUILTY OR NOT GUILTY!
NOT GUILTY!
HURRAY! HURRAY! WONDER WOMAN GOT HER ACQUITTED!
ORDER! NO DEMONSTRATION, PLEASE!

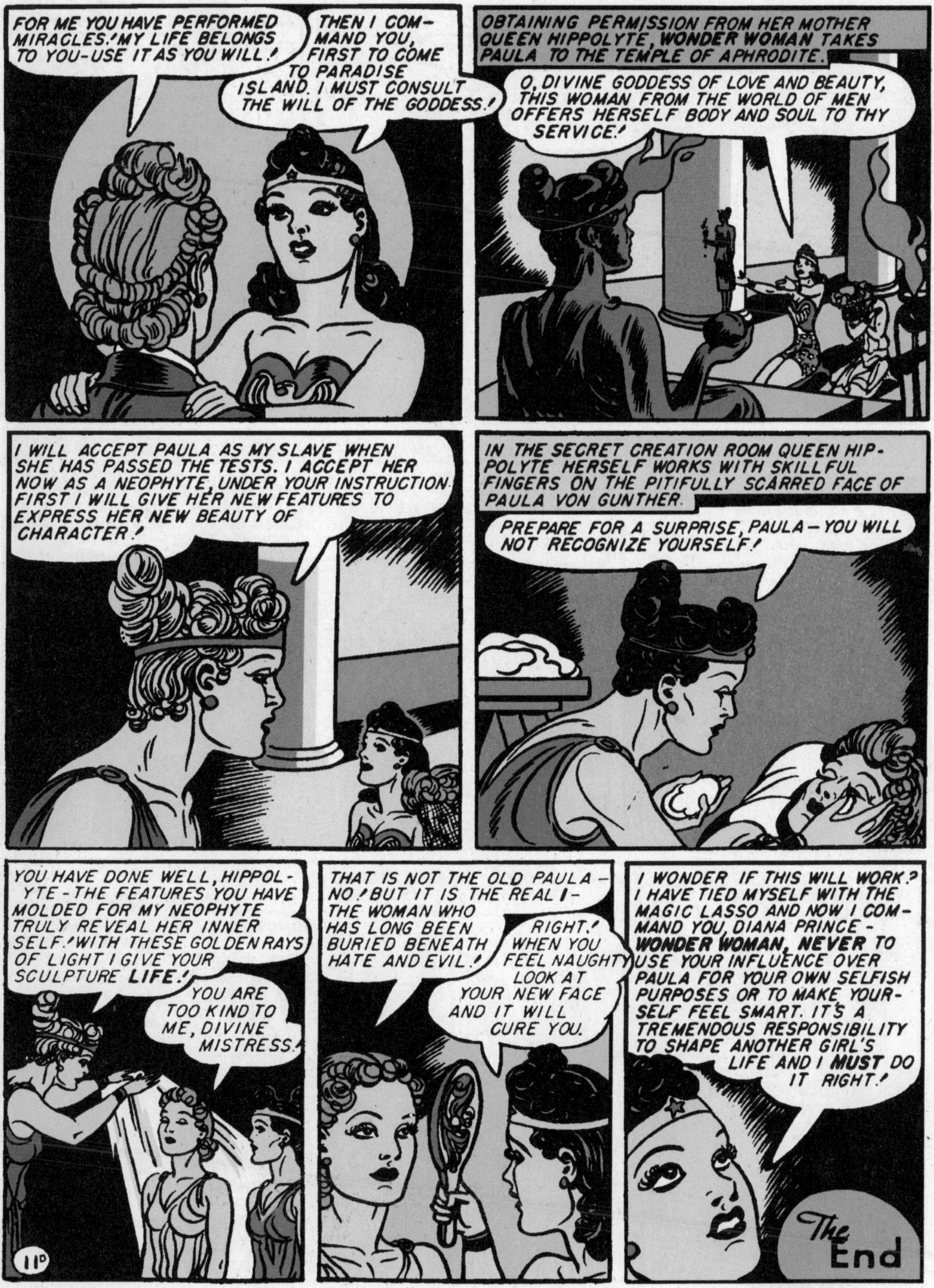
FOR ME YOU HAVE PERFORMED MIRACLES! MY LIFE BELONGS TO YOU-USE IT AS YOU WILL!
THEN I COMMAND YOU, FIRST TO COME TO PARADISE ISLAND. I MUST CONSULT THE WILL OF THE GODDESS!
OBTAINING PERMISSION FROM HER MOTHER QUEEN HIPPOLYTE, WONDER WOMAN TAKES PAULA TO THE TEMPLE OF APHRODITE.
O, DIVINE GODDESS OF LOVE AND BEAUTY, THIS WOMAN FROM THE WORLD OF MEN OFFERS HERSELF BODY AND SOUL TO THY SERVICE!
I WILL ACCEPT PAULA AS MY SLAVE WHEN SHE HAS PASSED THE TESTS. I ACCEPT HER NOW AS A NEOPHYTE, UNDER YOUR INSTRUCTION. FIRST I WILL GIVE HER NEW FEATURES TO EXPRESS HER NEW BEAUTY OF CHARACTER!
IN THE SECRET CREATION ROOM QUEEN HIPPOLYTE HERSELF WORKS WITH SKILLFUL FINGERS ON THE PITIFULLY SCARRED FACE OF PAULA VON GUNTHER.
PREPARE FOR A SURPRISE, PAULA—YOU WILL NOT RECOGNIZE YOURSELF!
YOU HAVE DONE WELL, HIPPOLYTE-THE FEATURES YOU HAVE MOLDED FOR MY NEOPHYTE TRULY REVEAL HER INNER SELF! WITH THESE GOLDEN RAYS OF LIGHT I GIVE YOUR SCULPTURE LIFE!
YOU ARE TOO KIND TO ME, DIVINE MISTRESS.
THAT IS NOT THE OLD PAULA-NO! BUT IT IS THE REAL I-THE WOMAN WHO HAS LONG BEEN BURIED BENEATH HATE AND EVIL!
RIGHT! WHEN YOU FEEL NAUGHTY LOOK AT YOUR NEW FACE AND IT WILL CURE YOU.
I WONDER IF THIS WILL WORK? I HAVE TIED MYSELF WITH THE MAGIC LASSO AND NOW I COMMAND YOU, DIANA PRINCE-WONDER WOMAN, NEVER TO USE YOUR INFLUENCE OVER PAULA FOR YOUR OWN SELFISH PURPOSES OR TO MAKE YOURSELF FEEL SMART. IT'S A TREMENDOUS RESPONSIBILITY TO SHAPE ANOTHER GIRL'S LIFE AND I MUST DO IT RIGHT!
The End